p^{343}

Developing
Language Skills
in the Elementary Schools

Developing

Language Skills

in the Elementary Schools

second edition

Harry A. Greene *Professor Emeritus of Education, State University of Iowa*

Walter T. Petty *· Associate Professor of Education, Sacramento State College*

Allyn and Bacon, Inc.

Boston, 1963

Preface

THE FIRST EDITION OF *Developing Language Skills in the Elementary School* was used by many students in teacher education programs and by in-service teachers and supervisors. Particular satisfaction was expressed by these users with the research orientation of the book, the detailed description of the elementary school language curriculum, and the careful attention given to specific methods and techniques useful in developing and evaluating language skills. In this second edition these features have been retained and strengthened. There are even more references to specific investigations and studies supporting the theory and practices suggested than in the earlier edition. There are also many additional suggestions as to techniques and methods to be used by the teacher of language skills.

A chapter on reading as a receptive language skill is included in this edition, and the interrelationships of all of the language skills are dealt with extensively. Each chapter in this edition is introduced with a short preview of the content of the chapter and a statement of the purpose of it. Each chapter concludes with questions for thought and discussion which summarize and review the chapter's content. Other additions to this edition include a discussion of linguistics, new material on listening, and an expanded emphasis upon certain evaluative techniques.

This edition continues to emphasize the authors' belief that the effective teaching of language in the elementary school rests upon a professional approach resulting from the thoughtful consideration of basic educational issues, together with a thorough and specialized knowledge of the field of language. The point of view that language is a tool of expression is again stressed. Language is regarded as a skill field dependent for its effectiveness on the formation of correct habits. The authors believe that a child acquires mastery of language by using it. He learns about sentences, not by talking about them, but by constantly forming them and writing them correctly; he learns desirable usage, not by studying confusing and easily-forgotten rules, but by repeating the usages until they become habitual. These beliefs lead therefore to the view that language skills must be developed in connection with a school program and subject matter sufficiently rich in content to provide interesting activities and thus to stimulate extensive expression.

In developing these beliefs, citing evidence for them, and suggesting teaching procedures the authors have followed a logical organization they believe useful both for students in teaching and experienced classroom teachers. Part One, Educational Point of View as it Affects Language Teaching, introduces the important problem areas in the teaching of expressional language skills. It then presents the nature, origin, and functions of language, various current concepts of language, and issues in and forces affecting the development of the language program.

Part Two, Objectives of the Language Program, presents in detail the desired outcomes of instruction and learning in language expression for the different grade levels and skill areas. Part Three, Techniques and Methods for Developing Language Skills, gives actual teaching procedures by which the program outlined in Part Two can be achieved in terms of child growth and mastery. Both Parts Two and Three deal with oral and written language and with listening and treat separately the informal pre-third grade program and the more formal program for grades three and above. Both parts also treat the development of the specific oral and written skills separately as well as together in chapters dealing with skills common to both forms of expression.

Part Four, Special Aspects of the Language Program, is concerned with the special problems of grammar teaching, creative expression, reading in the language program, and the use and evaluation of textbooks and workbooks. Finally, Part Five, Evaluation of Language Teaching, concludes the book with an introduction in some detail to the general problems of measuring and evaluating the effectiveness of the different aspects of the instructional program and the quality of the resulting products. The final chapter provides specific information and procedures for evaluating language teaching.

To the many experienced teachers and supervisors, colleagues, and students in the institutions in which the authors have taught, grateful acknowledgements are again expressed for the contributions they have made directly or indirectly to this book. The authors are especially indebted to the many graduate students and other students of language teaching whose research over several decades is quoted and summarized here as the basis for objective answers to many of the complicated and perplexing issues in language instruction.

H. A. G.
W. T. P.

Contents

Developing
Language Skills
in the Elementary Schools

part 1

Educational Point of View

as it Affects

Language Teaching

EACH OF THE PARTS COMPRISING THIS VOLUME HAS A SPECIFIC FUNCTION to perform in relation to the total language program. The chapters comprising each part are organized to develop these specific functions. The two chapters in this part stress the importance of the thorough, professional preparation of teachers and supervisors of language, beginning with the acceptance of a workable philosophy of education, and on through a thorough understanding of how effective language habits are acquired and how they become a part of the individual's daily social performance.

1

Teaching the Language Skills:

A Professional Approach

THE PURPOSE OF THIS CHAPTER IS TO INTRODUCE THE STUDENT AND teacher to a professional approach to the teaching and supervising of language through the consideration of the following basic issues:

a. The four fundamental areas of professional information required by teachers and supervisors.
b. The contribution of educational point of view to the curriculum, methods, materials, and results of instruction in the language classroom.
c. Education for social needs versus education as discipline.
d. The dependence of curriculum content on educational point of view.
e. The relation of instructional materials and methods to point of view and the current psychology of learning.
f. The importance of an adequate program for the evaluation of results of instruction.
g. The teacher and the teaching of language.
h. The meaning and the problems of supervision.

In addition to the normal supply of desirable physical, mental, and emotional qualities, you as a teacher or supervisor must have extensive professional knowledge and technical skill in the areas you teach and supervise. You must have well-founded and defensible opinions on at least four important educational problems: point of view or educational philosophy, the nature and sources of curriculum content, methods of instruction, and evaluation of results. These are problems which require thoughtful consideration; problems of concern to anyone with genuine personal or professional interest in the welfare of children and of our schools. No teacher or supervisor dedicated to the development of language skills in children may seek answers to these problems casually. Opinions and answers which are well-founded and may be defended require diligent pursuit. This book is concerned with these problems and with beliefs in regard to them which have resulted from experience and a thorough examination of the research evidence.

3

FUNDAMENTAL AREAS OF
PROFESSIONAL INFORMATION

The manner in which each individual forms his opinions with respect to these basic educational issues may vary widely. Some may evolve their answers from experience in the classroom, some from study and research, some from reading and other professional sources of teacher information. Since these four problem-areas are of such great professional significance, and an understanding of them is so essential to a comprehension of the plan of organization and the point of view of this book, they are discussed in detail in the following pages.

POINT OF VIEW

Point of view, the first of the four problem-areas with which the teacher and the supervisor must be thoroughly familiar, is basic to the entire educational program. It raises the question of *why* in education. Why do we as a nation give education such high rating among the important values of life? Why do we spend so much effort and money on our educational program? What are we trying to accomplish? What are desirable goals? How can we tell when we have achieved these goals?

For most of us the answers to these questions are secured in one of two ways, either by formulating answers from our own critical thinking and experience, or by adopting statements formulated by others who have given them critical thought. The answers we give determine the entire direction and character of our educational program. Without acceptable and clearly defined answers, without an operating point of view, the goals of instruction cannot be formulated. The tone and color of the answers determine the nature of the goals, and they in turn determine the selection of the skills and subject matter needed to achieve them. The content of the curriculum has a direct bearing both upon the methods of instruction to be used in attaining the goals and upon the methods employed in evaluating the extent to which these goals have been attained.

The pages of history are filled with examples of the effects of changes in the purposes and outcomes of the educational programs of nations. The glory of Greece was the culmination of a national philosophy, channeled through its educational system, stressing beauty, art, music, and

4

literature. Rome became a world conqueror as a result of a national philosophy that expressed itself in the goal of training its youth for military service. The rise of Germany as a military power prior to 1914, Nazi Germany under Hitler, Italy under Mussolini, Japan before Pearl Harbor, and Russia under the Communists are all examples of the way in which national philosophies translate themselves into educational programs designed to strengthen specific points of view or purposes. The leaders of all of these nations knew exactly what they were doing when they regimented and controlled the training activities of the youth of their times.

Even within the history of our own nation, the records show many significant changes in philosophical and psychological points of view that have influenced educational policies. Around the turn of the century an extensive series of experiments revealed the failure of *formal discipline* to function as a principle of learning. This theory of learning, popular around 1890 to 1910, held that certain school subjects had the power to impart disciplinary training to the mind quite apart from the content value of the subjects themselves. The new ideas that arose from experiments in learning at that time have caused important changes, mostly for the better, in the purposes and desired outcomes of our program of education.

Education as discipline. An economical way of evaluating the nature and extent of our own national adjustments educationally may be to examine quickly two contrasting definitions of education found in the literature of the periods involved. In the formal period, which roughly may be considered to have ended its major influence during the first decade of the current century, the generally accepted purpose of education was the discipline of the mind. The followers of this concept of learning held that the human mind was composed of a number of separate functional centers—such as memory, reasoning, will, persistence, neatness, and many others—that could be developed most effectively by having the individual learner work hard at any of a number of selected formal activities. What the individual studied or learned was not important, except that to be worthwhile it had to be difficult. The specific knowledge or skills resulting from these activities were secondary products. Only the general or formal training mattered, for through the general training the several disciplines or functional centers of the mind were developed. Learning was general rather than specific. Reasoning, as a functional area of the mind, was developed by any difficult process or activity calling for the exercise of reasoning. Memory was the result

5

of working on the recall of any type of difficult material. Each function was looked upon as a storage tank which was kept filled by the right amount of mental activity and from which the desired reaction could be obtained simply by the opening of the correct valve.

The practical effect of this theory of learning was the introduction of many difficult, abstract, and formal subject-matter activities into the curriculum. Notable among these subjects thought to provide the desired mental activities were Latin, foreign language, mathematics, science, and certain aspects of English. These subjects continue in the curriculum but largely have been modified so that they can be defended on grounds other than their disciplinary effects. This is not true for Latin and English grammar, and some aspects of the others, and it is not unusual even today to hear defenses which stress disciplinary values.

Education for meeting social needs.   The interest of psychologists in formulating a defensible theory of learning to replace the discredited theory of formal discipline, combined with the contributions of sociologists, brought into being early in this century an entirely new educational philosophy. Many educators have felt that this modern point of view was most effectively expressed in the teaching of John Dewey.[1] This point of view, in contrast with that of the formalists, holds that the function of education is to help the individual take his optimum place in society. In order to attain this goal, the school must give him mastery of the knowledge, habits, attitudes, and skills that an analysis of adult social situations shows he is likely to be called upon to use. Thus the individual, instead of being trained to reason in general areas, must be taught to reason in specific situations. Instead of developing ability to spell in general he must learn to spell the words he will be called upon to use in written expression in later social situations. Instead of trying to learn the mechanics of the structure of the sentence by diagramming he must learn to construct sentences himself. Instead of memorizing general rules governing language usage he must develop automatic responses to usage situations. Learning thus becomes specific rather than general, a change that has brought about extensive and vital revisions in the content of the school curriculum.

This social conception of education gives emphasis to cultural values as well as to vocational values. The nature of the social needs is very largely determined by the values held by society, and many statements have appeared which have attempted to translate these values into defini-

[1] *The School and Society,* 1900; *The Child and the Curriculum,* 1902. Chicago: University of Chicago Press.

6

tions of the purposes of education. The following is believed by the authors to be a reasonably acceptable expression of the modern social point of view in education: *Education has as its essential purpose the preparation of the individual to do in a better way all of the desirable things he will do anyway.*

This statement, gathered from many sources, accepts in a realistic and practical way the social responsibility of the school for preparing the individual, within the limits of his ability, to meet the demands which society may make on him as a child and as an adult. It makes no attempt to divert him from his own fields of interest or to make him something he has no desire to be. It obligates our educational program to prepare the future citizen, doctor, lawyer, merchant, teacher, farmer, banker, hewer of logs, or digger of ditches in such a manner that he may perform his functions at his own best level of efficiency. Moreover, this point of view enables the curriculum worker to proceed in an objective, scientific manner in the determination of the specific elements of greatest social usefulness in each subject-matter field.

CURRICULUM CONTENT

The determination of the socially important knowledge, attitudes, skills, and abilities which the future citizen should master is the second of the four major educational problems for which each teacher must find an answer. This is the question of the *what* in education. Perhaps for the majority of teachers the textbook constitutes the curriculum, but for those who are not dependent upon the textbook for subject matter as well as instructional techniques, an unusual fund of information and skill in knowing where to look is called for. Such a teacher must be unusually well trained and experienced in applying the techniques of subject-matter evaluation and selection. In turn, it is vital for the teacher dependent upon the textbook to know how to evaluate the subject matter and methods presented in the text.

The acceptance of the social point of view of the purposes of education clearly defines the areas in which the teacher and his supervisor must look for vital elements of the curriculum. Since the individual must be equipped to meet the specific demands with which life may confront him, the place to look for the types of training he will need must be in life itself. For example, the vocabulary comprising the spelling curriculum should include a limited list of words which the individual needs to use when he writes, not a long list of uncommon and difficult words. Logically,

7

the place to look for these words is in vocabularies compiled from the actual written communication of children and adults in meeting their own expressional needs. The modern arithmetic course of study emphasizes the skills and abilities utilized most frequently by children and adults in meeting life situations calling for quantitative thinking. The language program similarly stresses those skills most frequently needed in situations calling for inter-communication of individuals.

The recognition of the fact that learning is highly specific rather than general has brought about many significant changes in the content of the curriculum. In general, useless and unnecessarily difficult concepts and skills have been omitted from instructional emphasis in favor of those commonly used in meeting important social needs. For example, the spelling vocabulary of today suitable for use in the elementary school grades may comprise a list of only three or four thousand relatively simple words of high social usefulness. In fact, a limited list of under one thousand words will be found to carry most of the vocabulary load in written expression. Contrast the instructional problem of the teacher and the learning problem of the child in mastering this limited word list with that of coping with the ten thousand or more words, many of high difficulty, formerly included in the spelling curriculum. When spelling was believed to be a general ability, the words included for instruction were chosen more for their difficulty than for their utility. Some socially useful words offer spelling difficulties, but difficulty alone should not be the criterion of their selection.

A comparison of the arithmetic curriculum of twenty-five years ago with that of today reveals that many abstract, difficult, and useless processes have been omitted from the modern program with a corresponding increase in emphasis on skills that can be justified by their social usefulness. The same situation is found in almost every school subject, although it must be admitted that in some areas—such as mathematics, foreign language, and English grammar—the formalists have waged a persistent battle in defense of the disciplinary values of their subjects.

The modernization of the school curriculum in general and of the expressional language arts in particular tends to be slowed by two factors. The first of these is the unwillingness of many educators and teachers to discard an accepted point of view even though it may have been proved unsound, obsolete, and indefensible in the light of the experimental evidence. The second factor is the fact that in many areas of learning, notably the language arts, the complexity of the field itself limits the techniques by which the socially useful skills can be determined. This difficulty is readily illustrated in the areas of oral and written expression. The evidence shows that while approximately ninety-five per cent of all language activity is oral, the research and the instructional emphasis in most language programs is almost entirely on the written skills. Doubtless this comes about because of the technical difficulties encountered in research in oral language, and the relative ease of identifying the written language skills.

The existence of these two serious limitations on the improvement of the instructional program requires the highest degree of teacher-supervisor-administrator cooperation in the formulation of an acceptable point of view and in the selection of suitable techniques to be used in any program of curriculum development. Since this volume is concerned chiefly with the expressional language skills, the details of the curricular problems of the language teacher are treated primarily in this book.

METHODS OF INSTRUCTION

Educational point of view, curriculum content, and the currently acceptable principles of learning used to promote the child's mastery of the approved curriculum content combine to affect the selection of instructional methods in a given subject. This is the question of the *how* in education. In general the answer to this question is best found through critical development of point of view and experimental investigation of learning. The teacher must be well-informed about research and critically receptive of what it tells him concerning instructional procedures in the classroom. Questionable methods of instruction are more often the results of an obsolete philosophy of education or an out-dated theory of learning than they are of the content of the curriculum itself. The history of the teaching of the expressional language arts affords good illustrations of both of these points. The primary goal of language instruction, that of developing skill and effectiveness in oral and written expression, was as generally accepted by the teacher thirty or forty years ago as it is by the present-day teacher. Many of the desired outcomes would be approved by both groups. Their differences in classroom procedure would be accounted for almost entirely by the radically different theories of learning involved. The teachers who believe in the functional center theory of learning—and apparently some still do—accept a formal method of approach. These, by and large, are the teachers who are still convinced that the teaching of formal grammar is the correct approach to effective

9

language expression. Perhaps it is because of the many teachers of this type in classrooms today that instruction in language has improved so slowly. The teachers who are convinced that mastery of language is not a general function of the mind acquired through memorizing formal rules and generalizations but rather the result of specific habit formation are in harmony with the best modern theory of learning. The classroom procedure of the modern teacher depends upon the introduction of activities which stimulate the child to express himself and through repetition bring about the formation of the desired habits. The indirect approach, depending upon formal grammar, sentence diagramming, and memorization of rules, is based upon a theory of learning that is largely obsolete. The experimental evidence long available offers strong support for the use of direct methods rather than formal methods in the teaching of language.[2]

EVALUATION OF THE RESULTS OF INSTRUCTION

The fourth of the fields of information in which the teacher must be well-qualified concerns the procedures and the instruments by which the results of instruction may be evaluated. This is the question of the *how well* in education. It represents an area in which much research has been done and many volumes written in the fifty years since the introduction of the idea of educational measurement to the teachers of this country.

The term *evaluation* is used here to include all types of devices and techniques by which the results of classroom instruction may be described objectively. The broader concept of measurement expressed by evaluation is particularly helpful in the appraisal of the results of instruction in language expression. Within its scope it includes the standardized tests and scales commonly considered as synonymous with measurement of achievement. In addition, it gives a proper place to many of the widely used and often subjective procedures used by teachers in describing such qualities of expression as style, interest, variety, organization, choice of subject matter, choice of words, and many others. Standardized tests may perform reasonably well in the measurement of pupil and class achievement and growth in such areas as usage, punctuation, capitalization, sentence sense, and spelling. However, teachers often find such a great difference between the apparent learning of certain skills, as shown by high scores on objective tests, and the actual mastery of the skills, as shown by pupils' usage in their own writing and speaking, that many doubt the

[2] Harry A. Greene, "Direct versus Formal Methods in Elementary English," *Elementary English Review*, 24:273–285; May, 1947.

validity of objective tests. Most teachers are convinced that evaluation of the effects of instruction in language expression involves much more than the use of standardized tests and scales.

There are times and places for the use of the standardized tests and scales as measures of achievement, status, and growth of individual pupils and classes, as the basis for diagnostic and remedial work, and as a means of evaluating the results of a special instructional or supervisory program. There are also times and places for the use of the teacher-made test, the check list for teacher guidance, and the cooperative check list prepared by teacher and pupils for the purpose of setting up standards and for revealing individual pupil and class growth. Detailed consideration of the problems of evaluation is given in Chapters Seventeen and Eighteen.

THE TEACHER AND THE TEACHING
OF LANGUAGE

Teachers of the expressional language skills face the same general types of problems encountered by their colleagues in other subject-matter fields. Any difference lies in the fact that for language teachers the problems are best stated definitely in terms of language skills and activities. The philosophy of the school must be translated into a specific point of view and statements of purposes for the teaching of spelling, handwriting, written expression, oral expression, usage and grammar. The content of the language curriculum must be broken down into readily identifiable and socially important expressional language skills. Accepted theories of learning must be adapted to meet the specific problems involved in learning to spell useful words, to capitalize and to punctuate correctly, to acquire new words and word meanings, to pronounce words correctly, to master correct habits of usage, to develop a pleasing style in writing and an effective platform manner. Classroom methods that have been found to be generally effective must now demonstrate their value in particular situations and under experimental conditions. Standardized and teacher-made tests and other evaluative devices must meet narrow rather than general criteria of validity. Drill, practice, and remedial exercises must be designed to meet individual and specific learning situations.

Teachers of English in the elementary school often seem to be dissatisfied with the results they obtain in the class, but they also appear to resent any suggestion that their vague objectives, their obsolete psychology of learning, their shop-worn and formal methods may be important contributors to their dissatisfaction. These teachers appear to want formal methods, perhaps because formal methods simplify their teaching problems. Modern methods depend upon imaginative planning to provide life-like activities for the stimulation of pupil expression. Formal methods mechanize teaching. It is far easier for children to analyze or diagram ready-made sentences than it is for them to produce interesting and varied sentences of their own. Moreover, for many teachers the use of modern methods would mean discarding a disproven theory of learning which for years they have found satisfying and acceptable. This step they apparently are unwilling to take. All that is necessary to establish the truth of the above statements is to check the contents of any of a long list of language textbooks that have appeared in the past five years. They contain many pages of material whose inclusion is difficult to justify in the light of the experimental evidence now available. The authors and publishers probably did not set out to compromise. Undoubtedly they had intended to produce a program that would show constructive leadership in language teaching, but they have been forced for economic reasons to conform to the demands of conservative pressure groups.

Perhaps this conservative point of view among certain teachers and supervisors of elementary school language should not be surprising. Naturally student teachers in training are usually impressed by the scholarship and success of their instructors in methods courses. Young teachers can hardly be blamed for imitating their instructors when they begin work in their own classrooms. If, as students, they were given a faulty philosophy and psychology of learning, they are likely to follow them in their own teaching. If they were taught by formal methods, and formal approaches were used in the demonstration lessons they observed, they will almost certainly follow that pattern. Teacher training institutions must, therefore, accept a share of the responsibility for the conservative views of many of the current generation of teachers.

In many universities and colleges, the methods courses are still general in character and content. This means that many of those responsible for training our teachers still believe that English teachers learn to teach in general, rather than learn to teach English. Such general methods courses are offered, not by subject-matter experts with a rich background of educational training and experience, but by individuals who believe that general and formal training in method is all that is necessary for the teacher. Many older teachers in our schools were trained in this type of program and still believe in it. Thus a vicious circle seems to perpetuate a conservative point of view among language teachers. Fortunately, many of our training institutions have accepted the modern theories of learning, and have shifted the emphasis in their training from general to special methods courses. The best of these courses are offered by qualified subject-matter experts with advanced professional training in principles of curriculum construction, in modern psychological principles of learning and up-to-date classroom procedures, as well as in the use of the best methods and instruments for evaluating the results of teaching. In such institutions and courses lies the best hope for the gradual improvement and modernization of the point of view of elementary school teachers of language.

THE SUPERVISOR AND THE TEACHING OF LANGUAGE

It is no accident that the words *teacher* and *supervisor* appear together so frequently in this volume. The interests and responsibilities of the teacher and the supervisor are so closely related that it is doubtful if the two services should be considered as separate activities. It may be closer to the truth to treat them as different levels of the same process. Usually the teaching and supervisory activities are pursued by different individuals, but their final goals are the same and they face almost identical problems. As a matter of fact, many teachers are supervisors in the very real sense of the term, and most supervisors are primarily teachers.

THE MEANING OF SUPERVISION

The authors recognize that current educational terminology tends to identify the supervisor as the "consultant," [3] but insist that the supervisor has a role other than that of the "do-gooder," which appears to be the single operating principle of some consultants. Actually, the modern supervisory officer is a highly trained specialist who almost invariably has established himself as a superior classroom teacher. [4] With his back-

[3] See Herman G. Richey, "Growth of the Modern Conception of In-Service Education," *In-Service Education,* Nelson B. Henry, ed., Fifty-sixth Yearbook of the National Society for the Study of Education, Part I. Chicago: The University Press, 1957, p. 61.

[4] Robert Beck, Walter Cook, and Nolan Kearney, *Curriculum in the Modern Elementary School,* Englewood Cliffs, N.J.: Prentice-Hall, Inc., 1960, 2nd ed., Chapter 23.

13

ground of training and experience the modern supervisor is thoroughly appreciative of the qualities of good teaching. He is able to lead the way in the classroom by constructive suggestions and by demonstration of his own mastery of the techniques for attaining the goals of his program. This type of leadership most teachers appreciate and are glad to follow. The more completely the teacher and the supervisor understand each other's responsibilities and problems, the smoother their professional relationships will become. One of the purposes of this volume is to help effect this type of understanding.

Established supervisory principles, as sound today as when they were first written, are the following:

1. Good supervision is based upon sound educational theory and practice, growing out of a judicial blending of science, philosophy, and ordinary educational experience.
2. Good supervision is democratic.
3. Good supervision is creative (and not prescriptive) both in the discovery and validation of educational facts and relationships and in applying these to specific situations.
4. Good supervision proceeds by means of an orderly, cooperatively planned and executed series of activities.
5. Good supervision is known by the results it secures.
6. Good supervision is guided by professional goals and standards.[5]

A consideration of these six principles leads to the general conclusion that good supervision depends not only on *what* is done, but also on *who* does it and *how* it is done. Teacher acceptance or rejection of supervisory programs may depend as much upon the personality, tactfulness, and methods of the supervisory staff as it does upon the teacher's professional attitude or understanding of the desired goals.

A universally acceptable definition of the purposes of supervision is obviously difficult to express. The following statement, gleaned from many sources, is submitted in the hope that it may stimulate the reader to formulate a statement of his own: *Educational supervision has for its purpose the improvement of the conditions under which children learn and teachers teach.*

This statement is recognized as being extremely general and possibly lacking in many of the specific elements demanded by most supervisors and teachers. Within its framework, however, may be developed all of the essential qualities and activities of good supervision. It makes room for the administrative, financial, physical, and public relations aspects of

[5] From A. S. Barr, "Supervision," *Encyclopedia of Educational Research,* rev. ed., Walter S. Munroe, ed. New York: The Macmillan Company, 1950, p. 1372.

the school as a community enterprise. It does not attempt to define sharply the distinctions between the administrative aspects of supervision and the supervisory aspects of administration. The activities involved blend or separate depending upon the type of organization or the size of the school. In the small school system the superintendent or the principal responsible mainly for administrative activities may also carry supervisory responsibilities. It is even conceivable under this statement that the building janitor might be performing a supervisory function when he does anything that improves the physical conditions, such as heating, lighting, and ventilating within the classroom. In the larger school systems the supervisory functions become highly specialized.

The purpose of supervision as stated above is broad enough to include such important features of good teaching and supervision as the improvement of the mental, moral, and social atmosphere of the school. In fact it is in these intangible areas that the good supervisor frequently leaves his most important mark on the attitudes of the pupils and the spirit of the school and community.

This conception of the functions of supervision also provides the basis for the consideration of the four general professional problem-areas which every teacher and supervisor must face and for which they both must produce the answers if they are to be professionally equipped to direct the learning of children or to supervise the instructional program in the classroom. Not only must the teacher and the supervisor each have solutions which are satisfying to themselves as individuals, but they must be able to bring their ideas into harmony with each other and with the overall policy of the school.

MAJOR NEEDS FOR SUPERVISION

The preceding section on the meaning and general purposes of supervision as related to the classroom teacher should provide a suitable foundation for the consideration of the major needs for supervision, both as a general process in the educational scene, and as a program specifically applied to the improvement of instruction in language expression.

To clarify and to put into operation the local educational point of view. Just as the philosophy of a nation is its educational lodestar, the educational attitude of the local community determines the direction its educational program will take. Genuine community interest and belief in the importance of its schools expresses itself in liberal financial support,

15

adequate and modern school plants, well-trained and adequately paid teachers and supervisors, high quality instructional equipment, and up-to-date textbooks and courses of study. General indifference to the welfare of its children reveals itself just as obviously in the poor quality of the community's educational program. At each of these two extremes the problems of the supervisor may be quite different, but in each case his responsibility is equally clear. The favorable attitude toward education in the one community may be the result of inherent and traditional belief in schools. Quite as often it is the outgrowth of the continued expression of faith and foresight of a single individual or a small group of educational leaders.

The definition and clarification of the locally acceptable educational point of view is one of the supervisor's most important functions, regardless of his own special fields of interest. Complete agreement of teachers with the educational point of view of the community as expressed through the supervisory program is necessary if the program is to be really effective. There are times, however, when this conformity should not be made compulsory. Educational progress is made by trying out new ideas. The supervisor should be openminded. If a teacher has a new idea, he should propose an acceptable digression from the program, which, with the cooperation of the supervisor, can be subjected to experimental evaluation. From this type of cooperative effort come the greatest values of the supervisory program.

To coordinate the instructional program.   Since the teacher in his individual classroom is able to view only a small part of the total instructional program, he is constantly in need of guidance as to instructional emphasis, time allotments, standards of achievement, rates of progress, types and frequency of drill, and many other factors that the supervisor with his broader view is able to provide. Supervisory guidance is necessary also to maintain a proper balance in emphasis between subjects and within related areas of the same subject. A teacher who is especially qualified in arithmetic or elementary science may unintentionally slight other fields in favor of his major interest. A teacher who is primarily interested in written expression may seriously under-emphasize the oral language skills.

The need for supervisory attention to the coordination of instruction is especially serious in the teaching of language. Language is a skill area with relatively little subject-matter content. Language activities based upon language become formal, often deadly, and the desired language habits are not formed. Naturally the activities most useful in stimulating language expression must be centered around fields which are especially rich in content. Not all subject-matter fields are equally well suited to stimulate language activities. Certain areas of elementary science or the social studies are particularly useful for this purpose, although this does not mean that all language activities must arise from these situations. Many other subject-matter areas, such as art, music, or mathematics, should be used as the sources of activities to stimulate language expression. However, it is necessary to guard constantly against the possibility that interest in the subject matter may overshadow the importance of the language, so that instruction on the language skills is under-emphasized. Most language textbooks attempt to maintain a proper balance of emphasis on subject matter and skill, but the teacher who is following an activity program of his own in his language teaching should make constant reference to the course of study or the textbook to make certain that the proper language skills are being emphasized.

To select, evaluate, and grade curricular content. The supervisor and the teacher must work in close cooperation in choosing suitable basic and supplementary books, especially in situations where books are the teacher's main source of information on content, grade placement, and method. The books should be checked against the best available criteria for suitability of (1) content, (2) difficulty, and (3) suggestions on method. In subjects that permit it, tabulations should be made showing the amount, type, and distribution of drill provided for the fixation and maintenance of skills. Such tabulations, of course, are difficult to make, but language books can be subjected to this type of analysis. Perhaps this is a problem for the textbook selection committee rather than the individual teacher or supervisor, but both should be aware of its possibilities.

To point out weak spots in the instructional program. Critics of teachers and of the results of teaching are so widespread and so vocal that it often seems as if not much remains for the supervisor to accomplish in pointing out weaknesses in the educational program. It may not be out of order to note in passing that many of the published criticisms cover vague and general issues. Moreover, many of the criticisms are voiced by individuals who have little or no professional background for the opinions they express. This does not mean, however, that there are not real weak spots in the program which teachers and supervisors would do well to identify. In fact, they should be the first to sense the weakness, to criticize it, and to correct it.

Among the important areas in which the supervisor might properly

17

look for weak spots would be the personal and professional qualities of the teachers themselves, the content they present to their pupils for learning, the methods of teaching they follow, and the procedures and devices they use to evaluate the results of their teaching. If the textbook or the curriculum is weak, new instructional material may be adopted or produced. Careful interviewing of prospective teachers and the use of a period of trial employment prior to permanent assignment will do much to screen teachers for personality defects as well as for inadequate training. A great deal can be done to improve the professional qualities of the teacher through supervisory encouragement to pursue in-service training courses. Other means of improving the professional qualifications of teachers include special methods courses, taught by educationally qualified subject-matter experts; the study of methods textbooks under supervisory direction; the use of teachers' manuals accompanying textbooks; and courses and texts designed to give the teacher an understanding of the possibilities and limitations of standardized and teacher-made tests.

To provide stimulation for professional improvement. Under the pressure of the daily grind of classroom preparation and instruction the teacher may find it difficult to keep abreast of the many new materials and procedures in his field. As a matter of fact, it is practically impossible for a worker in a single subject-matter field to check, not to mention read, all of the currently available published material. The preparation of abstracts of articles and books presenting new points of view, new statements of goals and objectives, improvements in methods, modern instructional materials, and new types of evaluative instruments is one of the most valuable services the supervisor can render his teachers. Attendance at educational meetings, conferences, and demonstrations in the teachers' fields of interest should be encouraged. Opportunities to visit and observe other teachers of language at work in the classroom should also be provided. Obviously not all of the new and good ideas thus gained can be adapted and used by the classroom teacher, but just knowing of their existence provides real professional stimulation.

The classroom teacher and the supervisor cannot know too much about each other's problems. They are mutually dependent upon a workable philosophy of education and a defensible theory of learning as the foundation of curriculum content, classroom methods, and evaluation techniques. A successful educational program requires a close understanding between teacher and supervisor of the common ground on which their professional activities are based.

18

EXERCISES FOR THOUGHT AND DISCUSSION

1. What are the four basic areas of professional information in which teachers and supervisors must be well grounded?

2. What do you consider the best way for you as a teacher to acquire a workable educational philosophy?

3. In what specific ways does educational point of view determine the content of the school curriculum? Illustrate.

4. Describe and illustrate ways in which educational point of view has influenced the curriculum in your lifetime.

5. Present arguments for and against formal discipline as an educational objective.

6. What is the basic justification for the acceptance of the social utility principle as one guide in curriculum construction? Why is it not an adequate single guide to curriculum content?

7. Illustrate ways in which the content of a specific subject area, as spelling, can be directed to meet social needs.

8. Show how methods of instruction are directly affected by educational point of view.

9. In a similar way show how methods and materials of instruction are related to the currently accepted psychological principles of learning.

10. How do *you* believe effective language usage habits are developed?

11. Why is it essential for the teacher to know how to evaluate the results of instruction in the classroom?

12. What differences do you see between good teaching and good supervision?

13. How would you as a teacher define supervision?

14. Enumerate and illustrate four of the major contributions good supervision should make to you as a teacher.

SELECTED REFERENCES

Association for Supervision and Curriculum Development, *Group Processes in Supervision.* Washington: National Education Association, 1948.

AYER, FRED C. *Fundamentals of Instructional Supervision.* New York: Harper and Brothers, 1954.

19

BARR, A. S., BURTON, W. H., and BRUECKNER, L. J. *Supervision: Democratic Leadership in the Improvement of Learning.* New York: D. Appleton–Century Company, 1947.

BARTKY, JOHN A. *Supervision as Human Relations.* Boston: D. C. Heath and Company, 1953.

BECK, ROBERT; COOK, WALTER; and KEARNY, NOLAN. *Curriculum in the Modern Elementary School.* Englewood Cliffs, N.J.: Prentice-Hall, Inc., 1960, Chapter 23.

BLEWETT, JOHN, editor. *John Dewey: His Thought and Influence.* New York: Fordham University Press, 1960.

BURTON, WILLIAM H., and BRUECKNER, LEO J. *Supervision.* New York: Appleton-Century-Crofts, 1955.

Commission on the English Curriculum, National Council of Teachers of English. *The English Language Arts.* New York: Appleton-Century-Crofts, Inc., 1952.

———. *Language Arts for Today's Children.* New York: Appleton-Century-Crofts, Inc., 1954.

DE BOER, JOHN J. "Earmarks of a Modern Language Arts Program in the Elementary School," *Elementary English Review,* 31:485–493; December, 1954.

DUTTON, WILBUR H., and HOCKETT, JOHN A. *The Modern Elementary School.* New York: Rinehart and Company, 1959.

GREENE, HARRY A. "Principles of Method in Elementary English Composition." *Elementary English Review,* 14:219–226; October, 1937.

HASS, C. GLENN. *In-Service Education Today.* The Fifty-sixth Yearbook of the National Society for the Study of Education, Part I. Chicago: The University of Chicago Press, 1957, Chapter 2.

HERRICK, VIRGIL E., and JACOBS, LELAND B., eds. *Children and the Language Arts.* Englewood Cliffs, N.J.: Prentice-Hall, Inc., 1955.

JORDAN, ARTHUR M. *Educational Psychology.* New York: Henry Holt and Company, 1956.

LIEBERMAN, MYRON. *The Future of Public Education.* Chicago: University of Chicago Press, 1960.

LOWE, JOE. "Status of the Work of the General Elementary Supervisor in Indiana." Unpublished doctoral thesis, Indiana University, 1952.

OTTO, HENRY J., and others. *Principles of Elementary Education.* New York: Rinehart and Company, 1955.

PEEL, E. A. *The Psychological Basis of Education.* New York: Philosophical Library, Inc., 1956.

PETTY, WALTER T. "Orienting a New Teacher." *CTA Journal,* 53:30–31; May, 1957.

————. "The Supervisory Bulletin Today." *Educational Administration and Supervision*, 43:157–162; March, 1957.

RAGAN, WILLIAM B. *Modern Elementary Curriculum*. New York: Henry Holt and Co., revised edition, 1959.

REPLOGLE, VERNON L. "What Help Do Teachers Want?" *The Education Digest*, 16:9–11; October, 1950.

SHATTUCK, MARQUIS E., Chairman. *The Development of a Modern Program in English*. Ninth Yearbook of the Department of Supervisors and Directors of Instruction. Washington: National Education Association, 1936.

SPEARS, HAROLD. *Improving the Supervision of Instruction*. Englewood Cliffs, N.J.: Prentice-Hall, Inc., 1953. Chapters 1–10, 13, 15, and 18.

STROUD, JAMES B. *Psychology in Education*. New York: Longmans, Green and Company, 1956.

WEY, H. W. "Difficulties of Beginning Teachers." *School Review*, 59:32–37; January, 1951.

WHITEHEAD, M. J. "Teachers Look at Supervision." *Educational Leadership*, 10:101–106; November, 1952.

2

Language and

the Language Program

THE NATURE AND THE EFFECTIVENESS OF A PROGRAM OF INSTRUCTION
in language are the results of the operation of two basic factors. The first
of these factors is implicit in the nature of language itself—how it is
learned and how it is used. The second factor is the educational philosophy that is operating in the period of time in which the program is
developed. It is the purpose of this chapter to discuss and evaluate these
elements as they relate to the content of the curriculum and the methods
of teaching in the elementary school language program.

THE PHILOSOPHY OF LANGUAGE

Man has accomplished nothing quite so wonderful as the development
and the use of language for communication. Through language, man ob-
tains social responses from individuals and groups; through language he
is stimulated to reaction; through language he acquires understanding,
attitudes, ideals; with language he thinks and solves problems; from
language he finds inspiration and secures emotional release. Language
makes possible the operation of business and government; it holds the
keys to achievement, security, and international understanding. Our
schools are fundamentally language schools; the schools' programs are
basically affected by the nature, origin, and use of language.

THE NATURE OF LANGUAGE

Language, according to the first definition in Webster's New International Dictionary, is "audible, articulate human speech as produced by
the action of the tongue and adjacent vocal organs." This is a very limited
conception of language and hardly an adequate one for the purposes of

22

this discussion, since it restricts language expression to audible, hence oral expression, and definitely indicates that only the human animal can produce it. A second and, for our purposes, somewhat more acceptable definition in the same source describes language as "any means, vocal or other, of expressing or communicating feeling or thought." This definition implies, that "expressing or communicating" is not an instinctive but a conscious act, a distinction of considerable importance in defining language. In a general sense, then, it may be said that *the intentional or conscious use of any sound, sign, or symbol to transmit a fact, an idea, a feeling, or an emotion from one individual to another may be classified as language.*

An involuntary cry of pain or fear, the bark of a dog, the wailing of a hungry baby, all are sounds that may be heard and may attract the attention of a human being within hearing range, but they are not necessarily language. If the baby wails *because* he has found that if he makes enough noise he will be given food, if the dog barks *because* he has learned that when we hear him we will open the door and let him into the house, then these sounds might logically be classified as a kind of language. A small pile of sticks arranged in a certain manner near our front gate might not be a symbol, but if it were left by a beggar as a sign to the next one passing that here lives a kind-hearted housewife who will feed a hungry man, then it *is* language. The intent with which the sounds or symbols are used determines whether or not they are language as an instrument of communication.

In a most interesting and stimulating discussion of the nature and origins of language, Charlton Laird has described man as a "languagized mammal." [1] The following brief quotation will clarify the point made by the writer:

A cow may be able to communicate in a cowlike way by bawling and dogs may be able to express themselves by looking soulfully from one end while wagging the other, but man is probably more significantly distinguished from his fellow creatures by his complicated means of communication than by any other differences. In short, man as we know him could not exist without language and until there was a language. Civilization could not exist until there was written language, because without written language no generation could bequeath to succeeding generations anything but its simpler findings. Culture could not be widespread until there was printed language.

Perhaps the notion that language is the principal quality that distinguishes man from the other animals is merely man's way of expressing

[1] Charlton Laird, *The Miracle of Language*. Cleveland: The World Publishing Company, 1953.

23

his idea of his superiority among the animals. On the other hand, it may well be that man's ability to communicate so effectively with others of his kind *is* his chief claim to distinction.

Most observers believe that animal cries and actions are instinctive and are not the result of thought or an attempt to communicate the thought to others. Watching a mother hen call her chicks under her wings at the approach of danger, or observing a colony of ants at work in their tunnels under glass, or following a mother quail as she lures you away from her nest by appearing to be crippled raises some question that man has a corner on the thinking process. Does the mother hen *think* danger when she calls to her chicks? Is the dog's bark a conscious request to open the door? Regardless of what we like to believe about reasoning as man's prerogative, it still appears that animals do produce signs, actions, and sounds that are interpreted by other animals. For animals, such actions are believed to be largely instinctive and spontaneous. Whether there are conscious or intentional elements in them is a difficult question to answer.

Man's use of language for communication has been acquired through long periods of imitation and practice. Human communication through speech sounds or symbols is largely unnatural rather than natural, conscious rather than instinctive. In man, language expression makes constant unnatural use of physical equipment apparently designed for other purposes. For example, body posture and movements, facial expressions, and movements and position of the hands are constantly used to express meanings in sign language where other language barriers exist. Even more strikingly unnatural uses of parts of the body are found in the making of speech sounds for oral communication. Air, forced through the voice box (larynx) by the lungs, causes vibrations of the vocal cords which are varied in quality, volume, and pitch by muscular adjustments in the lungs, throat, larynx, tongue, jaws, teeth, palate, and lips. Through constant repetition certain characteristic sounds have come to be associated with certain meanings, feelings, or actions. Similarly, certain marks, signs, and symbols have acquired specific meanings through association and now constitute the basis for written expression.

ORIGIN OF LANGUAGE

Theories of the origin of language open interesting areas for speculation but lead to no very definite conclusions. No single theory nor all combined explains all that we need to know about how language came into being. One theory explains the origin of language as the direct gift from the Creator. While nothing is said about language as such in the story of the creation, it is difficult to understand how this event could have taken place without language being involved in it, especially after the coming of Eve. Perhaps the confusion of tongues at the time of the building of the Tower of Babel supports the belief that language appeared at the time of the creation, but it just as strongly justifies the belief that language and man evolved together. Many legends found in different cultures explain language as the conscious invention of some heroic individual. The theory that the skills of communication were the spontaneous products of human nature evolving through the ages is the explanation now most generally accepted. Chance vocalizations and sounds came to take on special meanings. No one knows what these first words or symbols were, but it is quite probable that they were closely related to natural sounds.

Numerous explanations of the origins of words have been advanced. Naturally one such theory is that the first words were derived from the vocal imitation of sounds in nature. Such words as *bow-bow, roar, splash, rumble, flash, hiss, gurgle* may readily have come from such sources. Another group of words, such as *oh, ha, pshaw* is explained as originating from involuntary exclamations of man under emotional stress. Other words and their meanings are thought to have evolved through the social adjustment brought about by the gregarious nature of man. Perhaps such words as *stop, go, help, march, halt, heave-ho* might be accounted for in this manner.

FUNCTIONS AND PURPOSES OF LANGUAGE

Language, the means by which ideas, thoughts, feelings, and emotions are best communicated, is a vital part of every activity in which each of us engages. Certainly each of us talks with many people in the course of a day, but we also use language in many other ways. In addition to letters, newspapers, books, and magazines, we are constantly obliged to read street signs, billboards, menus, and directions. We regularly listen to oral language in public gatherings, as well as over the telephone, the radio, the television set. We fill out application forms, write checks, write letters, make notes, and keep diaries. We ask questions, relate stories, tell jokes, and discuss news, jobs, politics, and the weather. In short, language in some form is an essential part of everything we do.

For the child, the need for language is just as real as it is for the adult.

25

The very young child, even before he is able to talk, listens and comprehends much of what he hears—more, in fact, than we as adults often suspect. The pre-school child faces many situations in which talking and listening are necessary. All children constantly ask questions and make statements prompted by the experiences they have had—things they have seen, done, heard, or read, and things that have happened to them, their families, or their friends. The school itself confronts the child with many additional situations in which talking, writing, reading, and listening are necessary. In fact, practically all of his learning depends upon his success in meeting these language situations. All of these, and many others, result in each child having both the urge and the need to use the skills of communication.

Language plays an important role, not only in learning, but in all aspects of the school program. Every activity of the school requires some form of reception and expression of facts, ideas, thoughts, and feelings. The preparation of almost every lesson in school requires first that facts and ideas be read and comprehended, and then that they be assimilated and used in expressional situations. When a child tells about a story he has read, makes a report on a unit of social studies, prepares his arithmetic paper, or meets in a committee to plan a project, he is using language. On the playground, language is necessary for giving directions, for explaining rules, and often for playing the game itself. It is difficult to think of any phase of the school program in which language does not play a vital part.

COMMUNICATION

Human beings live in closely-knit social groups, and it is natural for them to communicate with each other. Universally they talk, and almost invariably they utilize some form of recorded or written expression. The Congo tribes, the Ecuadorian Indians, the residents of Los Angeles, Brooklyn, London, Moscow, Cairo, Hong Kong, or Tokyo all talk, all communicate by means of language. The language forms used depend entirely upon the culture-area in which the individuals are located. While human beings are almost certainly not the only living creatures capable of communication, man by his use of auditory and visual symbols—speech and writing—has greatly extended the range of his powers of communication. Language in the full sense of the term is much more than the production of sounds and symbols, to be heard by the ear or seen by the eye. It involves the use of the higher mental processes; it involves thinking. The richness of the development of our language forms, as compared with the level of communication between animals, is the result of the thought processes involved. Man has associated ideas, thoughts, and actions with symbols that can be written or spoken. The wide variety of these associations account for the extent to which man's language enables him to communicate his thoughts, ideas, and feelings to others. *Communication, then, is the first function of language.*

Communication has been described as the art of making one person's ideas the property of two or more.[2] This statement clearly indicates the power that language exerts in the thinking, creating, sharing aspects of man's activities. As soon as primitive men began to live together, first in families, and then in tribes, there was a need for some means of making their intentions and desires clear to one another. Warnings of danger had to be given and sources of food reported; orders had to be given for group protection from enemies. Probably the earliest language originated through the use of natural signs—cries, gestures, and facial expressions which at first were made spontaneously in response to natural situations to indicate needs, emotions, feelings. From these early and often accidental beginnings, meanings were refined for the signs and sounds. Vocal utterances, substituted gradually for manual signs, were found to be more effective, especially in combat and in the dark. Gradually man recognized the need for the creation of graphic symbols (writing) to represent the natural signs. Down through the ages language has been developed and refined until a rather intricate but reasonably effective means of communication has evolved. This process of development and evolution of our language is still going on and will doubtless continue to do so as long as man's small segment of the universe survives.

Communication involves at least two persons, one to present the idea or thought by means of speaking or writing, and one to receive the idea or thought by means of reading or listening. The effectiveness with which the actual communication takes place depends entirely upon the knowledge of the language and its skillful use by both of the individuals involved. The individual who has a good command of language and its use for communication will be able to express his ideas and convey the desired meaning to someone else. Likewise, if the reader or listener has an adequate command of language, he will be able to comprehend the intended meaning speedily and correctly.

The teacher of language faces the very difficult task of creating in the

[2] From an abstract of a speech by Dora V. Smith, Professor of Education, University of Minnesota, given at the Forty-first Annual Conference on School Administration and Supervision, State University of Iowa, and reported in Epsilon Bulletin, Phi Delta Kappa, Volume 32, 1957.

classroom the types of conditions that make communication easy and natural. In some way he must encourage the very shy child who fears to express himself or fears that he has nothing of interest to say and who therefore will not talk. He must also control the opposite type of child who feels that he must talk constantly even though he has little to say. Activities capable of stimulating both the shy and bold child to find his own field of interest and to express himself must be provided. In the following statement the authors have found an excellent summary of the communicational function of language as well as a source of helpful hints to the teacher in securing the right atmosphere for effective communication.

The function of language is communication of things of value between persons appreciative of the values, but possessing them at different levels of control. This statement places no premium on the manner of the communication. It may be in words, in signs, in symbols, or in actions. The important feature is the fact that someone has had an experience that he has enjoyed, and after thinking about it wishes to share it with somone else. He feels, moreover, that having personally had the experience, he knows more about it than his listeners would be expected to know, and is thus qualified to speak on the subject. At the outset, the proper speaker-audience atmosphere is established.

To the classroom teacher such an approach suggests that activities designed to stimulate expression must be varied in nature and offer different types of appeals to different children. From these activities each child must be able to find some special interest in which he feels that he can become better informed than any of his fellows. This gives him personal status and enables him to speak with an element of authority. Nothing is more destructive to a speaker's ease and effectiveness than the discovery that his topic was not very important in the first place, that his audience considers it uninteresting, and that they know as much about the topic as he does.

The practical implication here should lead the classroom teacher of language to provide multiple activities to be experienced by small groups of children. In this way a curious if not highly interested audience would be assured for each speaker. Perhaps some shy child may find that he does have something to say that both he and his audience are interested in discussing, and that he can tell his audience many things about his topic that they do not know. Older teachers will readily recall the deadly oral-reading class of former times in which each child reading from the same books watched the page of his book with eagle eyes (but not much comprehension) hoping to catch the "reader" in an error so that he could take over. What a stupid waste of audience motivation!

THE VEHICLE OF THOUGHT

The second major function of language is its use *as the vehicle of thought.* Psychologists have long recognized the important role that language plays in our thinking processes. Thinking involves the mental manipulation of symbols which represent certain meanings. The symbols are of two kinds: mental images and language symbols. Here, again, the development of a fairly complicated primitive society contributed to the early growth and development of language. Language of the type needed for purposes of communication was essentially the same language required to stimulate or permit thinking or reasoning to take place. It was probably not too difficult for primitive man to learn to think in terms of mental images as he planned to go into the jungle to hunt an animal for food. But the process of living with others of his kind brought the need for rules, generalizations, laws, customs—the development of social mores. Such abstractions as truth, honesty, love, honor, courage were not easily expressed or comprehended by means of mental images. As man evolved, his society became more and more complex and new concepts and experiences required the creation of new and more elaborate language symbols to represent them in his mind. These symbols have become the tools by which the individual forms an opinion or draws a conclusion; they are the means by which new meanings and new principles are constructed in his mind. This process of manipulating ideas is thinking and requires the association of the symbolic forms of language with the various meanings the racial culture has given them.

TRANSMISSION OF CULTURE

The third or preservative function of language is equal in importance to its other two functions as the tool of communication and the vehicle of thought. This function of language is clearly identified in the last two sentences in the quotation from Laird's *"The Miracle of Language"* on page 23. In the legends and folktales passed by word of mouth from one generation to the next we have learned what little we know about the primitive culture patterns of certain races, but these sources are not dependable. Tellers of folktales were usually imaginative individuals inclined to color their stories differently with each repetition. Written lan-

29

guage was necessary in order to keep the records straight. Doubtless Laird is right in his statement that "civilization could not exist until there was written language, because without written language no generation could bequeath to succeeding generations anything but its simpler feelings. Culture could not be widespread until there was printed language."

Many of man's ideas, bright or dull; his thought, brilliant or biased; his deeds, heroic or cowardly; his mistakes, stupid or profitable are accessible to us today as a result of the literature he has left us. This trail has been left principally by language, although art and music, also forms of expression, have made their contributions. *Through recorded language man has shared the accumulation of human experience and conveyed it to posterity.* It would be difficult to imagine what it would be like to live without being able to profit from the experiences and contributions of our ancestors recorded in history and in literature. Without language we would be isolated; we would not be able to share the thoughts and ideas of others living during the same period as ourselves. We would know nothing of history, nothing of the marvelous literature of our own and other cultures. The preservation of the record of man's thoughts and deeds is vitally necessary to education and to the future development of man and society.

MODERN CONCEPTS OF LANGUAGE

The three social functions of language discussed above make it very clear that a reasonable mastery of the language skills is of prime importance to our educational thinking and planning. It enables us to think clearly and logically, to communicate these thoughts to others, and to preserve them for the use and guidance of future generations. Language is not a separate subject in the school curriculum to be studied for content only, or for cultural or disciplinary purposes. It is a tool that is needed constantly in every walk of life. It is an absolute necessity in the conduct of our business and social affairs, the preservation of our ideas and ideals, and the expansion and growth of social responsibilities in the future. Moreover, in view of the recognized importance of language and cultural barriers in world affairs it may well be necessary to world survival.

LANGUAGE IS A SKILL SUBJECT

Like arithmetic and other subjects, the skills in language form an extremely important body of knowledge which each individual must master in order to meet all types of school and life situations. Language should be thought of as a tool, the mastery of which frees the mind of the user from any fears that what he desires to communicate may not be understood, or that because the communication is not free from error those to whom it is directed will doubt the competency of the speaker or writer.

LANGUAGE SKILLS ARE LEARNED

Learning to express oneself correctly is a personal and individual matter that cannot be left to incidental teaching. The pupil must learn that mastery comes only through his understanding of his own needs and his own honest efforts to improve through the exercise of the skills. The teacher should recognize that expressional skills are learned, not instinctive; that they are the results of specific habits produced by practice under proper motivation, not the products of general training.

LANGUAGE LACKS ITS OWN SUBJECT MATTER

For many teachers the teaching of language is complicated by the presence of a great many specific skills and the absence of language subject matter as such. Most other curricular fields have subject-matter content. The science class may study the weather and learn about recording weather conditions, the relationship of weather and climate, the causes of changes in the weather, or the importance and accuracy of weather forecasts. These are the subject matter of the science class. The social studies class may study the people, geography, and history of Canada. Again, these are the content of the course. On the other hand, language by its very nature as a skill area is obliged to use as subject matter the child's activities in his other school subjects, his home and community enterprises as the means of exercising and fixing his language skills. There is a large body of skill material in language, but the content material must come from other sources.

LANGUAGE USAGE IS A MATTER OF HABIT

Correct language habits are acquired by practicing the use of acceptable forms rather than by discussing them or memorizing rules and generalizations supposedly governing their use. Such practice provides pupils with extensive experience in responding correctly to language situations and ultimately sets up a sensitive mental attitude toward language. If

31

a pupil does not recognize language errors when he hears or sees them, he is not likely to correct his own errors. Conscience, the "still, small voice" that guides us in moral situations, may be developed into an important factor in determining rightness or wrongness in language usage. A background of good language habits gives the individual an attitude toward error in language and this attitude may provide a protection against the recurrence of careless language usage.

EARLY ENVIRONMENT AFFECTS LANGUAGE HABITS

The early environment of the child is of great importance in establishing his language habits. The young child learns most of his language through imitation of the speech he hears constantly. For many a child the models he is obliged to imitate leave much to be desired either in the usages they favor or in their own attitudes toward good language usage. The child's parents, other adults whom he respects, or his closest pal may ridicule his efforts to use correct language to the point that he himself goes on the defensive with such a comment as "What's wrong with 'he don't'? My dad says it and he gets along OK!"

DETERMINING THE LANGUAGE CURRICULUM

In a world of almost instant communication, the importance of language is increasingly being recognized. The ideas men have about language and its importance and its learning are basic in the determination of what is taught in the language programs of the schools. This section gives consideration to the issues faced in the establishment of a philosophical basis for the curriculum.

THE NATURE OF THE CURRICULUM

Traditionally the school curriculum in a general sense comprises those elements of the cultural and social experiences of the race that are thought to be of sufficient importance to preserve and to pass on for the guidance and improvement of succeeding generations. Through the years these experiences have become organized into the special subjects taught in the school. We have tended to think of the curriculum in terms of the "three R's" and many times have mistakenly considered them to be something constant and unchanging. Obviously, the curriculum is not static; it is much broader than the "three R's," broader than any subject-matter content to be learned. Only when the content becomes absorbed as a part of the experience of the learner does it become important in the curriculum. As one writer has expressed it, "The curriculum exists only in the experience of the children; it does not exist in textbooks, in the course of study, or in the plans and intentions of teachers . . . In order to evaluate the curriculum of a school, it is necessary to observe carefully the quality of living that goes on in it." [3] Clearly it is the living experience with it that makes subject-matter content real and important to the child.

This broadened concept of the curriculum makes it desirable to clarify the meanings of the terms *curriculum* and *course of study*. It has been suggested that the course of study bears approximately the same relation to the curriculum as the carefully marked road map does to the tourist's experiences on a cross-country trip. The map itself is important mainly to the extent that it marks a route that leads to enjoyable and profitable experiences.

If we accept the modern view that *the curriculum of the school is composed of all the experiences and activities in which children participate under the direction of the school,* it follows that the language curriculum comprises all of the situations in which individuals communicate —that is, listen, speak, write, or read. In addition to the regularly scheduled activities in the language class, it includes all sorts of activities that take place outside of the language classroom, such as: greeting and entertaining parents and other guests, giving reports in the social studies class, listening to directions on the playground, writing a note of thanks for a birthday present, or reading instructions for doing arithmetic problems. In short, the language curriculum includes every type of communicative activity in which pupils engage.[4] The language course of study can then be thought of as the guide for the teaching and learning of the language skills, as well as the related attitudes and understandings necessary to these situations.

[3] William B. Ragan, *Modern Elementary Curriculum.* New York: The Dryden Press, Inc., 1953, p. 4.
[4] *Language Arts for Today's Children,* The Curriculum Commission of the National Council of Teachers of English. New York: Appleton-Century-Crofts, Inc., 1954, p. 320.

HOW SUBJECT MATTER IS CHOSEN

In the early types of schools from which our present system of free public education has evolved, discipline, both mental and physical, appears to have been the primary function of the school. According to the theological teaching of the period the child could be brought to anything like human status only under the most rigid types of discipline. The school with its cheerless atmosphere, its stern master, its birch rod, its knuckle-rapping, and its dunce cap resembled a prison more than any other social institution of the time. Learning was largely pure memorization motivated by fear of punishment. Furthermore, *what* was learned was not so important as the *discipline* that accompanied the learning.

Subject matter was chosen primarily for its difficulty, not for its utility. Actually the chief concession to utility in the curriculum of early days was the emphasis on reading in order that the child might receive proper religious training from the Bible. Later writing, spelling, church catechisms, prayers, and hymns were added. Little attention, however, was paid to the utility content of these subjects except in the cases of those contributing to religious training. Writing was formal, slow, decorative. Legibility and speed in writing, being utilitarian functions, were regarded as secondary. Spelling dealt with large numbers of words of extreme difficulty but of little or no utility in the written expression of the day. In arithmetic the problems were selected for their contributions to mental discipline, not to their usefulness in daily life. As our system of public education developed, new subjects were added. Latin, foreign languages, mathematics, and science among others were taught and defended because of their disciplinary values. All were quite difficult to learn and were, therefore, good training material for mental discipline. This was in complete conformity with the theories of learning of the period.

In the schools of not so long ago, children learned in arithmetic class to compute the volume and weight of the amount of timothy hay that could be stored in a barn loft of given size; in geography they learned the names of the major cities along the Tigris and Euphrates rivers; in history they learned the names of the Pharaohs of Egypt; in English class they learned numerous rules governing usages thought to be important; they learned how to diagram sentences. Fortunately times have changed somewhat, and we are no longer greatly concerned about the weight of a cubic foot of timothy hay. We find there is little demand for us to compute volume; it can be read from a table so much more easily. We

34

have reason to suspect that the rules of English grammar are of little or no benefit in our oral and written expression. We are becoming convinced that while any moderately intelligent individual can in due time learn to diagram sentences, he might much better spend that time in writing well-constructed, varied, interesting sentences, if that is what we really want him to learn to do. Not so long ago we were concerned with teaching the child in our language class when to use "shall" and when to use "will." We kept him struggling with "can I go" and "may I go"; "it is I," "it is me." Now we spend little or no time in teaching these subtle and generally useless differences in usage. Current usage by the man on the street and contemporary writers and speakers recognizes no difference in the use of these words.[5,6]

Subject matter changes with the times. As long as a language is alive, as long as a culture is evolving, fashions in correct usage will change as do the fashions in dress. Members of an earlier generation commonly used *et* as the past form of the verb *to eat*. In that period it was considered correct usage, but today we would take a second look at the individual who used it in his conversation. As old forms become obsolete, new forms and usages appear. Certainly we do not wish to follow every language fad, but our teaching must keep reasonably in step with the times. In our own age, the advent of atomic energy, jet planes, "wonder drugs," and television has brought about the need for new vocabulary, new concepts, and new attitudes, not to mention occasion for new worries. A comparison of *Webster's Third New International Dictionary, Unabridged* with its edition twenty-seven years earlier will reveal a surprisingly long list of changes in language in the period involved. Perhaps the editors of the new edition are less conservative than those of the earlier one, but an unabridged dictionary generally does not drop usages until their uselessness has been established, nor add new words and concepts until their social values are demonstrated by extensive usage. This is doubtless as it should be. It operates as a governor to control the speed with which our language changes take place.

[5] Sterling A. Leonard, *Current English Usage,* English Monograph No. 1, National Council of Teachers of English. Chicago: National Council of Teachers of English, 1932, p. 497.
[6] Albert H. Marckwardt and Fred G. Wolcott, *Facts About Current English Usage,* English Monograph No. 7, National Council of Teachers of English. New York: Appleton-Century-Crofts, Inc., 1938, pp. 77, 83.

ADJUSTING SUBJECT MATTER TO
SOCIAL NEEDS

Wise and thoughtful men from the time of Confucius in the fifth century B.C. down through Herbert Spencer in the nineteenth and John Dewey in the twentieth century A.D. quite properly have criticized the schools for their failure to prepare the individual adequately to meet the problems of life. Yet it is only in relatively recent years that steps have been taken to remove some of the major causes of these criticisms by eliminating large sections of certain disciplinary and useless material from the curriculum and replacing them with functional subjects.

It is inevitable that the curriculum should be somewhat out of adjustment with the environment that it is supposed to reflect in the activities and experiences provided by the school. Since these elements of life about us must be experienced before their importance for future generations can be evaluated, they are likely to be from two to ten years behind the environment in which the young learner finds himself. Actually this lack of adjustment of curricular content to life outside the school is brought about in two ways. The first is the failure of the curriculum to keep up with the changing demands of society and to anticipate these needs. The second is the result of a type of educational inertia (conservatism) that insists on retaining in the curriculum much that is obsolete.[7]

The over-crowded condition of our schools and the resulting shortage of adequately trained teachers has meant that much of the teaching has taken place from textbooks rather than from more flexible courses of study. This also undoubtedly contributes to the lack of adjustment of the curriculum to current social needs. Even if the authors of textbooks were able to include only subject matter of current social importance, the content of the books is likely to be out of adjustment with the social needs by the time they are printed and put into the hands of pupils and teachers. Then too, the producers of textbooks may be guilty of lagging somewhat behind current social demand and practices. This may result from their own conservative point of view or from a somewhat natural desire to stay in line with the types of textbooks that teachers seem to prefer. Too often teachers are inclined to teach *as* they were taught and *what* they were taught. Add to all this the fact that frequently textbooks,

[7] See J. Galen Saylor and William M. Alexander, *Curriculum Planning: For Better Teaching and Learning,* New York: Rinehart and Company, Inc., 1954, chapter 3, for a discussion of this problem.

once adopted, are retained in use in the system long after their prime of life is over, and it is not difficult to see why the classroom at times appears to be so badly out of step with life.

The problem of determining which of the current social needs are sufficiently important to justify inclusion in the curriculum is a difficult one to solve. For example, when Sir Winston Churchill was chided by his editors for ending a sentence with a preposition, this able statesman replied: "This is the sort of pedantic nonsense up with which I will not put!" Shall we, then, continue to teach our pupils this rule to which he objected? This is only one of the many similar problems that the curriculum builder must answer. Determining whether to retain or eliminate the teaching of a skill becomes a difficult problem to solve by objective methods. Too often it becomes a matter of opinion, and frequently a matter of *whose* opinion is involved. Certainly a teacher should consider the needs of his own particular students. Furthermore, he will find it profitable to study the published reports of such groups as the National Council of Teachers of English and the National Conference of Research in Elementary English for the best up-to-the-minute thought on these issues.

THE IMPORTANCE OF THE LANGUAGE CURRICULUM

Our schools are fundamentally language schools, but it is difficult to determine objectively the values held for language instruction by an examination of school programs. One index of society's estimate of the importance of a subject should be indicated by the amount of instructional time and emphasis allotted to the subject in the school program. Unfortunately, it appears that no nation-wide surveys of time allotments to elementary school subjects have been made since the study by Mann in 1928.[8] Results from a number of state studies of time allotments have indicated a trend toward the reduction in the number of minutes per week devoted to instruction in the "three R's." [9] The constant pressure of special subjects for inclusion in the curriculum in the period since the study by Mann would readily account for this trend.

Important recent data adapted from a comprehensive study in a single state are summarized in the table on the next page in an attempt to indi-

[8] C. H. Mann, *How Schools Use Their Time*. Teachers College Contributions to Education, No. 333. New York: Columbia University, 1928.

[9] Virgil E. Herrick, *Handwriting in Wisconsin*. Madison: School of Education, University of Wisconsin, 1951, p. 17.

cate something of the current emphasis given to language arts in the elementary school. This table shows for grades one to six the percentage of time allotted to each of the specified subject-activities in a school week of 1,650 minutes. Naturally, reading demands a heavy share of the school week in grades one, two, and three. Only in grades five and six does the time allotted to social studies exceed that given to reading. In no grade does the time allotted specifically to language instruction equal that given to either reading or to social studies. Only when the time allotted

Average Percentage, in One State, of Time Per Subject in Grades 1 to 6 [10]
(Based on 1,650 minute week)

Subject	Grade					
	1	2	3	4	5	6
Reading	33.3%	27.2%	21.3%	15.8%	13.4%	12.2%
Recess	9.1	9.1	7.6	6.1	6.1	6.1
Social Studies	6.1	6.1	9.1	13.7	16.7	18.2
Physical Education	4.9	4.9	5.4	5.4	5.4	5.4
Language	6.1	6.1	6.1	7.6	7.6	8.5
Arithmetic	5.2	7.5	9.1	10.6	12.2	11.6
Music	4.9	4.6	4.9	4.9	4.9	4.9
Handwriting	4.2	4.6	4.2	3.6	2.4	2.4
Literature	4.2	4.2	4.2	4.6	4.2	3.6
Science-Health	3.6	4.9	4.6	5.4	6.1	6.1
Spelling	3.0	4.6	4.6	4.6	4.2	4.2
Individual Aid	3.6	3.6	3.6	3.6	3.0	3.0
Starting Period	4.6	3.6	3.6	2.7	2.4	2.4
Active Period	3.6	3.6	2.7	2.7	2.7	2.7
Art	3.6	3.0	4.2	4.2	4.2	4.2
Library		2.4	3.0	2.7	2.7	2.7
Student Council			1.8	1.8	1.8	1.8

to handwriting and spelling is combined with oral and written expression does language appear to receive a proper instructional emphasis so far as time allotments reveal it. In grade three, the beginning of the systematic program of instruction in language, the combined percentages of time allotted per week to all expressional language activity is 19.1 per cent. The proportion remains practically at that level throughout grades four, five, and six.

[10] Adapted from table of time allotments in *Resource Ideas for Planning Classroom Programs.* Bulletin prepared by committee under chairmanship of Arthur C. Anderson, State Department of Public Instruction. Published by the State of Iowa, Des Moines, 1955.

Another indication of time and instructional emphasis on the language arts is given in a sample fourth-grade schedule for a city in Illinois. Two periods are given to language arts in this fourth grade, a twenty-minute period in the forenoon and a forty-five-minute period in the afternoon. According to the accompanying table of time allotments, this total of 315 minutes, including oral and written expression, handwriting, and spelling, represents 19.8% of the school week of 1,590 minutes.

The results of these comparisons lead to the conclusion that the Iowa and the Illinois data when treated for comparability are in rather close agreement as to the amount of instructional time given to the language

Fourth-grade Time Allotments in a City System [11]

Subject	Time in minutes	Percent
Reading [a]	300	18.8
Language Arts [b]	315	19.8
Arithmetic	250	15.7
Social Studies	230	14.5
Science	90	5.7
Phy. Ed.–Health	150	9.4
Art	90	5.7
Music	90	5.7
Recess	75	4.7
Total	1,590	100.0

[a] Includes library.
[b] Includes oral and written expression, handwriting, and spelling.

arts. They also indicate that, on the average, time allotments to the expressive language arts run a close second to the time set aside for reading in the elementary school. This unmistakably places the expressive language arts high in the list of socially and educationally important elementary school subjects.

CONFLICTING IDEAS OF LANGUAGE AND ITS FUNCTION

For years language was considered a static, unchanging subject. Many teachers have been taught to believe that there is only one correct lan-

[11] Adapted from table in *School Briefs*. Chicago: Scott Foresman and Company, May, 1956.

guage, and that this "correct" language if mastered will equip the individual to use language as he needs it in any situation. Fortunately this view is passing. Most of us are aware of the changing aspects of language. We recognize that there is no strictly correct language. We recognize that an acceptable usage in one situation is not necessarily suitable in another. It is probable that each of us (even the staid college professor) has several types of language that he uses: one for the classroom lecture on his pet subject; one for the golf course; one for the social gathering at his club; one for starting the car on a cold wintry morning. The average person, for example, may not say "It is I," or "For whom are you looking?" on the street or in his home, but he might be sensitive enough to do so in a formal social gathering or in an important professional conference. The level of language that is used depends upon the situation. Slang and colloquial expressions which are quite acceptable in daily conversational exchanges, or in friendly letters, may be completely out of place in a formal speech or in a letter of application for an important position.[12]

The typical elementary school classroom of forty years ago was not only formal, cold, and rigid, but also a silent one in which children were obliged to be seen but were not encouraged to be heard, except when asked to recite memorized facts. There was little or no freedom for children to use language naturally. Language lessons were mechanical and formal with most of the activities written rather than oral. Such written work kept the children busy, and when they were busy, they were quiet. Since it was assumed that the children already knew how to talk when they came to school, oral language activities were not necessary. The purpose of language lessons in this period was to establish a pattern of "correct" language usage—a pattern which while actually correct was often extremely stilted and artificial. Perhaps in this is the true source of the antagonistic attitude toward approved language usage that exists in the minds of many persons today. The psychology of learning upon which this method of teaching was based optimistically held that there would be an effective transfer of the principles and practices of correct usage from the stilted, artificial, and formal language situations to activities in real life in which good language habits were important and necessary.

Fortunately, this point of view has undergone a rather complete change. Today we recognize the social importance of language. We

[12] See Robert C. Pooley, *Teaching English Usage,* New York: Appleton-Century-Crofts, Inc., 1946, chapter 3, for a discussion of "correct" language.

realize that language is the basis for practically all social activity. We believe that a classroom must be free enough to encourage children to act and talk naturally, yet sufficiently controlled that all may be able to listen and to think freely. We know that the best language development comes when there is extensive opportunity for thinking, experiencing, and talking both at home and at school. This social emphasis implies that the language program is more than a few short isolated language lessons. If children are to learn to use acceptable language habitually, they must be given every opportunity for practice in using both written and oral expression in meaningful, lifelike situations.

OBJECTIVES AS DETERMINING SUBJECT MATTER

Teachers of language traditionally have shown a tendency to stress written expression and to neglect the oral skills. The importance of oral language in communication was recognized, no doubt, but apparently it was assumed that instruction in written language skills transferred directly to oral language situations. Modern principles of learning, supplemented by a large amount of evidence from research, now convince us that this was a mistaken assumption. Just as mistaken was the assumption that good language habits would transfer from stilted, unreal, formal situations to those lifelike activities in which the child or the adult would be expected to use good language.

If we accept the idea that communication is the primary objective of the language program, and if it is true that learning to express oneself is an individual accomplishment acquired by personally practicing expressional skills, then it would seem that the effective way to teach language would be to provide many types of real and lifelike situations in the school, in which the child would find it necessary and advantageous to learn to listen, to read, to write, and to speak in accordance with the accepted standards of the time.

THE SOCIAL UTILITY PRINCIPLE

The modern school is faced with the almost hopeless task of trying to teach something of everything to everybody. The rapid increase in our school population, combined with the general acceptance of the belief that secondary education and higher education as well as elementary training are the privilege of all, have created a most difficult series of

41

problems. Our educational resources are being taxed to the point that we now know the schools cannot teach everything to everybody. We must, therefore, select what we teach.

The selection of the elements of the curriculum that are most worth teaching has become an increasingly vital educational problem as we have moved past the middle of the present century. It is rather discouraging to note, however, that it has taken the schools almost a century to accept and put into operation the social principles underlying the curriculum first stated by Herbert Spencer.[13] Gradually schools have been forced to meet the challenge of their critics that the training offered did not prepare the individual to meet life situations in a practical way. More recently the growing pains of bulging classrooms and the need for economy of teacher time and effort have compelled schools to eliminate much dead timber from the over-loaded curriculum. Educational leaders of the present generation and the one just past have aroused an active interest in the application of the social approach to a revitalized curriculum. Skills, knowledge, attitudes, and experiences seeking entrance into the curriculum are challenged by the question: Will their mastery better equip the individual to meet the needs of his adult life and enable him to become a worthy member of society? During this period many elements that were firmly imbedded in the curriculum have been rooted out by the same challenge. Actually the point of view that the skills taught in the school must be those of greatest social need, is not confined to language alone but plays an important part in all modern educational thinking.

The acceptance of the belief that the function of the school is the provision of experiences which enable the individual to adjust himself effectively both as a child and as an adult, practically forces the adoption of the social utility principle in the construction of the language curriculum. According to this view, decisions regarding what should be taught in the area of language must be based upon an analysis of the skills, abilities, and experiences that people encounter and use in life situations. Numerous such analyses have been made, resulting in statements of outcomes and catalogs of skills in language which are much more specific and objective than any made in previous times. For example, the modern spelling vocabulary is composed of a relatively limited number of words of high utility in the writing of children and adults. The instructional emphasis on handwriting is now on the develop-

---

[13] Herbert Spencer, *Education: Intellectual, Moral, and Physical.* New York: D. Appleton and Company, 1860.

ment of reasonable speed with high legibility. In arithmetic rarely used skills are eliminated in favor of problems known to be of high utility in life. While the language program unfortunately has not given up formal procedures readily, encouraging signs are noted. Recognition of the social utility principle is revealed in the marked shift in emphasis in language instruction from written to oral skills. Letter writing, as a form of written expression high in social importance, is receiving the instructional emphasis it deserves. The use of formal drills and rules governing the usages and the mechanical skills of expression are all given their proper places in establishing habits of good usage. The language program today is making every effort to place the instructional emphasis on the skills and usages that carry the social burden of expression. Frequency of use of language skills in normal social situations affords one objective index of their importance. The more often a usage appears, the greater its social utility, and the more important it becomes as an element in the language curriculum. Frequency alone, however, is not enough. Many usages with relatively low frequencies still deserve places in the curriculum, not because they are frequently needed, but because when they are used the need for them is crucial.

The evaluation of the social utility of a language skill, ability, activity, or experience is based on the principle that *whatever is taught must fill an important need in life* both inside and outside the school. Importance is defined in terms of the answers to these four questions:

1. How frequently is this skill or ability needed and used in the life activities of children and adults?
2. How crucial or vital is this skill or activity when the need for it arises?
3. How universally is the skill encountered in all types of life activities?
4. Does the skill show evidence of meeting a permanent need? [14]

No elaborate statistical study is required to convince even the skeptic that the ability to carry on an intelligent conversation with ease is constantly needed by most persons in day-to-day activities. The ability to converse is also a universal need in all cultures and localities; there is reason to believe that it is as permanent as civilization. On the other hand, many of us as adults may not need to give an oral report on a unit of science or social studies material, or prepare a detailed topical outline. Yet in the school activities of the child these skills may be extremely

[14] L. Thomas Hopkins, "Needs and Interests: A Sufficient Basis for the Elementary School Curriculum," *View Points on Educational Issues and Problems*, Annual Schoolmen's Week Proceedings. University of Pennsylvania Bulletin, Vol. 39:104–111; 1952.

crucial as well as frequent. Almost everyone is obliged constantly to write notes and friendly letters, but the need to write a letter of condolence or an answer to a formal invitation may be rare for most of us. The low frequency of the need does not make it any less important for us to be able to meet each of these situations correctly. When the need to write a business letter arises, the need is usually great and often crucial, as in the case of a letter of application for employment. An error in form or a mistake in spelling might mean that the application would be discarded. These examples illustrate the way in which the criterion of social utility may be applied in selecting or eliminating content in the language curriculum.

The importance of skills which otherwise meet the primary criteria of frequency, cruciality, universality, and permanence may be affected by the secondary criteria of suitability and difficulty as expressed in these two questions:

1. Is the skill sufficiently worthwhile for learning?
2. Is the skill of suitable difficulty for learning at this level?

The relation of high social frequency of a skill to its difficulty of learning seems to be in reverse order. That is, the skills that are frequently needed in life situations are usually quite easy to learn. It is not at all clear, however, whether they are easy to learn *because* they are commonly used, or are widely used because they are so easy to learn. The difficulty of making use of a skill might be enough to exclude it from instruction, but in most cases it merely means that instructional emphasis on it is postponed until later in the maturity and experience of the learner. Lack of suitability of a skill of reasonably high social frequency, such as the use of slang or profanity, would naturally justify its exclusion from the curriculum.

FACTORS AFFECTING THE SOCIAL POINT OF VIEW

There are certain limitations to the social utility principle as the main philosophical basis for the determination of the language curriculum; there are factors affecting the principle that apply limitations. These factors and the limitations are discussed in this section.

ADULT AND CHILD NEEDS

Any survey of the language skills and abilities needed in life situations must take into account the fact that there may be needs that are peculiar to adult situations but are not among the language needs of the child. They may, for example, represent cultural needs of adults in particular social settings. Most adults have certain positions in society that they feel they must maintain. Frequently these positions call for particular levels of language usage considered by their colleagues to reflect this social position. Even though their frequency of use may be relatively minor, certain of these cultural language habits and abilities must be included in the more advanced levels of the language curriculum. Their importance or cruciality to the persons involved is great, and in our volatile democratic society we cannot be certain which children in the classroom will in time encounter this need.

Children, on the other hand, frequently need skills and abilities in a particular language situation that may occur very rarely in adult life. Almost invariably these needs arise out of a school-stimulated activity. The fact that they occur as a child need makes them important, and, to the child or the children involved, particularly crucial. Children in school take part in plays, entertainments, and other activities that seldom are found in the activities of the average adult. Children make oral and written reports on special school activities. They need to understand and be able to spell the vocabularies of various subject-matter areas. Such activities are of great value in the school curriculum, but the particular skills involved are associated far more with the child's in-school needs than with his life as an adult. The language program must take into account these child needs, whether they arise out of a local school situation or out of particular and immediate needs created by out-of-school activity.

LIMITATIONS OF THE SOCIAL UTILITY APPROACH

In spite of the great contributions of social utility to the development of a functional language curriculum, there is a danger that its too-rigid application might result in a lowering of the general plane of language usage. Extensive studies indicate that the typical adult does not have an adequate notion of what constitutes acceptable English usage. Ac-

45

cordingly, then, a cross-section of the normal usage of adults might result in a serious lowering of usage standards.

While it is certain that the English language must be in a continuous state of adjustment to meet the demands of social usage, it is also true that there must be certain leavening forces at work to prevent the too-rapid decline of these usages below the level of social acceptability. It is here that the school, the functional grammar of a living language, the dictionaries, the handbooks, and the style manuals of publishing houses exert their influence for the improvement of language usage.[15,16,17]

The practical application of the social utility principle encounters other serious obstacles. Language is universal; it enters into practically every life activity in which we engage. Even the most comprehensive analysis of language usage must of necessity be based on only a limited sampling of the usages in all of life's activities. The samples that have been taken thus far have naturally been those that are easiest to obtain. For example, the frequencies of the words used correctly and in error in friendly letters and notes are relatively easy to obtain by working from copy in which the context has been destroyed. Samples showing context are almost impossible to secure, especially in the important areas of confidential social and business correspondence. Moreover, the samples of letters included in most of these vocabulary studies have been secured from persons who have had some reason to save letters. It is possible that these letters are not truly representative of the countless letters that are written.

Any attempt to record the oral language activities of children or adults assumes a certain artificiality, especially if the persons involved know that their language is being recorded. In most such studies the activities are school-stimulated; this fact takes them out of the desired lifelike setting. Attempts to record oral language activities without the knowledge of the speakers introduce many complicated problems. All of these factors made it extremely difficult to obtain samples of oral language for analysis.

[15] Harry A. Greene, *A Criterion for the Course of Study in the Mechanics of Written Composition*. Studies in Education, Vol. VIII, No. 4. Iowa City: State University of Iowa, 1933.

[16] Robert A. Hall, Jr., *Leave Your Language Alone!* Ithaca, N.Y.: Linguistica, 1950.

[17] Robert C. Pooley, *A Handbook of Current English Usage*. Bulletin, No. 3, Series XXX; Greeley, Colo.: Colorado State Teachers College, June, 1930.

LIMITATIONS TO OBJECTIFYING THE LANGUAGE CURRICULUM

Application of the social utility principle is faced by many practical limitations in precisely and objectively determining language uses and needs. If oral interviews are arranged, the language is likely to be artificial and stilted. If people find that what they are saying is being recorded or transmitted, the entire pattern of their vocabulary and usage is likely to change. Recordings made without the individual's knowledge involve great difficulty and expensive equipment. In general, such studies are institutional projects and are not usually undertaken by the individual research worker. In spite of these difficulties, however, numerous attempts have been made to objectify the oral language course of study by determining the types of oral language situations adults and children face in ordinary life activities and what oral language usage is necessary in these situations.[18,19]

Attempts to record the conversations of adults in normal situations have met with some success, but large groups have been omitted from any such analyses because of the casualness of their language activities, and the mechanical difficulties of voice pick-up. More success has been achieved in recording the discussions of children. Hundreds of thousands of running words of oral language activity of elementary school children have been recorded and analyzed as the basis for curricular material.

Interviews and questionnaires have been widely used in determining the frequency and types of oral language situations which adults and children meet in life. Individuals in various occupational groups are asked to list or describe oral language situations in which they have been involved. While this method may have some validity, the results often reflect opinion and wishful thinking rather than fact. Other attempts have involved the actual observation of the activities. This method proves to be rather satisfactory with children, especially while they are in the classroom, but the results must be discounted because of the classroom stimulation involved. With adults it has not proved to be a practicable method.

Efforts to objectify the written language curriculum have been more successful. These attempts have been of two main types. The first type

[18] Emmett A. Betts, *An Evaluation of Certain Techniques for the Study of Oral Composition*. Studies in Education, Vol. 9, No. 2. Iowa City: State University of Iowa, 1934.

[19] T. K. Goltry, "An Analysis of Sentence Structure in Oral Composition." Unpublished doctoral dissertation, State University of Iowa, 1935.

of investigation has endeavored to determine the written language needs of persons engaged in various occupations.[20,21] These data generally have been secured by asking the individuals interviewed to list the written activities they actually engage in over a specified period of time. From such data have been determined helpful lists of language activities which occur most frequently, and to some extent the activities which are considered most crucial. One special merit of this procedure is the fact that the individuals interviewed reported the actual activities they engaged in, not those they thought they might use in such a situation.

The second type of investigation of written language needs has centered around studies of errors made by many different individuals in their written language activities.[22,23] Hundreds of thousands of running words of the writing of school children at different grade levels, in widely scattered geographical areas, and on systematically controlled topics have been analyzed. These tabulations of usages and mechanical skills have resulted in important information concerning the skills and abilities that occur most frequently, that seem to present the greatest difficulty in written expression, and that by their nature seem most crucial.

GRADE PLACEMENT OF LANGUAGE SKILLS

FACTORS IN GRADE PLACEMENT

The grade placement of the specific oral and written skills included for instruction in the elementary school language program is dependent to a large degree upon the general principles which accounted for their appearance in the curriculum in the first place: frequency, cruciality, difficulty, and suitability. Despite the lack of objectivity in certain of these principles, it is believed that they can be effectively applied to grade placement in the language field.

[20] Charles S. Pendleton, *The Social Objectives of School English*. Nashville, Tenn.: George Peabody College for Teachers, 1924.

[21] J. W. Searson, "Research in Constructing the Elementary School Curriculum," Third Yearbook of the Department of Superintendence. Washington: Department of Superintendence of the National Education Association, 1925, pp. 285–286.

[22] Ruth Aaro, "Types of Errors Found in Business Letters," *National Business Education Quarterly*, 14:23–28; May, 1946.

[23] James W. Evans, "The Social Importance and the Pupil Control of Certain Punctuation Variants." Unpublished doctoral dissertation, State University of Iowa, 1929.

48

The social criterion of the *frequency* of use of the skills in life situations both in school and outside of the school by children and adults affords a reasonably objective approach to grade placement. The determination of *cruciality,* on the other hand, is almost entirely a matter of subjective judgment. The *readiness* of the pupil at a given age or grade to learn the skills and to use them in his expressional activities is based almost entirely on inferences from other objective data on the mental and physical maturity of the child. Certain psychological principles as well as the opinions of experienced teachers lead to the belief that there is a best order or *sequence* for the presentation of language abilities in certain areas, so that skills acquired later may strengthen rather than interfere with previous learnings. The practical limitations of time in the classroom and pages in the textbook combine to provide reasonably objective answers to the question of the *number* of skills which should be presented for learning at any one age or grade level. Direct evidence appears to be almost entirely lacking on the problem of the real learning *difficulty* of language skills. At present the best guide is in the form of objective but relatively crude data on the persistence of errors in certain usages. It should be noted that persistence of error may very well be due to factors other than the innate difficulty of the particular skills.

PRINCIPLES FOR USE IN GRADE PLACEMENT

The following principles are suggested for consideration in the grade placement of activities and skills comprising the elementary language program: [24]

1. *The frequency and cruciality of the specific skills in the language activities of adults.*   This factor gives immediate and proper recognition to the school's responsibility to prepare the individual to respond effectively to the most important language situations he will encounter as an adult. Other things being equal, the more frequently these skills are needed by the adult in life situations, the more immediately they should appear in the language program for instruction. Similarly, skills with social importance, even though low in frequency, should be taught early in the program.

2. *The frequency and cruciality of the specific skills in the important language activities of children both in and out of school.*   Consideration

[24] Harry A. Greene, "Principles of Method in Elementary English Composition." Elementary English Review, 14:219–226; October, 1937.

of this principle protects the curriculum worker from the criticism that school-stimulated activities are not adequately recognized in the language program.

3. *The readiness of the pupils to make use of the specific language skills at different age and grade levels.* The mental and the physical maturity of the individual child combine to determine his readiness to learn. The importance of pre-school and kindergarten training in developing pupil readiness for learning in specific fields is generally recognized. This principle suggests that when the child reaches the point in his development at which he undertakes to use a particular skill, he is probably ready to learn it, and that is the proper time to teach it.

4. *The relation of the skills to each other in terms of facilitation and interference in learning.* There is considerable evidence that there is an optimum sequence for the presentation of certain language abilities, so that the skills acquired later may strengthen rather than interfere with previous learning. A careful consideration of the steps in learning in certain areas, coupled with a consensus of the opinions of experienced teachers of language, is the best guide here.

5. *The number of different skills which it is psychologically sound and administratively practicable to present to the pupil for learning at any age or grade level.* Experience has shown that when a limited number of closely related skills are studied, they are learned more readily and retained longer than when widely varied learning situations are involved. Common sense indicates that complete mastery of a few skills is to be preferred to partial mastery of many. Psychologically the child can absorb only a certain amount in a given learning period. Practically, the pages of the textbooks and the numerous demands on the time of the teacher allow only so much space and time for the language program.

6. *The learning difficulty of the specific skills selected for instruction.* In general, the easier language skills to learn are the ones with the higher frequencies of usage. Logically, the easier skills are the ones presented earliest in the language program, both because they are easy to master and thus encourage the learner, and because they generally have high social usage frequencies. Unfortunately, objective evidence is almost completely lacking on the innate learning difficulty of most language skills. The best that is now available is a limited amount of relatively crude data on persistence of errors in certain usages. While direct evi-

dence on the learning difficulties of many skill areas is lacking, helpful inferences can be made from the indirect evidence.

Attempts by different individuals to apply these principles in the actual grade placement of content and skills in the language course of study would almost certainly result in wide disagreement at many points. The subjective nature of many of the principles would make such disagreements unavoidable. Even in the case of principles with reasonable foundations of objective evidence, there would be inescapable differences in the interpretation and in the weighing of the facts. In spite of these weaknesses and limitations, however, it seems desirable to present these principles for what they are worth and to suggest their critical use in the checking of the grade placement of instructional material in current textbooks and other curricular sources. The teacher or the supervisor may find them useful in his own preparation of instruction units, or better still, he may find them sufficiently provocative to stimulate him to more concise and objective statements as guides in the grade placement of language experiences, activities, and skills.

RELATIVE SOCIAL IMPORTANCE OF ORAL AND WRITTEN LANGUAGE

Early man had no need to write and had no special need for records. He needed principally to communicate with those in his immediate environment. As time passed, however, he began to feel the need to communicate with those more distant, both in time and space. He needed to send messages in more tangible form than mere words. Later he found it desirable to leave a record of his thoughts and actions for the guidance of others of his race. From these needs written language as we know it developed. Now the daily use of oral and written language is so commonplace that we rarely give a thought to the relative social utility of either form of language expression.

Obviously, oral language is used much more extensively in the activities of daily life than is written language. All of us converse daily, discuss plans and events, give and take directions, tell about experiences and ideas, and report progress and results in some personal enterprise. There may be many days when some of us do not write a single word, but virtually everyone does some talking every day. For most of us, oral language is the indispensable tool of expression.

Because of difficulties of administration and the unreliability of estimates of observers, not many dependable investigations have been made
of the proportion of time adults spend in each form of language expression. However, such studies as have been reported indicate that approximately 95 per cent of all communication is oral.[25]

SCHOOL EMPHASIS ON ORAL AND
WRITTEN EXPRESSION

Traditionally the school has emphasized written language. In classrooms
of an earlier day, children were not expected to speak except when called
upon to recite, to read, or to report. About all the oral language that
was used was for formal recitations. Free conversation in the classroom
was unheard of and was generally feared by teachers because of the
disciplinary problems involved. The quiet classroom was considered the
good classroom. The school learning activities of the day were carried on
almost entirely by writing. In complete disregard of the actual life needs
for language, classroom emphasis was almost entirely upon written language. In far too many classrooms today this is still the common practice.

Happily, however, this heavy emphasis upon written language in
elementary school classrooms is gradually declining. Today's schools
make a special effort to provide extensive oral language activities. Free
conversation periods are encouraged. New textbooks in language, by
their emphasis on oral language skills, have led many conservative
teachers to change their own emphasis in the language classroom. We
are coming to recognize that in school, as in life outside the school,
we communicate through oral means.

REASONS FOR CONTINUED HEAVY EMPHASIS
ON WRITTEN EXPRESSION

In spite of the adjustments that have been made in our schools to give
proper recognition to oral language needs, it is still true that the relative
emphasis upon written and oral expression is misplaced. Some of the
reasons for this emphasis are discussed below.

[25] R. L. Lyman, *Summary of Investigations Relating to Grammar, Language and
Composition,* Supplementary Educational Monographs, Number 36. Chicago: The
University of Chicago, January, 1929.

52

Pre-school mastery of oral language. The fact that the child normally enters school with ability to use many of the important oral language skills for purposes of communication is perhaps one reason why teachers turn their classroom emphasis as soon as possible to the written skills. They seem to have mistakenly assumed that the child has acquired an adequate mastery of oral expression and that no further instructional or maintenance program is required. This assumption, of course, is not supported by the facts in the case.

Disciplinary dangers in oral activities. A good language class is not necessarily a quiet, well-disciplined class. The process of acquiring oral language skills is likely to be an active and noisy one, but active and noisy classes are not necessarily badly disciplined. Nor do most of the disciplinary problems arise in the language class. Many physically-subdued classes produce their share of disciplinary cases. Language teachers must learn to discriminate between the lack of classroom control and the noisy hum of children at work learning to use a vital group of skills.

Training of teachers. The fact that many of our schools still emphasize written expression to an extent out of proportion to its importance in life may be due in part to the type of training received by our language teachers. Most teachers teach as they were taught in their own elementary school training and in their methods courses. Since they were taught language largely as written expression, they naturally assume that is the way to teach it. Our programs for the education of elementary teachers too often slight the teaching of elementary language in favor of reading, science, social studies, or arithmetic. This is not to say that the methods courses in science, social studies, arithmetic, and other areas are not of great importance. But teachers in training learn far too little about how to teach functional language expression. According to a report on the training of elementary teachers in an educationally prominent mid-western state, "only two of the nine colleges list a specific course in methods in the teaching of language; in these colleges it is a required course and carries four credits. It is presumed that in the remaining seven colleges, methods in language are combined with methods in other subject areas." [26] The authors are prompted to add parenthetically the words: or are not included at all.

[26] Robert C. Pooley and Robert D. Williams, *The Teaching of English in Wisconsin.* Madison: University of Wisconsin Press, 1948.

53

Course of study and textbook emphasis. While a comparison of courses of study and textbooks of recent date with those of the previous generation may show a considerable increase in the emphasis on oral language, there is still much room for improvement. Actually many texts published within the past ten years would require extensive instructional readjustment to provide the desirable balance. For many teachers the textbook *is* the course of study; they cannot be blamed for following the instructional pattern of the book. Moreover, it is doubtful if many teachers would be qualified to undertake the adjustments necessary to give the proper oral and written language emphasis, even if they were convinced that it was necessary.

Seatwork or busy work. A teacher with a class of thirty-five or forty active youngsters has many demands on his time and attention. It is such a constant problem keeping all the young minds and hands busy and learning that the harried teacher may be forgiven for turning to seatwork or busy work, rather than to well-designed practice material, for temporary relief. Seatwork may be defined as mechanical activities which a child may do independently at his seat. These activities usually do not call for oral expression; in fact, they may even suppress it. The primary purpose of such material is to keep the child occupied and quiet while the teacher gains time to work actively with others in the class. The activity may have some relationship to language expression, usually in written form, but too often it is primarily busy work of a type that does not present much of a new challenge to the learner. Seatwork involving written work too often calls for much repetitious activity that may not represent an important learning experience for the child. The teacher should never forget that each child is an individual, and that each one faces particular language needs. Unfortunately seatwork is almost invariably the same for all children participating in it and hence does little toward caring for individual differences.

Assumed transfer of written skills to oral. There are still many teachers who believe that skill in written expression transfers to oral activities and that competence in oral expression is gained economically through this transfer. Faith in this view is shown by the following statement from a recently adopted course of study: "Precision in the use of words and clarity in the composition of sentences are also learned best through the trainings associated with written communication." [27] While

[27] *Communication: A Guide to the Teaching of Speaking and Writing.* Minneapolis: Minneapolis Public Schools, 1953, p. 8.

it is true that skill in the use of words and the writing of well-constructed sentences may be expected to result from written activities, the assumption that these written-language skills transfer in a significant degree to oral situations is decidedly open to question. The results of research indicate that the opposite may be equally true. Habits of speech—good usage, sentence construction, and organization—do transfer to written language activities.

CURRENT PRACTICES

In a study published in 1948, Pooley and Williams reported that "in both city and rural schools teachers tended to dominate the classroom more than they should, despite the many opportunities that oral English instruction provides for permitting pupils to plan, direct, and evaluate their own lessons. Panel groups, round tables, club meetings, dramatizations, and prepared programs—to cite a few of the devices that have been used with great success—were only very infrequently observed. Teachers dominated completely 83 percent of the oral English lessons in rural schools and 62 percent of those in city lessons." [28] They further reported that 24 per cent of the language lessons in the rural schools and 38 per cent of those in city schools were oral lessons. This finding clearly shows an unrealistic emphasis upon written language, a tendency made more serious by the unwarranted teacher-domination of oral language lessons.

Situations similar to the above would almost certainly be found in most sections of the country today. It must be admitted that time allotment studies may not show a true picture of language activities, since language expression appears in some form in practically all classes throughout the school day. Much of this language activity, however, is in the form of an exercise in which the child raises his hand if he wishes to respond to the teacher's question, is called upon, and recites. This procedure undoubtedly has its values, but certainly it should not be considered as time spent in promoting the development of the skill of oral expression.

Suggested instructional emphasis. The following statement appears as a principle in the teacher's manual of a recent language textbook series: "The affairs of daily living demand oral expression largely. Therefore, the language program in all grades should give major em-

---

[28] Pooley and Williams, *op. cit.,* p. 68.

phasis to the improvement of oral expression." [29] This appears to be the established point of view of textbook writers and curriculum workers today. The question is not whether oral language should be emphasized, but rather how much the instructional emphasis should be increased. Courses of study as well as language textbooks are not in agreement on this point. For example, one teacher's guide states quite definitely that "oral language should be utilized in all situations; it should not be entirely relegated to any one period of the day; however, certain periods should be set aside for a definite attack upon specific language skills." [30] Certainly language is used throughout the day and most of this language is oral, but much of the oral expression can have little instructional meaning unless definite time is allotted for this purpose. One course of study recommends "that written language occupy not more than 10 percent of the work in the lower grades, 35 to 40 percent in the intermediate grades, and up to 70 percent in the upper grades. The exact amount for each grade-level must necessarily be affected by individual pupil or class conditions." [31] This seems to be a realistic approach and one that will call for definite instructional emphasis upon oral language and not assume that children are learning oral language skills simply because they are speaking.

INTERRELATIONSHIPS OF
LANGUAGE SKILLS

The language curriculum in the elementary school generally consists of segments of speaking, writing, and listening selected from the total body of skills often called the Language Arts. The other principal language art is reading, most often taught as a separate subject. At the high-school level the language arts tend to be combined into what is commonly called English. At the elementary-school level it is not unusual, too, for particular facets of writing—spelling and handwriting—to be taught somewhat separate from the remainder of the language program. Regardless of how language may be broken down for instructional purposes,

[29] Mildred A. Dawson, *Language for Daily Use.* Teacher's Manual for Grade Five. Yonkers-on-Hudson: World Book Company, 1951, p. 3.

[30] *Trends in Elementary Education,* A Teacher's Guide. San Diego: San Diego County Schools, 1945, p. 54.

[31] Artley, A. Sterl, and others, *Interrelationships Among the Language Arts.* Champaign, Ill.: National Council of Teachers of English, 1954.

however, the resulting segments are all highly interrelated, and it is not possible to keep them from being integrated and merged. Even the most superficial consideration of language teaching leads to the conclusion that very rarely does any language skill function independently of the others.

The interrelationships among the language areas are many, varied, and in numerous ways highly intricate.[32] Generally speaking, however, much of the interrelationship is due to the presence of common elements in each area or facet, and to the fact that an experience affecting one will influence other facets. For the teaching of language skills such an interrelationship is of basic importance. A teacher who tries to teach a child to read without recognizing the importance of listening and speaking skills to success in reading will meet with frustration. A teacher who thoughtfuly recognizes the interrelationships of language skills may well discover that a reading problem really hinges upon a listening difficulty, or an immature speech pattern. Too, the teacher who is sensitive to interrelationships will not wait until confronted by a problem to note the commonness of elements, but will so direct lessons in all of the facets as to keep in mind the carry-over effects. For instance, a lesson in letter writing will give attention to the skills of spelling, handwriting, and sentence construction, and may call for the use of listening and reading skills.

LISTENING AND LANGUAGE

The infant's first contact with language is through listening; it is his sole contact for approximately the first year of his life, and it remains throughout his life a major factor in all of his activities. He comes to school with a learned pattern of speech based upon what he has heard, a pattern which is of basic importance in the school's efforts to instruct him in speaking, reading, and writing. For example, recognition that speech is learned through imitation—through listening—points up the need for hearing good speech and shows the futility of attempting to make substantial changes in speech habits by approaches other than listening. The skills in listening are also involved in instruction in the other aspects of language. Instruction in reading, speaking, and writing are often given by the teacher by speaking, and speaking and oral reading by the child call for the use of listening skills by his audience.

[32] Iowa Elementary Teachers Handbook, Vol. 4, *Oral and Written Language*. Des Moines: Iowa State Department of Public Instruction, 1944, p. 61.

57

Listening and reading are especially close in that they are both receptive aspects of language and that there appears to be a commonality in the particular skills involved.[33] However, in spite of the obvious similarity, the relationship between the skills in the two areas is not so high as might be expected.[34] There are perhaps greater intricacies of relationship present than surface appraisal would indicate.

READING AND LANGUAGE

The second of the receptive aspects of language is reading. This facet of language calls for the use of listening, writing, and speaking, both in its learning and in its teaching. A basic relationship is shown in that reading performance varies significantly with proficiency in speaking. Too, as stated above, reading skills and listening skills are positively correlated. Deficiency in reading skill is a limiting factor in the building of vocabulary and in the understanding of concepts upon which writing, as well as speaking, are so dependent. What is read is frequently the substance or the point of departure for writing; and any instruction in writing should be built upon the principles that what is written has been written for someone to read.

A particular aspect of writing that is closely associated with reading is spelling. Much learning of spelling takes place through reading, and attention to the form and sounds of words as they are learned in reading assists in the accurate spelling of these words when they are written.

SPEAKING AND LANGUAGE

The linguist would say that "speaking is language," but our intent here is to note further the relationships between this facet of the total language arts, or of "language" used as a general term, and the other facets. Speaking is a language skill that develops early in the child's life, preceded only by listening—the facet through which speech is learned; every act of speech is an act of listening for someone else. Every act

---

[33] Edward Pratt, "The Experimental Evaluation of a Program for the Improvement of Listening in the Elementary School." Unpublished doctoral dissertation, State University of Iowa, 1953.

[34] Harry Goldstein, *Reading and Listening Comprehension at Various Controlled Rates.* Contributions to Education, No. 821. New York: Columbia University, 1940. Gus P. Plessas, "Reading Abilities and Intelligence Factors of Children Having High and Low Auding Ability." Unpublished doctoral dissertation, University of California, 1957.

of speech is limited by the vocabulary the child has learned through listening and reading. Every product of writing is dependent upon the speech fluency and the knowledge of words and ideas of the writer. Again, the skills necessary to effective speaking are many of the same skills needed for effective reading, listening, and writing.

WRITING AND LANGUAGE

In the child's earliest school experiences he finds words to read: the names of objects in the room, his name on his desk and beside a coat hook, the names of other children. He early learns to write many of these words. Before long he is writing his own ideas—ideas which have come from reading and from listening. Writing and speaking, the expressive phases of language, are obviously interrelated. While writing tends to be more formal than speech, fluency in one direction affects the other. Particularly is this the case with fluency in writing; what a child writes, and the words he uses, are not likely to go beyond his facility in speaking.

EXERCISES FOR THOUGHT AND DISCUSSION

1. Evaluate the adequacy of the definitions of language given in this chapter.
2. Discuss the relative importance of the three social functions of language.
3. Distinguish between the terms *curriculum* and *course of study*.
4. When the social utility principle is applied, how is subject matter chosen? Illustrate this in a particular field, as spelling or writing.
5. What can be done to give adequate emphasis to the language arts subjects in proportion to the importance of the language arts curriculum?
6. What are the major limitations of the social utility principle in curriculum building?
7. What factors have seriously complicated the objectification of the language curriculum?
8. Discuss and evaluate the six principles for grade placement of language skills as presented in this chapter.
9. In the light of the relative social importance of oral and written expression, what needs to be done to bring about the proper balance of instruction in the average classroom?

10. Show how listening, reading, speaking, and writing are each closely interrelated with language as such.

SELECTED REFERENCES

Child Development and the Curriculum. Thirty-Eighth Yearbook of the National Society for the Study of Education, Part I. Chicago: The University of Chicago Press, 1939.

Commission on the English Curriculum, National Council of Teachers of English. *Language Arts for Today's Children*. New York: Appleton-Century-Crofts, Inc., 1954. Particularly Chapter 11.

Experience Curriculum in English. A Report of the Curriculum Commission of the National Council of Teachers of English, W. Wilbur Hatfield, chairman. New York: D. Appleton–Century Company, Inc., 1935.

FRIES, CHARLES C. *American English Grammar*. English Monograph No. 10, The National Council of Teachers of English. New York: D. Appleton–Century Company, Inc., 1940.

―――. *The Structure of English*. New York: Harcourt, Brace and Company, Inc., 1952.

GREENE, HARRY A. "Improving the Elementary English Curriculum," *Elementary English Review*, 12:74–77; March, 1935.

―――. "Principles of Method in Elementary English Composition." *Elementary English Review*, 14:219–226; October, 1937.

HERRICK, VIRGIL E., and TYLER, RALPH W., eds. *Toward Improved Curriculum Theory*. Supplementary Educational Monographs, No. 71. Chicago: The University of Chicago Press, 1950.

JESPERSOM, OTTO. *Language: Its Nature, Development, and Origins*. New York: Henry Holt and Company, 1922.

LAIRD, CHARLTON. *The Miracle of Language*. Cleveland: The World Publishing Company, 1953.

Language Arts in the Elementary School. Twentieth Yearbook of the Department of Elementary School Principals, Vol. XX, No. 6, July, 1941. Washington: National Education Association.

MC CARTHY, DOROTHEA A. "Language Development in Children," in *Manual of Child Psychology*, Leonard Carmichael, ed. New York: John Wiley and Sons, Inc., 1946, Chapter 10.

MC GEOCH, J. A. *The Psychology of Human Learning: An Introduction*. New York: Longmans, Green and Company, 1942.

MENCKEN, HENRY L. *The American Language.* New York: Alfred A. Knopf, 1936.

MILLER, G. A. *Language and Communication.* New York: McGraw-Hill Book Company, Inc., 1951.

PEI, MARIO. *The Story of Language.* Philadelphia: J. B. Lippincott Company, 1949.

PHENIX, PHILIP H. *Philosophy of Education.* New York: Henry Holt and Company, 1958, Chapter 23.

Psychology of Learning. Forty-first Yearbook of the National Society for the Study of Education, Part II. Bloomington, Ill.: Public School Publishing Company, 1941, Chapters 3, 5–7.

SCHLAUCH, MARGARET. *The Gift of Tongues.* New York: Viking Press, Inc., 1942.

SEEGERS, J. CONRAD. "Language in Relation to Experiences, Thinking, and Learning." *Teaching Language in the Elementary School.* The Forty-third Yearbook of the National Society for the Study of Education, Part II. Chicago: The University of Chicago Press, 1944. Chapter 3, pp. 36–51.

SMITH, DORA V. "Growth in Language Power as Related to Child Development." *Teaching Language in the Elementary School.* The Forty-third Yearbook of the National Society for the Study of Education, Part II. Chicago: The University of Chicago Press, 1944.

———. "Basic Considerations in Curriculum-making in the Language Arts." *English Journal,* 37:115–126; March, 1948.

———. "The English Curriculum in Perspective—the Elementary School," *Elementary English Review,* 23:45–55; February, 1946.

SPENCER, HERBERT. *Education: Intellectual, Moral and Physical.* New York: D. Appleton and Company, 1860.

STRATEMEYER, FLORENCE B., FORKNER, H. L., and MC KIM, M. G. *Developing a Curriculum for Modern Living.* New York: Teachers College, Columbia University, 1947.

part 2

Objectives of the

Language Program

THIS PART, COMPOSED OF FOUR CHAPTERS, SETS FORTH THE INSTRUCTIONAL objectives of the language program from the time of the child's first experiences with language in the home, through the informal beginnings of instruction in the primary grades, to the development of such mastery of the oral and written language skills as is possible in the elementary-school grades. The purpose in these chapters is to identify concisely the major instructional objectives of the elementary-school language program.

3

Informal Beginnings of the

Language Program

THE PRINCIPAL ISSUES INVOLVED IN THE PRE-THIRD-GRADE LANGUAGE
program are considered in this chapter with the emphasis centered on
the following:

a. Language as communication in the pre-school years.
b. Objectives of the language program in the kindergarten and primary
grades.
c. Oral language in the pre-third grades including dramatization and
creative expression.
d. Objectives of the written language program in the pre-third grades.

The elementary-school language program actually begins with the
informal expressional experiences the child encounters in the home,
the pre-school, and the primary grades. There are many opportunities
in the kindergarten and in the first and second grades for the informal
guidance of language development, but this guidance is best accomplished
when related to the objectives of the total language program. The program in both oral and written expression for these grades and its relationship to pre-school language development and that in the lower grades
are considered in detail in this chapter.

LANGUAGE IN THE PRE-SCHOOL YEARS

LEARNING TO COMMUNICATE

Language is such an important key to the child's mental life that it is
natural for emphasis on its mastery to begin for him almost as soon as
he is born. His first cries are simple instinctive responses to conditions
that are unsatisfactory to him but do not represent language as we ordinarily think of it. The infant soon learns, however, that his cries will

65

bring someone to discover and perhaps remove the causes of his un-happiness. This is one of the first steps in the difficult process of learning language. Soon his cries take on characteristics easily identifiable by those near him as indications of hunger, anger, pain, or other feelings. Communication is beginning, and his language habits will soon be estab-lished.

The child's natural impulse is to vocalize and to imitate those around him. Sooner or later, depending upon his maturity, he begins to make sounds similar to the words he hears others use. Although his first attempts produce little more than meaningless, unintelligible sounds, gradually they develop into words which name things or people in his own familiar world. By the time the normal child has reached the age of eleven months to a year, he may be using simple word-sounds with meaning. Usually the first words are repetitions of single syllable sounds, such as *ma-ma, da-da, bye-bye*. By the time he is two years of age he will have added a fund of simple name words, action words, and descrip-tive words which he is learning to string together into meaningful but often incomplete sentences. Before he reaches the age for kindergarten, the average child is able to speak in simple sentences, the complexity of which depends upon his mental maturity, language aptitude, and experiences.[1,2,3] Soon he is keeping up a constant stream of chatter, talk-ing to someone or to no one but himself, simply bursting with ideas he must express by means of these new skills that he has acquired and that demand to be exercised. All of this means, of course, that his lan-guage habits are gradually becoming established.

Since the child tends to imitate those about him, he naturally learns to speak the language and the kind of language he hears. His vocabulary, usage, and pronunciation are inevitably patterned after those of his parents or others in his immediate environment. When his mother uses "baby talk" in speaking to him, he is willing to adopt that style of speech, if that is what she wants. This does not imply, however, that in the family circle in which correct and precise English is always used, the child will learn immediately to pronounce words correctly and to

[1] Madorah E. Smith, *An Investigation of the Development of the Sentence and the Extent of Vocabulary in Young Children.* University of Iowa Studies in Child Welfare, Vol. 3, No. 5, 1926.

[2] Dorothea A. McCarthy, "Language Development in Children," in *Manual of Child Psychology,* 2nd ed., L. Carmichael, ed. New York: John Wiley and Sons, 1954.

[3] Mary K. Smith, "Measurement of the Size of General English Vocabulary through the Elementary Grades and High School," *Genetic Psychology Mono-graphs,* 24:311–345; 1941.

enunciate properly. Unfortunately children seem to pick up faulty language usages much more readily than they do the correct habits. No child immediately learns to say words exactly as he hears them said, whether they be "baby talk" or flawless English. His vocal mechanism must mature and become adjusted to making the required and meaningful sounds. This adjustment is a gradual process and varies with different children; but as the child grows, he learns to say the words he has heard, and to say them as he has heard them said. Thus the young child readily develops habits of good usage or bad, adopts the language of his close environment, whether it be English, Scandinavian, German, French, Spanish, or Italian.

FACTORS IN LANGUAGE READINESS

The family environment of the child plays an important part in the speed with which he develops language facility. For instance, an only child tends to have closer association with adults than does one who has brothers and sisters; it is probable, therefore, that he will develop a larger vocabulary and greater facility in expressing himself.[4] Similarly, the child whose parents talk to him a great deal develops facility earlier, while one who has spent his pre-school years in an orphanage may tend to be retarded in language development. Slowest to develop are twins, who associate so closely with each other that they have a minimum of contact with others.[5]

It should be obvious that in order to acquire an extensive vocabulary and new ideas about which to think and talk, the child of pre-school age needs to be given many rich experiences. The child who plays alone or only with other children in his own home has a limited number of opportunities to gain new ideas and concepts. If, however, he goes to the park, visits the zoo, takes vacation trips, travels extensively with his parents, or even accompanies his mother on a shopping expedition, he acquires a wealth of new sights and sounds, and the words that relate to them. The child whose parents read good books to him gains experiences available in no other way. Learning to communicate is an accomplishment that is markedly affected by the child's environmental status. The environment in which the child is reared before coming to school is de-

[4] Edith A. Davis, "The Development of Linguistic Skills in Twins, Singletons with Siblings, and Only Children from Ages Five to Ten Years." Unpublished doctoral dissertation, University of Minnesota, 1937.

[5] E. Day, "Development of Language in Twins: Comparison of Twins and Single Children," *Child Development,* 3:179–199; September, 1932.

pendent to a large degree upon the social and economic status of his parents. Numerous studies have shown that there is a positive correlation between the socio-economic status of parents and the linguistic progress of children.[6,7,8,9] This suggests for the language program of the school the desirability of giving primary children an environment rich in experiences and activities.

Not all language habits are the results of environmental factors, however. Children vary in the speed and ease with which they learn and develop language skills. Some children learn to talk at an early age and make more rapid progress in all language skills. Other children may be late in learning to talk even though they may show considerable evidence of language understanding. A child who is late in starting to talk may listen carefully and absorb a great deal of language meaning before he actually begins to talk. Children of this type may later become as competent in language as some of those who started talking at an earlier age. There are some children, however, who never become adept in the handling of the language and who are thus handicapped in their social development all their lives.

There are several reasons why some children may have inadequate language readiness. Mental immaturity may be partially responsible for the inadequacy. Certainly there is a maturation in language development as there is in other mental and physical qualities. A child simply may not have developed to the point of fully understanding the meanings of words and how they are put together into sentences. This does not mean, necessarily, that he will never achieve an understanding of words and sentences. He may remain slow in learning throughout his school experience, but his language development may respond rapidly to the stimulation of good language experiences in the primary grades.

Girls generally are ahead of boys in most phases of pre-school lan-

[6] John E. Anderson, "Child Development and the Growth Process," in *Child Development and the Curriculum*, Thirty-eighth Yearbook of the National Society for the Study of Education, Part I. Bloomington, Ill.: Public School Publishing Company, 1939, p. 33.

[7] John J. DeBoer, "Some Sociological Factors in Language Development," *Elementary English Review*, 29:482–492; December, 1952.

[8] Mahmoud Roushdi Khater, "The Influence of Social Class on the Language Patterns of Kindergarten Children." Unpublished doctoral dissertation, Department of Education, The University of Chicago, 1951.

[9] Fred Rosenthal, "Some Relations Between Sociometric Position and Language Structure of Young Children." Unpublished doctoral dissertation, University of California, 1956.

guage development.[10] This fact would seem to be the result of two factors.[11] First, girls mature physically at an earlier age than boys, and thus are ahead of boys in most aspects of their growth. Second, society expects certain interests and actions from girls and others from boys. Girls spend more time, both before starting school and later, talking to their mothers, "listening in" while their mothers talk with neighbors and guests, and looking at books and listening to stories. Naturally girls are exposed to more and probably better language experiences than are boys. Boys are expected to spend most of their waking time out of doors in physical activity at home or on the playground. They associate with other boys and men who are not always too much concerned about the quality of their language habits.

Children who have experienced the most desirable environmental conditions for language development prior to entering school will have acquired habits that pay rich dividends in later life. The generally downward social pressures of much of television, most comic books, the playground, and even the school may tarnish some of their language usage. But if, in the first three or four years of their lives, they have heard good language and have formed habits for its use, the school language program has an excellent chance of overcoming social pressures which tend to lower the language standards.

THE LANGUAGE PROGRAM OF THE KINDERGARTEN AND PRIMARY GRADES

LANGUAGE OBJECTIVES OF THE PRE-THIRD GRADES

Language experiences take place throughout every day a child is in school. These experiences occur in some form of reception or expression of language in practically every other subject-matter area. This is reason enough for the language program to be considered the core of the entire school curriculum, rather than a separate subject to be encountered only

[10] Mildred C. Templin, *Certain Language Skills in Children: Their Development and Interrelationships.* Institute of Child Welfare Monographs Series, No. 26. Minneapolis: University of Minnesota Press, 1957.

[11] Dorothea A. McCarthy, "Some Possible Explanations of Sex Differences in Language Development and Disorders," *Journal of Psychology,* 35:155–160; September, 1953.

during an altogether too-brief period of the school day. While the allotment of a specific period of the school day to systematic language instruction is necessary for effective teaching of specific language skills, the need for the development of efficiency in communication is so important that some phase of it engages the major portion of the child's school program during the primary years. Laying the foundations of readiness for later systematic training in the language arts is the primary responsibility of the kindergarten teacher. Helping children develop interest, readiness and beginning skill in reading, writing, speaking, and listening becomes the principal task of the first and second-grade teachers.

Children enter school, either in the kindergarten or the first grade, with widely different backgrounds of capacity, maturity, readiness, and experience. Not only do they differ from each other, but the same child may reveal surprising differences in readiness and interest in different fields of activity. He may love color and form and be skillful with his hands in art class but show no interest in learning to read or to write. He may be relatively mature in his understanding vocabulary, yet immature in making certain speech sounds. He may early have developed skill in telling a story and in holding an audience, yet be careless in his language usage. The primary grade language program must recognize these individual differences at the outset and meet them with experiences specifically planned to develop such skills as the child will need to adjust himself properly in his present and later life activities.

The preparation of a statement of desired outcomes would seem to be a logical and obvious step in planning a program of language instruction at any level. Since this early and informal experience with the mastery of the skills of communication is so important in the entire school and social life of the child, the teacher of the primary grades must have a clear understanding of the desired aims and objectives. To have a workable program, the teacher must have a firsthand knowledge of the kinds of language activities in which children and adults normally engage. He must identify the many different types of demands which the school makes on the child for the use of language skills. From these demands he must select the ones encountered most often by the adult in his activities. These activities are real, and the classroom experiences provided for the child must be just as realistic. The functional language program must be built "as close as possible to the reality of extra-school and post-school life, without deception and pretense . . ." [12] Five important

[12] *An Experience Curriculum in English.* A Report of the Curriculum Commis-

general objectives of the language program in the pre-third grade years are summarized here.

Spontaneity of expression. At the top of the list of objectives in the teaching of language to young children is the development of fluency and naturalness in expression. The desire to express himself is instinctive in the child, but quite often his willingness to do so must be encouraged by giving him many satisfying experiences with these activities. No matter how many ideas he may have or how much language skill he may possess, there must be a desire to impart these ideas to others. One of the most important elements in the development of fluency and spontaneity in expression is an abundance of experiences that will provide the child with plenty to talk about. Fluency comes from having had many interesting and personal experiences. Some pupils will come to school with a rich background of experience, but most of them will need the stimulation of an understanding teacher in addition to many satisfying school experiences to help develop the desired spontaneity.

Socialization. A second major objective is the socialization of the child. Each child, upon entering school, is in every sense of the word an "individual." Many of these children will not be interested in listening to others, in taking turns talking, or in trying to learn to feel comfortable while talking to an audience. The pre-school child progresses through three distinct phases in his socialization through language: (1) egocentric speech, in which he talks to himself; (2) parallel speech, in which several children playing together talk at the same time, no one either giving or expecting response from another; (3) socialized speech, in which children speak and respond *to* one another.[13] It is the task of the kindergarten or primary teacher to guide pupils in learning to talk freely and easily, to listen courteously to others, and to acquire habits of using socially accepted phrases such as "thank you" and "excuse me." They must learn to share ideas, as well as materials, and to develop a sense of responsibility, both as individuals and as groups.

Enunciation and voice control. A third objective is the development of ability to enunciate words properly and to achieve voice control. Baby talk, lisping, stuttering, and incomplete enunciation are definite handicaps in mastering language usage. Moreover, if they are allowed to per-

---

sion of the National Council of Teachers of English, W. Wilbur Hatfield, chairman. New York: D. Appleton–Century Company, 1935, p. 134.

[13] Arthur T. Jersild, *Child Psychology.* Englewood Cliffs, N.J.: Prentice-Hall, Inc., 1954, pp. 412–415.

sist, they may well become sources of embarrassment and difficulty in conveying thoughts and ideas. Indistinctness or an unpleasingly high voice is likewise a major handicap in developing ability and fluency in language. It should be an objective of the early language program to work toward the development of an easy and a pleasant manner in speaking, good voice control both as to volume and tone, and an interest in accurate articulation and clear enunciation when speaking.

Correct usage. The establishment of acceptable habits of language usage is a fourth objective of the language program in the kindergarten and primary grades as well as one of major importance in later grades. Since many children will enter school with poor but firmly established habits of usage, it is extremely important that the teacher begin at once the task of eliminating errors insofar as is possible. This is by no means an easily accomplished feat. The child who has heard and imitated incorrect usage in the home for five or six years will continue to hear and probably to imitate the same incorrect forms. The teacher must furnish at all times a correct model and attempt to instill in the child the desire to use his language correctly as well as fluently. If the child can be made to recognize the social importance and the personal satisfaction to be gained from correct usage, the first major battle is won. Naturally, the teacher must not attempt to correct every error he hears, or the child may become overly self-conscious and grow fearful of expressing himself. Consequently, the number and kind of corrections must be gauged to the needs of the individual child, and an attitude of constructive helpfulness rather than constant criticism must be assumed by the teacher.

Organization of thought. A final and extremely important objective is the development of skill in the organization of ideas in expression. Organization is necessary to the effective presentation of ideas in the sentence and in the paragraph and in oral as well as written form. One of the early experiences of the kindergarten pupil is that of learning to arrange pictures in the correct order to tell a story. Later he will be able to use words in relating the events in a story or experience in sequential order. This will, of course, be brief and simple in the early grades and will gradually include more items and details as the child matures in his ability to arrange material into an organized pattern or plan, to eliminate extraneous information, and to relate new information to that already acquired.

GRADE-TO-GRADE OBJECTIVES

Since the language program in the primary grades is an informal one and since children enter school with such widely varying backgrounds of readiness and experience, it is almost impossible to assign specific language skills for mastery at a particular grade level. The net result is that kindergarten, first-, and second-grade teachers emphasize practically the same language skills, the chief difference being in the intensity of the emphasis. The objectives from grade to grade are very similar in nature. The language program in the first grade is an extension and refinement of the readiness program in the kindergarten with informal emphasis on a few simple skills. The second grade program is a further extension and refinement of that of the first. In fact, one survey of a large group of superior first- and second-grade teachers showed that if all the language skills they listed as taught in their grades were taught to the point of mastery, there would be little language left for teaching in grades three, four, five, and six.[14] The grade-to-grade objectives in language actually do not change appreciably; it is the increase in the instructional emphasis from grade to grade that makes the difference.

Growth in expressional power is a gradual and continuous process of development. Every primary teacher knows that some of the more able pupils in a given class may be far ahead of some pupils in the grade above who have been slower to develop their language skill. One case in point is the matter of correct usage. Overcoming speech errors is quite as often a matter of individual growth on the part of the child as it is a class problem. For this reason, and taking into consideration the fact that the language program at this level is extremely informal, it is difficult to list with assurance the specific items of incorrect usage that should be eliminated at the kindergarten, first-grade, or second-grade levels. It must be recognized that all children at any particular grade level should not be expected to achieve correct usage goals at the same rates. Normally, approximately one-fourth of the children in a grade group should master the specified skills rapidly and easily. A slower group of approximately one-fourth of the class will find considerable difficulty in attaining the goals, while the remaining half of the class will master the material after a normal period of instruction.

It is believed that as a result of the informal language program recom-

[14] Helen A. Brainard, "Identification of Pre-Third Grade Language Skills." Unpublished master's thesis, State University of Iowa, 1933.

73

mended in grades one and two, the child, by the end of the second grade, should be able to:

1. Talk freely and easily in discussion with others or before a group.
2. Use good enunciation and pronunciation, and a natural and pleasant speaking voice.
3. Listen attentively and courteously.
4. Use sentences in voicing his thoughts orally and to a more limited extent in writing.
5. Copy sentences from the board correctly.
6. Develop a simple sequence of ideas, both orally and in writing (at least a brief paragraph).

In addition to these abilities it is reasonable to expect that he will have:

7. Acquired a rich fund of ideas through experiences, books, pictures.
8. Developed his vocabulary by participating in activities and by listening to and reading stories.
9. Become sensitive to many social amenities, and learned to perform simple introductions.
10. Developed the desire and ability to write the following:
    a. short invitations and thank you notes,
    b. a short account or a story of a real or imaginary experience,
    c. an announcement and a short, friendly letter.

ORAL LANGUAGE IN THE
PRE-THIRD GRADES

ORAL LANGUAGE EMPHASIS

Since the child enters the kindergarten with virtually no skill in written language, it is obvious that the beginning language program will be devoted largely to further developing the oral language skills he brings to school. Little progress can be made in the written forms of language until he has acquired a rich vocabulary of words and meanings, and has developed considerable skills in oral expression as such. In addition to being the logical approach to informal instruction in language, this procedure gives proper recognition to the great social importance of oral expression as an integral part of the entire language program.

The oral language program in the primary grades includes story telling, oral reporting (including "show and tell" and "sharing"), dramatic

74

play, simple dramatizations, giving directions, telephoning, and similar activities.[15]

SPONTANEOUS ORAL EXPRESSION

Children come to school full of interest in their immediate experiences. They bubble over with things to tell. Conversing, "sharing," and discussing are a natural and integral part of the program in the kindergarten and primary grades. As the children converse about their experiences, engage in games, and discuss activities, projects, and excursions, unlimited opportunities are presented for accomplishing the objectives of the language program. While enjoying games on the playground, they may be learning to follow directions, to take turns, and to act cooperatively as a group. Even the lunch period offers opportunity for informal conversation in small groups. All these new activities and contacts of the children add to their background of experiences and ideas. With each new experience must come new meanings, new words to describe and explain it. Since the knowledge of words and word meanings is essential in both the expressive and receptive aspects of language, vocabulary building is vitally important to the early language program. Therefore, all activities of the group should be utilized to furnish both additional words and new meanings for words already familiar to the child.

As children work and play together, they learn to express their ideas in sentences, to listen while others talk, and to arrange their thoughts in order. Socialization comes as a result of many activities. Merely being a part of the group is the first step. Later, the children will learn also to perform simple introductions, use polite language, and act as hosts or hostesses to guests.

DRAMATIZING

One of the earliest types of dramatization is dramatic play, in which children assume roles and attempt to experience how it feels to be the

---

[15] The greatest share of language activities in the primary grades consists of informal conversation and discussion between teachers and children and among children themselves. Too often the value of this informal emphasis upon learning language is overlooked, or at least neglected, although it is probably a very important factor in forming good language habits.

75

father, the mother, the storekeeper, or the pilot. Spontaneity and creativity are the chief characteristics of this play. In a more formal sense children pantomime actions of a story told or read by the teacher, or they may create the actions and words of a story they know well. Using puppets for telling a story also calls for dramatizing and allows for spontaneity and creativity.

Dramatization is usually distinguished from dramatic play by the child's deliberate and planned assumption of a role. However, young children are interested in all forms of dramatizing and there is little need for making such distinctions. All dramatizing provides for the oral use of language, but the dramatization that calls for some planning gives opportunity for the teacher to focus instruction upon the program's objectives.

It should be emphasized, however, that the planned forms of dramatization, while they should be encouraged, should not be so formal that spontaneity and creativity are sacrificed. There is little need in the primary grades for dialogue to be memorized and recited by children. The important aspects of planned dramatization for oral language development are the socializing effects and the organizing of action and events into proper sequence. The children should be taught to have definite ideas as to the sequence of action and events, but the words should be spontaneous and original. This should be true even when such dramatization is part of a program planned for parents and other classes.

STORY TELLING

Story telling is done both by teacher and by pupils. The enrichment of the children's experience background and vocabulary is one of the major purposes of having the teacher read and tell stories. These objectives should always be paramount in the primary grades.[16]

The development of good taste in literature is a further objective that should not be overlooked. Furthermore, story telling gives the teacher an opportunity to serve as model for the children in speaking. The stories should be told with interest and enthusiasm. The teacher should choose, from a wide acquaintance with various types of children's stories, those that are suitable to the backgrounds and interests of the class.

After listening to a wide variety of stories and reproducing many of them in dramatic form, the children themselves will begin to tell stories

[16] The specific objectives of these language activities are discussed in greater detail in the following chapter.

they have read or heard. This activity helps to develop such desirable language skills as:

1. Recalling events in proper sequence.
2. Using descriptive words and phrases.
3. Speaking loudly and distinctly enough for all to hear.
4. Avoiding fragmentary and run-on sentences.
5. Using gestures to add interest and audience appeal.
6. Speaking easily and without self-consciousness.

CREATIVE EXPRESSION

Creative expression begins in the kindergarten with the telling of bits of personal history and experience, known to most teachers as "sharing." The skills listed above apply also to this type of activity. Creative expression, both oral and written, should be a vital part of the language program at all levels, for the greater part of the expression of the adult is spontaneous and original. This does not mean that planning is not involved. The child should learn early that he will speak more interestingly and coherently if he knows exactly what he is going to say before he starts talking. This does not mean memorization, but it does imply definite planning for *what* is to be said and *how* it is to be said.

Final steps in creative oral expression are the telling of original stories and poems. All expressional activities should at first be brief. A first poem may consist of only two lines. Obviously the children must become acquainted with the concepts of rhythm and rhyme before attempting to produce even a two-line jingle. If poems are carefully chosen and well presented, a child will react very favorably. As soon as he learns to talk in connected phrases, the pre-school child may be heard at his play repeating over and over in singsong fashion a phrase or a sentence which has appealed to him. Rhythmic games will help to develop still further the feeling for rhythm. The children may experiment with new rhymes to accompany a familiar tune or a favorite game.

CORRECTING ERRORS

The successful teacher is always watchful of pupils' oral errors in expression. The most important steps in overcoming these errors are: (1) to make clear to each child wherein his trouble lies; and (2) to help him to develop a desire to correct it. Many habitual errors in pronunciation and usage are the result of repeatedly hearing incorrect forms until the individual loses all sensitivity to the error. Peculiarities in speech and the misuse of certain words thrive unmolested until someone reveals the error to the user. Directing the child's attention to these errors may be done in several ways. First, the teacher should always set a good example and should strive to become an informal model for the class. Since children learn many of their language habits through unconscious imitation, teachers and supervisors should at all times furnish the best possible example. Second, the teacher should always correct errors unobtrusively and tactfully. Criticism should at all times be friendly and constructive. *Never do anything that will lead the child to become fearful of expressing himself.* Finally, children must be led to establish for themselves standards for speech and language usage. They will react strongly to the approval or disapproval of their associates. This furnishes the strongest motive for improvement in speech and usage—the desire to do well in order to merit the approval of teacher and classmates.

THE PRE-THIRD GRADE ORAL LANGUAGE PROGRAM

The chief responsibility of the kindergarten, first grade, and second grade teacher so far as the language program of the school is concerned is the development of attitudes of readiness toward the learning of language in preparation for the systematic emphasis on the subject which normally begins in the third grade.

The program of instruction in oral language in kindergarten, first grade, and second grade may be summarized as follows:

Kindergarten. In addition to creating a pleasant climate for the physical and mental maturation of the child, the kindergarten should stimulate his curiosity about language by providing interesting activities involving language skills in which he may have an active part. He listens to stories and poems. He gives information about himself. He reports news items which his teacher places on the board for the class to see. He helps dictate an invitation or a letter of thanks which the teacher copies for the class. In these ways he learns enough about the mystery of language to become interested and curious but not enough to satisfy his desire to learn more about it in the next grade.

The primary purpose of most of the language activity in the kindergarten is the rapid enrichment of the child's word and meaning vocabulary rather than the mastery of specific language skills.

First grade. In addition to carrying forward any skills begun informally in the kindergarten, the first-grade child should at least be taught to:

1. Express ideas clearly in short sentences.
2 Distinguish between telling and asking sentences.
3. Use the polite forms of *please, excuse me, thank you, good morning* and *good night*.
4. Say *yes, no,* and *what,* rather than *yep, yeh, uh-huh,* and *huh*.
5. Use *I have no* or *I haven't a* rather than *I haven't no*.

Second grade. In addition to the skills taught in the first grade, the second grade child should at least learn to:

1. Arrange sentences in proper sequence.
2. Pronounce *d, t,* and *g,* clearly as endings of words.
3. Avoid monotony of tone in reporting information in which there is no emotional stress.
4. Determine the two or three most important ideas involved, before relating a story.
5. Use the word *and* correctly in series.
6. Tell a story connectedly by selecting interesting beginning and ending sentences.
7. Use *haven't any, have not* (not *haven't got,* or *ain't got no*); use *them* and *those* correctly; use *went* and *gone* correctly.
8. Recommend a book orally, giving the author, title, and some point of interest.

WRITTEN LANGUAGE IN THE
PRE-THIRD GRADES

WRITTEN LANGUAGE EMPHASIS

Written language in the primary grades is a natural and gradual outgrowth of the oral language activities. In addition to facility in expression, a knowledge of vocabulary, an awareness of what constitutes a sentence, and many new concepts and meanings are necessary in written expression. Further, in order to communicate by writing, the child must learn to spell the words he wishes to use; he must acquire the physical skill necessary to do the writing itself.

The written language program in the primary grades is necessarily limited by the children's lack of mastery of the mechanics of spelling and handwriting. Kindergarten teachers correctly stress activities that aid in the development of the child's control of the larger muscular systems of the body. Many of the smaller muscles, such as are required in writing, develop slowly, and need time to mature. Kindergarten and first grade programs recognize the physiological immaturity of children of this age. Accordingly, only general manual activities are undertaken at this time. Pencils with large soft leads, and crayons are used mainly for the purpose of training the child in coordinating the movements of his hands and eyes. No writing, as such, should be expected of the kindergarten child, and relatively little should be required of the first grade child during the first half of the year. Ordinarily some formal spelling instruction begins in the second grade. This means that the writing vocabulary of most children in grade one, and for much of grade two, is quite limited. During these grades the teacher should be ready to encourage the child's attempts at written expression by helping him at all times with the spelling of the words he wishes to write.

Manuscript writing is now quite generally recommended as the form of writing to be taught to the first grade pupil.[17] The following reasons are advanced in support of this practice:

1. Print script, or manuscript writing, is easier than cursive writing for the beginner to learn. Only simple curves and straight lines are required in the formation of letters.
2. The normal six-year-old lacks the motor coordination necessary to do connected, or cursive writing. This motor control develops later.
3. The formation of letters in manuscript writing is similar to the form of letters and words encountered in reading.
4. Print script is typically more legible than cursive writing.
5. Primary pupils derive great satisfaction from their rapid progress in mastering manuscript writing.
6. The use of manuscript writing appears to contribute to achievement in reading and spelling.
7. Primary grade pupils using manuscript writing produce more and better written language products.[18]

The introduction of cursive writing may properly take place in the latter part of the second grade or in the beginning of the third grade. The transfer from manuscript to cursive writing form can usually be made very economically in a month to six weeks. The social utility of cursive writing is sufficient reason for its inclusion in the curriculum as soon as the children develop the necessary motor coordination to master it economically.

[17] Print Script. See Chapter 19 for samples of manuscript writing.
[18] See Selma Hill, "Comparison of Cursive and Manuscript Writing as it Affects Language Problems in the Primary Grades." Unpublished master's thesis, State University of Iowa, 1937; and reports by: Gates and Brown, *Journal of Educational Research,* Vol. 20, 1929; Turner, *Elementary School Journal,* Vol. 30, 1930; Arrington, *National Elementary Principal, 20th Yearbook,* Vol. 20, No. 6, 1941, pp. 469–472; and Frank N. Freeman, *What Research Says to the Teacher: Teaching Handwriting.* Washington: National Education Association, 1954, p. 26.

THE PRE-THIRD GRADE PROGRAM
IN WRITTEN LANGUAGE

Before written work is begun, the children have used oral language in and out of school for five or six years as a means of communication. They have built up a store of experiences and ideas. They have acquired the vocabulary, the control of the sentence, and the various other abilities and skills that make possible the oral expression of ideas for ordinary purposes. Directed instruction in oral work has made the children language conscious, has set up certain usage standards, and has made a good beginning in the establishment of proper language attitudes, abilities, skills, and habits.

General preparations for beginning written work are made very early in the first grade. The children observe the teacher as names, assignments of duties, records and notes are written on the blackboard. As soon as the children acquire a small, basic reading vocabulary, they begin to observe the written forms of words; they read sentences; they engage in cooperative class enterprises, such as making experience charts that are dictated to the teacher for writing on the board; and they are taught to notice sentences, capital letters, and periods.

The program of instruction in written language in the kindergarten, first, and second grade may be summarized as follows: [19,20]

Kindergarten. The kindergarten has met its responsibilities in the primary grade language program by providing pleasant and stimulating activities contributing to the child's mental and physical maturity. Because gaining control over his body and its larger muscles is much more important at this time than learning to write, no written work by the pupils is suggested. The children observe the teacher, however, as written records are placed on the blackboard and are thus made curious about writing and ready for the beginning of the written language program in grade one.

The teacher may later copy on the board sentences dictated by the children. Letters may also be written cooperatively by class dictation. Attention may be called to the use of capital letters with names and with the first words in sentences, as well as the use of the period at the end

[19] Helen A. Brainard, "Identification of Pre-third Grade Language Skills." Unpublished master's thesis, State University of Iowa, 1933.

[20] Hazel Sechler, "A Course of Study in Language for the Pre-third Grades." Unpublished master's thesis, State University of Iowa, 1936.

of the simple sentence stating a fact. Later in the year some of the more ambitious and able children may be encouraged to learn to print their own names.

First grade. During the first half of the year most written work in grade one should be done cooperatively, the children dictating as the teacher writes it on the board. In this the children are given an opportunity to learn about the content and form of written announcements, news items, stories, notes, and letters. The teacher should call attention to capital letters and periods in sentences. The form for the simple informal note should be presented and taught. In addition to carrying forward any skills begun informally in the kindergarten and thus far in the first grade, the child should now be able to copy form and content from the blackboard. By the end of the year the normal first-grade pupil should at least have learned to:

1. Write his full name correctly.
2. Write the date correctly after finding it on the calendar.
3. Copy words and simple sentences correctly.
4. Write one, two, or three short sentences about one thing, using good form.
5. Use capital letters and periods correctly with sentences.
6. Use periods correctly after numbers indicating words in a spelling list or questions in a reading or language exercise.
7. Write a simple announcement of a program to be given, telling time, place, and purpose.

Second grade. In addition to carrying forward the skills begun informally in the kindergarten and developed systematically in the first grade, the second grade now begins a rather extensive written language program. At the outset, the pupils should continue to do much of their written work cooperatively. Greatest emphasis should be on the writing of friendly notes, with some attention also to notices, announcements, labels, forms, and very short stories.

By the end of grade two, the child should at least have learned to:

1. Use manuscript writing to produce legible copy at reasonable speed.
2. Write the name of his school, using capital letters where required.
3. Write the name of his home city and state using abbreviation for state if permitted.
4. Fill in correctly a simple completion exercise or information form.
5. Capitalize correctly the names of persons, places, cities, which children use in writing.
6. Capitalize correctly the names of the days of the week and the months, and holidays.
7. Use correctly *Miss, Mr.* and *Mrs.*

8. Arrange his written work neatly; use good straight margins; and write in straight lines.
9. Place in correct form the following items of a simple note or friendly letter: salutation, first word of body, complimentary close, signature.

EXERCISES FOR THOUGHT AND DISCUSSION

1. Discuss the dangers of the mother using "baby talk" during the child's early formative years.
2. What are some of the major socio-economic factors which seem to affect the child's linguistic progress during the pre-school years?
3. List and evaluate a series of contributions made by the kindergarten to the language development of the child.
4. Discuss and evaluate the grade-to-grade objectives of the language program in the primary grades.
5. Suggest a number of ways and means of stimulating spontaneous oral expression in the primary grades.
6. What should be the teacher's attitude toward the correction of pupils' expressional errors?
7. What would you add to the lists of oral and written language skills given in this chapter for the pre-third grades?
8. Discuss methods by which kindergarten, first, and second grade teachers can best develop language readiness for the later more formal language program.

SELECTED REFERENCES

BROWN, DOROTHY L. and BUTTERFIELD, MARGUERITE. *The Teaching of Language in the Primary Grades.* New York: The Macmillan Company, 1941.

Bureau of Elementary Education, Department of Education. *Teachers Guide to Education in Early Childhood.* Sacramento: California State Department of Education, 1956.

CARROLL, JOHN B. "Language Development." *Encyclopedia of Educational Research,* third edition, Chester W. Harris, ed. New York: The Macmillan Company, 1960, pp. 744–752.

DAWSON, MILDRED A. *Language Teaching in Grades 1 and 2.* Yonkers-on-Hudson: World Book Company, 1957.

Early Childhood Education. Forty-sixth Yearbook of the National Society for the Study of Education, Part II. Chicago: National Society for the Study of Education, 1947.

HEFFERNAN, HELEN. *Guiding the Young Child.* Boston: D. C. Heath and Company, 1951.

Knowing When Children Are Ready to Learn. Washington: Association for Childhood Education, 1947.

Ohio State University Laboratory Schools. *How Children Develop.* School Series, No. 3. Columbus: The Ohio State University, 1946.

Portfolio for Kindergarten Teachers. Prepared by Elizabeth Neterer. Washington: Association for Childhood Education, 1945.

SHANE, HAROLD G., REDDIN, MARY E., and GILLESPIE, MARGARET C. *Beginning Language Arts Instruction with Children.* Columbus, Ohio: Charles E. Merrill Books, Inc., 1961.

SMITH, DORA V. "Growth in Language Power as Related to Child Development." *Teaching Language in the Elementary School.* The Forty-third Yearbook of the National Society for the Study of Education, Part II. Chicago: The University of Chicago Press, 1944.

WATTS, A. F. *The Language and Mental Development of Children.* Boston: D. C. Heath and Company, 1947.

WILLS, CLARICE DECHENT and STEGEMAN, WILLIAM H. *Living in the Primary Grades.* Chicago: Follett Publishing Co., 1956.

4

The Program in Oral Expression

and Listening

THE MAJOR ASPECTS OF THE TOTAL ELEMENTARY-SCHOOL PROGRAM in oral expression and listening as represented by the following major topics are presented in this chapter.

a. The basic oral language skill areas.
b. Socially important oral language situations.
c. Outcomes of the program in oral expression.
d. Listening in the language program.

Early man learned to speak long before he learned to express his thoughts in written form. Even though it may seem to be ancient, writing is a modern invention when compared with oral language. It is only because history is largely in recorded form that the immensely long span of centuries man needed to use speech before he learned writing may be overlooked. Similarly, the years that a child speaks before he writes should not be minimized in the language program. Furthermore, man, in his life activities, spends a far greater amount of time in talking than he does in writing. Many authorities estimate that at least ninety-five per cent of language usage is oral. In addition, oral language activities are the source of much written expression. This chapter emphasizes the formulation of an effective elementary school oral language program, outlines and presents the details of such a program, and relates the special role of listening to oral language.

ORAL LANGUAGE SKILLS

The need for a planned oral language program in the schools is strongly supported by the fact that many individuals, even though they may have sound and constructive ideas, are unable to express them effectively.

Many are actually afraid to stand before a group of their associates and read an announcement, make a report, or present an opinion. Such individuals may be seriously handicapped in their social effectiveness and in their business or professional activities as well. It is vital, therefore, that the school provide a well-organized program which requires oral language and teaches its use effectively. While it is desirable to keep oral language situations in the school as natural and spontaneous as possible, it is nevertheless necessary to plan for systematic teaching and practice of the skills discussed in this section. Competence in these skills is necessary for oral expression.

ARTICULATION, ENUNCIATION, AND PRONUNCIATION

It is difficult to find dictionary statements of the meaning of these three words that do not define each word in terms of the others. Since this is the case, it seems desirable here to attempt to clarify the distinctions that the common use of these abilities in oral language seems to justify.

Articulation is the process of uttering speech sounds as distinct sounds, syllables and words. It implies the proper separation and relation of the sounds within the words and between words. In the sentence, "Although May didn't *want to* go in the water, she *was swimming* in the lake," careless articulation might make it sound like this: "Although May didn't *wanna* go in the water, she *waswimming* in the lake." Careless articulation undoubtedly accounts for many common language faults, such as: "cancha," "doncha," "didja," and many others.

Enunciation, on the other hand, refers to the fullness or distinctiveness with which the utterance is produced. In the sentence above, the omission of the g sound in swimming (swimmin') would be an error due to indistinct enunciation. The typical American habit of dropping the final *d*'s, *t*'s and *g*'s as the terminal sounds of common words is a matter of carelessness in enunciation.

Pronunciation is related to articulation and to enunciation, but refers especially to the utterance of sounds in syllables and words. Further, a social connotation is attached to this skill in that the sounds must be uttered in an accepted order and with an accepted accent or emphasis. For example, the sounds of the letter symbols *a, d, l, t, u* may be clearly enunciated by the speaker in saying the word "adult," but if the accent is placed on the first part of the word, (as "ad'ult") the preferred pronunciation would not be given the word. Again the sounds of the letters *a, c, e, h, i, l* and *t* each may be clearly enunciated by the speaker in saying the word "athletic," but adding an extra *a* sound between the *h* and *l* causes the word "athletic" to be mispronounced "athaletic."

The mastery of these three closely related abilities is largely a matter of normal development and the hearing words spoken repeatedly in an accepted conventionally correct manner, and using them frequently enough to make them sound and feel right. If children have normal speech apparatus and normal hearing, they will tend to acquire the pronunciation and enunciation of their parents and others with whom they come into contact. Since the speech used by teachers and others at school become important models, every care must be taken to insure that children do hear words correctly pronounced, clearly enunciated, and well articulated. The children not only must hear words so spoken very often; they must also have many opportunities to repeat the words, correctly pronounced and distinctly enunciated.

Studies of the growth and development of children show considerable variability in the ages at which children master certain physical and mental skills. This same principle is true in the acquisition of skill in the production of sounds. One study showed an interesting table of the ages at which most children are able to articulate certain sounds: [1]

> 3.5 years—p, b, m, w, h
> 4.5 years—t, d, n, g, k, ng, y
> 5.5 years—f, v, s, z
> 6.5 years—sh, zh, l, th as in thin, th as in then
> 8.0 years—s, z, r, wh
> (s's and z's are listed twice because of distortions
> in these sounds when children lose their front teeth)

Another study concluded that growth and maturation eliminate many sound errors in the first four grades but that maturation does not effect noticeable improvement in the speech sounds of children in higher grades.[2] Thus it would seem to be of great importance that children be consistently encouraged to avoid routine causes of speech errors.

The problems in children's production of sounds which occur most

---

[1] I. P. Davis, "The Speech Aspects of Reading Readiness," *Newer Practices in Reading in the Elementary Schools,* Seventeenth Yearbook of the Department of Elementary School Principals. Washington: National Education Association, 1938, p. 283.

[2] V. Roe and R. Milisen, "The Effect of Maturation upon Defective Articulation in Elementary Grades," *Journal of Speech Disorders,* 7:44; March, 1942.

often are those of articulation. Articulatory defects are listed by Ogilvie as:

1. Substitution of one sound for another; for example, a child says *wed* for *red, wiwy* for *lily,* or *fum* for *thumb.*
2. Omission of sounds; for example, the *s* sound may have some of the characteristics of the *sh* sound.[3]

Attention very often needs to be given to proper enunciation of each syllable in these expressions:

did you	gave them
don't you	gave him
why don't you	how are you
what did you	how do you do
didn't you	would you
did he	let me
give me	let him
give her	let her
came to meet you	shouldn't have
could have	she may have

Children from homes in which a foreign language is spoken often have difficulty with the inflections and rhythm of our language. Too, a few children in each classroom may not use their lips and other speech organs correctly when they talk. Special opportunities must be provided for the improvement of the speech of children with these difficulties.

AUDIENCE SENSITIVITY

The oral language program should focus upon effective communication. A pupil speaks because he has something to say, because he needs to express an opinion, because he wishes to present facts or information. He has something to say *to someone;* therefore an audience situation is implied. This audience may be a single classmate, a group of classmates, or any number of parents, friends, or other visitors. Oral communication quite obviously is not a one-way street. It requires not only that the speaker must have something to say, but that he must say it in a way that will evoke proper responses from his listeners. Children should be made aware of their double responsibility in oral language situations. The speaker must be conscious of his audience and sensitive to their needs, interests, and desires. The listener must give courteous attention

[3] Mardel Ogilvie, *Speech in the Elementary School.* New York: McGraw-Hill Book Company, Inc., 1954, p. 236.

to the speaker, and respond to what has been said in an acceptable way.

We should encourage children to think and possibly disagree with the speaker while at the same time showing tolerance and respect for his opinion. In addition, the program should include:

1. Giving quiet, courteous, and alert attention to the speaker.
2. Responding as appropriate with facial expression to show interest.
3. Making other appropriate responses, including laughter and applause.
4. Asking pertinent questions in order to amplify or clarify the speaker's comments.
5. Observing common courtesies in questioning.

VOICE CONTROL

The teacher is responsible for aiding each child in developing the following abilities and good voice habits:

1. Volume and voice control adequate for various communicative activities.
2. The ability to pitch his voice appropriately for different situations.
3. A clear voice tone.
4. A speaking tempo which facilitates the reception of ideas by his listeners.

Some children seem always to speak too loudly, while others can scarcely be heard even when they are near. Many children have not learned to adjust their voices to the size of the room. Some children speak in monotonous tone; others pitch all their speaking in a shrill tone. Some voices are resonant, pleasant and clear; others are nasal, breathy, hoarse, or thin. Some children speak so rapidly that the meaning of the communication is lost; others speak so slowly the result is the same. These are a few of the problems the classroom teacher may encounter and must solve. If the problems appear to be serious, he should secure the help of specialists. Until such help is an actuality, or if the problems are such that he can handle them, the teacher is obligated to help each child learn to speak in a voice that is naturally pleasing, rhythmical, and can be clearly understood.

Teachers play an important part in determining the emotional climate in the classroom, and hence in determining the voices used by the children. Teachers with calm and relaxed personalities give encouragement to children to be calm and also to speak in low-pitched voices. Teachers should continually evaluate their own voice quality and ways of speaking as well as their classroom personalities.

POSTURE

Many of you may recall hearing, "Now stand up straight when you talk;" and if you do recall such a statement from one of your teachers of an earlier day, you probably also remember how stiff and unnatural you became after such an admonition. This stiffness carried over into what you were saying, too. Happily this stress upon posture in relation to oral language activities has changed somewhat today. Good posture is important, but should not be considered as taking priority over quality of expression. An individual's good posture while speaking adds to what is being said, creates a better impression on the audience, and makes the audience more receptive to the communication, but it will not do so if the posture is an unnatural one. A speaker's stiffness and awkwardness are more often than not the result of nervousness. When oral activities are experienced frequently, the pupil soon learns to forget his nervousness, particularly if the atmosphere of these activities is warm and spontaneous rather than formal. Negative criticism of a speaker should be extremely rare in the elementary school. Rather, the class itself may set up standards toward which they will strive, and the teacher may offer casual, friendly suggestions for improvement, both to the group as a whole and to individuals in the group.

MANNER

Manner, of course, combines all the previously mentioned matters of voice, articulation, posture, and audience attitude, along with gestures and that indefinable something which is in the speaker's own personality. No longer do we teach oral language in the manner of the old-fashioned elocution class in which a child memorized formal speeches and learned exactly at which word to wave his arm mechanically or step forward on one foot like an obedient robot. The good speaker combines naturalness with a sincere interest in both his subject and his listeners. Surely it was the warmth and sincerity of Lincoln's own personality, as well as the power of the words he spoke, which have made the Gettysburg Address familiar to every school child. Had he recited it as monotonously and as meaninglessly as do many of those same school children when they are forced to memorize his words, it would certainly have been lost to us today.

True ease in speaking can result only from constant practice in all of the various types of situations in which the individual as a child or as an adult will find himself called upon to speak.

SPECIAL ORAL LANGUAGE SITUATIONS

CONVERSATION

Conversation is the form of oral language activity most frequently used by both adults and children. Children ordinarily have acquired some skill in carrying on a conversation before they come to school. Not only have they listened to conversations at home, but most children have participated in them many times. In general, when a child comes to school, he has a favorable attitude about conversation. He wants to converse and regards conversation as something in a sense apart from school activities. This is a favorable situation for the acquisition of attitudes, skills, and abilities that will later be useful in all forms of oral and written language expression.

Conversation is generally defined as an exchange of thoughts or ideas about one or more topics between two or more speakers. It is well to note in this definition the words *exchange* and *thoughts*. Qualities of a good conversationalist include the ability:

1. To think clearly.
2. To use English effectively.
3. To speak to the point.
4. To discuss without arguing.
5. To stimulate others to talk.
6. To discover common interests.
7. To describe situations and events.

The good conversationalist should also show good judgment, tact, conviction, a wide range of interests, originality, good memory, broadmindedness, adaptability, and sincerity. Certainly this is a big order and one which cannot entirely be filled in the elementary school.

When a child feels secure, is happy, and is spared situations which cause undue anxiety, he tends to speak with ease. Likewise, power over language aids emotional and social adjustment. The child who has developed the ability to participate effectively in conversation gets greater satisfaction from his activities which involve other people and has better chances for satisfactory growth than the child who does not have this ability. In the primary grades, emphasis should be placed upon first helping the child to feel comfortable in the conversational group and then creating within him a desire to participate fully. Oral language teaching at this level, besides developing the child's ability to converse naturally and spontaneously, should include such skills as selecting the proper time to talk and the proper time not to talk, talking about something of interest, sticking to the subject, enunciating clearly, and showing consideration for the rights of others by taking turns in talking and listening.

The objectives of teaching conversation in the middle and upper grades, of course, include all those of previous levels, but with greater emphasis upon developing each child's sense of responsibility to the group and upon showing respect for and giving encouragement to others. It is reasonable, too, to expect the upper-grade child to be able to carry on a sustained conversation with considerable skill and assurance.

The elementary school does not have the responsibility for producing polished conversationalists, but the children should be given many opportunities to take part in conversation in many different forms, in order that they may develop to the maximum of their abilities. A program of instruction based upon the following principles should accomplish this goal:

1. Conversation is a two-way process between a listener and a speaker, who exchange ideas in turn.
2. Conversation involves listening to the contributions of others and reacting to them.
3. Conversation is not random talk but involves real interaction about a subject of mutual interest.
4. Courtesy should prevail in the behavior of the participants even though the conversation may be very informal.
5. Good conversationalists have a responsibility to themselves and others to be truthful and considerate in their remarks.
6. Good conversationalists at all times attempt to avoid aggressive or argumentative attitudes. After all, conversation is a friendly discussion, not a verbal battle.

In addition to building a program upon the above principles, specific attention needs to be given to the acquisition of the following habits and abilities by each pupil before he leaves the elementary school:

1. A realization of the value of being informed on many suitable topics to talk about.
2. The ability to be enthusiastic during conversation.
3. A knowledge of and the ability to use a pleasing vocabulary.
4. The ability to be a good listener.
5. A knowledge of sources of interesting material.

92

6. The ability to observe common courtesies in conversation.
7. The ability to change the topic of conversation tactfully.
8. The ability to talk without the use of distracting mannerisms.
9. A knowledge of when and where it is not appropriate to talk.
10. The ability to follow up an introduction with remarks designed to make all parties feel at ease.
11. A sensitivity to the appropriateness of topics for certain occasions and people.
12. The ability to use speech acceptable to the particular conversational situation.

The language abilities and habits listed above represent the content children should learn through an instructional program in conversation, and are common to other aspects of oral language, such as story-telling, making announcements, using the telephone, and the like.

Particular emphasis also needs to be given to the observance of courtesies in conversation. Among those deserving special attention are the following:

1. Knowing how and when to interrupt the person talking.
2. Knowing how to disagree with the speaker's statement.
3. Avoiding completing the speaker's statement.
4. Not being too demonstrative.
5. Not monopolizing the conversation.
6. Avoiding unpleasant topics.
7. Not whispering in the presence of others.
8. Including all members of the group in one's remarks.
9. Expressing likes and dislikes moderately.
10. Avoiding being too personal.
11. Speaking in a soft voice.
12. Not contradicting the speaker's statement.
13. Avoiding futile argument.
14. Knowing what to do when two people begin talking at the same time.
15. Showing consideration for persons entering the group after conversation has started.
16. Avoiding hurting the feelings of others.
17. Not listening to conversations not meant for one.
18. Not using unfamiliar language.
19. Avoiding unusual mannerisms and affectations.
20. Not repeating needlessly.

The listing of general goals or standards in the early phases of teaching conversational skills should be followed by noting individual goals for improvement. These individual goals should be limited in number and should represent a possible achievement for each child. Attainment of these individual masteries should be discovered through observation by the teacher of each child's conversational efforts and successes. Such evaluations need to be carefully and regularly made to pinpoint individual goals.

DISCUSSION

Group discussion is the most frequently used classroom means for carrying on learning in any area. Through guided discussion children gain information, learn to deal with facts and problems, and develop the ability to express themselves effectively. Discussion not only occupies a key position in the school program, but has a very prominent place in adult activities as well. When a group has a common interest that requires planning, a solution, or agreement, a discussion will develop naturally.

Discussion differs from conversation in that it has a more purposeful goal. This goal is generally understood and in school situations has been agreed upon by both teacher and pupils. In the lower grades, the goal is perhaps less apparent to the pupils than to the teacher but is still present.

Discussing is definitely not the same as arguing. In a discussion, the purpose is to secure information, to arrive at a better understanding, to answer a problem. In an argument, the participants are defending a point, sometimes without factual support, hoping to convince through sheer weight of verbal attack. Generally speaking, the school has little responsibility to develop skill in argumentation, and quite often it is necessary for the teacher tactfully to change arguments into discussions.

The following goals for instruction in discussion are designed to teach the children to:

1. Stay on the topic.
2. Take turns talking.
3. Listen courteously to others.
4. Attempt to make worthwhile contributions.
5. Make concise statements and ask clear questions.
6. Speak so that all may understand.
7. Respect the opinions of others.
8. Support statements with facts.
9. Avoid repetition through careful listening.
10. Distinguish between relevant and irrelevant material.
11. Distinguish between fact and opinion.
12. Reach a suitable conclusion.

In addition, the speaking skills and abilities cited in the first sections of this chapter as well as those needed in conversation apply also to discussion. These objectives are basic and must always be considered in planning any language activities. Then too, of particular importance is the establishment of a definite problem. The final definition of the problem rests ultimately with the teacher at all grade levels, but progressively through the grades the pupils should be encouraged to assume more and more of the responsibility for setting up specific problem goals for discussion. Topics for discussion should be within the range of experience of the children and should be about things of interest and importance to them.

Many natural situations arise in the classroom for discussing real problems, such as planning a party or a program, deciding how best to keep the playground clean or finding specific answers to questions arising in social studies or science lessons. In the discussion of problems, pupils need to learn that, in addition to setting a definite purpose for the discussion, they must stay on the topic. They should learn to recognize and to handle differences of opinion regarding the interpretation of facts and the drawing of conclusions, to distinguish between important and unimportant details and issues, to avoid repeating what others have said, to respect authority, and to discriminate between sources of information.

TELEPHONING

Much conversation takes place over the telephone. Adults talk with their friends, place orders for supplies or services, and call police, fire departments, or doctors in emergencies. Children use the telephone, too. They talk with friends, answer the telephone for parents, and converse with relatives. Many adults and some children use the telephone skillfully; others antagonize their listeners—and the telephone company. The importance of the telephone as a medium of communication is emphasized in the following statement:

> More than forty-four million telephones form a voice highway over the entire nation. This fact indicates that the telephone is a very important medium of communication in which the school and home have a responsibility for developing habits of courtesy, for considering the rights of others by limiting conversations and by calling at appropriate times, for providing practice in using the telephone in case of emergencies such as calling the police, the fire department, or the ambulance, or in making long distance calls.[4]

[4] The Commission on the English Curriculum, National Council of Teachers of English, *Language Arts for Today's Children*. New York: Appleton-Century-Crofts, Inc., 1954, p. 378.

Attitudes and abilities important to everyday life that are emphasized in teaching the use of the telephone are: [5]

1. Formulating messages, inquiries, orders, and other detailed information as concisely as possible before making a call.
2. Identifying the speaker clearly and courteously when making or receiving a call.
3. Explaining clearly and courteously the purpose of a call that is made.
4. Speaking courteously and graciously as if one were speaking to the person face to face.
5. Allowing the person who made the call to close the conversation.
6. Asking permission to use another person's telephone.
7. Placing calls at convenient times for the person one is calling.
8. Avoiding monopolizing a party line.

In addition to the above social objectives, distinct speech, a well-modulated tone of voice, brevity and pointedness are desirable language objectives. Certain specific telephoning techniques also must be learned, such as using the directory to find numbers, getting the operator or dialing a number, making emergency or special service calls, and placing long-distance calls.

In the primary grades, learning about telephoning provides a meaningful opportunity to teach (1) the courtesies of "please," "thank you," taking turns, and listening; (2) self-confidence and spontaneity of expression; and (3) creativeness in oral expression. In the middle and upper grades, instruction in telephoning provides opportunity to teach (1) further courtesies of conversation; (2) the informational or research skills of alphabetizing and getting specific help through the use of the Yellow Pages of the telephone directory; (3) calm reaction in emergencies, such as calling the police, the fire department, a hospital; and (4) the speech skills of articulation, enunciation, pronunciation, pleasing voice, and correct word usage.

STORY TELLING

Children of almost all ages love stories, whether the teacher tells them or whether the children tell stories they have read or create stories of their own to tell. Through stories children are drawn into a world of beauty, imagination, and action with which they identify themselves according to their past experiences. They are intrigued by the sounds,

---

[5] *An Experience Curriculum in English.* A Report of the Curriculum Commission of the National Council of Teachers of English. W. Wilbur Hatfield, chairman. New York: D. Appleton-Century Company, 1935, p. 143 (adapted and supplemented).

the feelings, and the sights that the words of the story convey. They enjoy the humor of an unexpected ending, a strange-sounding word, a funny character. They live the experiences of others in a world of adventure.

Although story telling is primarily for enjoyment, other goals of oral language may be inconspicuously injected into the experience without spoiling the fun. By first listening to the teacher tell a story and then telling it himself, a child learns how to put ideas in sequence and how to compose sentences and emphasize meaning with his voice. Children who have had frequent opportunities of listening to and telling stories are better able to appreciate desirable techniques of telling a story than are children who have had no such experiences.

Story telling should be carefully planned, with special attention paid to the creation of the right classroom atmosphere. The children must feel relaxed, at ease, and expectant. They must feel that they are participating in an enjoyable activity. The stories selected may be realistic or fanciful; reproduced or original. They may be stories about friends, pets, things they have seen; places they have been; stories about imaginary characters; anecdotes or "cuties" as the TV announcers call them, with a suitable point of wit; stories about things seen in movies or on television; stories based on pictures they have seen, or books they have read. In order to tell about things—to tell stories, children need opportunities to hear stories, to read stories, to go places, and to do things. It is noticeable, too, that the one who tells stories well works at it constantly, trying his skill frequently on others.

The language objectives of story telling are similar to those in other oral expression, as well as to enrich children's vocabularies through use of new words and meanings, give specific assistance in developing freedom and ease of expression, and teach the appreciation of simple and sometimes homely experiences and the enjoyment of creating interesting stories just for fun.

DRAMATIZATION

Story telling leads directly to dramatization, for all children love to see stories acted out and to take part in the acting. In the lower grades, dramatization should be very informal and might more properly be thought of as play activity than as dramatization in the sense that adults think of it. Such dramatic play is inherent in many child activities. It provides the spontaneity and natural enthusiasm which move children to express feelings and thoughts. The pre-school child and the child of the primary grades sits in the cockpit of his airplane built of blocks or orange crates. He *is* the pilot. He talks as he thinks the pilot would talk. He does the things he thinks the pilot would do. Through such activity the child furthers his learning of language. He seeks facts, information, and materials which provide new relationships and meanings for him. He experiments with new words, new ideas, and new ways of saying and doing things.

As a child becomes older, he consciously pretends he is someone else. Through broadening interests and experiences, dramatic play begins to shape itself into a pattern that gradually becomes dramatization. There is a steady progression from individual, spontaneous play to ever-widening group play, from unpatterned to patterned play, and from completely free expression to the selection of action and dialogue. The older child is no less creative, but is more interested in reproducing exact dialogue, in organizing a series of events, and in writing the script for class plays or puppet shows, or for make-believe radio, telvision, and motion picture shows.

Specific goals of dramatization and dramatic play activities should include the following:

1. To provide opportunities for each child to gain socially: the timid child to become less timid, the aggressive child to learn to accept a minor role, the less academically inclined to achieve recognition.
2. To pronounce words distinctly and correctly.
3. To avoid errors in usage.
4. To speak so that he may be easily heard by his audience.

REPORTING

Reporting is an oral language activity used primarily in the middle and upper grades and is an outgrowth of the "sharing" or "telling" activity of the primary grades. As the child progresses through the primary grades into the intermediate and upper grades, he finds that much more attention is given to the selection of topics for reports than had been given to the "shared" topics in earlier grades when the major emphasis was upon freedom of expression and spontaneity. The middle and upper grade child should learn to stick to his topic and to show by his presentation of a report that he has planned his contribution with care.

The needs for oral reports vary. The members of a committee may report to the entire class. School council members may report to the classmates they represent. A child may report on a book he has read, a trip he has taken, or an interview that he has made. Reports often are given as part of social studies or science lessons, or similar classroom activities. Reporting puts more responsibility upon the pupil than does conversation or discussion. Reporting calls for more of a formalized audience situation and thus requires that a pupil collect his thoughts and ideas so that his concise report will have audience appeal.

Giving reports helps a pupil gain self-confidence, and feel that what he has been doing has been worth while and of interest to others. He learns that if his report is to be successful, he must plan what he is going to say and try to make it interesting to listen to. Reporting as a school activity should be so planned that pupils will feel honored to be asked to give the report. Pupils must learn that good organization, language usage, posture, and speech will increase the effectiveness and interest of their reports.

GIVING ANNOUNCEMENTS, DIRECTIONS, EXPLANATIONS

Making announcements and giving directions and explanations are oral language activities frequently encountered in school and life situations in the experiences of both children and adults. School announcements are made by children relative to lost and found articles, school programs, exhibitions, and parties. Frequently children give directions for playing games or for performing some classroom task. They explain how they found a particular item or fact in a book. Outside of school, children make announcements at Scout meetings, club meetings, and parties. They give directions to one another in their play, and they explain their hobbies to anyone who will listen. Adults are called upon to make announcements at social gatherings and public meetings, to give directions to motorists, and to make explanations to employees or employers as a part of their work. Thus there are many occasions in which both children and adults are called upon to use directly the skills and abilities which are needed if announcements, directions, and explanations are to be effective.

The skills and abilities necessary for making announcements and for giving directions and explanations are similar to those needed in other oral language situations. The language used must be properly organized and must be presented in terms which will be understood by the audience. All of the essential information relative to who, what, when, where, and how should be given. Correct language certainly should be used but attention must be paid to the particular language of the situation. Since

99

these language situations are generally limited in time, specific attention must be paid to conciseness and clarity and the manner in which the communication is made.

INTERVIEWING

Increasingly, attention is being given to interviewing as an oral language situation that enters frequently into the lives of both children and adults. The interview as a method for securing information is being stressed in social studies and science; the interview has a prominent place in television programs of news and information; interviewing, of which the panel presentation is one variation, is used in club programs. Interviewing not only calls for the use of many speaking and social skills; it also shows the importance of careful listening. The necessity for schools to provide a direct program of instruction in the various aspects of this activity was pointed out by Broening over twenty years ago: [6]

The interview has become a very useful technique with the present-day emphasis on the students' having actual contact with the activities about them . . .

Are we helping our students to ask important, direct questions, so that they can bring back the information desired? Are we stressing the necessity of quoting statements exactly as they were made? Are we insisting on courtesy at all times? Are we teaching students how to make a tactful and pleasing entree and introduction to the person being interviewed?

Skills and abilities to be developed for successful interviewing include:

1. Knowing clearly the purpose of the interview.
2. Preparing for interviews by finding background information and leads for questions.
3. Taking notes.
4. Observing courtesies as to appointment times, questions asked, and appreciation for the interviewee's time and information.

Children also need to experience being interviewed. Those who have taken trips, done particular kinds of research, or otherwise have information not known to others in the class may be interviewed.

CONDUCTING MEETINGS AND CONFERENCES

Formal and informal conferences and meetings call for the use of language. Usually these language activities are oral and take the form of

[6] Angela M. Broening *et al., Conducting Experiences in English*. New York: Appleton-Century-Crofts, Inc., 1939, p. 128.

conversation, story telling, announcements, panel discussions, and informal talks. These have previously been discussed. The formal type conference calls for more precise language situations. Certainly most such conferences call for the language activity engaged in by a presiding officer or conference moderator. In the school, children at an early age participate in similar activities in the room organization. A room organization calls for a presiding officer and subordinate officers and in turn for the oral language abilities and skills necessary to fulfill the duties of these positions. Children enjoy taking part in such organizations, and many worthwhile attitudes and understandings may be acquired in addition to those normally related to the language program.

Parliamentary procedure is designed to help groups carry on their activities in an orderly manner. Knowledge of this procedure, if used properly, will aid in teaching respect for the social rights of others, as well as the proper procedures for arriving at specific group decisions.

Needless to say, the teacher should know parliamentary procedure thoroughly in order to teach it. From this knowledge he will be in a position to teach habits of orderly procedure in all group activities. The form of the procedure should be suited to the age and ability level of the children but attention should be given to the development of advancing levels of skill in order to secure a degree of proficiency that will be useful to the child throughout his school and later adult life.

CULTIVATING THE SOCIAL CONVENTIONS

Most activities of child or adult life that require the use of oral language also call for an observance of social amenities. Good manners and social graces are based upon a consideration for others. Such consideration flourishes in a friendly, amiable atmosphere; desirable social behavior is picked up for the most part by imitation. At times, however, it is necessary for the school to introduce situations that call for a new concept of thoughtfulness and for the use of the conventional forms and procedures followed in making introductions, giving an apology, or replying to a greeting. Opportunities for the observance of social amenities occur daily in most classrooms.

Many children need to be helped in the simple matter of exchanging informal greetings. Not knowing the proper thing to say in response to a greeting may make the individual appear rude or indifferent when all that is wrong is that he is trying to cover up the fact that he is embarrassed. Proper forms of greeting and responses to greeting are quickly

101

mastered as a result of a few simple lessons. Later the children enjoy the experience of showing off their new skills by exchanging greetings with teachers, other adults, and children around them. The custodian, the bus driver, the principal, as well as the teacher and the children all help set the school's tone of friendliness. As habits of greeting and saying good-bye to people in a gracious manner are acquired, the children grow in ease and self-confidence.

Situations are constantly arising at school and at home in which introductions are necessary. Lack of acquaintance with the somewhat formal conventions of making introductions, of acknowledging an introduction, of being introduced may make for unnecessary embarrassment. Children need to learn how to introduce parents and friends and how to reply when others are introduced to them. There may be those who will criticize the school for accepting responsibility for teaching these elementary social conventions. However, a brief observation of the manner in which many adults stumble through such a simple act as the introduction of two friends will still the criticism. Names are mumbled or given in the wrong order. Simple explanatory remarks that might help to put the individuals at ease are omitted. Confidence and ease in the use of these social skills come only through practice. It is apparent that in too many cases the children do not learn them at home, so the responsibility returns to the school, and the language program is the logical place in which to develop the self-confidence, assurance, and ease that comes with their mastery.

CHORAL SPEECH

Choral speech is much more than a mere pleasure device for school groups or a means of entertaining visitors to school programs. Choral speaking is group oral expression and may lead to: (1) the improvement of voice quality, (2) the development of improved habits of enunciation and articulation, (3) the improvement of habits of pronunciation, (4) the freeing of children from unhealthy inhibition and excessive shyness toward expression, and (5) a recognition of the importance of the audience and group effort in such forms of communication. In addition to these values, choral speaking is considered by many to be a good way to teach appreciation of poetry and prose selections.

Choral speaking can be used with children of all ages. It teaches them to listen, to remember, and to interpret words and word patterns. Most selections for choral speaking provide opportunity for learning to keep voices modulated—an important first step in developing good speaking habits. At about the third to sixth grade level the children become interested in choral speaking with themes of adventure or mystery. This interest can be directed toward improvement of diction, voice quality, vocabulary, and understanding of meaning.

CREATIVE ASPECTS OF ORAL LANGUAGE

Children are characteristically happy, imaginative, and creative. To the young child the ever-changing world is full of wonder, excitement, and adventure. Children as young as four and five often use surprisingly beautiful forms of expression as they indicate their awareness of all there is to feel, to hear, to see, to touch, and to smell in the world around them. Children should be encouraged at all times to give oral expression to their reactions to their world.

The most important requisite to creative expression is an environment based upon a friendly, relaxed, happy relationship between teacher and children and among the children in the group. It is the sheer joy of creation as experienced by each child, not content or form itself, that is the primary goal of creative expression.

Opportunities for developing the creative aspects of oral language can be provided by:

1. Helping children develop a sensitivity to the rhythmic and beautiful elements of their own and others' speech.
2. Providing children with many opportunities for sensory experiences to translate into words.
3. Providing many and varied opportunities for children to talk freely about their experiences.
4. Developing a feeling for words by reading and listening to poetry, rhymes, and rhythmic prose of particularly descriptive and moving language.
5. Encouraging each child to contribute his bit to the pleasure of creative expression.[7]

OUTCOMES OF THE PROGRAM IN
ORAL EXPRESSION

By the time the child has completed the elementary school language program at the end of the sixth grade, he should have developed a

[7] The creative aspects of oral expression are discussed in detail in Chapter 15.

reasonable mastery of the following oral language abilities, knowledge, and skills:

1. Ease in speaking before a group or with individuals.
2. Ease in giving or receiving a compliment.
3. Absence of annoying mannerisms while speaking.
4. Courtesy in giving attention to speaker.
5. Pleasing voice, careful enunciation and pronunciation.
6. Clearness in making meaning known in a talk.
7. Interest in presenting meaning in a talk.
8. Ease and confidence in meeting a stranger, or accepting an introduction.
9. Ease and confidence in introducing strangers.
10. Ease and assurance in being greeted and returning a greeting.
11. Ease and courtesy in asking and answering a question.
12. Absence of listening in or rudely interrupting in groups.
13. Absence of glaring errors in oral language usage.
14. Sincerity and absence of affectation in all speech.
15. Ability to tell a simple story interestingly.
16. Ability to tell a simple incident or to make a simple explanation.
17. Ability to give directions simply and clearly.
18. Attitude of listening courteously as a member of an audience.
19. Ability to make a simple announcement concerning a lost or found article.
20. Ability to ask a favor with tact and courtesy.
21. Ability to place a telephone call, or answer a telephone call courteously.
22. Ability to conduct an assembly, make the announcements, and introduce the numbers.
23. Ability to carry on an interesting conversation, observing common rules of courtesy, and having something interesting to contribute.
24. Ability to ask for and engage in a conference with the teachers, or with some other individual in regard to problems of school concern.
25. Knowledge of where to get material of interest, types of magazines, stories, references, and other information.
26. Knowledge of the accepted thing to do in common social situations.
27. Knowledge of the elements that make a talk interesting.
28. Knowledge of the factors that make a pleasing voice.
29. Skill in remembering important items, anecdotes, jokes, and other items of use in making speeches and conversations interesting.
30. Sensitivity to the effect that posture has on speech.
31. Habit of standing well and breathing properly as aids to speech.
32. Correct enunciation, aiming directly at eliminating these recurring errors:

Say:	"I don't know"	not	"I daknow"
	"Can't you"	not	"Can'tcha"
	"He and I"	not	"Him-n-me"
	"Let me be"	not	"Lemme be"
	"We are coming"	not	"We're comin' "
	"What's the matter"	not	"Whasa matter"

SKILLS AND USAGES COMMON TO BOTH ORAL AND WRITTEN LANGUAGE

In addition to the specific language skills found primarily in oral expression, there are many that are essential to both oral and written language. The skills and usages common to both oral and written expression are summarized in Chapter 6. The instructional techniques used in teaching the common verb and pronoun usages, the functional skills of grammar, the rhetorical skills involved in sentences, the problems of thought organization in sentences and larger units, as well as those related to vocabulary growth and enrichment may vary somewhat depending on whether the expression is in oral or written form. However the skills themselves are so nearly identical that they may be treated in common regardless of the purpose of the program. The reader who is particularly interested in the program and the methods of instruction in oral expression is advised to follow the reading of this chapter with Chapters 6, 9, and 11. In this way a logical and complete picture of the program and the teaching techniques of the oral expressional skills may be obtained.

LISTENING IN THE LANGUAGE PROGRAM

Listening, as a communication skill, is recovering from a long period of neglect and is now receiving increasing attention in the elementary school program. Probably one practical reason for this increased emphasis is the sudden realization of the amount of time people spend in listening. Rankin reported that of the time people spent in communicating each day, approximately 45 per cent is devoted to listening, 30 per cent to speaking, and the rest to reading and writing combined.[8] Listening is particularly related to speaking. It is a forerunner of speaking and throughout a person's life bears a reciprocal relationship to it. In spite of its acknowledged importance, apparently no one is advocating today the addition of another course to an already crowded elementary curriculum. There is, however, considerable feeling that the listening skills should "be developed in a general language arts context and, indeed, in the total 'living-and-learning' setting of the elementary school." [9]

[8] Paul T. Rankin, "The Importance of Listening Ability," *English Journal,* college ed., 17:623–630; October, 1928.
[9] Commission on the English Curriculum, National Council of Teachers of

105

THE NATURE OF LISTENING

We regularly hear many sounds to which we are not actively listening. Listening implies more than just hearing. Listening involves giving active and conscious attention to sounds of auditory expression for the purpose of gaining some meaning from it. We may listen to someone speaking, to the music of a fine orchestra, or to the traffic sounds outside our windows. In each case, if we are really listening, we expect or may be expected to make some reaction to the sounds we hear. If we merely hear the sounds, no overt reaction may take place. We must comprehend the special meanings of the sounds we hear and relate them to our past experiences. We must give attention to what is being presented or some important detail may be missed and our comprehension of the situation may suffer.[10]

Speaking and writing are commonly called the expressive phases of language, and listening and reading the receptive phases. While this generalization is true, neither listening nor reading should be regarded as passive activities. In both reading and listening the reader or listener is actively engaged in the perception and comprehension of ideas and facts and is consciously or emotionally reacting to them, relating what he reads or hears to his background of experience. Further, while listening or reading, he may be formulating a response, or deciding on a future course of action. The reader or listener is actively, personally, consciously involved in the activity.[11]

We know that every child enters school with some degree of listening ability, just as he possesses some skill in expressing himself orally. There is a mistaken idea held by some that listening power increases with the individual's maturity. The known evidence indicates that unless the individual is given an understanding of the nature of listening, and the

English, *Language Arts for Today's Children*. New York: Appleton-Century-Crofts, Inc., 1954, p. 71.

[10] Recently the term *auding* has been used to mean the recognition, meaning gaining, and reaction that occurs in listening. (See, for example, D. P. Brown, "Auding as the Primary Language Ability," unpublished Ed. D. dissertation, Stanford University, 1954.) However, the April, 1961 issue of the *Review of Educational Research* on "Language Arts and Fine Arts" makes use of the term *listening* again, after the 1958 issue had used the term *auding*.

[11] Robert Larsen and D. D. Feder, "Common and Differential Factors in Reading and Hearing Comprehension," *Journal of Educational Psychology*, 31: No. 4; April, 1940. Merle Catherine Watkins, "Factors in the Relationships of Listening, Reading, and Intelligence of 260 Second Grade Students of Des Moines, Iowa," unpublished master's thesis, Drake University, 1960.

skills which are necessary to its effective use, there is little likelihood that either maturity or incidental instruction will make him an accurate and critical listener. He must be taught how to listen and how to utilize the results of listening in determining his future actions. Pratt, in a report on an experimental program in the teaching of listening skills, described listening as the act of receiving oral language.[12] He pointed out that this type of listening involves at least the three following steps:

1. The recall or deduction of meaning for spoken word symbols.
2. The comprehension of ideas represented by different combinations of these word symbols, and
3. The ability to use the ideas presented to build understanding by adding to, modifying, or rejecting previous learning.

TYPES OF LISTENING

The Commission on the English Curriculum defines the types of listening as follows: [13]

Passive or *marginal listening* is prevalent today as many children study with the radio on. In fact, there is often a deliberate "tuning out" of what is heard with just enough consciousness of the language or sound to bring the child back to attention when a favorite radio personality comes on. Similarly, in classroom or home the tone of voice of teacher or parent may flash the danger signal which alerts the child whose attention has been wandering. The way one listens to background music while reading differs markedly from the type of listening one does when evaluating critically a proposed plan for action which affects one personally or professionally.

Appreciative listening is involved when the hearer settles down to enjoy a dramatization, a story, or a poem. The process of developing new or original solutions to problems presented through the spoken word may be termed *creative listening* or the act of entering imaginatively into the experiences, the setting, and the feelings of the characters in a story which is being told orally or produced on screen or stage.

Attentive listening is needed in situations in which accuracy of comprehension is involved, as in directions, announcements, and introductions. Probably there is a different mind set in situations in which the hearer participates, such as in conversation and discussion; this might be called *responsive listening*.

Analytical listening takes place, for example, when the listener weighs what is heard against personal experience and is alert to attempts of the speaker to sway his opinion by the devices of propaganda. This kind of lis-

---

[12] Edward Pratt, "The Experimental Evaluation of a Program for the Improvement of Listening in the Elementary School." Unpublished doctoral dissertation, State University of Iowa, 1953.

[13] *Language Arts for Today's Children*, p. 80.

tening must be developed by older elementary and high school pupils in order that they may evaluate what they hear.

There are other classifications of types of listening which might be made such as: appreciational, informational, and critical; [14] or attentive, purposeful, critical, and responsive.[15] Regardless of the classification that might be made, however, the point of concern is that listening is a specific ability. It is obvious that we listen to particular sounds, for particular purposes; we do not *just* listen.

THE SKILLS OF LISTENING

Listening skills take many forms depending upon the purpose of the activity. In the language program we are principally concerned with the skills necessary for the accurate and thoughtful reception of speaking, although other listening in the language program includes listening to music and sounds for the setting of mood in creative expression. The necessary listening skills can be broadly separated into two classes: (1) those concerned with accuracy of reception, and (2) those concerned with reflective listening. Pratt and Greene further identify these skills:[16]

1. Word perception
   a. Recall of word meanings
   b. Deduction of meanings of unknown words
2. Comprehension of ideas
   a. Noting details
   b. Following directions
   c. Organizing into main and subordinate ideas
   d. Selecting information pertinent to a specific topic
   e. Detecting clues that show the speaker's trend of thought
3. Using ideas to build understandings
   a. Evaluating an expressed point of view or fact in relation to previous learning
   b. Making justifiable inferences

Suggested procedures for the development of these skills are presented in connection with the development of other oral expressional abilities in Chapter 9.

[14] Ralph G. Nichols, "Ten Components of Effective Listening," *Education,* 75:292–302; January, 1955.

[15] Earl J. Dias, "Three Levels of Listening," *English Journal,* 36:252–253; May, 1947.

[16] Edward Pratt and Harry A. Greene, *Training Children to Listen.* A Monograph for Elementary Teachers, No. 80. Evanston, Ill.: Row, Peterson and Company, 1955.

EXERCISES FOR THOUGHT AND DISCUSSION

1. Discuss the similarities and differences in articulation, enunciation, and pronunciation.
2. Summarize a number of ways in which you as a teacher can develop proper audience sensitivity and correct audience attitudes in your classes.
3. List and evaluate the major oral language skill areas stressed in this chapter.
4. Which of the outcomes of the program in oral expression listed in this chapter should, in your judgment, receive major instructional emphasis? Defend your list.
5. What is the practical thing to do about the time to give instruction on those skills common to both oral and written expression?
6. Discuss the relative social significance of the four types of listening emphasized here. Add other types that occur to you.
7. Prepare a list of listening skills to supplement the one given in this chapter.

SELECTED REFERENCES

ARBUTHNOT, MAY HILL. *Children and Books*. Chicago: Scott, Foresman and Company, 1957. Chapter 10.

BAKER, ZELMA W. *The Language Arts, the Child, and the Teacher*. San Francisco: Fearon Publishers, 1955. Chapter 2.

BERRY, ALTHEA. "Listening Activities in the Elementary School." *Elementary English Review*, 23:69–79; February, 1946.

BROWN, CHARLES T. "Studies in Listening Comprehension." *Speech Monographs*, 26:288–294; November 1959.

Commission on the English Curriculum of the National Council of Teachers of English, Dora V. Smith, chairman. *Language Arts for Today's Children*. New York: Appleton-Century-Crofts, Inc., 1954. Chapters 4 and 5.

Creating a Good Environment for Learning. Association for Supervision and Curriculum Development. 1954 Yearbook. Washington: National Education Association, 1954.

EARLY, MARGARET J. "Communication Arts." *Encyclopedia of Educational Research*, third edition, ed. Chester W. Harris. New York: The Macmillan Company, 1960. Pp. 306–312.

An Experience Curriculum in English. A Report of the Curriculum Commission of the National Council of Teachers of English, W. Wilbur Hatfield, Chairman. New York: D. Appleton–Century Co., 1935. Chapters 1, 2, 13.

GREENE, H. A. "English—Language, Grammar, and Composition." *Encyclopedia of Educational Research,* rev. ed. New York: The Macmillan Company, 1950.

HATCHETT, ETHEL L. and HUGHES, DONALD H. *Teaching Language Arts in Elementary Schools.* New York: Ronald Press, 1956. Chapters 5 and 6.

HATFIELD, W. WILBUR. "Parallels in Teaching Students to Listen and to Read." *English Journal,* 35:553–558; December, 1946.

HERRICK, VIRGIL E. and JACOBS, LELAND B., eds. *Children and the Language Arts.* Englewood Cliffs, N.J.: Prentice-Hall, Inc., 1955. Chapters 1, 6, and 7.

KELLER, PAUL W. "Major Findings in Listening in the Past Ten Years." *Journal of Communication* 10:29–38; March 1960.

LOBAN, WALTER; RYAN, MARGARET; and SQUIRE, JAMES R. *Teaching Language and Literature.* New York: Harcourt Brace and World, Inc., 1961. Chapter 4.

MC COWEN, A. "Opportunity to Develop Skill in Communicating Ideas." *Elementary English Review,* 19:99–104; March, 1942.

MC KEE, PAUL. *Language in the Elementary School.* Boston: Houghton Mifflin Company, 1939. Chapters 2 and 3.

MULGRAVE, DOROTHY I. *Speech for the Classroom Teacher.* Englewood Cliffs, N.J.: Prentice-Hall, Inc., 1946.

NICHOLS, RALPH G., and others. *Selected Bibliography of the Literature on Listening Comprehension.* St. Paul: the Author (Department of Rhetoric, University of Minnesota), 1957.

OGILVIE, MARDEL. *Speech in the Elementary School.* New York: McGraw-Hill Book Company, Inc., 1954. Chapters 2, 5, 6, 7, 8, 9, and 10.

PRATT, EDWARD, and GREENE, HARRY A. *Training Children to Listen.* A Monograph for Elementary Teachers, No. 80. Evanston, Ill.: Row, Peterson and Company, 1955.

PLESSAS, GUS P. "Reading Abilities and Intelligence Factors of Children Having High and Low Auding Ability." Unpublished doctoral thesis. Berkeley: University of California, 1957.

SMITH, DORA V. "Learning To Listen, Listening To Learn in the Elementary School." *NEA Journal* 47:100–101; February 1958.

Teaching Language in the Elementary School. Forty-third Yearbook of the National Society for the Study of Education, Part II. Chicago: The University of Chicago Press, 1944. Pp. 64–65, 77–81, 199–200.

Toward Better Speech, Curriculum Bulletin, 1952–53 Series, Number 5. New York: Board of Education of the City of New York. Pp. 23–108.

VAN RIPER, CHARLES, and BUTLER, KATHARINE G. *Speech in the Elementary Classroom.* New York: Harper and Brothers, 1955, Chapters 1 and 2.

5.

The Written Language

Program

IN THIS CHAPTER THE ESSENTIALS OF THE PROGRAM IN WRITTEN expression are formulated around the following topics:

a. The similarities and differences in oral and written expression.
b. Specific written language skill areas, including spelling, handwriting, manuscript form, punctuation, capitalization.
c. Skills in specific written language situations; letter writing, outlining, filling in forms.
d. Writing announcements, memoranda, reports.
e. Using printed sources.
f. Self-editing and proofreading.
g. Rhetorical skills.
h. Creative writing.

The many technical and specialized skill areas which are part of written expression emphasize the necessity for a systematic instructional program, even though written expression is secondary to oral expression in the extent to which it is used. Traditionally, school English programs have emphasized written expression, and through this emphasis have endeavored to improve both written and oral expression. Such an approach will not accomplish that objective, although there are many common skills, as is pointed out in the following chapter.

SIMILARITIES AND DIFFERENCES IN ORAL AND WRITTEN EXPRESSION

Written expression and oral expression are alike in many basic elements, but they are also different in a number of important respects beyond the forms in which the expression takes place. They are alike in the sense that certain grammatical and rhetorical skills contribute to the

111

successful use of either form of expression. They are unlike in the types of special situations in which they are needed. Oral expression depends upon certain physical qualities involved in sound production. Written expression in turn depends heavily upon the development of certain mechanical skills. Written expression is not aided by other factors such as voice tone, inflections, accent, gestures, and the physical appearance or manner of the individual; oral language may be. Oral language is volatile and intangible; a word once uttered disappears except in the mind of the speaker or hearer. Written language, being at least temporarily recorded, comes under much closer scrutiny than does oral language; it can be reviewed and edited. In oral expression, the editing is over when the sentence leaves the speaker's lips.

The language used in writing is generally more formal than that used in speaking. Sentences in written expression are likely to be longer and more complex, and the particular words and expressions used are likely to be less colloquial than those used in oral language activities. In written language, attention must be given to spelling, handwriting, punctuation, capitalization, and manuscript form—skills that naturally do not require emphasis in the oral program. The chart of language skills on page 146 shows the elements in which the oral and the written language programs are alike and unlike, and also shows the emphasis and organization of the discussion in Chapters 4, 5, and 6 of this volume.

WRITTEN LANGUAGE SKILLS

SPELLING

As children record or communicate their ideas or facts by writing, they need the ability to spell correctly. Writing is done for the purpose of transferring information from the writer to his audience. While it is possible, in some instances, to communicate in writing without all of the words being correctly spelled, such communication lacks something in its effectiveness. The ability to spell correctly not only gives the individual confidence and independence in his writing and makes for more effective communication, but it also represents a reasonable if not necessary courtesy to extend to the reader.

In general practice, the instructional program in spelling centers in a textbook or a workbook; in some schools, the spelling vocabulary is taken from the daily work of the children. But in either case, too often the spelling instruction is limited and not really correlated with the general program in language. The goal in spelling is, of course, to teach children to spell the words they are most likely to need to spell in their life activities as children and as adults. This goal is based upon an acceptance by our society of certain more or less standardized ways in which words are spelled in order to communicate effectively the thought or information we are writing about.[1]

The goal described above sets only the general pattern for the spelling program. This goal must be expressed in more specific objectives if it is to be achieved. The following basic objectives should be understood by every teacher or supervisor planning a spelling program:

1. To develop in each child an attitude that
   a. recognizes that correct spelling is important to effective communication.
   b. creates a desire to spell correctly all the words he writes.
   c. instills a desire to spell correctly an increasing number of words and to understand and use words more effectively.
2. To develop in each child the habit of
   a. always being concerned about the correct spelling of the words used in writing.
   b. proofreading his writing carefully.
   c. using reliable sources to determine the correct spelling of unknown or doubtful words.
   d. following a specific study procedure in learning the spelling of new words.
3. To develop in each child the ability to
   a. recognize all the letters of the alphabet in capital and lower case forms in both printed and handwritten materials.
   b. write all the letters of the alphabet in a legible manner in both capital and lower case forms.
   c. alphabetize words.
   d. hear words accurately as they are spoken.
   e. pronounce words clearly and accurately.
   f. see printed or written words accurately.
   g. group and connect the letters of a word properly.
   h. use properly any punctuation elements important to spelling.
   i. use a dictionary, including the use of diacritical markings and guide words.
   j. use phonetic aids in arriving at the proper pronunciation of unfamiliar words.
   k. use the most effective spelling rules.
   l. use effective procedures in learning to spell new words.

Vocabulary. If a child is to write effectively, he must learn to spell the words he uses. This means that the child must be taught to spell a core vocabulary of the words most useful in written communication. The selection of this writing vocabulary is important because upon it depends the teacher's success in developing the desired attitudes toward

---

[1] See discussion of the social utility principle in Chapter 2.

correct spelling as an important element in written communication.

In the selection of words for a spelling program, both for the beginning speller and for the more advanced one, the research on adult and child writing vocabularies should be utilized. The basic vocabulary of a modern spelling workbook or textbook should include the words most used by children and adults in writing activities. These words have been selected on the basis of frequency counts of words written by adults in their daily-life writing and by children in school compositions, letters, and informal writing in and out of school. Numerous investigations have been made to determine these words. The most comprehensive study of the writing vocabulary of adults was made by Ernest Horn and published in 1926.[2] The best known of the frequency counts of children's writing was made by Rinsland and published in 1945.[3] Numerous other word lists have been derived from these early frequency counts. One of the more recent of these is that compiled by Fitzgerald from numerous child and adult writing vocabularies.[4] Important too as a spelling vocabulary source (though not originally intended for that purpose by the author) is *The New Iowa Spelling Scale*.[5] This source lists 5,507 words which elementary school children are commonly called upon to spell and indicates the percentage of children who at the beginning of each grade may be expected to spell each word correctly.

Naturally the reports of frequency counts of words used in writing show much variation. However, numerous spelling authorities have called attention to the fact that the commonest words written by children are also commonly used by adults.[6] Fitzgerald reported a concurrence of 1,972 words in comparing the most common 3,000 words used by children in letter writing and the most common 4,000 words used by adults as reported by Horn. Breed, reporting the results of several of the spelling vocabulary investigations, stated that 2,500 words constitute 96.7 per cent of all words used by adults and that 59.17 per cent

[2] Ernest Horn. *A Basic Writing Vocabulary; 10,000 Words Most Commonly Used in Writing*. Monographs in Education, No. 4. Iowa City: State University of Iowa, 1926.

[3] H. D. Rinsland. *A Basic Writing Vocabulary of Elementary School Children*. New York: The Macmillan Company, 1945.

[4] James A. Fitzgerald. *A Basic Life Spelling Vocabulary*. Milwaukee: Bruce Publishing Company, 1951.

[5] Harry A. Greene. *The New Iowa Spelling Scale*. Iowa City: Bureau of Educational Research and Service, State University of Iowa, 1954.

[6] See summaries in: James A. Fitzgerald, *The Teaching of Spelling*, Milwaukee: The Bruce Publishing Company, 1951; Gertrude Hildreth, *Teaching Spelling*, New York: Henry Holt and Company, 1955; and Ernest Horn, "Spelling." *Encyclopedia of Educational Research*, third edition, Chester W. Harris, ed., New York: The Macmillan Company, 1960, pp. 1337–1354.

of the words in studies of adult and children's usages are common to both.[7]

Children should learn to spell the words they most often will need to spell as adults. They also ought to learn to spell the words necessary for their immediate and future school needs, as well as for their own needs for writing out of school. These words, then, should form the basic vocabulary of the spelling program. Most present-day spelling books are based upon this point of view and contain not more than 4,000 words in their basic lists, although some include additional words in supplementary lists.[8]

Early in the language program children need to learn to spell the words they are currently using in their writing activities in school. To some extent, then, the specific spelling words to be learned must be determined by local curricular emphasis. Children should learn the words specifically required for their individual needs as they arise. The teacher or local school staff certainly should not be responsible for the compilation of the basic spelling vocabulary. Not only is this an expensive and technical task, but it might lead to grave omissions in the basic vocabulary. Moreover, the results of extensive research in this area are already available to the teacher.[9]

The total number of words to be taught in the spelling program is perhaps not so important as is the stress upon spelling in all writing activities and upon the supplemental spelling skills of proofreading, using the dictionary, and learning to apply spelling generalizations.[10] Furthermore, teachers and curriculum workers must make adjustments in the list of words to be taught in order to care for the needs and abilities of slow and gifted learners. When such adjustment is needed, it should be done on the basis of evidence of the relative importance of the words in the basic list for a specific grade level or for the school. Teachers should turn to the reports made by Horn, Greene, Fitzgerald, and others for this help and not attempt to decide subjectively the importance or suitability of a particular word. As Horn says: "It is important to remember that it is impossible to teach all the words which children need in their writing, much less all words needed by adults."[11] It should be

---

[7] F. S. Breed. *The Selection and Gradation of the Spelling Vocabulary,* Sixteenth Yearbook of the National Elementary Principals Association. Washington: National Education Association, July, 1937.

[8] Ernest Horn. *What Research Says to the Teacher: Teaching Spelling.* Washington: National Education Association, 1954.

[9] Greene, *op. cit.;* Horn, *A Basic Writing Vocabulary.*

[10] Horn, *Encyclopedia of Educational Research, op. cit.,* p. 1344.

[11] Horn, *op. cit.*

noted that Horn mentions the impossibility of *teaching,* not the impossibility of a child or an adult *learning,* the words needed in his writing.

Abbreviations. Most formal writing that children and adults are called upon to do requires the writing out of certain words that might in some instances be abbreviated. Children should learn to write out words rather than abbreviate them unless common practice permits the use of abbreviation in the particular situation. Such abbreviations as A.M. and P.M. are commonly used in sentences. Other abbreviations which should be learned but are written as complete words in sentences are: *doz., qt., in., ft., yd., lb., bu.,* and the names of the days of the week and the months of the year. *Mr., Mrs.,* and *Dr.* are abbreviated in writing if they are used as titles with proper names. Abbreviations for the names of some states and for street, *st.,* and rural delivery route, *R.D.,* may properly be used in letter writing.

The relatively few abbreviations selected for teaching should be taught as they are needed. This means, for example, that second grade children, as they learn about the writing of informal and friendly letters, will need to learn the abbreviations *Mr.* and *Mrs.* Many of the other abbreviations which children should learn later and which they may have occasion to write, in school, such as *doz., ft.,* and others, should be taught as the need arises in science, arithmetic, or other classes. However, care should be taken that the occasions for using such abbreviations do arise somewhere in the elementary school program.

Contractions. In informal oral expression we commonly use many contractions that are very rarely used in most written language. Contractions that are commonly used in informal writing may be taught in elementary school, but probably more attention should be given to discouraging their over-use. The spelling of contractions often causes difficulty for many children. The fact that some contractions omit one letter and some use the apostrophe to replace more than one letter might be one cause of difficulty. Then too, certain contractions are sometimes confused with a possessive pronoun of similar spelling, such as *it's* being confused with the possessive *its.*

Generally, in grade three children begin to learn to use the apostrophe in the spelling of such contractions as *isn't* and *aren't.* In grade four the practice of using the apostrophe to replace the *o* in a negative verb form continues. Such contractions as *wasn't, weren't, hasn't, couldn't,* and *don't* are usually taught. In addition, in grade four contractions such as *you'll, I'm, it's,* and *we've* are also taught. In grade five are taught contractions which omit more than one or two letters, such as *you'd*. Also taught in grades five and six are *can't, haven't, doesn't, didn't, we're, you're, who's, they're,* and *wouldn't*.

HANDWRITING

Observation of a typical elementary school classroom will reveal some disturbing conditions relative to handwriting and to the entire written language program. Children are likely to be sitting in all sorts of positions at their desks, with pencils and papers clutched in various ways, and with the papers upon which they are writing at unusual or incorrect angles. This too-typical situation would seem to be the result of improperly applying a sound principle. Today in schools the principal objective of handwriting is communication. Children write in order to communicate; in order to communicate, the handwriting must be legible. Thus, we no longer stress meaningless drills in handwriting instruction but strive mainly to produce legible copy. The misapplication of the principle of use and need has come about through the neglect of sound principles of instruction in handwriting. The principal factor that is overlooked is that handwriting is a developmental process that requires more than just a few years of the child's total period of growth. This simply means that attention must be given in schools to the proper development of this skill. Handwriting cannot be once taught and then dropped from the instructional program. Production of legible copy at a reasonable speed can be maintained only as a result of constant practice.

A handwriting program that gives adequate emphasis to the teaching of the necessary skills and their maintenance should be built around these basic goals:

1. To encourage pupils to use handwriting as an effective means of expression and thought.
2. To help each child discover how skill in handwriting will serve his needs.
3. To strive for neatness and legibility with moderate speed in all the writing activities of pupils.
4. To establish adequate practice periods which will provide training in handwriting at all grade levels.
5. To analyze handwriting faults of individual pupils and seek their correction.
6. To develop in all pupils a sense of personal pride, self-appraisal, and self-improvement in the handwriting skills.
7. To develop correct posture and the proper use of writing tools.

Such goals are directed at the development of attitudes which foster learning of the skills of handwriting. More specific objectives of the

117

actual mechanical skills are suggested by the definition of good writing in one curriculum guide.[12]

Good writing must be legible; it must have:
1. Correct letter formation
2. Good spacing between letters and words
3. Uniform slant
4. Satisfactory alignment
5. Correct size letters

Good writing must make a pleasing appearance; it must have:
1. Careful arrangement of work
2. Neatness
3. Smooth, even line quality

Good writing must be easily written; to write easily, one must have at all times:
1. Good posture (body, arms, hands)
2. Correct position of materials (pen, book, paper)
3. Free movement (not exclusively arm movement)
4. Rhythm (properly stressed strokes and pauses)

Good writing must show life and dash in quality of line and spacing; this is accomplished by:
1. Making strokes rapidly
2. Decreasing the duration of pauses, letters, and words

Manuscript vs. cursive. The educational controversy over the teaching of manuscript (print script) writing versus the teaching of cursive writing has been waged for more than a quarter of a century. Some of the questions concerning the basic problem seem to have been resolved, but other problems are still live topics of discussion. Most modern schools have accepted the practice of teaching manuscript writing for the child's initial writing experiences, but the extension of the manuscript form as the only or principal means of writing throughout the grades and high school is still a topic of considerable debate. Some schools continue to teach manuscript writing throughout the grades and give no instruction in cursive writing. Other schools continue instruction on manuscript after beginning the teaching of cursive writing. The actual number of school systems following either of the latter two practices is at this time limited.

Manuscript writing undoubtedly is easier to teach to six- and seven-year-old children than is cursive writing. Children in the first and second grades, because of their limited control of the small muscles, are better able to make the simple circular and straight line movements needed for manuscript writing than they are the more intricate and varied movements needed for cursive writing. Studies have shown, too, that manu-

[12] "Language Arts Guide, Grades K–6," Jefferson County Schools, Lakewood, Colorado, 1960, pp. 127–128.

118

script writing seems to favor the development of fluency of expression in the primary grades.[13] Since fluency of language expression is a major goal of the language program, the extension of the use of manuscript writing, particularly into the third and fourth grades, has become the major item of the current controversy.

The point here is that since society still demands that the schools teach cursive writing, the change from the manuscript form to the cursive form should be made at such a point in the school program and in the development of a child as will least interfere with language expression. Since the language program in grades one and two should be largely oral, it would seem that this transfer should be made near the end of the second grade and thus before the more formal written language program begins.[14]

Handedness. Left-handed writers seem to be a perennial classroom problem to many teachers. Much of this concern is unwarranted, however, and due to a lack of understanding of how to help the left-handed child adjust to a skill that is performed by most children with the right hand and for which instructional material is geared to right-handed children. There is confusion often as to whether a left-handed writer should be changed to a right-handed one.

The first thing for the teacher to realize is that no one is entirely left-handed nor entirely right-handed. Furthermore, as Cole points out: [15]

It is essential that a teacher be totally indifferent in the matter of hand preference. She must regard a preference for the left hand over the right hand as no more disturbing than the possession of blue eyes instead of brown. This should not be taken to mean that the teacher is not expected to make instructional adjustments to meet the problem.

Most authorities agree that hand dominance is fairly well established by the time children reach school age. They further recommend that the child who is dominantly left-handed be trained to use the left hand for writing and not changed to the more common right-handed pattern. There are some children, of course, who will come to school with a wavering dominance. For these few children it is recommended that encouragement be given to using the right hand, since this is largely a right-handed world. Where the left-handed dominance is strong, the concern of teachers should be in the direction of helping the child learn to

[13] See footnote 18 on page 80.

[14] Helen Heffernan, and Bernard Lonsdale, "Learning to Speak, Read, and Write," *Teachers Guide to Education in Early Childhood*. Sacramento: Bureau of Elementary Education, State Department of Education, 1956, chapter 11, p. 371.

[15] Luella Cole, "Instruction in Penmanship for the Left-handed Child," *Elementary School Journal*, 39:436–448; February, 1939.

write with greater ease, legibility, and speed than he might otherwise be able to do if left to his own solution of the problem.

MANUSCRIPT FORM

Many of you undoubtedly can recall being confused at various times in your school lives over the many contradictory practices regarding the matter of form in written work. There were inconsistencies regarding the width of the various margins on a page of written work, the placement of the title, or the names on papers to be handed in. We still note many such inconsistencies in manuscript form today. For most children, these inconsistent teachings are sources of confusion and lead to time spent in explanations that could better be spent in improving written language abilities.

There are no set rules for manuscript form. There are some generally accepted ideas such as margins at top and bottom and at the right and left on the paper, but the width of these margins will vary with the person prescribing the form. To avoid needless confusion some schools have agreed on certain items of form to be followed within the system.

The following items concerning manuscript form are suggested for consideration and for agreement by the teachers in a school system. An excellent practice is for the school to compile a handbook on form, style, and usage for the guidance of the teachers and the pupils.

Kindergarten	No written work, but the teacher should call the attention of the children to material which involves form. For example, attention could be called to the attractiveness of neat work, to margins in books and newspapers, to titles of stories, to attractive arrangements of work on paper.
Grade one	a. Margin at left and right
	b. Spacing at top and bottom of page
	c. First word of a paragraph indented
	d. Second line of paragraph brought back to margin
	e. Writing all work to be handed in carefully, on one side of the paper.
Grade two	a. All outlined above for grade one
	b. Spacing between title and body of a composition
	c. Indenting the number as well as the first word if the paragraph is numbered
	d. Placing the name and date correctly on paper

Grade three
    a. All outlined for previous grades
    b. Correct form used in writing several sentences in one paragraph
    c. Leaving last line of a ruled sheet blank
    d. Avoiding crowding at end of a line

Grades four, five, and six
    a. All outlined for previous grades
    b. Placing of all work on paper with attention to beauty as well as correctness
    c. Use of correct paper for particular writing occasions

One school recognized the lack of agreement on many matters of form by including in its language guide this entry.[16]

Heading for Written Work

That a uniform heading be used for all written work by all pupils in the elementary schools the committee recommended that the following forms be used:

Grades 2–6

School _____ Name _____

Date _____ Grade _____

Grade 1

Name _____

PUNCTUATION

Errors in punctuation are the most frequent type of mechanical errors in writing. Studies which have analyzed the writing of elementary and secondary school children and of adults show that errors in punctuation persist through all educational levels. These studies indicate that, in general, skill in punctuation is difficult to acquire, or it has not been well taught in schools. Perhaps the greatest cause of this difficulty is that too little attention is given to the punctuation items of greatest social importance and too much effort is wasted upon items of little, if any, importance.

The task of determining the relative importance of punctuation items is to the classroom teacher like the selection of words for the basic spelling list. Exact information is difficult to come by and a "guess" may be wrong. An analysis of language textbooks is likely to be unreliable, since the authors of such books do not agree as to the importance

[16] Jefferson County Schools, *op. cit.,* p. 158.

121

of various items.[17] Textbooks which based their punctuation program on such studies as that by Evans, however, may give reliable evidence of the social importance of various punctuation items.[18] Evans made a frequency count of punctuation variants used by pupils in grades four through eight in a wide variety of writing activities. His study showed that thirty variants account for an average of 80 per cent of the punctuation needs in each of the grades. The specific variants or items he reported are:

1. A period is used to mark the end of a complete sentence which is neither mandatory, interrogatory, nor exclamatory.
2. The colon is used after several words used as the salutation of a business letter.
3. A comma should be used after the complimentary close of a business letter.
4. The apostrophe is used in forming the possessive case of singular nouns.
5. The apostrophe is used to indicate the omission of a letter from the interior of a contraction.
6. The comma is always used before the abbreviation "etc." when the latter is in the interior of a sentence.
7. A comma is used to separate independent clauses joined by "and" if there is a change of subject.
8. The interrogation point is used at the end of a whole sentence used as a question.
9. The comma is used to set off a dependent "if" clause preceding the main clause.
10. The comma is used to separate nouns in series when they are not connected by a conjunction.
11. A direct quotation at the end of a sentence may be separated from its preceding introductory material by a comma.
12. Quotation marks are used before and after a direct quotation at the end of the sentence.
13. The period is placed inside the quotation marks at the end of directly quoted discourse.
14. A period is used to separate dollars and cents.
15. A comma should be used after the salutation of an informal letter.
16. A comma is used after the last word of a series of words, phrases, or clauses, or letters not connected by a conjunction.
17. The semicolon may be used between two coordinate clauses which are not connected by a conjunction.

[17] See Paul Cesander, "A Study of Pupil Usage as a Factor in the Grade Placement of Certain Items of Punctuation." Unpublished doctoral dissertation, State University of Iowa, 1931; also reported in Harold G. Shane, *Research Helps in Teaching Language Arts,* A Report for the Association for Supervision and Curriculum Development. Washington: National Education Association, 1955, p. 59.

[18] J. W. Evans, "The Social Importance and Pupil Control of Certain Punctuation Variants." Unpublished doctoral dissertation, State University of Iowa, 1939.

18. A colon is placed after a single word used as the salutation of a business letter.
19. Quotation marks may be used to enclose the titles of books.
20. A period should be placed inside quotation marks. (This variant covers situations not involving quoted conversation.)
21. A period is used after the abbreviations "Mr." and "Mrs."
22. A comma should be used after the complimentary close of an informal letter.
23. Parentheses may be used to enclose sums of money in business letters.
24. The comma is used to separate prepositional phrases in series when they are not connected by a conjunction.
25. A comma may be used to separate any other elements which might otherwise be improperly joined in reading.
26. Commas are used to set off a noun in apposition in the interior of a sentence.
27. A comma is used to set off a noun in apposition at the end of a sentence, title, or quotation.
28. The colon may be used before enumerations.
29. A comma is used to separate independent clauses joined by "but" or "only" if there is a change of subject.
30. The comma is used to set off certain introductory phrases.

These punctuation items were determined on the basis of an arbitrary criterion, the authority as to "correct" word usage, namely custom and practice, which are generally considered to be based upon the need of a particular punctuation item as an aid to clear communication. However, opinions vary as to this need. Greene, for example, analyzed the manuals of style of seven publishing houses on the assumption that the editorial departments of such organizations would be authoritative sources for the evaluation of the many different punctuation usages.[19] This assumption was partly borne out, but of the total of 124 items checked only 57 were found to be included in four or more of the editorial manuals. Thus, it would seem that wide disagreement is likely to be present in comparisons even among "authorities."

On the other hand, there is definite realization that punctuation is an effective aid to written expression, and hence, certain punctuation skills must be taught. Both the Evans and the Greene studies show that a limited number of items are recognized as important and widely used. These items are those which are technical aids to the types of writing children and adults are called upon to do and accordingly should be the basis of the program in punctuation.

The following is a suggested list by grade levels of punctuation items that should receive instruction in the elementary school:

[19] Harry A. Greene, *A Criterion for the Course of Study in the Mechanics of Written Composition.* Studies in Education, Vol. VIII, No. 4. Iowa City: State University of Iowa, November 4, 1933.

Grade one
    a. Period at the end of a sentence which tells something
    b. Period after numbers in any kind of list

Grade two
    a. Items listed for grade one
    b. Question mark at the close of a question
    c. Comma after salutation of a friendly note or letter
    d. Comma after closing of a friendly note or letter
    e. Comma between the day of the month and the year
    f. Comma between name of city and state

Grade three
    a. Items listed for grades one and two
    b. Period after abbreviations
    c. Period after an initial
    d. Use of an apostrophe in common contractions such as isn't, aren't
    e. Commas in a list

Grade four
    a. All items listed for previous grades
    b. Apostrophe to show possession
    c. Hyphen separating parts of a word divided at end of a line
    d. Period following a command
    e. Exclamation point at the end of a word or group of words that makes an exclamation
    f. Comma setting off an appositive
    g. Colon after the salutation of a business letter
    h. Quotation marks before and after a direct quotation
    i. Comma between explanatory words and a quotation
    j. Period after outline Roman number

Grade five
    a. All items listed for previous grades
    b. Colon in writing time
    c. Comma to indicate changed word order
    d. Quotation marks around the title of a booklet, pamphlet, the chapter of a book, and the title of a poem or story
    e. Underlining the title of a book

Grade six
    a. All items listed for previous grades
    b. Comma to set off nouns in direct address
    c. Hyphen in compound numbers
    d. Colon to set off a list
    e. Comma in sentences to aid in making meaning clear

CAPITALIZATION

Capitalization, like punctuation, is a mechanical element of written language about which considerable evidence concerning needs at various grade levels has accumulated. These needs have been identified by examining examples of spontaneous writing and by examining the particular capitalization items for proper order of treatment and relative difficulty. Courses of study and textbooks in language are often quite definite in listing grade requirements in the area of capitalization. However, it is well to remember that such listings are merely guides for the introduction of drill upon the items and that within a classroom there will be considerable variation in skill in capitalization, as there is in language usage. This means, therefore, that items of capitalization called for generally in grades two and three should be mastered by an individual child before items which may be listed for grades five or six.

The following list of minimal capitalization skills by grades is suggestive only, but it does take into account the needs of children in writing and the relative difficulty of the various items.

Grade one	*a.* The first word of a sentence
	b. The child's first and last names
	c. The name of the teacher, school, town, street
	d. The word I
Grade two	*a.* Items listed for grade one
	b. The date
	c. First and important words of titles of books the children read
	d. Proper names used in children's writings
	e. Titles of compositions
	f. Names of titles: "Mr.," "Mrs.," "Miss"
Grade three	*a.* Items listed for grades one and two
	b. Proper names: month, day, common holidays
	c. First word in a line of verse
	d. First and important words in titles of books, stories, poems
	e. First word of salutation of informal note, as "Dear"
	f. First word of closing of informal note, as "Yours"
Grade four	*a.* All that is listed for preceding grades
	b. Names of cities and states in general
	c. Names of organizations to which children belong, as Boy Scouts, Grade Four, etc.

125

    d. Mother, Father, when used in place of the name
    e. Local geographical names

Grade five
    a. All that is outlined for previous grades
    b. Names of streets
    c. Names of all places and persons, countries, oceans, etc.
    d. Capitalization used in outlining
    e. Titles when used with names, such as President Lincoln
    f. Commercial trade names

Grade six
    a. All that is outlined for preceding grades
    b. Names of the Deity and the Bible
    c. First word of a quoted sentence
    d. Proper adjectives, showing race, nationality, etc.
    e. Abbreviations of proper nouns and titles

In addition to teaching the proper use of capital letters, attention must be directed toward the importance of eliminating unnecessary capitals in all writing. In particular the practice of capitalizing words for purposes of emphasis should be avoided.

USAGE

Using good language is largely a matter of habit, but it is unsafe to assume that habits formed in one situation will transfer without loss to another, no matter how similar the two situations may appear to be. The child who uses good language in speaking situations may have a good start toward good usage in written expression, but he may also make errors in oral work that he does not make at all in written expression. The reverse of this is also true. Because of the importance of teaching acceptable usage, and because usage is of concern to both oral and written expression, the discussion of this program is presented in the following chapter.

SKILLS IN SPECIFIC WRITTEN
LANGUAGE SITUATIONS

LETTER WRITING

The writing of letters is one of the most important written language activities of life and on that account should receive major instructional emphasis in the elementary school. Almost everyone at some time needs to write friendly letters, informal notes, and business letters. Instruction in letter writing should include letters of all types. Experience with each letter form should be carried to the point of giving the child complete confidence in his ability to produce a letter adequate in both content and form.

If instructional emphasis is to be given to language situations in proportion to the social burden they carry in expression, letter writing should be emphasized constantly in written language instruction. The pupil should consider at all times what is said in the light of the purpose for which the letter is written. All teaching of letter writing in any grade must always emphasize content. Interest factors in social letters and essential items in business letters should be carefully discussed and clearly understood by the class. The child should consider that without good content a letter is nothing, and that items of form are an important but secondary matter.

It is most important that the children in all grades acquire correct attitudes toward letter writing. These will come largely through informal discussion and the teacher's wise use of real situations. Among the important attitudes are the following:

1. Answering questions that have been asked.
2. Implying or expressing respect and esteem.
3. Expressing earned congratulations.
4. Expressing sympathy when needed.
5. Inquiring about matters of concern to the reader.
6. Expressing good wishes.
7. Keeping the letter tidy.
8. Enclosing a stamped envelope when requesting a reply from uninterested parties.
9. Never reading another's letter except upon request.
10. Selecting appropriate materials (pen, paper).
11. Mailing letters promptly.
12. Writing and typing the signature when the typewriter is used.
13. Placing the return address on the envelope.
14. Reading letters before mailing.
15. Making social letters as interesting as possible.
16. Being concerned about the quality of writing and the correctness of spelling.
17. Answering invitations.
18. Giving reasons when refusing invitations.
19. Not writing letters in anger.
20. Answering letters with relative promptness.

127

In addition to these attitudes toward letter writing, children need to develop certain abilities which contribute to good letter writing. Among those that are peculiar to letter writing are the following:

1. A realization that a letter is a means of communication.
2. A realization that a letter has different parts.
3. A sensitivity to the situations in which a letter should be written.
4. A knowledge of the purpose of each of the different parts of a letter.
5. The ability to capitalize, punctuate, and place correctly the heading, salutation, ending, and signature.
6. A knowledge of the relative position of each of the parts of a letter.
7. The knowledge of what should be included in each part of a letter.
8. The ability to space the various parts of a letter properly.
9. A knowledge of the appropriateness of different types of salutations, addresses, and endings in terms of the addressee and the type of letter being written.
10. The ability to spell correctly certain words of great importance in letter writing such as: dear, Mr., Mrs., Miss, gentlemen; names of cities, states, months; friend, sincerely, truly, sir, etc.
11. A knowledge of what is appropriate to say in a letter in terms of the circumstances of the writing.
12. A knowledge of the factors that make a friendly letter interesting.
13. A knowledge of worn expressions to be avoided in letter writing.
14. The ability to keep the content of a business letter appropriate and to arrange the necessary information correctly.
15. The ability to write and place the address correctly on the envelope.
16. A knowledge of the appropriateness of writing materials to the purpose and type of letter.
17. The ability to write and place the return address on the envelope, and an understanding of its importance.
18. A knowledge of how to enclose money in a letter, and how to write dollars and cents.
19. A knowledge of how to fold a letter.
20. The ability to capitalize names of firms.
21. The ability to write simple informal and formal invitations and acceptances.
22. A knowledge of the location of the first word in the body of a letter.
23. A knowledge of what types of invitations deserve formal answers.
24. A knowledge of sources of information relative to correct procedure in regard to invitations.
25. A knowledge of abbreviations to use in titles, addresses, etc.
26. Certain attitudes of fundamental importance in letter writing such as (1) neatness, (2) handwriting conscience, (3) spelling conscience, (4) promptness in mailing letters, and (5) answering letters.

The form in which a letter is written is largely a matter of custom, which to a large degree is determined by the purpose of the communication. Two types of acceptable forms for friendly letters are in common use: the block form, and the indented form. With both of these forms, punctuation at the end of the lines is usually omitted. Some elementary teachers prefer to teach the indented form for pen-written letters. Because of the wide use of the typewriter in all forms of communication the authors recommend that the block form be taught in initial instruction on letter writing. The teacher should explain to the child that the block form is one of two equally acceptable forms. The block form works equally well for pen-written or for typed letters, and for simple friendly or business letters. It has the additional advantage of simplicity and ease of learning, due to the fact that the child is able to concentrate on a single form in the early stages of learning. The indented form may be introduced in the fifth or the sixth grade with the explanation that this form is also acceptable. It should be emphasized that either form may be used, but that one form or the other should be followed consistently throughout the writing and addressing of a single letter.

The accompanying illustrations show the acceptable block form for the simple friendly letter (Sample A) and for the return and main address of the envelope (Sample B). These samples also indicate the proper names and positioning of the parts of the letter. Sample C illustrates acceptable form for the pen-written or the typewritten business letter. Sample D shows the indented form of the pen-written or typewritten business letter with inside address.

Sample A: Friendly Letter

(street and number) _____

(city and state) _____

(date) _____

(greeting) _____

(body) _____

_____

_____

_____

_____

(closing) _____

(signature) _____

Sample B: Envelope

(sender)   _____

                     _____

                     _____

(addressee)   _____

                                 _____

                                 _____

                                 _____

**Sample C: Typed or Pen-written Business Letter,
Block Form**

(heading)   _____

                                             _____

                                             _____

(inside address)   _____

                         _____

                         _____

(salutation)   _____ :

                     _____

                     _____

(body)   _____

                     _____

                     _____

(closing)   _____

(signature)   _____

130

Sample D: Typed or Pen-written Business Letter,
Indented Form

(*heading*)   _____

                                              _____

                                            _____

(*inside address*)   _____

                    _____

                      _____

(*salutation*)   _____ :

                  _____

                  _____

(*body*)   _____

                  _____

                  _____

                  _____

(*closing*)   _____

(*signature*)   _____

These items include the majority of specific abilities that children should acquire in the elementary school and that should be considered the particular objectives of the aspect of form in an instructional program in letter writing.

OUTLINING

The ability to outline should be taught in the elementary school as a necessary aid to study, and to the planning of all types of oral and written expressional activities. Children and adults who are skilled in outlining can properly organize written material for reference purposes.

Outlines may be made of work to be done, of a story that is to be told, or a report that is to be presented to the class. Simple beginnings in outlining may be made in the primary grades as either a part of language or reading instruction, thus introducing the children early to the idea of classification and organization. For example, in the kindergarten the children might dictate lists of items such as the following to the teacher to be written on the blackboard:

Fruits	*Vegetables*
Oranges	Lettuce
Apples	Carrots
Grapes	Potatoes

Young children should make simple outlines of such things as a story to be told or dramatized, a trip that is to be taken or was taken, materials needed for a project. In the intermediate grades these types of outlining activities should be continued in greater detail.

The objectives of the written language program in teaching outlining should include the following: [20]

Primary grades (1–3)

a. To learn that an outline is an aid in clear and orderly thinking.

b. To be able to outline important material under proper headings and to discard minor details.

c. To be able to arrange ideas in proper sequence.

d. To be able to determine the main topic of paragraphs in a selection of more than one paragraph.

e. To realize the significance of sub-topics for an outline of material read.

f. To be able to number and punctuate a series of main topics.

g. To learn to capitalize the first and important words of main topics.

h. To be able to use the capital Roman I, II, etc., for main heads.

i. To know that the period is omitted after a title or after main headings (except when sentences are used), and that a period should be used after a Roman number.

Intermediate grades (4–6)

a. To continue practice on all primary objectives.

b. To learn to write outlines correctly with main topics and first and second sub-topics.

[20] Adapted from Iowa Elementary Teachers Handbook, Vol. 4, *Oral and Written Language*. Des Moines: Iowa State Department of Public Instruction, 1944, pp. 89–91.

        c. To see the values of outlining for comprehension and organization of thinking.
        d. To form the habit of making an outline when it is needed in connection with speeches and reports.

Upper grades (7–8) *a.* To continue and refine use of former objectives.
        b. To learn to outline correctly in the complete form of main topics and subheads.
        c. To know the vocabulary used in outlining, for example: Topics, heading, major, main, sub, subordinate, sequence, indent, irrelevant.
        d. To develop definite habits of using outlines when they will be helpful.

It is well to remember that outlining should be regarded as a means to an end and not an end itself. It is a means of organizing in a logical and developmental way the related elements of a topic. The child should learn very early that while an outline is a valuable aid in organizing, there are times when the material will not go together as he first planned it. Then the best thing to do is to abandon the original outline and to organize it as is indicated by the new idea.

Outlines may be made in topical form or in sentence form. For the younger children the sentence form is undoubtedly easier to follow. If the sentence form is used, it should be pointed out that the period must be placed at the end of each sentence as in any other written work. The important thing for them to learn is to use one form consistently within the same outline. There is no one acceptable form for outlining, but some major principles such as the following may be used in developing the form for use in a particular school:

1. The outline should have an introductory and a concluding topic or sentence.
2. Each major topic should be of comparable importance and directly related to the subject of the outline.
3. There must be at least two sub-topics under each major topic.
4. The same form for numbering, lettering, indenting, capitalizing, and punctuating should be used throughout the outline.
5. There should be no punctuation after the topics unless they are complete sentences.

The following outline form is offered as a general guide for either a topical or a sentence outline carrying three main topics with sub-topics. If sub-topics are indented, their subordinate value becomes apparent.

133

Suggested outline form

I. First main topic
   A. First sub-topic
   B. Second sub-topic
II. Second main topic
   A. First sub-topic
   B. Second sub-topic
III. Third main topic
   A. First sub-topic
   B. Second sub-topic

FILLING IN FORMS

All of us as adults are frequently called upon to fill in forms of one kind or another. We fill in the information called for on a test booklet, on the application for a driver's license, or on an order blank. There are many situations in day-to-day activities in school in which children are called upon to fill in forms. These situations should be utilized for language instruction. It is important, if forms are to be filled in accurately and completely, that children attain certain attitudes concerning these tasks. The following attitudes pertain particularly to filling in forms:

1. Realizing the necessity of filling out blanks accurately and neatly
2. Realizing the necessity of following directions fully and accurately
3. Giving information in the form that is called for
4. Striving to give all the information called for
5. Using every effort to make the completed work look attractive

Situations in school which involve the filling in of forms may include the following:

1. Writing a money order
   a. To a picture company for pictures to be used in booklets
   b. To a cotton mill for cotton to be used in a display
   c. For seeds for a school garden
   d. To a manufacturing company for material to be used in social science
   e. To a publishing company for a magazine subscribed to by the class
2. Information blanks
   a. Questionnaires regarding personal history or health
   b. Enrollment cards
   c. Library loan card
   d. Call slip for books at the library
   e. The heading of a standardized test
   f. An application blank for membership in a magazine club
   g. A book plate for textbooks

134

3. Forms concerned with banking
   a. A deposit slip for school savings account
   b. An application card for a bank in the school savings organization
   c. A withdrawal slip
4. Mail order forms
   a. A subscription blank
   b. A coupon for samples or free booklets as advertized in magazine
   c. An order to a firm for books to be used in reference work

ANNOUNCEMENTS, NOTICES, LABELS, TITLES, SIGNS

The writing and posting of announcements and notices, and the making of signs, labels, and titles are activities that arise constantly in the elementary school. The teacher should be ever alert to utilize all situations for teaching the skills involved in these activities. These language situations call for correlation with art and with handwriting as well as with many other activities of the school.

The objectives of the program should include the following:[21]

Primary grades:	*a.* To discover that announcements and notices posted on the bulletin board often contain valuable information and should be read
	b. To acquire skill in writing a clearly understandable statement of a school event, including the essentials of time, purpose, and place
	c. To know where and how to get permission to post a notice at school
	d. To know the proper location of various kinds of notices
	e. To know the form of capitalization and punctuation that should be used
	f. To study attractive arrangement and correct spacing
	g. To learn that some kinds of labels, signs, and notices should be designed to catch the eye
	h. To learn that appropriateness, accuracy, and brevity are the three major tests of good notices and announcements
Intermediate and upper grades:	*a.* To continue refinement of all previous objectives
	b. To be able to make a clear statement of all essentials in the wording of notices, announcements, and advertisements

[21] *Ibid.* Adapted.

In the primary grades the use of labels, signs, and poster and chart titles should be widespread. Labels are often used for identifying and arranging room furnishings and personal belongings. In the intermediate grades similar types of labels and signs are frequently used to identify and display articles collected by the class and by individual pupils. In the early grades the labels and signs are generally made by the teacher in terms of the decisions of the class about their content. As pupils become capable of doing so, individual pupils should be given this responsibility.

MEMORANDA, RULES, RECEIPTS, MINUTES

Throughout the elementary school children have need to write memoranda of various sorts, rules for games or other activities, and various kinds of records, including receipts and minutes. Generally, the occasions for such writing will come up in numerous types of classroom activities. Similar occasions also arise in the lives of most adults and hence represent an important need for written language instruction.

McKee classifies most of these activities under the heading of *Keeping Records*.[22] He includes:

1. A class activity such as a yearbook in which experiences and information are recorded.
2. Special topic books such as "Our Iron and Steel Book."
3. Rules, standards, or posters which children compose as the need arises.
4. The "Recipe Book" in which children record brief and accurate directions relative to the performance of some task.
5. The class newspaper.

Elementary school children are particularly interested in nature and in science. It is not difficult to motivate them to keep records on such things as the following: [23]

The time the sun sets at different seasons of the year
When the birds go south; return north
The dates of the planting and appearance of flowers and of different crops
Changes in the amount of water in streams and ponds and the causes thereof
The action of wind vane, thermometer, barometer, compass
Weather calendars

[22] Paul McKee, *Language in the Elementary School*. Boston: Houghton Mifflin Company, 1939, p. 184.
[23] *The Language Arts: A Handbook for Teachers in Elementary Schools*. Bureau of Elementary Curriculum Development, New York State Education Department, 1957, p. 26.

136

The changing position of the stars
Relation of community industries to soil, climate, waterways
Habits of wild animals and pets
How animals and plants adapt themselves to their surroundings
Height and weight records; the relation of these to proper food, sleep, exercise

The writing of such records offers excellent opportunity for instruction in written composition as well as in the basic value of the records themselves. The records that children keep should be accurate, definite, and written in the children's own words so they will be understood and be of actual value. The proper teaching of the use of records should convince the children of the importance of language and its correct use.

REPORTS

This area of the written language programs should include the writing of summaries, directions, and reviews, as well as the writing of reports. These types of writing are important in carrying out the activities which generally comprise a part of social studies and science programs in the school. They are also quite important in the affairs of ordinary adult life.

In the kindergarten and first grade, children should begin reporting activities by dictating to the teacher brief sentences and paragraphs that describe some experience they have had, a unit of work they have carried out, or the directions relating to some familiar procedure they have found interesting. In the second and third grades some of the report and summary work should be done by the children themselves. In the intermediate grades children should write summaries of an increasing number of paragraphs, recommendations of books read, reports on excursions taken or projects developed, and directions relative to classroom trips and activities.

The objectives for the various grade levels should be similar to the following:

Primary grades
    a. To begin to express observations in written form either by pictures or story.
    b. To learn to make accurate observations and reports.
    c. To develop the ability to note essentials clearly and in order.
    d. To learn the importance of the use of definite, descriptive language.
    e. To see the value of concrete experiences as a means of learning.

137

         f. To learn habits of persistence in tasks of long duration.

Intermediate grades   *a.* To prepare summaries of increasing length.

         b. To learn the importance of planning in advance the steps in an activity.

         c. To learn the correct form for keeping minutes of a meeting.

         d. To train accurate observation and reporting, using as much descriptive language as possible.

         e. To learn to use a few key words which will recall data afterwards.

         f. To learn to organize for a particular purpose.

         g. To be able to use related materials to stimulate interest and achievement.

         h. To develop the habit of noting the source of material and giving credit for its use.

         i. To learn to select only appropriate material and to transfer it accurately.

Upper grades   *a.* To continue to refine and extend all previous objectives.

         b. To acquire skill in taking notes that give a comprehensive record of a procedure, speech, or process.

         c. To learn to take notes on important points while reading, listening, or observing.

USING PRINTED SOURCES

Children should learn in the elementary school to make and to use bibliographies. They should learn the origin of the word *bibliography* and learn to observe correct bibliographical form in listing references in their writing. A systematic program of training in the construction and use of a bibliography and in correct bibliographical form is necessary if we expect children to work efficiently and independently in using this aid to the use of books.

The techniques to be taught in writing bibliographies may be summarized as follows:

1. To give completely and accurately all necessary information, as author's name, page numbers, and date of copyright.
2. To use alphabetical order whenever suitable.
3. To write first the author's surname, followed by a comma.
4. To underline all titles of books or magazines.
5. To develop habits of absolute accuracy on references and forms.

138

A suggested bibliography form for grades one to six is the following:

Author, A. B., *Bibliography Form.*

For the upper grades and junior high school, the following form is recommended:

Books	Author, A. B., *Bibliography Form as Practiced by the Publishers.* Boston: Hale University Press, 1962.
Magazine articles	Author, A. B., "The Standardization of Bibliography Forms." *School Review,* 26:348–357, July, 1935.

A part of the language program in written expression is the proper use of material written by others. Children should be taught how to use the exact words of others. They should learn how to quote and to record the particular source of the material quoted. They should also learn to be honest enough to give credit for an idea even though the exact words of another are not quoted. Much of this instruction will come about through emphasis by the teacher and by having pupils practice this skill in their notetaking and information-gathering activities.

SELF-EDITING AND PROOFREADING

SELF-EDITING

In spite of the best efforts of teachers of language, many pupils develop a surprising lack of concern toward learning to speak and to write in ways that are acceptable to society. This indifferent attitude is mainly responsible for the large number of persistent errors of form and usage in written and oral expression. Combatting such an attitude is one of the chief battles of the English or language teacher from the elementary grades through college.

Undoubtedly a major cause of the lack of attention many pupils give to improving their language expression is that there is no apparent or pressing motive for doing so. Often the pupil sees no purpose in the writing that he is called upon to do in school and hence can see no point in editing it carefully or in re-writing it. Teachers must remember that there is no place in the language program for careless, sloppy, routine writing of a busy-work nature. Written expression and its improvement should be approached from the viewpoint of having some idea, experi-

139

ence, or feeling of importance to share with someone else. As children feel that they have something worth while to write about, they will recognize that the quality of their writing is important in the accomplishment of communication.

Children should be taught to develop a feeling of personal responsibility for the quality of their written work; they should feel that it is important, that it has a purpose, and that they have said clearly and correctly what they intended to say. They should feel responsible for proofreading their written work, for correcting errors, and for copying it neatly and legibly before allowing anyone else to see it. Attitudes which should be encouraged may include the following:

1. An awareness of the need for deciding what is to be said before even beginning to write.
2. The realization of the fact that the "first draft" is mainly for the purpose of getting ideas into some concrete form.
3. The consciousness of the fact that neatness in written expression is like neatness in appearance, and that each of us is judged by one as well as by the other.

PROOFREADING

Studies have definitely shown that pupils do not learn to write correctly and effectively when teachers put the corrections on paper, but that they do improve when pupils make corrections for themselves. This means that teaching an editorial attitude toward one's own work and the ability to proofread carefully should both be part of the instructional program in written language. The goal is to establish proofreading as a habit with each child.

Research also shows that better writing is accomplished by placing the major emphasis first upon content, then stressing organization of ideas, vividness, and fluency. From this beginning emphasis upon content, the writing is improved with attention to form and how things are said. Each article that is written in school should be checked, edited, and revised, but by the pupil himself, with specific help from the teacher.

RHETORICAL SKILLS

An important group of grammatical and rhetorical skills including usage, sentence sense, sentence structure, clarity of treatment, interest factors, organization of content, vocabulary and word choice contribute equally to both oral and written expression. In order to avoid unnecessary duplication of emphasis the treatment of these skills is postponed for presentation in Chapter 6, "Skills Used in Both Oral and Written Expression."

CREATIVE WRITING

A feeling of freedom in oral expression, which should be the major language goal of the primary grades, sooner or later comes to maturity in creative writing in the form of poems, stories, plays and articles, or compositions. Such forms of expression, if not dominated by direction or by imitation, are creative." [24]

Man's social and scientific advancement is largely the result of his imagination and originality. The school should encourage the child to use his imagination and originality at all times. The business of the school in teaching writing is not to train professional writers, but to develop each pupil's capacity to value his experience—real or vicarious, and to translate his experience into words. Hatfield states the following objectives in stimulating creative expression:

1. To help pupils recognize the value of their own experience.
2. To amplify the range of pupils' experience.
3. To improve the quality of observation.
4. To aid pupils to fit words to the details of experience.
5. To help pupils discover suitable forms for the transfer of experience to others. [25]

A somewhat different list of objectives for encouraging children in their efforts at creative expression is the following:

1. To develop individual personality by furnishing opportunities for the expression of feelings and ideas.
2. To provide a means for using leisure time profitably by making children more independent and self-reliant in the field of language expression, which in turn would enrich their lives.
3. To draw out and promote any natural ability that children may have in language expression.
4. To help children appreciate good literature through their own attempts at

---

[24] Creative aspects of written language are discussed fully in Chapter 13.

[25] *An Experience Curriculum in English.* A Report of the Curriculum Commission of the National Council of Teachers of English, W. Wilbur Hatfield, chairman. New York: D. Appleton–Century Company, 1935, pp. 112–113.

literary production, which usually leads to better understanding of the writings of others.[26]

Both of the above statements, which have much in common, emphasize particularly the value of creative expression for its own sake and with no thought of utilitarian or practical aspects. The second group of statements, with which the present writers are in agreement, points up the contributions of creative expression to other more practical language activities.

In addition to recognizing real purposes for creative expression, certain conditions are essential for its satisfactory stimulation. First, the pupil himself must feel a desire or urge to share his thoughts and feelings with others. A major factor in the development and encouragement of this urge is to be found in the quality of the child's immediate environment. Naturally, this environment must be rich and stimulating. Beauty in and near the classroom, artistic displays, science tables, lovely music, and shelves of attractive books are all parts of this stimulating environment. Beyond this, the child needs to sense a sympathetic attitude toward his efforts, friendly encouragement in his attempts, serious consideration of his productions, and above all, a feeling of security and normality in his expressional efforts.

EXERCISES FOR THOUGHT AND DISCUSSION

1. List and discuss the most important likenesses and differences in oral and written expression.
2. Evaluate the basic objectives of the spelling program given in this chapter.
3. If you were selecting a basic vocabulary for a spelling program in your school, where would you look? Why?
4. What are the essential criteria for good handwriting? How well and how fast should the individual write?
5. Present arguments for and against manuscript writing as the basis for the child's initial writing instruction.
6. How would you handle the handwriting problems of a left-handed first-grader in your room?
7. Check the grade listing of punctuation skills in this chapter. What skills would you add or delete?

[26] Adapted from Paul McKee, "Creative Writing," Language Service Bulletin. Boston: Houghton Mifflin Company, no date, p. 3.

8. Criticize in a similar way the listing of capitalization skills.

9. Discuss the importance of training the child to give credit to sources of information he uses. Present methods for accomplishing this.

10. Present suggestions for developing habits of proofreading and self-editing on the part of pupils.

SELECTED REFERENCES

Communication, A Guide to the Teaching of Speaking and Writing. Minneapolis: Minneapolis Public Schools, 1953.

DAWSON, MILDRED A., and ZOLLINGER, MARIAN. *Guiding Language Learning.* Yonkers-on-Hudson: World Book Company, 1957.

FITZGERALD, JAMES A. *A Basic Life Spelling Vocabulary.* Milwaukee: The Bruce Publishing Company, 1951.

GREENE, HARRY A. *A Criterion for the Course of Study in the Mechanics of Written Composition.* Studies in Education, Vol. VIII, No. 4. Iowa City: University of Iowa, November 4, 1933.

————. "English—Language, Grammar, and Composition." *Encyclopedia of Educational Research,* rev. ed. New York: The Macmillan Company, 1950, pp. 383–396.

————. *The New Iowa Spelling Scale.* Iowa City: Bureau of Educational Research and Service, State University of Iowa, 1955.

Guide For the Teaching of Language Arts. San Francisco: Elementary School Division, San Francisco Unified School District, 1955.

HORN, ERNEST. *A Basic Writing Vocabulary: 10,000 Words Most Commonly Used in Writing.* Monographs in Education, No. 4. Iowa City: State University of Iowa, 1926.

————. *What Research Says to the Teacher: Teaching Spelling.* Department of Classroom Teachers and American Educational Research Association. Washington. National Education Association, 1954.

MC KEE, PAUL. "An Adequate Program in the Language Arts." *Teaching Language in the Elementary School.* Forty-third Yearbook of the National Society for the Study of Education, Part II. Chicago: The University of Chicago, 1944. Chapter 2.

————. *Language in the Elementary School.* Boston: Houghton Mifflin Company, 1939.

RINSLAND, HENRY D. *A Basic Vocabulary of Elementary School Children.* New York: The Macmillan Company, 1945.

SHANE, HAROLD G. *Research Helps in Teaching the Language Arts.* A Report of the Association for Supervision and Curriculum Development. Washington: National Education Association, 1955.

6

Skills Used in Both Oral and

Written Expression

THE PURPOSE OF THIS CHAPTER IS THE DISCUSSION AND EVALUATION of the large and important body of skills required by and common to both oral and written expression. The main topics emphasized in this chapter are:

    a. Classification of language skills.
    b. Current English language usage.
    c. Errors in verb and pronoun forms.
    d. Errors of redundancy, vague antecedents, double negatives.
    e. Grammatical skills; functional grammar.
    f. Rhetorical skills; sentence structure; clarity; interest; organization; vocabulary.
    g. Using sources of information; the library, dictionary, reference books.
    h. Notetaking.

Many aspects of language expression, oral and written, are similar and are supported by many of the same basic principles. The principles support the over-all language program and give identity to skills and objectives that are essentially the same for both speaking and writing. Of course there are certain learning experiences and related skills that fall into one category or the other, as has been brought to the reader's attention in the two preceding chapters. The purpose of this chapter is the discussion and evaluation of the large and important body of skills required by and common to both oral and written expression.

CLASSIFICATION OF LANGUAGE SKILLS

The similarities and differences in oral and written language are concisely shown by the chart on page 146. This chart identifies specific skills

144

needed in oral expression and the special situations where it is characteristically used, as well as making a similar identification for written expression. In addition, the chart shows those skill areas which are indispensable to both forms of expression. It both summarizes the language program is discussed in this chapter and in Chapters 4 and 5, and forecasts the treatment of the development of these expressional skills in Chapters 9, 10, and 11.

ENGLISH LANGUAGE USAGE

The English language is a live, growing, changing language. Current social usage is the principal criterion for what is acceptable or correct; only a small part of what is called "good usage" derives its justification from any historically grounded or logical principle. Language is largely a personal matter; each person uses it to express his own individual thinking. Correctness is a relative matter in communication. The nature of the language used in a communicative act is dependent upon (1) the meaning to be communicated, (2) the purpose of the communication, and (3) the effect desired in the communication.[1]

We want the child to become sensitive to and to appreciate the factors which govern usage choices. We want him to recognize that there are language forms and constructions that are associated with particular social groups or with particular occasions for using language. It is necessary, however, to make the child aware of the acceptability and nonacceptability of certain usages considered important in society in general. Such matters as the use of the correct or acceptable verb form, pronoun, or antecedent are important to both oral and written expression.

Teachers and writers have long recommended that the number of usage items for instructional emphasis in the elementary school should be limited. Pooley makes these observations to support this principle: [2]

1. The constant repetition of a relatively small number of errors constitutes over 90 per cent of the usage problem in the elementary grades.
2. A large number of "errors" listed in textbooks and language work books are not errors at all, but are colloquial English appropriate to the speech and writing of young children.

[1] Robert C. Pooley, *Teaching English Usage.* New York: Appleton-Century-Crofts, Inc., 1946, p. 27.
[2] *Ibid.,* p. 179.

145

Chart of Language Skills

Oral skills	Oral and written skills	Written skills
Articulation	Usage	Spelling
Enunciation	Verbs	Handwriting
Pronunciation	Pronouns	Manuscript form
Audience sensitivity	Redundancy	Punctuation
Voice	Antecedents	Capitalization
Posture	Grammatical skills	Proofreading
Manner	for self-editing	Special Situations
Special situations	Vocabulary	Letter writing
Conversation	Use of Sources	Outlining
Discussion	Dictionary	Filling in forms
Telephoning	Reference books	Notices and an-
Story telling	Index	nouncements
Dramatization	Table of Contents	Labels, signs
Reporting interviews	Bibliographies	Memoranda, rules
Announcements	Credit to sources	Receipts, signs
Assemblies	Rhetorical skills	Minutes
Conferences	Sentence structure	Written reports
Social conventions	Clarity	Creative writing
Choral speech	Unity	
Creative Expression	Interest	
Listening	Organization	

Evidence for the above statements is found in the studies of Charters, O'Rourke and others. Charters reported that forty per cent of all errors made by children were in the forms of fifteen common verbs, chiefly in the confusion of the past and past participle forms: see, come, run, write, begin, break, drink, lie, do, go, give, take, ring, sing, sit.[3] Brown and Butterfield in reporting the O'Rourke study state the most serious errors are found in: [4]

1. Past tense of see, do, come, go, run.
2. Perfect tense of see, do, come, go, run.
3. Those (not them) apples.
4. You were; you weren't; he, she, it isn't.
5. I'm not; we were; we weren't; they were; they weren't; weren't they.

[3] W. W. Charters and Edith Miller, *A Course of Study in Grammar Based Upon the Grammatical Errors of School Children of Kansas City, Missouri.* University of Missouri Bulletin, Vol. XVI, No. 2, Education Series 9, 1915.
[4] Dorothy L. Brown and Marguerite Butterfield, *The Teaching of Language in the Primary Grades.* New York: The Macmillan Company, 1941, p. 86.

6. I, we, you, they haven't.
7. My father and I (not me and my father) went to the store.

Similar concentration of errors on relatively few usages was indicated by Goltry in a study of several hundred thousand running words of electrically-recorded oral compositions by school children.[5] He reported that the following 19 items having frequencies of ten or more in his tabulations accounted for ninety per cent of the total of all such errors:

	Frequency:
1. Use of expletive *there* with subject and verb not agreeing in number	78
2. Use of subject and verb not agreeing in number	55
3. Use of past participle for past tense	14
4. Use of *lay* for *lie, set* for *sat, laid* for *lay, lie* for *lay*	12
5. Use of *have got* to denote possession	18
6. Use of pronoun which does not agree with antecedent in number, person or gender	39
7. Use of *you* in impersonal sense	26
8. Use of adjective for adverb	49
9. Use of *like* for *as* or *as if*	18
10. Use of *lot* or *lots* meaning much or many	150
11. Use of *kind of* and *sort of* meaning rather	57
12. Use of *quite a bit* and *quite a lot* meaning considerable	10
13. Use of *made out of*	33
14. Use of *cause* for because	23
15. Use of *oh, well,* and *why* to introduce sentences	398
16. Use of *reason is because*	26
17. Shift of tense within sentence	114
18. Use of double subject	24
19. Use of sentence with indeterminate grammatical construction	106
Total	1,250

An interesting comparison of teacher attitudes toward certain questionable usages with those of a large group of editors and authors was suggested in an article by Norman Lewis.[6] The same procedures and directions used by Lewis were followed by the writers in securing responses from 107 classroom teachers in their education classes. The directions are quoted below as a means of showing the type of approach used:

Here are nineteen expressions about which there is today a good deal of controversy, and we'd like your opinion as an educated adult, of their acceptability in everyday speech.

[5] T. Keith Goltry, "An Analysis of Sentence Structure in Oral Composition." Unpublished doctoral dissertation, State University of Iowa, July, 1935.
[6] Norman Lewis, "How Correct Must Correct English Be," *Harpers,* 198:68–74; March, 1949.

Do not be influenced by whether these usages do or do not violate formal grammatical rules. Rather, indicate, by affirmative vote, that you would be willing to use the expression listed or that you believe such an expression has become sufficiently current in educated American speech to be labeled *acceptable* usage; by a negative vote, that the expression is *unacceptable* in educated circles.

	% Acceptable by editors and writers	% Acceptable by 107 teachers
1. His attitude makes me *mad*. (Synonym for angry)	68	45
2. I *will* pay your bill if you accept my check	90	93
3. The reason I am worried is *because* I think she's ill	48	61
4. The work is different *than* mine	31	37
5. We had a *nice* time at the party	88	85
6. *Can* I have another helping of dessert, please?	40	24
7. I encountered *less* difficulties than I had expected	23	40
8. Everyone put on *their* coat and went home	45	18
9. How much money have you got?	65	37
10. *Due* to the storm, all trains are late	65	87
11. She has an *awful* headache	77	65
12. We *only* have five left. (Position of *only*)	44	41
13. Let's not walk any *further* right now	58	44
14. We must remember *to accurately check* each answer	53	51
15. He's one person I simply won't do business *with*	86	69
16. Go *slow*	86	55
17. It is *me*	62	36
18. She acts as if she *was* my wife	34	24
19. *Who* did you meet?	43	44

The results appearing in the two columns following the sentences above indicate the percentage of each group of judges considering the statement acceptable under the conditions stated in the directions. It is evident from this study that the teachers are somewhat less willing to forget their grammatical prejudices than are the less grammatically inoculated judges. Teachers were noticeably more sensitive to usages such as are represented by sentences 1, 6, 8, 9, 15, 16, and 17. They were less sensitive to the questionable usages in sentences 3, 7, and 10.

A more recent study by Womack confirms the fact that the battle of levels of acceptable usage has not been won in spite of support given this approach in English journals, by the National Council of Teachers of English, and by published sources of authority.[7] Womack questioned

[7] Thurston Womack, "Teachers' Attitudes toward Current Usage." *The English Journal*, 48: April, 1959, pp. 186–190.

over 300 randomly sampled members of the National Council of Teachers of English with regard to the acceptability in formal or informal speech and formal or informal writing of fifty items of usage. The usages selected are as follows:

The split infinitive
the case of the noun or pronoun before the gerund
seven items of agreement between subject and verb and pronoun and
    antecedent
one . . . he
. . . is when . . .
these kind
data is . . .
preposition at end of a sentence
either of three
shortest of two
dangling participle (not an absurd one)
myself used in the nominative
between you and I
who are you waiting for?
drive *slow*
as if he *was*
it is *me*
aren't I . . .
Jones was younger than *him*
building's roof
after discussing the heroine, most of the young women expressed no desire
    to be *her*
it looks *like* it will rain
the boy felt *badly*
can in the sense of permission
very *nice* people
fixed in the sense of repaired
different than
awful colds
New York is *further* east than Chicago
try *and* finish
due to in the sense of because of
has *proven*
raised instead of *reared*
Americans *have got* to make democracy work
some students do not know *if* they can . . .
divided *between* three
the *reason* . . . was *because* . . .
the students *enthused* about . . .
the state *hung* the murderers
the old man *laid* down on his bed . . .
. . . cannot help but . . .

149

the swimmers *dove* into the pool
the soldiers fulfilled the *dying wish* of the commander

Womack stated that an item-by-item comparison of the teachers' views with published information in such sources as Leonard's *Current English Usage,*[8] Marckwardt and Walcott's *Facts About Current English Usage,*[9] "Current English Forum" in *The English Journal* or *College English,* and *Webster's New Collegiate Dictionary* reveals that in general the majority of the teachers still reject most usages that published information tends to support as acceptable.[10]

In spite of the resistance to change indicated above, standards of acceptable English usage are shifting. More and more language is regarded as a living, growing, changing instrument, flexible and adaptable to modern life—a life that often calls for direct, vigorous, idiomatic forms of expression. As Dawson points out, "The ultimate goal in teaching correct usage of words is the establishment of a strong personal preference for comfortably informal, effective language free from flagrant errors." [11]

Evidence of the shifting standards of English usage are reported by Marckwardt and Walcott, with the constructions cited below being accepted by 75 per cent of good speakers and writers,[12] and by such recently published sources as the scholarly *Webster's Third New International Dictionary.*

1. I had rather go at once.
2. You had better stop that foolishness.
3. This is the chapter whose contents causes most discussion.
4. He did not do as well as we expected.
5. You just had a telephone call.

Did they leave any message?
6. The women were all dressed up.
7. One is not fit to vote at the age of eighteen.
8. Our catch was pretty good.
9. I can hardly stand him.
10. Jane was home all last week.
11. I'd like to make a correction.

[8] Sterling A. Leonard, *Current English Usage,* English Monograph No. 1 of the National Council of Teachers of English. Chicago: National Council of Teachers of English, 1932.

[9] Albert H. Marckwardt and Fred G. Walcott, *Facts About Current English Usage,* English Monograph No. 7 of the National Council of Teachers of English. New York: D. Appleton–Century Company, Inc., 1938.

[10] Published information clearly supports all but two of the usages (between you and I and intransitive *laid*).

[11] Mildred A. Dawson, "Correct Usage, Including Capitalization and Punctuation," *Teaching Language in the Elementary School.* Forty-third Yearbook of the National Society for the Study of Education, Part II. Chicago: The University of Chicago Press, 1944, p. 165.

[12] Marckwardt and Walcott, *op. cit.,* pp. 27–31.

12. I felt I could not go further.
13. I've absolutely got to go.
14. That is a dangerous curve; you had better go slow.
15. There are some nice people here.
16. Have you fixed the tire?
17. I don't know if I can.
18. The room is awfully cold.
19. You had to have property to vote.
20. The kind of apples you mean are large and sour.
21. The real reason he failed was because he tried too hard.
22. They went way around the orchard.
23. We got home at three o'clock.
24. There is a large works near the bridge.
25. None of them are here.
26. We'll try and get it.
27. We only had one left.
28. Factories are mostly closed on election day.
29. He moves mighty quick on a tennis court.
30. It is me.
31. Who are you looking for?
32. Drive slow down that hill.
33. There was a bed, a dresser, and two chairs in the room.
34. They invited my friends and myself.
35. Can I be excused from this class?
36. Haven't you got through yet?
37. Everyone was there, but they all went home.
38. He went right home and told his father.
39. A treaty was concluded between the four powers.
40. I wish I was thin.
41. I've no doubt but what he will come.
42. My folks sent me a check.
43. He came around four o'clock.
44. I have got my own opinion on that.

VERB FORMS

The language program in the elementary school should provide for the elimination of those errors in verb usage that appear most frequently in the speaking and writing of the children. This means that periodically the teacher should check the class informally as to the specific errors in verb form being made in oral and written work. As a result of this examination, the most frequent and most obvious errors should receive corrective instruction. Every possible effort should be made to prevent the use of the incorrect verb forms in any and all expressional situations throughout the school.

The above does not mean that other errors in verb usages should not be corrected. It does mean that only a limited number of errors should receive the major attack by the entire class. Most of the other errors will be traced to individuals who in each case should be encouraged to eliminate these errors as a personal matter.

The following verb form errors generally need to be eliminated in the elementary school:

1. Errors in tense

come for *came*
have *did* for have *done*
run for *ran*
done for *did*
rung for *rang*
give for *gave*

seen for *saw*
has *went* for has *gone*
ask for *asked*
have *rode* for have *ridden*
has *took* for has *taken*

2. Incorrect word

knowed for *knew*
git for *get*
et for *ate*

ain't for *isn't*
onct for *once*
throwed for *threw*

3. Confusion of words

leave for *let*
set for *sit*
lay for *lie*
awful good for *very good*

learn for *teach*
guess for *think*

4. Predicate not agreeing with subject in number

we *was* for we *were*
they *is* for they *are*
they *was* for they *were*
girls *helps* for girls *help*
he *don't* for he *doesn't*

there *is* for there *are*
you *was* for you *were*
May and John *is* going for May and John *are* going.

5. Miscellaneous verb errors

have got or *has got* for *received*

hadn't ought for should *not* or *ought not* [13]

PRONOUNS

Children should learn that a pronoun is a convenient and useful substitute for the name of something. Pronouns are used to eliminate tiresome repetition of nouns. By their use the effectiveness of oral and written language is increased. Since correct usage in oral language tends to result in the correct expression when written, particular attention should be paid to the use of correct pronouns in the oral language program.

McKee cites the study by Harap in listing the pronoun errors occurring most frequently in oral and written expression.[14]

1. Subject not in nominative case. *John and me are going to camp this summer.*
2. Predicate nominative not in nominative case. *It is him. It is me.*
3. The use of wrong cases of pronouns after *than* and *as* and *as well as.* He *is taller than me. This misfortune falls more heavily upon you than I.*

[13] Adapted from listings by Robert C. Pooley, *op. cit.,* p. 180, and Maude McBroom, *The Course of Study in Written Composition for the Elementary Grades,* Monographs in Education, First Series No. 10. Iowa City: State University of Iowa, December, 1928, pp. 58–59.
[14] Paul McKee, *Language in the Elementary School.* Boston: Houghton Mifflin Company, 1939, pp. 288–289.

4. Object of a preposition not in objective case. *Mother gave the ball to John and I.*
5. Object of a verb not in objective case. *Mother sent John and I.*
6. *Whom* for *who; who* for *whom.*
7. Wrong formation of compound pronouns. *They hurt theirselves.*
8. Use of objective for possessive with gerund. *I'm tired of him complaining.*
9. Disagreement of pronoun with its antecedent. *Will everyone bring their paper.*
10. Confusion of *its* and *it's. Its hard to tell. The dog hurt it's paw.*
11. Use of *which* for *who* and vice versa. *He is the man which I meant. This is a dog who knows his trick.*
12. Lack of clear reference of pronoun to antecedent. *Mary told her friend that she was mistaken.*

As stated previously, however, more recent studies indicate acceptability of a number of these items in some forms of expression. For example, in the case of *It is I* or *It is me,* Pooley states that "in formal literary, and solemn style the pronoun *I* is used; in cultivated colloquial usage, custom has also established the pronoun *me.* The tone and purpose of the speech or writing must in all cases determine the choice of the pronoun." [15]

An Experience Curriculum in English lists these pronoun usages for mastery in the elementary school: [16]

1. You (not *youse*); *himself* (not *hisself*); *themselves* (not *theirselves*)
2. My *father and I* (not *me and my father*) went to the store
3. Masculine, *he;* feminine, *she;* neuter, *it*
4. *Yours* (not *yourn*); *his* (not *hisen*); *hers* (not *hern*)
5. *Who* for persons, *which* for all other objects

REDUNDANCY

Among the errors of redundancy which studies have shown to possess high frequency of occurrence and persistency of difficulty are the following: [17]

1. *This here, that there* for *this, that.*
2. *Where is it at?* for *Where is it?*
3. *John he* for *John.*
4. *He went and threw it* for *he threw it.*
5. *Go get it* for *get it.*

[15] Pooley, *op. cit.,* p. 71.

[16] *An Experience Curriculum in English,* A Report of the Curriculum Commission of the National Council of Teachers of English, W. Wilbur Hatfield, chairman. New York: D. Appleton–Century Company, 1935, p. 247.

[17] McKee, *op. cit.,* p. 294.

Teachers will immediately recognize many of the errors cited above as common errors in the speech and writing of elementary school children. Children can be taught to avoid these errors if the mistakes are consistently corrected wherever found.

ANTECEDENTS

Another type of error in usage which should receive some attention in the elementary grades is that of using a pronoun not in agreement with the noun or noun equivalent to which it refers. For example, *Each must do their own work,* rather than *Each must do his own work.* The strongest case in holding to agreement in number between a pronoun and its antecedent is that in which the pronoun is definitely either singular or plural and the noun or noun equivalent is either singular or plural. In the case of the indefinite pronouns *everyone, everybody, either, neither,* and so forth, the referent pronoun takes the singular or plural depending upon the meaning intended, although in most cases the usage established is singular.

Naturally the worst errors in lack of agreement should be corrected first. Teachers should recognize that not all errors in usage can be eliminated in the elementary school. Language authorities tend to agree, for example, that the use of *their* or *they* when the antecedent is *everybody* or *everyone* should not receive direct teaching attention in the elementary grades. Such errors as *Everybody had their hat* or *Everyone said that they were going* should probably be reserved for attention in the junior-high school and high school grades.[18]

DOUBLE NEGATIVES

Errors in the use of double negatives are not numerous but are generally rather firmly established language habits. The following should receive particular attention at the elementary school level:

1. *Can't you have no* for *can't you have any.*
2. *Haven't no* for *haven't any* or *have no.*
3. *Isn't no* for *is no* or *isn't any.*
4. *Don't know nothing* for *don't know anything* or *doesn't know anything.*

[18] Pooley, *op. cit.,* p. 181.

The following types of errors in expression are common enough that instruction directed toward their correction is generally necessary in the elementary school:

1. The use of needless introductory words, as *then, well, so, listen, why.*
2. Needless repetition of words, caused by rapidity of speaking or simply carelessness, as *That's what he said. He said that.*
3. Use of illiteracies, as *yourn, hern, youse.*

GRAMMATICAL SKILLS

Most parents and practically all educators agree that the elementary school teacher accomplishes at least a minor miracle as he stimulates and guides his young charges through their inaccurate and often illiterate language usage toward the development of socially accepted language habits. In this undertaking the teacher faces a serious challenge; the basic patterns of language usage have been set in early childhood and still continue to be influenced by the same factors that established them.

The elementary school language program has two major goals: (1) the development of effective expression in the language activities in which children and adults engage, and (2) the development of the related attitudes, abilities, and skills contributing to expressive efficiency. The place that grammar assumes in this program is determined by the contribution it makes to acceptable habits of expression. The extent of such contribution is discussed fully in Chapter 12. At this point it is enough to say that scientific investigations have failed to show that a knowledge of grammar is effective in the elimination of language usages which are generally not acceptable. In the process of constructing sentences and paragraphs, however, children must manipulate the various elements of the sentence; and in this manipulation they will likely learn the relationships of those elements as well as the appropriate grammatical terminology for describing them.

NEED FOR PURELY FUNCTIONAL GRAMMAR

If grammar is regarded as the descriptive framework of the language, then the speech and writing of persons may be described by grammatical terminology. Grammar in this sense puts no prescription on language, makes no judgments concerning the "correctness" or "incorrectness" of usage items. As language habits change—as they certainly do change —the fallacy in reliance upon a prescriptive grammar becomes evident.

The elimination of any undesirable habit is not necessarily achieved by the learning of rules and definitions. Most children in the elementary school have neither the capacity nor the background of experience which would enable them to understand abstract principles or rules of grammar and to apply them to specific cases. There is no reason, therefore, for teaching grammar as such unless the ideas taught can be used almost immediately by the child himself as independent aids for improving his speech and his writing. Grammar taught in such a manner is functional and practical because it is learned not merely *for* use but *in* use.

WHAT IS FUNCTIONAL IN THE ELEMENTARY GRADES?

In teaching language expression, emphasis should at all times be upon the child's clear presentation of thought; as this requires an understanding of the basic structure of the English sentence, the grammar of that structure will be learned inductively. As Hatfield says, "They simply learn by normal desirable manipulation of a sentence element which the teacher calls by its proper name, exactly as they have developed the concepts and learned the words bell, school, truth." [19] Elements which do not arise naturally and which are not needed in the formulation of a child's expression are probably not sufficiently important to justify being taught.

RHETORICAL SKILLS

Effective language expression, both oral and written, is based largely upon mastery of the sentence. The sentence is the principle unit of thinking, communicating, and recording. Larger or smaller units are composed respectively of sentence multiples or sentence parts. The importance of the sentence in language instruction can scarcely be overemphasized. While any discussion of the importance of the sentence must first of all be concerned with its content, the writer or the speaker of a sentence who wishes to be really certain that his sentence conveys his thought to

[19] *An Experience Curriculum in English,* p. 228.

his reader or listener must know and use many specific skills of sentence construction. These skills comprise the subject matter of this section. Instruction in the attainment of these skills is discussed in Chapter 10.

SENTENCE STRUCTURE

Adequate sentence sense and sentence mastery must be developed before ideas and feelings can be expressed in effective and meaningful ways in either written or oral form. It is a common criticism that far too many pupils pass through the entire language program without gaining a clear conception of the meaning of a sentence. Many of these pupils can recite a memorized definition of a sentence taken from a textbook, but their real understanding of the elements that make up a sentence or that determine sentence quality is either extremely vague or entirely lacking. Thus they are unable to construct good clear sentences of their own or to examine and edit their sentences critically.

Sentence sense. The sentence fragment is one of the most common types of language errors. Most sentences must express a thought which can stand alone, without reference to other sentences, in order for the meaning to be clear. If the thought is not completely expressed, the reader or listener may be confused and forced to guess at the speaker's or writer's intended meaning. A second type of sentence difficulty also is a result of not understanding that a sentence is basically a two-part unit with a subject (that to which the speaker or writer wants to call attention) being stated or definitely understood and a predicate (that which is said about the subject). The so-called *run-on* sentence, instead of saying too little, tries to say too much and results in an expression which also may be confusing. Children must be taught that in the expression of their ideas they must be careful to make sense. Failure to do so is generally traceable to two causes: (1) the child himself knows or thinks he knows so well what he is trying to say that he does not take the trouble to fill in necessary details and to use the language skills he knows to convey his ideas fully; or (2) the child does not know the essentials of a sentence and does not understand the subject-predicate concept that is essential to every sentence.

With a receptive school climate and active and proper instruction, children will attain early in their school experience the ability to tell a sequence of events, experiences, or facts in functional and structurally complete sentences. They begin to learn to vary the order of words in sentences as they acquire freedom and flexibility of thought and expres-

157

sion. Maturity in sensing relationships in time, space, and circumstance brings increased language maturity, particularly in the use of introductory adverbs, connectives, and prepositions. Experiences with oral sentences form a background for written work. The child who uses oral sentences well usually has less difficulty in constructing good sentences in his written expression. The development of sentence sense should be stressed from the moment the child first enters school and should be continued until he leaves school or learns to use sentences uniformly well.

Omissions. As suggested above, children's thinking sometimes runs ahead of their writing and speaking with the result that vital points are omitted from their sentences. Then, too, children often lose sight of their reader or listener or they assume that what has been omitted is known to everyone. Naturally, the result is sentence fragments or sentences lacking words or phrases necessary for understanding. The realization that the thought must be conveyed completely for the reader or listener to understand will help prevent such omissions in sentences.

Loose "ands." The word *and* is a conjunction which is used to connect words, phrases, or clauses. The overuse of *and, but* or any conjunction, a common practice of young children, detracts from effective sentence structure. A conjunction should be used only to connect words, phrases, and clauses of *equal* importance or rank. A clear understanding of the sentence is necessary to avoid the misuse of connectives. The simple sentence is most commonly used at every grade level and should be thoroughly understood before a child is urged to use complex and compound sentences. Moreover, in most elementary school writing and speaking the simple sentence will satisfy the majority of the child's need.

Run-ons. A common type of error in sentence structure is that of a series of more or less rambling and complete statements unseparated by punctuation or capitals. This type of error, common in the early elementary grades, rapidly decreases in occurrence after the fourth grade.

CLARITY

The effective expression of an idea or thought is dependent upon the clearness of the understanding that the speaker or writer himself has of that idea or thought. Concise statements are not likely to be made by one who is confused in his own thinking about what he is attempting to express. Sharply defined sentences are the product of clear thinking, which in turn is based upon a wide background of experience and knowledge of that subject.

The essentials of speaking and writing with clarity are listed by McKee as follows:

1. Selecting the right symbol with which to present a given meaning to a reader or a listener. This symbol will be the symbol that will best stimulate the listener or reader to make the meaning intended by the speaking or writer.
2. Organizing a series of right symbols into phrases, clauses, types of sentences, paragraphs, and longer selections that will best stimulate the listener or reader to make the meaning intended by the speaker or writer.
3. Utilizing an attitude of concern about the degree of clarity and exactness with which one presents his meaning in language.[20]

The location of modifiers and antecedents in a sentence very often has much to do with making the meaning clear. All of us have been confused by lack of clarity in such sentences as: "John told Harry that the postman had brought a letter for him." Not only confusing, but also often amusing, is the misplaced modifier. The sentence, "John said that the letter had been brought by the postman which he found in the mailbox," cannot help but conjure up a humorous view of the postman's head sticking incongruously from the letter slot of a mail box. Such sentences as "He counted three beautiful paintings coming down the stairs," or "She dropped the letter she was carrying to her mother in the mud," are intriguing to pupils because of their humorous aspects but may lead to a serious consideration of word order. Children need to learn that whether a sentence is in natural or inverted order, whether it begins with its subject or with a modifying clause or phrase, its meaning will be clearer if modifiers are placed next to, or as close as possible to, the words they modify, and if pronouns are so placed that they clearly indicate their proper antecedents.

UNITY

Oral and written expression should be so organized that each sentence and paragraph is related to and a part of the principal idea or ideas of the content. Each sentence should have unity within itself, with no content that is not related to the principal thought. Each paragraph should be built around the main idea being expressed and should include no ideas which are extraneous to the principal one. The words and phrases

---

[20] Paul McKee, *Language in the Elementary School*, p. 16.

of each sentence and the sentences of each paragraph should be placed in proper sequence to convey logically and clearly the thought or idea intended. Each phrase, word, or sentence should be properly connected with the remainder of the content to relate fully the idea being expressed.

INTEREST

Children must learn about the important role that interest plays in completing the communication process. First, of course, pupils must come to realize that a listener or reader cannot be expected to maintain interest in what is written or being said unless the writer or speaker is himself vitally interested and desires to convey this interest to his audience. He must know what he is talking or writing about and say it in acceptable language. Acceptable language will, of course, be correctly structured, and will make proper use of the principles of unity and clarity. Furthermore, the pupil should learn to make use of colorful and interesting words as well as variety in sentence structure.

The content of speech and writing should be understandable and interesting to the audience. However, factors other than the content itself may be used to arouse the interest of the listener or reader in a subject in which he has previously found no interest. Illustrations and anecdotes may be used to arouse interest and to increase understanding. The use of similes, metaphors, and colorful and forceful words also serves to increase both interest and understanding. All of these factors help to make ideas concrete, interesting, and well-stated. Conciseness and concreteness must be present or attention of the audience may wander or disappear completely.

ORGANIZATION

Children must recognize that in order best to present an idea or thought, the material must be organized so that it is interesting, sticks to the point, presents facts in proper sequence, and can be clearly understood. The problems of organization of thought occur both in sentences and in paragraphs. These problems are generally the following:

1. Not sticking to the subject.
2. Not relating events in proper time sequence.
3. Not relating ideas to a problem or a purpose.
4. Generalizing or not interpreting experience.

160

Primary in importance in organization is sticking to the point. In oral language situations this means limiting the scope of a topic of discussion, the content of an announcement, or the theme of a report, and relating the ideas and thoughts expressed to that limited scope. Another feature of good organization is the presenting of material in the most effective sequence. Such sequence may involve a series of events in which time is a factor or events in which there is a cause and effect relationship. Other important considerations in organization are the beginning and ending sentences, especially in short announcements, reports, or talks. The beginning sentence is the topic sentence and introduces or sets the topic. The final sentence presents the conclusion and again relates to the topic specifically.

The problem of organization is related to outlining, and ability to outline correctly indicates maturity in organization. Organizing ideas should be taught, however, before the mechanics of outlining. That is, children should learn early to make lists, to classify, to organize. From this experience, skills in outlining and more formal organizing will develop quite naturally.

VOCABULARY

Many people go through life with a very limited supply of words which they use in both speaking and writing. Consequently their talking and writing is colorless, often boring, and sometimes not clearly understandable. This is often the result of the repeated use of a few words, the lack of appropriate, exact, and interesting adverbs and adjectives, and in general, the lack of an adequate supply of usable words.

The possession of a wide vocabulary gives one an advantage in expression. A broad vocabulary is essential for using language as a vehicle for the communication of meaning. Further, a rich, colorful, concise vocabulary helps to make both talking and writing interesting. The school must at all times emphasize the development and the proper use of the vocabulary which each child uses in his expressional activities. Promoting the growth of writing, speaking, reading, and listening vocabularies is a most important function of the school's language program. Children understand many more words than they use for speaking and writing; and, as reading skills develop, they learn to read more words than they use for either speaking or writing. The writing vocabulary is likely to be the smallest of the four, and consequently in greatest need of enrichment and development.

161

By the time the child enters school he has acquired a fairly large speaking vocabulary. Early studies of the pre-school child place the total of words known at about 2,500. Some recent studies indicate that the figure may be nearly ten times that number.[21] At any rate, before entering school, most children have large and usable vocabularies acquired largely through sensory experience. The child has heard the names of things; he has learned the names of things seen; he has learned through observing, touching, seeing, feeling, smelling, tasting, and hearing. The school language program must be seriously and constantly concerned with all phases of children's vocabularies.

Choice of words. Children should learn early to choose words which mean exactly what is intended. They should learn that some words are more suitable for certain types of oral and written expression than are others. They should learn that much can be added to their expression through the use of words which are particularly colorful or vivid. The following points concerning choice of words should be kept in mind:

1. Colloquial speech is the comfortable, clear, idiomatic, forceful type of speech used in the informal situations of life, whether in school or not.
2. Bits of expressive slang may be used at times to give "punch" to a speech.
3. Teachers should guard, however, against illiterate and crude expressions that are unacceptably local or provincial.
4. There are occasions for both children and adults when *formal* expression is required. For example: assembly programs, reports.
5. Oral expression activities can be used to broaden the vocabulary by placing on the board words that are used and suggesting more graphic synonyms for use.
6. Literature can be a source of unusually apt expressions and well chosen words. Let the pupil dramatize these expressions with the purpose of drafting them into his own vocabulary.

Vocabulary enrichment. Children's vocabularies may be enriched by the addition of new words, and the addition of new meanings to words they already know. There is no point in adding to the vocabulary of a child merely by teaching just any new word that occurs in a word list. Words taught should be those that the child is likely to need and use. The same applies to learning the meanings of words. Those which should be learned first are the meanings which will be of greatest importance to the child in terms of use and needs.

The development of vocabulary should be a continuing job for the

[21] Mary K. Smith, "Measurement of the Size of General English Vocabulary Through the Elementary Grades and High School," *Genetic Psychology Monograph,* 24:311–345; 1941.

school, beginning in the kindergarten. Complete dependence cannot be placed upon the incidental improvement of vocabulary by the provision of an environment which facilitates such development, but type of learning is of basic importance. In addition, attention must be given to the direct teaching of new words and new meanings (See Chapter 11).

USING SOURCES OF INFORMATION

In order to accomplish the growth of vocabulary as well as to foster interest and growth in reading, children also need instruction in the use of the library. Skill in the accurate and speedy location and use of reference books, periodicals, newspapers, fiction, and other printed material is essential to success in virtually all areas of the school curriculum. Skill in gaining information from observations, interviews, films, and talks must also be developed if children are to learn efficiently at school.

THE LIBRARY

Carefully planned instruction in the use of a library is essential if children are to know how to use it effectively and to carry over this knowledge to later school and adult activities. The amount and type of instruction depend upon the library facilities available, both school and public, and the degree of familiarity the children already have with libraries.

Elementary school children should learn that:

1. Books are arranged in a systematic fashion (either Dewey Decimal or Library of Congress classification) and that this classification system is an aid to the user of the library.
2. The card catalog is an index of all books in the library, arranged by name of author, title of the book, and subject of the book.
3. Books are shelved numerically from left to right, section by section.
4. Fiction is arranged alphabetically by the names of authors.
5. Other materials, such as filmstrips and records, picture files, atlases, etc., are in special areas.

In addition to the necessary knowledge suggested above, children need to know how to:

1. Check out and return books to the library.
2. Find directions for locating books by use of the card catalog.
3. Use dictionaries, encyclopedias, atlases, and similar reference sources.
4. Use special reference sources such as *Reader's Guide.*

163

5. Make use of bibliographies.
6. Take notes.

Behavior in the library, and care and appreciation in handling books are the result of direct instruction, supervised practice, and good example. Speaking softly, walking quietly, and asking for help from the librarian when needed are all important to efficient use of a library. Teachers should also teach young children to handle books only when their hands are clean and to turn pages carefully. Insistence upon these practices with older children is not out of order.

THE CARD CATALOG

McKee lists these items concerning the use of the card catalog for teaching in the elementary school: [22]

1. An understanding of the purpose, contents, and value of the card catalogue.
2. An understanding of the meaning of the letters on the drawers.
3. Skill in finding a word in an alphabetical list.
4. Skill in using guide cards.
5. An understanding of the arrangement of cards in the drawers.
6. An understanding of the meaning of each piece of printed matter on each of the following type of cards:
   a. the author card
   b. the title card
   c. the subject card
   d. the author-analytic card
   e. the title-analytic card
   f. the subject-analytic card
7. An understanding of the meaning and use of "see" and "see also" on cross reference cards.
8. An understanding of the use of Library of Congress cards.

THE DICTIONARY

Every person should learn to use a dictionary in his speaking and writing as well as in his listening and reading. Its use for checking pronunciations and clarifying meanings is often taught in schools in connection with the reading program as one means of developing independence in word recognition. However, as is pointed out by Trabue, "Dictionary training for the interpretation of reading materials will not necessarily enable the individual to use the dictionary effectively in facilitating his

[22] Paul McKee, *The Teaching of Reading in the Elementary School*. Boston: Houghton Mifflin Company, 1948, p. 429.

own expression." [23] Using the dictionary as an aid to expression must be taught deliberately, definitely, and specifically for this purpose.

The following is a listing of the dictionary skills which should be taught, with the approximate grade levels at which they should be introduced and practice given on their use.[24]

1. Learning the names of letters, recognition of each (Grades 1, 2, 3)
2. Learning alphabet, consecutive arrangement of letters (Grades 1, 2, 3)
3. Learning location of letters in alphabet with relation to each other (Grades 1, 2, 3)
4. Finding in any alphabetical arrangement words beginning with certain letters (Grades 1, 2, 3)
5. Arranging words alphabetically; beginning with different letters; beginning with the same letters (Grades 3, 4)
6. Appreciation of dictionary as a tool and interesting source of much information (Grades 3–6)
7. Understanding that the dictionary is built on alphabetical order by first, second, third letters, etc. (Grades 4, 5)
8. Familiarity with relative position of letter sections; d's come in first third of the dictionary, y's in final third, etc. (Grades 4, 5)
9. Using guide words to locate material on a page (Grades 4, 5)
10. Understanding that words are listed by root forms (Grades 4, 5)
11. Using the dictionary to find the correct spelling of a word (Grades 4, 5)
12. Learning the use of diacritical markings and key words as aids in pronunciation (Grades 4, 5)
13. Learning the meaning and use of accent (Grades 4, 5)
14. Learning the meaning and the use of respelling to show pronunciation (Grades 4, 5)
15. Learning the meaning and the use of syllabication (Grades 4, 5)
16. Using the definition best suited to the context (Grades 4, 5)
17. Using the dictionary for correct use of homonyms (Grades 4, 5)
18. Using the dictionary as a key to various meanings of a common word (Grades 4, 5)
19. Understanding abbreviations in the dictionary (Grades 5 and above)
20. Using synonyms and antonyms to clarify meaning (Grades 5 and above)
21. Using the dictionary to get related forms, irregular plurals, irregular verb forms (Grades 5 and above)
22. Using cross references for additional information (Grades 5 and above)
23. Understanding significance of word derivation, prefixes, suffixes, etc. (Grades 6 and above)
24. Learning about special features of the dictionary; e.g., table of measure, atlas, etc. (Grades five and above)

[23] M. R. Trabue, "Use of the Dictionary," *Teaching Language in the Elementary School*, p. 187.
[24] Adapted from listing in Iowa Elementary Teachers Handbook, Vol. 2, *Reading*. Des Moines: Iowa State Department of Public Instruction, 1944.

GLOSSARY

Many children's books have a glossary of new words used in the stories or lessons. A glossary is used in the same way as a dictionary. It is a help with the pronunciation and the meaning of the new words which are found in that book. In doing research, children should learn to look for a glossary and to use it when they encounter a word which is unfamiliar to them.

REFERENCE SOURCES

The use of an encyclopedia, atlas, almanac, and similar reference source involves many of the same skills needed for effective use of a card catalog, a dictionary, or a glossary. In addition, the use of reference sources involves the ability to locate within the topic the particular paragraph or sentence that will give the child the specific information he is seeking. Such an ability involves the skill of skimming, which is taught in relation to the basal reading program, but should be reinforced here and used in connection with gaining new ideas for use in expression.

Specific items to be taught concerning the use of an encyclopedia, the most commonly used reference source, are listed by McKee as follows: [25]

1. An understanding of the contents, purpose, and value of an encyclopedia.
2. An understanding of the form in which the material in an encyclopedia is arranged.
3. Skill in finding a word in an alphabetical list.
4. An understanding of the location of the index in an encyclopedia.
5. An understanding of the meaning of guide letters on covers of volumes.
6. An understanding of the placement of topics made up of compound words.
7. An understanding of the different types of encyclopedia.
8. Skill in using pronunciation keys.
9. Skill in locating on the page the particular information needed.
10. Skill in using cross references.
11. Skill in using guide words.
12. An understanding of the purpose of bibliographies given at the close of articles.
13. An understanding of the meaning of certain marks such as boldface type, parenthesis, italics, etc.
14. An understanding of how to keep an encyclopedia up to date.
15. The attitude of depending upon the encyclopedia as one of the more valid sources of printed information.

[25] McKee, *op. cit.,* p. 429.

INDEX

As children use books for pleasure and for the location of pertinent information, they should be shown the importance of the index as an aid in securing new ideas. The index of a book should be taught as a tool for research in that book; in reading the book, a pupil should learn to use the index as a means of locating information on a given topic. In written expression, the pupil should learn to prepare an index for a record, report, or summary he has made.

The following skills and information concerning the use of an index should be taught:

1. The difference between topics and sub-topics.
2. What the different punctuation marks in the index mean.
3. How maps, graphs, tables, or diagrams are shown in an index.
4. The use and significance of the key or direction at the beginning or the end of the index.
5. Different types of arrangement of sub-topics.
6. How the pages of the most important discussions on the particular topic are shown.
7. Whether or not pronunciation is indicated in an index.
8. How to look under more than one topic if necessary to find the information wanted.

TABLE OF CONTENTS

As soon as reading from books begins, pupils should learn how to use the table of contents in locating a particular story to be read. While children will eventually begin to learn to use the index of a book and will recognize that it is generally much more useful as a tool for locating information, the table of contents is still useful for finding a particular story or major heading in a book.

NOTETAKING

Children should be taught to take notes as they go on social studies excursions, conduct scientific experiments, and search out information for answering problems. Such notes will generally be brief and should be used as aids in recalling facts and information for later outlining and still later expressional activities. One curriculum guide gives these suggestions for notetaking: [26]

[26] *Arts and Skills of Communication for Democracy's Children,* Vol. II. San Bernardino: San Bernardino County Schools, no date, p. 280.

167

1. List only the important facts—the main ideas.
2. Abbreviate long or difficult words.
3. Use a different page or piece of paper for each question.
4. Write plainly so that the notes may be read by the writer.
5. Be sure there is enough information for discussion.

EXERCISES FOR THOUGHT AND DISCUSSION

1. Make a critical examination of the three groups of language skills in the chart on page 146. What changes would you want to make in the classification of skills? What other skills would you add?

2. Without looking at the two columns at the right, record your personal reaction to the suitability of each of the 19 usages suggested by Norman Lewis and listed on page 148. Discuss the usages with which you disagree most sharply.

3. In your judgment is the general level of language usage improving or deteriorating generation by generation? Defend your answer by examples.

4. Discuss what the term "functional grammar" means to you. How does a mastery of functional grammar differ from the establishment of correct habits of usage?

5. Suggest a number of devices which you as a teacher might use to improve sentence structure in the written expression of your pupils.

6. Devise a series of exercises designed to give your pupils practice in organizing words and phrases within sentences to give clarity of meaning, variety, and interest.

7. You need to give your pupils practice in organizing sentences in correct and effective order within the paragraph. Devise such a series of exercises.

8. Discuss the problems of vocabulary enrichment from the standpoints of (1) an increased number of usable and colorful words, and (2) the number of meanings per word. Check the dictionary to discover the large number of different meanings given for many common words.

SELECTED REFERENCES

Arts and Skills of Communication for Democracy's Children, Vol. II. San Bernardino, Calif.: San Bernardino County Schools, no date.

DAWSON, MILDRED A. *Teaching Correct Usage.* Language Arts Notes, Number 6. Yonkers-on-Hudson: World Book Company, 1956.

——. *Training Pupils to Study*. Language Arts Notes, Number 3. Yonkers-on-Hudson: World Book Company, 1955.

DEAN, LEONARD F. and WILSON, KENNETH G. (editors). *Essays on Language and Usage*. New York: Oxford University Press, 1959.

Experience Curriculum in English. A Report of the Curriculum Commission of the National Council of Teachers of English, Wilbur W. Hatfield, chairman. New York: D. Appleton–Century Company, 1935.

GREENE, HARRY A. "Direct versus Formal Methods in Elementary English." *Elementary English Review*, 24:273–285; May, 1947.

HILDRETH, GERTRUDE H. "Interrelationships Between Written Expression and the Other Language Arts." *Elementary English Review*, 31:40–48; January, 1954.

Iowa Elementary Teachers Handbook, Vol. 4, *Oral and Written Language*. Des Moines: Department of Public Instruction, 1944.

Iowa Elementary Teachers Handbook, Vol. 2, *Reading*. Des Moines: Department of Public Instruction, 1944.

MARCKWARDT, ALBERT H. and WALCOTT, FRED G. *Facts About Current English Usage*. English Monograph No. 7, National Council of Teachers of English. New York: D. Appleton–Century Company, Inc., 1938.

MC KEE, PAUL. "Grammar—Why, How, When?" *McKee Language Service Bulletin*. Boston: Houghton Mifflin Company, no date.

——. *Language in the Elementary School*. Boston: Houghton Mifflin Company, 1939.

POOLEY, ROBERT C. *Teaching English Usage*. New York: Appleton-Century-Crofts, Inc., 1946.

——. *Teaching English Grammar*. New York: Appleton-Century-Crofts, Inc., 1957.

Teaching Language in the Elementary School. Forty-third Yearbook of the National Society for the Study of Education, Part II. Chicago: The University of Chicago Press, 1944.

WOFFORD, AZILE. *The School Library*. New York: The H. W. Wilson Company, 1959.

part 3

Techniques and Methods of

Developing Language Skills

THE FIVE CHAPTERS COMPRISING THIS PART DEAL WITH THE INSTRUCTIONAL problems of methods, techniques, and materials required by the teacher and supervisor in attaining the specific objectives set forth in Part Two. Emphasis is placed on the general theoretical and psychological background of language methods. Practical approaches to classroom procedures are accompanied by extensive samples and examples of materials of known utility established on the basis of research evidence.

7

General Considerations in the

Teaching of Language

THE PURPOSE OF THIS CHAPTER IS TO PRESENT AND EVALUATE CERTAIN general issues which serve as background to the proper understanding of how learning in language takes place and to the effective development of methods of teaching as presented in the four chapters that follow. The discussion is organized around the following main topics:

    a. The organization of subject matter for language learning.
    b. The psychology of learning language.
    c. Motivation of learning.
    d. Recognizing individual differences.
    e. Classroom adjustments for individual differences.
    f. Organizing units of instruction in language.
    g. General issues underlying effective expression.

This chapter, being the first in the section on instructional procedures for developing language skills, presents an overview of the principal issues in the teaching of language, and gives consideration to the causes of the issues as well as suggesting the way toward the adoption and utilization of teaching methods based on the best experimental evidence and expert judgment.

THE ORGANIZATION OF SUBJECT MATTER

In spite of the fact that educational discussions have long been filled with references to the term *integration,* there is still confusion as to its meaning. The basic idea of the term, regardless of definitions that may be associated with it, is simply that school subjects are not taught in complete isolation, but are related one to another. In studying the subject matter in any given area, the child has opportunities for experiences that

173

contribute to an understanding of that field but that in general are considered other school courses. For example, the child may employ in one subject skills that are ordinarily taught as separate school subjects, such as reading, or writing, or composition. All that the child does in connection with understanding and using the original subject matter is closely related in his activities and experiences. This deliberate relating of all of the child's learnings is termed *integration*.

Perhaps part of the difficulty arises from a confusion of the meanings of the terms *correlation* and *integration*. In a correlated program the school subjects retain their traditional identities but aspects of one subject are related to another whenever possible. In an integrated program the subject-matter lines are almost completely broken down, with the result that the subject of language may not appear at all on the daily schedule, but expressional and communicational activities in all areas are considered a part of the language curriculum. Educationally there is much to be said for both practices. Both imply a closeness of emphasis when applied to subject relationships in the classroom. Both bring the pupil into close contact with rich experiences and ideas to be communicated. Doubtless there are many schools in which a reasonable degree of correlation of other school subjects with language is effected. Because of the difficulties of programming and the special demands on the teachers under this type of program, only a few schools achieve a satisfactorily integrated program.

The following statement describes integration as it is understood and widely practiced today:

To illustrate, a child may be studying subject matter in connection with a topic in social science, such as *transportation*. He reads geographies or histories or other books to get his information. He may even need to have some practice in how to gather information, how to outline, or how to comprehend what he reads. Thus, reading is related. He may write letters to steamship companies to get additional data. He may summarize the facts he has gathered into a few simple statements. He may find that he needs practice in writing letters or in composing clear summary sentences. Thus, composition is involved. As he writes his sentences, both spelling and penmanship enter in, and needed additional practice in those subjects may be brought to light. Thus, two other fields—spelling and penmanship—are related. He may decide to make a frieze illustrating the progress in types of water transportation. The art teacher comes to the rescue with suggestions on how to make the drawings. A lesson may grow out of this for the whole class on how to label drawings, how to arrange material for a frieze, or on methods of shading or coloring. Thus, another field—art—is related. The object, of course, is not to relate the fields, but to use every means to understand the original problem, *transportation*, and to make it meaningful. This, then, is integration.[1]

Certainly some degree of integration seems necessary if a child is to recognize the importance of language in all the other activities of school and life in which he engages. The child must learn that the language skills are the tools by which he receives and transmits ideas in connection with all of his daily activities, in school and out. The subject matter of these activities is the content around which a successful language program operates. If the child wants to discuss a television program with his friends, or bring one of these friends to his home and introduce him to the family, or call his mother on the telephone, he has his own subject matter to write or talk about as a part of the language program. Perhaps he is already engaged in making a report in a unit on the community, or in writing sentences in social studies that summarize facts about children in other lands, or in writing rules of healthful living about how to avoid catching a cold. He has no need for additional subject matter to write or talk about as a part of the language program. What he needs is instruction in the skills of how to write better, to talk better, or to think better about this subject matter, which is a part of his own activities. The successful language program uses as the basis of instruction the content or subject matter of the child's own activities, his school subjects, the unit the class is working on, or some home or personal experiences. The emphasis is always upon his activities and experiences and his expressional needs arising out of them.

THE PSYCHOLOGY OF LEARNING LANGUAGE

The capacity of the human mind to accept and to adjust itself to new conditions, to modify its responses to meet novel situations, to solve problems—that is, to *learn*—is second in importance only to its capacity to grow physiologically—to *mature*. These two characteristics are considered by many psychologists as the two major aspects of the human mind. While physiological growth toward maturity takes place from within as a natural process, learning is the result of external environmental factors and experiences.

[1] Harry A. Greene, Maude McBroom, Ruth Moscrip, and Norma Gillett, *Manual for Building Better English*. Evanstown, Ill.; Row, Peterson and Company, 1947, p. 19.

Maturity sets the limits to learning but does not determine the character of the learning or the use that is made of it by the human mind. Learning cannot take place effectively in many fields until the organism reaches a certain level of maturity. The moth or butterfly bursts from its cocoon when ready. To force the opening of the cocoon is to mutilate the organism; the struggle to emerge from its prison is required to give it full maturity. The time when the young child learns to talk or to walk is determined not by the calendar but by his physical maturity and his mental readiness. Learning to walk, to talk, to ride a tricycle, to coordinate his eyes in reading, or to use his hands in writing are all abilities whose appearance and rates of development are limited by maturity. Teachers at all grade levels will do well to note the implications of this fact in establishing times and rates of learning and in setting up standards of expectancy of progress and of quality of product.

LEARNING — A PROCESS AND A PRODUCT

Learning has been defined in various ways by psychologists and educators, but all agree that as a characteristic capacity of the human mind it is basic to the educative process. In general, *learning is the process of change that occurs in the individual as he acquires new, useful, and desirable adjustments to his environment through experiences and activities suited to his desired goals and to his level of maturity.* As a process, learning is an active and highly personal matter. Establishing the conditions or experiences necessary for efficient learning is the function of the home, the school, and the classroom teacher. The *product* of learning comprises the evidence of the new and useful adjustments acquired by the individual through the learning *process.* Actually it is the process, rather than the product that is important. Teachers frequently become confused on this point, however, and look upon the products of activity, such as the number of examples worked, words spelled, stories written, sentences correctly capitalized and punctuated, as evidence of the final success of the learning process. As a matter of fact, they are really only good indicators of the degree of skill of the learner at the time. "Teachers ought to be especially concerned with how the learner acts and his actions change rather than with what he produces. . . . The true products of schoolroom activity are found in improved mental and motor processes." [2] While an appreciation of the learning process in

[2] Ragsdale, C. E., "The Learning Process," in *The Implications of Research for the Classroom Teacher,* a joint yearbook of the Department of Classroom Teachers

176

general may be helpful to the teacher of language, the teacher's chief concern may well be with the end product, the development of effective mastery of the expressional abilities as shown in the child's habitually correct use of language.

LEARNING TO COMMUNICATE

It is fortunate that man is equipped by nature and by instinctive desire to produce the various sounds, signs, and symbols we know as language. Moreover, he seems disposed to communicate by means of language sounds and symbols. There is no reason to conclude, however, that he is predisposed to learn or to use a specific language. The young child instinctively uses his organs of speech to make sounds—sounds having no relationship to any particular language pattern or form. A child of Spanish parents transplanted at an early age to this country will learn to speak our language as readily as he would speak Spanish. His inherited tendency is to vocalize, to speak, but not to express himself in a specific language such as Spanish or English. Language is a social instrument, and as such it is acquired, and its meaning is determined by social means. The meaning of any specific language symbol, being purely arbitrary, is defined in terms of the particular culture-area in which it is found. It is given meaning by man, and usually is understood with difficulty out of its cultural context. Quite often little inherent relationship exists between the language symbols and the meaning conveyed.

PRINCIPLES OF LEARNING IN LANGUAGE

Learning to speak and write a language provides no exceptions to basic laws of learning. The principles or laws of learning that are of particular importance to the learning of language are commonly referred to as the *law of exercise* and the *law of effect*.

The law of exercise. In general, the law of exercise means that the more often a reaction is made to a situation the easier it is for the response to take place. Since this principle may operate for bad as well as for good, it is important that it be understood. The old adage that "practice makes perfect" expresses the same general idea and has the same dangers. It is true that practice increases the probability that a response will be made, but whether it is a desirable or an undesirable

and the American Educational Research Association. Washington: National Education Association, 1939.

response depends upon *what* is practiced. The individual learns precisely those skills on which he practices and not something else. Practice provides the opportunity and the motivation for the repetition of the desired activity. Whether improvement results from repetition is dependent upon the kind of practice and the follow-up that is given to this practice. Good classroom procedure sets the stage for learning experiences to take place under the best possible conditions.

Instruction designed to give the child an understanding of the new facts and skills presented for learning is necessary, but it is no substitute for repeated exercise of the skill itself. Not only is systematic drill required to enable the learner to secure some immediate mastery of skills

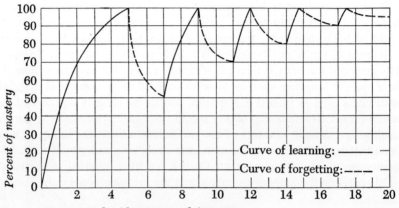

Time periods of learning and forgetting

presented for initial learning, but constant practice distributed in many short drill periods is necessary if the initial mastery is not to be lost through forgetting. The curve of learning efficiency in a new skill rises rapidly at the outset of instruction under the stimulation of interesting activities and motivated drill. Dropping the emphasis on the skill for even a short period permits forgetting to operate, with the result that the curve of mastery falls off at approximately the same rapid rate as it rose in the initial stages of learning. Not all that was learned initially is forgotten during the early periods of forgetting, but the curve of mastery does continue to drop at a decreasing rate until additional drill is presented to reverse it. After a round of practice has been given, the curve of efficiency may rise again to a point as high as it was originally. An interval of forgetting will cause it to drop again but at a slower rate than before, and it will not fall as low as it was before re-learning took place. With each repeated period of re-learning and forgetting, the curve of efficiency returns to maximum more quickly and falls off more slowly than in the early stages of learning. Finally after many properly distributed short periods of drill a sufficient amount of over-learning may take place that the curve of mastery falls only slightly after a long period of forgetting. Here is the justification for a systematically planned program of maintenance drills.

The law of effect. The second of these important principles of learning states a fact that most teachers know. Satisfying and pleasing results from first responses encourage the individual to repeat the reaction, while unpleasant results tend to discourage the repetition of the response. This, too, is a double-edged instrument which the teacher constantly uses in the classroom to encourage good language habits by favorable comment and to discourage poor habits by bringing to bear social pressures against them. The effective learning situation in language is one in which the individual is able repeatedly to produce the expected response under pleasant conditions.

Transfers in learning. The transfer of expressional skills from the classroom to other life-like communicational activities follows certain simple rules which many teachers unfortunately do not seem to understand. Ordinarily, transfers in learning take place from the general learning situation to the specific or new situation, to the extent that certain identical elements are found in both. A skill may be developed to high efficiency in the classroom and then fail to transfer to similar expressional activities, however, because the teacher failed to show adequately how the skill operates in a life-like situation. A pupil who follows every rule of neatness in the preparation of written material for his language classes may be careless in the form of the papers he hands to his arithmetic teacher. He may speak correctly in the classroom, but carelessly on the playground. It is unfortunately true that unless and until these identical elements in similar situations are pointed out for him by his teachers, a pupil may fail to make these ordinary transfers in learning. It is equally unfortunate that many teachers fail to sense this failure of their pupils to apply to life situations the skills they acquire and use in the classroom. The need for this constant assistance from the teacher in making such applications out of the classroom of skills acquired in the classroom, points up the necessity for persistent attention to language in all subject-matter fields and in all situations.

MOTIVATION OF LEARNING

RELATING SKILLS TO LIFE NEEDS

The child confronted with a real reason to write or to say something has the best possible motivation for learning the needed language skills as well as for continuing to practice them. It is possible for the observant teacher to find many life activities of the children in his class which can be the basis for instruction in the language skills. Children will spend much effort in learning how to prepare the script for a real radio broadcast, in learning to write articles for the school newspaper—if the articles really appear in the paper—and participating in other similar activities that have true purpose and meaning. Sometimes the teacher will need only to help define the real-life language situations that are present always when human beings are associated with one another. At other times the teacher may need to create language situations which are similar to those in life outside the school. Children are thus impelled, by their own desires and for genuine communicational motives, to engage in the language activity in which the desired skills can be taught.

A good language program constantly provides experiences that are closely related to the child's personal and social needs and which enable him to associate language symbols with meaning and use them in purposeful activities. In letter writing, for example, children soon learn to pay attention to letter form, to the spelling of the words used, and to the capitalization and punctuation required, if they first fully understand that the letters to be written are to serve real purposes, that they will really be sent, and that there is a need to communicate as effectively as possible with each person who will read them.

GIVING SKILLS A LIFELIKE SETTING

Just as the language skills that should be taught are those that are most closely related to life needs, so should the setting for the teaching of these skills be as nearly lifelike as possible. The average school classroom may not be very similar in appearance to the child's home but for several hours of the day school activities *are* life for him. Not all life activities are carried on in the home. Many take place in other settings. Again, the effectiveness of the transfer of ability or knowledge from

180

one situation to another is directly proportional to the similarity of elements of the two situations. This means that language instruction should be given in settings which are lifelike, or possess elements similar to those found in real life. In fact, much instruction in the use of language can be given in true settings without the children knowing that they are receiving such instruction. It is doubtful, however, that an artificial setting such as a school or classroom post office, even though there might be similarity to a real post office, would be successful for motivating an interest in letter writing. With so many opportunities for the writing of real letters it is unnecessary to resort to attempts such as this to create a lifelike setting. Simply recognizing that one of the children has moved to another city presents an opportunity for letter writing in a real setting.

Of much greater importance than just the social setting for language instruction is the intellectual and emotional climate in which it is carried on; how it is conducted; what is learned; and the materials used. It is the teacher who creates the classroom atmosphere most conducive to learning. It is the teacher who generates interest in projects, problems, and class activities, and who ultimately motivates the desire for learning the language abilities. The teacher's interest in the children and his respect for their contributions help each child to feel respected, liked, wanted, and needed. The teacher's friendliness, patience, and faith help each child to feel at ease, confident of some success, and free from the fears and tensions that block expression and learning. The teacher's knowledge of each child's cultural background, development, and ability makes possible the selection and adjustment of materials, facilities, and procedures to fit his needs. The teacher's enthusiasm, cheerful encouragement, and careful planning lead pupils to want to learn and to continue to be interested in learning.

UTILIZING AND EMPHASIZING AUDIENCE VALUES

Although learning a language is generally considered to be an individual matter, the use of language itself is a social activity, and language at once becomes a social instrument. It is a means of conveying the ideas and thoughts of one person or a group of persons to some other individual or group. Thus, the audience to which all speaking and writing is directed must be considered, a fact which should direct and motivate all who would speak or write. The audience expects and is entitled to gain

181

something from listening or reading; therefore, what is written or spoken must be of interest to the audience or the collective audience mind will be closed to any reception. This is one of the most powerful factors involved in motivation.

RECOGNIZING INDIVIDUAL DIFFERENCES

Each child is an individual possessed of qualities which make him different from all other individuals. While this is readily recognized as a true statement by most people, a look into a typical classroom would indicate that many teachers and educators apparently do not take it seriously. They prescribe instructional procedures and establish standards of achievement as if they expected them to fit all children. Children within a given school group differ in mental capacity, sex, size and physical development, motor control, sensitivity of sense organs, amount of pigmentation in the skin, and in many other aspects of mental and physical development. They not only differ in innate capacity for learning, but at any point in their growth show wide differences in achievement.

Language development follows the pattern of all other capacities and abilities in revealing extremely wide individual differences among children at all ages. Even at the beginning of their school experiences, children may vary by several hundreds or even thousands of words in such an area as the number of words in their vocabularies. Startling ranges of mental ability will be found within any given school grade. In one instance, the authors found pupils of a ninth-grade class ranging in mental ability from below seventh grade to above twelfth grade mental ability. As might be inferred from such extreme ranges of capacity, individual differences are marked in all phases of oral and written language. Such a simple procedure as the examination of pupil scores made on the parts of any good analytical test of language abilities will offer convincing evidence of the spread of individual differences in groups of pupils, whether classified by age or by grade. It must be clear that the teacher of a class made up of individuals ranging over six or seven years (or grades) in language abilities faces a hopeless task if he is expected to bring all members of the class up to the same levels of mastery.

182

TEACHER IDENTIFICATION
OF PUPIL NEEDS

It is relatively easy to secure a reliable estimate of the range of individual differences that may be expected in a classroom, but it is another matter to obtain a clear, detailed picture of the individual children with whom a specific teacher must deal. General facts of individual differences must be interpreted in terms of concrete realities as the teacher works with all of the children in his classroom in the various day to day situations. The teacher must deal with each child in his class as a person and not as a statistic.

The teacher in today's crowded classroom rarely has a program which is flexible enough to care for all the individual differences he encounters. There are many types of language experience which all children should receive in school if they are to become useful members of society. However, language is such an individual matter that much of the instruction must be carried on in small groups and directly with individual children.

In order for a teacher to care for the individual language needs of the members of his class, a continuing program of evaluation and observation must be carried on to determine individual needs and the range of differences. Examples of specific techniques and methods of determining needs and differences are the following:

1. Observing and recording speech, reactions, and general behavior, especially in language and literature activities.
2. Using a check list or inventory in evaluating speech, language abilities, and attitudes.
3. Tabulating errors which occur frequently in the children's informal and formal conversation and other language activities in the room and on the playground.
4. Making recordings of samples of speech; analyzing and checking the results.
5. Using teacher-made and standardized tests which measure abilities and achievements in language skills.

PUPIL IDENTIFICATION OF OWN NEEDS

Most children recognize that the ability to communicate effectively is needed by everyone, though they may not recognize the importance of the various skills that are a part of effective communication. The extent to which a particular skill seems important to an individual child varies

183

as does the extent of his mastery of that particular skill. The problem of getting a child to identify his own particular needs is a major one for the language teacher.

Stimulating the individual pupil to identify his own needs—the skills on which he particularly needs to work—is a basic motivational procedure and one that will pay rich dividends to the teacher. Children should be guided by teachers to use the papers they write and the talks they make in all of their classwork as a basis for judging the progress they are making in expression. By such procedure a child will be constantly working on his own errors, examining his own papers, and searching out means of improving his own productions. Other means by which pupils may evaluate their work and reach their own conclusions as to their need for improvement are the following:

1. Using a check-list, preferably one that the pupil has helped to devise.
2. Working as one of a pair or small group to identify areas which need improvement by his partner or others in the group.
3. Looking at the material in a folder which contains samples of his work and records of his achievement.
4. Plotting or recording his own standardized test scores and comparing them with the results of previous testing.

CLASSROOM ADJUSTMENTS FOR
INDIVIDUAL DIFFERENCES

The school program is operated on the assumption that the teacher accepts each child as he is, and proceeds with a plan of instruction that will take care of his individual needs but at the same time will promote the greatest amount of growth possible for all of the children in the class. The following suggestions are concerned with adjustments in the school program that may be made to care more adequately for the wide range of individual differences in language ability.

ABILITY GROUPING

The division of class groups according to ability is a procedure used in an attempt to reduce the range of individual differences within the classroom and thus to simplify the instructional problems involved in meeting the requirements of all types of ability. In theory this practice is sound, but for some reason the experimental evidence shows that while it is successfully used in reading, it has not lived up to its theoretical possibilities in the field of language instruction. Possibly language ability includes a more complicated variety of specific skills than those upon which ability grouping in reading is based. Part of the difficulty may lie also in the inadequacy of the instruments used for grouping in language. Ultimately this will undoubtedly be remedied by the development of tests and measuring instruments which will discriminate more accurately for smaller differences in individual abilities in language.

Yet children differ to such an extent in abilities to use some language skills that it is a waste of time for all of them to be working on the improvement of the same skill at the same time. The answer may lie in a flexible form of grouping, grouping which may be modified or readjusted frequently. Pupils may be placed in small groups according to their immediate interests or their current needs for instruction. Since interests and needs are constantly changing, such grouping plans would of necessity be flexible.

LANGUAGE LABORATORY

The laboratory plan of instruction in English skills has long been a successful technique in college and high school classes. Its use in the elementary school has been limited, however; so many of the language skills are introduced in the elementary school that teachers have felt that in general all pupils need the same basic instruction. The evidence concerning individual differences in language ability at any school level would indicate, however, that even though much class-wide and group instruction may be given, there is a need for the individual method of attacking the problems as provided through a laboratory plan.

Basically the plan consists of having each pupil write something that is meaningful to him. As the writing is taking place, the teacher moves from pupil to pupil offering help, making suggestions, and encouraging the efforts being made. Each pupil is doing something that has purpose for him and the attention of the teacher is given only to the things the child needs to correct or to improve in order to achieve his purpose.

In addition to the suggestions above, a number of special activities as listed below have value in individualizing instruction.

INDIVIDUALIZING PRACTICE AND REVIEW EXERCISES

A major problem in instruction for the language teacher is the provision of needed exercises for drill and practice to aid in the fixing of habits, and yet keep such practice so individualized that a pupil will not be concentrating on material he already knows and uses correctly. Children, themselves, particularly in the middle and upper grades, can be held responsible for the identification and recording of their own errors, thus relieving the teacher of many of the complications involved in giving individual attention. Many children can also be held responsible for using the indexes of textbooks and workbooks to locate practice material for their individual needs. Dawson makes two useful suggestions for the provision of individual practice and review material: [3]

A workable and extremely simple procedure that will provide some measure of individualization in practicing correct usage is as follows: From old, discarded language textbooks and workbooks, clippings from teachers' magazines, and files of teacher-made exercises, develop a set of practice materials that the pupils may use during their free time. Each exercise is placed in an envelope and labeled. The various envelopes are then filed in a substantial box as wide as the envelopes are long. Any pupil who needs practice on a certain phase of correct usage or a specific language skill may then go to the file and select from it a practice exercise related to his known needs. The teacher or a competent pupil may check the accuracy of his work. When the pupil has completed an exercise satisfactorily, he signs his name on the enclosing envelope. Although this procedure can be considered no more than supplementary, it can be helpful because practice is suited to individual needs and the pupils tend to enjoy selecting exercises and doing them on their own initiative.

One procedure in individualizing written drills involves the collection of numerous exercises by cutting up various workbooks. The lessons should be arranged according to kind; for example, put all lessons on the same type of capitalization together. Each sheet is mounted on stiff paper. (If a desirable lesson appears on each side of the sheet, the sheet can be so mounted that part of each side is exposed.) A table of contents, showing the arrangement (probably alphabetical order by type) and sheet numbers, can be mounted on stiff paper. On another sheet have a widely spaced alphabetized list of the pupils' names so that the items each pupil needs may be listed and a cumulative record made of the exercises he has completed satisfactorily. A strong box of suitable size and shape may be used for a file.

SELF-EDITING, REWRITING, AND PROOFREADING

Many of the errors made in language expression are the result of carelessness and a lack of correct habits. It is important, therefore, for teachers to train the children to proofread their own papers, to see that what

[3] Mildred Dawson, *Teaching Language in the Grades.* Yonkers-on-Hudson: World Book Company, 1951, p. 290.

186

they have written conveys the meaning intended and that their work is free from mechanical errors. Such teaching presupposes that the writing is purposeful and that the pupils will feel the need individually to do as well as possible. Such a practice should help children to evaluate their own work and to set higher standards for themselves individually.

Habits of proofreading and self-editing of all written work should lead the child logically and directly to the discovery that the complete rewriting of his product invariably results in its improvement. Rewriting should be distinguished from merely recopying the proofread original production, a process which actually has only doubtful value. A readiness to rewrite a product will develop only when the individual is brought to the conviction that nothing but his best effort will satisfy him. This is a state of mind that the teacher must be instrumental in developing. So important is it that it should be stressed from the very beginnings of language instruction in the primary grades. By creating a feeling of pride in the quality of his workmanship and by convincing him that his product is valuable enough in itself to justify his best effort, the teacher can make the child ready to accept teacher-editing, his own self-editing, and rewriting as the best means of improving his self-expression.

VARYING DIFFICULTY OF ASSIGNMENTS

It is a waste of time for all children to be working on the same task in most instructional situations in language, since individual differences are generally so great. It is difficult, however, for the teacher to manage a classroom in which the pupils are working on different things. In our school systems the same textbook is generally used for all children, and too often these texts do not make provision for individualizing assignments. It is possible to vary the difficulty of assignments in the English class by having the entire class working on the same general topic (for example, giving reports in a social studies activity) and yet doing things of different degrees of difficulty concerning that topic.

An example is the following: [4]

. . . all members of a class might be preparing reports for a social studies unit but the reports might be of differing degrees of difficulty. One child might be seeking information for a report on the foods the pioneers ate; another might be writing the conversation two wagon masters might have had before leaving with their wagon trains; a third might be preparing a critique of a western television show; and a fourth might be tracing routes on a map. The

[4] Walter T. Petty, *The Language Arts in Elementary Schools.* Washington, D.C.: The Center for Applied Research in Education, Inc., 1962, p. 8.

task of each child depends upon his interest and his ability. The child searching for names of foods may have limited reading and writing skills, so he is essentially engaged in finding words and listing them. The child writing conversation must have read extensively, and must be fairly skilled in writing. Each child's task should challenge him, however, and in order to be of value in teaching language skills, should call for the use of some of these skills—particularly those he needs most.

PROGRAMMED INSTRUCTION

A recent innovation, and one which has as yet received only limited use in language instruction, programmed instruction provides facts and questions in amounts that a pupil presumably can assimilate and master before moving on to others.[5] These items may be presented mechanically, such as by showing one frame of a film at a time, or in a more or less standard textbook fashion. A programmed textbook (or series of "visuals") differs from regular textbook and film materials in that the learner must finish one step (answer a question, for example) before moving on to the next. The programmed materials are designed for individual use also, which is not entirely the case with the textbook.

SPECIAL ACTIVITIES

The classroom teacher should be continually looking for ways in which individualized language instruction may be given. One way is through the use of special activities, perhaps in combination with some of the other procedures mentioned in this section. Some such special activities are the following:

1. Having each pupil keep in a notebook a record of the words misspelled in his writing. These words should be studied in his spare time. Other suggestions for recording in a notebook are usage errors and points to remember concerning punctuation and capitalization.
2. Spelling the difficult words which the pupils are not supposed to know; that is, writing the words on the board as they are asked for.
3. Having children who do good work in language help others who have difficulty.
4. Allowing children who finish assignments first to make copies of work to be preserved or posted on bulletin boards.

[5] The only instance of programmed instruction in the language area that the authors have found is in spelling, and was reported by Douglas Porter, "Some Effects of Year-long Teaching Machine Instruction," in *Automatic Teaching: The State of the Art,* Eugene Galanter, ed. New York: John Wiley and Sons, Inc., 1959.

5. Giving incidental individual correction of errors, particularly usage errors in the primary grades.
6. Allowing pupils to choose their own topics for reports and writing activities.

In addition to these possibilities, many language teachers have found that special activities of a non-language type are greatly enjoyed by the more able students when their language goals have been attained. The real appeal of these special activities seems to lie in the fact that they provide live, interesting, novel activities which the pupils may anticipate with pleasure, rather than the typical "more-of-the-same" drill on language.

ORGANIZING UNITS OF INSTRUCTION
IN LANGUAGE

The preparation of an instructional unit in language for a given age or grade level requires that practical questions such as the following be answered. What kinds of language activities should the unit provide? In what amounts, and at what performance levels should these be provided? What emphasis should be given to the selected general abilities? What specific skills of speech and writing should be emphasized at this level?

The critical problem is to build an instructional unit for the particular grade or age level so that it bears the correct relation to the units of other preceding and following levels and is properly adjusted to the current language needs of a particular group of children. These language needs are usually determined from the children's language activities in school and outside of school. All kinds of language situations must be considered as to the use of both general abilities and specific skills.

From the standpoint of the classroom teacher of language it is suggested that the instructional unit should meet at least these general requirements:

1. The unit should include the most important socially useful facts, skills, attitudes, and usages suitable for instruction at this age and grade level.
2. It should present these important facts in situations designed to motivate and simplify their teaching and to guarantee their mastery by pupils of this age and grade level.
3. It should provide rich sources of experience through literature and pupil activities as the bases for expression.

189

4. It should make clear to the child the standards by which certain debatable usages are judged to be acceptable.
5. It should introduce adequate motivation and drill to guarantee mastery of the essential habits and skills presented for instruction.
6. It should include evaluative and testing devices suitable for use with pupils of this age and grade and with skills of the types in the unit.

For the pupil, the instructional unit should be organized to accomplish at least these specific purposes:

1. The unit should practically guarantee the development of efficiency in language habits through accurate and speedy handling of the elemental language skills needed in the basic child and adult life situations.
2. It should contain material designed to promote clearness and completeness in thinking as the basis for clarity in language expression.
3. It should stimulate freedom and fluency of expression under all types of situations. Specifically it should stimulate the use of a rich, varied, colorful, and suitable vocabulary.
4. It should encourage the pupil in his efforts to develop a desirable personality in speech and a pleasing style in writing.
5. It should provide for personal creative production and expression of his own individuality.
6. It should stimulate the development of: desirable pupil attitudes toward good English, and its improvement as a personal matter; a proper appreciation of the effect of purpose on the conditions of speaking and writing; and an understanding of the value of self-criticism and rewriting in producing quality and style in expression.

The facts, skills, attitudes, usages, and activities to be included in the instructional unit should at least meet the following criteria:

1. The unit should be organized around content and needs selected from the socially useful adult activities suitable for instruction at this grade or age level.
2. It should give preference to skills which rate high in the child's own language needs.
3. It should include certain crucial skills even though their social frequencies may be relatively low.
4. It should take into consideration both the skills with high social frequencies and the errors made in the use of these skills by the children of this age and grade level.
5. It should give emphasis to the correction of bad language habits in the areas of socially important skills.
6. It should give special emphasis to the mastery of skills not ordinarily perfected out of school but which are essential to creative work in language expression.
7. It should be so organized that the language skills suitable for this age and grade level are taught in connection with activities from a wide range of subject-matter fields.

8. It should give emphasis to the oral and written skills in close accordance with their importance as shown by analyses of social demands on language.
9. It should be composed of timely and teachable material as determined by experimental use with similar age and grade groups.
10. It should take into account the content of tests, drills, texts, and courses of study as supplementary guides to suitability of skills and their placement.

GENERAL ISSUES UNDERLYING
EFFECTIVE EXPRESSION

In addition to the consideration of such teaching problems as the organization of subject matter, how learning occurs, motivation, individual differences, and the development of units, attention must be given to a number of other general issues of basic importance to teaching. These issues are discussed in this section.

ASSUMPTION OF TRANSFER FROM ORAL DRILL TO WRITTEN DRILL

Many of the basic elements of spoken communication are identical with those of written communication. Skill in the construction of concise and clear-cut sentences, the ability to develop ideas and to organize them for convincing and entertaining expression—these are the essentials of communication, either oral or written. Too, items of usage tend to be the same in both oral and written language, although written language often is more formal. Extensive use of properly constructed drills in oral usage may help to correct many errors found in both forms of expression. However, such drill should not be expected to correct the mechanical errors which are so important to effective written expression. Although oral drill on items of usage will improve both oral and written usage, it is a fallacy to assume that skills which are identifiable only with written language will be learned. If we expect children to learn to write well, we must provide proper motivation and many opportunities for them to write. Moreover, we must provide drill specifically designed to establish the desired habits in the mechanics of expression.

PROPER EMPHASIS ON CONTENT AND FORM

Quality in language expression, whether oral or written, depends upon two important elements: content, and form. Content is concerned with the number and the quality of the ideas or thoughts expressed, while form involves the mechanics or skills of presentation. Both of these are essential, but neither should receive exclusive emphasis in a language program. The child, struggling to express an original idea or feeling, should turn to his teacher as a friendly, sympathetic, understanding guide for his venture into new and uncharted regions. The teacher's first duty as a guide is to stimulate further the child's thinking, to clarify his ideas, and to help him to organize them. When the child has arranged his ideas to the best of his ability, the teacher should then, and not until then, turn the child's attention toward the improvement of the mechanics and form of expression. The principle is first to stimulate fluency of expression and then to stress the mechanics of expression.

RICH SOURCES OF CONTENT

It is almost axiomatic that no one can be fluent either in writing or speaking on a subject about which he knows little. Dawson and Zollinger suggest that there must be *intake* as well as *outgo*.[6] In order for expression to be effective and interesting, there must be reception through many rich and varied activities and experiences. Every adult well knows that it is likely to be embarrassing if not actually dangerous to attempt to talk or write about something outside his realm of experience. But if he has directly and personally participated in an event or activity, or has experienced it vicariously, he will at least have some ideas or thoughts and can talk or write about the subject within the range of his experiences with it.

LIFELIKE SITUATIONS TO MOTIVATE EXPRESSION

Children are best motivated to master desirable habits of expression when they themselves sense the need and are convinced that it serves a real and lifelike purpose. Most children are highly imaginative but at the

[6] Mildred A. Dawson and Marian Zollinger, *Guiding Language Learning.* Yonkers-on-Hudson: World Book Company, 1957, p. 9.

192

same time are slow to accept obvious artificiality. Too often pupils interested in a problem in science or social studies which has a real meaning to them are forced to put aside this genuine motivation and use material from a textbook as the basis for learning about discussion or some related expressional skill. Pooley expresses this point concisely: [7]

The conscientious teacher of English will be alert to use natural settings for spoken exercises and will teach correctness, good usage, and good manners in oral English through and by means of the subjects and topics which the children *really want to talk about.*

In general, the same conditions apply to written language. The need for writing should arise out of the natural activities for which the writing serves a purpose.

CREATIVENESS BEFORE CORRECTNESS

Special emphasis needs to be given in the language program to the development of children's creative abilities. The basis for creativity and fluency is a wealth of rich experience and strong emotional feelings which result in a rush of ideas and emotions that the child feels compelled to express in verbal form. In order for this spontaneous type of creativity to be properly encouraged there must be, first, a complete absence of strain in the creative situation, and, second, an abundance of opportunities for enriching and stimulating experience. No child can be creative when his imagination is not stimulated or when his major attention must be given to form. Such shifting of attention to the mechanics of expression may readily provide the strain that stifles the real creative spark.

LANGUAGE LEARNING AS DIRECT, NOT INCIDENTAL

The development of skill in the use of language is heavily dependent upon the subject matter of other fields if the learning of language is to be meaningful and interesting to the learners. However, this in no sense suggests that the mastery of specific language skills should be left to incidental teaching. The child himself need not be aware that in his pursuit of his interesting activities in other subject-matter fields he is developing control of vital language skills, but the teacher should never lose sight of the specific language skills which may be introduced and taught in each and every activity situation.

[7] Robert C. Pooley, *op. cit.,* pp. 206–207.

In spite of the many school programs that claim to depend upon the incidental teaching of the necessary language skills, the evidence indicates that the vast majority of effective language programs are not developed on an incidental basis. Every socially important skill of expression must be identified, taught, reviewed, and maintained by systematic drill and practice exercises in order to develop an adequate mastery. The evidence in support of this statement is the long record of failure of formal, indirect, or incidental methods to produce adequate control of the expressional skills.

CORRECT USAGE THE RESULT OF HABIT

The smooth, flowing, effective use of good English in childhood or in adult life rests upon a firm foundation of good habits of expression so thoroughly established as to be automatic. The speaker who must hesitate as he searches for a particular word, who must pause to choose the correct usage, who is obliged to retrace his steps to reconstruct his sentence misses his opportunity to express himself effectively. The following statement by Pooley expresses this point of view concisely.[8]

For all ordinary purposes of communication the proficient adult is generally unconscious of language choices; appropriate words, idioms, and constructions flow along unimpeded by conscious effort. Only in unusually formal or difficult situations does he become conscious of the need for closer discrimination in his language choices. Even then, good habits, augmented by experiences gained in observation of the speech and writing of others, carry him through. The laying of sound habits is therefore the first step in teaching good usage.

This statement represents the consensus of most language experts on the most effective methods of learning to use our language acceptably. It rests primarily upon the basic psychological principle that correct habits are developed and made automatic through the repeated exercise of the desired responses under good motivating conditions.

LANGUAGE HABITS FOLLOW GENERAL LAWS OF LEARNING

In the language-learning process, habits of correct usage are the result of continuous repetition of the desired reactions. Speaking or writing acceptably is an automatic reaction, the result of countless firmly established and interrelated habits. These habits are best established when the child is motivated to correct his errors in language through the recog-

[8] *Ibid.,* p. 177.

nition that for him such correction is needed and is important. The teacher has the responsibility for providing many opportunities for the practice of the correct expressions and for guiding the child into regarding socially acceptable or correct language expression as desirable.

The use of effective motivation must be emphasized at all times. An undesirable usage habit may continue in spite of repeated drill unless the pupil himself desires to break the habit. Teachers all too frequently use drill after drill without motivation or instruction, and without provision for consistent use of the correct forms in all subsequent language activities. Dawson suggests this formula: "Motivate; make a clear impression; repeat again and again with no intervening use of incorrect forms; consistently put the correct form into practical use." [9]

RULES GUARANTEE NO CONTROL OVER USAGE

Research accumulated over the past fifty years consistently lends support to Hoyt's conclusion stated in 1906 that "there is about the same relationship existing between grammar and composition and grammar and interpretation as exists between two totally different subjects, as grammar and geography." [10] Numerous recent studies, substantiating this conclusion and pointing out the lack of a positive relationship between a knowledge of the rules of grammar and a pupil's ability to express himself, are evaluated in a later chapter. It may be significant to note here that the more recent studies show that the above statement is true in the case of the mechanical skills such as punctuation and capitalization as well as in language usage.

Unfortunately, knowing a rule does not insure that it can be recalled or that it will be applied when needed. Too often, of course, rules are taught formally and merely memorized as indisputable facts; rarely are they derived inductively. Probably there is a place in language instruction for inductively derived principles when children have developed the necessary reasoning ability. Certainly, for most children, this is not in the elementary school grades.

NEED FOR LANGUAGE CONSCIENCE

Skill in language expression develops through the proper exercise of desired habits. This implies that the necessary skills are identified by the teacher and recognized by the pupil and that suitable opportunities are

[9] Mildred Dawson, *Teaching Language in the Grades,* p. 280.
[10] Franklin S. Hoyt, "Studies in English Grammar," *Teachers College Record,* 7:500; November, 1906.

provided for the exercise of the correct responses. Here the goal is to set up in the pupil's mind an attitude toward language error, since only when he is made sensitive to error does he watch carefully enough to prevent its recurrence. As Green has pointed out:

> Until a child *desires* to speak English correctly, all teacher efforts to realize that objective will fail . . . . The most important factor of all—in fact, the deciding factor—is this: the child must want to say the correct form. This will to prefer the correct to the incorrect must come as a resolve within the child to want to choose the proper words, to listen to himself and hear what he says, to correct it if he says the incorrect, and to *take pride* in speaking English correctly . . .[11]

There is a possible danger in developing so much sensitivity to error that the child may become over-sensitive regarding his mistakes to the point of self-consciousness in his use of language. This would be unfortunate, of course, for it would retard his expression. A major goal of the language program is to develop fluency, and in most cases this is possible along with the development of a language conscience.

EMPHASIS ON SOCIALLY IMPORTANT SKILLS

Consistently throughout this book the authors have expressed the point of view that the school should teach those elements of language which have the greatest social value. Research has identified many of the most common sources of difficulty in language expression as well as the errors in expression which occur most frequently. Language situations which are of major importance in the lives of children and adults have been identified and now receive direct attention in school instruction. The skills needed most in language expression should be among those selected for teaching. Greene gives this example:

> . . . one of the significant comma rules indicates that a comma should be used to set off a substantive in direct address. The following sentences illustrate this rule:
>
>> "Tom, for once you are correct."
>> "For once, Tom, you are correct."
>> "For once you are correct, Tom."
>
> It will be noted that two of the illustrations require the use of one comma, while the other requires the use of two. It seems obvious that each of these variations must be taken into account in making an appraisal of pupil mastery of these skills, for each is a specific learning situation . . . the usage represented by the first example accounts for almost exactly one-half of the

[11] Ivah Green, "Motivation for Correct English." *Elementary English,* 22:50–51; February, 1945.

usages of this type by elementary school children. In general, it may be concluded tentatively at least that emphasis on the variations when the person addressed introduces the sentence and when it closes the sentence will account for about 85 percent of the occasions when it will arise. From the standpoint of efficiency in the development of these skills, drill emphasis on the first and third type of sentence shown above would be most productive, since they appear to bear the major social burden in this particular area of skill.[12]

ALL ACTIVITY AS LANGUAGE ACTIVITY

Language as a means of thinking and communicating is so much a part of the total life activity of the child that we cannot expect a brief period of instruction in the classroom to make its use really effective. Children may very well develop a language consciousness which they use in the English class; they may completely recognize their language needs; however, unless they are constantly stimulated to do so, they may not carry these over to other activities. Improvement in language usage can be expected only when correct usages are insisted upon by all teachers in all written and oral expression. Pooley summarizes this principle as follows:

The English language is not a subject to be taught and dropped; it is a series of skills to be established for all the needs of life. Correctness can only be established when it is maintained consistently and constantly, nor may lapses in the essential items be tolerated at any time. Stated more positively the principle is this: the habits and attitudes instilled by language instruction must function without lapse or deviation in every use of language throughout the school day, and so far as possible, in out-of-school hours. Only by unremitting watchfulness can old habits be broken and new ones established.[13]

EMPHASIS ON AUDIENCE VALUES

Adults express themselves because they feel their expression has some importance for their audience. A child will learn to stand on his feet and think out loud by being placed frequently in situations in which he is obliged to do just that. He will learn to write by writing. In today's school a pupil speaks because he has something to say; the message is of first importance. As this principle is held to, the child will have an audience. The audience will expect some interesting information or some entertainment as he speaks. The same holds true for written expression. Children naturally look forward to having someone read what they have

[12] Harry A. Greene, "Principles of Method in Elementary English Composition." *Elementary English Review*, 14:219–226; October, 1937.
[13] Robert C. Pooley, *op. cit.*, p. 183.

written if they feel that their writing has real purpose, and that they are really sharing an idea or giving information. Throughout all language instruction, the emphasis should be on this principle: that what is said or written must be of value to an audience. The converse should be stressed too: that an audience should be interested, since what they are to hear or read is of interest.

FREEING THE CHILD FROM MECHANICAL HANDICAPS

In the lower grades, children in general express themselves much less fluently in written form than they do in oral form. Mechanical handicaps, such as inadequate skill in spelling and handwriting, account for much of this difference. Teachers may do much to free lower-grade children from such handicaps by writing on the board words the children need in their writing but are not expected to know.

DIRECTED DRILL IN PLACE OF REWRITING

The practice of having teachers mark errors, changes, and corrections in the pupil's written expression and then hand it back for re-copying is still prevalent in many classrooms in spite of evidence which indicates that the value of such a procedure is distinctly open to question. Modern practices in language programs stress proofreading by the pupil and the recognition of his own individual errors. From this recognition of individual needs a program of individualized drill on the more formal usages and skills may be compiled which will result in increased mastery. Such a program is based not only upon the sound principle of individualized instruction, but also upon high motivation through the pupil's personal interest in his own language improvement.

Drill exercises in any form are often criticized by advocates of incidental teaching. Such criticism may be justified, according to Tidyman and Butterfield since "much work of this type has been futile in the past; and it will probably continue to be futile, unless the teacher observes faithfully certain basic principles." [14] The justified criticism, however, is directed at drill that is not planned or directed and does not observe these basic principles: [15]

[14] Willard F. Tidyman and Marguerite Butterfield, *Teaching the Language Arts.* New York: McGraw-Hill Book Company, Inc., 1951, p. 389.
[15] *Ibid.,* p. 390.

198

1. Instruction and drill should be an outgrowth of a purposeful activity which reveals need for a particular skill.
2. Correct and incorrect forms should be presented together, properly labeled to show right and wrong.
3. Oral work should be provided so that the correct form will *sound right*.
4. Drill periods should be short, intensive, and frequent.
5. The cause of the error should be determined and attempts made to have the pupil understand the principle involved. Such explanation and subsequent understanding must be adjusted to the maturity of the pupil.

EXERCISES FOR THOUGHT AND DISCUSSION

1. Compare the dictionary meanings of the term *integration* with the educational interpretation as given here. In a similar way, compare the meanings of *integration* and *correlation*.

2. Discuss the classroom implications of the two major aspects of the human mind: the power to learn and the power to mature.

3. Formulate a defensible definition of learning as a mental process providing the basis for language mastery.

4. What does the evidence show concerning the hereditary aspects of a particular language?

5. Enumerate and discuss the major principles of learning operative in the mastery of language.

6. Discuss the three great motivators that function in learning to use a language effectively.

7. What can the classroom teacher do to adjust instruction to the needs of the slow and the bright pupils within a class?

8. Discuss the six general requirements which a language instructional unit should meet for the classroom teacher.

9. Evaluate the ten criteria which it is suggested the facts, skills, attitudes, and activities included in a language instruction unit should meet.

10. Restate in brief form as a principle each of the fifteen general issues underlying effective expression given in this chapter.

11. As a result of your study of this chapter prepare a series of concise statements which might be used as principles of method to guide you in the teaching of language in the elementary school.

SELECTED REFERENCES

DAWSON, MILDRED A. *Teaching Language in the Grades.* Yonkers-on-Hudson: World Book Company, 1951.

DAWSON, MILDRED A., and ZOLLINGER, MARIAN. *Guiding Language Learning.* Yonkers-on-Hudson: World Book Company, 1957.

An Experience Curriculum in English. A Report of the Curriculum Commission of the National Council of Teachers of English, W. Wilbur Hatfield, chairman. New York: D. Appleton–Century Company, 1935.

GILLETT, NORMA. "A Correlated Curriculum in Composition and the Social Studies." *Elementary English Review,* 80–86; March, 1937.

GOOD, CARTER V., ed. *Dictionary of Education.* New York: McGraw-Hill Book Company, Inc., 1945.

GREENE, HARRY A. "Direct versus Formal Methods in Elementary English." *Elementary English Review,* 24:273–285; May, 1947.

———. "English—Language, Grammar, Composition." *Encyclopedia of Educational Research,* rev. ed. New York: The Macmillan Company, 1950.

———. "Principles of Method in Elementary English Composition." *Elementary English Review,* 14:219–226; October, 1937.

HERRICK, VIRGIL E., and JACOBS, LELAND B., eds. *Children and the Language Arts.* Englewood Cliffs, N.J.: Prentice-Hall, Inc., 1956.

HORN, ERNEST. "Language and Meaning." *The Psychology of Learning.* The Forty-first Yearbook of the National Society for the Study of Education, Part II. Bloomington, Illinois: Public School Publishing Company, 1942.

JENKINS, FRANCES. *Language Development in Elementary Grades.* New York: Thomas Nelson and Sons, 1936.

JERSILD, ARTHUR. *Child Psychology.* Englewood Cliffs, N.J.: Prentice-Hall, Inc., 1947.

Language Arts for Today's Children. Prepared by the Commission on the English Curriculum, National Council of Teachers of English, Dora V. Smith, chairman. New York: Appleton-Century-Crofts, Inc., 1954.

MC KEE, PAUL. *Language in the Elementary School.* Boston: Houghton Mifflin Company, 1939.

PETTY, WALTER T. *The Language Arts in Elementary Schools.* Washington, D.C.: The Center for Applied Research in Education, 1962.

POOLEY, ROBERT C. *Teaching English Grammar.* New York: Appleton-Century-Crofts, Inc., 1957.

————. *Teaching English Usage.* New York: Appleton-Century-Crofts, Inc., 1946.

STROUD, JAMES B. *Psychology in Education.* New York: Longmans, Green and Company, 1956.

Teaching Language in the Elementary School. Forty-third Yearbook of the National Society for the Study of Education, Part II. Chicago: The University of Chicago Press, 1944.

TIDYMAN, WILLARD F., and BUTTERFIELD, MARGUERITE. *Teaching the Language Arts.* New York: McGraw-Hill Book Company, Inc., 1951.

8

Developing Language Skills

in the Primary Grades

THIS CHAPTER, THE SECOND OF FIVE CHAPTERS DEALING SPECIFICALLY with language methods, considers the techniques of developing language readiness and the beginnings of instruction in expressional skills in the primary grades. The discussion centers around the following topics:

a. The role of early training in language.
b. The relation of handedness to expressional skills.
c. Instructional emphasis on oral language; conversation, discussion, story telling, dramatizing.
d. Speaking and hearing poetry.
e. Listening as a language skill.
f. Speech development.
g. Instructional emphasis on written language.
h. Spelling.
i. Written language group products.
j. Manuscript writing.
k. Dictated group reports.
l. Copying letters.
m. Creative expression.

The time the child spends in the kindergarten and first and second grades, and for some children the third grade, is a period of transition from the informal language activities of the home to the more formal language program of the later grades. The language activities before the third grade are primarily those that have to do with maturing the organs of speech, developing spontaneity and fluency in speaking, becoming socially adjusted individuals, and beginning to learn the mechanics of writing. The kindergarten provides stimulating experiences contributing to language readiness, while grades one and two are highly important foundational periods for later more formal emphasis and teaching. Because of the differences in the objectives of the primary grades program and the later language program, the instructional methods differ significantly.

THE ROLE OF EARLY TRAINING
IN LANGUAGE

The child's language training truly begins the moment he hears a spoken word. In the home the mother talks and sings to him, not with any expectation that he will immediately use language but simply because this is her way of communicating with him. Through the process of constant repetition the child begins to associate certain words and sounds with things that happen to him. Later he attempts to reproduce the sounds he has heard and gradually develops the beginnings of an understanding of language.

LEARNING A LANGUAGE

The physical apparatus necessary for the production of speech sounds —sounds which in their varied arrangements account for numerous languages used by the world's people for communication—is usually all present when the child is born. Using this speech apparatus for vocal communication is a very complex act; much practice is required for the child to develop control of the intricate patterns of muscular reactions necessary. Given the various structures necessary for speech—lungs, chest muscles, diaphragm, a larynx with vocal chords, lips, tongue, and cheeks—the child will probably learn to make speech sounds. The vocalizations during his first days of life tend to be distress signals without meaning other than that he is completely helpless. Studies indicate that infants do make definite speech sounds which in many instances can be identified. However, these sounds are not necessarily the sounds used in the language spoken by the adults in his environment.

The young infant is fascinated by his ability to vocalize. He will play with his vocal apparatus, blowing, gurgling, and sputtering, simply for the sensory pleasure it affords him. Soon he comes to realize that he is the producer of the sounds he hears, and will intentionally repeat them over and over with evident enjoyment. This manipulation of vocal chords is the beginning of speech, a beginning which is activity for pure pleasure to the infant without any relationship to a language or to the concepts for which various language symbols stand.

203

INITIAL SPEECH HABITS

Since children acquire their early impressions of language by listening, the wise parent will take every precaution to see that even the youngest child hears good speech. A child will pattern his own language after the words and sounds he hears. Baby talk and "talking down" to the child, instead of talking with him, may hamper both his desire and his ability to use language. The child develops very rapidly during his pre-school years, and his language ability will definitely tend to reflect the influence of his early home environment.

The development of desirable language habits before coming to school is not only dependent upon hearing good language but also upon the closely related factor of the parents' attitude toward language. A publication of the Chicago schools suggests that parents of pre-school children provide special opportunities for vocal experimentation during the child's play-time, bath-time, and fun-time.[1] Parents should also encourage the child's beginning verbalization through smiling, humming, talking, singing, reciting nursery rhymes, and playing word games with him. The child should have frequent opportunity for talking to toys, pets, and other little children. Not the least of the parents' responsibility is that of learning to accept without comment or ridicule the quantity and quality of the child's beginning speech.

During their pre-school lives many children experience various parental and other cultural pressures that may adversely affect their language fluency and their facility in speaking. The child who has continuously been told to "keep quiet" or who has been ignored in his attempts to tell something important is not likely to have a high degree of fluency in speaking. He has been conditioned by pressures. We must convince him that we are interested in his thoughts. The child who has played alone, who has been kept from natural association with other children, may also be quiet and retiring. His habits of usage, however, may be more acceptable than those of another youngster who has played on the neighborhood "lot" for several years, and who has succumbed to the language habits of his playmates.

Clear and distinct speech does not necessarily come easily to a child. He spends time trying to imitate others—sometimes not too successfully. If he is pressured by parents to speak more clearly and with less hesita-

[1] Adapted from *Teaching Guide for the Language Arts,* Chicago: Chicago Public Schools, pp. 13–14.

tion, he may become frustrated to the extent that actual stuttering will begin. On the other hand, the child who continually hears "baby" talk from his parents may receive pressure from his peers because of it. If he is allowed to speak baby talk, not only is he likely to fail to communicate with his playmates but he is almost certain to be ridiculed for the failure.

HANDEDNESS

In the development of the various phases affecting language skills in the elementary school, the competent teacher will observe many individual differences in the attitudes and aptitudes of his pupils. Probably no more common and easily observable deviation from the so-called norm exists than the trait of left-handedness. The incidence of left-handedness is estimated in the current literature as ranging from 2 to 8 per cent of the population.[2] There is likely to be a higher percentage in the lower grades, with a falling off as children progress through school and are influenced by pressures of conformity. Teachers of an earlier day were greatly concerned with changing children from left- to right-handedness. For many children, particularly those with firmly established left-hand dominance, learning to write with the right hand was extremely difficult. Recently there has been much concern about the production of emotional upsets and possible speech defects if hand dominance is changed; that is, if a child who is accustomed to performing most tasks with his left hand is suddenly called upon by his teacher to perform a more difficult task than usual with his right hand.

The question as to whether a baby is born with a predisposition to either left- or right-handedness has not been answered definitely. The prevailing authoritative opinion, however, is that the development of a particular hand dominance is environmentally influenced.[3] In most cases, it is well established by the time the child reaches school age. The teacher should definitely be aware of hand dominance in each child but should learn to regard preference for the left hand over the right as no more disturbing than differences in eye or hair coloring.

Relation of handedness to speaking. Except for the conventions of our civilization, it matters little which hand is dominant. It follows, too, that a normally endowed left-hander should be as fluent and skillful

[2] Betty J. Wills, "Handedness," *Encyclopedia of Educational Research*, rev. ed. New York: The Macmillan Company, 1960, p. 613.
[3] *Op. cit.*, p. 614.

in speaking as a right-hander of similar mental and physical endowments. Many cases of speech malfunction do occur, however, due principally to:

1. Physiological factors. These might be in the nature of a lesion, tumor, or other brain injury in the side of the brain opposite the dominant hand.
2. Psychological factors. Impatient, unscientific, and unsympathetic attempts to change a strong hand preference, as well as similar approaches to other problems of children, may result in mental confusion, instability, and loss of confidence, all of which may affect speech.

The left-handed child should have no more reason for a speech handicap due to physiological factors than would the right-handed child. As to the psychological factors, the story is somewhat different. In a right-handed society, being left-handed is a deviation from the norm. It is easy for a left-handed child to recognize this, and if he receives particularly unsympathetic notice from parents, teachers, and classmates, emotional problems are likely to occur.[4] These problems may lead to speech problems just as any emotional problems, whatever the cause, may do.

There has been much concern about creating possible speech defects by forced changes in hand dominance. Particular speech problems, such as stuttering, are most pronounced during the period of establishing dominance. These problems may be caused and cured by the methods used in training hand dominance. It is most desirable for the child to develop a dominant handedness at as early an age as possible, even though delay in accomplishing this may be a result of some deeper neurological inadequacy which may in itself affect speech.[5] Ojemann, some years ago, summed up the evidence on changing by saying that ". . . under ordinary conditions the danger of producing speech disturbance, after the speech habits have been formed, by training a left-handed child to write with the right hand, is very slight." [6] However, most authorities would not recommend a change where the dominance is strong, the speech habits not fixed, or emotional problems already present.

Relation of handedness to writing. Hand dominance is usually well established by the time children reach school age. Psychologists generally recommend, therefore, that the child who is dominantly left-handed at the time of school entrance be trained to use the left hand for writing.

---

[4] Lawrence T. Dayhaw, "Guiding Handedness in the Development of the Child." *Education,* 74:196–199; 1953.

[5] Margaret M. Clark, *Teaching Left-Handed Children.* New York: Philosophical Library, Inc., 1959, p. 22.

[6] Ralph Ojemann, "Studies in Handedness: III. Relation of Handedness to Speech," *Journal of Educational Psychology,* 22:125; 1931.

Determining hand dominance should not be left to casual observation. Tests such as overarm and underarm throwing movements, putting pegs in holes, locking and unlocking a padlock, cutting with scissors along an irregular line, winding cord onto ball, and screwing and unscrewing a top on a bottle or jar, may be used. Eye dominance can be determined readily by rifle-sighting or by the hollow tube test. From such testing, over a period of several attempts with each item, dominance will generally be shown. Hildreth claims that a child ". . . should not be classed as definitely right- or left-handed unless he shows dominance in 75 per cent or more of all observations made of his hand usage." [7] If a child has a wavering or weak dominance, he should be encouraged to use his right hand. If he can be so encouraged, he should be taught to use his right hand for writing.

INSTRUCTIONAL EMPHASIS ON
ORAL LANGUAGE

The most natural way to communicate is through oral language; for young children communication is necessarily oral. They have little or no ability to write, and should not be forced into writing until fluency of expression and physical ability to do so have been developed.

INFORMAL LANGUAGE IN PLAY AND ACTIVITY PERIODS

Language is a part of all the activities that a child engages in, both in school and out. He spends more time each day playing informally and taking part in various activities not directed by the school than he does in the formal and informal school program. Naturally, the school can do little about teaching language in those situations over which it has no control or direction. It can do something, however, about the informal language situations that are part of the school program. The play periods at school are usually under the direction of a teacher. The teacher thus has as great a responsibility for developing language attitudes and skills at those times as he has at any other time during the school day. The same responsibility holds for music, physical education, and art periods,

[7] Gertrude Hildreth, *Readiness for School Beginners.* Yonkers-on-Hudson: World Book Company, 1950, p. 62.

which are much less formal than other parts of the program. Language habits are not produced in the language period alone; they must be taught at all times that the teacher is with the children.

It is difficult to think of any school activity in which language does not, of necessity, play a large part. It is the medium through which a child both receives and gives his thoughts and ideas. Children talk freely to one another as they play or work together in games, in drawing and constructing, and in planning and discussing. Language is the key to all learning activities and the basis for the teaching of other skills. Skills in reading, listening, spelling, and handwriting, the other areas of the language arts, are directly related to and dependent upon the skills of oral and written expression. The skills necessary for these and for other areas of the curriculum are acquired only if some degree of skill in expression is first present.

The teacher of the primary grades must be concerned with teaching language in all of the informal and formal activities of the school. Of course, this does not mean that he should stop the playing of a game to correct errors in usage which some of the children are making. In many instances it would be virtually impossible to call a halt to the activity because of the enthusiasm and spontaneity of the children. The teacher should, however, note the errors made, and whenever possible the child making the error as well. This can be done on a regular chart in many instances; in others the teacher will need to rely on his mental notes until such time as written notes can be made.

The noting of errors in usage, in sentence construction, and in the social use of language is of particular importance in the primary grades, however, since only a few errors should receive major attention. By carefully noting those errors which are made most frequently by the majority of the children in a class, the teacher can select for correction those which are the most serious and the most frequent.

Most improvement in primary children's use of language will come through the use of an audience situation, the children's imitation of the teacher, and incidental individual correction. Since spontaneity of expression is the first consideration in teaching language during these years, attempts at correction of errors in many language activities will have to be done in such ways as to avoid embarrassment to the child. Spontaneity will probably not be inhibited by suggestions for improvement that are given in a kindly and unobtrusive manner. For example, the teacher may remark on the side to Tom, "You *saw* it, Tom. Say, 'I *saw* the dog.'"

CONVERSATION AND DISCUSSION

There are many periods of the day in the primary grades in which language is used in a more formal sense than in play and activity times. There are many occasions for conversing about class activities and for discussing plans for things to do. Many primary grade teachers start the day off with a "Talking Time" in which matters of interest are discussed. Here is an opportunity to help children practice the amenities and skills of good conversation, and if the topic of interest goes beyond the conversational stage (see chapter 4 for distinctions made between conversation and discussion), to help them stick to the point and to take turns in discussing.

Sometimes the morning "Talking Time" will take the form of a "newspaper" in which children report items of interest to the group and the teacher serves as the reporter by writing the news on the chalkboard. At such times teaching largely consists of making decisions as to content—whether what is being reported is of general interest, whether it is news or already known, and whether the item is appropriate for "their newspaper." Opportunity is also present at such a time for the teacher to provide individual incidental correction of language usage, to help a child phrase his thoughts and to organize them in a systematic way, and to call attention to certain aspects of written language by saying such things as, "Who can tell me what I need to put at the end of this sentence?" "Tell us that again, but one sentence at a time," and, "That's a big word. What letter do you suppose it begins with?"

Throughout the school day there are many occasions for planning. Children and teacher must plan for games and activities on the playground, for cleaning up after the art period, for various daily housekeeping tasks, for activities for part of the group while the others are working with the teacher, and for numerous special events, excursions, and changes in the daily schedule. There are also many occasions for conversation and discussion that arise relative to extending and clarifying concepts. A new word met in a reading lesson may lead to a considerable exchange of ideas; some knowledge gained in science may need clarifying. The above are merely suggestive of the many opportunities in the primary program which utilize conversation and discussion and which may serve the teacher in guiding language development.

ORAL REPORTING

In the primary grades this oral language activity usually takes place under the names "Show and Tell" and "Sharing." Periods for oral reporting give each child opportunity to tell about things of interest to him, thus fostering the major objective of spontaneity of expression. The period also provides the teacher with an occasion to focus attention upon the expressional facility of each child and to help him with his most perplexing language problems.

The "Show and Tell" activity has a considerable advantage over simply "sharing" in that the child who is showing something—a new sweater, a turtle, a sea shell, a book—has something on which to direct his attention and thus keep from thinking about himself and any hesitancy he may feel about talking. Then too, the act of showing something tends to make the oral expression organized; when something has been shown and features of it mentioned, there is no need to ramble on, as is sometimes the case with "sharing."

Not all "showing and telling" and "sharing" must be prefaced by the child first marching to the front of the room. Sharing may occur quite informally if the classroom climate is one of mutual respect. Children may show or share things with only a small group; they may indeed show and share with only the teacher. The teacher, however, should strive continually to achieve with each child the objectives of spontaneity of expression, socialization, enunciation and voice control, correct usage, and organization of thought. Oral reporting which is not being directed at the achievement of one or more of these objectives should be avoided.

Principles for the primary teacher to observe in oral reporting (see chapter 9 for instructional details to observe with older children) are:

1. Encourage the child to talk to the group rather than to the teacher.
2. Have each child report on or show only one thing.
3. Encourage questions and comments on the report.
4. Insist upon attention and good listening. The teacher must listen too.
5. Provide adequate time for each child to report.
6. Do not formalize the schedule of "turns" too much; some scheduling is necessary, but always provide for the special occasion.
7. As a child progresses in achieving spontaneity, give greater attention to usage and organization of the content of the expression.

It is generally a good idea not to interrupt a child when he is speaking. In order to correct an error in usage such as "I *seen* him last night," the teacher may say after the report is concluded, "We are glad you *saw* him, so you could tell us about it." More direct help may also be given to the child in private. After the reporting period the teacher may simply take the child aside and after pointing out positive aspects of his report, restate correctly the sentence in which the error occurred and have him repeat it several times. When this has been done, the child should then be complimented on his new achievement.

STORY TELLING

Story telling in the primary grades includes: (1) reproduction of stories which the child has read, or heard told, either incidentally or by his mother, teacher, or someone else, for the purposes of entertainment or information giving; (2) original stories, stories created by the child; and (3) stories related to the child's personal experiences. The creative aspect of story telling is discussed later in this chapter, and with all of the above, in the following chapter. Story telling by primary grade children and how it is taught are discussed here along with the closely related areas of dramatization and poetry.

Story telling is not limited to fanciful and imaginative stories—heard and retold or made up—but includes the relating of personal experiences. In this sense story telling is closely related to many of the activities that take place in "Show and Tell" and "Sharing." Relating personal and original experiences represents for the younger child the most potent approach to more advanced forms of story telling.

The creative quality of expression may appear early in various phases of the child's language development. It will grow in extent and effectiveness if given encouragement. It must be developed through the use of familiar personal experiences. The child relives his experiences and interprets them if he has the opportunity to express his own thoughts and feelings. Jimmie is giving vent to some feelings as he tells his fellow first-graders about George:

George

This cat is sort of gray. He plays with a spool. How funny he looks! George sits in the big chair. One day he caught a mouse. Another time what do you think he did? Ran away!

Yesterday George put his paw into the bowl of milk he was drinking and spilled it. Bad pussy!

Jimmie has learned by the time he tells about George, the bad pussy, that a story has a title. In the kindergarten, Donald hasn't learned about

211

titles, but his story has sequence and he's telling about something with which he is familiar:

> Once upon a time, on a rainy day, two cows were outside and the crops were all ready. The farmer picked his crops and took them to town to sell because he needed some money to buy a new horse. His old horse had a broken leg and was sleeping in the barn.

Some stories told by primary children are longer than others and more fanciful. Margaret May, a seven-year-old, has considerable story-telling ability. Her story reflects her experiences:

> There was a queen in a big castle. She had lots of things, but she wasn't happy. The king tried to make her happy, but she wouldn't be.
> One day he gave her some awfully pretty jewels. She said, "Thank you, but I'm still not a bit happy."
> So the king brought some Hawaiian girls to dance for her. But she didn't like that either.
> So the king brought some funny old clowns, too. They did silly things. But she didn't like that either.
> The king didn't know what to do.
> That night a fairy came with a map. She said there were some nice kids that had no homes and if the queen had some kids, she would be happy. [Margaret explained that the map showed where the children could be found.]
> The king brought the kids to the castle. Oh golly, when the queen saw all those kids she was so glad she clapped her hands.

Some children need more encouragement and stimulation to tell original stories or experiences. Creating a pleasant atmosphere in a room filled with things of interest to children is a major first step in leading them into relating their experiences. Children are also helped by having something to show as they talk. Pictures are often very helpful to children in telling an original story.

Perhaps the most common form of story telling in the lower grades is the telling of stories which the children have been told, most often by the teacher. It is important to emphasize again that successful teaching of story telling can best be accomplished through a great deal of informality. If possible, children should gather in an informal group, very often sitting on the floor, with evident expectancy that something pleasant is about to happen. There should be no feeling of a standardized way of doing things, no emphasis upon technicalities and memorization of details. The teacher should always remember that a child tells a story because he is enthusiastic about something interesting that he wishes to share with others, and that an audience listens to stories for the purpose

212

of enjoyment. Suggestions as to the content and method which may be used in teaching story telling at the several primary levels follow:

In the kindergarten: Story telling may include two types of stories—those told by the teacher to the class, and those told by individual children to others. In the first type it is essential for the teacher to have a wide acquaintance with various types of children's stories.[8] The teacher should select stories that have strong appeal to kindergarten children and must know the story well enough to be able to feel the humor or other quality a particular story may possess. He should have some skill in shortening stories and in preparing children for listening to a particular kind of story. For the second type of story, that told by one of the children, preparation must be made so that the child knows his story well before attempting to tell it. A story of this type should be brief; it should be planned by the child and approved by the teacher before presentation.

In the first grade: In this grade some attempt can be made to establish standards. For example, in preparing for story telling these points may be talked over with the children and perhaps written on a chart: (1) Know your story well. (2) Look at your audience. (3) Have a natural attitude. (4) Speak clearly and not too rapidly. There will be little if any desirable growth in story-telling ability without the sensible use of standards and criticism. The standards which are used should be set by the children themselves as their understanding of the importance of doing things well develops. The first grade should see the beginning of the development of this understanding.

Very often the story-telling period in grade one may start with the teacher and the pupils simply talking about story telling. The children may discuss the kind of story telling that they have heard at home and in the neighborhood. They will be able to help with the planning and will suggest the types of stories that may be told at school.

After this or a similar introduction, actual story-telling hours may be begun. Most success will be achieved at first by dividing the children into groups of four or five each. After they have selected a chairman and are organized to proceed, each group may simply begin telling their stories. The children should take turns telling their stories to others in the group. After such an introductory procedure the entire class may again discuss story telling, talking over the stories they have heard and suggesting

[8] One good source of old and new stories and poems for children, with indicated grade level, is *Story and Verse for Children* by Miriam B. Huber, New York: The Macmillan Co., 1955. See the selected bibliography for other suggestions.

standards to observe which will improve their story telling ability. After this general discussion stories may again be told in small groups. This time as each child finishes telling his story, the chairman should ask for comments and criticism of the story and the way it was told, in line with the standards that have been established. Each child should have a later opportunity to show that he has improved in the areas of criticism.

Also in the first grade, stories may be told for the enjoyment of the entire class. Perhaps stories might be told as a part of a program which has been planned by the pupils and the teacher for the class's entertainment or for the entertainment of the children of another grade; or perhaps each group might choose one of its members to tell his story at a time set aside for such activity.

In the second grade: In this grade a procedure for teaching story telling, similar to that suggested for the first grade, may be used. The practice of evaluation of performance each time a story is told should be continued. Standards should be agreed upon by the pupils and the teacher, to be used as the basis for evaluation of stories and the way they are told. In addition to the standards suggested for the first grade, these might be appropriate: (1) pronounce words correctly (2) speak distinctly (3) avoid the use of unnecessary "ands."

McKee suggests that the type of lessons for use in the second grade include:

1. A lesson in which plans are made for story-telling in small groups, and in which a review is made of points learned in the first grade about telling stories
2. Lessons in which stories are told in small groups by individual children to entertain the audience, and new standards developed
3. Drill lessons in which individuals tell stories in small groups in order to determine points in which they are well equipped, points in which they are weak, and to discover improvement made on specific difficulties
4. Lessons in which stories are told for fun by individuals to the entire class
5. Lessons in which stories are told in order to select children to take part in a special program
6. Lessons in which the teacher tells suitable stories to the children.[9]

DRAMATIZATION

Brief dramatizations of stories children read, hear, or tell should be a basic part of the story-telling activity in the primary grades. Dramatiza-

[9] Paul McKee, "Story-Telling," *McKee Language Service Bulletin.* Boston: Houghton Mifflin Company, no date, p. 6.

tion is a natural outgrowth of children's thinking about their particular interests, and they engage in it in their play, both at home and in school.

Kindergarteners enjoy dramatizing Mother Goose Rhymes and short stories about animals. Often simple masks are used; this delights and encourages the shy child to take part. First show a filmstrip of Mother Goose or a familiar story. Talk about the story as it is presented. Re-show the filmstrip and let different children participate in describing what is happening on the screen.[10]

At the first-grade level children are interested in choosing the characters in a story whom they would like to represent. Many, of course, want to be the same character. This calls for taking turns, and in some cases, for dramatizing only a part of a story or doing the entire story in segments.

The first grade children were reading a story, "The Funny House." They decided that they should play the story. After the characters were chosen, a house was constructed by placing a blanket over a heavy cord and this was dropped over the children. Each child played a role and one was chosen as the narrator.[11]

Dramatization or less-structured dramatic play will not arise without opportunities for them to do so. As one state guide points out: "A lush environment with opportunities for varied experiences invites dramatic play. Trips, sensory experiences, manipulative materials, reading and listening to poetry and stories, and listening to selected radio programs encourage this form of expression. Encouraging children to use their imaginations will free them to 'use their wings.' A costume box adds to the fun and effectiveness of dramatic play. Teachers tell how donning a mask, throwing a rug or a skin over the head or handling a simple property seems to help the child lose his identity and interpret the part he is playing with an unanticipated vigor and reality." [12]

Dramatization in the primary grades should not be done solely for the purpose of performing for parents or others. While occasionally a dramatization may be performed for an audience, the emphasis is upon the development of language skills that it provides and the pleasures it affords to the children who participate. At this level, the audience is the group itself; it is an audience with which the child is familiar and not one which may inhibit his expression. If a dramatization seems to be such that it

[10] *Language Arts Guide for Yolo County.* Woodland, Calif.: County Superintendent of Schools, 1953, p. 7.
[11] *Learning Through Action.* Aberdeen, S. Dak.: Aberdeen City Schools, no date, p. 42.
[12] *Language Arts for the Elementary Schools of Utah.* Salt Lake City: Utah State Department of Public Instruction, February, 1954, pp. 204–205.

215

would appeal to children in another grade or to parents, and if the idea of performing for others appeals to the children, it may be polished up to be presented. This does not mean learning lines and parroting them verbatim on cue, but rather getting the "feel" of the dramatization and a particular part. When children have the feel of what they are doing, it will go well and the interpolating and ad libbing will be normal and natural.

SPEAKING AND HEARING POETRY

Most people enjoy the feeling of saying poetry and of hearing it spoken. This is particularly true of children. Children enjoy hearing their teacher read poetry about things with which they are familiar and poetry that stimulates the senses and stretches the imagination.

May Hill Arbuthnot says in *Time for Poetry:*

Undeniably, poetry with its emphatic melody and rhythm has the power of evoking in its hearers strong sensory imagery and emotional responses. The happenings of everyday life are lifted out of the commonplace by the small perfect frame of words that poetry gives them. The child finds in verse what the adult finds—an exhilaration that comes from the compatibility between ideas and the movement of lines, and from the little shiver of delight that these qualities induce. More than any other type of literature, poetry trains the child's ears to the cadence of words and develops his sensitivity to the power and music of the English language.[13]

Poetry is read to children to give them a feeling for our language; to help them appreciate that it may have rhythm and rhyme. Poetry, if carefully chosen and well read, teaches the child to listen carefully and appreciatively. It teaches him new words, new ways of saying things, and new ideas and feelings for his own expression.

One first grade teacher tells her children to close their eyes and listen carefully to see how many lovely things they can "see" as she reads this poem.

> Of speckled eggs the birdies sing
> And nests among the trees
> The sailor sings of ropes and things
> In ships upon the seas.
> The children sing in far Japan
> The children sing in Spain

[13] *Time for Poetry,* May Hill Arbuthnot, ed. Chicago: Albert Whitman and Company, 1952, introduction.

> The organ, with the organ man,
> Is singing in the rain.[14]

The children then tell all the lovely things they saw. They tell them in words and phrases, and some in complete sentences. The children may repeat the poem in unison with the teacher. Sometimes an individual child will say a line or two of the poem.

The qualities of poems that appeal to young children are those which are similar to the qualities of stories they enjoy: plot, action, humor, mystery, and surprise. Young boys and girls imagine they are the child who says:

> I'm going out to fetch the little calf
> That's standing by the mother. It's so young,
> It totters when she licks it with her tongue,
> I shan't be long.—You come too.[15]

Children like poems that paint pictures for them. For the children to see the pictures the poems paint, the poems must not be too far removed from their experiences. Not all young children see the subtle comparison in Carl Sandburg's "Fog" but those living near the ocean would see it.

> The fog comes
> on little cat feet.
> It sits looking
> over harbor and city
> on silent haunches
> and then moves on.[16]

In the early grades before facility with the mechanics of writing is developed, poems can be written as a joint effort of teacher and children. This example, from a first grade, describes how this may be done.

Teacher: Isn't the snow beautiful? What's it like? Like—what?
Children (in turn): Tissue paper stars, woolly sheep, little popcorn balls, millions of pearls, white angels flying, white ferns, fairies dancing, fuzzy—and so on.
Teacher (recording): Tell me now in sentences what it looks like to you.
Pupil 1:   When the snow falls out of the sky it's kind of fuzzy.

[14] From *Arts and Skills of Communication for Democracy's Children,* Vol. 1. San Bernardino, Calif.: San Bernardino County Schools, no date, p. 72.

[15] From *Collected Poems of Robert Frost.* New York: Henry Holt and Company, Inc., 1939. By permission of the publishers.

[16] From *Chicago Poems* by Carl Sandburg. New York: Henry Holt and Company, 1916. By permission of the publishers.

Pupil 2:   The branches on the tree look wrapped in lambs'
                             wool.

And so on. Later the children's impressions were put down in blank
verse under the title:

A Snowy Day

One day we looked out of the window.
We saw the beautiful snow falling.
It fell like rain upon the drain.
The rain turned to snow.
It fell on the trees.
The snow was like diamonds.
The snow glistened and sparkled.
It sparkled like stars in the sky.
It looked like stars falling.
The trees were weary and cold.
And the snow covered them like a white blanket.
The snow was white as a polar bear.
It was white as a sheep's coat.
When people walked on the white snow
It s-cr-unched down.
We could make a snowman.
We could make a snow bunny
I loved the snow when it fell.
It was so nice and white.[17]

Children naturally love to play with words, to feel their power and
rhythm, to experiment with using them. Not all of this needs to be done
by the group. One kindergartener composed this "Slide Song" and his
teacher wrote it for him:

Down, down
Yellow and brown.
Here comes someone down the slide! [18]

Young children enjoy repeating poetry in unison. Group reading or
choral speaking helps to improve voice quality and clear speech. It also
provides opportunities for the shy to participate without embarrassment.
A teacher has to read or repeat a poem to primary children only once or
twice, allowing them to say as much as they can after each reading, and
they will know it. Children sometimes enjoy solo parts instead of repeating the entire selection in unison.

[17] *Communication: A Guide To the Teaching of Speaking and Writing.* Minneapolis: Minneapolis Public Schools, 1953, p. 19.
[18] Richard Buck, Kindergartener, 1955–1956. Ella School, Marysville, California.

Pussy-Cat, Pussy-Cat

All:	Pussy-cat, pussy-cat, where have you been?
Solo:	I've been to London to visit the queen.
All:	Pussy-cat, pussy-cat, what did you there?
Solo:	I frightened a little mouse under the chair.

Such a poem may be repeated several times with different children taking the solo part, boys taking the first line, girls the third.

PERSONAL EXPERIENCE ACTIVITIES

Children must have an abundance of opportunities for experiences which will give them something to communicate. This does not mean that a continual round of field trips into the school yard and neighborhood should be embarked upon. Naturally the school program should stress firsthand observation and participation in enrichment activities. But many firsthand observations can be made in the actual classroom or on the way to and from school. Children with very little encouragement will bring butterflies, worms, Indian relics, rocks, and innumerable other objects into the classroom.

Some activities that will lead to subjects of conversation, reporting, and discussion may be found in nature. Such continuing projects as keeping an aquarium or terrarium, keeping indoor gardens of various kinds, caring for classroom pets, keeping weather charts, and helping in planning daily activities are all subjects interesting and real to children. Many other activities are seasonal in nature or occur as the subject matter of social studies changes throughout the year. The following is a representative list of opportunities for personal experiences that will lead to much more language activity:

1. Noting temperature differences in sunshine and shade.
2. Collecting leaves of different kinds.
3. Looking at frost under a magnifying glass.
4. Watching flying formations of birds.
5. Feeding birds in winter.
6. Collecting nuts, rocks, seeds, etc.
7. Observing soil erosion.
8. Planning and obtaining the contents for Junior Red Cross Boxes.
9. Making puppets to play out a story.
10. Observing variations in growth of different seeds.
11. Caring for a classroom pet.
12. Daily observing of an ant house or a termite box.

219

13. Feeling various materials, such as velvet, fur, aluminum foil, and sand.
14. Tasting substances, such as berries, nuts, pickles.

Children may not have enough personal experiences to draw upon for language expression, or they may hesitate to draw upon the experiences they do have. For such children the needed stimulation for language activity can come through the use of pictures that the child will associate with some experience he has had. This stimulation may lead him to relate an experience or to ask questions through which the teacher can guide his participation in activities leading to further learning and interest. Often, too, pictures in the form of filmstrips, slides, and films can be used as almost real substitutes for firsthand experiences.

LISTENING

The fact that every communicative act requires reception as well as expression should always be kept in mind by the teacher planning oral language activities. The presence of an audience of one or more persons who are really desirous of hearing the expression is the most effective motivation for good oral expression. Most young children, while interested in themselves and what they are doing and saying, can be taught to listen and be good members of an audience.

Good audience behavior is a form of social courtesy which should be practiced and learned as are other courtesies and skills. Children themselves are interested in audience standards and readily cooperate in setting up proper standards of audience behavior. Such standards will emphasize:

Listening courteously and attentively
Expressing enjoyment and appreciation
Avoiding interruption
Offering constructive criticism or asking intelligent questions.

One second grade developed these standards: [19]

A Good Listener

Looks at the person talking
Keeps hands quiet
Doesn't talk
Thinks about what is said

An audience that feels a need for listening and has the skill for doing so effectively will behave in the manner desired. Effective listening to

[19] West Acres School, Mrs. Morley, teacher; West Sacramento, Calif.

220

children's oral expression will generally occur as attention is given by the teacher to the following principles.

1. Readiness for the listening activity must be established. The stage must be set, which includes deciding upon the purpose and relating the attainment of this purpose to previous learning and experience. The stage-setting phase may include creating a need to listen through the use of materials and situations which secure the pupils' attention. A teacher may gain attention for the stage setting by using puppets, charts, pictures, sudden noises, or an unusual action. Sometimes the stage may be set for the listening simply by discussing what to listen for. Usually more prompting is necessary. The teacher may need to say, "How many of you have heard this story?" Or, "The words in this song are sung very fast. See if you can hear every word."

2. Appraisal of the speaking is necessary. Usually this may be in terms of purpose and may be in the form of questions, in the same manner as following the reading of a story—using such questions as, "Did you think that would happen? What did Bill tell us? Can you name the three games Mary said they played? What do you suppose would have happened if . . . ?"

3. Recognition should be given to an audience which has listened effectively. Praise should be given the children when they have listened carefully and perceptively.

4. The teacher himself must demonstrate good listening and audience participation. In doing so it is necessary to avoid giving faked attention (which pupils easily detect), demanding pupil attention, and making repeated statements when such repetition is needless.

The teaching of listening is discussed more fully in the following chapter in connection with the oral language activities in the elementary grades above the primary level; however, the following suggestions from one language guide suggest appropriate listening activities for the primary grades.[20]

1. Remembering action words.
   After the children have listened to a story, have them list certain action words that help tell the story. For example, after one story the children may recall the following words and tell what they remember about the story: bark, running, rumbling, jumped, piled, raced, fell.
2. Summarize a story.
   The teacher reads a short story to the group and has the pupils retell the plot in one sentence. Use stories on the reading level of the group.

[20] Selected from "Language Arts Curriculum Guide, K–6," Jefferson County Public Schools, Lakewood, Colorado, 1960.

3. What happens next?

Read aloud part of a story which is unknown to the pupils and have them suggest what will happen next.

4. Telling back.

Read a story to the group and ask the children to retell it in their own words.

5. Following directions.

The group may be divided into two or three teams. The teacher gives a series of directions, perhaps three or four specific things to do. A child is then selected from each group to carry out the directions. Each child who can follow the directions accurately and in order scores one point for his team.

6. Listening to conversation.

Reading aloud the conversational parts of a story may help children to listen for dialogue or for characterizations.

7. Taping a story.

If a tape recorder is available, children may be asked to record stories they have made up themselves. The class will then listen to the stories and ask questions.

SPEECH IMPROVEMENT

The teacher in the primary grades will encounter many children whose speech development has not attained the "norm" for the age group. Such lack of speech maturity is not of special concern, however, unless the speech is inadequate for communication. The kindergarten child who says *thay* for *say* and *thoap* for *soap* usually has no difficulty communicating, but the child with a lisp or a stutter will encounter problems. Too, whenever a speech deviation, no matter how minor, causes undue self-consciousness, communication is interfered with.[21]

Classroom teachers should help children make sounds correctly by helping them hear sounds accurately and by showing them how the sounds are made. Although the teacher must notice all speech deviations, care must be exercised in handling many of them. It is usually the safest practice to seek the aid of a speech correctionist if one is available. Generally the specialist will suggest specific procedures for the teacher to follow with the children needing help and will deal with the more serious cases himself.[22]

[21] Jon Eisenson and Mardel Ogilvie, *Speech Correction in the Schools.* New York: The Macmillan Company, 1957, Chapter 2.

[22] See Chapter 9 for further suggestions.

INSTRUCTIONAL EMPHASIS ON
WRITTEN LANGUAGE

Children look forward to being able to write; writing is one thing they expect to learn in school. Often they come to school for the first time with some ability to print and perhaps to scribble in a style resembling cursive form, and they expect to use the skill they have and to develop it further. Of course, there are many occasions for using written language in the first and second grades, and even some in the kindergarten, where the teacher does the writing for the group. This practice is of great value, but it does not satisfy the children's desire to write nor does it satisfy the genuine need of each individual child to learn to write well.

Writing should, of course, be taught when the children are ready to learn it; that is, when they have achieved the muscular coordination necessary for letter formation, when they feel a need to write their thoughts, and when they have the necessary emotional and mental maturity for learning the skills. Most children in the first grade have sufficient physical, mental, and emotional maturity to begin to learn some form of handwriting. There are exceptions, of course, and the child who is not ready should not be forced into writing. There is no question regarding the motivating effect of a need to write as a factor in deciding when handwriting should be introduced. Up to this point children have become accustomed to having their needs satisfied through the use of vocal language. Parents and teachers answer their questions and supply them with physical needs; this is satisfactory to most children. As pointed out above, there is interest in writing but a real need to learn to write as a means of communication has not been felt. The teacher, then, must create this need; otherwise neither the necessary readiness for learning the skill nor the mastery of the skill itself will be achieved.

The kindergarten and first-grade teacher should share responsibility for developing in children:

1. A recognition of how writing serves people and how it can serve them.
2. The desire to use writing to meet their needs.
3. The desire to use writing for pleasure.
4. The attitude that writing is a satisfying means of self-expression.
5. The oral vocabulary and forms of spoken expression which later can be transferred into writing.
6. The visual-muscular coordination requisite for the skill of handwriting.

In these grades, the first written expression will be done by groups, with the teacher doing the actual writing. At first the teacher may need

223

to point out situations which call for practical writing and may need to make suggestions as to what might be written. With experience in this type of writing, children will rapidly begin to contribute their own ideas and suggestions as to what should be written. Often after such group compositions the teacher will duplicate copies for each child. If some of the pupils express a desire to do so, they may write their copies. The children can then put their names on their copies, if the writing is a letter or invitation, or add illustrations if the writing is a chart.

Mechanical limitations. The fact that handwriting is closely associated with the growth of manual dexterity is sometimes overlooked. Manual dexterity usually develops slowly and by stages. The eye-hand controls needed for handwriting may be developed through other manual skills; drawing, clay work, finger painting, sewing with yarn, weaving, cutting out and pasting, coloring, constructing toys from wood, and rhythmic responses to music all help to develop these eye-hand controls.

Spelling. Inability to spell needed words and the recognition of this inability by the child is another handicap to writing in the primary grades. Systematic instruction in spelling usually does not begin until the second grade and then only for those children who are ready for it. The child who is interested in writing and is ready to do it feels individually the need to spell the words he wishes to use. While spelling correctly is desired by society, and the teaching of correct spelling is and should be a major goal of the elementary school language program, a child should be able to write without an initial spelling handicap. In view of the emphasis upon content rather than form in these early grades, words that he does not know how to spell should be spelled for him and misspellings that occur in words he has not had an opportunity to learn should be pointed out but not criticized.

MANUSCRIPT WRITING

Manuscript or print in the elementary grades has gained steadily and rapidly in educational acceptance and use in the United States since it was first introduced in about the year 1922. It would probably not be an exaggeration to say that at least since 1931, except in somewhat isolated instances, no child in the primary and elementary grades of school has been taught to write initially by the cursive method.[23]

[23] Beula P. Beale, "Trends in Handwriting," *Baltimore Bulletin of Education,* 21:29–32; September, 1944.

Manuscript writing is now being taught as a communication skill in the primary grades and used widely in all elementary grades. Various claims have been set forth concerning the advantages of this form of handwriting:

Effect on reading. One of the chief advantages of teaching manuscript writing in the primary grades is the generally accepted fact that it facilitates reading because it resembles the print in books. With the current heavy emphasis on reading, along with considerable controversy concerning currently used methods of teaching, any device which can be used to improve that very important skill is worthwhile and valuable. There is no question but that print script writing does look quite like the print which children see daily in their reading. In like manner, children become used to reading what someone else has written through their charts, original stories written down by the teacher, and bulletin boards. In other words, the established psychological principle of going from the known to the unknown works efficiently and easily in this situation.

Effect on language expression. We are most interested in developing language communication in the primary grades as a matter of content rather than form. We want children to express themselves, to contribute their ideas and feelings, and not to be hampered any more than is necessary by various mechanical manipulations. Manuscript writing fits into this program very well. First of all, manuscript writing is easy to learn because of the simple strokes. Thus immediate use can be made of the skill without extensive drill on movement. Secondly, the letter forms are so simple that each child can see his difficulty and by comparison with letters he sees in books correct it himself. Manuscript writing is thought by many to be less fatiguing than cursive writing and more suited to the child with poorer muscular control. Manuscript writing facilitates beginning writing; a child may learn to write, have something to write about, and by using manuscript writing can do so.

WRITTEN LANGUAGE IN GROUP PRODUCTION

The basic form of written language in the kindergarten and first and second grades is the group production. In the kindergarten and early first grade, the teacher will write for the children as they dictate what to write. In later first grade, the children can begin to work in groups, giving their ideas to the teacher for the first recording and organization. Later still the group can compose much on their own with the teacher helping only in selecting words that are easy to write and in keeping the sentences short.

Group composition is widely used in all of the primary grades. It gives the children experience in finding ways to express ideas in written work, and of course, in its beginning stages, satisfies the children's desire to express themselves while they are handicapped by lack of skill in the mechanics of writing.

Dictated stories. Stories dictated by the group usually precede or follow closely some group activity such as a trip, a film, a party, or even a story, song, or something a little different that takes place in the classroom. If the class is planning a field trip, the teacher might think it wise to discuss class behavior before leaving. The suggestions again should be recorded by the teacher. These rules should guide the children on the trip; since they are written, they are likely to be remembered better than if just talked about. If the children are taking a trip to the dairy, they might have questions about cows, milk, and how the milk gets to their doorsteps in the mornings. The teacher might record their questions on chart paper.

> Where does milk come from?
> How does it get in the bottles?
> How does it get to the store?
> How does it get on our doorstep?

After the trip the children will have much rich experience to draw upon for writing activities. In the discussion following, they should find the answers to their questions and the teacher should record this information, perhaps in story form. In addition to finding answers to the initial questions, the children will probably learn about milking machines, pasteurization, and the sterilization of the containers. Thus many new words and concepts will be learned and will be included in the group stories that are written.

If the children in the example cited above are early first-graders, the teacher probably would have to point out the need for writing down questions and possibly make suggestions as to what might be written; the children could then make selections from his suggestions. The same would be true in the composing of stories after the trip.

Children need guidance in the composition of group stories. If they are going to write about what they saw at the dairy, the teacher will usually guide the story's development with questions: Where did we go first?

226

Where are the cows kept? What does the milking machine do? etc. In recording the children's responses and putting them into story form, the first writing may not be well organized. The teacher may need to say, "Let's go back over this and decide which sentences we need to keep in our story and how they should be arranged." Every effort should be made to make the final story the product of the children's thinking rather than of what the teacher wants, although with good guidance and stimulation of thinking the two may be the same.

Some attention should be paid in group writing, even from the very first productions, to the mechanical skills. As the teacher uses a capital letter, he may say, "I'm making a capital letter to begin my sentence." Later he may say, "How do I begin this sentence?" The same approach may be used with periods and other punctuation and with margins, position of title, and, with less direct attention, to the spelling of words.

Sometimes the teacher may make copies of stories written and give one to each child so that he may put his name on it and identify it as "his" story. Kindergarten children may be satisfied just to have the story read back to them, but sometimes they want their own copies of a story such as this one:

Our Halloween Party

We had a Halloween party.
We had cookies and milk.
Mothers sent the cookies.
Thank you, Mothers.
Some visitors came.
We had fun! [24]

Whenever possible group stories should be kept by each child to enrich his vocabulary and language ability. When these stories are short, they may be duplicated as suggested above, or if the children are in grade two, they may be copied by the children and placed in a story booklet.

Dictated summaries and reports. When children have achieved some ability in using manuscript form and some knowledge of the uses of capitalization and punctuation, they will be ready to write directly from teacher dictation of a story, report, or summary. Generally this will occur in the mid-second grade. The first step is again one of group production. The teacher writes on the board the composition of the children. Attention is called to the spelling of words that are unfamiliar, to the punctuation needed to give the meaning desired, to the necessary capitalization, and to the order of the composition for clarity, exactness, and interest.

[24] Kindergarten group, 1955–56. Ella School, Olivehurst, California.

After the composition has been written it should be read over carefully by the teacher while the children listen for the organization of the story or report. Next, the sentences should be read one at a time while the children pay particular attention to spelling, punctuation, and capitalization. After this initial familiarization procedure is completed, the children should write each sentence—or possibly each phrase if a sentence is long—immediately after repeating the sentence read by the teacher. The teacher should inspect pupils' papers immediately after each sentence is written to be certain that it has been written accurately. When an error is found, it should be immediately discussed with the pupil and then corrected by him.

Within a few weeks after learning to write from this type of dictation, some of the children will be able to write a dictated story that they have not composed or seen. This procedure will not be suitable for use with all second graders, but those who are capable should be given this type of training.

Copying letters, notes, invitations. In slightly more advanced group composition in the first and second grades, children will compose brief letters and notes, make lists, write invitations and news notices, and engage in other similar practical writing. Teacher guidance will be needed in selecting words that are easy to write and in keeping sentences short. Such compositions will be limited generally to three or four lines, but may be longer if required by the content. At the time of the children's copying the note, letter, or other composition, the teacher should rewrite the original copy, presenting it word by word or phrase by phrase as the children write. By doing this, the teacher is given another opportunity to call attention to punctuation, capitalization, paragraphing, hyphenating divided words at ends of lines, and other similar writing skills.

Sometimes some individuality in the written message may be provided when the children are able to do the handwriting without close teacher guidance. For example, several messages may be suggested by the children as appropriate for "get-well" cards being sent to an absent classmate: "Get well soon," "Come back soon," "I miss you," "We miss you at school." From the suggestions which the teacher has written on the board the child may select the one he likes and write it on his card.

Copy work can take many forms, from copying a simple label or name in the kindergarten or early first grade, to copying a report of possibly two short paragraphs in the second grade. In all copy work, the standard of work should be absolute accuracy in the reproduction.

CREATIVE EXPRESSION

In the fall, one kindergartener drew a picture showing the falling of leaves and then dictated to his teacher the following poem:

> The limbs get heavy
> and fall off the tree.
> The stems of the leaves get heavy
> and fall off too.[25]

In a first grade the children were suggesting titles for each other's paintings:

Two pictures in particular inspired picturesque language. For the first, these titles were suggested: "The Diamond," "Under the Sea," "Sea Shells," "Strange Things," "Funny Fishes." "Rainbows Under the Sea" was finally chosen, with the artist's approval. For the second, these: "Star-lighter," "Angel Queen," "In the Night," "Christmas Angel," and finally, "Bless the Tree," which was finally chosen.[26]

As these examples show, most creative expression in the kindergarten and grades one and two is oral. The goal is not a finished poem or story but a real expression of the creative thinking of children. Such creativeness, as has been frequently mentioned, is dependent very largely upon two factors. These are (1) opportunity for experiences which lead to the learning of many new words and expressions to the extent that they are understood and can be used, and (2) provision for many occasions to be creative. These two factors, in a certain sense, represent the main objectives of the language program in the primary grades, whether evaluated in the long-term practical mastery of the language skills for use in later life, or in the short-term purpose of producing fluency and creativeness in these early years of the child's school life. From either standpoint, it is imperative that the primary teacher follow the proper instructional techniques in attaining these goals early in the child's life.

Beyond this point in the child's language experience the teacher's problem is one of coaxing and fanning into flame the small spark of creativeness that may have been generated in the few who are gifted with the necessary abilities and the imagination to express themselves creatively. Of equal importance, of course, is the provision of the fuel

[25] Lynn Smith, Kindergartener, 1955–56. Ella School, Marysville, California.
[26] *Communication, A Guide to the Teaching of Speaking and Writing.* Minneapolis: Minneapolis Public Schools, 1953, p. 19.

229

of rich experiences and the warm and friendly atmosphere in which the flame may burn unstifled.

Brief references to creative expressions have appeared at several points in previous chapters of this book as well as in this chapter. Creative expression is much too important an area of communication to treat adequately or economically in brief references. Since the problems of stimulating and developing creative expression in the elementary-school grades are essentially the same except for the expected differences in the quality of the products, the reader is referred to Chapter 13 for further discussion of the instructional techniques suggested for this important language area.

EXERCISES FOR THOUGHT AND DISCUSSION

1. How important is the child's early home language training as a factor in his later progress in language expression?

2. Since it is doubtful that a baby is born with a predisposition to be right- or left-handed, what practical steps would you as a parent take immediately after his birth to direct his handedness?

3. What reason would you advance for not attempting to change the handedness of a child after he reaches the age of school entry?

4. Evaluate the significance of the instructional activities in oral language outlined in this chapter. Discuss fully the three you consider most important to the teacher.

5. Discuss the probable effects of the speaking and hearing of poetry on the later language development of the primary school child.

6. Suggest a series of clues or steps for the child to note as he learns to listen. Explain how he may be taught to identify them.

7. What is the responsibility of the classroom teacher with regard to speech correction work?

8. What arguments can you advance for and against the teaching of manuscript writing in the primary grades?

9. Evaluate the practice of dictating stories, group summaries, and letters and notes for developing written expressional skills in the primary grades.

10. Outline steps you as a teacher may take to make creative expression really productive in the primary grades.

11. As a result of your study of this chapter prepare a series of concise statements which might be used as principles of method to guide you in your teaching of language in the primary grades.

SELECTED REFERENCES

APPLEGATE, MAUREE. *Easy in English*. Evanston, Ill.: Row, Peterson and Company, 1960.

BAILEY, MATILDA, and others. *Language Learnings*. New York: American Book Company, 1960.

BROWN, DOROTHY L., and BUTTERFIELD, MARGUERITE. *The Teaching of Language in the Primary Grades*. New York: The Macmillan Company, 1941.

CLARK, MARGARET M. *Teaching Left-Handed Children*. New York: Philosophical Library, Inc., 1959.

COLE, LUELLA. *Handwriting for Left-Handed Children*. Bloomington, Ill.: Public School Publishing Company, 1955.

Communication: A Guide to the Teaching of Speaking and Writing. Minneapolis: Minneapolis Public Schools, 1953.

DAWSON, MILDRED A. *Language Teaching in Grades 1 and 2*, rev. ed. Yonkers-on-Hudson: World Book Company, 1957.

GANS, ROMA and others. *Teaching Young Children*. Yonkers-on-Hudson: World Book Company, 1952. Chapter 8.

Guiding Growth in Written Expression, Vol. I: Young Children. Los Angeles: Division of Elementary Education, Office of County Superintendent of Schools, June 1956.

Handwriting Committee. *Handwriting Today*. Cambridge, Mass.: New England School Development Council, September 1954.

HILDRETH, GERTRUDE. *Readiness for School Beginners*. Yonkers-on-Hudson: World Book Company, 1950.

MORRISON, IDA E., and PERRY, IDA F. *Kindergarten-Primary Education*. New York: Henry Holt and Company, 1961.

OGILVIE, MARDEL. *Speech in the Elementary School*. New York: McGraw-Hill Book Company, Inc., 1954.

SHEEHY, EMMA D. *The Fives and Sixes Go to School*. New York: Henry Holt and Company, 1954.

231

9

Developing Speaking

and Listening Skills

THIS CHAPTER, THE THIRD OF FIVE WHICH PRESENT METHODS AND techniques for developing the communicative skills, deals with teaching oral expression and reception in the intermediate and upper elementary grades. The following topics are emphasized in this chapter:

- a. Developing good speech habits.
- b. Improving enunciation, pronunciation, and articulation.
- c. Achieving audience sensitivity.
- d. Improving voice quality.
- e. Developing self-confidence.
- f. Instructional techniques in oral language.
- g. Developing skills in special oral language situations.
- h. Observing the social amenities.
- i. Developing listening skills.
- j. The teacher's listening.

The development of skill in speaking and listening is the result of a carefully planned and purposeful program of teaching. Such of these skills as are acquired incidentally do not result in the mastery necessary to effective communication. Systematic and continuous instruction must be provided in order to develop and reinforce the basic attitudes, skills, and abilities needed for speaking and listening and to implement their use in meaningful communication situations.

IMPORTANCE OF GOOD SPEECH HABITS

SPEAKING EASE THROUGH LIFELIKE SITUATIONS

While the practical importance of doing actual telephoning, conversing, and reporting is not to be denied, merely providing plenty of opportunity

232

for talking will not solve the problems involved in effectively performing in situations calling for oral language. More specific measures are necessary. This means that in the oral language program the child must master the speech skills necessary for good articulation and enunciation; he must learn to pronounce words correctly; he must learn to be sensitive to his audience; he must learn to speak in a controlled and well-modulated voice; he must use in his speaking words that express his ideas clearly and yet are acceptable to society. These are a few of the special skills he needs if his oral expression is to represent his thinking and is to be really effective communication. At the same time true ease in speaking can result only from constant practice in all of the various types of situations in which the individual, as a child or as an adult, will find himself called upon to speak.

In attempting to develop the attitudes and skills of oral language the elementary teacher should constantly remember that:

1. In all matters of oral presentation, the teacher himself must set a good example.
2. Frequent and varied oral language situations must be provided.
3. The atmosphere of the classroom must be happy and friendly, so that reticent children will not be afraid to speak.
4. All criticism should be friendly and constructive.
5. Standards for speaking should be set up cooperatively by the pupils with help from the teacher.

IMPROVING ENUNCIATION, PRONUNCIATION, ARTICULATION

Most teachers recognize that many of the learning activities related to oral language are impeded by indistinct utterance, careless pronunciation, uninflected or improperly inflected speech and incorrect phrasing. However, some of these teachers fail to recognize their own responsibility in the problem. Too often the teacher is careless about his speech and the children are thus emulating a model who aggravates the problem. One recently published teacher's manual in discussing this problem states:

Consider for a moment the effects of a too loud, harsh, strident voice on a class group. One of two reactions will ensue: the children will be frightened into submission; or they will become defiant, disorderly, and discourteous. Neither of these reactions is conducive to profitable learning. Contrast this behavior with the effects produced by a pleasing, well-modulated voice that gives evidence of strength of purpose with no hint of weakness. Almost at once there is a feeling of security evidenced by the relaxed and responsive

233

attitude of the children. This reaction can be traced directly to the teacher's poise, friendliness and self-discipline, which are reflected in her voice.[1]

In addition to avoiding a harsh, strident, or angry voice, the teacher should correct any of these deviations of which he is guilty:

1. lisping
2. nasalization of vowel sounds
3. *ng* errors
4. dentalization
5. pedantic speech [2]

The teacher may consistently encourage good enunciation, pronunciation and articulation by:

1. Using a pleasing, friendly tone of voice.
2. Speaking distinctly.
3. Enunciating clearly and naturally.
4. Pronouncing words in a conventional and easy manner.
5. Encouraging children to feel free to talk at proper times.
6. Providing opportunity for children to talk freely.

Almost all children will profit from some types of direct help with speech. The child who comes to school from a highly favored home and speaks clearly and well is an exception. Many children, even from homes where the parents' speech is satisfactory, will need help with some speech skills. They may have no serious handicaps, but some emphasis on the learning of these skills will help them improve the quality of their speech. Often, too, there are entire neighborhoods or areas in which slurred or careless speech is characteristic.

As was pointed out in Chapter 5, many of the speech errors in the classroom are those of improper articulation. The teacher will do well to observe these points in connection with instruction in articulation:

1. Make certain that the sounds which are taught represent real difficulties to the children in the class.
2. A given sound should be taught at the time or in the grade where the difficulty in its utterance occurs.
3. The teacher should continually strive to present examples of good articulation in his own expression.
4. Attention should primarily be given to the special difficulties of individual children rather than to a given sound that is supposed to represent a problem to every child in the class.
5. Motivation must be such that the children will realize that good articula-

---

[1] *Toward Better Speech: A Manual for Teachers of all Grades.* Curriculum Bulletin, 1952–53 Series, Number 5. New York: Board of Education of the City of New York, p. 7.

[2] *Ibid.*

tion is important in all oral expression and is not to be confined to just those times when the problem is being directly attacked.

Children in the middle and upper grades who have persistent difficulty with articulation and enunciation should be brought to the attention of a person specifically trained in speech correction. However, some children may simply never have learned to make certain sounds correctly. In such cases the teacher should make a direct attack on the problem by:

1. Showing the child how the sound should be made by means of illustration and demonstration.
2. Forming the sound clearly while the child observes the action of the lips and tongue.
3. Having the pupil examine his own imitative attempts by use of a mirror.
4. Following this procedure in practice exercises:
   a. Repeat the sound several times.
   b. Speak syllables that include the sound.
   c. Speak short sentences in which the sound is used with some repetition, including sentences made of words of high social utility which children actually use in their own expression.
   d. Utilize exercises which facilitate breathing and the use of lips and tongue.[3]

Differences in pronunciations based upon acceptable speech in various geographical areas should not be regarded in the same way as careless and slurring speech. However, differences in speech among educated persons are not so wide as those among persons with less education. No educated person from one state or area in this country should have difficulty in understanding an educated person from a different area. The teacher should encourage the child to use the cultivated pronunciations of the particular area in which he lives but to accept and respect the pronunciations of individuals from different regions.[4]

The child acquires many of his habits of pronunciation by imitating others. The pronunciation, of course, varies according to the occupations and social standing of the people he encounters. For many children this may cause confusion. Some may use definitely colloquial pronunciation and others may use the pronunciation of formal platform speech. A comparison may be made between the wearing of different kinds of clothes for different occasions to the levels of pronunciation. The use of colloquial pronunciation, like wearing overalls, is perfectly appropriate

[3] See Charles Van Riper and Katherine G. Butler, *Speech in the Elementary Classroom,* New York: Harper & Brothers, 1955, for additional suggestions.

[4] The classroom teacher should have some familiarity with a pronouncing dictionary such as *A Pronouncing Dictionary of American English* by John S. Kenyon and Thomas A. Knott. Springfield, Mass.: G. and C. Merriam Company, 1949.

235

in many situations. But men also wear tuxedos and full dress suits, which may be compared with formal usage. However, most of the time people wear comfortable, everyday clothes, and most of the time people also use the informal level of language. The important characteristics, in both informal dress and speech are that they are comfortable and practical but that within the bounds of both wide variations exist.

ACHIEVING AUDIENCE SENSITIVITY

Communication means reception as well as expression. Thus all communication involves an audience, either seen or unseen. In oral language communication the audience is usually present and generally can be seen. Thus its attitude toward the speaker is a reaction that the speaker can see or sense. If the speaker is properly sensitive to his audience, he can adjust his entire approach, his manner of presentation, the content or the organization of his material. The experienced, audience-sensitive speaker knows as soon as he faces the audience whether or not he should read his prepared speech or talk informally to his audience.

A basic element of audience sensitivity appears when the communication is deliberately planned in advance of the presentation to appeal to the special interests of the audience. This type of preparation requires no last-minute adjustments in content or in preparation to attract or to hold the audience. One fifth-grade textbook reminds the pupils to "keep your audience in mind when you give a report orally. Boys and girls who are listening like to have the speaker look at them when he is talking . . . Speak clearly and distinctly so your listeners will understand each word." [5] The same textbook suggests that these points be remembered by speakers:

1. Choose a subject that will interest your audience.
2. Plan to tell the things that will interest others.
3. Tell things in the right order.
4. Speak clearly and distinctly.
5. Speak in a voice loud enough for the size of the room where you are speaking.

Children are born critics and, consciously or not, judge the one who is speaking sometimes even before he has begun to speak. Their thoughts may not be expressed in words, but their inner feelings are evidenced by their emotional response to a speaker: bright, smiling face, attentive

[5] Thomas C. Pollock and John J. Forester, *Using Language, Grade 5.* New York: The Macmillan Company, 1954, p. 127.

posture; or noticeably inert posture; constant talking, etc. The effectiveness of speech, like TV programs, is gauged by audience reaction. This reaction is not the responsibility of the speaker alone but is shared with the audience. Since in the classroom the audience usually includes the teacher, he should remind himself frequently of this fact and consider his own reactions.

IMPROVING VOICE QUALITY

The tone and quality of a child's voice is dependent upon mental and emotional attitudes as well as upon physical factors. A child who speaks freely and without fear and hesitancy generally has a voice which shows satisfactory quality and control.[6] Thus, again, there should be an emotional climate which is free from tension. Except for those children who have speech difficulties of a physical nature, spontaneous speech is seldom of poor quality. When normal children are embarrassed or emotionally upset, however, they may speak in shrill or monotonous tones. When language activities are characterized by an atmosphere which invites spontaneous expression, children are likely to speak with the appropriate intonation called for by the activity.

As has been suggested, teachers should evaluate their own voice quality and ways of speaking as factors reflecting their classroom personalities and the resulting emotional climate. A teacher might well make use of a recording in order to discover how his own voice actually sounds. Successful solution of voice problems is dependent on the realization that a voice may be unpleasant or that because of its quality it interferes with communication. This is as true for children as it is for teachers.

In addition to making use of a recording instrument there are several ways in which a teacher can make a child aware that he is talking too loudly, too harshly, or in an unpleasant voice. One way, of course, is for the teacher to say simply, "Let's keep the voice down"; or "Speak softly this time." Sometimes this procedure is criticized as discouraging fluency of expression. Such a remark will not make the child self-conscious if spoken in an encouraging tone and accompanied by a warm and friendly smile. Another way is for standards to be established by the class for a speaking situation, with suggestions about voice tone included. The teacher may interject the idea of voice quality by playing parts of several

[6] Edith B. Mallory and Virginia R. Miller, "A Possible Basis for the Association of Voice Characteristics and Personality Traits." *Speech Monographs* 25:296–304; November, 1958.

recordings of speaking voices. Then he might ask, "Which ones did you *like* to hear speak?" "Why do you suppose you liked his voice?" "Do you know someone whose voice you especially like?" After some discussion, he may ask "What are some of the things we might do to make our voices more pleasant when we talk to the class?" These points should be listed on the board to become the standards for the next speaking situation, which preferably should follow immediately, At the end of the speaking activity the class should evaluate themselves in terms of the standards they have set up and see if they need to add more points to the ones they have. These should be left on the board as a reminder, and after the list has been completed a chart might be made showing the complete list of standards.

Another procedure may involve having the child talk with other children and discovering how he sounds. For example, the teacher might say:

During the next three minutes, I want each of you to talk with as many others in the room as you can. Your job is to find the person whose voice sounds the most like yours. You've heard about people who look alike but are not twins; well, you won't find anyone whose voice is just like yours, but you'll find someone whose voice is more like yours than anyone else's in the room. As soon as you've found your "sound alike," come up to the front of the room. Let's see how many pairs we can get.[7]

The child whose voice has not developed the expected natural qualities will also profit greatly from participating in choral speech activities discussed in a later section of this chapter. He will tend to modulate his voice, to control its pitch, tempo, and volume to blend with those around him.

AVOIDING PHYSICAL MANNERISMS

One speech authority points out that speech is of two kinds, *visible* and *audible*.[8] The teacher, as well as the pupil, needs to realize that speech is both seen and heard. Quite often bodily actions convey meanings to the audience and add to or detract from what is said.

The elementary school teacher is not concerned with developing highly

[7] Charles Van Riper and Katharine G. Butler, *Speech in the Elementary Classroom*. New York: Harper & Brothers, 1955, p. 175.

[8] Harley Smith, "Bodily Action—Part of Speech," *Guides to Speech Training in the Elementary School,* A Report of the Elementary Committee of the National Association of Teachers of Speech. Carrie Rasmussen, chairman. Boston: Expression Company, 1943, pp. 33–39.

accomplished platform performers who make full use of meaningful physical expression. However, he is responsible for the elimination of annoying mannerisms which detract from effective communication. It is almost impossible for anyone to speak without using some body movements; these movements should be natural and in harmony with the speaking activity. Annoying physical mannerisms which should be eliminated include such undesirable activities as:

1. Fidgeting
2. Head jerking
3. Hand twisting
4. Eye blinking
5. Twitching of mouth, face, or body
6. Constant and inconsistent changing of facial expression
7. Unchanging facial expression
8. Overdone physical movement

Basic in the elimination of most annoying mannerisms is the elimination of self-consciousness. It is not possible to have a child stop certain muscular movements just by asking him to do so. His nervous movements are expressions of his emotional state. Physical activities are helpful in cases where the problem is one of lack of coordination. Particularly helpful activities for this purpose in the language program are: rhythmic games, pantomime, creative dramatics, memorized plays, puppet and shadow plays, monologues, dialogues, imitations, and demonstrations.

DEVELOPING SELF-CONFIDENCE

It is relatively easy for an aggressive, confident child to assume leadership, and it is perhaps natural for him to monopolize language and play activities. The development of assurance in other children may not be easy, nor may it be accomplished incidentally. It is the responsibility of the teacher, particularly in the kindergarten and primary grades, to identify and to draw out the shy, retiring child. The teacher should watch for special interests or abilities of such children and provide opportunities for them to participate actively at first and later to take leadership so that this shyness may be overcome. If opportunities of this type are not provided in the elementary school, the shy and retiring child is virtually certain to grow into an adult who is handicapped both socially and professionally by his inability to speak before a group of his peers.

INSTRUCTIONAL TECHNIQUES IN
ORAL LANGUAGE

The child learns to speak the language that he hears. By listening and imitating he acquires a knowledge of words and how they are put together in order to communicate with other persons. Much of this he has learned before he comes to school. The school has the instructional task, however, of improving and developing these expressional skills until each child has the competency to meet with assurance the oral language situations that life calls for.

A BASIC INSTRUCTIONAL APPROACH

From the third grade throughout the remaining years of the elementary school, emphasis in the oral language program should be placed upon specific expressional abilities and skills rather than upon spontaneity of expression, the major goal in the primary grades. This means no lessening of encouragement to free expression or reduction of emphasis upon content rather than form. It means that children in the middle and upper grades should now begin to learn to be discriminatory in their speaking. They should know when to speak and when not to speak. They should be concerned with making their speaking as effective as possible. Of course any child in the middle or upper grades who has difficulty in talking or who has not achieved the goal of spontaneity retains this goal, and the teacher places the more discriminating aspects of the program in the background for this particular child.

Since teachers must be concerned with teaching both freedom of expression and the skills and techniques for making this expression most effective, an instructional approach is suggested which first focuses on one aspect of the expression and then upon the other. This approach calls for two types of lessons: expressional and corrective. Expressional lessons deal mainly with *what* is said rather than *how* it is said. The expressional lesson must be one in which a real purpose for communication is present. Thus this type of lesson calls for organization of ideas, fluency and skill in speaking, and effective use of voice, the skills which are the prime concern of the training or correctional lesson.

240

EXPRESSIONAL LESSONS

In most language programs the differences between the two types of lessons are indicated by the ways in which they are used. Children discuss plans for a science field trip, converse about some event on the playground, report answers found to their questions on a social studies problem, tell a story that they read or heard, or introduce their parents to the teacher or principal. These are expressional activities. Some of the techniques applicable to all expressional lessons are discussed in the following paragraphs.

Audience-speaker relationship. In every expressional lesson it is important that attention be given to the audience. An attentive, interested audience is a strong motivational factor encouraging the child to make his expression as effective as possible. In order for an audience to be attentive and willing to listen, the content of the expression must be something they want to hear. It must be organized clearly and concisely. It must communicate something that the audience wants to know or is receptive to becoming interested in. Of course, the teacher should encourage the audience to be attentive. This usually may be done by giving actual attention to what has been said immediately after a child has finished talking. This may be done by the initiation of a discussion, by asking questions for further clarification, by commenting upon the sources of the speaker's information, and in other similar ways.

Imitating and practicing. Children learn much about speaking by observing and imitating others. Thus, if the teacher wants a child to learn to give an effective oral report, he must present a model for him to observe and imitate. This model may be the teacher, or it may be a pupil who has shown special skill in the particular activity. In another instance a model may need to show how to make introductions—what actually should be said. We can't expect the child to learn to speak effectively by reading about how to do it. We need to show him and then to let him practice it.

Improving usage habits. Teachers should incidentally and tactfully try to improve habits in usage and to correct bad habits in manner of speaking throughout the school day. This needs to be done with special skill and tact, particularly with those children for whom the greatest concern is freedom of expression. Without such correction, bad habits

241

will become fixed through practice. The correction of poor language habits is an individual matter for each child and in general is a practice which should be used for those habits which are the most seriously in need of correction. The teacher should never interrupt the child's line of thought as he is speaking, but the necessary corrections should be made as soon as possible, and under conditions that will not embarrass the speaker.

Activity planning. Both teacher and pupils will profit from planning expressional activities. The teacher should carefully plan each expressional lesson. He should clearly formulate the purposes that he hopes to stress and plan directly for the accomplishment of these purposes. Thus the child will know what he is attempting to do and can plan accordingly. He must select and organize the facts and ideas he desires to communicate and then plan the best method of doing it. In the very first activities, the planning should be done by the teacher and the children working together. Some children will need individual help with planning their expressional activities.

Evolving standards. Standards for each particular expressional activity should be established by the pupils. These standards may be an outgrowth of criticism of a previous lesson, they may be established after observing a model, or they may be the result of a discussion lesson. The standards should be the pupils' own statements, even if they fall below the goals of the teacher or the textbook. Standards should be treated as statements undergoing constant change as the pupils feel the need. If they are too low for one lesson, the pupils will realize this and change them as similar lessons and activities recur. Standards should be recorded in writing, possibly both by the teacher and the pupils. Certainly they should be written by the teacher, at first on the board, and later on a chart where they can be seen and referred to.

Group criticism. Criticism is easy and natural for children, though often they are needlessly harsh or cruel in their comments. For this reason, lessons which are directed particularly at the development of appreciation or enjoyment should not be subjected to such appraisal. Frank and friendly criticism, however, may be a part of many expressional lessons. In order to avoid unnecessary embarrassment, critical discussions must be carefully controlled at all times both by the children and the teacher. At the beginning of the school year, and particularly with younger children, the teacher should make most of the comments and

242

these should be mostly favorable in nature. The object is, of course, to develop in each child a willingness to accept criticism from someone else. Gradually the child may be taught to criticize himself as well as others. He needs to learn that criticism involves pointing out good features as much as it does picking out flaws; so far as possible, criticism should be stated in positive rather than in negative or destructive terms. For example, the child should learn to say "John's report was interesting but would have been easier to listen to if he had practiced pronouncing some of the words ahead of time," rather than to say, "John sure mispronounced a lot of words in his report; about a dozen, I'd say."

CORRECTIONAL LESSONS

From the expressional lessons, the teacher derives the content for the correctional lessons. The purpose of correctional lessons is to improve pupil mastery of particular expressional skills or abilities. The object of a specific lesson may be the review of a skill that has received attention previously, or it may be a new skill on which instruction can now be given because certain basic or underlying skills have been mastered. The following procedures are suggested for the effective use of correctional lessons.

Evaluation and diagnosis. From an evaluation by the teacher or class of previous oral expressional activities, specific errors, bad habits, or special language weaknesses are identified. This process of identifying expressional weaknesses and determining what needs to be done to correct them is diagnosis. The accuracy of the diagnosis is determined to a large degree by the nature and the refinement of the evaluative instruments available. (See Chapter 18.) In certain areas, such as oral expression, in which objective devices are extremely limited, the diagnosis must depend almost entirely upon subjective evaluation obtained from teacher-pupil judgments.

Identification of individual deficiencies. Diagnosis, in order to provide a reasonable basis for corrective work in oral expression, must identify with considerable accuracy the exact deficiencies of each individual. Moreover, as a strong motive for improvement, each child should be encouraged to recognize his own oral language weaknesses. Perhaps this can be done by relating his deficiencies to the standards which have been adopted by the class. The teacher should prepare a chart showing each individual child's language errors, bad habits, or needs, in order that those of primary importance may receive first attention.

Purposive drive. The diagnosis of needs must be related to a *corrective* instructional *drive* in this class with *these individual pupils now.* Children are not greatly motivated by a purpose that is far off in the distant future, or that lacks specific objectives.

Immediate attack. An immediate, frontal attack must be made upon the specific errors or habits that need correction. Errors made last month or even last week are too far in the past to be the subject of a correctional lesson today. The attack on an error made yesterday should be begun as soon as possible, not later than today, but preferably yesterday.

Individual errors. Children should be stimulated and encouraged to discover for themselves the identity and the causes of their own most frequent and important errors in oral expression. This in itself provides an important motive for learning how to correct them without delay.

Corrective practice. After children recognize the individual errors they are making and learn how these errors may be corrected, properly designed practice must be provided to establish the new habit. The chapter on textbooks (Chapter 15) and the one on workbooks (Chapter 16) give help in using these materials in the establishment of habits. Often, however, because of the heavy emphasis on written responses in these materials, insufficient practice is provided on skills which are entirely or mainly oral in nature. Thus the teacher may want to have one child practice his pronunciation with another child, practice a particular usage skill in a small group whose members are working on the same item, or immediately proceed to another expressional activity which will call for the use of the skill or habit on which the child has been working.

DEVELOPING SKILLS IN SPECIAL ORAL LANGUAGE SITUATIONS

Learning to speak before an audience is a process of blending important knowledge, skills, and attitudes regarding oral expression with experience in using these abilities. Provision of frequent and continuous opportunities for speaking is one of the most productive factors in the development of the individual's oral language ability. A child learns to be at ease and to speak effectively by standing on his feet and speaking, just as he learns to swim by swimming, to pilot a plane by flying. The importance of speaking experience in the development of oral language abilities is well summarized by Hatfield:

> Experience is the best of all schools. Certainly no one learns so thoroughly, and few learn so rapidly, in any other. And experience need not be a dear school, if it is competently organized and is conducted by a capable teacher who illuminates each situation in prospect and in retrospect. . . . The school of experience is the only one which will develop the flexibility and power of self-direction requisite for successful living in our age of swift industrial, social, and economic change.[9]

In line with the stress that should be placed upon the provision of extensive experience in the exercise of the oral language skills this report also gives an excellent summary of procedures to be followed by the teacher in developing all types of language abilities.

The actual experiences in communication which go into the curriculum should be representative of the present experience of most pupils outside the English class—in other school classes, in clubs, on the playground, at home, at the store. Many of these may depend for their reality upon the social situation in the English class itself, but they should parallel quite closely the experiences that do and will occur elsewhere.

A curriculum of actual experiences in communication implies typical (not invariable) classroom procedures somewhat like these: (The order of the activities would vary with circumstances and pupils.)

1. Making the pupils conscious of a present, worthy occasion for communication. Sometimes this occasion must be created by the teacher; frequently it needs only to be brought to attention.
2. Letting pupils attempt to meet the situation by speaking or writing.
3. Giving advice and assistance as the pupils prepare (if the occasion permits preparation) and as they write (if the occasion calls for writing). This includes helping them to perceive the techniques which they can use to advantage.
4. Helping pupils to realize that the excellence of their work must be measured in terms of the effect of their efforts upon their audience, and pointing out the causes of their (usually partial) success or failure.
5. Introducing at any favorable time specific practice in a skill which the pupils realize the worth of but which they may not have mastered.
6. Noting growth, chiefly by comparing success on this and previous similar occasions.[10]

---

[9] *An Experience Curriculum in English.* A Report of the Curriculum Commission of the National Council of Teachers of English, W. Wilbur Hatfield, chairman. New York: D. Appleton–Century Company, 1935, p. 3.

[10] *Ibid.,* p. 135–136.

CONVERSATION

In terms of social importance, conversation is the most fundamental speaking activity of children and adults. As such, it should receive much more than the incidental attention frequently given it in the typical language teaching program. Apparently some teachers regard conversational activities merely as the source of minor disciplinary problems, since such activities call for individual freedom of expression. However, even if a teacher has no fear of losing control of the class, he may nevertheless be influenced by the possibility that his fellow teachers may misinterpret the freedom and noisy activity in his classroom. The teacher will do well to remember that the quiet class is not always the good class, and that the actively interested class, even though noisy, may readily be the best class.

Since conversation is a more spontaneous activity than most other oral language activities, it should be exploited by the teacher. Throughout the school day many topics arise which arouse pupil interests and stimulate the desire to communicate ideas and thoughts to others. Usually these topics will be related to purposeful activities of the classroom program. Conversing about them is the natural thing for the pupils to do. The teacher, therefore, should consider their appropriateness and whenever possible allow the pupils to develop this spontaneous conversational situation. When the conversational situation does not arise spontaneously, it may be necessary for the teacher to plan a more formal approach to the subject.

In either the spontaneous conversational situation or the planned approach, attention is centered first on the content of what is being said. For example, if the children are talking about where to store their art materials, attention is given first to answering the implied question. Answering the question is the purpose of the conversation. As the conversation progresses, however, attention may be diverted from the subject matter to the best ways of carrying on a conversation. The teacher may ask if any of the pupils have noted that some contributions are better than others and why this is so. Points appropriate to the ages of the children may be noted, discussed and placed upon the board or upon a chart. The number of different points should be limited and only the key ones should be recorded, so that the purpose of the conversation will not become lost in concern about technicalities in conversational skill.

Children have so many interesting experiences both in and out of school that the teacher should never be at a loss to find opportunities for teaching and practicing the conversational skills. Sometimes, however, some of these opportunities are overlooked or are not examined carefully enough to determine whether there is real purpose in conversing about a particular topic. Situations occurring in most classrooms which may be utilized for conversation include:

1. Making plans for the class
    a. for the day or a portion of it.
    b. for the week's activities
    c. for long-range purposes, e.g. "things we must do before visiting the Indian museum"
    d. for special occasions, e.g. "what we'll do at the farm tomorrow" or "what we'll need at our party"
2. Pictures in books or magazines
3. Newspaper items and articles in books or magazines
4. Special interests such as hobbies, games, TV and radio programs
5. Behavior in patricular situations, such as in committees working on problems in social studies or science, or coming into the room from recess.

In the teaching of conversation it is well to remember that it is an activity of some intimacy and that such intimacy is difficult to achieve in a formal physical setting. The shy child who will not talk from the isolation of his seat may find it easy to talk in a conversational group of four or five children where it is possible to talk in a low voice and feel secure in the physical nearness of others. In addition, the desks and chairs may need to be rearranged so that the children will face one another. Even in a small group, too, a self-confident child may need to be chosen to keep the conversation rolling and to urge the participation of all members of the group.

DISCUSSION

Instruction in discussion is related in many ways to instruction in conversation, but discussion is generally somewhat more formal than conversation. Generally the discussion group is larger than the conversation group and the discussion group usually has a leader. A discussion question frequently evolves from a conversation.

Basic to instruction on the discussion skills is the clear recognition of the problem in all its parts by all the children. Each child, if he is actually to participate, must be conversant with the problem. This, of course does not mean that he must know everything about the problem, but he must know enough so that he can make a contribution. Knowledge of the problem or topic implies that individual and class preparation is necessary. At this point the teacher will need to teach research skills, such as using the encyclopedia, dictionary, maps, and other reference sources. He will need to help children relate their experiences to the topic. He will need to stress that a problem is answered with facts, not emotions, and that facts must be collected and evaluated.

It is important for a teacher not to permit the more talkative children in the class to dominate the activities. In order to prevent this it may be useful to keep a "participation index" to indicate the distribution of children's contributions.[11] Such an index is simply a tabulation of the number of times each child contributes to a discussion. In some instances perhaps such an index could be kept by a pupil or by several pupils and serve as an added device for relating the discussion to previously established standards.

Discussional activities are important, too, in teaching cooperation. A discussion problem is solved or clarified by the participation of all. Discussion implies reaching a common viewpoint or a better understanding of a problem. It implies tolerance and good sportsmanship.

Leadership training is a part of the instructional program in discussion. Many, but not all, children in a classroom need practice in the leadership skills that are necessary for the discussion leader. Leaders must be taught how to open a discussion, how to draw out thinking and information through skillful questioning, how to summarize main points, and how to handle sharp differences of opinion in a tactful manner.

There are many situations in the school day which may be utilized for teaching discussion skills. Some representative situations or problems include:

1. The program for Education Week.
2. How to raise money to buy a phonograph for the classroom.
3. How best to organize the pet show.
4. What things about a movie make it good.
5. Classroom housekeeping.
6. A book everyone in the group has read.
7. An experience shared by all.
8. How to converse, use the telephone, etc.
9. How different people talk.
10. What a fifth-grade pupil should know about the Constitution.

The following is one teacher's report on a class discussion:

[11] Dorothy G. Petersen and Velma D. Hayden, *Teaching and Learning in the Elementary School.* New York: Appleton-Century-Crofts, Inc., 1961, p. 121.

When the boys and girls in our third grade class returned to the room after the lunch hour some were quite indignant because one of the boys had thrown a rock at another. Since we are very particular at our school about rock throwing, the children know it is something they shouldn't do.

I asked the accused if he really had thrown the rock. He said he had but because the other boy had said a certain area on the playground belonged to him and no one else could walk there. Some of the children thought that was funny and laughed. I asked what seemed funny and they replied that the playground belonged to all and no one person could claim part of it as his alone.

This seemed a good opportunity to discuss property and belongings. One child said, "That is just like saying that the school cafeteria belongs to only one person and no one else could eat there." I asked if children should share their lunches just because they shared the cafeteria. They promptly replied that that was different. That each should eat his own lunch because a lunch is meant for only one child.

We continued our discussion by naming a number of objects, buildings, and other things, and deciding whether each was something which might be used by only one or should be shared by a number of people.

Later we talked about places where it would be proper and safe to throw rocks. One boy said that his father and he sometimes spent an hour or so throwing rocks into a river near their home. We agreed that it would be good exercise and training to throw rocks under some conditions.[12]

TELEPHONING

Telephoning is an oral language activity in which most of us are almost constantly involved. It is not, of course, an activity that is ordinarily carried on in the school itself. Children from an early age learn to use the telephone at home, and even before learning to use it themselves are fascinated with the idea of talking into an instrument and hearing a voice answer. Consequently they are anxious to learn to use it themselves. Generally parents are glad when a child can answer a telephone or make a call and do either in a polite and competent manner. Teachers should take every advantage of genuine opportunities for children to acquire experience and skill in the use of the telephone. In planning a class excursion a call may be necessary to secure permission to visit a farm or a plant. Further calls may be necessary to complete the arrangements. Children may be allowed to call the homes of absent classmates or they may call to order the refreshments for a class party.

Most of the actual situations involving the use of the telephone generally arise out of school. In fact, many schools place definite restrictions on the use of the school telephones. More often than not a teaching situa-

[12] As reported by Mrs. G. W. McCready, Sonora, California.

tion in the use of the telephone at school is a dramatized or imaginary situation, depending upon the maturity of the pupils. Typical telephoning situations which may be recalled or dramatized for teaching purposes include the following:

1. Answering a call intended for oneself.
2. Answering a call for another member of the family.
3. Calling a message to a friend.
4. Telephoning a message for someone else.
5. Giving a tradesman an order.
6. Making emergency calls to fire station, police, hospital, or other special services.
7. Conversing with a friend over the telephone.

For supplementary experience in the use of the telephone one fifth-grade textbook suggests that children take turns acting out these situations:

1. A girl calls a friend to invite her to a party.
2. A boy calls a classmate to find out the time and place of tomorrow's baseball game.
3. A boy or girl calls an ice cream company to order ice cream for a class party.
4. A boy or girl telephones the public relations department of a railroad company to arrange for the showing of a film for a school assembly program.
5. A girl or boy telephones the library to see if it has a certain book.[13]

STORY TELLING

Story telling is an ancient art which was once almost universal. Today few people are good story tellers in the usual meaning of the term. This fact is not difficult to understand when the demands of modern life are considered. Skill in telling stories develops through use, and use responds to demand. The facts are that the many readily available story books and radio and TV programs leave little time for the children to listen to stories except in school and even less time to learn to tell stories themselves. The time left for the story teller to practice his art is extremely limited. Something very important in the lives of both children and parents is lost when the radio, TV, and hi-fi are allowed to displace the bedtime story.

There is no one way to tell stories. Successful story tellers have their

[13] Thomas C. Pollock and John J. Forester. *Using Language,* Grade 5. New York: The Macmillan Company, 1954, p. 30.

own ways of telling their favorite stories. They may even vary their methods to meet the demands of different types of stories. Similarly there appears to be no single best way of teaching story telling. Some of the following general suggestions may be helpful to the teacher and the class in a story hour.

1. The practice of relating the story itself closely to the experiences of the story teller and his audience is a sound and widely-used principle. A child cannot be expected to tell a story well unless he himself is fully informed about the events, situations, and content of the story. In the first place, he would not *want* to tell it if it didn't interest him and if he didn't feel that his audience, because of a background of similar experiences, would be equally interested.

2. The general atmosphere of the place in which the story is told is an important factor in successful story telling. Outside distractions should, so far as possible, be eliminated; the room should be quiet; the audience should be comfortably at ease. Since story telling is intended to be a thoroughly enjoyable experience—one in which all pressures and cares are laid aside—a calm air of informality should prevail in the room. The children will generally prefer to sit in a circle, perhaps on the floor, grouped closely around the speaker. Children enjoy watching the speaker closely during these story hours, and then too, the good story teller likes to be able to look directly at everyone in his audience.

3. The pleasure of a story telling experience depends so completely upon the masterful presentation of the story that the importance of a careful preparation prior to telling the story cannot be overemphasized. The story must be so well known to the teller that every detail can be seen in his mind's eye. He must sense the mood of the story and plan ways to convey that feeling to his audience. The words he will use must be well chosen. Sometimes these will be his own words, and at other times they will be the words of the characters in the story.

4. Realistic standards and friendly criticism should be part of every story telling experience but they should never be so exacting as to mar the pleasure of the occasion. Standards are needed to serve as reminders to the story teller. They should, of course, be ones that he has helped prepare, and must be easily possible of attainment. Criticism should be used, too, but in a friendly, sensible manner. The prime objective of this activity is to develop successful story tellers, and to encourage them to be willing to tell stories. Finding too much fault with a child's story telling efforts is a poor way to encourage him to try again.

5. As in the case of all other language abilities, the story telling skills

251

must be established through actual learning of the skills and repeated practice calling for their use in lifelike activities. This principle has been emphasized repeatedly throughout this book and should require no further elaboration here.

Brief statements of standards or "sign-posts" which seem to sum up these story telling principles are suggested by one speech authority.[14]

1. Know your story well.
2. Picture the story to yourself.
3. Know the mood of the story, and try to transmit that mood to your audience.
4. Tell the story in your own words.
5. Use natural gestures that add interest to the story.
6. Learn the use of the pause.
7. Speak quietly, enthusiastically, distinctly, conversationally.
8. Look directly at your audience.
9. Work for a pleasing voice quality.

Since the child cannot grasp all of these standards at once, only one or two points at a time should be emphasized. Many of them, such as manner of speaking and using natural words, are taught in other aspects of the language program. Others may be taught incidentally, or, as someone has said, "caught" from the teacher story teller.

A real love of stories and some ability in telling them on the part of the teacher is essential to teaching story telling to children successfully. The teacher is the model, and the one who, because of the obvious pleasure he gets from telling and listening to stories, instills this feeling in the children. The number one item in importance for the teacher and the children is the selection of the story to tell. In doing so, make a distinction between stories for the individual child and for a group of children. Select a story with a relatively simple and uncomplicated plot that will appeal to children's interests. Look for stories that fire the imagination; stories that bring laughter; those that stir some understanding of desirable qualities like courage, love, and beauty; stories that show respect for good; stories that have high adventure and daring.

After the story has been selected, the story teller should turn his attention toward the mood or feeling he plans to develop.

1. Beginning with the basic plot, and developing it from there, the speaker should plan ways in which he can create the desired mood or feeling.
2. Go to work at once on those devices and steps necessary to create this

[14] Genevieve Arnold, "Story-Telling," in *Guides to Speech Training in the Elementary School,* A Report of the Elementary Committee of the National Association of Teachers of Speech. Boston: Expression Company, 1943, pp. 67–68.

mood, such as the voice, the language, the gestures, the timing, the inflection.[15]

3. Get the attention of the audience with a striking beginning statement.
4. Learn the importance of timing and the use of the pause in getting and holding the attention of the audience.
5. Use gestures sparingly and only as an aid to suggestion.
6. Learn to mimic and to imitate animals, voices, and sounds in general.

From the negative point of view there are a number of points to avoid in story telling. This list is suggestive.

1. Avoid introducing non-essentials and side issues.
2. Alter stories for special occasions with care.
3. Do not use unfamiliar words when familiar words will work.
4. Avoid questioning children during the story telling.
5. Too much use of illustration has a distracting effect.
6. Do not overdo having the children draw a picture about what they've just heard. The value of this is debatable. Most of the things we hope they will visualize can't be drawn.
7. Avoid intensive discussion of the story immediately after its telling. This also appears to be of questionable value since the discussion tends to disrupt the pupils' own line of thinking about the story.
8. Do not make the mistake of insisting that every story be correlated with something else in the school program. Much story telling should be just for enjoyment.

Most story telling periods are the result of the teacher's or some pupil's telling a story to the rest of the class. The purpose of this activity may be pure enjoyment, a moral teaching, or the stimulation of the imagination. The improvement of one story telling activity over an earlier one is generally achieved by teacher and pupil together deciding what is in need of improvement and then working on these needs cooperatively and again appraising the effort. If these procedures do not satisfactorily accomplish the purpose, special activities or lessons such as the following may be needed.

1. Lessons in which stories are told in small groups by individual children. The smaller audience may give the necessary confidence the story teller needs.
2. Lessons in which new standards are developed.
3. Practice lessons in which individuals tell stories in small groups in order to determine points on which specific improvement is needed.
4. Practice lessons in which each class member participates, such as: practice in making a long story short.
5. Lessons for telling suitable jokes and anecdotes.

[15] See Ruth Sawyer, *The Way of the Story Teller.* New York; The Viking Press, 1942.

6. A lesson in which plans are made in small groups for the next story-telling experience. Usually this will include a review of points previously learned about telling stories.

The following helpful hints on story telling should also be kept in mind. The first sentence of the story should tell something important that helps to get the story moving and also starts the listener wondering what is going to happen. Early in the story some hint should be given about the ending. The events in the story should be told in the order in which they are supposed to have happened, and no unnecessary sentences should be used. Whenever possible, the actual words of the characters in the story should be used. The surprise or the most exciting event in the story should come near the end.

It is wise to keep in mind that story telling may be varied by using a flannel or felt board, puppets, or other regalia. The use of these aids will assist pupils in remembering the story, in establishing rapport with the audience, and in gaining enough self-confidence for telling the story. Any of these aids may be used by a teacher for building interest in story telling.[16]

Children should be encouraged to be constantly on the lookout for stories to tell. Many excellent ones about Hallowe'en, Thanksgiving, Christmas, and other holidays and special occasions often appear in magazines. The children should also be encouraged to tell stories they have read in their supplemental reading. It is generally a good idea for the teacher to require a conference with the pupil concerning the worth and appropriateness of his story before he is permitted to tell it to the class. Sometimes a committee of pupils may assist the teacher with the screening of stories.

DRAMATIZATION

In the middle and upper grades the informal play activities of the primary children are gradually replaced by more formal dramatic activities. Dramatizations are planned activities ranging from those set in very flexible patterns to those in which every detail is worked out before the performance. A dramatization is often characterized as having a written script, being prepared for performance for an audience, and calling for the memorization of lines and possibly extensive rehearsal. With children in the elementary school not all these characteristics need prevail.

[16] See Joseph Wagner and Robert W. Smith, *Teacher's Guide to Storytelling*, Dubuque, Iowa: Wm. C. Brown Company, 1958, for many suggestions.

With encouragement children are capable of great creativity and these abilities are important in dramatization.

Children like to create and they like to act. No form of self-expression calls forth so much enthusiasm, gives so much genuine joy or develops so much originality, imagination, and readiness for responsibility as does well-planned dramatic activity. Naturally, the first dramatic efforts of children should be those that are still very closely related to the spontaneous play activities of kindergarten and the first and second grades.

The teacher in the intermediate and upper grades faces a major problem, however, if the pupils have not experienced much informal play and creative dramatics in the preceding grades. The introduction of dramatization through charades, action songs, and choral speaking will help to break down undue reserve and will build interest in further dramatic activities. In the activities suggested the pupils are motivated by the rhythm of chant, song, or verse, and the action is focused upon pantomime. With enough of this preparation, and with a real mood of enjoyment, the reluctant pupils will become ready for the more formal dramatizations.

Dramatizations in the middle and upper grades include those calling for scripts and those calling for no scripts. The scripts may be commercial ones, or they may be written by the teacher, or by the children themselves. The first productions should call for no script and should consist simply of acting out very well-known stories. Beginning with no scripts is a fundamental technique used by teachers in producing more formal dramatizations, too.

The following is a suggested procedure for teaching dramatization:

1. The dramatization should be based on material thoroughly known by the children. The teacher and the class should discuss each character in the dramatization: how each character feels toward each other one, and why he feels so; how each character looks, walks, talks, etc; what each scene is like; what the dramatization is saying.

2. The children should cooperate in planning the setting, the costumes (if any), and the stage scenery. Whenever possible this planning should be extended to include the actual making of the costumes and scenery. These activities offer valuable opportunities for the development of responsibility and ingenuity, the use of special talents, and the "drawing-out" of the shy child.

3. After children thoroughly understand the dramatization, the first rehearsal should be begun without script. Various children should be tried for the different characterizations. Emphasis should be upon the

255

way the child creates the character. What the child has the character do should be based upon his understanding of the dramatization and the part he is playing. The words and actions should be those of the child.

4. The next step is the actual casting of the characters. Since most productions may be repeated several times, it is generally possible to plan for several complete casts. The children who are interested in stage management, scenery design, or costuming should be put in those positions. Of course, the emphasis as far as language arts is concerned is upon language expression, but in the average classroom there will be enough jobs necessary to present a play that each child can do several things that he wants to do.

The most appropriate stories for dramatization are those of the finest literary quality with simple plots. The plot should have a thread of interest, reach a climax, and have a happy ending. It must be clean-cut and call for vivid imagery; it must be short, interesting, and written within the range of the children's experience. Since the emphasis in the elementary school should be upon spontaneous expression, the dramatization should not call for complicated staging, scenery, and costumes.

In addition to the dramatization of stories, including those written by the children themselves, there are many situations which may be dramatized and thus provide a means for teaching speaking and listening skills. Situations such as those suggested by the following are excellent for dramatization:

1. Introducing people.
2. Answering telephone calls correctly.
3. Eating different kinds of food.
4. Delivering a message.
5. Entertaining visitors.
6. Going on a shopping tour.
7. Holding a club meeting.
8. Extending greetings or saying good-bye.
9. Giving directions.
10. Conducting an interview.

Puppetry is another form of dramatics that is very popular. Children often express themselves more freely through puppetry than through other dramatic activities. Since they are manipulating dolls, they have little opportunity to become concerned with fear of the audience. Then, too, the activity seems more "make-believe" and the children may become more thoroughly a part of the story.

Puppets include *stick puppets* which are made of cardboard and fastened to long sticks, *shadow puppets* which are made the same way as stick puppets but are not colored and have holes in the faces of the figures for eyes, and *hand puppets* made from solid, three-dimensional materials, paper bags, socks, and papier-mâché.[17]

Marionettes are string-controlled dolls with head, body, legs, and arms worked from above. Upper grade children enjoy making these figures and planning performances for them. The skilled story teller may use marionettes as aids in getting his story across to his audience. Using puppets and marionettes calls forth much creativity on the part of children. Much of the dialogue is spontaneous and this is to be preferred over a written script.

CHORAL SPEAKING

Choral speaking is more than a group of persons speaking in unison. It is an activity that is dramatic in nature and which resembles a singing choir in its make-up of blended voices and controlled expression. Choral speaking is not difficult to teach but it must be done carefully, since children do not move into choral speaking as easily as casual observation might indicate. Much of the success of choral speaking rests upon the careful selection of the material used. Ogilvie suggests that the material for choral speaking groups should meet these requirements:

1. It should interest the children.
2. It should be within their intellectual and emotional understanding.
3. It should possess literary value.
4. It should possess thought that is universal.
5. Its form should be adaptable to choral speaking.[18]

A teacher can have little hope for success with choral speaking unless the children have a background of experience resulting from extensive listening to the reading and speaking of selected prose and poetry. Often as the children have listened to the teacher, particularly in the lower grades, they have been encouraged to join in saying some lines of a poem they have heard often. From this background the teacher can lead them readily into actual choral speaking. First selections are generally nursery rhymes that children know well.

Choral speaking involves much interpretation. Children should be encouraged to decide whether a line should be said rapidly or slowly,

[17] For directions for puppet making and use, see: Mardel Ogilvie, *Speech in the Elementary School.* New York: McGraw-Hill Book Company, Inc., 1954, chapters 2 and 3.
[18] Ogilvie, *op. cit.,* p. 107.

whether the voices should be soft or loud, and other factors which make for an interesting and pleasant experience for themselves and an audience. Different ways of speaking should be tried with each selection. Perfection in performance should not be expected at once.

Voices in the elementary school may be divided into two groups, light and heavy, or into three groups, light, heavy, and medium. With very young children whose voices are developing, no attempt should be made to group pupils according to voice quality. As children mature, and as they learn to enjoy a poem thoroughly, they will themselves often suggest some voice grouping. A teacher who listens to his pupils talking and reading every day knows their voices—the high voices, the low, and the in-between. There should not be great difficulty in grouping them for the most effective speaking.

After trying out and discussing various interpretations, the teacher and the children together set the pattern for interpretation of each selection. The teacher then has the responsibility as the director for indicating the rhythmic pattern, the starting and stopping points, and the tempo, and for keeping the voices in unison. The teacher and pupils talk over their articulation, pronunciation, blending of voices, and the effect of their interpretation. All should remember that choral speaking is a cooperative, group, communication activity.

Types of choral speaking have been identified by Abney as:

1. Refrain—which requires a single soloist who reads the narrative, with the class joining in refrain.
2. Two-part or antiphonal—two groups balanced, one against the other; light voices versus dark; boys versus girls. Question-and-answer poetry, or poems of contrasting moods are good in this arrangement.
3. Line-a-child or sequential—interpretation of one or two lines by a number of individuals, leading up to a climax in which unison voices are often effective.
4. Part arrangement—in which maturing voices are grouped in choirs and blended somewhat as an orchestra.
5. Unison—in which all voices speak all lines as one.[19]

While choral speaking is an activity performed principally for the pleasure it gives, the opportunities for dealing with problems in oral expression should not be overlooked. Choral speaking can also give children a feeling for the quality of words and can give them a better appreciation of poetry. Of course, there is no guarantee that good taste and

[19] Louise Abney, "Poetry—Interpretation," in *Guides to Speech Training in the Elementary School,* A Report of the Elementary Committee of the National Association of Teachers of Speech. Boston: Expression Company, 1943, p. 73.

good voice and speech habits will prevail, but attention to the preceding suggestions should make choral speaking a profitable oral language activity.

REPORTING

The oral report is a relating, telling, or narrating of ideas about which the pupil has gathered information. Reporting is a major language activity in the elementary school, sometimes being used quite informally and at other times more formally. Included in this discussion of teaching procedures for reporting are those for the similar activities of presenting reviews, summaries, directions, and procedures.

Important school and life situations calling for the giving of reports include:

1. Providing information from sources or material not accessible to all
2. Summarizing results of independent observation
3. Securing an answer to a definite question raised in class
4. Making available results of council or class government activities
5. Summarizing results of individual or group excursions
6. Announcing recreational activities—concerts, plays, games
7. Evaluating books enjoyed
8. Selecting important current events
9. Summarizing progress of science experiments
10. Reviewing class newspaper progress

In the teacher's planning for oral reporting, specific attention should be given to the teaching of the skills that will help make oral reporting a profitable language experience. Basically, these skills are (1) the selection of appropriate material, (2) the collection and organization of this material, and (3) the actual presentation of the material to a group. The development of these skills and their practice should, in general, follow the suggestions for oral language teaching discussed earlier in this chapter. Particular points for a teacher to keep in mind at this time are the following:

1. Encourage the condensing of materials from sources.
2. Do not allow the direct copying of materials.
3. Base reporting activities upon the needs of the individual and the group.
4. Assign topics according to individual interests.
5. Stress the importance of good beginnings and endings of reports.
6. Supervise note taking occasionally.
7. Train pupils to give full credit for ideas, materials, and quotations used in reports.

259

8. Use group and individual evaluation of reports.
9. Use reporting activities to discover individual pupil weaknesses in usage, organization of ideas, voice control, and other important oral skills.

Even though some reports are quite informal, children need to be taught the definite steps in preparing a report. In every case, however, it should be stressed that communication is the purpose of the report and that the effectiveness of communication is enhanced by good form. Steps for the pupil to follow usually should include:

1. Making a list of questions which might be asked about the subject on which he is reporting.
2. Consulting reference sources and making notes for the answers to these questions.
3. Looking over his notes and deciding how the report should be organized. This includes first dividing it into main divisions and then preparing a complete outline in order that details may be arranged in their proper places. For many reports this outline may be very simple. In fact, throughout most of the elementary school the teacher should stress the importance of a simple outline.
4. Thinking about the length of time required for giving the report; reorganizing or cutting the outline if necessary.
5. Giving particular attention to ways to begin and end his report with interesting statements.

Discussing what makes for a good oral report is an appropriate topic for a class discussion and is in itself, as was suggested in an earlier section of this chapter, an effective teaching technique. From an exchange of ideas major points of agreement among the pupils appear and may be recorded. One class agreed on these requirements which were written on a chart as a reminder in the preparation of reports.

1. Choose a topic.
2. Find books and materials.
3. Select the information for the report.
4. Organize the information.
5. Make notes to use.

Sometimes reporting activities may be improved by the use of devices and materials to supplement the speaking. For example, the following have been found to be helpful:

1. Using pictures or cut-outs on a flannel board.
2. Referring to a diagram or chart previously prepared.
3. Having a partner pantomime what the child is reporting on.
4. Recording a report on a tape-recorder and having the class guess who gave it.

5. Stimulating interest in a report by placing something related to the topic on display previous to the time the report is given.
6. Displaying some object related to the report and telling about it.

GIVING ANNOUNCEMENTS, DIRECTIONS, AND EXPLANATIONS

The skills required in these activities are similar to those in reporting. Attention must be given to organization, to clarity, to unusual factors of interest, and to the inclusion of the essential facts. Teachers need to emphasize brevity particularly while retaining all the necessary details. Too often an announcement is made or directions or explanations given without the inclusion of all essential details.

Teaching the making of announcements and the giving of directions and explanations is best done through real situations. Children may be given opportunities to make announcements about programs, events, exhibitions, games, lost and found articles, rules, and other subjects to their own classmates, to other classes, in assemblies, and to neighborhood adult groups. Announcements may be made at school club meetings, and often one or more youngsters may be called upon to make announcements or to act as the master of ceremonies at school or club programs.

INTERVIEWING

Many opportunities occur for children to conduct interviews. For example, they may interview the teacher who has taken a trip or has a special interest or hobby; they may interview a new child about where he formerly lived; they may interview parents who have special fields of interest, hobbies, or professions; they may interview school personnel about their work, or community workers like the grocer, postman, and fireman. Particular attention and practice should be given to:

1. Allowing the individual who arranged the interview to introduce the subject and close the interview.
2. Teaching the interviewer to stick to the topic of the interview.
3. Developing sensitivity regarding the amount of time used by the interviewer.
4. Creating a feeling about when an interview should be closed.
5. Discovering something about appropriate times for making appointments.

The interview should be conducted in a courteous and friendly manner, with the interviewer listening carefully, contributing worthwhile

261

questions, taking notes, and expressing appreciation for the information being received. Further, the child conducting an interview must learn to plan ways to utilize the information he has received.

PARTICIPATING IN MEETINGS

Experiences that occur almost daily in the classroom may be utilized to show the children the need for orderly procedure. The teacher and pupils may discuss various ways of conducting meetings and the rules that may be appropriate. From such discussion the children will discover the value of rules in eliminating waste of group time and energy. A wall chart or a mimeographed guide may be the outgrowth of such discussion. The following is a sample one curriculum guide suggests:

Rules governing parliamentary procedure

1. The chairman calls the meeting to order.
2. The secretary reads the minutes of the previous meeting.
3. The chairman asks for corrections or additions to the minutes. After corrections or additions have been made, the minutes are then accepted.
4. The chairman calls for business to come before the meeting.
5. The group proceeds with the business of the day. (See making and voting on motions.)
6. The meeting is adjourned.

Making and voting on motions

1. The member who wants to make a motion rises and addresses the chairman by saying, "Mister (or Madam) Chairman."
2. The chairman recognizes the member by repeating his name.
3. The member proposes the motion by saying, "Mister Chairman, I move that . . ."
4. Another member seconds the motion by stating, "I second the motion." (All motions must be seconded before they can be discussed or voted upon.)
5. After the motion has been seconded it is stated in full by the chairman as follows, "It has been moved and seconded that . . ."
6. The chairman calls for discussion.
7. The chairman calls for a vote by saying, "All in favor say 'Aye.' Those opposed say 'No.' "
8. The chairman announces the result of the vote by saying, "The motion has been carried" or "The motion has been lost." [20]

---

[20] *Toward Better Speech,* Curriculum Bulletin, 1952–53 Series, Number 5. New York: Board of Education of the City of New York, 1955, p. 77.

Abiding by the rules of simple parliamentary procedure is not too much to expect from children in the intermediate and upper grades. Children generally enjoy such procedures because they sense that they are the same ones used by their elders. There are many opportunities for the organization of clubs and for all pupils to preside at meetings as well as to make nominations and motions and to take part in discussions.

OBSERVING THE SOCIAL AMENITIES

Every person must know something about how to extend and receive greetings, how to make introductions, how to show courtesy to others when speaking or listening to them, and how to apologize for breaches in social conduct. Learning to do these things is generally recognized by children as important, but sometimes outside motivation needs to be supplied. One way to stimulate interest in social conventions is by a discussion of customs of other people, periods, and places. For example, pupils become very much interested in greetings such as the following used in different parts of the world:

1. Eskimos rub noses when they meet.
2. French, Austrian, and some other European men kiss each other's cheeks.
3. In many European countries, men greet ladies by kissing their hands.
4. Japanese clasp their own hands and bow several times.
5. The Bakuba tribe in the Belgian Congo say "hello" and "goodby" by clapping their hands.
6. In this country it was once proper for girls to curtsy and boys to bow when greeted by another person.

Acting as a host or hostess is an important life activity that may profit from training. Occasions for gaining experience and confidence in these roles arise frequently in school. Visitors may come to the room and be greeted by a room host and hostess. The host and hostess may introduce themselves to the guests and in turn introduce the visitors to others in the room. Such activities, through careful teacher guidance, help the children become aware of the use and value of the commonly accepted forms of courtesy.

As an outgrowth of extensive discussion and practice, the child must become accustomed to observing the rather rigid conventions followed in making and in responding to introductions. He must learn the proper forms of expression to use in common social situations, such as his being introduced to another child, or to an older person, or his having to introduce an older person to another older person. The most effective

263

time to teach children about making introductions is just prior to a real occasion when they need to use the skills. This provides immediate and effective motivation for learning. Discussion of the skills is helpful, but it is not enough to give the child the needed experience and assurance. If numerous real situations are not available, imaginary social situations calling for many repetitions of the skills should be dramatized until the children develop the required feelings of ease and confidence.

The following general rules to be followed in making introductions should be learned by the boys and girls and practiced until each type of introduction is carried through with complete assurance.

1. Speak each person's name plainly to avoid embarrassment to either party. It is not improper for either party to ask for names to be repeated if they are not understood at the time of the introduction.
2. In introducing two persons who are complete strangers, the person making the introduction should tactfully add some remark which may start a conversation.
3. If the individual is obliged to introduce himself to another he should be certain to tell his name and add some personal, identifying remark.
4. When introducing a relative be sure to give his or her last name somewhere in the introduction.
5. One of the following formulas will help the individual to master the form of introductions:

       _____, this is _____
                  or
       _____, I'd like you to meet _____

In the first blank in each form, the child is to use the name of the person he wishes to honor. In the second blank he is to use the name of the other person.

The following rules may be used to help the one doing the introducing decide which person he wishes to honor:

1. In introducing a man and a woman (or a boy and a girl) the name of the woman or girl should be given first.
2. In introducing an older and a younger person, the name of the older person should be said first. If those being introduced are nearly the same age, either name may be given first.
3. In introducing an individual to your class or club meeting, mention the class or group first.

Many occasions arise naturally for using the social skills. Children may introduce friends and parents to the teacher and class. Many class groups appoint members to act as hosts and hostesses for special occasions or for a day or week; they answer the door, introduce visitors, and generally are in charge of the social obligations of the class. Sometimes one class may visit another and practice extending greetings and making introductions. Children may usher at school events. Other special occasions, such as class parties, call for the use of many social skills. Children may also practice courtesies in out-of-school activities by replying correctly to greetings on the street, responding to introductions at church, and greeting people and introducing themselves when engaged in such activities as collecting paper in the Boy Scout drive or selling Girl Scout cookies. Particular attention needs to be given in this day and age to courtesy to older persons. Giving an apology in a gracious manner is something that is difficult for many of us to do. Occasions for its use do occur, however, and learning to do it properly is a part of the responsibility of the language program.

Unlikely as this may seem to some of you who may read this discussion, teachers themselves sometimes forget to practice in their own home and school activities many of the courtesies they know. Perhaps this is the place in the language program for the teacher to recognize that in this area the most important "method" is for him to "practice what he preaches." In addition to the suggestions on teaching the social conventions and common courtesies given in this section, the teacher will find many excellent special references on courtesies and the social conventions as well as concrete hints and techniques for developing these skills in the teachers manuals and the language texts for the upper elementary grades.

DEVELOPING LISTENING SKILLS

For generations, teachers of the language arts have conscientiously accepted their responsibility for developing skill in reading, writing, and speaking, but too often they have been seemingly unconcerned with the importance of the listening skills. The idea that children must be taught how to listen is gaining increasingly wide acceptance. Today, supervisors and teachers are very much aware of the importance of skillful listening in the language program. Through skillful listening, thinking is stimulated, information is gained, oral language skills are improved, and creative appreciation is increased.

While many teachers now appreciate the need to do something about listening, few appear to know exactly what to do.[21] Until very recently

[21] Miriam E. Wilt, "A Study of Teacher Awareness of Listening as a Factor in Elementary Education." Unpublished doctor's dissertation, Pennsylvania State College, 1949.

the only listening instruction we gave children was "Pay attention" and "Listen carefully." We have demanded silence and attention but have been surprised to find that acquiescence to these demands did not guarantee listening.

The teacher's first task in giving instruction on listening skills is to make the children aware of the importance of careful listening. They must learn that skillful listening is important, not only to children in school, on the playground, and at home, but also to adults in almost every life activity. They must learn that listening skills can be developed, that they result from the formation of good habits which are easily learned, and that this mastery will reward them with a richer, more meaningful life.[22]

As a second step the teacher should stimulate the sense of hearing, or auditory acuity in the children. For example, the teacher might ask individuals in the class to name all the sounds they can remember hearing at a circus, in a hospital, or at an airport or railroad station. Each sound may be written on the board as it is mentioned, for the class to think about. Perhaps some pupils will be interested in writing a story which is based on the activities suggested by the words on the board. These pupils can read their stories to the class when they are completed. Similar exercises based on familiar situations will contribute to the development of a keen appreciation of the sense of hearing, and make children more alert to sounds they have previously taken for granted.

The third step is the provision of abundant opportunities for meaningful listening. A wide variety of opportunities for listening experiences must be introduced into the classroom if the children are to learn to adapt the kind of listening they do to the type that will best serve the purpose of the activity.[23] Thus, the program should call for listening to music, to poetry, to stories, to reports, to descriptions, etc. It should call for listening for specific purposes, for appreciation, for information, and for critical evaluation.

Related to the above is the fourth task, that of teaching children about the specific skills of listening and how each is necessary for a particular purpose or kind of listening.[24] Furthermore, emphasis must be placed

---

[22] Robert Canfield, "A Study of the Effects of Two Types of Instruction on the Listening Comprehension of Fifth Grade Children." Unpublished doctor's dissertation, Syracuse University, 1960.

[23] A good source of ideas for listening situations is David H. Russell and Elizabeth F. Russell, *Listening Aids Through the Grades.* New York: Bureau of Publications, Teachers College, Columbia University, 1959.

[24] See Chapter 4, pages 105–108, for a discussion of the skills necessary for effective listening.

on the development of these skills through specific teaching rather than merely giving attention to the superficial aspects of listening. The skills must be known to the teacher, and in a general way by pupils. The teacher must know the best procedures for developing each of the skills.[25]

A fifth responsibility of the teacher is to give the children many opportunities to talk about things that interest them. As they share experiences, hobbies, books, and information that are of genuine interest, with encouragement they will see the point of practicing the skills of listening as others practice the skills of speaking.

A final step involves the teacher himself: Teach the children to listen to you. This does not mean that you should "out-shout" them or speak in such a low voice that you are inaudible. It does mean that the tone should be low enough to force youngsters to stay alert in order to keep up with what is going on. It is advisable, too, to warn the children that the practice of not repeating instructions, explanations, or announcements will be followed in the class. In addition, the teacher should make every effort to make the classroom activities so interesting that all the children will want to listen.

LISTENING FOR ENJOYMENT AND APPRECIATION

Appreciative listening includes (1) enjoying the content of the material and the quality of the delivery of the speaker; (2) responding to a mood or setting; (3) identifying the character of a person from his lines or the dialogue in a play; (4) enjoying music, poetry, and dramatic bits; (5) understanding the use of body postures, gestures, asides, satire, and voice inflections; and (6) creating visual images of verbal descriptions. The objective of this type of listening is enjoyment. The securing of information or the critical evaluation of it is incidental to the major purpose. However, because the purpose is one of enjoyment it may be unsafe to assume that children will actually listen. They may not know the purpose, nor realize how skill in listening will help in achieving it.

In most listening for enjoyment, there is a need for physical comfort. We don't enjoy something unless we are comfortable. In the classroom, this means attention to such factors as ventilation, lighting, seating, absence of distractions, and the creation of a pleasant relaxed atmosphere. It may include the easing of emotional conflicts, making arrangements to

[25] See, for example, Paul C. Burns, "Teaching Listening in the Elementary School." *Elementary English,* January, 1961, pp. 11–14; and Robert Canfield, "Approaches to Listening Improvement," *Elementary English,* December, 1958, pp. 525–528.

facilitate hearing, or merely making sure that phonograph or tape recorder is in good working condition so that the activity may not be delayed or interrupted.

The following steps in the teaching of appreciational listening will suggest useful general procedures for the language teacher to follow.

Clearly defining the purpose of the listening experience. The purpose of the listening activity should be one that the children will understand and appreciate. For example, the teacher might make this introductory statement of purpose: "We have talked about river steamers and have seen pictures of them; now let's listen to this recording of music played on river steamers and see if this is the kind of music we would expect to hear on a steamboat."

Giving preliminary attention to unfamiliar vocabulary. The teacher should know the vocabulary that is used in the material to be heard. Unusual words that possibly will be heard by these children for the first time should be discussed and related to known words and previous experiences. This, of course, must be done with care, for it can be carried too far. For example, to appreciate a lovely poem, to derive meaning and pleasure from listening to it, does not require a complete understanding of each word. The sounds of the new words may, for some children, be the greatest source of pleasure in the activity.

Giving preliminary attention to the recall of related experiences. The teacher should attempt to relate what is to be heard to something that is known. This is really only a stage in making assignments that good teachers have always used. However, in listening for enjoyment and appreciation this must be handled with caution, for children may derive real enjoyment without complete understanding of all of the subtle elements involved.

Using guides as aids in attaining the listening purpose. Listening guides directing the attention of the children to particular features of the material may sometimes be prepared in advance and given to the pupils shortly before the listening lesson begins. Such devices should not be used often, however, for they tend to over-formalize this type of listening activity.

Replaying the production to heighten enjoyment. A second experience in listening to a beautiful musical selection, an exciting tale, a stirring speech, a marvelous poem invariably brings out elements of enjoyment that were not appreciated the first time. The value of this procedure may

268

be brought home to the children by asking them to list the new elements discovered in the second listening period that they did not notice in the first.

The following report of a portion of a listening experience designed to aid in developing creative writing ability is illustrative of the points presented above.

Presentation. Read aloud and discuss Walt Whitman's, *I Hear America Singing.* Listen to recording of *Ballad For Americans* (R8) in order to discuss the things people do to earn their living.

Discuss the fact that we are living in an American city, where many wheels are turning and many people are busy turning those wheels, and that we can hear the sounds of people and machines at work from our windows. Plan to write an original verse or paragraph describing how the city sounds to us and our feelings about it.

Exploration. Listen to the sounds from the schoolroom. (There should be a minute of listening, then naming of sounds heard.) As the children name the sounds, the teacher writes the words on the chalkboard. Then there should be another listening period for purposes of further identification.

Procedure. The ideas are shared and enlarged upon during a discussion period. When the time comes for individual writing, each child develops the idea that appeals to him and tries to express it in his own way. During this writing time, there is no interchange of ideas. However, the teacher should make the children feel free to ask for individual assistance if they need it. Since this writing should be a joyful and spontaneous experience, the children should not be forced to write. Those who do not write should engage in a quiet activity.

Stenographic Report of the Lesson

Children:	Rumble, rattle, roar, purr, slither, squeak, roll, chug, whistle, skid, sizzle, hiss, squeal, whiz, zoom, hum, sigh, squawk, scream, call, shout, wail, chime, ring, clang, whine
Teacher:	Now let's listen again for a minute. We may hear more. (All listen for a minute.) What things made the sounds we heard? What did we hear these things do?
Children:	Cars—rumble, rattle, roar, purr, slither Trains—roll, chug, whistle Tires—skid, sizzle, hiss, squeal, squeak Planes—whiz, roar, zoom, dash Buses—hum, signal, squeak, groan, whisper Trucks—rumble, roar, thump, rattle, pound, clatter Pneumatic drills—rat-a-tat Sea gulls—mew, squawk, scream

269

People—call, shout
Children—shriek, scream, bubble, whoop, yell, cry, wail
Signals—clang, clatter, toot, screech, wail, squawk
Boats—whistle, toot
Bells—ring, chime, clang, clatter
Electric saws—whine

Teacher: What adjectives can we use to describe these sounds?

Children: *Low* rumbles, *loud* roar, *soothing* purr, *high* squeak, *steady* click, *loud* squawk, *steady* roll, *mournful* whistle, *impatient* chug, *fast* squeak, etc.[26]

CRITICAL AND EVALUATIVE LISTENING

In Chapter 5, the skills necessary for the reception of speech are designated as (1) word perception, (2) comprehension of ideas, and (3) using ideas to build understandings. Any listening activity that calls for listening to speech requires skill in perceiving the meanings of words, and to a certain extent, the comprehension of ideas. Even in appreciational listening the words must be heard, and enough of them understood to convey some meaning. Some factors associated with comprehension are required also, such as organizing the content heard into a pattern that gives joy or appreciation.

In addition to the approaches to the teaching of listening suggested in previous sections, particular attention must be paid to the setting of the purpose. The children should learn to think, "What is the speaker aiming to do?" They want to know what they should get from this listening and how this information will be used. Perhaps prior to the listening experience they might formulate questions that would be answered if they listened, and thus they might find it easier to focus on the purpose. The setting of standards such as the following will be useful.[27]

To Be Good Listeners

Be attentive.
Think of what the speaker is saying.
Be ready to discuss what you have heard.

[26] *A Guide for the Teaching of Language Arts: Kindergarten–Eighth Grade.* San Francisco: Elementary School Division, San Francisco Unified School District, 1955, p. 82.

[27] Adapted from: Louise Willson Worthington, "Oral Reading? Certainly!" Ginn and Company Contributions in Reading No. 16.

Using supplemental activities such as notetaking, outlining, writing summaries, and using reference sources to check on the reliability of the information heard will help pupils to organize their thinking and remember what they have heard.

In critical or evaluative types of listening, skills are needed that relate what is perceived and comprehended to previous learning, as are skills that use this understanding in making inferences and arriving at new ideas. These skills are similar to those of analytical and critical reading, and like them should be taught after the primary skills have been learned. These, however, are skills which are of basic importance. Many of us perceive and comprehend words which we have heard spoken without making use of them ourselves. It is in the process of reflection and critical examination that new ideas and understandings are built.

The skills necessary for critical listening are taught in much the same manner as are those necessary for appreciational and informational listening. The children must understand the purpose for which they are listening; they must be able to relate what is heard to previous activities and learnings through a recall of experiences, concepts, and vocabulary; and they must have guide lists at times to help them follow through on the purpose. While critical and evaluative listening can and should be taught at every opportunity in the school program, the skills necessary for effective listening of these types, as well as the more elementary types, may be developed effectively by using specific lessons designed for these purposes.[28] The following is an extract from the directions for one of these lessons.

To the pupils: If we learn in geography that India, which is less than half the size of the United States, has more than twice as many people as the United States has, we can use that fact in our thinking. If the statement we have learned is true, we can be very sure that many people in India live under rather poor conditions. We can also make sure that farms are small. Inferences are not facts that have been stated. They are ideas judged to be true because certain conditions have been stated and, from experience or past learning, we know what the results are likely to be. I am going to read a paragraph to you. When I have finished, I will suggest two inferences. I will ask you to tell me which inference is the better on the basis of information in the paragraph.

This lesson, which was taught to sixth-grade children, continued with the teacher reading a short paragraph from which inferences might be

[28] Edward Pratt and Harry A. Greene, *Training Children to Listen.* A Monograph for Elementary Teachers, No. 80. Evanston, Ill.: Row, Peterson and Company, 1955.

271

drawn. This and similar lessons on the other skills necessary for effective listening were found to be successful in developing these skills.

COURTESIES IN LISTENING

The courtesies which are important to listening are known to most teachers but they too often are not practiced by the teachers themselves or taught to the children. The teacher is a model, one who is imitated in many ways, and one of the ways is how he listens. If an oral language activity is important, if the speaker is saying something that his audience wants to hear (and this should be the case, otherwise he wouldn't be speaking), then the teacher as well as the pupils should grant the speaker the courtesy of listening attentively. The child can hardly be expected not to "doodle," try to read a book, or draw a picture, if he observes his teacher sorting materials or marking papers during a listening period.

The most important courtesy is being attentive. Attentiveness is more than merely appearing to listen; it is becoming involved in such a way with the speaker that his every phrase, inflection, and gesture is noted and reacted to. This reaction—as insignificant as it might be with respect to physical movement—is sensed by the speaker; hence no one can really appear to listen and not actually do so. Such pupil-developed standards as the following are helpful to effective listening.

1. Relax and be comfortable.
2. Try to determine the plan or organization of the talk.
   Listen for the cue words or phrases, e.g.
   a. "There are three main points . . ."
   b. "The most important problem is . . ."
3. Listen for a summary of the talk or discussion.
4. Take notes on informational material.
5. Ask speakers for more information on certain points or for clarification of a point.
6. Compare what is being heard with what is already known about the subject.[29]

Other courtesies that should be taught include disagreeing in a polite manner with the speaker and waiting for the speaker to finish before expressing the disagreement.

[29] Ursula Hogan, "An Experiment in Improving the Listening Skills of Fifth and Sixth Grades Pupils," M. A. Seminar Study, June, 1953. University of California, Berkeley.

FURTHER SUGGESTIONS FOR TEACHING LISTENING

There are many daily opportunities in the elementary classroom for teaching one or more of the listening skills. Some of these are:

1. Listening to tape recordings of reports of trips, weekend experiences, and other classroom activities for the purpose of determining which speaking skills need improving.
2. Listening to sound-motion pictures for specific purposes related to social studies or science.
3. Listening to the other voices in choral speaking in order to understand the total effect of the presentation.
4. Listening to directions for the purpose of not missing any step involved. For example: "Billy, please get the green book from the corner of my desk; put it on the reading table. Then come here for the work sheets for your group and distribute them." (Expect the directions to be followed, too!)
5. Listening to a child reading a carefully prepared selection.
6. Keeping TV and radio logs of listening habits and discussing standards of choosing programs.
7. Listening to a tape recording of a talk. Cut it off before the talk is completed and then ask the pupils to state what the speakers' conclusion will be. (Move from simple to difficult on this one.)
8. Telling chain stories.

THE TEACHER'S LISTENING

As someone has said, teachers are notoriously in love with the sound of their own voices. A teacher who is so engrossed with his own speaking, his own ideas, may be unsuccessful in teaching listening. In planning a program for developing listening skills in pupils, it would be well for a teacher honestly to respond to such questions as:

1. Is it because of *me* that children do not pay attention? Could they be shutting out my voice for some reason?
2. Am I defeating good listening by talking too much?
3. Do I realize that children have difficulty listening attentively for a long period of time and that they can be encouraged to listen by being given fresh, original motivation?
4. Do I use changes in pitch, loudness, and rate in my own speaking?
5. Do I expect children to concentrate upon too many items at one time? Perhaps they need time to think about each one.
6. Do I give children time to think when I ask questions—to find the answer to one question before another is asked?

7. Are my explanations clearly presented and correctly timed? Do I repeat an assignment the necessary number of times? Do I get the full attention of the class before giving an assignment?
8. Do I try not to repeat what each child says but rather require the group to concentrate on the speaker?
9. Am I taking too much time in explaining to one child while others lost interest?
10. Do I have a democratic type of discipline in my room, knowing that children work better when there is neither an atmosphere of chaos nor one of strict authoritarianism?
11. Am I relaxed and unhurried in my speaking and in my movements?
12. Do I try not to repeat phrases or expressions so often that they become ineffective and monotonous?
13. Do I express appreciation for what children say? Are their opinions treated with respect?
14. Do I make myself available for listening? Do children feel free to come to me with their problems and know that they will have my undivided attention?
15. Am I setting a good example by being an attentive listener? [30]

EXERCISES FOR THOUGHT AND DISCUSSION

1. Elaborate and illustrate the five principles that elementary teachers must keep in mind in developing proper oral language attitudes and skills.
2. How would your treatment of difficulties in enunciation, pronunciation, and articulation in these grades differ from what you proposed for these same problems in the primary grades?
3. Suggest steps designed to make your pupils more directly aware of the need for sensitivity to the demands of the audience situation.
4. Report on the practical value of tape recorders for the study of voice quality in your classes.
5. Develop a rough scorecard for rating the elementary school pupil on his efforts in oral expression. Stress such factors as enunciation, articulation, pronunciation, audience attitude, mannerisms, voice quality, usage, etc.
6. Evaluate the importance of correctional lessons in a program for the improvement of usage habits.
7. Draft a set of classroom standards for courtesies and skills in using the telephone.

[30] Checklist used at Scenic View School, Englewood, Colorado. Helen Chancellor, principal.

8. Discuss choral speaking as a device for bringing out the expressional skills and possibilities of the extremely shy child. What other major values does it have?

9. Build a case for heavy emphasis on interviewing and reporting in the oral program of the upper elementary grades.

10. Plan a series of exercises suitable for classroom use designed to give your pupils a wide range of experience with the common social amenities.

11. Illustrate each of the six aspects of appreciative listening presented in this chapter.

12. Summarize in concise form the essential elements of this chapter which may serve as principles of method for the teacher to follow in the development of the speaking and listening skills.

SELECTED REFERENCES

ANDERSON, VIRGIL. *Improving the Child's Speech.* New York: Oxford University Press, 1953.

ARBUTHNOT, MAY HILL. *Children and Books,* revised edition. Chicago: Scott, Foresman and Company, 1957. Chapter 10, "Verse Choirs."

BACUS, OLLIE. *Speech in Education: A Guide for the Classroom Teacher.* New York: Longmans, Green and Company, 1943.

BLANK, EARL. "The Effectiveness of Creative Dramatics in Developing Voice, Vocabulary, and Personality in the Grades." Unpublished doctor's dissertation, School of Drama, University of Denver, 1954.

BROGAN, PEGGY and FOX, LORENE. *Helping Children Learn.* Yonkers-on-Hudson: World Book Company, 1955, pp. 51–124.

Commission of the English Curriculum, National Council of Teachers of English, *Language Arts for Today's Children.* New York: Appleton-Century-Crofts, Inc., 1954. Chapters 4 and 5.

DURLAND, FRANCES C. *Creative Dramatics for Children.* Yellow Springs, Ohio: The Antioch Press, 1951.

EARLY, MARGARET J. "Communication Arts," Encyclopedia of Educational Research, Third Edition (Chester W. Harris, Ed.). New York: The Macmillan Company, 1960, pp. 306–311.

Iowa Elementary Teachers Handbook, Vol. 4. *Oral and Written Language.* Des Moines: Iowa State Department of Public Instruction, 1944.

JOHNSON, WENDELL, ed. *Speech Problems of Children.* New York: Grune and Stratton, 1950.

Language Arts in the Elementary School. Twentieth Yearbook of the National Elementary Principals Association. Washington: National Education Association, 1941.

Learning to Speak Effectively. Washington: Association for Childhood Education International, 1943.

MUNKRES, ALBERTA. *Helping Children in Oral Communication.* New York: The Bureau of Publications, Teachers College, Columbia University, 1959.

NEVILLE, MARK A. "Listening Is An Art: Practice It," *Elementary English,* April, 1959, pp. 226–233.

New Intermediate Manual. Cincinnati: Cincinnati Public Schools, 1954. Chapters V–XV.

OGILVIE, MARDEL. *Speech in the Elementary School.* New York: McGraw-Hill Book Company, Inc., 1954.

PETTY, WALTER T., "Listening: Directions for Research," *Elementary English,* 39, No. 6: October, 1962.

POOLEY, ROBERT C. *Teaching English Usage.* New York: Appleton-Century-Crofts, Inc., 1946. Chapter 9.

POPOVICH, JAMES E. "A Study of Significant Contributions to the Development of Creative Dramatics in American Education." Unpublished doctor's dissertation, School of Speech, Northwestern University, 1955.

PRATT, EDWARD, and GREENE, HARRY A. *Training Children to Listen.* A Monograph for Elementary Teachers, No. 80. Evanston: Row, Peterson and Company, 1955.

PRONOVOST, WILBERT L. *The Teaching of Speaking and Listening in the Elementary School.* New York: David McKay Company, 1959.

SAWYER, RUTH. *The Way of the Story-Teller.* New York: The Viking Press, Inc., 1942.

SIKS, GERALDINE BRAIN. *Creative Dramatics, an Art for Children.* New York: Harper and Brothers, 1958.

SMITH, DORA V. "Learning to Listen—Listening to Learn in the Elementary School." *NEA Journal,* 47:100–101; February, 1958.

Teaching Language in the Elementary School, Forty-third Yearbook of the National Society for the Study of Education, Part II. Chicago: The University of Chicago Press, 1944.

TOOZE, RUTH. *Storytelling.* Englewood Cliffs, N.J.: Prentice-Hall, Inc., 1959.

Toward Better Speech. Curriculum Bulletin, 1952–53 Series, Number 5. New York: The Board of Education of the City of New York, 1953.

VAN RIPER, CHARLES and BUTLER, KATHERINE G. *Speech in the Elementary Classroom.* New York: Harper and Brothers, 1955.

10

Developing Specific

Written Language Skills

THIS CHAPTER, THE FOURTH OF FIVE PRESENTING INSTRUCTIONAL methods and techniques, deals with the development of the special skills which contribute to effective written expression. It is also concerned with written language in specific expressional situations including the content of the expression in these situations. The following subjects and topics are emphasized in this chapter:

- a. The broad skill areas of spelling, handwriting, manuscript form, capitalization, and punctuation.
- b. Instructional techniques in written language.
- c. Importance of extensive writing experience.
- d. Specific written language situations; letter writing; outlining; reporting.
- e. Using printed sources; alphabetizing and indexing; handbooks and style manuals.
- f. Credit for material used.
- g. Self-editing and proofreading; re-writing.
- h. Rhetorical skills.

The attainment of power and beauty in language expression requires that attention be given to both the content and the form of expression. Children must learn to organize their thinking, to choose appropriate ideas and information, and to develop the content of their expression in genuinely communicative ways. They must also speak and write accurately and according to acceptable conventions of form.

METHODS OF TEACHING WRITTEN
LANGUAGE SKILLS

SPELLING

Being a good speller is not simply a matter of being able to spell many words correctly, or of making a perfect score on a spelling test. The good speller is the individual who recognizes the importance of correct spelling, who endeavors to spell correctly each word that he writes, and who is equipped to learn how to spell new words independently. He knows that correct spelling will improve the quality of his written expression. He believes that the spelling words he is called upon to learn are important words that he will need to use frequently in his written work. In other words, the good speller has toward spelling an attitude conducive to learning to spell socially useful words both through direct instruction and incidentally. Thus, while one objective of the spelling program is to teach children to spell the words in a basic writing vocabulary list, that is not the sole objective. The development of a favorable attitude toward spelling is also of great importance.

Good attitudes toward spelling may be developed with continuous attention to these suggestions.

1. The teacher himself should regard spelling as important, as something that really matters. He should endeavor to spell correctly all words that he writes; when he has doubt as to the spelling of a word, he should use a dictionary to check himself.
2. Children should be shown that the words they are learning to spell are words that they consistently use in writing and have need to spell. Simple investigations directed at their own and their parents' and friends' writing will show this.
3. Children should be required to learn to spell only those words which spelling tests and actual writing situations have shown that they are unable to spell. The studying of words that are already known is a major deterrent to the development of favorable attitudes.
4. Each child should learn to use a specific and efficient method of learning to spell a word.
5. The teacher should encourage in the class a spirit of mutual pride and co-operation in spelling achievement. Children may help one another study, proofread for spelling errors, and give encouragement to those needing it.
6. The teacher should require a high standard of neatness and accuracy in all written work. The standards should be developed cooperatively by teacher and pupils and should be consistently observed.
7. The teacher should emphasize individual and class progress in spelling improvement and make pupils aware of their progress. Records of progress may be kept by the pupils themselves and any achievement appraised in the light of earlier efforts.[1]
8. The teacher should immediately attack any negative attitudes toward spelling by encouraging and stimulating the children's efforts. Fault-finding should be eliminated in favor of determining the cause of spelling failure.

[1] See: Ernest Horn, *What Research Says to the Teacher: Teaching Spelling.* Department of Classroom Teachers and American Educational Research Association. Washington: National Education Association, 1954, pp. 19–21; and James A. Fitzgerald, *The Teaching of Spelling.* Milwaukee: The Bruce Publishing Company, 1951, chapter 3.

278

A good attitude toward spelling is basic to a successful program but merely desiring to spell correctly will accomplish little unless certain habits such as the following have been established:

1. *Being concerned about the spelling of words used in written expression.* For the child, this means teaching him to think "Is this word spelled correctly?" and "Am I sure?" This habit is established by the development and maintenance of standards in written work and by repeatedly calling attention to the standards by the teacher.

2. *Carefully proofreading all written work.* This means examining each word carefully to see if it is spelled correctly. The teacher must insist that a misspelled word is a mistake in spelling, whether the child knows better or not, and that the only way to avoid the making of such mistakes is to proofread for spelling errors.

3. *Checking the spelling of all words about which the child is in doubt.* The pupil should ask the teacher the spelling of such words, or when skill in use of the dictionary is developed, he should consult that authority.

4. *Using a specific procedure for learning the spelling of new words.* Such a procedure may vary from child to child (as is discussed later) but the steps he follows should be known by each one.

Although spelling is sometimes integrated with the language program, even to the extent of following the spelling lessons in the language textbook, it is taught in most classrooms in periods set aside for the purpose and with a spelling book which largely determines the methods used and the words taught in those periods. These words generally represent the basic writing vocabulary that children and adults need to learn to spell correctly in order to communicate effectively. Some schools, while providing for special periods for spelling, do not use a textbook or workbook but make their own spelling lists. A few schools leave spelling largely to incidental learning; that is, they do not provide periods specially devoted to spelling instruction. Horn says on this point:

Whether it is practicable to teach spelling only in connection with the other language arts is a debated question. The evidence indicates, however, that what is done with spelling in connection with other language arts needs to be supplemented by direct, systematic instruction in spelling periods, especially in the case of pupils of below average spelling ability, and for all pupils in the learning of difficult words.[2]

Two general plans of instruction in spelling have been identified and are most often followed in spelling programs. These are the *test-study*

[2] Ernest Horn, *What Research Says to the Teacher: Teaching Spelling*, p. 15.

and the *study-test* plans. Evidence resulting from the comparison of the two plans clearly favors the test-study plan as the most efficient and satisfactory approach to achieving the objectives of the spelling program.[3] Teaching spelling by this plan means that the teacher tests the pupils first and thus determines the words that each pupil does not know how to spell. Thus interest in spelling is not lost by those pupils who know how to spell all or many of the words in the spelling lesson. The test-study plan of spelling instruction consists of these features:

1. A preliminary term or monthly test is given to determine the general level of spelling achievement of the class and of the individuals within the class.
2. A test on each weekly (or other instructional period) assignment is given before instruction is begun on that assignment. This test is preceded by the teacher's pronouncing the words as the pupils look carefully at each one and then pronounce it themselves. Words which have special writing difficulties should be written on the board by the teacher as he pronounces them. Any word which, in the teacher's judgment, may not be understood by the pupils should be explained, discussed, and used in a sentence.
3. The words that each pupil misspells on this pretest are identified by the child and become his study list for the lesson.
4. In learning to spell each word, each child uses the steps that have been worked out by the class, or by the teacher and himself if modifications have been necessary to fit his particular needs.
5. A final weekly or lesson test is used to determine for each child the degree of mastery of the spelling lesson.
6. Each child keeps his own record of spelling achievement on a chart or similar device.
7. Any words that the child misspells on the final test are recorded by him in a special review word list.
8. Each child studies the words in his review list in the same manner as he studied them in their original presentation.
9. At regular intervals testing of the review words for each child is done until all such words are mastered.
10. A final term or monthly test is given to measure the progress made since the administration of the first test.

The study-test plan is organized in a similar manner. A major exception is that the pretest called for is eliminated and the pupils begin the study of the words as the first step in the weekly lesson. This means that all the words in the lesson become the study list for each pupil whether he needs to study them or not.

Modern spelling books incorporate the findings of research in list-

[3] James A. Fitzgerald, *The Teaching of Spelling.* Milwaukee: The Bruce Publishing Company, 1951, p. 41.

ing the steps in learning to spell a word. The steps involve visual, auditory, and kinesthetic imagery as well as an emphasis on recall, and are, in general, the same in each recently published book. Most of the children will need to follow all the steps, although many of the best spellers will learn the word primarily by visual imagery, and thus quite rapidly. The poorer spellers will probably need special help and encouragement with the various steps. They should be particularly encouraged in the use of the steps which involve recall, since the ability to recall the correct spelling is the ability that is needed in actual writing.

In spite of the fact that most spelling books list the steps in learning to spell a word, and suggest that pupils refer to these steps often, the best procedure is for the teacher and the class to memorize the steps and use them without reference to the book. Teachers can guide children into thinking about how a word should be studied and from this guidance and the resulting discussion the children can themselves state the necessary steps. The statement of the children can then be written on a chart and hung in a place in the room where it can be readily referred to. Through their experience in studying words, the children may want to modify or revise their statement from time to time. This should be encouraged if any of the steps generally suggested have been omitted in the children's statement or if local conditions or individual problems seem to warrant some change. Each child should be encouraged to determine for himself whether the steps listed by the class are those he should follow or if some modification would be an aid to him.

The following method of studying the spelling of a word is suggested as a guide for the teacher in the development of the statement of the steps by the class.

1. Look at the word carefully and pronounce it correctly. If you are not sure of the pronunciation, look it up in the dictionary or ask someone who is sure to know. Say the word slowly and clearly, looking at the word while it is being said. Stress each syllable of the word in sequence.
2. Cover the word or close your eyes, pronounce it, and think how it looks. Try to visualize just the way the word is written as you repeat each letter in sequence to yourself. Be particularly sure you know how the middle of the word looks.
3. Look at the word again to be sure that you said it correctly and visualized each part. If you did not, start over at 1.
4. Cover the word and then write it, thinking carefully how the word looks. Check the accuracy of your spelling. If you misspelled the word begin again at 1.
5. Repeat this two or more times without looking either at the book or at your previous attempts.
6. Write a sentence using the word.

281

Many spelling textbooks or workbooks present the weekly list of words in context; that is, the words are introduced by their inclusion in a story or paragraph. This procedure, within limits, has value in making sure that pupils know the meanings of words to be learned. However, research has shown that the most efficient and economical method of presenting spelling words is through a list. This does not imply that meaning is of no concern; but it is well to remember that if the words are carefully selected, they will be words which are known to children or words whose meanings are readily learned since the words will be used in the child's writing. Too much attention to a contextual presentation may simply be a waste of the pupil's time.

On the matter of time, principles of learning and research in spelling indicate that not more than 75 minutes per week should be devoted to the spelling period. With a favorable attitude on the part of the teacher and pupils a spirited attack upon the learning of the words is most successful and prevents dawdling.

Attention should be given in the spelling instruction to the correction of the tests. Most modern spelling books call for the giving of two or more tests each week. These tests should be regarded as learning exercises as well as measures of spelling achievement. Horn states that "when corrected by the pupils and the result properly utilized, the test is the most fruitful single learning activity per unit of time that has yet been devised." [4] To utilize properly the testing procedure, the teacher should show children how testing identifies the words they need to learn to spell, how it is a learning exercise that calls their attention to how a word is spelled and calls for the necessary recall that is spelling. Pupils should correct their own tests and record their own scores with only occasional rechecking by the teacher to see that the pupils' checking has been carefully done.

Some spelling textbooks or wordbooks call for the learning of more spelling rules than do others. The number of rules that can be used effectively by the pupils is limited and of questionable value. In the primary grades it is better to teach each word as an individual problem and not attempt to show relationships of sound and sight as a part of the spelling program. Brighter children, at all grade levels, make generalizations themselves but the slow learning child does not easily do this. It is simply much easier to teach separately the spelling of each word than to try to teach enough examples of the application of a rule to give it meaning. There is no value in teaching a rule unless it is helpful to pupils in learn-

[4] Ernest Horn, *Teaching Spelling*, pp. 17–18.

ing to spell the words they need to write in the most economic and efficient manner.

Research has shown that the following rules have few exceptions in application and are, therefore, of practical value.

1. Words ending in silent *e* usually drop the final *e* before the addition of suffixes beginning with a vowel, but they keep the final *e* before the addition of suffixes beginning with a consonant.
2. When a word ends in a consonant and *y*, change the *y* to *i* before adding all suffixes except those beginning with *i*. Do not change *y* to *i* in adding suffixes to words ending in a vowel and *y*, or when adding a suffix beginning with *i*.
3. Words of one syllable or words of more than one syllable accented on the last, ending in a single consonant preceded by a single vowel, double the final consonant when adding a suffix beginning with a vowel.
4. The letter *q* is always followed by *u* in common English words.
5. English words do not end with *v*.
6. Proper nouns and most adjectives formed from proper nouns should always begin with capital letters.[5]

In teaching these rules the following procedures should be utilized:

1. Each rule should be taught inductively; that is, the teacher must develop it in connection with the study of the word it covers.
2. Only one rule should be taught at a time.
3. Both the positive and negative aspects of the rule should be taught.
4. Each rule must be systematically reviewed and applied.
5. Emphasis should be upon the use of the rule rather than the formal memorizing of its verbal statement.

Related to the problem of teaching spelling rules is the issue of the relationship of phonetic knowledge and spelling ability. Attempts have been made to assign "regular" spellings to some sounds. This has been shown to be naïve and unfruitful even though it is recognized that the child who has a good phonetic knowledge is apt to be a good speller. Of course, he is likely to be a good reader and ability in reading is highly correlated with ability in spelling. The teacher should give considerable emphasis to phonetics in his reading program but should approach the teaching of direct sound-letter relationships with caution. A number of investigations have shown that children may very well give a "correct" letter representation to a sound based upon the way that sound is spelled

[5] Ernest Horn, "Spelling," *Encyclopedia of Educational Research*. Revised edition. New York: The Macmillan Company, 1950. The rule relative to English words not ending in *v* is in the latest edition of this encyclopedia (1960) but was not in the 1950 edition.

in some other word and yet not spell the word correctly.[6] Proper procedure for making use of phonetic relationships is to pronounce the word correctly, noting how (in that word) each sound is spelled. This practice will gradually increase the pupil's knowledge of sound-to-letter relationships, but will also show him the unreliability of two much dependence upon phonetic generalizations.

In addition to the cautions suggested above relative to spelling rules and phonetic generalizations, observations of the authors and others lead to the following suggestions concerning practices in spelling instruction that should be avoided.[7]

1. The teacher should probably not waste time calling attention to known hard spots in words. While known hard spots for many words have been determined, a more positive approach is needed. Attention should be focused upon looking carefully at the word as it is pronounced rather than upon watching for a particular place of possible error.
2. The practice of writing words in the air is of doubtful value. This practice takes time and does not give the child a realistic image of the word. Supposedly this practice is to give a kinaesthetic impression of the word, but the result is questionable, since the arm and hand movements are generally not the same as in writing a word. A kinaesthetic impression may be useful to a few very poor spellers, but such impression could better be gained through finger-tip impression in sand or on the chalkboard.
3. Children should not be required to make repeated writings of words without intervening attempts at recall. The practice of having a child copy a word five times, or ten times, encourages poor habits and attitudes.
4. The teacher should avoid condemning children for asking how to spell a word. Of course, this does not mean fostering the habit of some children who always ask, particularly for the spelling of words that have been in their spelling lessons. However, asking how to spell a word is an expression of concern with spelling correctly and should lead to using the dictionary and other sources for checking spelling.
5. When a word is spelled by the teacher for a child, this spelling should be given in written form on a slip of paper or on the chalkboard—rather than orally. The effort of the teacher should always be to get the child to look at the word and thus gain a visual impression.
6. The teacher should not use the studying or writing of spelling words as a form of punishment. This practice will certainly not aid the spelling program, and it is even highly doubtful if it serves as a very meaningful punishment.

[6] See, for example, Walter T. Petty, "An Analysis of Certain Phonetic Elements in a List of Words of Persistent Spelling Difficulty," unpublished doctoral dissertation, State University of Iowa, 1955.

[7] Adapted from Walter T. Petty, *Improving Your Spelling Program*. San Francisco: Chandler Press, 1959, pp. 24–25.

Any successful spelling program must give attention to the individual needs of pupils, since the range in spelling achievement in any grade is as wide as the range of individual differences in any other school subject. This is not as difficult a problem as it may appear at first glance. Pupils should study only those words they cannot spell. Thus if a child spells all the words correctly on the first test, he doesn't need to study spelling that lesson. Whether his correct spelling of the words happened by chance or not will be established by the review test. For the child who has high spelling achievement on initial tests, one course of study suggests the use of activities such as the following to supplement the program:

1. Selecting synonyms and antonyms from words in a list
2. Using words in sentences to show varied meaning
3. Learning plurals, particularly of troublesome words as they are encountered
4. Finding root words in large words
5. Adding prefixes and suffixes to root words and noticing their effect on meaning
6. Studying history of interesting words and reporting in class
7. Using words in some form of creative writing
8. Making titles or slogans for the bulletin board
9. Doing purposeful dictionary exercises
10. Making individual spelling graphs
11. Making word charts: synonyms, antonyms, homonyms, contractions, abbreviations
12. Forming derivations from weekly list
13. Listing words in early lessons for practice in alphabetizing
14. Learning words from local unit list
15. Studying library card catalog and telephone books to discover importance of correct spelling
16. Proofreading compositions to find spelling errors
17. Building compound words
18. Collecting samples of homonyms and interesting word usage from other sources in the school, such as library books, readers, newspapers
19. Adding to individual dictionary words which are of special interest.[8]

With a carefully planned spelling program, and an enthusiastic teacher, there need be very few poor spellers in any classroom. For the child who has difficulty with spelling these suggestions should be followed: [9]

[8] *A Guide to the Teaching of Spelling Grades Two to Six.* Long Beach, Calif.: Long Beach Public Schools, 1951, p. 8. See also Walter T. Petty and Gus P. Plessas, "Challenging Superior Spellers," in *The Elementary School Journal*, 58:154–157; December, 1958.

[9] See also Gus P. Plessas and Walter T. Petty, "The Spelling Plight of the Poor Reader," *Elementary English*, 39:463–465; May, 1962.

1. Emphasize the importance of the words to be learned. Teach only a minimum list and make certain that the words taught are important. (See the section on spelling in Chapter 5.)
2. Teach no more words than the pupil can successfully learn to spell. Success is of major importance and the poor speller has probably had much experience with failure in learning to spell the words in the weekly lessons. Difficulty in spelling a word is not necessarily determined by its length or by the frequency or infrequency of its use. For assistance in determining the difficulty children have with common words, and in selecting those with which they may have success, the teacher should turn to a source such as *The New Iowa Spelling Scale* [10] in which the results of hundreds of actual spelling attempts by children are reported.
3. Give more than the usual amount of time to oral discussion of the words to be learned.
4. Note any bad habits of study the pupil may reveal. He must be shown that the bad habit is harmful and may be preventing him from achieving success in spelling.
5. Check and perhaps modify his method of individual study.
6. Provide many varied writing activities which call for using the words he has learned to spell.

HANDWRITING

As with the teaching of spelling, the teaching of handwriting is most effective when both the teacher and the pupils regard the skill as important and desirable to learn. The teacher shows this attitude by using care in his own handwriting. He must make certain that it is legible and represents an acceptable model, since some children will inevitably imitate the way he writes. Children will learn that handwriting is important if they recognize that when theirs is illegible, what they have written cannot be read, and therefore their attempt at communication has failed. In addition to a favorable attitude, favorable conditions for learning are important.[11] Children learn to write best when:

They write something that is meaningful to them and have definite ideas that they want to convey;
They are permitted considerable liberty in making handwriting adjustments;
They advance to each new step in the writing process without too great an expenditure of time and effort as they show readiness to succeed in it;
They have a strong personal incentive to improve their writing;
They are physically comfortable, emotionally secure, and have proper materials with which to work;
They have thorough teaching as it is needed and ample opportunity to practice under continuous supervision;

[10] Harry A. Greene, *The New Iowa Spelling Scale*. Iowa City: The Bureau of Educational Research and Service, State University of Iowa, 1955.
[11] See Petty, *op. cit.*, p. 18, for suggestions.

286

They progress at their own rate of speed, and instructional procedures are individualized;

They are encouraged to evaluate their own progress in terms of their previous achievements and present needs.[12]

Most schools teach handwriting in a special period, although properly, as with all the other language arts, attention is given to it throughout the school day. Some schools have no special period assigned to handwriting but give attention to individual problems as the need arises. Each child must be given opportunity and encouragement to develop his individual style, to detect his own illegibilities and poor writing habits, to practice systematically and efficiently those aspects of writing in which he shows his greatest need. He must learn how letters are formed and how they are connected into words, and he must be able to refer to suitable handwriting models in his practicing. In most schools this teaching is done through the use of a handwriting workbook. The handwriting workbook should be used by the pupil as a reference source giving information about how to make letters, how to join them, how to hold the hand, and the like. The teacher's manual, which usually accompanies the workbook, should be used by the teacher as an aid in securing teaching suggestions to help each child.[13]

The handwriting period should be spent mainly in practice upon the specific problems of the different children. One teacher built her year's handwriting program upon "a tripod of (1) diagnostic procedures, (2) remedial work, and (3) motivation." [14] Her first step was to evaluate the children's writing using standardized rate and quality scales. From this evaluation and the use of a chart for diagnosing handwriting faults, problems of slant, uniformity of alignment, letter formation, and spacing were identified for each child. The next step was to attempt to determine the causes of the handwriting faults. Such items as poor posture, improper paper position, inadequate lighting, and other factors were established as some reasons for the handwriting defects. Other defects were determined to be the result of psychological causes, including lack of interest, desire for affectation, and lack of confidence. The greatest number of causes as determined by this teacher, however,

[12] *Practices and Problems in Handwriting,* Educational Research Bulletin of the Bureau of Reference, Research and Statistics, Number 9. New York: Board of Education of the City of New York, September 1947, p. 22.

[13] Commercial materials for use by both teacher and pupil vary rather widely in suggestions to teachers and pupils, including form of letters. See Virgil E. Herrick, "Comparison of Practices in Handwriting Advocated by Nineteen Commercial Systems of Handwriting Instruction." Madison: University of Wisconsin, 1960.

[14] Sister M. Laurentia, "Teaching Penmanship in the Fourth Grade," *Catholic School Journal,* 59:27–29; March, 1959.

were related to improper and inadequate teaching. The remedial work she attempted consisted of frequent comparison of pupil writing rates and quality with the scale norms for the grade; the writing of timed sentences; close attention to posture, manner of holding the pen, pressure on the paper, position of the paper, and to regular inspection of written products for evenness of spacing, slant, and size of letters. The greatest amount of teaching was devoted to showing children how to make letters that have to be closed, that are half-space size, that require over- and under-curves, and that have to begin and end in certain positions in order to connect properly with adjoining letters.

As the teacher in the program described above discovered, the most important element in the instructional program is motivation. The motivational approaches she used included:

1. Emphasizing the value of legible and rapid writing.
2. Using handwriting functionally through a school program calling for much writing for genuinely communicative reasons.
3. Periodic comparison of handwriting products with handwriting scales.
4. Keeping charts and graphs showing individual and class progress.

Some persons might regard the foregoing program as one of too much rigidity. However, evidence from research favors individualized analysis and remediation.[15] The degree of competition implied might be questioned, also. Again, as Freeman points out, competition in itself is neither bad nor good—used in moderation it has a place in motivation.[16] Chief attention can be the competition the child may have within himself in striving to write well because the skill is useful.

General suggestions for teaching handwriting have been well summarized as follows in one teaching guide:

Writing should be viewed as being a means of expression and not an end in itself.

The best available conditions as to seating, lighting, posture, hand position, and position of paper should prevail.

In general, writing periods should be scheduled to follow periods of quiet activity rather than periods of strenuous movement.

Short writing practice periods should be provided often to fix letter forms and to make writing automatic.

[15] See for example: Leslie L. Bradley, "A Diagnostic and Remedial Study of Handwriting Difficulties," master's thesis, University of Chicago, 1933; and Dorothy Leggitt, "Perceptual Learning in Penmanship." *Elementary School Journal,* 40:764–770; May, 1940.
[16] Frank N. Freeman, "Teaching Handwriting," *NEA Journal,* 43:482; November, 1954.

In addition to textbook materials, practice should grow out of the needs of the pupils in practical writing situations. However, these practical writing situations should come under the teacher's guidance.

A chart showing progressive levels of achievement will help a pupil evaluate his performance.

Samples of children's writing should be collected at intervals for analysis of difficulties by the principal as well as the teacher.

The opaque projector is a useful aid in helping the class to analyze errors by projecting samples of work on the screen and having the writer and others point out good as well as poor writing characteristics.

The teacher should strive to write well on the chalkboard, on charts, or on paper, in both manuscript and cursive forms.

Constant attention by the teacher is required to establish good habits.

A checklist of letters on which individuals need special help has been used effectively by some teachers.

Too much stress on details—such as, the tail of the "q" is too long, or the "o" is not round enough, or the "t" is too tall—tends to make handwriting less interesting to your pupils. Rather than stress these difficulties, ask the child to refer to the wall charts to make his own comparison.

Handwriting should have speed enough to enable children to express themselves as they think.

Display each child's handwriting on the bulletin board sometime during each semester.

A child will try harder if he knows you will mark his paper and return it to him. In marking the papers, however, be sure he understands what the markings mean. Guide the student in:

1. Correct spacing between letter and words.
2. Uniform slant and correctly formed letters.
3. Improper position of the body for writing the page.
4. Careful joining together of letters in the formation of words.
5. Increased ability to use movement in all writing.[17]

Modern practice does not hold to one particular form of handwriting but insists rather that each child be allowed to develop some individuality in style. Thus, little stress should be placed upon having each child make letters by a particular pattern. However, studies of handwriting quality point out that poor handwriting is the result of lack of attention to certain factors of uniformity which make for legibility. The most commonly cited factors causing poor handwriting are:

1. Improper position of the hand in writing.
2. Improper position of the paper.
3. Improper position of the body for writing.
4. Poor letter formation, such as poor habituation in letter form, wavering or angular letters, and lack of distinct strokes.

[17] *Handwriting*, A Guide for Elementary Teachers. Downers Grove, Ill. Downers Grove Public Schools, April 1956, pp. 2–4.

5. Poor control of the arm, hand, and finger muscles.
6. Poor alignment and spacing, including inconsistent slant, cramped or scrawled writing, and lack of uniformity of lines.[18]

Myers in a comprehensive survey of research and practice in handwriting says: "Probably the most scientific studies on position as applied to handwriting have been made by Freeman." She then cites Freeman's findings: [19]

1. Statistical investigation indicates:
    a. The writer should face the desk squarely—side position causes spinal curvature.
    b. Both forearms should rest on the desk for approximately three quarters of their length—if one elbow is unsupported, spinal curvature is produced.
    c. The paper should be directly in front of the writer—paper on one side of the middle line requires different adjustment of the two eyes, causing eye strain, twisting of the head and body, which produces curvature.
    d. Paper tilted so the lower edge makes about a 30 degree angle with the edge of the desk.
2. Statistical and experimental evidence indicates:
    a. The forearm should form a right angle with the base line of the letters—this position is more common among good writers than poor writers.
    b. The hand should be held with the palm down—good writers do not incline the hand with more than a 45-degree slope to the wrist. Poor writers tend to rest the hand on its side. (Flat wrist produces strain.)
    c. The hand should rest on the third and fourth fingers.
    d. Forefinger should rest lower down on the pen or pencil than the thumb.
    e. Penholder should be grasped loosely, with the fingers moderately curved.
    f. The writing movement should be a combination of arm and fingers, the arm for the forward progress, the fingers for the individual letters.
    g. The writing movement, particularly in the early stages should be divided into a series of units of movement, separated by very slight pauses. It is not continuous and uniform in speed.
3. Experimental and observational evidence indicates:
    a. Downward strokes should be toward the body or nearly perpendicular to the edge of the desk. The slope produced will thereby correspond to the angle of the tilt of the paper—forward for right-handers, back slant for left-handers.

Legible letter formation is developed through practice in the making and connecting of the letters, comparison of the results of this practice with acceptable models, and the establishment of rhythm in writing. Rhythm is also related to speed of writing, and both are highly correlated

[18] Virgil E. Herrick and Leland B. Jacobs, *Children and the Language Arts.* Englewood Cliffs, N.J.: Prentice-Hall, Inc., 1955, p. 275.
[19] Emma Myers, "A General Review of Handwriting Instruction." Unpublished master's thesis, State University of Iowa, 1954.

290

with age. The question of rhythm in writing has been of concern for some time but in most schools the use of rhythmical exercises set to music or counting has been discontinued. Hildreth says: "The employment of rhythmical aids is increasingly discounted. The length of time taken to write different letters of the alphabet in any form varies with letters. The use of a uniform rhythmical count for all children fails to recognize the individual needs of children." [20]

However, Myers, commenting on this statement, says "the point and purpose of counting [may] have been lost to many teachers of handwriting. It seems quite clear that guidance in finding the rhythmical movement for each letter is needed. Once the timing of the different parts of a letter is worked out, some counting to regulate the repetition of the rhythm of the letter can be used to encourage speed or rate of writing." [21]

Too much stress cannot be placed upon the teacher's ability to diagnose handwriting difficulties and to develop this ability in the pupils of his class. Before improvement can be expected in the handwriting period, the pupil must be concerned about his handwriting and be able to determine how he needs to improve.[22] Further, it is important to remember that most handwriting problems are mental and require patience, continued effort, frequent successes, and encouragement for the relaxation and assurance necessary for actual improvement. Constructive criticisms and quick commendation of improvments made are inspiring to pupils and help them overcome their writing difficulties.

MANUSCRIPT FORM

A neat and attractive paper, whether it is a letter, a report, an announcement, a story, or a theme, is an implied courtesy to the reader and helps to increase the effectiveness of the expression. Modern schools are very properly interested in developing the individuality of a child. However, some teachers and supervisors mistakenly consider that giving the child detailed instruction on what constitutes a neat and acceptable paper inhibits his individuality and personality development. Actually this is not the case. Children apparently have no such feeling that their per-

[20] Gertrude Hildreth, *Learning the Three R's*. Minneapolis: Educational Publishers, Inc., 1947, p. 604.

[21] Emma Myers, *op. cit.*

[22] Theodore L. Harris and Virgil E. Herrick, *Children's Perception of the Handwriting Task*. Madison: University of Wisconsin, Department of Education, February, 1959. (Mimeo.)

sonalities are being stifled. They need to be taught certain routine matters such as form in writing, and they appreciate understanding what is expected of them. In later school work and in adult writing activities, they will appreciate having been obliged to learn how to prepare neat and attractive papers.

A search of current courses of study and curriculum guides reveals extensive evidence of this apparent indifference to form and appearance in written expression. Many of these sources make no mention of the physical appearance of the written expression. One exception to this is a source that prescribes the following form:

Title
(Omit one line after title)

· Indentation _____

  · _____

  · _____

· New paragraph _____
Keep all paragraph indentations equal.
Childs' name and other information may be given either at the top or the
  bottom of the page.[23]

Another source suggests that the training in format be such that the child, with continued teacher guidance,

maintains margins and indentations
uses prescribed heading according to school policy
writes with an awareness of standards for neatness
writes titles correctly
writes correctly heading, salutation, and closing of friendly letter
addresses envelopes
uses correct form in writing poetry [24]

Guides of an earlier period reflect more attention to form and appearance of written expression, possibly showing more standardization of procedure, or perhaps showing a more critical analysis and a better understanding of what is actually helpful to teachers.

1. Leave at least a one-half inch margin at the left and at the right of all
   written work.

[23] From *Child Growth Through Language Experience,* The Language Arts Committee, Tracy Rose, general chairman, South Bend, Indiana: The South Bend Board of Education, September, 1952, p. 147.
[24] *Language Arts,* Course of study, Grades 1–6. Curriculum Bulletin, Number 4, 1954–55 Series. New York: Board of Education of the City of New York, 1955. p. 52.

2. Leave a space of at least one inch at the top of a beginning sheet. Leave a space of at least one-half inch at the top of all other sheets.
3. Do not write on the last line of a ruled sheet, and on an unruled sheet leave at least one-half an inch at the bottom of the page.
4. Write on one side of the paper only in all written work which is to be used as a final copy to be handed in or preserved.
5. Indent each paragraph at least three spaces beyond the left margin.
6. If a paragraph is numbered, the number should be indented.
7. No lines should be left unfilled at the right except at the end of a paragraph or in outline form.
8. Do not crowd writing at the end of a line.
9. Do not draw a line for the margin.
10. Put no periods after titles.
11. Do not underline or capitalize for emphasis words in the body of the material.
12. Abbreviations within a sentence should be avoided.
13. When it is necessary to begin a sentence with a number, use a word and not a figure.
14. All written work to be read by others should be spelled correctly and written legibly and neatly.
15. No paper containing blots, untidy erasures, or unevenly torn edges should ever be handed in.
16. No written work should be posted which contains misspellings or other types of errors.[25]

The importance of neat and attractive papers is recognized by most teachers and supervisors. As is the case with many other similar technical matters, there is disagreement even among the so-called experts as to the most desirable practices or the ways to develop them. Different types of manuscript forms contain many acceptable elements. The important factor here is to avoid confusing the child by introducing contradictory practices as he moves from teacher to teacher. In teaching children to make their written work attractive and neat, it is suggested that at least these points be observed:

1. Teachers and supervisors within a school system should formulate statements [26] of agreement on certain matters of manuscript form and appearance, such as:
   a. position of name and date on the paper
   b. placement of the title of a report or other written material
   c. preferred size and type of paper to be used

[25] Maude McBroom, *The Course of Study in Written Composition for the Elementary Grades,* Monographs in Education, First Series, No. 10. Iowa City: State University of Iowa, December 1, 1928, pp. 100–101.
[26] Note: These statements should avoid conflict with matters of manuscript form suggested in the language textbooks in use.

    d. use of one or both sides of the paper
    e. extent of top, bottom, and side margins
2. Within the limits of the above school-wide agreements, the teachers and pupils should include matters of manuscript appearance in the statements of standards they establish for their own written work.
3. Following the establishment of the standards of manuscript form and appearance, the children should be expected to observe them in all their written work. This practice is likely to have a more positive effect on the favorable development of the child's personality than the anything-goes policy proposed by some teachers.

CAPITALIZATION AND PUNCTUATION

Instruction in the mechanics of capitalization and punctuation is most effectively given as the need arises. In the kindergarten and first grade, a child needs to know about capitalizing his name when he first writes it. He needs to know that the names of the months and the days of the week are capitalized when he first makes a weather calendar. Children discover their needs through actual activities. Thus, the need for the various capitalization and punctuation skills are brought to the children's attention through their writing activities. With the help of the teacher, they will notice, as they read what they have written, that difficulties in understanding arise without the help of the capitalization of some words and the use of some punctuation marks. One course of study effectively expresses the functions of punctuation in this way:

> Children soon learn that punctuation marks act as traffic signals to help them on their way. The best learning for the use of these comes from having the child read his own work and find the places where they are needed for clarity. Periods, commas, question marks can be introduced when the need to use them arises. When added practice is needed, make that practice meaningful to the children.[27]

From the initial discovery of need by the children the next step is the presentation of a model. That is, if a report has been written and contains many errors in punctuation and capitalization, the teacher should rewrite the material on the board or chart using correct punctuation and capitalization. This procedure emphasizes the need for the teacher himself to be careful in his own use of the punctuation and capitalization skills.

Special emphasis has been directed in this volume to the importance of developing fewer skills and of teaching more efficiently those that are

[27] *Using Language.* Wilmington, Del.: The Division of Elementary Education, Wilmington Public Schools, 1955, p. 121.

presented. Studies, such as the one by Evans, show that children tend to have many of the same needs for using specific punctuation items at every grade level and that their ability to meet these needs shows little improvement as the grade level advances.[28] This apparently means: (1) that children have not discovered the importance of these items; (2) that the items have not been adequately introduced; (3) that there have not been enough review and drill upon the items to establish their use; or (4) that not enough attention has been given to their use in genuine writing situations.

An interesting presentation of appropriate and inappropriate capitalization is this example at the third-grade level.

The children were keeping a diary on "Signs of Spring." At the top of each page (18 x 24 brown paper) was placed a picture and below it a title—"Robin Redbreast Returns," for example. Care was taken to show that in a title every important word began with a capital letter. After the children had chosen titles for their other pages, and written them on the back, the teacher said, "Did you begin every word in your title with a capital letter? Look and see!" Within the same project, the word April was repeated and the children reminded, "Names of months, also, begin with a capital letter."

One day one of the children drew the attention of the class to these two entries in the class diary:

April 15—	Today I saw a robin. It was sitting in the treetop and singing a song to me. (Barbara)
April 17—	I saw my friend Robin Redbreast. He flew to a tree. And then he flew away. (Rachel)
Tom:	How does it happen that sometimes robin is written with a small *r* and sometimes with a capital?
Teacher:	You are a boy, aren't you? If I write boy on the board, I write it with a small b. If you write boy in your stories, you write it with a small b. However, if I talk about a certain boy—Tom, for example—I write it with a capital letter. Or, if I were talking about any robin, as Barbara was, I'd use a small letter. If I were talking about one particular robin that comes regularly to a tree in my yard, which I regard as a friend and to which I have given a name, as Rachel did, I'd use a capital letter.[29]

The use, lack of use, or misuse of items of punctuation and capitalization is, or develops into, a habit with children. Since they do not or-

[28] J. W. Evans, "The Social Importance and the Pupil Control of Certain Punctuation Variants." Unpublished doctoral dissertation. State University of Iowa, 1939.
[29] *Communication, A Guide to the Teaching of Speaking and Writing.* Minneapolis: Minneapolis Public Schools, 1953, p. 38.

dinarily know how to write before coming to school, the school must take the responsibility for the establishment of the undesirable habits in the use of the mechanics of writing. Teachers should understand and practice the formula for habit formation, which is: (1) motivate, (2) make a clear impression and (3) repeat with no intervening exceptions. Emphasizing fewer items and creating realistic situations demanding their use will greatly aid motivation. A clear impression of what is correct is made by using a model, by discussing the problem, by showing by example the correct and incorrect, and by drilling upon the technicality. After the correct use of an item is established, it should be insisted upon.

The two examples which follow indicate appropriate drill or practice exercises for establishment of desirable habits of punctuation and capitalization.

Write each sentence and use capital letters wherever they are needed:
1. last christmas i visited a circus in florida.
2. it was uncle john who took me.
3. our circus will be at glenwood park.
4. will mrs. jones take us on monday? [30]

A. Write the following sentences, using commas where they are needed:
1. Alice are you coming?
2. Where did you get the stamps Bob?
3. Come here Helen and show me your ring.
4. I think Mother that I may be late.
5. Dick please hand me my glove.

B. Now write three sentences that you might use if you were talking to the following people and addressed them by name:
1. Miss Dale   2. Mother   3. Neil [31]

The following suggestions for developing capitalization and punctuation skills should prove useful to the teacher:

1. Observe all written work carefully, noting errors made, and perhaps tabulating the types of errors. This observation should be used as the basis for further teaching and review.
2. Use many proofreading drills which emphasize the types of situations that seem difficult for the pupil to handle.
3. Insist that pupils critically edit and proofread whatever they write.
4. Use dictation drills calling for the using of certain skills or for the avoidance of excessive punctuation and capitalization.
5. Give children work exercises which require them to verify their use of

[30] Mildred A. Dawson, and others, *Language for Daily Use. Grade four.* 4th ed. Yonkers-on-Hudson: World Book Company, 1959, p. 264.
[31] Harry A. Greene, and others, *Building Better English.* Grade Six. Evanston, Ill.: Row, Peterson and Company, 1947, p. 121.

capitals or certain punctuation items. The purpose of such exercises is to acquaint the pupils with irregularities in practices and with sources commonly used as standards.

6. Compile for each child (or mark and have him compile) a list of words which he frequently fails to capitalize, or which he frequently over-capitalizes. Give him exercises emphasizing these situations and acquaint him with the rules covering such situations.

7. Have each pupil edit his own or others' papers with special reference to capitalization. Sometimes this can be done individually; at other times the child should work in a group.

8. Emphasize the importance of careful use of capitals and punctuation in all the pupils' work. Stress continually the importance of good form in writing.

9. Have pupils check their own writing after a dictation exercise. Emphasize self-diagnosis of difficulties.

10. Stress the relation of sentence structure to punctuation, and both to clarity and smoothness of expression.

11. Give special attention to handwriting if that is the cause of some capitalization faults.

12. Give frequent short diagnostic tests on the major capitalization and punctuation items. Have the pupils check their own work.

13. Make all drill and practice periods short and related to specific needs. For example, use a five-minute individualized drill period near the close of the day on errors observed during the day.

USAGE

Written language, because it is recorded and can be re-examined, tends to be more formal than oral language. Improvement in usage in written expression depends to a large degree upon improvement in these matters in oral expression. However, many teachers assume the same sort of transfer from written to oral expression; they mistakenly spend much time in written drill on usages and expect improvement in oral usage habits. The fallacy here lies in the fact that so much more time is spent in speaking than in writing, and since the speaking activities are more likely to have a genuineness that the written drill exercises frequently do not have, oral habits receive far more effective practice.

The problems of developing skill in the usages common to both oral and written expression are discussed in detail in Chapter 11. It must be pointed out, however, that there is a real need for specific instructional attention to be given to the correction of usage errors in written expression. The best attack on a learning problem is one that is direct and specific. Thus, if errors are made in written expression, these errors must be attacked directly where they are found. Part of this emphasis, at least, must be through written activities and written practice exercises. Brueckner and Bond point out, as have others, that there are two methods of attack on language errors that are known to be successful.[32]

. . . One is to give the learner oral practice in using correct forms of expression so that they will come to sound right to him. When this occurs, he will use them habitually in oral and written expression. Having children fill in blanks in written exercises ignores the use of sound, which is the most potent factor in improving usage. Hearing the right form frequently at school is the most effective antidote for hearing the wrong form frequently at home and on the playground. Another method involves placing right and wrong forms before the learner in such a way that he is required to make a conscious choice of the right form by referring to some guiding principle or example which he should be led to discover.

This section deals directly with the organization of the language program for the most effective teaching of written expression and suggests procedures to facilitate this teaching.

INSTRUCTIONAL TECHNIQUES IN WRITTEN LANGUAGE

EXPRESSIONAL LESSONS

As was suggested in the discussion of the development of oral language skills on pages 240 to 244 in Chapter 9, two types of lessons are required to bring about adequate mastery of the skills of written expression. The first of these, the so-called expressional lesson, deals primarily with the creation of lifelike activity situations in which the content and motivation for extensive written expression will arise.

Learn to write by writing. Too often teachers assume that children's writing will improve through a discussion of the need for improvement and a concentrated program of carefully selected drill exercises. Nothing could be further from the truth. While corrective exercises are of value if their need is understood by children, it is contrary to good psychological practice to expect real improvement except through a program that calls for much natural and meaningful writing experience. If a child has a real purpose for writing, he will write, and ultimately he will be anxious to make this writing as effective as possible.

[32] Leo J. Brueckner and Guy L. Bond, *The Diagnosis and Treatment of Learning Difficulties.* New York: Appleton-Century-Crofts, Inc., 1955, p. 342.

Throughout this book emphasis has been placed upon developing skill in language expression through natural and meaningful activities which are needed and used by children and by adults in lifelike situations. Learning to write effectively is a developmental activity that must receive constant attention throughout the school program. The importance of learning to write by writing is summed up in this statement from a United States Office of Education publication:

Children learn to write by writing. There should be opportunities for every child to write every day in ways that are purposeful. This will not be writing of a formal sort, but rather for many purposes: writing a question on the board, taking notes to answer questions on a problem, writing directions for going on a trip, keeping a record of the weather, writing a letter, ordering merchandise, making an outline for a play, making a bibliography of books containing stories about dogs, writing a fanciful story, or any one of a hundred or more activities that children find interesting and useful.[33]

Evolving standards. When a writing situation develops for the first time, the teacher should guide the child in the examination of a suitable model. Examples and models are given in textbooks, but real examples preferably written by children of about the same age or grade level are much better. The teacher should attempt to accumulate a file of such model materials for use when particular types of written language situations are introduced. A good plan is to have each child prepare his own model from one worked out on the board by the teacher and the children. He can then keep his model in his desk and refer to it when needed.

From the examination of a model, or from the discussion of a previous experience, standards should now be set up for the writing activity. These standards will vary from one activity to another and should evolve in detail and achievement as children develop facility in written expression. At first, the standards developed by a third-grade class for writing reports might include:

1. Write complete sentences.
2. Capitalize the first word of each sentence.
3. Put a period at the end of each sentence.
4. Leave margins on your paper.

Activity planning. Just as oral expressional ability develops in advance of written expressional ability, attention must be given to the oral planning of what is to be written. Children need to understand thoroughly

[33] Helen K. Mackintosh and Wilhelmina Hill, *How Children Learn to Write.* Bulletin 1953, No. 2, U.S. Department of Health, Education, and Welfare. Washington: U.S. Government Printing Office, 1953, pp. 10–11.

the purposes to be served by their writing before they begin to set down their ideas or the information they have secured. This is of decreasing importance as children advance in grade level, but if needed it must not be neglected even though the children may be in upper grade classes. A decision must be made as to whether a formal letter or an informal note is needed, whether a report should be written or merely a record kept, whether simple notes should be taken or an outline made. One sixth grade undertook the worthwhile project of organizing the school's periodicals, which might otherwise have been discarded.[34]

Teacher and pupils planned together from the start. The pupils' activity was directed by repeated questions: How shall we proceed? What shall we do next? What jobs need to be done and who will do them? How much time each week shall we devote to the problem?

It was decided to limit the work on the problem to three eighty-minute periods a week. The teacher's remark that some record of work and procedure would be needed as the activity broadened brought forth from the class a suggestion that they keep a diary. The pupils agreed to keep a record of the activities in which they participated, on large sheets of paper attached to an easel. A guide for writing the diary entries was then set up.

After the decision has been made as to the purpose of the writing and the type that is needed, the actual writing must be organized. In the lower grades this may be done cooperatively. Sentences may be suggested by children, written on the board by the teacher, revised as necessary, and arranged in proper order. In the later grades this planning is generally done individually but only if the child can competently do so. Many children will need help with this organization. The teacher may work with a small group or with individuals in helping to complete the planning.

Self-editing and group criticism. After the first writing has been completed the next step is to refer to the standards and to check the written product against those standards and other factors making for good writing that the pupils know about. Teaching the child to edit his own writing takes time, and while a child can learn much in a year's time about correcting his own papers, real skill in this procedure is developed over several years. One practice that has been found to be successful is described by Dawson:

[34] Ann Sutcliffe, teacher, and Mildred S. Kiefer, supervisor, Whittier School, Phoenix, Arizona, reported in *Language Arts for Today's Children,* The Commission on the English Curriculum of the National Council of Teachers of English. New York: Appleton-Century-Crofts, Inc., 1954, pp. 285–6.

The writer has found socialized correction to be an effective means of eradicating individual language weaknesses. Here compositions are copied on the blackboard with all defects and errors duplicated. The pupil-author makes what improvements he can; his classmates then cooperate in suggesting other improvements while this same pupil-author makes revisions on his original paper. He thus is helped to see the exact spots where he needs to make improvement. Usually a lesson in socialized instruction includes a composition with very few errors. This is considered first in order that the entire class have creditable composition practices brought to mind. Then, two or three compositions with typical errors are improved. The next day all papers are returned to their writers. Each pupil tries to make the same type of improvements that were made in the socialized correction lessons of the previous day. There is provided a checklist of questions to guide this self-correction. These questions have been based on the errors that were located in the directed socialized correction lesson.[35]

A more efficient procedure to accomplish the same results is to show each pupil's paper to the entire class by means of an opaque projector. The group criticism should always be constructive and the teacher should take the lead in pointing out the good points about each composition.

Correcting errors.   The final procedure in an expressional lesson involves correcting the errors in the writing. The final product should be as nearly free from errors, as well organized, and as near the maximum development of content as the child can make it. To achieve this goal, rewriting may be necessary, but this should not always be done; sometimes moving on to the next expressional lesson after having identified deficiencies and errors will achieve the best results. Unquestionably the best incentive for achieving the final product that represents effective and acceptable writing of a child is that the writing must be highly purposeful. To write successfully each child must gain respect for the social value of correctness in writing.

CORRECTIONAL LESSONS

The content for the second type of lessons on written expression arises from the writing produced in the expressional lessons. Correctional lessons are designed to bring about individual pupil mastery of the specific skills and abilities required for effective written expression. Types of procedures suitable for use at this level are suggested here.

[35] Mildred A. Dawson, *Individualization in the Language Arts,* Language Arts Leaflet Number 3. Yonkers-on-Hudson: World Book Company, 1949, p. 1.

Evaluation and diagnosis. One teacher's manual lists some of the most common causes of poor written work among children as follows:

1. They write too much, not necessarily too frequently.
2. They write material which involves highly specialized skills for which they have had no preparation.
3. They don't thoroughly understand what they are to do in the writing.
4. They have no models or standards of good work to which to refer.
5. They do not know wherein their own work is poor, so they do not know how to improve it.
6. They don't care how their work is done, for usually it is not going to be used in any way.[36]

Evaluation and diagnosis of language expression is discussed fully in Chapter 18. The identification of errors to be considered in corrective teaching is, of course, basic to these lessons. No time should be spent on language lessons of a correctional or remedial nature unless there is evidence that the lessons are needed by certain individuals. Naturally, all such lessons should be on the specific items that need correction.

Identifying individual deficiencies. While some correctional lessons may be conducted on a group basis, most attention must center on correcting individual deficiencies. As a result of the group criticism and discussion among the teacher and the pupils, each child should begin to identify the areas of written expression upon which he needs the most improvement. The teacher should begin a systematic inventory (see Chapter 7, page 184) of each pupil's deficiencies the first week of school and continue it regularly throughout the year. The record should be open to pupils' examination and suggestion, and possibly for them to make entries.

Corrective Practice. Corrective practice in those skills which are distinctly applicable to written expression has been discussed in the earlier sections of this chapter; those which apply to both oral and written expression are discussed in Chapter 11. The corrective practice should be only on those items upon which it is obvious that practice is needed. The practice period should be short, specific, and directed toward a real need that the pupil himself has identified.

[36] Harry A. Greene, and others, *Building Better English,* Manual and Key, Grade 3. Evanston, Ill. Row, Peterson and Company, 1947, pp. 22–23.

IMPORTANCE OF EXTENSIVE
WRITING EXPERIENCE

STIMULATION OF DESIRE TO WRITE

It is usually quite easy to stimulate the normal child to want to write if there is in the writing a purpose that is apparent to him and that is an outgrowth of an activity and experience of his which has shown the need for expression. He will write when he has something to say, and when he feels that someone will read and appreciate or learn from what he has written. A child will write a report readily enough, for instance, if he feels that the information he will include in it is needed in a social studies problem and will be of interest to others in the class. He will gladly keep a record if he is convinced that this record will actually be referred to later and therefore there is a need to be certain the details are not forgotten. He will write a summary of a science experiment if he enjoyed working on it and knows that the summary will be sent to his parents.

Oral discussion of situations which may call for writing reports, summaries, and records, must be related by teacher guidance to the activities of the class. Questions such as: "Do we know everything we should about life in an Indian village before we show the fifth-graders about it?" "Should different ones see what they can find out about Indian cooking, shelter, and ceremonies in the village?" "John, you visited the reservation at Tama last year; what do you remember about the ceremonies?" "Do you suppose you could write down those things and perhaps find others and prepare a report each of us could read?"

The key to all useful suggestions for stimulating written expression is the genuineness of the need for the writing. "Ever since we began expecting children to write only when they had a genuine need or the earnest desire to do so, we have found them eager to write well. In that mood they have been sensitive to our guidance and suggestion." [37] Children usually have much to write about; the teacher, through careful guidance and planning of class activities must help them see the need.

The task of stimulating expression is relatively simple if real attention is given to needs. Consider the needs for writing in the day of a ten-year-old.

[37] Alvina Treut Burrows, and others, *They All Want to Write*. Englewood Cliffs, N.J.: Prentice-Hall, Inc. 1955, p. 3.

A day's activities in a classroom offer many situations requiring the use of writing skills. In one day, a ten-year-old in a fifth grade class used writing to:
Put the plans for the day in the log book of the class
Record the weather conditions on a chart
Write arithmetic problems made from the information found in a super market advertisement
Take notes from two reference books for a report in social studies on lighting in colonial times
Make the bibliography for his reference sources
List the characters and the properties needed for the dramatization of a reading story
Compose an invitation to be sent to another class inviting them to the play
Note the discussion topics in Student Council so that he could report back to the class
Outline the main ideas found in a science article on the invention of the electric light bulb
Make a word picture of a person for the other children to guess during a class game
Ask permission from his parents to accompany his class on a trip to the Town Hall [38]

IMPORTANCE OF ACTIVITY—EXPERIENCE

Most of us would be appalled if we were called upon to write a report on the subject "Functions and Relations in Mathematical Sets." Even after considerable reading, we probably would be unable to write a paper that would be either of much interest to a reader or satisfying to ourselves. In the first place, many of us would not know how to find information on the topic; it is simply too far removed from our experience. Then too, many of us would not be much interested in the topic, since our lack of information may indicate little interest in mathematics.

In evaluating the importance of experience in teaching written language it may be well for us to go back for a moment to a consideration of how children learn language. Language is a means or tool for thinking, communicating, and recording. Words are symbols, which alone, or with other words, represent concepts or ideas. The meanings of these concepts or ideas may be different for different people. A commonality of meaning to two or more individuals depends upon the common elements in their experiences. The child in learning language imitates others in learning the language symbols, or words, and through experiences associates these symbols with objects and ideas. He learns

[38] *Using Language.* Wilmington, Del.: The Division of Elementary Education, Wilmington Public Schools, 1955, pp. 116–117.

new words and concepts through relating new situations to experiences he has had. Thus the experiences in the school must be related to the child's previous experiences. Of course, the experience background of each child is different from that of any other. How valuable a school activity may be as an experience for a particular child, then, becomes very difficult to determine. Our best guess generally is that the interests a child shows are clues to his experiential background, and our best procedure is to extend this interest as far as possible.

Children in the middle and upper grades, of course, have had many experiences. They have many interests. There is much they could write about. Just because they have advanced above the primary level, however, we should not assume that it is not the school's business to provide activities which give them further experiences. Even if a child develops fluency and spontaneity of expression in the first and second grades, we cannot be assured that this fluency will be maintained. In fact, we can be assured that it will not be maintained unless he has the opportunity to learn many things that he wants to tell others about and feels that he knows enough to do so.

The further the child progresses in the elementary school, the greater is the danger that his language period may degenerate into one of exercise-doing, learning words in columns out of context, or studying language forms divorced from the use he is making of language the rest of the day. Special care, therefore, needs to be exercised to continue the kind of rich program of well-motivated enterprises common in the lower grades in order that the growth of language may continue in relationship to the development of meaning and that the challenge of a social purpose may motivate expression. Then the needed remedial drill and positive instruction in word knowledge and linguistic forms may be related directly to the problems which confront the pupil in his daily use of language.[39]

Sometimes there is a mistaken tendency for teachers to think that providing activity is the same as providing experience. This may be due to a teacher's interest in having children "learn by doing." Of course, the principle of "learning by doing" is a valid one, but the kind and extent of the learning depends upon what is done. While every activity may have a purpose, this purpose may be unknown or meaningless to the child—and, we suspect, sometimes unknown and unimportant to the teacher. Activities do need to be provided, and sometimes this in-

[39] Dora V. Smith, "Growth in Language Power as Related to Child Development," *Teaching Language in the Elementary School*. The Forty-third Yearbook of the National Society for the Study of Education, Part II. Chicago: The University of Chicago Press, 1944, p. 59.

305

volves considerable contriving on the part of the teacher to relate these activities to the desirable experiences that society says the school should provide. Not all these activities need be first-hand experiences, however; they may involve the use of books or other audio-visual materials. They must be activities which are of interest to the children and are made meaningful to them by being related to experiences they have had earlier.

DEVELOPING SKILLS FOR SPECIAL WRITTEN LANGUAGE SITUATIONS

There are many writing situations which are specific in nature and which call for the development of skills and abilities of basic social importance. The teaching of these special written language skills is considered in this section.

LETTER WRITING

Many different types of letters need to be written, including such personal letters as those of invitation and reply, sympathy, regret, thanks, apology, congratulations, and friendship, and business letters dealing with requests, orders, application, and complaints. Included also in letter writing are the special skills of writing business and personal telegrams and night letters, writing of postcards, and addressing of cards and envelopes.

Letter writing is most effectively taught as an integral part of an activity going on in the classroom. Children must understand the need for the writing of a letter and the importance of content, form, and courtesies before economical learning will occur. Teachers must be on the alert for opportunities which require the writing of real letters. Some frequently occurring opportunities that call for the writing of the various kinds of letters are the following:

Invitations:	To friends to visit the classroom
	To parents to come to a program
	To another class or school to come to a play day
	To the principal or supervisor to observe an activity
Replies:	Of acceptance to an invitation from another class or a parent
	Of regret at not being able to come to a program

Sympathy:	To a sick classmate or teacher
	To a teacher or family of a classmate after a death or accident
Greetings:	To others at school on a holiday
	To the principal and other teachers on birthdays
	To various friends on special occasions
Friendly letters and postcards:	To another classroom or school
	To a former pupil
	To last year's teacher
	To a student in a foreign land [40]
Thank-you notes:	To someone for talking to the class
	To friends and relatives for presents at Christmas
	To another class for the use of some books
	To a parent for the loan of materials
	To the principal for some special favor
Requests:	To a company or individual for information
	To a shop keeper for materials
	To someone for permission to visit his business or home
	To the principal for permission to take a trip
Orders:	To a business for class supplies
	For a magazine subscription
Applications:	For a position on the school paper
	For a job in school office
	For summer work
	For after school jobs
Complaints:	About an article in newspaper
	About a practice on the playground

The above are only a few suggestions. Most language textbooks give other suggestions and the alert teacher will think of many more. The important point is that there are actually many occasions for the real practice of letter writing and that these occasions occur naturally in a classroom which has many activities under way.

Content. Every letter should be written for a purpose. In the lower grades the teacher should spend considerable time with the pupils discussing the purpose of letters in general and more specifically the purpose of a particular letter that they are planning to write. The same practice should be carried on periodically throughout the middle and upper grades. Teaching the children about the purpose of letters in

[40] A good source of names of pen pals is: Youth of All Nations, 16 St. Luke's Place, New York 14, N.Y.

general and the specific purpose of a particular type of letter is naturally dependent upon a lifelike situation calling for the writing of a letter. The children must discover that in order to continue the interesting activity in which they are engaged, a letter must be written for the required information or material. They must understand that in another situation courtesy demands the writing of a letter of thanks or sympathy. These attitudes are not too difficult to develop if the situations are genuine and lifelike and if the children are convinced that the letters they write will actually be mailed.

A discussion of letter writing should focus upon the content necessary to achieve the letter's purpose. Decisions should be made as to the details to be included. If the letter is an order for some material, the amount should be listed, and the use that will be made of it if the material is free should be stated. The letter should also indicate when it is needed, and to whom it should be sent. These details should be organized into a logical sequence; in beginning letter writing they should be listed and organized on the board. Special attention will need to be given to good beginning and ending sentences. In the writing of friendly letters particularly, attention should be given to phrasing the thoughts in interesting and vivid ways. Other suggestions for developing ideas and attitudes about content in letters are the following:

1. Read to the class interesting letters recorded in literature, such as Roosevelt's *Letters to His Children*.
2. Analyze letters received as to their organization, why they are or are not interesting, and whether they do or do not achieve the purpose intended.
3. Encourage pupils in upper grades to plan what they want to say and possibly to make an outline of the content of a letter before writing it.
4. Help children to think of other interesting words and phrases to be used in place of the somewhat trite ones commonly used in both business and personal letters.
5. Have children exchange letters written and then analyze each other's letters.
6. Have children read letters aloud to the class. The children should then decide how certain ideas could be stated more clearly and interestingly.

Form. Children learn most about form in letter writing by seeing and studying good models. Most textbooks contain samples of different types of letters, but unfortunately a letter reproduced on the printed page of a textbook does not resemble the original letter in many respects. The content may be reproduced verbatim and in script, but the size of the paper stock, the widths of margins, the lengths of lines, the size of the writing, and the spacing between the lines must all be restricted to meet the specifications of the printer, not the standards of a correctly written letter. As a supplement to or perhaps an antidote for these textbook models, the teacher should develop with the class a correct letter form from content dictated by the children. Following the class acceptance of the letter form, the teacher and the class should consider the size, shape, and color of letter paper suitable for a letter of the type represented by the model. Proper paper should be secured, and each child should produce a teacher-approved copy of the model letter for his personal use. As instruction on letter writing progresses, similar personal models should be prepared for the return and outside addresses on the envelope. The model letters should then be folded properly, inserted in the envelopes, and attached to textbook or notebook covers for convenient reference at any time.

This procedure is particularly helpful in the grades in which the initial instruction on letter form is given, but it is also important in the higher grades to give emphasis to the importance of form and to recall to pupils' minds the various details of form in the correct perspective. For many children this personal model letter may be their first or only experience with a correctly written friendly or business letter. It is no wonder that children write cramped, crowded letters with narrow margins on paper of an improper shape, size, or color if they never see a letter model that looks more like a letter than those shown in many of the language textbooks.

Children should understand the purposes of various parts of a letter. Questions such as these should be asked:

"Why does a letter have a heading?" (It tells the reader where the letter came from and on which day it was written.)

"What does the greeting do?" (It is courteous and establishes contact with the reader. It is like saying, "Hello.")

"What do we put in the body of a letter?" (We put the message in the body of the letter.)

"How do we end a letter?" (A formal or informal closing ends the letter. It is like saying, "Good-bye.")

"What comes after the closing?" (The signature comes after the closing. It is necessary to tell who wrote the letter.) [41]

Letter form may also be taught by:

1. The teacher dictating a letter and the pupils putting it into correct form.
2. Exchanging letters between pupils for correction of matters of form.
3. Placing models on charts in order that pupils may refer to them.

[41] *A Guide for the Teaching of Language Arts.* San Francisco: Elementary School Division, San Francisco Unified School District, 1955, p. 24.

4. Placing on the bulletin board copies of business and personal letters which show good form.

Courtesies. Throughout the entire school program teachers should be watchful for opportunities to point out to the children the courtesies which should be observed in the writing and receiving of letters. These courtesies are listed and discussed in Chapter 5 and will not be repeated here. Courtesies may be best taught through showing the need for them. The teacher's concern for letter-writing courtesies may convince the children of their importance. The idea should be stressed that it is discourteous to send a letter that is carelessly written or illegible, disregards details of good letter form, is written on inappropriate paper, or contains errors in spelling and usage. The teacher should strive to develop in pupils a feeling of what is courteous and appropriate rather than continually tell them that particular courtesies should be practiced.

OUTLINING

An outline is a special form of written product that is a means to an end and not really an end itself. Children in the kindergarten and primary grades begin to become familiar with outlining when the teacher lists items on the board and later encourages the children to list them in sequential order. The first formal teaching of outlining generally comes in the fourth or fifth grades. One guide gives these directions for making an outline in the fourth grade: [42]

1. Pupils develop their outlines under the leadership of their teacher.
2. In answer to leading questions, the pupils tell the teacher which items are to be included in the one-paragraph report.
3. The teacher writes the items on the board, listing them in outline form.
4. The pupils copy the outline, observing the following points:
   a. The title is written on the second line. A line is skipped after the title.
   b. The first word and every other important word in the title begins with a capital letter.
   c. Each item in the outline is numbered to show the order in which it belongs. Either Roman numerals or Arabic numerals may be used.
   d. The number is written at the margin. It is followed by a period.
   e. The first word of each item in the outline begins with a capital letter.

Until the ability to outline is well developed, pupils should work together on composite outlines and then copy them individually. One of the best materials to outline in the beginning is a story that is well known to the pupils, so that they will have a good understanding of the se-

[42] *Language Handbook,* Houston Public Schools, Curriculum Bulletin, Number 53CBM15, 1953–1954. Houston, Texas: Houston Public Schools, p. 99.

quence. Many stories are so written that the major and minor topics can be easily distinguished. The purpose of such an outline may be to dramatize the story to another class.

In teaching outlining, the teacher should stress the point that any task worth doing is worth planning in advance, and that outlining is valuable as an advance plan for the creative or practical expression of pupils as well as in gleaning meaning from the writing of others. The value of outlining must be demonstrated to pupils. One suggestion is to have them write stories, one without and one with an outline, and then compare the stories in a class evaluation period.

Outlining should be taught as the need for it arises, and reviewed occasionally throughout the year, but it should be taught thoroughly and in suitable complexity of form for each grade as it is introduced. Frequent reference to the values of outlining will encourage the pupils to make regular use of outlining skills in both their oral and written work. In the intermediate and upper grades the teacher may properly point out to the pupils that they need not become slaves to the outline. After all, an outline is one form of organization of content. If in their actual creative work they hit upon a new plan of organization that is better than the original, they should not hesitate to leave the old outline and follow the new organization.

FILLING IN FORMS

To fill in the necessary information called for by the various forms most people encounter frequently, is a language skill of some importance. The major concerns here are accuracy and neatness, attributes which are acquired only through considerable practice. In the primary grades, children need oral drill in answering such questions as: "What is your name?" "How old are you?" "How old will you be at your next birthday?" Later this sort of exercise may be expanded into a game in which children see which ones know all of the personal history a particular form, such as a standard test blank, may require. Of course, this activity should be introduced as a need occurs, but to give the proper kind of teaching the teacher may need to stimulate interest by preparing different types of forms to be completed. One teacher suggests this procedure for teaching the skills necessary for filling in forms: [43]

1. Introduce by pointing up situation in school where use of form is required, such as sending for material, absence excuse, or test form. In a discussion period set up questions.

[43] Reproduced with permission of Mrs. Mary Bowen, Folsom, California.

311

    a. What kinds of forms are there and how are they used?
       Why are they used?
    b. What do we need to know to fill out a form correctly?
       Are there any special words we need to know the meaning of?
2. Have the children bring in as many forms as they can find. Discuss these and practice filling them out. The teacher may need to bring in forms that the children won't locate. The discussion emphasis should be on the use of the forms and the need for neatness and accuracy.
3. Have the children construct a form to be used, such as for a picnic to gather information about who will need a ride, who can provide a ride, what type of food they'll bring, which games they'll want to play, etc.

ANNOUNCEMENTS, NOTICES, LABELS, TITLES, SIGNS

A wide variety of writing activities may be included under this heading, all of which have to do with concise, short written phrases or statements. Again the emphasis needs to be upon accuracy and neatness, but also upon including all essential details in the shortest possible statement. Special teaching suggestions are the following:

1. Oral practice is needed before writing. Children should practice giving oral directions, making oral announcements, or suggesting orally labels and signs.
2. Oral discussion is needed concerning the appropriateness of the wording of written labels, signs, and notices, as well as the appropriateness of places where the notices are to be posted.
3. Study the weaknesses of notices, signs, and labels used in stores, along the highways, and in the school. Try rewriting some of the weakest of these in form to serve their purpose more effectively.

MEMORANDA, RULES, RECEIPTS, MINUTES

Many of the suggestions in this chapter for teaching other forms of written expression apply equally well to the writing of memoranda, rules, receipts, and minutes. The writing of minutes can best be taught in connection with a situation in which minutes are needed, as in a club or committee meeting. Most committee activities in the middle and upper grades may include the writing of minutes. Children should take turns writing the minutes. Following the procedure of a committee and keeping a record of its work makes for more efficient and businesslike committee activities. For the teaching of memoranda writing, the teacher may read or tell interesting material on some worthwhile topic. As this is done the children may write brief notes on four or five main points which were treated. In the writing called for in these situations, emphasis again should be upon accuracy, the inclusion of all necessary detail. In the interests of accuracy, careful listening is essential.

REPORTING

There are many occasions calling for the writing of reports in the elementary school. Children will willingly report when the topic of the report is one of personal interest and when they are confident that the report serves a purpose to an audience.

The many situations in the elementary school which call for the writing of reports and summaries should be utilized for teaching purposes. The following, dictated by kindergarten children to their teacher, is an example of a report on a sweet potato plant:

We brought a potato to school. We put it in a jar. We filled the jar with water. Long roots grew. Soon we saw buds. Now there are leaves on our potato.[44]

The writing of a report may serve as a challenge to the exceptional child, or to one who has developed some special interest or hobby. A child will painstakingly search for information about a topic that he is particularly interested in. An example is the following report made by a fifth-grade boy:

Thomas Alva Edison

Edison is generally known as the greatest inventor in history, because his inventions have had so much effect on our lives. His electric light bulb, phonograph, and motion picture machine have become known all over the earth.

Edison was born at Milan, Ohio. He was always trying out things that he had read or thought about. His parents always liked to recall the time they came upon 6 year old "Al," as he was called, sitting upon a bunch of eggs. He had seen a goose hatch eggs. Why couldn't he?

When he was seven years old his family moved to Port Huron, Michigan, where Al entered a public school. His teacher considered him a dunce, and he left school after three months. His mother became his teacher. He loved books and his father paid him twenty-five cents for each book Al could report on intelligently. The boy's memory was remarkable. He rarely forgot any useful bits of information he had read.[45]

[44] *Communication, A Guide to the Teaching of Speaking and Writing.* Minneapolis: Minneapolis Public Schools, 1953, p. 35.
[45] Excerpt from report by Bob, Grade 5 in *Using Language.* Wilmington, Delaware: Division of Elementary Education, Wilmington Public Schools, 1955, pp. 104–105.

313

In addition to these suggestions and those given earlier which apply to all similar types of written language situations, the following are particularly suitable:

1. Stress the importance of conciseness of expression, the need to base the report on research or accurate observation.
2. Discourage the typical tendency of children to copy the work of others. Point out that this is plagiarism, and is the same as stealing from another.
3. Help children to choose important facts, to arrange the material in logical or chronological order, and to construct effective opening and summarizing sentences.
4. Cooperate with the children in discovering colorful and accurate descriptive words and expressions.
5. Have the class practice making observations. For example, see who can remember the most different objects, people, incidents seen on a trip.

USING PRINTED SOURCES

Since books and other printed materials as sources of information are equally important in the pupil's preparation for either oral or written expression, these materials are discussed in detail in Chapter 11. However, certain aspects of the use of printed sources are of particular concern to written expression, and accordingly are considered briefly in this chapter.

The principal reference sources in the elementary classroom are the encyclopedias, dictionaries, supplementary textbooks, and books and pamphlets on special subjects. Children need to learn to use all of these sources. To do so properly they must know about alphabetizing, indexing, the table of contents; and further, they must know how to skim-read, to pick key words and ideas, and to take notes and make outlines. Much of the learning required calls for using writing in the learning process.

ALPHABETIZING AND INDEXING

In order to learn about alphabetizing, children need practice in putting words in alphabetical order. They need practice in writing simple tables of content, indexes, and headings for paragraphs. In these activities real situations should be utilized. When children put together a book of pictures they have collected, for example, they will need a table of contents and perhaps an index. In answering questions or preparing reports, children will need to use reference sources. From these genuine needs, then, the skills for the efficient use of the sources are taught. Language textbooks suggest exercises for teaching these skills.

On a sheet of paper place the guide words *likelihood* and *limerick* in the same position in which they would be at the top of a dictionary page. Copy from the list below only the words that would be on that page.

1. lilac	3. like	5. lily	7. limit	9. lime
2. light	4. likewise	6. limb	8. lingo	10. line [46]

Pick out the key word in each question below.

1. How is radio important in flying?
2. For what are airships used?
3. Where is Randolph Flying Field?
4. How does radar help a pilot?
5. How are gliders used in flying?

Make a list of the key words in the five sentences above. Talk over your lists in class. Did you all choose the same words?

Now take the questions that your class raised.

Decide in class which word in each question is the key word. Underline the key words.[47]

HANDBOOKS, TEXTBOOKS, AND STYLE MANUALS

Particularly important as reference sources in written expression are books prepared as guides to good writing. The best known handbook for the use of children (primarily in the upper grades) is the *Handbook of English for Boys and Girls* which was prepared by a committee of the National Conference on Research in English.[48] This excellent handbook, now out of print, provided many helps for more effective writing and speaking. So far as the authors know this is the only commercial attempt to provide such a handbook, although it is not unusual for a school system to develop local guides for upper grade pupils in mimeographed form for a limited number of items. Children may also compile in their own handbooks the models of letters and other forms of written expression suggested earlier. To these compilations of models may be added various suggestions regarding punctuation, capitalization, and usage.

[46] Thomas C. Pollock and John J. Forester, *Using Language*. New York: The Macmillan Company, 1954, p. 222.

[47] Harry A. Greene, and others, *Building Better English, Grade Five*. Evanstown, Ill.: Row, Peterson and Company, 1947, p. 22.

[48] C. C. Certain, ed. *Handbook of English for Boys and Girls*. Chicago: Scott, Foresman and Company, 1939.

315

Such a handbook could be indexed and receive much use as well as pride in developing it.

Generally the best sources available in most classrooms as references for good writing are the newest textbooks in English. Too often, of course, the adopted textbook is not used as a reference source, but is more or less literally followed section by section, page by page. The superior teacher, however, will make use of the textbook, or perhaps several textbooks, by having pupils independently examine each book as a reference source.

Of special assistance to the teacher in many matters of written expression in the intermediate grades and above is the *University of Chicago Manual of Style*.[49] This manual and others similar to it may also be used by the better pupils in upper-grade classes. All children should learn to turn to available authoritative sources for guidance in their writing.

CREDIT FOR MATERIAL USED

Teachers should begin in the lower elementary grades showing children the necessity for complete honesty in giving credit for ideas and information obtained from others and used in their language work. Many children develop a vague feeling that there is something wrong about using the ideas of others, with the result that they copy material and try to hide the fact that it is copied when actually the hiding is the only thing wrong with this practice. None of us, children included, can be expected to know all about everything. In fact, most people have very few completely original ideas. We simply learn many things from others and after a time, of course, are not able to identify the actual source of the idea or information. However, when we are able to identify the source we should do so, and this fact should be stressed to children at an early age.

Generally in written expression credit to sources is supplied in footnotes and bibliographies. Models for footnotes and bibliographies are suggested in Chapter 11 and other such models may be secured by reference to handbooks, textbooks, and style manuals. Children should learn to follow these models and to refer correctly to the sources they have used.

[49] *A Manual of Style*. Chicago: The University of Chicago Press, 1949.

SELF-EDITING AND PROOFREADING

An aspect of language teaching that too often is neglected is that of self-editing and proofreading. Children may recognize the need for writing in a special situation; they may be presented with a model and evolve their own standards; they may be cautioned about possible errors to be avoided; and finally, they may actually write and turn the product in to the teacher or perhaps to others to read and at no time reread it themselves or give thoughtful consideration to what they have written. Pupils who practice proofreading and self-editing are limited to those who have been forced into it by persistent teachers. From the beginning of instruction in written expression the pupil should be encouraged to depend upon himself, both in finding his own errors of expression and in correcting them. He should learn to examine carefully what he has written in terms of selection of the ideas or information, effectiveness of organization, clarity of expression, and courtesy to the readers, including legibility of writing, correct spelling, punctuation, and usage.

From a genuine situation it is relatively simple to guide the pupil into an attitude of concern for achieving success in his writing. This is generally developed by reference to standards which have been established by the class, and later to standards the pupil himself has set. A child might develop these criteria, for example, which would serve as standards for his self-editing: [50]

1. Is my story told in good order?
2. Does each paragraph tell about one topic?
3. Is each sentence in a paragraph about the topic?
4. Are there any words I should change because they are uninteresting or or don't say what I mean?
5. Is each sentence a good sentence?

Harmful habits of writing are certain to develop from inadequate attention to proofreading. McKee has stated this point effectively as follows:

If he does not do this thinking and changing or rewriting, the chances are good that his first draft will have supplied him with harmful practice in writing poorly. It is by this correcting, improving, and changing or rewriting that the pupil learns to write well. He learns to write well, not so much by

[50] Walter T. Petty, *The Language Arts in Elementary Schools.* Washington, D.C.: The Center for Applied Research in Education, Inc., 1962, pp. 76–77.

writing first drafts about many different topics as by the right sort of proof-reading and rewriting of what he has written.[51]

In *They All Want to Write* a positive attitude toward editing and proof-reading is advocated through attention to improvement in the writing after editing has taken place.

The contrast between the finished copy and the corrected rough draft, with its erasures, crossed out words, arrows and stars for insertions, was gratifying. The fourth-grade reporters were proud of their well-organized, accurate results and infinitely pleased with themselves and their new accomplishments.[52]

Some simple proofreading skills should be taught when children first begin to write. In the first or second grade the child should be taught to read over what he has written; to check to see if the first words of his sentences are capitalized; to see if there is a period at the end of each sentence. It is not enough for the teacher to say, "Proofread what you have written"—an admonition meaningless to young children and ineffective to older ones without instruction in how proofreading is done. In the early stages of teaching proofreading the teacher and children may develop standards or lists of appraisal questions from which they may together select and correct errors. As children progress through the grades, however, they should be encouraged to develop for themselves criteria as suggested above for observance in proofreading and self-editing. The habit of depending upon the teacher to lead them through an evaluation of their work is almost as harmful as that of depending upon the teacher to make the corrections. Therefore, in spite of the fact that the teacher must give guidance in proofreading, attention should be directed toward developing habits that will enable the child to depend upon himself.

Class or individually developed criteria for proofreading should at first be limited to only one or two details. Later these may be expanded to include further items of organization, form, and mechanics. Group developed criteria which might be used at first should include such questions as:

Have I written sentences?
Have I capitalized the first word of every new sentence?
Have I put a period at the end of each sentence?

[51] Paul McKee, "An Adequate Program in the Language Arts." *Teaching Language in the Elementary School*, Forty-third Yearbook of the National Society for the Study of Education, Part II. Chicago: The University of Chicago Press, 1944, pp. 34–35.
[52] Alvina Treut Burrows and others, *They All Want to Write*. Englewood Cliffs, N.J.: Prentice-Hall, Inc., 1955, p. 65.

Criteria to be used later might include such additional questions as:

Have I indented the first word of each paragraph?
Have I left good margins?
Does each paragraph tell about one topic?
Does each sentence in a paragraph tell something about the topic?
Does each sentence begin and end correctly?

Pooley suggested the following procedure for use in the high school, which with modification is applicable in the elementary grades:

A carefully worked out technique of proofreading can do a great deal to improve standards of written work and correctness in composition. For some reason it is very difficult to get students to reread their own work with a critical and corrective eye. The best procedure is one which is worked out with the group as a whole. When a set of compositions is ready to be handed in, the teacher should follow an accepted procedure of proofreading. The first step is to check the title of the paper, to make sure that it is correctly placed on the paper, has capital letters where capital letters are required, and that it is correctly punctuated. The next step is to scan the paper for paragraph form. Each paragraph should be properly indented; the first sentence in the paragraph should naturally begin with a capital letter; and there should be some kind of break in the composition to show the changes of thought. The next stage is to check the whole paper for accuracy in spelling and then for accuracy in word usage. Pupils that are dubious of the acceptability of certain phrases, or are unsure of the idiom they have employed should ask help of the teacher before handling the paper in. In some cases it may be advisable to have the reactions as a kind of double check on accuracy. This proofreading, if followed without fail at the time each paper is to be submitted, will have a vigorous effect, first in stimulating pupils to give their own papers a critical checking before they are handed in and in developing an attitude of respect for correctness and accuracy in all work.[53]

RHETORICAL SKILLS

The rhetorical skills necessary to good sentence structure and to clarity, unity, and the organization of ideas in written expression are discussed in Chapter 11, since these skills are of equal importance in both oral and written expression. However, as written language tends to be more formal than oral language, attention to rhetorical skills should receive a proportionally greater amount of emphasis in the written program. Before considering that this discussion of methods of teaching written

[53] Robert C. Pooley, *Teaching English Usage*. New York: Appleton-Century-Crofts, Inc., 1946, p. 232.

expression is complete, the reader should read all of Chapter 11 and give special attention to the methods of developing the rhetorical skills of sentence structure, clarity, unity, interest, organization, and vocabulary as presented there.

EXERCISES FOR THOUGHT AND DISCUSSION

1. Show why a sampling of words from such sources as the dictionary would result in a meaningless and useless word list.

2. Discuss the relative merits of the *test-study* and the *study-test* plans of teaching spelling.

3. On the basis of your conclusions in Exercise 2 present the essential steps in the method of study you would use in your spelling classes.

4. Why is it essential for each individual pupil to master a specific method of learning to spell new words?

5. How would you proceed in determining the quality and the speed of handwriting that represent reasonable social standards?

6. What would you do to clear up some of the difficulties of the left-handed writer who curves his left wrist and writes upside-down over the top of the paper?

7. What specific differences in physical position at the desk should there be for the left-handed and the right-handed writer?

8. Discuss the pros and cons of requiring that a uniform style of manuscript form be followed through all grades in a school system.

9. Evaluate the thirteen suggestions for developing capitalization and punctuation skills given in this chapter and select the six most helpful ones for discussion.

10. Distinguish between expressional lessons and corrective lessons. What relative emphasis should be given to each in the language classroom?

11. Outline a program designed to stimulate your pupils to proofread and self-edit all of their written work for both content and form, to correct their copy, and then to re-write it in final form.

12. As a result of your study of this chapter prepare a series of concise statements which you might use as principles of method to guide you in your teaching of written expression.

SELECTED REFERENCES

ALPERT, FAITH, and others. "Effect of Proofreading on the Mechanics and Structure of Writing." Unpublished master's thesis, Boston University, 1956.

BAKER, ZELMA W. *The Language Arts, the Child, and the Teacher.* San Francisco: Fearon Publishers, 1955. Chapter 10.

BURROWS, ALVINA TREUT, and others. *They All Want to Write.* Englewood Cliffs, N.J.: Prentice-Hall, Inc., 1955.

COLE, LUELLA, "Reflections on The Teaching of Handwriting." *The Elementary School Journal,* 47:95–99; November, 1956.

Communication, A Guide to the Teaching of Speaking and Writing. Minneapolis: Public Schools, 1953.

CROSSLEY, ALICE. "Can We Help Children to Write?" *Journal of Education,* 139:3–32; February, 1957.

DAWSON, MILDRED A. *Teaching Language in the Grades.* Yonkers-on-Hudson: World Book Company, 1951. Chapters 11 and 12.

FITZGERALD, JAMES A. *The Teaching of Spelling.* Milwaukee: The Bruce Publishing Company, 1951.

FREEMAN, FRANK N. *What Research Says to the Teacher: Teaching Handwriting.* Department of Classroom Teachers and American Educational Research Association. Washington: National Education Association, 1954.

GRAY, WILLIAM S. *The Teaching of Reading and Writing,* UNESCO. Chicago: Scott, Foresman and Company, 1956.

GREENE, HARRY A. "English—Language, Grammar, and Composition." *Encyclopedia of Educational Research,* rev. ed. New York: The Macmillan Company, 1950.

———. *The New Iowa Spelling Scale.* Iowa City: The Bureau of Educational Research and Service, State University of Iowa, 1955.

Guide for the Teaching of Language Arts. San Francisco: Elementary School Division, San Francisco Unified School District, 1955.

Handwriting, A Guide for Elementary Teachers. Downers Grove, Ill.: Downers Grove Public Schools, April 1956.

HERRICK, VIRGIL E. "Handwriting and Children's Writing." *Elementary English,* 37: 248–58; April, 1960.

HERRICK, VIRGIL E., AND JACOBS, LELAND B., eds. *Children and Language Arts.* Englewood Cliffs, N.J.: Prentice-Hall, Inc., 1955.

HORN, ERNEST. "Spelling." *Encyclopedia of Educational Research,* 3rd. ed. New York: The Macmillan Company, 1960.

———. *What Research Says to the Teacher: Teaching Spelling.* Department of Classroom Teachers and American Educational Research Association, Washington: National Education Association, 1954.

Iowa Elementary Teachers Handbook. Vol. 4, *Oral and Written Language.* Des Moines: Iowa State Department of Public Instruction, 1944. Section II.

MACKINTOSH, HELEN K., and HILL, WILHELMINA. *How Children Learn to Write.* U.S. Office of Education, Bulletin 1953, No. 2. Washington: U.S. Government Printing Office, 1953.

MC BROOM, MAUDE. *The Course of Study in Written Composition for the Elementary Grades.* Monographs in Education, First Series, No. 10. Iowa City: State University of Iowa, December 1, 1928.

MYERS, EMMA. "A General Review of Handwriting Instruction." Unpublished master's thesis, State University of Iowa, 1954.

NORDBERG, H. ORVILLE. "Research and the Teaching of Written Expression." *California Journal of Educational Research,* 2:89–91; March, 1951.

PETTY, WALTER T. *The Language Arts in Elementary Schools.* Washington, D.C.: The Center for Applied Research in Education, Inc., 1962.

———. *Improving Your Spelling Program.* San Francisco: Chandler Press, 1959.

Practices and Problems in Handwriting. New York: Board of Education of the City of New York, 1947.

STRICKLAND, RUTH G. *The Language Arts in the Elementary School.* 2nd ed. Boston: D. C. Heath and Company, 1957. Chapter 13.

Using Language. Wilmington, Del.: The Division of Elementary Education, Wilmington Public Schools, 1955.

When Children Write. Washington, D.C.: Association for Childhood Education International, 1955.

11

Developing Skills Common to

Oral and Written Expression

THE TWO PRECEDING CHAPTERS HAVE PRESENTED PROCEDURES FOR THE developing of language skills which are exclusively either oral or written. This chapter, the last of five dealing specifically with problems of instructional techniques and materials, emphasizes the skills that are equally essential to both oral and written expression. The discussion is organized around these topics:

a. A functional approach to the mastery of usage.
b. An instructional program for improving usage.
c. Developing the rhetorical skills.
d. Sentence structure and sentence sense.
e. Interest factors.
f. Organization of content.
g. Vocabulary enrichment.
h. Using sources of information effectively.

A FUNCTIONAL APPROACH TO MASTERY OF USAGE

THE ROLE OF HABIT

Most teachers are well aware that the speech and writing habits of children with respect to usage persist year after year in spite of efforts to bring about improvement. Moreover, those usage habits which are less acceptable tend to be most difficult to eradicate, a condition for which several reasons have been suggested:

1. The habits which the child has acquired in the five or six years of his life before school entrance have become firmly fixed.
2. These habits tend to be strengthened even after coming to school, since

323

the child usually continues to live in much the same type of environment into which he was born.

3. The child whose usage habits are most in need of change is likely not to be interested in correcting them, since to do so would set him off from his social environment.
4. The school generally does not provide enough active language situations for real exercise of the correct habits.
5. Many of the lessons on usage taught in the school are ineffectively motivated and taught.

In addition to these reasons, and perhaps of even greater importance as a reason, is the emphasis the school typically gives to improving usage through written drill, even though the errors may be more prevalent in the children's speaking than in their writing. Pooley, in discussing workbook exercises states, "Usage practice must be heard and spoken to be effective . . ." [1] Dora V. Smith, on the same point says, "Since sound plays so large a role in errors in usage, *oral* drill should constantly supplement the written exercise." [2]

The problem, of course, is to eliminate the undesirable usage habits and to substitute more desirable ones. This is a difficult task, considering the fact that the school can do little about the influences of out-of-school environment. However, the school—every teacher—can do something about the reasons for the persistence of poor usage habits that are related to instruction.

A teacher can provide many active language situations for the genuine exercise of desirable habits. Every teacher should understand, as Blair points out, that "the chief cause of deficiency in oral and written expression is probably *lack of experience and practice in using correct forms.*" [3] He further states that "evidence from the field of psychology clearly indicates that pupils *learn to do what they do.* If a pupil learns a rule of grammar, he will be able to repeat that rule, but he will not necessarily be able to put the rule to use in his speaking and writing. Transfer of training takes place only between elements and situations which are approximately identical. *If pupils are to speak and write correctly they must be given practice in speaking and writing correctly.*" [4]

[1] Robert C. Pooley, *Teaching English Usage.* New York: Appleton-Century-Crofts, Inc., 1946, p. 184.
[2] Dora V. Smith, in *Educational Diagnosis,* Thirty-fourth Yearbook of the National Society for the Study of Education. Chicago: University of Chicago Press, 1935, p. 257.
[3] Glenn Myers Blair, *Diagnostic and Remedial Teaching.* New York: The Macmillan Company, 1956, p. 343.
[4] *Ibid.,* p. 355.

Every teacher must recognize, too, that it is a basic instructional procedure to apply remedial practice at the point of the error.[5] This fact makes it imperative that the exact errors a child makes in his language usage be identified, which in turn means carefully cataloging each pupil's errors for individual attention. Exercises dealing with usage errors that cause a child no difficulty may properly be omitted by that child. The teacher should keep a file of cards on which he jots down the usage errors made by each child. In this way practice exercises and language expression activities for each child may be centered on the errors recorded on his individual card.

Perhaps the most vital point involved in developing correct usage habits is motivation. Pupils must be stimulated to want to improve their English, or little good will result from teaching efforts. Teachers must utilize every possible device to relate the activities of the classroom to the basic goals of each individual pupil. A child must be made to feel that improving his English usage will benefit him personally. He must be convinced that his communication is more effective when he uses good English; that most people actually do use correct English and that these are the people with whom he will be associated. Efforts of the teacher to motivate pupils will of course be geared to each pupil's individuality. It is true, too, that efforts to improve usage in the lower grades will not depend so greatly on the pupil's actually feeling a need to make improvement, for he may be too immature to realize its importance. At this level, major dependence must be placed on simply changing usage habits through continuous incidental correction and the provision of genuine situations for speaking and writing.

AN INSTRUCTIONAL PROGRAM FOR
IMPROVING USAGE

A teacher who recognizes the role of habits in usage and the need for a direct and systematic attack on the problem, can achieve success by following these steps.

1. Appraise the usage problem of the class and of each individual in the class through the use of check lists and the cataloging of errors (as suggested above). Such cataloging should be for both oral and written usage. With the completion of this survey the errors found should be compared with those in lists (see Chapter 6) to determine which are really errors

[5] In addition to references cited in Chapter 7 on this point, see P. M. Symonds, "Practice Versus Grammar in the Learning of Correct English Usage," *Journal of Educational Psychology,* 22:81–95; February, 1931.

and which are simply colloquialisms that need little or no attention in the elementary school.

2. Select the most frequent and grossest errors for consistent attack. After they have been selected, make them known to the children with the reason for their selection. From the time of their selection allow no deviation or lapses from the correct forms at any time, even though this will call for diligent effort in the classroom and on the playground. When the new habits have become reasonably fixed, move on to the selection of other errors for attack.

3. Provide many opportunities to use the correct forms in natural communication. The activities suggested in Chapters 4 and 5, following the teaching procedures suggested in Chapters 9 and 10, should adequately serve to accomplish this end.

4. Make parents aware of the usages under attack and ask for their cooperation. This may be done at a group conference, at a PTA meeting, and by letter. Pupils may also write letters to their parents explaining what they are trying to accomplish with respect to improving usage.

5. Place as much responsibility for improvement as possible upon the children themselves. Have them make individual lists of troublesome items and individual charts of usages that they have mastered.

6. Build interest in words and expressions, and an enjoyment of the fitness of words in their uses (see the vocabulary section of this chapter).

In addition, a teacher must consistently be aware of the fact that if desirable habits are to be established, children must consistently *hear* good usage. They must recognize the errors they are making; that is, they must *hear* and *see* what their errors are. They must *learn* the correct usage; both how the words *sound* and how they *look*. Then, too, drills or exercises in usage may be used to help fix usage habits in addition to the natural communication activities. Written drills or exercises in usage do have certain shortcomings particularly in the way they ordinarily are made and used, but as is pointed out in Chapter 15 many of these shortcomings can be remedied. Too often drill materials are used before the child is properly motivated and before he adequately understands just what is correct and what is not. The effectiveness of usage drill or practice may be improved through an observance of these suggestions:

1. Use drill exercises to establish the correct usage through repetition.
2. Above the second grade, conduct lively drills for five or ten minutes at the end of the day, based on the needs of the children.
3. So far as possible base this drill on what have been found during that very day to be faults.
4. Vary the time of day for the drills.
5. Remember that drill is most effective when a genuine feeling of need exists.

6. Individualize drill by placing in sub-groups children making the same types of errors.
7. Make practice and drill periods short and specific.
8. Have pupils keep notebooks of their own most persistent usage errors.
9. Individualize drill by securing two or more copies of each of several language workbooks for the grade, and supplementing this material by mimeographed or duplicated exercises from other sources. Cut each book into separate sheets, and mount these and the duplicated exercises on stiff paper; arrange materials alphabetically according to type of error. This material may be used in conjunction with an inventory sheet of errors the individual children make.
10. Whenever possible use material familiar to children for content of drills, such as a recent field trip or seasonal interests.
11. Be certain children understand the purpose of the drill and any explanatory material that is a part of it.
12. Use the language textbook as a reference pattern as well as a source for drill exercises.
13. Supplement all written drill with oral drill. Use as much oral drill as possible.

In connection with planning and directing a corrective program on usage, the teacher will do well to keep in mind the following practical points concerning choice of words and word usage.

1. Some teachers become too pedantic about niceties in language expression. Colloquial language is the comfortable, clear, idiomatic, forceful type of expression used in the informal situations of life, whether in school or not, and in general should be accepted without too much pressure. On the other hand, teachers should guard against crude and illiterate expressions that are unquestionably provincial or unacceptable.

2. Teachers should recognize that there are occasions when a bit of expressive slang may be appropriate and can give "punch" to expression.

3. Children and teachers should both recognize that some occasions in the lives of both children and adults call for the use of *formal* expression, both oral and written. Such occasions as assembly programs, some reporting activities, and business letter writing are the most common examples.

4. Dramatization of unusually apt expressions and well-used words selected from good literature should be recognized as a useful aid to the pupil in adding them to his vocabulary.

VERB USAGE

Errors in verb usages occur frequently in the language expression of elementary school children and, for that matter, in the expression of most

327

other individuals. The errors are individual in nature and the teaching procedure for their elimination should be one of individual attack. That is, if one child consistently says "he brung," it is not likely that every child in the classroom will use the same expression, though there may be several who do so. The teaching emphasis then should be directed at the child making the error and on the specific error made, not at the entire class, or on the mechanical conjugation of the verb *bring*.

When an error in verb usage appears consistently in the child's oral or written expression, he should be shown and allowed to hear both the correct and incorrect forms. He should then select the usage which is correct—with the emphasis of the teacher being placed on "Doesn't this sound better?" The next step is to present drill materials and situations, oral and written, which call for practice in using the correct form. Finally, a practical situation is presented which calls for the recall and use of the correct form.

PRONOUN USAGE

The difficulty encountered most often in teaching usage, including that of pronoun usage, is caused by undue reliance on grammar. Pooley states that "this fallacy arises from the assumption . . . that a pronoun error (him and me went home) is corrected by teaching the declension of the pronoun." [6] The solution to the problem of establishing the correct use of a form is to be found in ear-training and meaningful practice rather than in "authority." Because of the immaturity of elementary school children, grammatical explanations mean very little and may be harmful in that they rob the children of time that could be spent in more profitable ways of developing acceptable usage. Ear-training simply means having the child listen to the correct and incorrect usages as spoken by others and *himself,* and then having him practice orally using the correct form.

Many recently published textbooks in English approach the teaching of correct pronoun usage through oral exercises as is illustrated in the following lesson.[7]

Hear it right.
The words *I, he,* and *she* are used correctly in these sentences. Listen as someone reads the sentence aloud. Listen to the sounds of *I, he,* and *she,* as they are used together and with the names of people. Notice that they are used with the words *are* and *were.*

[6] Robert C. Pooley, *op. cit.,* p. 181.
[7] Thomas C. Pollock and Florence B. Bowden, *Words Work for You.* New York: The Macmillan Company, 1954, p. 143.

1. *Bill* and *I are* brothers.
2. *She* and *I were* late.
3. *He* and *I were* skating.

4. *She* and *he are* cousins.
5. *Mary* and *she are* at home.

Say it right.
Write five sentences to read aloud to the class. Use these words:

1. *Jim and he*
2. *Father and I*
3. *Mary and she*

4. *he and I*
5. *she and I*
6. *she and he*

It is important to remember in teaching pronoun usage that while many errors are made in oral expression they are not necessarily the same errors that children make in writing. Studies indicate, too, that the kinds of pronoun errors made by all children in oral expression are limited in number. For example, Goltry reported that the use of a pronoun which does not agree with its antecedent in number or gender and the use of *you* in an impersonal sense were the errors he found occurring most frequently in his recordings of many thousands of words of children's oral language.[8] In a community in which the population is largely foreign born or extremely provincial, and certain kinds of errors exist, the class should work on the worst errors first. If children persistently say "him and me done our work," this should be attacked before errors in pronoun agreement. The first step is to eliminate truly illiterate usage. Constant correction of over-emphasis on many errors may tend to repress free expression.

ANTECEDENTS

Clarity in sentences is the result of selecting and arranging the words and phrases so that they express exactly the meaning intended. Failure to have the pronoun agree with its antecedent in number is a common error in children's sentences. The teacher may become so concerned with the observance of the rules governing the pronoun and its antecedent that he fails to recognize that the expression the child is using is perfectly acceptable in standard English usage.[9] For example, in the sentence *Each of them took their books home last night* the meaning is entirely clear but the rule governing the pronoun and its antecedent is not observed.

Clarity in expression involves more than agreement of pronoun with

[8] Thomas K. Goltry, "An Analysis of Sentence Structure in Oral Composition," unpublished doctoral dissertation, State University of Iowa, 1935.
[9] See, for example, Sterling A. Leonard and H. Y. Moffett, "Current Definition of Levels in English Usage," *English Journal,* 16:345–359; May, 1927.

its antecedent in number. Clarity in expression results when the user remembers that a pronoun is a word used in place of a noun or noun equivalent and that it has definite meaning only when the reader or listener knows what it stands for. For example, in the sentence *It was too large for him to carry,* we do not know what *it* was. If we know that *it* was a box, then the meaning is clear. Teaching the correction of this type of error does not involve learning a rule but simply realizing that the meaning must be clear if the communication is to be effective.

DEVELOPING THE RHETORICAL SKILLS

The rhetorical skills are concerned with how a sentence is constructed and made interesting, clear, and concise, and how this sentence is placed in relation to other parts of the expression. These skills were identified in Chapter 6 with some description and discussion of their use. This section deals with the development of skill in sentence construction, the use of interest factors, the organization of facts and ideas, and the selection and enrichment of the vocabulary used in expression.

SENTENCE STRUCTURE

At all levels of instruction in oral and written expression, teachers encounter the problem of helping their pupils form complete, clear, and interesting sentences. Too often this problem is approached without adequate understanding of what is involved. Good sentences are indicative of clear thinking. A clumsy, awkward sentence is likely to be the result of a struggle to express a vague idea or feeling that has been poorly thought out. Before starting to write or to speak a child should give thought to *what* is to be said and *how* best to say it.

One guide gives these suggestions for developing ability in sentence construction:

Sentence growth can be furthered at any time during the day and in any subject.

The teacher should speak or read to the children in a voice that shows "sentence sense."

The child should give one statement at a time and pause at the close of it. Use the word "sentence" informally at first.

Show how a sentence can be recognized by starting with a capital letter and closing with a mark of punctuation.

330

Help the child to recognize a sentence by dictating a sentence, reading it in a story or by having the child give a sentence in answer to a question. A child may tell one thing about an experience.[10]

What really determines whether or not a group of words is a sentence is not easily answered. Textbooks often define a sentence as follows: "A sentence is a group of words that in itself gives a whole thought." [11] The textbook from which this definition was taken follows with the statement: "A sentence is understood when read apart from the sentence that preceded it." [12] This, of course, is not entirely true, since many statements are perfectly good sentences but have little or no precise meaning apart from the remainder of the expression. The best examples are the sentences of one word each such as "Yes," "Go," or "Good."

Defining a sentence as a group of words expressing a whole or complete thought should be appoached with caution. Rather, a sentence should be thought of as a device for expressing an idea. With this in mind attention should be given to the idea and expressing that idea in a way that is clear and exact with no thought of a definition. With ample opportunity for expression, and with careful attention by the teacher in the guidance of expression to its greatest effectiveness, children will very early discover that a sentence always has at least a subject and a complete verb, either expressed or implied. They learn that there is always a word or several words present or implied which makes the group of words state something. They also learn that another word or several words is present or implied about which something is stated. They come to realize, also, that sometimes other elements must be present or implied to express the idea with clarity and exactness, and that the inclusion in a sentence of too many elements may lead to lack of clarity.

Sentence sense. There are no shortcuts to the understanding of the sentence. The desired understanding comes about only through constant and conscious effort on the part of teacher and pupil. The pupil learns that his sentences must make "sense"; that is, that they must not be vague or incomplete and that they must not try to tell so much that the meaning is confused or lost. The following suggestions for developing sentence sense should be helpful for most pupils.

[10] *Child Growth Through Language Experience,* The Language Arts Committee, School City of South Bend. South Bend, Indiana: The South Bend Board of Education, September, 1952, p. 149.
[11] Harold G. Shane, Florence K. Ferris, and Edward E. Keener, *Building Good English.* River Forest, Ill.: Laidlaw Brothers, 1956, p. 304.
[12] *Ibid.*

1. Provide children with ample opportunity for oral composition, especially in the primary grades.
2. Encourage pupils in their oral expression to form habits of using sentences that make sense, that are clear and complete.
3. Begin by emphasizing one-sentence statements, with the child understanding that his sentence must tell one thing and only one thing.
4. From the one-sentence composition move to the two- and three-sentence composition as sentence skill develops.
5. Continually expose pupils to good sentences that are read well by a good oral reader. This generally means that the teacher will read well-written materials frequently to the children in a voice that portrays "sentence feeling."
6. Encourage pupils to do considerable group composing and dictating of letters and other forms of written expression in the early grades.
7. Provide exercises in which each child tells one thing about some personal experience, such as an excursion, a project, or a picture.
8. Make frequent use of dictation exercises which require punctuation and capitalization.
9. Encourage children to answer questions with the expression of one complete thought.
10. Provide exercises in which pupils are required to distinguish between fragments and complete sentences.
11. Insist on pupils' proofreading their own writing.
12. Provide exercises for making sentences out of non-sentence groups of words.
13. Use matching exercises made up of short lists of complete subjects in one column and complete predicates in another.
14. Provide exercises for breaking up "run-on" sentences into correct sentences.
15. Develop the sentence concept through the use of contrast. Brief stories told by children may be written twice by the teacher in such ways that both good and poor sentence sense is shown. The two compositions should be compared, discussed, evaluated, and the poor form should be reconstructed.
16. Provide exercises for the organization of sentence elements into their proper relationships.
17. Give careful explanations of the various types of incorrect sentences with illustrations of each.
18. Make certain that the child is able to recognize verbs, which are really the core of every sentence, and around which all the other words are grouped as subject or predicate modifiers. Next see that he learns to find the subject of verbs and to see how a verb and its subject form all the framework of sentences. After this pupils can advance to the study of words which modify the subject and verb.

Omissions. A sentence is weak or incomplete if too little is said about the thought it attempts to express. Too often pupils do not know when the thought they are expressing is complete; that is, their own thinking is incomplete and not clearly in mind before the expression is begun. The natural result of such inadequate thinking is the omission of parts of the sentence necessary for complete understanding. For example, the words *The wind blew* may express a complete thought, but they also omit elements needed in the development of the essential idea. *The cold wind blew the snow into deep drifts* may better express the intended thought. The pupil using the first sentence may have used it because he had not thought about the details of what he wanted to say, or he may simply have neglected filling in the essential details for the reader or listener. This difficulty may be corrected by insisting that the pupil have a clear understanding of his ideas before attempting to organize them for expression. This leads to effective teaching of sentence sense.

Loose "and's." For young children a common fault in sentence construction is the repeated use of "and" to tie together a series of simple sentences. The otherwise interesting little story which follows is an example of this common error.

Yesterday was my birthday and I was eight years old and my mother and father gave me an electric train and we had a birthday cake.

While all sentences need not be simple sentences, children should be encouraged to express only one idea at a time in a sentence until they have firmly grasped the idea of sentence construction. This problem of loose "and's" is a part of the total problem of good sentence structure. With the development of sentence sense and the ability to use variety in word order the matter of too many *and*'s will gradually be eliminated.

Run-on sentences. The use of run-on sentences is the result of inadequate understanding of the sentence, inadequate understanding of the use of capital letters and end punctuation, or carelessness on the part of the pupil. Practice in finding sentences in a paragraph is one of the most effective means of correcting this bad habit. The example below shows this type of exercise.

The following sentences should be written in a paragraph. Decide where each sentence begins and ends. Then write the paragraph correctly.

the other day we saw a new streamlined train the cars were built of aluminum the whole train shone like silver it was running on the track along the river it went so fast we saw only a shining streak as it went by [13]

[13] Harry A. Greene and others, *Building Better English, Grade Five.* Evanston, Ill.: Row, Peterson and Company, 1947, p. 57.

333

Sentence clarity. Constantly reworking and rewriting his own sentences to make them express meaning clearly, concisely, interestingly, and accurately is the best procedure for the pupil to use in developing clarity in sentence construction. Particular attention needs to be given to the use of modifiers to help to build up an idea or to create a colorful picture, as the following example shows.

The children had returned from a study trip to the harbor. They wanted to write about their experiences, but many of them were not satisfied with the sentences they could write and asked the teacher for help.

Teacher:	Perhaps we could write a sentence on the board and then see how we can make it different and better.
John:	Here's one of mine. It's a sentence, but it doesn't tell much—"We saw the waves on the beach."
Teacher:	Yes, that is a good sentence to work on. Perhaps someone can make the sentence tell more about the waves.
Patty:	The waves tumbled over each other.
Sally:	The waves rushed to the shore.
Teacher:	Could someone put those two ideas about waves together?
John:	The waves tumbled over each other as they rushed to the shore.
Martin:	I know another way to describe the waves—sometimes they're lazy.
Patty:	Lazy, lapping waves.
Sally:	The waves lazily lapped at the white sands of the beach.
Teacher:	That has a nice sound and makes a good picture. Anyone else have ideas?
Pete:	Sometimes the waves are noisy—they thunder and pound on the rocks.
Teacher:	Would we say that noisy waves lapped at the shore?
Martin:	No, they dash and splash.
Patty:	The roaring, tumbling, pounding waves dashed against the rocks.
Louisa:	I think the waves look like they're dancing.
Margaret:	Little bent-over dancers with white lace caps.
Polly:	And the dancers just vanish and more keep coming.
Teacher:	Those are lovely ideas. Can someone put them together in a sentence?
Martin:	The white-capped waves danced to the shore and —and—
Polly:	Vanished in misty spray.

334

Teacher: I've written those sentences in my notes and I'll put them on the board so you can see them and use them if you wish.[14]

Variety and word order. Variety in word order comes from flexibility in thought and expression. Smith suggests that it be taught through appeal to the interest achieved by saying the same thing in different ways.[15] She gives these examples at the primary grades level:

There was a tiger walking around his cage at the zoo. There was a monkey hanging on a swing and jumping around. There was a polar bear splashing in the water.

There was a tiger walking around his cage at the zoo. A monkey was hanging on a swing and jumping around. Splashing in the water was a polar bear.

Children should be encouraged to take an idea and see how it may be expressed in differently arranged sentences, such as:

I saw the fishing boat leaving the harbor as I came down to the dock.
As I came down to the dock, I saw the fishing boat leaving the harbor.
The fishing boat was leaving the harbor as I came down to the dock.

This activity could be followed by a discussion of which sentence various children liked best and why. Language textbooks contain practice exercises for the development of sentences with changed word order which suggest that each sentence be rewritten by inverting the subject and predicate.[16]

1. The deer sped away into the forest.
2. The deep voice of the clock boomed solemnly over the sleeping town.
3. A tiny, red-roofed hut could be seen far down the valley.
4. A herd of buffaloes thundered across the plain.
5. A footsore and weary dog straggled behind the rickety cart.

INTEREST FACTORS

Listening to interesting stories and reading them are both ways by which children can become aware of the importance of factors which make

[14] *Arts and Skills of Communication for Democracy's Children,* Vol. II. San Bernardino, Calif.: San Bernardino County Schools, 1954, p. 263.
[15] Dora V. Smith, "Growth in Language Power as Related to Child Development," in *Teaching Language in the Elementary School,* Forty-third Yearbook of the National Society for the Study of Education, Part II. Chicago: The University of Chicago Press, 1944, p. 68.
[16] Mildred A. Dawson and others, *Language for Daily Use, Grade Six,* 4th ed. Yonkers-on-Hudson: World Book Company, 1959, p. 144.

for interest in their own expression. One language textbook suggests that children select stories they like from such collections as *Arabian Nights* and *The Jungle Book* and then discuss reasons why their stories were enjoyed. Points suggested for the children to consider are:

It tells about interesting characters and events.
The words in the story make me see and feel all that happens.
There is plenty of action.
The characters seem alive.
The characters converse.
No part is dragged out too long.
It has a surprise ending.[17]

Lessons similar to this can be used to show the importance of various factors that help to make oral and written expression interesting.

There are many factors which effect interest. Some are taught in incidental ways and some are developed through specific lessons, as suggested above. The factors of content concreteness, and the use of examples and similes are sufficiently important in all expression to justify special emphasis here.

Content. The first consideration in expression should be given to the selection of the topic. Expression should not be attempted unless the person attempting it has something to say, something about which he is informed and about which he can speak or write with authority and confidence—confidence and authority usually based upon experience. In developing the importance and use of interest factors the teacher must give attention to sources of content. In most instances, this means providing opportunities for children to enjoy direct or indirect experiences. On the basis of the background of each child, the teacher can guide him in the selection of the topic and the content that will result in expression that is both interesting and appropriate.

Concreteness. Words are either *concrete* or *abstract*. A concrete word is one whose referent can be touched or seen, while an abstract word refers to an idea. Not all words, of course, can be or should be concrete, and not all concrete words are of like definiteness. The word *ship*, for example, is less definite than is *cruiser*. In expression, interest and meaning will be improved through the use of the words and phrases which are as concrete as is possible. The following report given by a child after a study of airlines shows the use of concreteness in expression.

[17] Mildred A. Dawson and others, *op. cit.*, p. 230.

336

My picture tells you that on big airliners you can get your meals as you sit in your seat. The stewardess has a small kitchen, called a galley, where foods are kept cold and hot. The food is placed in light plastic dishes on a tray. For dinner, on my flight to New York, I had roast beef, potatoes, peas and carrots, a salad, ice cream and milk. You can see it here in my drawing. It was fun to be eating three thousand feet above the ground and in the clouds.[18]

The importance of concreteness in stimulating interest can be demonstrated to children through the comparison of materials. Exercises that call for listing words in order of their definiteness and or concreteness are helpful, too, as is the use of a dictionary to determine the exact meaning of a word. Particular attention should be given to the exact meanings of synonyms in order to use the one that expresses the meaning most definitely and concretely. The most effective means of developing skill in the use of concreteness in expression is by the actual construction of sentences and paragraphs and by constant critical editing and revision of the product.

Examples and illustrations. Expression is made interesting through the use of examples and illustrations, as the child who wrote about eating in an airliner showed by drawing a picture to accompany his report. Teachers sometimes insist upon the exclusive use of words for expression, or upon a conciseness of words which may or may not be the best way to express the idea or information. The judicious use of illustrations may help to secure interest and achieve understanding. The child who in a letter to his grandmother wishes to tell her that his puppy is getting fat should be encouraged to write something like this: "Our puppy is getting fatter every day, and now is as fat as that red pig of Grandpa's."

Similes. The use of similes is another way by which interest may be added to expression. The purpose of similes is to give enriched meaning to composition by expressing comparisons or likenesses which are themselves interesting and readily understandable. Similes are always announced by such words as *like* or *as*. Children should learn to use the simile idea in general for showing comparison as a means of adding interest and meaning to their oral and written expression.

These suggestions for teaching the use of similes, examples, and figurative expressions are representative of procedures teachers can follow to encourage variety and interest in expression.

[18] *Child Growth Through Language Experience.* The Language Arts Committee, Tracy Rose, general chairman. South Bend, Ind.: Board of Education, September, 1952, p. 129.

1. Encourage children to list interesting comparisons they encounter in their reading, in assembly programs, in television and radio programs, and at home, and to share them with other members of the class.
2. Encourage children to watch for opportunities to use examples, figures of speech, and interesting comparisons in their written and oral expression.
3. Have the children maintain a column on the bulletin board similar to the "Spiced Tongue" in the *Reader's Digest*.
4. Have the children practice completing sentences such as the following with the most interesting phrase:
The boat rocked as—.

ORGANIZATION

When a child begins to recognize relationships he is beginning to organize. Activities such as telling a story in proper sequence, putting together a puzzle, making a list of things seen on a field trip, or making an outline are all organizational activities. Organizational ability as a part of the thinking process must be developed before the child can become skilled in arranging the order of his facts in his written or spoken expression.

Sequence of ideas within the sentence. No set formula can be stated for the presentation of ideas within the sentence. Many dull and uninteresting sentences are the result of always placing the subject first and following it with the predicate. Actually almost any word or phrase may be used for the beginning of the sentence or for the ending of it so long as the resulting sentence makes sense and fully and clearly expresses the intended idea. Simple sentences may be made interesting by varying the ways in which they begin. Children should be encouraged to transpose an appositive to the beginning of a sentence, to place a word or phrase modifier at the beginning, and to use increasingly complex and compound-complex sentences. It is not expected, of course, that the children learn these terms or receive direct teaching on their use, but rather they should be encouraged in these and other natural ways to make their sentences interesting, varied, and meaningful.

Connectives. The run-on sentence construction appears far too frequently in the expression of children at every grade level. Young children often have difficulty in keeping their ideas distinct, while older children are not always sure of their punctuation and thus tend to run simple sentences together in a monotonous pattern. Children should be advised that although *and,* as well as other connectives, are perfectly good words, they should not be used too frequently. A positive approach to the problem of using too many connectives seems to be the best teaching procedure. The teaching emphasis should be upon the natural use of connectives as they are needed for clearly expressing the meaning intended. Children learn the use of other connectives than *and* or *but* by practicing such forms as *for, which, if, when,* and *because* when opportunity arises.

Some suggestions for teaching the proper use of connectives are:

1. Select and read to the class stories of generally equal interest; one in which all of the sentences are short, one in which all of the sentences are long, and one in which the sentences vary in length. Have the children decide which story they like best and why.
2. Select and write on the board several paragraphs having short choppy sentences. Have the children decide which sentences to combine and how to combine them.
3. Compile a list of connectives, such as:

and	since	wherever	as soon as
so	until	whenever	unless
but	where	that	then
if	when	because	
who	which	although	

4. Have each child bring to class some sentences from his own writing showing how he used good connectives in rewriting them.
5. Select a sentence, such as: "John was happy, *and* he began to laugh." Discuss the relationship of the two parts of the sentence leading to the selection of some other word for *and,* on to a complete reorganization of the sentence.
6. Through such exercises as the above, lead children to discover that:
   And is used to join ideas of equal importance.
   So, therefore, since, because show cause or reason.
   When indicates time.
   Whenever indicates time and repetition.
   But is used when there is something unexpected to follow.
   Who, which, that are good substitutes for *and he, and it.*

Order of sentences within paragraph. In order for children to use good paragraphing habitually, it is necessary to develop a feeling for the paragraph in much the same manner as sentence sense is developed. Children should learn about paragraphs as the need arises; that is, when they need to include a number of distinct topics within a single unit of expression. Actually this is not too difficult to teach in the primary grades if they have first learned to write single sentence paragraphs and later paragraphs of two and three sentences with the emphasis always being on the idea of beginning a new paragraph when a new idea or unrelated information is introduced. Teaching the single-sentence paragraph and later the paragraph of two or three sentences leads children to recognize that a paragraph has a main idea, or as someone has expressed it that sentences are like the branches of a tree—they all lead to the trunk, or main idea.

One teacher taught the organization of material into a report and at the same time developed the idea of good paragraphing by using the following procedure:

1. I took the information one child had obtained and wrote the statements on the board.
2. They read the statements.
3. They decided which statements belonged together.
4. They decided which group of statements should come first, second, etc.
5. They read the report with statements in correct order.[19]

Points to remember in teaching good paragraphing include the following:

1 Emphasize the function of the paragraph as an aid to clarity of expression.
2. Stress the importance of putting sentences in logical or sequential order.
3. Inspect and analyze each pupil's writing for improved sentence sequence.
4. Encourage children to watch for ways in which professional writers move skillfully from topic to topic and use paragraphs in their writing.
5. Demonstrate to children that the beginning sentence should be interesting enough to get the reader's attention and let him know what the paragraph is about and that the ending sentence is actually needed in the paragraph.

Notetaking. As children read, study, carry on experiments, participate in field trips, conduct interviews, listen to programs and reports, and watch films, there is an almost constant demand for notetaking. Notetaking is not something that is learned incidentally. It is an activity that calls for the use of learned organizational skills that are a part of logical and sequential thinking processes. Usually the development of these necessary skills begins in the kindergarten and first grade when the teacher writes lists of things to do, things to watch for on a trip, things seen on the trip, and things to be remembered. Other activities for the primary grades which begin the teaching of notetaking are: (1) drawing pictures to show ideas or facts, (2) building sand, block, and clay representations of ideas, (3) having children dictate descriptive labels, and (4) having children find pertinent passages. In the intermediate grades these activities are appropriate: (1) building more complex replicas, such

[19] *Using Language.* Wilmington, Del.: The Division of Elementary Education, Wilmington Public Schools, 1955, p. 63.

as models, pictures, diagrams, and illustrated maps, (2) individual or group dictation of memoranda or sentences based upon observation or reading, and (3) oral discussion of ideas and things to look for before individual notetaking is done. An illustration of this latter suggestion is given in one curriculum guide.

In the study of "Modern Press and History of Records" a group of children planned a study trip to a large city newspaper office. They discussed the important questions they wanted to ask and noted the things they wished to observe. These were listed on the board and included:

Who gives the reporters their assignments?
How does a linotype operate?
How many papers are printed in a day?
How does news come over a teletype machine?
How are pictures printed in a paper?
Where is the city desk located? [20]

Children should be taught to take accurate notes. In their reading they should learn to take exact notes but *not* to copy the exact words of the writer except as quoted material. Encouraging children to copy the exact words of a selection into their notes, as is suggested in some sources,[21] may really lead to unintentional plagiarism in their writing. Certainly children should exactly understand the idea, fact, or opinion of the writer, but copying the exact words can be done with little or no thought. Teachers should insist that the children indicate in their notes the exact source of the information.

Outlining.   From the time children first learn to write independently, they can be helped to jot down their ideas and organize them in sequence. This is the beginning of outlining and may be as simple as:

> I went to the park.
> I saw the animals.
> I had a balloon and ice cream.
> I came home on a bus.

Outlining should be taught for a specific purpose. Each occasion calling for the making of an outline should accomplish the maximum with the minimum of time spent on actual outline making. Thus the idea will become established that the making of an outline is an aid to another

[20] *Arts and Skills for Democracy's Children,* Vol. II. San Bernardino, Calif.: San Bernardino County Schools, no date, p. 280.
[21] See for example, Alvina Treut Burrows in Chapter 8 of *Social Studies in the Elementary School,* Fifty-sixth Yearbook of the National Society for the Study of Education, Part II. Chicago: The University of Chicago Press, 1957.

activity. The first teaching of outlining should be done on a group basis with the pupil activity being oral and the teacher doing the writing. The children should work out composite outlines together, and as needed, copy them individually. Some pupil activities in organizing facts and outlining that can be handled cooperatively are the following:

1. The dictating of a story which the teacher writes on a chart. The story is then cut into strips and the pupils arrange the sentences in outline form.
2. The listing of events that happened on an excursion in the order of their happening.
3. The outlining of some process in either logical or chronological order.

The teacher should always stress the fact that any task worth doing is worth planning in advance, and that outlining is valuable as an advance plan for many activities, even those in which language expression is not involved. Outlining should be developed thoroughly when it is introduced and reviewed occasionally throughout the year. Of course, the initial teaching of formal outlining is much more meaningful and acceptable to children if they have had an adequate background of training in organizing their own thinking, planning, and recording.

One curriculum guide suggests developing the concept of outlining through a particular experience, such as the cooperative planning of an oral report for an assembly program following a class visit to the International Airport.

Discussing highlights of the visit

Selecting main ideas to be presented in oral report

Writing these main ideas on the chalkboard as topic headings

Listing the important facts related to each of the topics as a series of notes. under each heading

Developing, according to standard form, a cooperative outline from the information recorded by arranging topics in order of importance, as determined by class, and organizing the related facts under each topic

Using the completed outline as a guide for presenting the oral report

Providing additional cooperative experiences in developing both sentence outlines and topic outlines

Stressing the correct use and placement of Roman numerals, subheading capital letters, Arabic numerals; capitalization and punctuation

Encouraging children to use language texts and chart models as reference aids in proofreading their outlines [22]

[22] *A Guide for the Teaching of Language Arts.* San Francisco: San Francisco Public Schools, 1955, p. 19.

VOCABULARY

The best means for enlarging and giving breadth and depth to a child's vocabulary is the provision of many opportunities for new, life-like, and interesting experiences. For example, kindergarten or first-grade children may be taken to visit a farm. From such an experience, the following words and perhaps many more might be added to their vocabularies:

milking machine	pasture	harvest	flock
tractor	manger	cattle	irrigate
barn	grain	orchard	
silo	crop	well	

Opportunities for direct experience may be given children in many ways and in all areas of the curriculum. All such experiences should provide for a heavy emphasis on the enrichment of the children's vocabularies. Here are some ways often used, particularly in the primary grades:

1. Through manipulative activities that involve handling various materials, tools, and equipment; learning new names and understanding directions; discussing plans and results.
2. Through social experiences within the classroom, such as the "show and tell" period, the daily news period, committee work that calls for planning and discussing, free conversation periods, or general class discussion.
3. Through developing the children's social responsibility for receiving and greeting guests, extending courtesies, and helping one another.
4. Through developing children's interest in the natural environment and in community activities by means of field trips that entail preliminary discussion of plans, training in observation, and eventual discussion of the total experience.
5. Through having children observe and handle specimens and articles brought into the classroom in connection with science or social studies.
6. Through arousing interest in setting up a class science museum or hobby display that involves classification, organization, and the making of appropriate labels.
7. Through encouraging children's interests in words and urging them to be more and more curious about words.[23]

Unquestionably it is possible that many activities which school children engage in that hold possibilities for vocabulary growth may not in fact accomplish this growth. Definite guidance in word study is necessary

[23] Adapted and expanded from list by Mildred A. Dawson, *Promoting Vocabulary Growth,* Language Arts Notes, Number 5. Yonkers-on-Hudson: World Book Company.

343

if maximum use of the activities in building vocabulary is to be secured. On this point Smith says:

Merely setting the stage is not enough. Conscious attention to the meanings of words and to their usefulness for the expression of ideas is imperative. The teacher is in a position to lead children to a precision and extension of language which, without her assistance, they could not achieve for themselves. Sometimes the problem is to learn words new to the child's experience. Sometimes it is to give specific application to general terms, as in the case of *water,* now applied to *river* and now to *lake.* Sometimes it is to build generalizations out of specific experiences. Often it is to derive new meanings for old words previously met in different contexts, as in the instance of the "tow" rope and the call for "succor." Frequently, also, it is to help redefine the child's use of language by seeking the most *exact* or the most *concrete* word to express an experience which he has just had or shared with others. For example, first-grade children, stroking a bunny which was visiting school at Easter, were asked to tell what the bunny *felt like.* "It feels nice," "It feels fine," "It feels swell" were the immediate responses of the children. Without the teacher's urging that they help us to understand still more clearly *what* the bunny *felt like,* they would never have achieved the "It feels soft" or "It feels like silk," which came triumphantly in the end.[24]

Some suggested ways for the development of real consciousness of the meaning and use of words are the following:

1. Listing on the board and on charts new words encountered in classroom activities, in reading, and in out-of-school experiences. Following the listing these should be discussed and examples of their use shown.
2. Keeping individual lists of new words that the pupils like and want to use. This should not be an assignment of so many words a day, or anything of the sort that becomes drudgery, but something a child wants to do because he is interested in the words.
3. Making charts of "quiet" words, or perhaps "sound," "gay," "sad," or "musical" words. Charts may also be made of words to use instead of commonly over-worked words and of words for special occasions or special interests, such as football games, space travel, camping trips, and so forth.[25]
4. Find words and phrases that prompt images, such as "dancing leaves," "a pacing tiger," "a shining beach."
5. Building words from root words by adding various prefixes and suffixes. For example, the root word *port* might be used and as many prefixes and

[24] Dora V. Smith, "Growth in Language Power as Related to Child Development," in *Teaching Language in the Elementary School.* The Forty-third Yearbook of the National Society for the Study of Education, Part II. Chicago: The University of Chicago Press, 1944, pp. 54–55.

[25] Marguerite P. Archer reports in "Building Vocabulary with a Fourth Grade Class," *Elementary English,* 37:447–448; November, 1960, that the class found 104 words that could be used instead of *said.*

suffixes as possible added to it. Some would be: *report, transport, portable, portage, porter, reporter, export.*

6. Noticing alliteration and rhyme in posters and slogans, in picturesque and descriptive phrases, and in reading in general.
7. Suggesting ideas and topics for written compositions and oral reports which will bring forth new words and words used in new ways. Topics such as the following may do this:

> The Freshness of Spring
> Across the Nation by Jet Airliner
> Sounds at Night
> What I Saw in the Park
> What a Duck Sees as He Flies South

8. Helping children to effectively use clues in their reading to get the meaning of new words.

Not only must the school language program be concerned with the development of a wide and well exercised vocabulary through provision of activities which give direct experience to the child, but it must also provide for vocabulary development and mastery through other means.

Reading widely.   The practicality of developing word mastery through actual experience is limited. One of the best answers to this limitation lies in extensive reading. Strickland describes reading as a means of developing vocabulary as follows:

Reading, reading, reading. The more the children read the more meanings they learn.
Reading things one is interested in
Reading easy things for fun
Reading anything and everything that adds to the value of the things one is doing or studying
Reading to build new interests
Reading newspapers, magazines, books, catalogs—anything that adds interest to living.[26]

Wide reading as a means of vocabulary mastery is limited, of course, by the extent of the development of the pupil's reading skills. Some children may spend three or more years in reaching a point at which they can read widely and independently, while others may do so in their second school year. A real recognition of children's reading needs means that a wide range of materials suitable for all levels of reading skill and for a variety of interests must be provided. Each book or article that a child reads with understanding will reinforce his reading vocabulary and will

[26] Ruth G. Strickland, *The Language Arts in the Elementary School.* Boston: D. C. Heath and Company, 1951, p. 199.

give him confidence and a sense of mastery in using words which he recognizes and understands but hitherto has hesitated to use in his expression. Children need systematic guidance in the selection of reading materials if their vocabularies are to be effectively broadened and their understanding developed.

Sometimes children read fluently but without discrimination or feeling. These individuals need to be taught to note words or phrases which seem particularly well chosen and appropriate. They should be stimulated to discover and think about the feelings that various words arouse and to note the difference between vivid and colorless expression in their reading.

Using new words and new meanings. A word is not mastered and does not become a real part of the individual's vocabulary until he uses it repeatedly with confidence. A basic part of the language program dealing with mastery of vocabulary is the development of the child's confidence in using new words. Many times the meanings of words can be explained by the teacher as material is read. At other times children may check definitions in the dictionary or discuss as a group the meaning of some new word. A good way to develop confidence in using new words is illustrated in the following report of a kindergarten class:

After the first snowfall the children brought a bowl of snow into the room and watched it melt and *evaporate*. They learned the word as they observed the fact.

Next day Linda said, "My daddy doesn't believe that water *evaporates*, but I'm proving it to him. I put some water in a glass and each day some has *evaporated* until it will be all gone.[27]

Real understanding of the meaning of a new word is shown in this report:

Ronnie shared his prized guinea pigs with the class. The children watched the little animals eagerly as they gnawed and nibbled. They held them close to feel the soft warm bodies. They listened to the characteristic "conversation" of the guinea pigs. They heard the scratching and digging of tiny claws.

When the young guinea pigs were born and were less than an hour old, excited voices called, "See how tiny his claws are!" "Feel the soft velvety fur." "The babies are really miniature guinea pigs, aren't they?"

This last comment came from Joe who had been working on a miniature adobe house and had been fascinated by the new word miniature. He was eager to experiment with it in many situations.[28]

[27] *Communication: A Guide to the Teaching of Speaking and Writing.* Minneapolis: Minneapolis Public Schools, 1953, p. 26.
[28] *Arts and Skills for Democracy's Children,* p. 234.

Calling things by right names. Many words are open to different interpretation by different individuals; it is necessary, therefore, that children learn to use the right words if they are to convey the meaning intended. Children must be taught precision in the choice of the words used in their expression, as these words act as a bridge for mutual understanding between themselves and their reader or listener. At the kindergarten and first grade levels the teacher may begin by teaching the correct names of familiar objects such as parts of the body or school equipment and the like. The same practice should continue at every grade level.

Children should also be taught to understand that many words have similar but not identical meanings and therefore should be selected with care. For example, in describing the idea of eating too rapidly, the teacher asked the children to express more clearly the sentence. "He ate much too quickly." Some of the results were:

He gobbled his food like a young turkey who hadn't been taught his manners.

He gulped whole pieces of bread. They almost choked him.

He swallowed so fast, the milk just wouldn't go down and he had to wait to catch a little breath.[29]

Pronouncing words clearly and correctly. Errors in word usage as well as in pronunciation which are made by young children are very often the result of hearing and imitating mispronunciations. Pronunciation errors may also be a result of lack of careful attention to the use of the word, to difficult sounds within the word, or to misunderstandings about the word; for example, when a child uses *brang* as the past tense of *bring* believing it should match with the past tense of *ring* or *sing*. If a child is hesitant about the pronunciation of a word due to any of these or other reasons, he will frequently avoid the use of the word in his speech and writing. He will simply resort to the use of a word that he is confident he knows and make no attempt to master the use of the new word.

The teacher's own example in matters of pronunciation is especially important as a model for the children to imitate. Children soon become aware of the teacher's desire for them to use standard, acceptable pronunciation and, if the teacher-pupil relationship is as it should be, children will develop a sense of obligation to use the standard form.

Using the dictionary. Although teaching the use of a dictionary is discussed in a later section of this chapter, it should be noted here that

[29] *Developing Children's Power of Self-Expression Through Writing.* New York: Board of Education of the City of New York, pp. 79–80.

347

the use of a dictionary to facilitate and expand the vocabulary demands the ability to find and select the information needed for a particular purpose and to ignore other unrelated information. For example, a child may need to check the spelling of a familiar word. He may want to know how a word is divided into syllables. At the upper grade levels he may want to select the applicable meaning from the several meanings listed. The pupil should be taught to regard the dictionary as a reference source that contains much more information than may be needed at any one time.

Teaching the vocabulary of a subject.   Whenever a new unit, a new topic, a new country, or a new problem in science or social studies is being studied, the words of that particular problem, many of which are new to most of the children, should be put on the board or on a chart, pronounced, and called to the attention of the children in as many ways as possible. No opportunity should be overlooked for using these words in meaningful sentences in both oral and written expression. In a new area of study children should never be allowed to stumble and mumble over words or to avoid using the exact and specific words. The words should be left in view on the board or chart in order that the children may refer to them as often as necessary.

USING SOURCES OF INFORMATION

Skill in using the library and its materials as well as other sources of information is of great importance to both oral and written expression. Children in the middle grades, particularly, find themselves in a new world of experiences in contrast to those encountered in the primary grades. Their environments have expanded; they encounter many new facts and practices. They need to be correct and specific about information. It is essential that they learn how to use the valuable printed resources of this new world.

Instruction in the skills of properly using different sources of information involves several principles worth noting. The teacher should:

1. Provide for individual differences in pupil's abilities, interests, and needs wherever possible by small-group instruction and by using instructional materials of varying levels of difficulty.
2. Deal with individual or small groups selected on the basis of common needs.

3. Be sure that the pupils understand the purpose of the instruction. They need to know exactly what technique is being stressed and how it will contribute to effective independent study and research.
4. Lead the pupils to acquire feelings of responsibility for really understanding what they study. He should discourage rote repetition of words not fully understood, a practice which leads to verbalism or answering in the words of the book.[30]

THE DICTIONARY

Most people are intrigued by words and it is natural for children to be attracted by the book that tells so many interesting things about so many words. Children also seem to have a natural affinity for names and pictures of objects arranged in alphabetical order. The dictionary is such a basic source of information that if it were possible to teach the use of only one reference source, it probably should be the dictionary.

Skill in using a dictionary develops slowly and requires the guidance of a sympathetic and wise teacher. Dictionary skill is developed over a period of years and its teaching is the responsibility of every teacher encountered by the child in his school career. In most schools, the fourth-grade teacher has the task of really introducing the use of a simplified dictionary to the children. Since real skill is based upon use, beginning in the fourth grade at least each child should have access to a dictionary, preferably his own, which is suited to his level of understanding. One of the surest ways to get anyone to use a dictionary (or any reference source) is to have it easily accessible. Few people will go to another room, look on a closet shelf, move a pile of books, or ask the teacher's permission to get a dictionary.

Alphabetizing. Some knowledge of the alphabet is acquired by many children even before they come to school. When the child starts school, he soon learns the letters in his name, if he has not known them before. As he learns to read and to write, he learns all the letters and learns more about their order in the alphabet. Learning the alphabet involves more than simply memorizing the order of the letters. It should mean knowing instantly where a letter comes in the alphabet, and which letters immediately precede and follow it. Some suggestions for teaching these skills are:

[30] Adapted from Mildred A. Dawson, *Training Pupils to Study,* Language Arts Notes, Number 3. Yonkers-on-Hudson: World Book Company, 1955, p. 2.

349

1. Asking questions at various times throughout the day which call for remembering the position of letters. Questions such as the following are appropriate:
What letter is before *i*, after *i;* before *y*, after *y?*
Is *f* near the first or the last of the alphabet?
2. Turning to words beginning with certain letters in a telephone directory, glossary, or dictionary.
3. Pointing to or saying any letter and asking the children to say the alphabet forward or backward to some other letter.
4. Arranging lists of words alphabetically. The first lists should be those in which each word begins with a different letter. Later exercises may be given which call for alphabetizing based upon the third or fourth letters of words.
5. Making alphabetical lists of children's names, names of cities, or names of objects. At first, attention should be given only to the first letter.
6. Arranging lists of words in which all words begin with the same letter.
7. Giving the children free time to turn freely through dictionaries and explore for themselves.
8. Dividing the dictionary into quarters and learning what letters are in each quarter.
9. Practicing opening the dictionary to certain letters.
10. Practicing on such exercises as "If you are looking for *j* and open the dictionary to *h*, which way should you turn to find *j?*

Guide words. After children become acquainted with the dictionary and have developed considerable skill in alphabetizing, they are ready to learn to use the guide words at the tops of the pages in the dictionary. They may be shown the value of these guide words by such questions as: "Are there any words which come after the right-hand word?" Children must be shown that to use the guide words efficiently they must have a thorough understanding of alphabetical order in order to be able to tell quickly when looking at a word if it would come before or after the guide word at the beginning of the page. The following two sample lessons should be helpful in teaching about guide words: [31]

Discussion: Notice the two words at the top of each page in your dictionary. The one on the left side is the same as the first word on the page. The word on the right is the same as the word which appears last on the page. These words are called *guide words.* Turn to a page in your dictionary and read the guide words. Look up the word *insect.* Between what two guide words is it?
Directions: You may read the words below when studying about *airplanes.* Each word in the list is in your dictionary. Find each of the words and write the two guide words on that page.

[31] Iowa Elementary Teachers Handbook, Vol. 2, *Reading.* Des Moines: Iowa State Department of Public Instruction, 1943, pp. 173–174.

Word	First guide word	second guide word
propeller	———	———
hangar	———	———
aviation	———	———
airdrome	———	———
wing	———	———
beacon	———	———
ceiling	———	———
goggles	———	———
parachute	———	———

The line below represents page 472 in a certain dictionary. *Nest* and *new* are the guide words on the page. Underline the words in the following list which would be found on this page of the dictionary:

nest	472	*new*
lake		nerve
net		Negro
neutral		nail
neglect		nettle
nesting		next
nestling		

Other dictionary skills. One of the principal uses of the dictionary by middle and upper grade children is for help in pronouncing words. These children need to be taught to use pronouncing keys and diacritical marks and to understand syllabication and accent marks. Diacritical marks are of value only as they help pupils with pronunciation. These skills should be taught in situations that call for their use.

Children need to be taught also to find meanings of words. In most instances, a child looks up a word not merely to learn the meaning, but also to determine the meaning in a particular context, or to use the word in a particular way. The following is a sample lesson for teaching this skill:

Directions: The dictionary often lists many meanings for one word. The use of the word in the sentence tells you which one to choose. Before each sentence below put the number of the meaning which fits that sentence. Make up four other sentences, using the word with each of these same four meanings.
sup-port' (su-port'), v. 1. To hold up; to keep from sinking or falling; as pillars support the porch roof. 2. To bear. 3. To take sides with; to back up; as, to support a candidate. 4. To provide with food, clothing, shelter, etc.; as, he supports his mother.

351

1. He could not support the suspense any longer.
2. Many people must support a man to get him elected to office.
3 He helped to support his family by working after school.
4. The shelf was supported by braces.[32]

REFERENCE SOURCES

As children begin their use of books, they should be taught to recognize the importance of the table of contents and the index of a book in locating particular items of information. This teaching should begin with the first books children use in the reading class. The teacher calls attention to the table of contents and shows how it is a guide to information in the book.

Index. The index affords a much more exact way of locating information than does the table of contents. The two major skills necessary to use an index are deciding upon the topic or key word to look for and using knowledge of the alphabet to locate that topic or word. Ability to organize material, skill in finding topic sentences, and knowledge of the meanings of words will all aid in the development of skill in deciding upon the topic or word to look for. Knowledge of the order of the alphabet is taught in the same manner as was discussed in the section on the dictionary.

Card files and reader's guides. Children will readily recognize that a card file or a reader's guide is organized in alphabetical fashion. They are quite likely to have difficulty with the abbreviations and references used. In most instances teachers should secure the assistance of a librarian in teaching about these items. Preferably this instruction should take place in the library where the files and guides are to be used.

EXERCISES FOR THOUGHT AND DISCUSSION

1. Evaluate the suggested instructional program for improving usage. What would you add to this program?
2. How can you avoid overstressing the niceties of language to the point that the pupil flow of language in the classroom dries up?
3. Suggest a series of exercises for giving children practice in separating sentence fragments from sentences.

[32] *Ibid.,* p. 175.

4. State clearly the distinction between the so-called "loose and" and the "run-on sentence."

5. Illustrate ways in which the proper use of introductory words and connectives adds interest through improving the organization of the paragraph.

6. Evaluate the eight suggestions for vocabulary enrichment given in this chapter.

7. Develop a series of exercises designed to give your pupils practice in alphabetizing, using the index, or using guide words in the dictionary.

8. As a result of your study of this chapter prepare a series of concise statements which might be used as principles of method to guide you in teaching language expression in your classroom.

SELECTED REFERENCES

Arts and Skills of Communication for Democracy's Children, Vol. II. San Bernardino, Calif.: San Bernardino County Schools, no date.

BENFER, M. C. "Sentence Sense in Relation to Subject and Predicate." Unpublished master's thesis, State University of Iowa, 1935.

BLAIR, GLENN MYERS. *Diagnostic and Remedial Teaching.* New York: The Macmillan Company, 1956.

Child Growth Through Language Experience. The Language Arts Committee, Tracy Rose, general chairman. South Bend: The South Bend Board of Education, September, 1952.

DAWSON, MILDRED A. *Promoting Vocabulary Growth.* Language Arts Notes, Number 5. Yonkers-on-Hudson: World Book Company, undated.

DEIGHTON, LEE C. *Vocabulary Development in the Classroom.* New York: Bureau of Publications, Teachers College, Columbia University, 1959.

DOLCH, E. W. "Vocabulary Development." *Elementary English Review,* 30:70–75; February, 1953.

EVANS, BERGEN and EVANS, CORNELIA. *A Dictionary of Contemporary American Usage.* New York: Random House, 1957.

GOLTRY, THOMAS K. "An Analysis of Sentence Structure in Oral Composition." Unpublish doctoral dissertation, State University of Iowa, 1935.

A Guide for the Teaching of Language Arts. San Francisco: Elementary School Division, San Francisco Unified School District, 1955.

HATFIELD, W. WILBUR. "The Shortest Road to Sentence Sense." *Elementary English,* 33:270–273; May, 1956.

Iowa Elementary Teachers Handbook, Vol. 2, *Reading.* Des Moines: Iowa State Department of Public Instruction, 1943.

Iowa Elementary Teachers Handbook, Vol. 4, *Oral and Written Language.* Des Moines: Iowa State Department of Public Instruction, 1944.

POOLEY, ROBERT C. *Teaching English Grammar.* New York: Appleton-Century-Crofts, Inc., 1957.

————. *Teaching English Usage.* New York: Appleton-Century-Crofts, Inc., 1946.

Teaching Language in the Elementary School, Forty-third Yearbook of the National Society for the Study of Education, Part II. Chicago: The University of Chicago Press, 1944.

Using Language. Wilmington, Del.: The Division of Elementary Education, Wilmington Public Schools, 1955.

part 4

Special Aspects

of the Language Program

CERTAIN SPECIAL ASPECTS OF THE LANGUAGE PROGRAM WHICH LIE OUTSIDE the specific fields of objectives and methods are treated in the five chapters comprising Part Four. The first of these evaluates the place of formal grammar in the program of elementary language instruction. Another stresses the importance of creative expression. A third places a proper emphasis on the importance of reading as a receptive language art. Two chapters present much-needed material for the use of teachers and supervisors in the selecting, evaluating, and using of textbooks and supplementary workbooks and practice materials in the classroom.

12

Grammar in the Elementary

Language Program

THE PURPOSE OF THIS CHAPTER IS TO CONSIDER THE TEACHING OF grammar as it affects the language program in the elementary school. The discussion centers around the following topics:

  a. The nature and meaning of grammar.
  b. The relation of grammar to language.
  c. Theoretical values of grammar.
  d. Evaluation of grammar as language method.
  e. The practical values of grammar.
  f. Grammar in today's language classroom.

THE NATURE AND MEANING OF GRAMMAR

The teaching of grammar in the elementary school is a subject of much controversy in spite of the sixty years of research evidence negating its value in improving oral and written expression. As a technical term, grammar has a number of meanings, unfortunately often not clearly understood. Furthermore, new meanings are being added constantly, along with the use of many modifiers, until we now have "traditional grammar," "functional grammar," "transitional grammar" in addition to formal grammar.

WHAT IS GRAMMAR?

The meaning of the word *grammar* depends upon the identity and the purpose of the individual using it. Grammar is variously defined in the dictionaries, seven different meanings being discussed in one unabridged dictionary. According to Good,[1] grammar is "strictly, the study of the

[1] *Dictionary of Education,* Carter V. Good, ed. New York: McGraw-Hill Book Company, Inc., 1945.

phonology, inflections, and syntax of a language. As commonly used, [grammar] is the part of language study that pertains to the different classes of words, their relations to one another, and their functions in sentences." According to this same authority, formal grammar is "logically organized principles and rules relating to the subject of English grammar." Formal grammar thus becomes identified as the scientific framework of language. Functional grammar, on the other hand, is described as "a method of learning correct usage in language through activity rather than through reference to rules." It should be noted, however, that *functional* is a relatively recently developed term as applied to grammar.

To the general public, grammar refers at one time to certain mechanical skills of expression, at another to correctness in expression, and at still another to the systematic study of the structure of language. In educational literature, grammar has been referred to as "the mechanics of English" and "English fundamentals." In some schools, grammar has come to mean all elements of English which deal with written expression. Nemec and Pooley [2] suggest that the use of the term *grammar* be applied to language structure, that matters of correctness be called *usage,* and that matters of form or custom in written or oral expression be called *convention.* The National Council of Teachers of English accepts these distinctions and defines grammar as "(1) the description of the formation of English sentences, including the relationships of words, phrases, and clauses to each other; and (2) the explanation of choices in those inflectional forms which still survive in modern English." [3]

Naturally the pro's and con's of the arguments arising from the lack of a common ground of understanding have resulted in much confusion and many misconceptions concerning the function of grammar in the teaching of language. As might be expected, believers in formal grammar have rushed to the defense of rules, classifications, parsing, and diagramming as being necessary both to the understanding of what is expressed by others and to the accurate expression of our own ideas. Apparently these individuals have mistakenly thought of grammar as the crystallized laws and rules to which usage and convention in language must conform rather than as "merely the organized description or codification of the actual speech habits of educated men. If these

[2] See Chapter 13 of *Children and the Language Arts,* Virgil E. Herrick and Leland B. Jacobs, eds. Englewood Cliffs, N.J.,: Prentice-Hall, Inc., 1955.
[3] The Commission on the English Curriculum of the National Council of Teachers of English, *The English Language Arts.* New York: Appleton-Century-Crofts, Inc., 1952, p. 284.

habits change, grammar itself changes, and textbooks must follow it. To preserve . . . requirements no longer followed by the best current speakers (or writers) is not grammatical but ungrammatical. It makes of grammar not a science but a dogma." [4] On the other hand, some teachers appear to have interpreted the findings of research concerning grammar to mean that all study of correct usage and form is to be eliminated from the language program. They have concluded mistakenly that the elimination of what they have called grammar means that no instructional emphasis is to be given such important elements as correctness, legibility, neatness, or other standards of acceptable usage or form. In practice neither of these widely divergent views can lead to a well-rounded, constructive program of language teaching in the elementary school.

RELATION OF GRAMMAR TO LANGUAGE

Even with the clarification that grammar is not spelling, punctuation, capitalization, or manuscript form, and that it is not usage, much controversy still exists as to just what should be included in grammar, and how what is included should be derived. If grammar is a description of the structure of language, the question immediately arises, "Whose structure?" or perhaps more accurately, "Whose description?"

Traditionally English grammar has been regarded as a fixed and unalterable body of knowledge concerning the structure of the language. The descriptive terminology used has been largely that derived from Latin grammar. Rules have been stated governing the use of words and parts of sentences—rules developed from a logical application of the Latin pattern to the English language. The assumption is made that language is uniform, that the same kind of language—"correct" language —should always be used, and that the rules concerning its structure are unchanging.

Two other points of view have arisen in the past half a century concerning the structure of the language. The first of these is that generally exemplified by the term "functional grammar." Functional grammar is not static in the sense that traditional grammar is—language change is recognized. Too, no attention is given to the so-called rules of grammar. The grammatical terminology, when used, is that which is used in the

---

[4] Albert H. Marckwardt and Fred Walcott, *Facts About Current English Usage*, English Monograph No. 7, National Council of Teachers of English. New York: D. Appleton–Century Company, 1938, pp. 133–134.

traditional descriptions of the language, though many of the traditional and formal descriptions are not dealt with. The emphasis being upon usage and sentence construction, in effect no grammar is taught except as it affects (directly) items of usage and sentence construction. This point of view is the one expressed in the quotation from *The English Language Arts* in the preceding section.

A third approach to the description of the language structure has arisen in comparatively recent years through the efforts of some linguistic scholars. Linguists refute the idea that the system of one language may be imposed upon another; thus they have rejected the idea that the language structure which may be described by Latin grammar will serve to explain the structure of English.[5] In addition, the inappropriateness of Latin grammar for describing the structure of English has led to dissatisfaction with Latin labels and nomenclature in general. The grammar of the linguist, then, using different terminology from that used in traditional and functional grammar, is known by such names as "the new grammar," structural grammar, structural linguistics, and descriptive linguistics.

The principal issue upon which these points of view are based is whether the structure of a language is inherent in the language itself or whether the structures of all languages are similar enough that they may be described by a common grammar. The evidence, however, is overwhelmingly in favor of the view that a language itself is systematic, that it is a system, and that while there are difficulties in describing that system adequately in a grammatical fashion, the grammar should *describe* the language that *is* rather then *prescribe* what it *should be*.

EVOLUTION OF GRAMMAR IN LANGUAGE TEACHING

The rise in the eighteenth century of a wealthy middle class of merchants led to the development of a systematic grammar. Aspiring to social prominence, these newly wealthy families employed tutors to help them gain refinement of diction and usage. The tutors based their judgments of correctness and elegance upon the system of grammar they knew best—that of the classics, particularly Latin. With the recognition of composition as a school subject about the middle of the nineteenth century, grammar continued to occupy a prominent position in the language curriculum. Because Latin and the other formal and disciplinary subjects still actively dominated the curriculum, it was natural for composi-

[5] *The English Language Arts*, p. 281.

tion and language instruction to be considered a content subject rather than a skill subject, with the study of formal grammar as its chief content. Instructional emphasis in the English classroom was devoted almost entirely to learning the tenses of verbs and the cases of nouns, diagramming and analyzing sentences, and memorizing rules. What little opportunity for oral or written expression the pupils enjoyed was in the form of memorized orations or declamations and the writing of formal themes and compositions. Long after the need for such activities as letter writing, reporting, and taking minutes of meetings was recognized, correct form was still considered a matter to be taught separately from production by means of drill and the repetition of rules.

This approach sought to make the English language fit the rules of Latin grammar. The grammarians of the day formulated rules for the regulation of the English language that failed even then to recognize the trends in usage actually found among people of culture and education —rules founded on the basis not only of Latin grammatical forms but on usage found in formal literary works and language which traditionally had been considered elegant. The shortcomings of this approach are evident, of course, to any student who has advanced beyond the comic-book stage in reading, since he will have discovered for himself that reputable writers and speakers do not always follow the rules laid down by the grammar books. Proof of this fact is so widespread that only a few examples need be cited here.

Many language textbooks still attempt to teach the distinctions between *shall* and *will* and between *can* and *may;* yet how often do we hear such distinctions made in the speech or writing of people of education and culture? Then, of course, there is the rule that a sentence must not begin with *and* or *but*. One need only refer to the Bible to discover how frequently sentences in this highly respectable source begin with "And it came to pass . . ."

Opposition to the imposition of Latin grammar rules upon English has been expressed from the time of Shakespeare to the present. With the rise of linguistic science it became even more pronounced. For example, Jesperson in 1894 proposed the thesis that change in language is improvement, not corruption,[6] and the English grammarian Henry Sweet wrote in 1891 that teachers generally fail to realize "how unsettled grammar still is." [7]

Parallel with the research and observation which were producing con-

[6] *Ibid.,* p. 275.
[7] James Sledd, "Grammar or Gramarye?" *The English Journal,* 49:301; May, 1960.

vincing evidence that language is more than merely a matter of rules, the experimental psychologists were developing new theories and practices concerning the learning process. According to the evidence advanced by the psychologists, we learn by doing. It would seem to follow, therefore, that we learn to speak clearly and acceptably by having much experience in speaking; we learn to write, not by analyzing and diagramming sentences, but by writing them and rewriting them. Since a true learning experience demands that the activity be purposeful, the skills necessary to produce correct usage must be employed in meaningful situations. That is, they must be taught as they are actually needed in the expressional experiences of the individual.

These changes in the language program have been gradual but definite —a process of evolution rather than revolution. It may best be described by an examination of its aims. At the inception of language instruction in our schools, its purpose was to develop in the pupil a complete mastery of the elements of formal grammar. Today, the primary goal of language instruction is communication; communication in all its aspects of reading, writing, listening, and speaking.

THEORETICAL VALUES OF
FORMAL GRAMMAR

In the evolution of the teaching of grammar, four statements of its value have been advanced. Brief discussions supporting or attacking each statement are presented here. In a later section of this chapter the experimental evidence supporting or denying these values is reported.

GRAMMAR AS THE ANALYTICAL STUDY OF LANGUAGE STRUCTURE, FORM, AND CLASSIFICATIONS

This statement of the purposes of the study of grammar holds that grammar provides the only effective basis for the mastery of the expressional skills; that only through the study of grammar, involving the mastery of language forms, the learning of rules, the parsing and diagramming of sentences, can the student learn to express himself acceptably. Proponents believe that a detailed understanding of the individual parts of the sentence leads to correct usage and to good oral and written expression.

In assuming this analytical approach they overlook the rather obvious fact that children learn to use language through imitation and habit formation long before they encounter any need to analyze its structure. Such an analytical approach is, of course, the invention of an adult mind and meets no child need. Those who still believe in the effectiveness of this type of grammar totally disregard what research reveals concerning the repeated failure of formal grammar to function as a disciplinary subject or to transfer to improved English expression. The findings of research have shown repeatedly that there is no more relationship between a knowledge of grammar and good usage in language than there is between any other two unrelated subjects, as, for example, geography and language usage.

It is difficult to discover many good reasons for the survival of this approach to learning the English language. The grammar of Latin fails to meet the requirements of English in many ways, just as it would fail to function for any other foreign language. From what sources then comes the demand for continuing the teaching of formal grammar in the upper elementary grades? High school teachers of English and of the foreign languages commonly complain that the pupils sent to them from the elementary schools are ignorant of even the minimal essentials of grammar required in their subjects. This view, of course, is based upon the belief that knowledge of grammar is essential to the improvement of expression, or upon the holding of objectives for language expression other then the improvement of this expression. Authoritative opinion and research evidence would indicate that the responsibility of the language teachers in the elementary school is met in full if they give major emphasis to the continuous use of acceptable language forms leading to the development of effective habits of expression. Their job is not to stress abstract knowledge about the structure or the rules of the language to ease the burden of a few teachers of special subjects.

GRAMMAR AS A DISCIPLINARY SUBJECT

This very popular statement offered in defense of formal grammar for many years, and apparently still the view of many so-called academicians and critics of the schools, holds that the study of formal grammar, like the study of mathematics or natural science, is of definite value in developing the mind and improving the thinking of students. Such disciplinary subjects are believed to provide mental discipline and develop the power to think in an orderly and logical fashion in any similar field of activity. Specifically it is assumed that the study of formal grammar will transfer directly to the individual's abilities to express himself verbally.[8] Present-day authorities give little support to this theory in any subject area. Educational psychologists naturally recognize that in the interests of economy of effort and of learning efficiency transfers must take place. However, they are convinced that if the transfer is to take place the circumstances must be right, and that transfers can be negative as well as positive. In order for the transfer to be favorable, the teacher must be alert to point out the similar or identical elements in the learning situations.

GRAMMAR AS MEANS OF ESTABLISHING CORRECT IDIOMATIC USAGE

A third conception of the function of formal grammar holds that its study would stabilize or fix the idiom and usage of the language. This theory is based on the mistaken belief that the grammar of a language *determines* the usage patterns rather than *reflects* them. Under this theory our common expressions would fall into grammatical patterns labeled as correct or as incorrect depending on whether they conform or fail to conform to the rules of grammar. Actually the contrary is true, as is witnessed by the usages and the idiomatic phrases which appear in our periodicals and in the way educated and cultured people express themselves.

In spite of the attempts of grammarians to crystallize the idiom of our language, the evidence shows that idiomatic usage is not established by the grammar but by the practices of the social groups using the language. As a live and growing language evolves, new usages appear, new forms of expression are developed and, if found effective, adopted by society. The grammar of the language must grow or become obsolete. Every writer or speaker with an important message to express strives to choose the words and to formulate the sentences which will most effectively achieve his goal. In this way the language grows and grammar reflects the changes.

[8] It is interesting to note that even today so many thoughtful and well-intentioned people, many of them teachers, still believe that general training which improves an analytical skill like grammar will similarly improve creative skills such as are involved in oral and written expression. These same individuals would be the last to contend that the ability to write prose will carry with it the corresponding ability to write poetry. Yet prose and poetry, both being creative, are certainly much more closely allied than grammar with either prose or poetry.

GRAMMAR AS METHOD OF DEVELOPING UNDERSTANDING OF THE SENTENCE

One of the most potent arguments for the continued study of grammar is that by learning the forms and functions of the individual parts of the sentence the reader will understand and find meaning in the sentence as a whole. This contribution of grammar to the understanding of the sentence has been exploited by some authorities as the first and fundamental purpose of grammar.[9] However, in order for an individual to understand and make use of grammar for this purpose, he would need to know the nomenclature and be able to identify the elements of the sentence with which he has to deal, and to apply generalizations of what he knows to the particular sentence. The latter implies a considerable degree of maturity, certainly more than is present in most children in the elementary school.

The experimental evidence on the value of the grammatical approach to the development of skill in the construction of effective sentences does not justify the confidence in its effectiveness expressed by the believers in formal grammar. Specifically the evidence from numerous investigations on the value of a knowledge of grammar and diagramming in connection with the development of sentence skills discourages the continuation of this type of approach in the elementary language program.

EVALUATION OF GRAMMAR AS LANGUAGE METHOD

The value of the study of grammar is examined in this section, with evidence cited in support or criticism of the various theories. The grammar teaching being appraised is that defined earlier as formal grammar, but support or criticism of the "new" grammar is cited where appropriate.

FORMAL GRAMMAR AS DISCIPLINE

Grammar as a teaching method in English remained secure and almost unchallenged in the school curriculum until the new science of psychol-

[9] *The English Language Arts*, p. 285.

365

ogy began to develop in this country around the turn of the century. Along about that time the efficiency of learning and the validity of the assumptions of transfers in learning supposed to take place under the disciplinary theory came under critical questioning. Actually the problem of transfer was not of special importance so long as the major function of school training was to transmit previously accumulated cultural elements. At that time the formal subjects, such as Latin, algebra, geometry, and natural history were studied for two reasons. First, the knowledge of these fields was the mark of an educated man. Second, mastery of these and other generally difficult subjects was believed to strengthen certain mental faculties and thus provide the desired mental discipline, the primary educational objective. The accomplishment of this objective was dependent upon general learning, not upon the acquisition of specific skills. Gradually the belief developed that a much more important function of education is the production of change in the behavior of the individual. Under this philosophy, learning became the acquisition of specific skills, not broad general abilities. The individual learned to read, to comprehend, to compute, to solve problems, to write, to spell useful words; not merely to remember, to reason, to visualize in general situations.

In 1890, William James, the father of experimental psychology, reported the results of experiments showing that transfer effects in memory, perception, reasoning and others of the so-called mental faculties were so slight as to discredit the claims of formal discipline and the functional theory of learning.[10] Numerous other studies in special subject areas followed promptly. As early as 1906 Hoyt reported that pupils in the seventh and eighth grades with no training in formal grammar did as effective work in writing compositions or in interpreting literature as did those with two years of drill on formal grammar.[11] A few years later, Briggs conducted a carefully controlled classroom teaching experiment designed to reveal the extent of the transfer of grammatical skills to language abilities of seventh grade pupils. He concluded that "these particular children after the amount of formal grammar that they had, do not, as measured by the means employed, show in any of the abilities tested improvement that may be attributed to their training in formal grammar." [12] This study offered conclusive proof of the failure of formal

[10] William James, *Principles of Psychology*. Henry Holt and Company, New York, 1890.

[11] Franklin S. Hoyt, "Studies in English Grammar," *Teachers College Record*, 7:467–500; November, 1906.

[12] Thomas H. Briggs, "Formal English Grammar as a Discipline," *Teachers College Record*, 14:251–343; September, 1913.

grammar to transfer to such readily identifiable language skills as the statement of a definition, the application of a definition, or the ability to correct errors.

GRAMMAR FAILS TO FUNCTION AS ENGLISH METHOD

During the early decades of the present century, critical students of the problems of teaching English were quick to question the practical contributions of formal grammar as a method in the teaching of English. Segel and Barr gave a formal grammar test and a test of applied grammar to a large group of pupils and after analyzing the data concluded that "formal grammar has no immediate transfer value so far as applied English grammar is concerned."[13] In the next two decades Rapeer,[14] Boraas,[15] and Asker [16] in three independent studies corroborated the earlier findings of Hoyt and led to the general conclusion that "knowledge of formal grammar influences ability to judge grammatical correctness of a sentence and ability in English composition only to a negligible degree." [17] This conclusion has been confirmed many times, one of the most recent studies having been carried out by Kraus in 1957.[18] On the other hand, Mallis [19] and Senatore [20] report favorable results with junior and senior high-school students in developing clearer writing and better statement of ideas through the teaching of "structural grammar." However, the present authors know of no studies made in the elementary school supporting the teaching of any grammar, including structural or linguistically based, having any appreciable effect upon expression. In fact, many linguists would make no claim that the teaching of linguistics

[13] David Segel and Nora R. Barr, "Relation of Achievement in Formal Grammar to Achievement in Applied Grammar," *Journal of Educational Research,* 14:401–402; December, 1926.

[14] L. W. Rapeer, "The Problem of Formal Grammar in Elementary Education," *Journal of Educational Psychology,* 4:125–137; March, 1913.

[15] Julius Boraas, "Formal English Grammar and the Practical Mastery of English." Unpublished doctoral dissertation, Department of Education, University of Minnesota, 1917.

[16] William Asker, "Does Knowledge of Formal Grammar Function?" *School and Society,* 17:109–111; January 27, 1923.

[17] *Ibid.*

[18] Silvy Kraus, "A Comparison of Three Methods of Teaching Sentence Structure." *The English Journal,* 46:275–281; May, 1957.

[19] Jackie Mallis, "Experiment with the New Grammar." *The English Journal,* 46:427–435; October, 1957.

[20] John J. Senatore, "SVO: A Key to Clearer Language Teaching." *The English Journal,* 46:419–424; October, 1957.

367

or any form of structural or pattern grammar has any effect upon expression.[21]

Although teachers have long defended the thesis that a knowledge of grammar is essential to the proper understanding of the sentence,[22] the study by Benfer indicated a discouraging lack of relationship between the ability to identify sentence fragments and sentences, and grammatical skill in identifying subjects and predicates.[23] A similar lack of correspondence between usage test scores and the knowledge of the grammatical reasons for the accepted usages found in a critical statistical study of a well-known grammar-usage test prompted two parallel studies.[24] Both of these involved the relationship of scores on a difficult and comprehensive test of punctuation skills and a knowledge of the rules governing the usages. Pupils with little knowledge of the rules made high scores on the usages and, with almost equal frequency, individuals with extensive knowledge of the rules made low scores on the usages.

In a comprehensive and carefully controlled experimental study by Butterfield, definitely superior results in the teaching of punctuation skills were obtained by direct teaching of the desired skills rather than by methods based upon the pupil's knowledge of the grammatical elements listed by English teachers as contributing directly to the punctuation skills.[25]

DIAGRAMMING FAILS TO PRODUCE MASTERY OF THE SENTENCE

The use of graphic analysis or sentence diagramming has long been a favorite teaching device of upper-grade teachers of language. Two different studies lead unquestionably to the conclusion that while diagramming responds nicely to training and is readily learned, it has very

---

[21] James Sledd, *op. cit.,* p. 298. This view is also advanced by Robert D. Williams in "Linguistics and Grammar," *The English Journal,* 48:388–392; October, 1959.

[22] That this thesis is still stoutly defended is shown by surveys of current practices in New York, Wisconsin, Illinois, and Georgia, reported by John J. DeBoer in "Grammar in Language Teaching." *Elementary English,* 36:413–421; October, 1959.

[23] Mabel Benfer, "Sentence Sense in Relation to Knowledge of Subjects and Predicates." Unpublished master's thesis, State University of Iowa, 1935.

[24] E. R. Butterworth, "Mastery of Punctuation Usages as Related to the Rules." Unpublished master's thesis, State University of Iowa, 1932. William A. Ortmeyer, "Relation of Punctuation Rules and Practices." Unpublished master's thesis, State University of Iowa, 1932.

[25] Claire J. Butterfield, "The Effect of Knowledge of Certain Grammatical Elements on the Acquisition and Retention of Punctuation Skills." Unpublished doctoral dissertation, State University of Iowa, 1945.

slight value in itself so far as production of sentence mastery is concerned. Many children enjoy the mechanical exactness of sentence diagramming. Teachers like it too, perhaps because it is a convenient form of busy-work. The only defensible reason for teaching children to diagram sentences should be the improvement it brings in their ability to create effective sentences. Unfortunately, the evidence shows that this is insignificant. Barnett, for example, demonstrated that children could be taught to diagram sentences rapidly and correctly, but that the skills thus acquired did not contribute in any significant degree to an improvement in pupils' language usage or in their abilities to read and comprehend sentences.[26]

Stewart examined this problem further in a comprehensive investigation involving twenty different school systems with classes selected and balanced in all essential respects.[27] Again the children in the experimental group demonstrated that they could be taught to diagram, but those in the control group, by spending the same amount of time given to the diagramming group, showed slightly more improvement in sentence mastery than did those who learned diagramming. These results raise a number of questions. Why spend valuable class time in acquiring a useless skill when the same time and energy would attain a useful objective? Is time spent in learning to diagram justifiable or is it mainly busywork? Why not proceed directly to the real goal of expression by having the pupils develop their sentence-writing skills by writing sentences arising out of their classroom activities?

ENGLISH GRAMMAR FAILS TO AID IN LEARNING FOREIGN LANGUAGES

While the argument that knowledge of English grammar is essential to the learning of foreign languages is still being advanced by some foreign-language teachers, leaders in the field of foreign-language teaching have long ago dismissed it. The evidence shows that foreign languages are learned as readily by those students with no knowledge of English grammar as by those with such knowledge.[28]

---

[26] W. W. Barnett, "A Study of the Effects of Sentence Diagraming on English Correctness and Silent Reading Ability." Unpublished master's thesis, State University of Iowa, 1942.

[27] J. Reece Stewart, "The Effect of Diagraming on Certain Skills in English Composition." Unpublished doctoral dissertation, State University of Iowa, 1941.

[28] Walter V. Kaulfers, *Four Studies in Teaching Grammar from the Socio-psychological Viewpoint.* Palo Alto, Calif.; Stanford University, 1945.

FORMAL GRAMMAR FAILS TO SATISFY
RESEARCH AND TEACHING GROUPS

In addition to the failures of grammar cited above, the attitudes of two influential professional groups on this problem should be given serious consideration. These organizations are the *National Council of Teachers of English* and the *National Conference on Research in English*. The second of these organizations in 1937 reported evidence substantiating earlier research showing the failure of grammar to function as a method of teaching language expression, and supporting the statement that "training in formal grammar does not result in a great gain in the writing of correct English or in the ability of the individual to recognize correct English in writing." [29] Hatfield, as chairman of the *Curriculum Commission of the National Council of Teachers of English* expressed the conviction of the commission that "all teaching of grammar separate from the manipulation of sentences be discontinued . . . since every scientific attempt to prove that knowledge of grammar is useful has failed." [30] Again, this same organization has recently taken the position that "labeling the parts of speech has proved in one research study after another . . . to be futile so far as its effect on speech and writing is concerned. Intermediate-grade pupils should have practice in the *use* of language, not in the classification of forms." [31]

VALUES OF GRAMMAR

The discussion of the meaning, history, and place of formal grammar leads to the conclusion that many of the claims made for it are unsupported by either the experimental evidence or the results. Grammar failed to function as a discipline, just as formal discipline failed as a theory of learning. It failed as a method of teaching, because it lacked the elements of good classroom method. It failed to develop effective language expression, because language is a skill field, not a subject-matter

[29] Harry A. Greene, "Principles of Method in Elementary English Composition," *Elementary English Review,* 31:485–493; December, 1937.

[30] W. Wilbur Hatfield, "What Grammar? And How?" *Virginia Journal of Education,* 29:318; May, 1936.

[31] *Language Arts for Today's Children.* Curriculum Commission of the National Council of Teachers of English. New York: Appleton-Century-Crofts, Inc., 1954.

area. Language is active, creative, not formal and analytical. Grammar failed at the curriculum level, because its methods slowed the growth and development of a live and growing language. The learning of rules, the study of the sentence elements, the diagramming of sentences, the study of the parts of speech, in addition to other formal methods, have not enabled language teachers to attain the desired objective of enabling the individual to express himself effectively. However, even though the results of research in the past fifty years have demonstrated that formal and indirect methods do not assure good, or even acceptable language expression, no one, least of all the present writers, would deny that a responsibly developed grammar does have a value in describing the structural framework of a language. An understanding of the function of this framework and an ability to work within it are of obvious value in learning to use the language effectively. Such understanding is not of equal value to all persons, however, nor are all elements of the framework of equal importance. Most importantly, there is little evidence to indicate that such understanding can be developed in the elementary school.

It is the conviction of the authors that the principal concern of the elementary school should be the teaching of usage rather than grammar; that is, the approach must be functional rather than formal. Any grammar program that makes use of structural linguistics, or anything else that passes as the "new" grammar may be as formal as that of the traditional grammar based upon Latin. There is no more reason for teaching a formal "new" grammar than for teaching a formal traditional grammar, considering the present lack of genuine evidence.[32] A functional grammar program consists of pupils meeting and mastering the essential language habits in situations that are as lifelike as possible in order that they may use them to communicate effectively in real life activities. The organization of the grammar program in this functional approach may be seen in the following principles:

1. Pupils develop language habits as they are needed in actual meaningful situations.
2. Only a limited number of skills of high social utility are presented for attack in the elementary school.
3. The pupil is led to discover his own deficiencies and is given practice only on those skills in which he individually has need of practice.
4. Clear, complete, effective expression is stressed at all times.
5. The pupils are led to a gradual awareness of the function of grammar in correct and effective expression.

[32] DeBoer, *op. cit.*, p. 419.

GRAMMAR IN TODAY'S LANGUAGE
CLASSROOM

Experimental psychology has shown that all learning takes place most readily when the motivation is strong. The functional approach in teaching usage, the common conventions, and essential language structure utilizes this principle by presenting the socially important skills for instruction as the need for them arises in the classroom. Take for example the simple matter of using capital letters. In most instances there is little question of which words should be capitalized. There are, however, many rules that cover these various kinds of words; at least the number would seem considerable to the child if all were presented to him at one time. Yet the rules or principles may be mastered without undue effort if the various needs are introduced as they arise in meaningful situations.

One of the earliest forms of written expression introduced in the language program is the writing of letters. Letter-writing is a valuable activity not only because of its high social utility, but also because it can be pleasantly motivated. Furthermore it introduces a surprising number of language skills, particularly those of capitalization and punctuation. Before the child has even begun to write, he has probably observed from his reading that people's names and new sentences begin with capital letters. As he writes his first letters, he has these concepts re-affirmed by the teacher and he also discovers that titles such as Miss, Mr., Captain, or Doctor are also capitalized when used with names, as is Dear in the salutation and as is the first letter in the complimentary close. As he addresses the letter—for in a properly motivated situation the letter will certainly be mailed—he learns that the names of the city and state to which it is to be sent are also capitalized. No rules are learned—the teacher simply shows that this is the correct procedure. Naturally the child is eager to be correct in order that the letter may reach its destination and that the receiver of it may be pleasantly impressed. In grade four when the social studies program includes the study of people of other lands, the child discovers that names of countries and the people who live in them are also capitalized, as are the names of rivers, mountains, and other place names. Perhaps a child may be stimulated to write a poem about children of another land. This is the time for him to learn by action as well as by observation that the first letter in each line of poetry should be capitalized. Gradually the concept of common and proper nouns becomes a part of the child's knowledge without his ever having learned a rule.

This is the fundamental concept behind the functional approach to grammar. No formal grammar is taught in the first six grades. Rather, the emphasis is on increasing the child's experiences and understandings, his abilities in securing and sharing information, his competence in meeting the usage needs of his life in school and out. Such grammatical elements as are mentioned are not presented in isolated form. The program consists in the development of language concepts beginning in grade one and growing continuously throughout the elementary school. Rather than beginning with the study of subjects and predicates, nouns and verbs, the child begins by writing sentences and then paragraphs. Emphasis is placed upon saying a thing clearly, completely, and interestingly. Gradually, he realizes that in order to be clear and complete a sentence must have two parts: the first tells who or what is the *doer;* the second expresses what is *being done*. In order that pupils and teacher may be able to talk about these parts without confusion, the terms *subject* and *predicate* may be introduced, and later *noun, pronoun,* and *verb*. Since interesting and colorful expression demands more than merely a noun and a verb, words that tell how, when, or where (*adverbs*) and those that tell what color, what kind, how many (*adjectives*) gradually become a part of the sentence concept. Later the techniques of rearranging the order of words for interest or clarity become a part of his knowledge.

Although no grammar is presented formally the pupils are gradually learning the grammatical concepts referred to above—concepts which can be fully grasped only after a long experience in trying to formulate sentences. Understanding of these concepts is thus gradual, and the technical naming of them, as such, may well be postponed until much later. Children actually begin their study of the sentence in the kindergarten when their teacher helps them begin and end these expressions of their thoughts. Very early, too, they learn to recognize that there are two parts to a thought expressed in a sentence. They do not call these parts subject and predicate, nor are they able to distinguish the parts of each. However, they are building toward an understanding (not a memorized definition) of the subject-predicate relationship.

It must not be assumed, however, that the functional approach to language instruction leaves the learning of language skills entirely to unplanned, incidental teaching. The program as a whole is carefully planned so that opportunities for motivated teaching and learning *will* arise, and activities are designed that will call for those skills which it is desirable for the child to learn. At each grade level the teacher will plan language activities to include both those skills that are prescribed for that grade by the state, city, or county courses of study and those that are discovered to need re-teaching for individuals or groups in the class, as revealed through the use of both standardized and teacher-made tests and other evaluative devices.

The following principles, as summarized by Tidyman and Butterfield, provide the fundamentals of the functional approach: [33]

1. Grammar is taught as needed in expressional activities.
2. New concepts are learned through a study of live language and therefore have meaning.
3. Terms and statements of rules *follow* ideas and understandings.
4. Observation of language plays an important role.
5. Familiar generalizations, recalled and applied in new situations, gain increasing clarity and breadth of application.
6. Development is orderly, systematic, and planned. Direction and rate of growth are determined by the teacher.

EXERCISES FOR THOUGHT AND DISCUSSION

1. Answer the question "What is Grammar?" as you understand it after having read this chapter.
2. Discuss the three current points of view regarding the relation of grammar to language.
3. Assemble arguments for and against the four theoretical values of formal grammar.
4. What does the evidence show regarding the contribution of formal grammar to mastery of the English sentence?
5. What is your personal attitude toward sentence diagramming as a useful technique in the language classroom?
6. What are the actual practical values of grammar? What place should it have in the elementary language program?
7. As a result of your study of this chapter prepare a series of concise statements which might be used as principles of method to guide you in your use of formal grammar in your language classroom.

[33] Willard F. Tidyman and Marguerite Butterfield, *Teaching the Language Arts.* New York: McGraw-Hill Book Company, Inc., 1951, p. 307.

SELECTED REFERENCES

ASKER, WILLIAM. "Does Knowledge of Formal Grammar Function?" *School and Society,* 17:109–111; January 23, 1923.

BARNETT, W. W. "A Study of the Effects of Sentence Diagraming on English Correctness and Silent Reading Ability." Unpublished master's thesis, State University of Iowa, 1942.

BENFER, MABEL. "Sentence Sense in Relation to Knowledge of Subject and Predicate." Unpublished master's thesis, State University of Iowa, 1935.

BORAAS, JULIUS. "Formal Grammar and the Practical Mastery of English." Unpublished doctoral dissertation, Department of Education, University of Minnesota, 1917.

BREDE, ALEXANDER. "Grammar Reconsidered." *Elementary English Review,* 16:86–90; March, 1939.

BRIGGS, THOMAS H. "Formal English Grammar as a Discipline." *Teachers College Record,* 14:251–343; September, 1913.

CARLSON, G. ROBERT. "Conflicting Assumptions in the Teaching of English." *The English Journal,* 49:377–386; September, 1960.

Commission on the English Curriculum. *The English Language Arts.* New York: Appleton-Century-Crofts, Inc., 1952.

COOK, LUELLA B. "Teaching Grammar and Usage in Relation to Speech and Writing." *Elementary English Review,* 23:193–198, 213; May, 1946.

DE BOER, JOHN J. "Grammar in Language Teaching." *Elementary English,* 36:413–421; October, 1959.

FRIES, CHARLES C. *The Structure of English.* New York: Harcourt, Brace and Co., 1952.

————. *American English Grammar.* English Monograph No. 10, National Council of Teachers of English. New York: D. Appleton–Century Company, Inc., 1940.

GREENE, HARRY A. "Direct versus Formal Methods in Elementary English." *Elementary English Review,* 24:273–285; May, 1947.

HATFIELD, W. WILBUR. "Using Grammar for Correctness and Style." *English Journal,* 31:137–142; February, 1942.

HAYAKAWA, S. I. *Language in Action.* New York: Harcourt Brace and Company, Inc., 1947.

HOYT, FRANKLIN S. "The Place of Grammar in the Elementary *Curriculum.*" *Teachers College Record,* 7:467–500; November, 1906.

KAULFERS, WALTER V. *Teaching Grammar from the Socio-psychological Viewpoint.* Palo Alto: The Leland Stanford University Bookstore, 1945.

————. "Grammar for the Millions." *Elementary English Review,* 26:1–11, 65–74, 107; January and February, 1949.

LAMBERTS, J. J. "Basic Concepts for Teaching from Structural Linguistics." *The English Journal,* 49:172–176; March, 1960.

LYMAN, R. L. *English Grammar in American Schools Before 1850.* Bureau of Education Bulletin No. 12. Washington: U.S. Government Printing Office, 1921.

MARCKWARDT, ALBERT H., and WALCOTT, FRED G. *Facts About Current English Usage.* English Monograph No. 7, National Council of Teachers of English. New York: D. Appleton–Century Co., Inc., 1938.

POOLEY, ROBERT C. "What Grammar Shall I Teach?" *The English Journal,* 47:327–333; September, 1958.

————. *Teaching English Grammar.* New York: Appleton-Century-Crofts, Inc., 1957.

SEGEL, DAVID, and BARR, NORA R. "Relation of Achievement in Formal Grammar to Achievement in Applied Grammar." *Journal of Educational Research,* 14:4–12; December, 1926.

STAGEBERG, NORMAN C., and GOODRICH, RUTH. *Using Grammar to Improve Writing,* Educational Service Publications. Cedar Falls: Iowa State Teachers College, June, 1953.

STEWART, J. R. "The Effect of Diagraming on Certain Skills in English Composition." Unpublished doctoral dissertation. State University of Iowa, 1941.

376

13

Developing Creative Expression

in Language

THIS CHAPTER DEALS WITH THE PLACE OF CREATIVE EXPRESSION IN the language program and the methods by which it may be developed under classroom conditions. The discussion emphasizes the following topics:

a. What is creative expression?
b. Creative expression in relation to the total language program.
c. Purposes of creative expression.
d. Stimulating creative expression.
e. Importance of rich experiences.
f. Creative oral expression.
g. Creative written expression.
h. The place of practical writing.

Creativity appears often in young children and may be given expression through many different media. The classroom teacher is concerned with creativity both as a product and as a process. The same concern with creativity is shown throughout society as men recognize the potential of a conflict in space and of having developed the power of mass self-destruction. The fostering of creativity, and the giving of expression to creativeness, are looked upon as routes to the ultimate in man's evolution. More and more we are recognizing creativity in areas that were formerly thought of as being largely routine. Similarly in the classroom there are many opportunities for creativity, even in simple activities. It is important for the teacher to recognize and encourage the creative efforts of children in their language activities. This chapter deals with the place of creative expression in the language program and the methods by which it may be developed under classroom conditions.

WHAT IS CREATIVE EXPRESSION?

In the fields of literature, music, painting, sculpture, and the dance the idea of creativity is readily accepted. But creativity is found in many activities not always recognized as requiring imagination. Usually we think of the activities of the store clerk as being largely routine and un-imaginative. Yet the store clerk may very well produce a new sales approach or a new method of displaying a product that represents real creative imagination, and the inventor surely does cause something new or different to come into existence. In a field like mathematics, too, new thinking shows a markedly changed point of view. Max Beberman is quoted as saying that "mathematics is as creative as music, painting or sculpture." [1] In our age, disturbed by atomic power and man-made satellites with their power for good or evil, all forms of creativity must be recognized and nurtured, no less in the field of creative language expression than in the many other areas of human mental and physical activity.

In the fields of art, music, or the dance, creativity is recognized as the tangible expression of the thought, imagination, and physical activity of the individual. A painting is an individual's production; it has not been done by someone else. In music the composition is the composer's. His arrangement of the composition or the way he plays it points up the creative aspect. We admit these differences in creative ability in such areas and yet recognize each individual's creativity. When we turn to the creative activities of the school, however, we encounter sharply varying points of view as to just what is creative.

The most critical problem in defining what is creative in language centers around the issue of whether or not the product has utility. Some hold that expression which is really creative is not affected by the utility of the product. Thus the writing of a friendly or business letter would not be classed as creative because it has practical and utilitarian value. The same would be true for an oral report concerning information of interest and benefit to an audience. Others, however, hold that whatever an individual says or writes in his own individual way is creative. Considered from this point of view any individual expression that a person makes is creative, whether or not it has utility, when it is not merely a repetition of the words of someone else. And, in the last analysis, of

[1] Helen Rowan, "The Wonderful World of Why," *Saturday Review,* November 2, 1957, p. 42.

course, any expression may be thought of as having utility even if it results only in giving emotional release to the expressor.

The point of view held by the authors is that creative expression does not necessarily lack utility and purpose. In fact, they believe that the practicality and utility of the product may be heightened through the creativity of imaginative and descriptive words and expressions, and the form in which these are put. Thus, a letter may be so written that the imagination is used, the senses are stimulated, and a true and artistic word-picture is painted for the reader. This is creativity; it is also practical and very effective communication. Another letter might be just as practical, and possibly just as communicative (at least of the principal ideas) and yet lack the sparkle of creativity. Both represent "practical" writing, but one shows creativity in a real sense and the other does not.

Some authorities hold that creative expression must be spontaneous. While a considerable amount of expression is spontaneous, still much spontaneous expression is not very creative. For example, a spontaneous answer may be given in response to a question and yet this answer may be merely a parroting of another's words. A spontaneous note may be written to thank someone for a present or a favor and yet no sparkle and imagination may appear in the expression. On the other hand, the person who thoughtfully writes a rhyme may be acting spontaneously, but he may also be acting because of some stimulation or motivation, direct or indirect. Spontaneity is closely akin to "voluntary," a criterion often stated as a measure of creative expression. Again, there is an element of truth here; much creative expression is voluntary. Yet if we could depend upon voluntary action to produce creative language expression we would not be devoting a chapter to the teaching of it nor would the teaching of language expression emphasize to such an extent the importance of an "intake" of experience.

Creativity of expression hinges upon many things, including an abundance of ideas and thoughts to express, which in turn is dependent upon a rich background of experiences with real meaning and vitality upon which to draw. The letter writer without many thoughts or ideas will only write "Thank you for the pair of socks sent me at Christmas," while the writer with more imagination and broader experiences may write "The red stripes in the socks you sent are picked up in the faint stripes in my new suit. Of course, I have to cross my legs for this to be noticed, but I do that often since it seems so striking." Few would argue that the latter thank-you note is not only more creative than the first, but it is also more effective communication because it says "thank you" in a nicer way.

For language expression to be creative it is believed that it must be:

379

1. *Original,* in the sense that it is based upon thoughts and ideas which are the person's own. These thoughts are not necessarily new, but they are stated in a way that is new to him, and they are not expressed in the exact way someone else expressed them or told him to express them.

2. *Based upon a real desire and feeling of need of the individual to express himself.* This desire or need does not necessarily come about spontaneously or voluntarily; in fact, every voluntary action is prompted by something, however remote from the immediate. It will not be creative if it is in any sense forced or stimulated against resistance.

3. *Different from the commonplace and unimaginative.* Creative expression has the sparkle and vividness which show that thinking, imagination, and something of the individual's personality and feeling have gone into it.

Creative language expression may take many forms. It may appear as a poem, a story, a play, a letter, a report, the minutes of a meeting, an interpretation made through a character in a story, or an announcement of a lost article made in an assembly. It may have the utility of attempting to recover that lost article, or of entertaining an audience through the interpretation of the character. On the other hand, it may be as lacking in utility as the note in the personal diary or the poem written to be seen by no one but the writer, or the joke made up and told by the maker. It may be a stanza jotted down hurriedly, or it may be prose produced after many hard hours of thought, self-editing, and polishing. In every case, however, if the expression is the individual's, if it shows imagination and is not commonplace, it may be really creative.

CREATIVE EXPRESSION IN RELATION TO THE TOTAL LANGUAGE PROGRAM

The functions of language have been identified earlier in this volume as (1) a means of communication, (2) a vehicle for thinking, and (3) a way of preserving ideas and information. In developing language expression we must develop those attitudes, abilities, and skills which will lead to the most effective use possible of language in the various functions it serves. No distinction is made between "practical" and "creative" language in our statements of objectives of the expressional aspects of the language arts. It is necessary to recognize, however, that all language expression is not equally creative. Sometimes a child is unable to express himself creatively because of an inadequate background of experience which forces him to borrow another's ideas or words. Sometimes, because of a lack of interest at the time, he simply does not have the inner feeling or urge to express his thoughts. Thus, while creativeness is greatly to be desired, it is almost inescapable that much of the language expression of the school program will be rather commonplace even though it may be practical and useful.

PURPOSES OF CREATIVE EXPRESSION

The primary purpose of all language expression is the stating of thoughts clearly and lucidly with the amount of emotion and feeling necessary to make such expression really effective. The major purpose of creative expression is no different. There are no hidden aspects; creative expression just goes further than the expression that is void of the feeling, emotion, and thinking of the individual. Clear and imaginative thinking, based upon real understanding, will lead to clear and creative expression if the opportunity is provided. Creative expression shows feeling and emotion to the extent that the thinking process has really been involved. The child who adequately understands something, who has involved his thinking processes because he is interested, will achieve satisfaction from this thinking and a desire to express it. The expression will really be his because it comes from within.

The forms which creative expression seems most often to take, by the very nature of creativeness, point to two purposes or values which should be particularly emphasized.

1. Creative expression serves as a release valve for pressure and tensions which are in the make-up of most of us. Often we are confused about various thoughts we have with regard to external conditions and possible effects. The release of these thoughts through language expression may provide a satisfaction and sense of relief. The release is likely to be creative, individual and original, in an attempt to meet, explain, and justify, if only to ourselves, these external conditions and effects. In general children, as well as adults, who suppress their feeling to too great an extent are often not happy and their personalities may not be developed to the potential possible. Perhaps this is a real justification for the keeping of a personal diary. It gives the individual a chance to unload, if only to himself.

2. Creative expression of a truly imaginative nature is a means of securing fun and adventure. There is real pleasure and satisfaction de-

rived from doing something which for us is new and original. The expression bolsters our ego and sense of self-worth, and we feel pleasure in our achievement and inventiveness. John, for example, almost "glowed" as a result of the praise from his fellow third-graders for his poem written after the class had discussed pets.

> Tabby is our mother cat,
> She's going to have a litter.
> With all those kittens at her side
> She'll need a baby sitter.

FORM AND CORRECTNESS

Many authorities in creative expression emphasize that correct language and the mechanical skills of speaking and writing should not be stressed in order that creativeness may not be lost. Certainly attention to the mechanics alone does not make a masterpiece; this is true for letter writing, poetry writing, giving an announcement, or any other form of language expression. On the other hand, correct usage, mechanical skills, and content are so interwoven in normal expression that it is impossible to separate one from the other completely or to say that one is of such importance that the others can be disregarded. Matters of form and correctness are not the ultimate goals in any expression. Emphasis should always be given to content first, but not content alone.

Children who can write and speak with real creativeness will want to use acceptable language and form. Indeed, a child who does not have some confidence in his own mastery of the skills of language usage is not likely to express his thinking and feeling through language media. If he has great difficulty in writing legibly, if he has too much hesitation in spelling, or if he has trouble saying some sounds, his expression will be suppressed, and what does come forth is not likely to represent his own individuality.

Most people, when they first try to create something in written form, pay very little attention to spelling, punctuation, agreement of subject and verb, etc.; their first concern is to get the idea down. Later they correct errors and rewrite where necessary. This practice places emphasis upon content first, but does not disregard correctness and form. Thus, in creative expression attention must be given to correctness and form; not to do so means sanctioning techniques that must later be unlearned. But correctness and form are not the first qualities to be considered in judging attempts made by children to express themselves creatively. The essential aspects are the ideas, the personal feelings and thoughts expressed, and the desire and urge for this expression. The child's ideas and his grasp of the content he is expressing are important elements in the quality of creative expression. Such a quality is more likely to be secured when children are free from the strain of consciously and continuously giving attention to correct usage and form. This aspect of strain will be absent if teachers will have children practice the essential skills and usages in drill situations until these become matters of habit.

STIMULATING CREATIVE EXPRESSION

A primary goal of the school is to help each child develop his personality to its greatest potential. As each individual develops, it is natural for him to desire to express, to give out of himself in some manner. He will struggle to express ideas and reactions which are his; he will strive to create in order to gain the approval of his fellows and the satisfaction of self-attainment, the feeling of personal worth that is his due. Thus, the stimulation of creative expression in children becomes a matter of letting them release inhibitions and fears and of providing satisfying acceptance for their efforts. The guidance of creativeness into channels acceptable to society becomes a major task of the school, the guidance of this creativeness into desirable language expression is a task of the language program.

The implication of the above statement is that the language program is as much one of guidance as it is of stimulation, and this is largely true for the children who are satisfactorily developing toward their respective potentials. It is not true for many others who seem always to need outside stimulation in order to carry on even the simplest activities. Some children may be surrounded by toys, games, and many things to do and learn and yet seem to be bored and lacking in interest in their surroundings. Others seem satisfied with string or a stick, and perhaps are creative with these simple devices. Then, too, most children must be able to identify themselves with their own experiences before they can be motivated to expression. Individual as well as classroom motivation must be presented in such a way that each child can identify himself with the given situation.

IMPORTANCE OF CLASSROOM ENVIRONMENT

The educational climate of the classroom is of major importance in bringing forth from each child his best creative expression. The classroom conditions must be such as to foster good will, respect, and friendliness on the part of both teacher and pupil. Every effort should be made to have each child feel relaxed, at ease, and an accepted and important member of the group. Such a climate respects each child's personality, his problems of adjustment to other members of the group, and the emotional and social effects of his out-of-school environment.

The establishment of this desirable environment is not a simple matter. It is, of course, largely dependent upon the teacher, but other school personnel and their attitudes on how children learn and what school should be like are also important. The principal of the school must encourage a teacher to have a happy, busy, and interesting classroom; the custodian must be interested in what the class does and be willing to accept disarrangement of furniture as part of the day's work. Parents must realize that children in school need to be active and that these activities and interests are of great importance to real learning. Physical materials in the classroom are also important. Little creative stimulation will come from a classroom that does not have many shelves of colorful and interesting books. Wall decorations and displays that are interesting and thought-provoking, materials for science and social studies in abundance, attractive furnishings, and other thoughtful and artistic decorative touches are all important in making the classroom a stimulating place.

Classroom environment that is attractive to the adult eye will not necessarily draw forth a child's expression. Children are highly sensitive to sham or pretense. There must be an air of honest freedom to which children sense that there is willingness and encouragement for them to follow desirable expressional impulses. This highly desirable classroom atmosphere will come chiefly from the children's feeling of freedom to think independently and to express their own thoughts and feelings without officious direction or criticism from their teachers or the other members of their classes.

PROVIDING EXPERIENCES

A child can be creative only within the realm of his own experiences. For example, after a discussion of the shape of the earth a group of fourth-grade children wrote about their observations. One child wrote, "The earth is round and full of bumps. The cars and buses have a tough time on the hills." This was a natural observation for a child who had lived his life in a rugged section of the country where transportation over steep dirt roads was the only life line to the rest of the world. In another class, also the fourth grade, the children discussed many places in the world they had been, looked at flat pictures, films, and filmstrips of different areas, and read about those places which seemed interesting. After these experiences Roy wrote:

> The desert is a lonesome place,
> Where abundant is the brush.
> Where big and little lizards pace,
> And all the winds say "hush."

Of primary importance in securing creative expression from children is an abundance of opportunities for them to gain ideas and impressions for themselves. The best provision for this comes through wide and varied real experiences in which the child himself observes and personally interprets materials and processes about him. Various suggestions have been given particularly in Chapter 10 and 11, for providing these experiences.

To secure expression showing real imagination and vividness, however, it is necessary to do more than provide the child with activities and opportunities for experience. Mauree Applegate suggests, "If you want your children to write . . . , you must take plenty of time to appreciate the little things that happen every day." [2] Many children, as well as some teachers, are unobservant and may not note the significance of the commonplace in their lives. They may fail to notice the intricacies of the dew-covered spider web in the plant by the school yard fence, the design formed by the shadows of the flag pole and the oak tree on the corner, and the eager look of the puppy waiting for his supper. The teacher must constantly encourage the children to be observant and to appreciate what they have observed. This is best accomplished by observing in a leisurely way and taking time to discuss the details of what has been seen or experienced.

Children may see, hear, taste, and feel things and yet gain only vague impressions. Teachers must talk over experiences with children. This process must be thought-provoking and related to other experiences the children have had. The teacher who calls the attention of the class to the

[2] Mauree Applegate, *Helping Children Write.* Evanston, Ill.: Row, Peterson and Company, 1954, p. 17.

flight of geese in the gray October sky has been observant and has shown the children something to watch for during that time of the year. Perhaps starting a list of things of beauty and interest to be seen in the sky will bring forth ideas such as the following:

> a streaking falling star
> a swooping swallow
> the trail of a jet plane
> the circling of a hawk
> the darting of the sea gulls
> the rolling thunder clouds

This need not be the end, and it may not be the time to suggest the writing of a verse or story. It will be thought-provoking and is likely to lead to further observations and additions to the list by the children themselves, and may bring forth an expression like fourth-grade Susan's "Clouds":

> I like to see the clouds
> Floating all around.
> Often they smile,
> Sometimes they frown.

Vicarious experiences may lend themselves as readily to creativeness as do experiences in which the child has actually participated.[3] For both types of experiences, it is important that as great a variety of means of perception as possible be activated. Creative expression is a reaction by the individual to his own experiences. To gain this, it is necessary to establish a vivid relationship between the words used for expression and the experiences themselves.

THE ROLE OF READING

Expression that is vapid and unimaginative is often an almost direct consequence of a background of little reading. The encouragement of reading is an avenue that every teacher can follow and is one that will be immensely rewarding in the creative expression that may result. Reading good language expression insinuates itself into the mind, awakens ideas, and gives impetus to expression. A reader finds pleasure, excitement, awe—feeling itself—through the many sensations aroused by his reading. Reading brings to a child the inheritance of the ages and an

---

[3] Neal R. Edmund, "A Study of the Relationship Between Prior Experience and the Quality of Creative Writing Done by Seventh-Grade Pupils." *Journal of Educational Research*, 51:481–492; March, 1958.

interpretation of the world in which he lives. It challenges his imagination and enriches his experiences—both essentials to creative expression.

A child must want to read and must have the skills necessary for satisfactorily meeting his needs in reading. The achievement of this goal for each child is the principal purpose of the reading program in schools. Even though a desire may be present, however, and much skill in word recognition and comprehension attained, most children will need guidance in reading selections which will given them actual intake to inspire expression. Basal reading textbooks provide some of this guidance, but the major responsibility falls upon the teacher to stimulate interest in reading, to help make reading choices, and to give encouragement to expanding efforts.

The basic test of the effectiveness of what one reads is the extent and kind of response one makes. Reading is not effective if feelings are not engendered, and if emotional or thoughtful response is not forthcoming. A discerning teacher, therefore, must guide the children's reading in ways that are satisfying, that bring forth feelings, that lead to expression.

AN APPRECIATIVE AUDIENCE

Securing the approval of one's fellows is a basic human desire. Appreciation of creative expression by an audience is no exception. Children like an audience, preferably an immediate one, for their speaking and writing. They will express themselves with more vitality and spirit if they are aware that the teacher, a fellow pupil, or the class is ready to receive their efforts in an appreciative manner.

Although not every child, nor all children in every situation will desire an audience for creative expression, everything possible must be done to cultivate the growth of children's confidence, their interest, and their expressional abilities. The child who is extremely shy and sensitive must be nurtured like a tender plant so that he will want to express himself creatively. When he does express himself to an audience, he should not be misled by being told his poem or story is good, when it is merely an imitation or is not well done. This does not mean, however, that the teacher will not be a receptive audience for him. His audience must be friendly and eager to give deserved praise and encouragement, recognizing that even the most feeble contribution is an attempt and as such is deserving of encouragement. Children cannot be expected to be as understanding of the effect of praise and criticism as the teacher should be. The teacher who has helped create a classroom climate of genuine friendliness and respect for every other individual will have no fear of harsh or unfair criticism from the children. The children will criticize, but their comments will be frank and fair, and appreciative of the effort made.

THE TEACHER'S ROLE IN CREATIVE EXPRESSION

It has been said that "creativeness cannot be taught; it can only be released and guided," [4] and that "all creative teaching is merely bringing the child to the threshold of his own mind." [5] Thus, it would seem not to be possible for the teacher to treat creativity as he would long division, American history, or the parts of speech. Since imitation is the child's method of learning language, not only its sentence structure and its vocabulary, but also its beauty, its power, and its elegance, the example the teacher sets in expression and appreciation is of utmost importance. Creativity is the bringing to life of an idea within the child. Thus the teacher has the task of being the model, of providing ways for his charges to gain and store up ideas and thoughts, and of maintaining an atmosphere which not only allows but encourages creativeness.

Worthwhile experiences. A child can be creative only within the realm of his experiences and environment. He cannot create from a vacuum. For the teacher this means providing many opportunities for worthwhile experiences, making the most of these experiences, and relating them to the child's other learning. Too often we think of field trips and excursions to places of interest as the only type of experience opportunities that may be presented. This is not true, of course, even though these experiences are important. The opportunities provided should be based upon things about which the children already have some knowledge, but the new contacts will help to eliminate the vagueness that they may have about the previous experiences. All such experiences should be very rich and above the quality of those they often have outside the school. The school experiences should be so designed as to improve and extend the range of experiences children have had. The fact that many opportunities for experiences come from the world of books should not be overlooked in even a minor respect by the teacher. Children gain many new facts and feelings from working with one another on projects and experiments in the classroom, and from dis-

[4] Mauree Applegate, *op. cit.,* p. 1.
[5] Frances C. Durland, *Creative Dramatics for Children.* Yellow Springs, Ohio: Antioch Press, 1952, p. 10.

plays, collections, films, filmstrips, records, and many other materials which can be made available by teachers.

Literary experiences. The teacher should provide many different types of literary experiences for the children, including much reading aloud of good literature by the teacher himself. He must use special care in selecting material to be read and should try to develop a sensitivity to children's interests. The reading, which should be carefully planned, should include presentation of something about the author and other information about the story and how it came to be written, in an effort to heighten the children's interest. The teacher may provide literary experiences by telling stories as well as by reading them, by suggesting books and stories to read, by preparing exhibits and displays about books, by leading and participating in discussions about reading the class has done, and by showing a sincere interest in reading.

Although literary experiences will lead to spontaneous creative expression, both oral and written, often the teacher must steer these experiences into actual creative effort. One guide suggests that a teacher begin a lesson on "made-to-order" stories by saying: [6]

We have read many stories and poems this term. We have had fun talking and listening. Today we might try to write some "made-to-order" stories. This is a story you make up from a list of words and phrases. On the board you will find the list of words. Listen while I read them to you.

> A tinkling sound
> Bright, inquisitive, blue eyes
> A faint blue line
> Whispering and swishing sounds
> Clickety–clackety
> A smooth round object

Now take this list of words and see how quickly you can get a story idea. Perhaps these words and phrases have already started you thinking. Remember, try to weave all the words and phrases into your story. Remember to start your story with a good opening sentence. Recall some opening sentences from the stories we have read this term. Don't let spelling or capital letters or periods interfere with your writing. Get your thoughts and ideas on paper. Remember your story must have a *beginning,* a *middle,* and an *ending.* In the beginning you start the action, in the middle part you develop the action, and the ending rounds the story off.

Meanings of words. Providing various opportunities to clarify meanings of words and concepts that children have some knowledge of but

[6] Detroit Public Schools, *A Guide to Instruction in the Language Arts, Grades 4, 5, and 6.* The Board of Education of the City of Detroit, 1959, pp. 167–168.

which they may not be able to define accurately and clearly is another activity of the teacher that will aid creative expression. Showing pictures or cartoons and the use of word games will encourage the children to use the words they have learned or have had clarified in their expression. See other suggestions on pages 343 and 348.

Choice of words. Teachers may do many things to develop an interest in, appreciation of, and taste for words and their use in creative expression. Following are a few of the procedures every teacher can follow:

1. Notice and bring to the classroom colorful phrases and apt words.
2. Bring in choice and unusual descriptions. Keep these and similar collections in a notebook, or perhaps in a file which children can add to and use.
3. Notice alliteration and rhyme in slogans and posters and call these to the attention of the children.
4. List on a chart "quiet" words, or perhaps "noisy," "sad," or "gay" words.
5. Use new words and phrases whenever possible in both speaking and writing.
6. With the pupils hunt for phrases and words that establish mood.
7. Try defining common objects with the pupils.
8. Keep a list of "tired" words (e.g., *pretty* and *nice*) and good substitutes for them.
9. Get children interested in foreign words, the derivation of words, and the tracing of changing meanings and spellings of words.
10. Dramatize the shades of meaning of words.

Varieties of creativeness. Creativeness breeds creativeness; children should try being more creative in all types of expression. Perhaps a child is not satisfied with the results in one endeavor. What of it? There are many other areas for creative expression. Remember, being creative does not apply only to the writing of poetry. Creative expression can be encouraged by providing for flexibility in the daily schedule in order that time may be taken to listen to a child's efforts, or to read and post his poem on the bulletin board. A classroom that has a rigid schedule rarely has a creative climate.

New ideas. When new ideas are discussed with children and the spirit of discovery and adventure is encouraged, surprising results may occur in creativity of expression and other learning too. The fifth-grade boy who reported to his father that "We talked about some pretty advanced chemistry today" and then explained how carbon monoxide is different from carbon dioxide, revealed that he considers his teacher a real friend, "smart," and almost his "equal."

Interesting topics. Interesting and stimulating topics that may be written or talked about should be suggested. For example:

How I feel in the dark.
What I do first thing in the morning.
How our backyard looks today.
Troubles I've had baby sitting.
What I love to touch (see, etc.)
Seeing the earth from a space ship.

Such topics might be kept in a file, as one teacher reports.[7] In addition, she has a picture file, a phrase file, and an opening sentence file. Two of the opening sentences she has filed are: "Mr. Jones had a car, and what a car it was!" and "Even the other ghosts were frightened!" A variation might be a file of opening sentences from children's own compositions. One of the authors has these opening sentences (among many others) that suggest things to express:

I was a pine seed.
I think a blade of grass is a very marvelous thing.
During Easter vacation, I went to Santa Cruz.
A clown is the nicest man to know.
My brother's dog is called Lucky.

Creative materials. Creative materials should be displayed on bulletin boards, in the hall, and in the lunch room. Creative writing may be duplicated and copies sent to the authors' homes and to their friends. Some teachers provide a poetry box or a display board for pupil self-posting of writing.

CREATIVE ORAL EXPRESSION

Creative language expression may occur in any of the situations and through any of the activities outlined for the oral language program in Chapter 4. The suggestions in Chapter 9 for methods and procedures for teaching oral expression, if properly used, bring out much of this creativeness. In this section, additional focus is given to creativity and further suggestions and examples are presented, particularly in the more imaginative areas of creative expression such as story telling and dramatization.

[7] Helen Danforth, "First Aid in Children's Writing." *Elementary English,* 37:246–247; April, 1960.

DRAMATIC PLAY

This form of creative expression, while usually identified with the pre-school and primary age group of children, may also be used by middle and upper grade children if the opportunity is provided and if the children feel free to utilize the opportunity. A sixth-grade class may give real creativity to an informal dramatization of "The Three Little Pigs" with the use of original versions of the replies the pigs give to the wolf puffing at the door, including such sixth-grade expressions as "blast off, chick," "go man, go," and "keep cool, toad stool."

Dramatic play is spontaneous and free of immediate adult suggestion and control. It calls for the shedding of the child's own normal personality inhibitions and the living of the role he is portraying. Most often it occurs away from the classroom, in a play situation in which the little girl is the mother and keeps house or the boy is the real Davy Crockett or Wyatt Earp.

DRAMATIZATION

Dramatization may take many forms; there is no hard and fast line between many of these forms and dramatic play. Children are naturally interested in what they call acting out things and will play their parts with fervor if they feel free to do so and have an understanding of the plot. Much dramatization may take place with little preparation if the story is a simple and familiar one. In these dramatizations, encouragement and full freedom should be given to the child's acting and talking for the character he is portraying in the way that he thinks the character would act and talk. Dramatizations that are longer or more complicated will call for more planning and perhaps the working out of lines and then memorization. However, the pupils themselves should do much of this preparation if the real creative values are to be obtained.

Stick, hand, and shadow puppets, marionettes, and pantomime are other forms of dramatization which have great creative value. Often the most creative of oral expression will occur through the use of puppets since the child will not actually be seen by the audience (nor see the audience himself) and will give of himself with less inhibition.

STORY TELLING

Story telling has been rather thoroughly discussed, together with techniques for teaching it, in Chapters 4 and 9; however, it is important to note that this is an aspect of oral language calling for vivid imagining, fanciful yarn spinning, and real originality. Children enjoy many forms of story telling. They enjoy telling chain stories in which the teacher or one of the pupils starts a story and after a time stops and asks another pupil to continue. As this process goes on, perhaps to every child in the room, it will often bring out much imagination and interesting words and phrases. A simpler version is the unfinished story which is completed by a single pupil. Sometimes changing the endings of stories in books will also bring out considerable creativity of expression.

CREATIVE WRITTEN EXPRESSION

Any form of written expression may be creative, but most often we think of creativity in writing as being in the form of poetry, or short stories. The sections that follow give some hints on techniques teachers have used successfully in bringing forth creativity, together with some examples of the results of their efforts.

POETRY AND RHYMES

Mauree Applegate tells the story of the forgetful gardener who plowed and cultivated a plot of ground but forgot to plant any seeds. She notes that even though he was forgetful, some seeds did spring up as a result of having fallen from parent plants. She compares many teachers and the conducive climates of their classrooms to the plight of the forgetful gardener, noting that "Reading poetry to the children, appreciating things together, giving the daily invitation to write, having a quiet hour each week, and providing a poetry drawer will grow more and better poetry" [8] and, further, that "one cannot travel to the stars in a wheelbarrow, or speak of his journey there in the words of the field." [9] Too often teachers turn children to the task of writing without enough limbering up with words and ideas orally first.

[8] Mauree Applegate, *op. cit.*, p. 29.
[9] *Ibid.*, p. 31.

393

A discussion of frosty nights near Christmas time by one teacher and her class brought forth such phrases as "Christmas magic," "breeze stirring lightly," and "elves with twinkling feet," and resulted for one pupil in:

The Magic of Christmas

Upon a frosty winter night
When the household was asleep,
There awoke the Christmas magic,
The Elves with twinkling feet
Stepped down from every Christmas card,
The carolers began to sing,
The dancers had a merry ball
And bells began to ring.

From a big card on the mantel,
St. Nick and his sleigh swooped down.
The Christ Child woke in the manger
And the angels gathered around.
The star in the sky shone brightly,
As the shepherds came down from the hills
And the breeze stirred ever so lightly
The mistletoe over the sills.

And now, from every Christmas card
Joyful voices ring,
And everyone within the room,
Joins in the Christmas sing.
Indeed it must be magic.
What else could it possibly be?
For I'm sure I heard those voices
Of Christmas gayety.[10]

The second grade had been studying the circus and had seen the animals and the crowds and excitement of the circus which had come to town. It was the topic of all the talking at school, and Arnold wrote:

When circus time is here,
People come from far and near
To see the animals dance and play—
It makes their lives so bright and gay.

The fifth-grade class enjoyed hearing Miss Clark read "City Rain" by Rachel Field and then talking about other things observed along the streets of the city during a rain storm. Following this experience, Evelyn wrote:

[10] Linda Higgins, eighth grade, C. E. Dingle School, Woodland, California.

The wind blows,
Leaves fall,
Red, yellow and brown.
The rain,
From a gray sky,
Plasters them
To the wet ground.

A form of poetry which is particularly satisfying to children is Haiku, one of the oldest types of Japanese poetry. Haiku generally has three lines consisting of seventeen syllables—five in the first and third lines, and seven in the second—although sometimes this formula is modified.[11] One child wrote:

My tiny puppy,
How mournful shine his sad eyes
Seeking, seeking me.

Sometimes just observing things will bring forth words and phrases that lead to almost spontaneous writing of poems. A dew-laden spider's web, a straight and sharp icicle, the activities in an ant hill or of a hive of bees, the drip of a leaky faucet, and so forth, will start words flowing.

PROSE WRITING

Much of the prose form of creative expression in the classroom will come through the writing of stories. Story writing techniques discussed in Chapter 10 point up the importance of proceeding from the cooperative blackboard story in the primary grades to the independent writing of stories of one or two sentences, then to the writing of a single paragraph, and finally to the writing of a complete short story. Stories may be stimulated in many ways. One first-grade teacher read a poem about owls. The children drew pictures of what they heard, told simple stories to one another, and finally, as a class, decided they would all like to write Christine's story:

Two baby owls were sitting in a tree. They could not see in the day time. They decided they should go home and go to bed.

In another first-grade class Garry wrote this story after the teacher's friend told about penguins, using Willie, the marionette penguin.

Willie is a penguin.
He likes water.

[11] Harold G. Henderson, *An Introduction to Haiku.* New York: Doubleday Anchor Books, 1958.

395

He likes fish.
He danced for us.

John, age eight, showed his maturity and his developing story writing ability as he told about the volcano.

One calm day in the jungle far away there was a village, and the village was very small.

Behind the village was a volcano, and the villagers did not know that the volcano was a volcano. The reason they did not know that the volcano was a volcano was because the volcano had not erupted for eight hundred years.

Days went by and after a while the volcano began to shake and then to throw hot rocks and lava down the volcano side.

It was a sad time for the people. They ran for their lives, leaving all behind but what they could grab up on the run.

Days later, after the eruption had stopped, the villagers returned. They found that the only two huts left were the one on the hill and the one in the tree.[12]

David, in the sixth grade, demonstrates real imaginative power in his story of how the wind came to be.

One day the Spirit of the Moon was walking along. He came to a large cave, and started to enter it. All of a sudden he felt that he had to sneeze! He went "Ah, ah, ah-choo" right into the cave. The back force of the sneeze was so great that when repelled it knocked over Moon Spirit.

He was so angry that he called the force a bad name! "Wind!" he yelled.

The Indians too, were afraid and brought him presents. Since the wind came from the north they called it the North Wind.

Not all prose writing must be in the form of a story. For example, one teacher has secured some creative and thought-provoking ideas from his sixth-grade children by having them write their interpretations of adages such as, "The best place to find a helping hand is at the end of your own arm," "The best way to climb a mountain is to begin at the bottom," and "A mind is like a parachute; it is useful only when open." [13]

Children may also write their reactions to situations of which they are reminded by statements such as, "Once I was very sad because . . . , " "I was almost frightened to death once when . . . ," and "How disappointed I was when . . . ." Or they may write compositions based upon the teacher's directions, such as:

You have invented a new soft drink. Write an article emphasizing at least four ways in which you might test it before offering it to the public.

[12] *Guiding Growth in Written Expression,* Los Angeles County Schools, June, 1956, p. 122.

[13] Walter V. Ashforth, 6th grade teacher, Orville Wright School, Sacramento, Calif.

What will be tomorrow's headlines? Do you know what will be in the paper tomorrow? Write the headlines and then explain why you chose each one.

PRACTICAL WRITING

Although all writing may be practical and have actual utility, generally we think of practical writing as including the writing of letters, invitations, responses; the writing of minutes of a meeting; and the writing of reports in social studies and science. The emphasis in this type of writing is upon clarity, graciousness, brevity, and organization perhaps more than is the case of prose written for entertainment. Practical writing does not have to be all "business"; in fact, clarity and effectiveness may be abetted through the use of humor, inventiveness, and attention to the interests of the reader.

The fourth-grade child who wrote the following letter was striving for courtesy and sincerely wished to thank a new-found friend.

Dear Mr. Bales:
Thank you for inviting us to your Conservation Center. We enjoyed seeing your animals very much.
Their cages were very clean. I think they enjoy having clean cages.
I like the baby deer best. It looked like it is growing antlers. Some of the students in my class fed him lettuce.
The horned owl looks very vicious. I don't see how the horned owl can eat such big animals. We would like it very much if we could come again.
Your friend,
Hester Hart

A favorite friend of the authors (at that time in the third grade) had a real reason for writing a letter, and write it without prompting or knowledge of his doing so by his parents or teacher. It was obviously meant to be interesting and appreciative.

Dear Mrs. Naglich:
Thank you for the stamp. I am very pleased to have my second stamp a foreign one!
I have a book from the library about how to collect stamps. I think stamp collecting is very interesting. I know your stamp is from Helvetia, Switzerland. I have heard of Helvetia before. My favorite country is Switzerland!
Sincerely,
Roy Petty

Children have many occasions to write reports on facts or experiences to share with their fellow pupils. Essentially these reports are aimed at conveying information, but they may convey something of the writer and his feelings at the same time. The pupil in the fourth grade who wrote about "Why We Celebrate Lincoln's Birthday" could have gotten his information directly from the encyclopedia and conveyed it to the class in about the same language as the encyclopedia used. Instead a creative approach was used, as is shown in this introductory paragraph.

Every time I lie by the fire and read I think that one of America's greatest presidents did just that. That man was Abraham Lincoln. He hated slavery, but he wanted to keep the states together. He said that "someday this country will be friends again." If you take this country and cut it into two pieces you will no longer have one country but two half-countries. Try to join each half to another country. It would not stay on. So the halves will have to join together again.

Gilbert, in the third grade, stuck fairly closely to the facts in writing his report, but it was creative for him.

The Story of Nautilus

The Nautilus traveled two years without refueling. It could stay under water for 60 days. It came back to get fuel. It got its power from atomic energy.

Children often have opportunities to do creative report writing if the teacher provides the chance to publish their own "newspaper." Karin was encouraged to go further and submitted her story to the city newspaper: [14]

On November 10th, 1955, a wild deer decided to be educated in the Howe Avenue Elementary School shortly before 9 A.M.
A couple of teachers, a janitor, and several children saw the deer. One boy tried to catch the deer and has a torn shirt and a bruised side to prove it.
Much to the school's regret, the deer got away through the south gate after running across the playground.

Numerous additional examples of the creative achievements of children with language could be presented in this chapter, but it is believed that the many specimens of children's writing scattered throughout the earlier chapters of this book, together with those presented here, should serve adequately to illustrate the philosophy and purposes of this chapter. The critical study of this discussion together with Chapters 9, 10, and 11 should give the teacher a sound point of view as well as constructive assistance in attaining one of the most important objectives of the language program, that of developing the attitudes and skills necessary to

[14] Reported in *The Sacramento Bee,* Tuesday, November 15, 1955.

the production of a high quality of creative language expression in the elementary school classroom.

EXERCISES FOR THOUGHT AND DISCUSSION

1. What in your judgment determines when language expression becomes creative? What criteria for creativity can you suggest?
2. How important relatively is creative expression among the other objectives of language instruction?
3. What are the major factors contributing to the stimulation of creative expression?
4. Evaluate the roles of the teacher, the classroom, activity-experiences, reading, travel, contact with art, music, and the theatre in stimulating creativity.
5. How do you get the poetically inclined youngster to produce?
6. What do you do with the child who insists he simply cannot write poetry?
7. Outline a series of suggested situations which might serve to stimulate your pupils to write either poetry or prose.
8. At the conclusion of your study of this chapter prepare a series of concise statements which might be used as principles of method to guide you in developing creative expression in your classroom.

SELECTED REFERENCES

APPLEGATE, MAUREE. *Easy in English*. Evanston, Ill.: Row, Peterson and Company, 1960.

BRACKEN, KATHRYN. "My First-Graders Write Original Stories." *Instructor,* 64:81; February, 1957.

BRADY, FLORENCE. "The Use of Marionettes in Literature." *Elementary English Review,* 22:182–185; May, 1945.

BURGER, ISABEL B. *Creative Play Acting*. New York: A. S. Barnes and Company, 1950.

BURROWS, ALVINA, and others. *They All Want to Write*. Englewood Cliffs, N.J.: Prentice-Hall, Inc., 1952.

CONRAD, LAWRENCE H., *Teaching Creative Writing*. New York: Appleton-Century-Crofts, Inc., 1937.

CARLSON, RUTH KEARNEY, "Seventeen Qualities of Original Writing." *Elementary English,* 38:576–579; December, 1961.

DANFORTH, HELEN, "First Aid in Children's Writing." *Elementary English,* 37:246–247; April, 1960.

DURLAND, FRANCES C. *Creative Dramatics for Children.* Yellow Springs, Ohio: Antioch Press, 1952.

EDMUND, NEAL R. "Writing in the Intermediate Grades." *Elementary English,* 36:491–501; November, 1959.

LEASE, RUTH, and SIKS, GERALDINE. *Creative Dramatics in Home, School, and Community.* New York: Harper and Brothers, 1952.

LOWRIE, JEAN. "Stimulating Creative Expression with Help from the Library." *National Elementary School Principals Bulletin,* 36:62–67; September, 1956.

PETTY, WALTER, and ANDERSON, TONI. "A Dramatization of a Familiar Story." *The Instructor,* 67: 47 *et seq.* September, 1957.

WALTER, NINA WILLIS. *Let Them Write Poetry.* New York: Holt, Rinehart and Winston, 1962.

WARNER, RUBY H. *The Child and His Elementary School World.* Englewood Cliffs, N.J.: Prentice-Hall, Inc., 1957, Chap. 3.

14

Reading as a Receptive

Language Skill

THE PURPOSE OF THIS CHAPTER IS TO GIVE PROPER EMPHASIS TO THE position that reading deserves in the total elementary school language program. Reading and listening represent the two basic receptive language skill areas. It is through reading and listening, coupled with the basic ability to observe, that information and ideas first received, and then become the substance for the expressive arts of speaking and writing. The emphasis in this chapter centers around the following topics:

   a. Reading and language.
   b. The objectives of reading instruction.
   c. A modern reading program.
   d. Essentials of the effective reading program.
   e. Practices and issues in the teaching of reading.
   f. Individual and group teaching approaches.
   g. The teacher and the teaching of literature.
   h. Methods and materials for teaching literature.
   i. Ways of presenting literature.

The teaching of reading, which has a unique place in the elementary school curriculum, is a complex problem that involves a more detailed consideration than can be given here, especially in view of the many useful textbooks now available on the subject.[1] However, since reading is of such importance to listening, speaking, and writing—the language skills whose development is the main concern of this volume—the authors feel that an overview of the teaching of reading, some consideration of particular issues and practices, and a discussion of the teaching of literature still need to be presented here.

[1] For example: John J. DeBoer and Martha Dallmann, *The Teaching of Reading*, New York: Holt, Rinehart and Winston, 1960; Arthur W. Heilman, *Principles and Practices of Teaching Reading*, Columbus, Ohio: Charles E. Merrill Books, Inc., 1961; David H. Russell, *Children Learn to Read*, 2nd ed., Boston: Ginn and Company, 1961; and Miles A. Tinker and Constance M. McCullough, *Teaching Elementary Reading*, 2nd ed., New York: Appleton-Century-Crofts, Inc., 1962.

READING AND LANGUAGE

Learning to speak with some assurance and skill, and learning to listen and understand speech, prepare a child to read, since he thus learns to comprehend ideas formulated into sentences, to determine word meanings from the context of sentences, and to interpret ideas expressed by means of word symbols. Getting meaning from print is relatively easy for the child who has skill in speaking and listening and who has had much experience in using these skills. Many of the difficulties children encounter in reading are highly related to their inadequacies in using oral language. When the language to be read is too far removed from the child's experiences, largely expressed through his use of language, problems in recognizing and understanding symbols are apt to arise. It is possible, of course, for a child to be proficient in language and still fail to read effectively because of difficulties in visual perception of symbols, emotional blocking, or other reasons. However, without adequate language proficiency, no matter how well he can perceive word forms and perform other functions related to effective reading, true reading will not occur since the content will be unintelligible to him.

THE OBJECTIVES OF READING INSTRUCTION

The ultimate purpose of teaching reading in schools is to develop in each child the abilities and skills necessary for using reading as a means of (1) securing information, and (2) deriving pleasure. The principal implication is that the school must teach a child to read so that he may then read to learn and to enjoy what he reads. Thus, the reading program may be thought of as consisting of three parts—which in a modern program are intertwined rather than built one upon another. These parts are: (1) developmental reading, (2) functional reading, and (3) recreational reading.

More specifically the goals of the reading program are:

1. The development of fundamental reading skills in:
   a. recognizing words.
   b. securing word meanings.
   c. comprehending and interpreting what is read.

    d. reading silently at speeds appropriate to the material and purpose of
the reading.

    e. reading orally.

    f. using books efficiently.

2. The provision of opportunity for rich and varied experiences through
reading.

3. The development of enjoyment through reading.

4. The development of lasting interest in reading voluntarily.

5. The acquisition of ability for using reading in resourceful ways to meet
particular needs and interests.

A MODERN READING PROGRAM

Reading in a modern program is not taught in isolation; children use
reading for gaining information and ideas and for enjoyment as they
are taught the skills of reading. The use of reading as a tool thus receives
emphasis from the very beginning of reading instruction. Reading naturally is a part of many school activities, and in a modern program the
use of reading is fostered and the skills are practiced whenever possible.
The reading program also takes into account the many differences among
the children in a class in reading interests and abilities. This recognition,
along with the use of reading throughout the school day, calls for a program which is considerably expanded from one which merely "has a
child in a reader."

    1. A modern reading program is based upon conditions which facilitate
reading. Such conditions include an abundance of attractive reading materials in the classroom, a well-equipped and well-managed library easily
accessible to every child, attention to reading in all school activities,
physical equipment in the classroom which is attractive and appealing
to children, and a vital interest in reading on the part of all teachers
in the school.

    2. The principal basis of a modern program is provided through basal
reading instruction. Basal reading instruction provides for the systematic
and sequential development of skills, including the skills which provide
readiness for initial instruction. The basal reading program is built
around the use of a series of textbooks which have been planned for
the sequential development of vocabulary and the various reading skills.[2]
These books are supplemented by manuals or guide books for teachers,

[2] David H. Russell, *The Basic Reading Program in the Modern School*, rev. ed.,
Contributions to Education, No. 1. Boston: Ginn and Co., 1959.

403

books which provide content enrichment and additional practice in using the skills taught, and workbooks. An adequate basal program provides for:

a. Continuity of growth in reading habits, skills, and attitudes.
b. A wide variety of reading activities closely related to the interests and needs of children at the various grade levels, including their needs in other school subjects.
c. A rather complete organization of the total reading program, including the incorporation of reading other than basal reading into that program.
d. The presentation of information and ideas of importance to many activities of children, both within and outside of the school.

3. Essential, too, in a modern program is the provision for work-type reading under the teacher's guidance in the content fields of the curriculum. The work-type reading should include the reading of textbooks in these content fields, as well as the reading of encyclopedias and other reference materials. Particularly important in work-type reading is learning to interpret maps, charts, tables, and graphs.

4. Independent reading of supplementary reading textbooks and other books under occasional teacher guidance must also be provided for. There are many occasions in the classroom for this type of reading, including the gathering of information in other subject areas, reading for pleasure, and practicing the use of reading skills.

5. Guided literature reading, including the reading of prose and poetry by the teacher, is also a part of a modern reading program. This aspect of the total program is developed more fully in later sections of this chapter.

6. Perhaps the ultimate phase of the reading program is the provision for free and voluntary reading by the pupils. In free reading the pupils read, often outside of class and without teacher guidance, materials of particular interest to them. This reading is largely for recreational purposes, but the functional aspect enters into recreational reading. Reading for recreation is not always just for enjoyment; much recreational reading includes the seeking of information and the development of ideas.

ESSENTIALS IN A READING LESSON

The teacher in a modern reading program uses a combination of methods with considerable flexibility in instructional techniques from day to day. The stress in teaching is upon reading to gain meaning and to interpret the ideas presented in print, and the various techniques all focus upon this endeavor. Most teaching methods and techniques, however, tend to be built around a fundamental instructional plan for all directed-reading activities. The essentials of such a plan are the following:

A. Developing readiness for the reading activity
   1. Through a discussion of experiences which are related to the content to be read
   2. Through the introduction of new words and new concepts and relating these to words and concepts which are already known
   3. Through stimulating interest in what is to be read and establishing purposes for the reading
B. Guiding the first or survey reading of the selection
   1. Through motivating questions related to the purpose or purposes
   2. Through noting the organization of the selection
C. Rereading for specific purposes, such as
   1. Answering specific questions
   2. Interpretive oral reading
   3. Finding specific words or explanations of particular concepts
D. Developing important habits and skills
   1. Through direct instruction and practice in using word recognition techniques, comprehension skills, and so forth
   2. Through the use of workbook and teacher-prepared materials
   3. Through evaluation of progress and the establishment of further instructional goals
E. Providing for enrichment
   1. By following up on activities begun during rereading
   2. Through relating what has been read to interests and needs in other curriculum areas
   3. By suggesting supplemental reading and other activities.

PRACTICES AND ISSUES IN THE TEACHING OF READING

Instruction in how to read and guidance in the use of reading skills involves varied methods and activities. Some of these that are of a controversial nature, or are of particular importance in the reading program, are discussed in the following sections. For a full development of these issues and practices, and many others, the student is advised to read a recently published textbook exclusively devoted to the subject of reading instruction.

READING READINESS

Attention has been directed in many places in this volume to the extent of the differences among children of the same grade or chronological age. Particularly are the differences present in language development—differences which very markedly exist even before the children first come to school. There are many differences also in mental development, physical health and development, personal and social adjustment, interests, and the amounts and kinds of knowledge the children have. The success a child has in learning to read depends to a very great extent upon many of these factors in his development and upon the amount and kind of his earlier learning.

Reading readiness is not an all or none proposition, nor does the term mean the same thing to all persons. Some regard readiness (in reading or any skill area) as a stage in maturation—physical, mental, and emotional. Others regard it as an expression of desire, purpose, or interest. Still others emphasize that readiness hinges largely upon information and abilities learned through previous experiences.[3] However, the evidence indicates that readiness for initial reading instruction is dependent upon (1) physical factors such as the child's ability to see and hear words clearly, (2) mental factors such as the ability to follow directions or to relate the sequence of events in a simple story, (3) social factors such as the ability to work with a group and to accept a teacher's direction, (4) psychological factors such as appearing well adjusted to schoolwork or showing interest in reading, and (5) experiential factors such as knowledge of the concepts and information which will be met in the reading experiences.

Reading readiness is actually only an expression of the old teaching rule that the teacher must begin at the child's level—the level of what he knows or can do—and build upon this. Reading readiness functions at all grade levels and in all reading activities. Progress in learning to read, or progress in achieving the next stage in reading skill, is most rapid and has the greatest chance for success when all factors affecting the readiness are optimum. At any stage in reading instruction many of these factors can be improved and developed; a teacher cannot just wait for the readiness to be achieved. Instruction can be provided through systematic programs to develop readiness factors in the areas of personal

[3] Gertrude H. Hildreth, *Readiness for School Beginners.* Yonkers, N.Y.: World Book Company, 1950.

and social adjustment, visual and auditory discrimination, language facility, habits of attention and work, eye movements, interests, and concept building through experiences.

There is some controversy concerning reading readiness, though most criticism of present-day programs comes from persons who are uninformed or have made "snap" judgments based upon chance observations.[4] Readiness programs simply recognize that a child has to be taught from the foundation of what he already knows and what he can already do. Programs in readiness for beginning reading endeavor to provide aid in the development of factors important to the first steps in learning to read.

Critics of beginning readiness programs have often voiced the complaint that some children are ready to learn to read, or perhaps may even be able to read, when they first enter school. It is true, of course, that some children are able to read when they enter school, but these are few in number. Durkin, for example, found that about one per cent of children entering the first grade in one California city were able to read.[5] Most kindergarten and first grade teachers would attest to the fact that a majority of children are not ready to read when entering the first grade and that these children benefit from a readiness program. Criticism directed at the much-too-common practice of having a six-week "readiness" period at the beginning of the year in the first grade and then instructing all the children in beginning reading is nevertheless justified. This practice simply does not recognize the purpose of reading readiness.

THE QUESTION OF PHONICS

Phonetic analysis is one of the most important of the ways by which unknown words may be recognized. This is an established and well-documented fact; as Heilman states, "there are no non-phonetic methods (in the teaching of reading) in use in America today." [6] In spite of this, however, the controversy continues, much of it resulting from misunderstandings and from the development of certain myths about phonic instruction. This controversy, and the vagueness of many who write and

[4] For example: Charles C. Walcutt, *Tomorrow's Illiterates: The State of Reading Instruction Today.* Boston: Little, Brown, 1961.

[5] Dolores Durkin, "The Precocious Reader: A Study of Pre-School Reading Ability," *California Journal for Instructional Improvement,* 2:24–28; December, 1959.

[6] Heilman, *op. cit.,* p. 241.

speak on it regarding the real issues, have often caused confusion among teachers concerning many of their instructional practices about which there should be no question. For example, first-grade teachers may feel hesitant about deliberately teaching the names of the letters of the alphabet to children, when the real issue is the teaching of the alphabet in sequence and in ways unrelated to the first-grade curriculum.[7] Children obviously need to know the names of letters and to recognize letters quickly and accurately. Another myth is built around statements concerning how many words a child must know by sight before he makes use of word-recognition techniques, including phonics. Often instructions to teachers in basal reading series and in textbooks on the teaching of reading will state that a child needs 75, 150, 50, or some other number of sight words before he is introduced to phonics. While the principle is true that ability to recognize some words at sight is needed before aids to word recognition may be used (since such aids or techniques call for the relating of an unknown word or a part of a word to a known word), it is not true that even in beginning reading instruction such knowledge and techniques may not be put to use. For example, the child who can recognize at the sight the words *can* and *mother* can be taught that *man* begins like *mother* and rhymes with *can*. Instruction in helpful methods of recognizing words should begin with even the earliest of reading lessons.[8]

Actually instruction in phonics begins in the readiness program with activities which call for discriminating between common sounds, similar words, beginnings of words, and rhyming elements. With the beginning of actual reading this instruction is expanded to the combining of visual and auditory perception of and discrimination between words and elements in words. Later various principles concerning the sounds of vowels, consonants, blends, digraphs, and diphthongs are introduced inductively and made a part of the tools which a pupil has to use in recognizing words.

The question is not "Should phonics be taught?" Nor is it even "When should phonics instruction begin?" These questions are easily answered: phonetic analysis is a useful aid and must be taught, and instruction should begin with the earliest of readiness activities and should be given whenever it will aid in recognizing words. The real questions center upon the extent to which drills on the sounds of letters are isolated from

[7] *Ibid.*, p. 215.
[8] Arthur I. Gates, "The Teaching of Reading—Objective Evidence Versus Opinion." *Phi Delta Kappan,* 43:197–205; February, 1962.

408

meaning; the teaching of the "sounding" of single consonants, such as *buh, cuh, duh,* and *tuh* for the sounds of *b, c, d,* and *t;* and instruction prior to actual reading activities in the sounds assigned to letters or combinations of letters in words. The reason for this is simple: these are false approaches. Gaining meaning is the reason for reading and no more drill on phonic techniques should be given than is necessary for learning the principles which are useful in gaining meaning. Consonants in isolation do not have sounds; the letters which represent them have names, but they have sound only when spoken with vowels. The teaching of sounds prior to actual reading does not recognize the purpose of reading and what it is as a process. The synthetic approach of teaching sounds is a mechanical procedure that results in facility in word calling rather than in reading.

WORD ANALYSIS SKILLS

Word analysis involves analyzing an unfamiliar printed or written symbol for clues as to its sound and meaning. Essentially word analysis is of two kinds—structural and phonetic—although a type of analysis may occur as words are recognized through such aids as pictures, the context itself, the configuration or appearance, and the recognition of familiar parts. Word recognition also occurs through looking for its pronunciation and meaning in the dictionary.

Structural analysis relates to the recognition and use of word parts or the visual characteristics of words as contrasted to the phonetic characteristics. For example, a compound word such as *football* may be recognized through first noting that the word *ball* is a part of it. Structural analysis also involves using knowledge of prefixes, suffixes, roots, inflectional endings, the division of words into syllables, and the effect of accent.[9] Structural analysis is useful in that it is based upon two fundamental facts about language: first, that a root word retains its basic meaning in derived and inflected forms and in compounds; and, second, that affixes to the root have meaning themselves or add to the meaning of the root in specific ways. Thus, by adding *s* to *boy* a specific meaning is denoted; the adding of *un* to *like* combines the meaning of the root and the meaning of the prefix to give the meaning of the new word; the meaning of the compound word *horseback* is easily determined from the meanings of the words which have been put together.

[9] E. A. Betts, *Foundation of Reading Instruction.* New York: American Book Company, 1954, p. 645.

It is important for teachers to remember that the attainment of skill in word analysis is not an end itself. The principal purpose for using this and the other skills in word recognition or perception, is the determination of what a word is and what it means. Pronouncing a word may do this if, when it is pronounced, it is known to the child. However, this is not always the case, nor is it always possible to determine a word's meaning—or the meaning in a particular context—by structural analysis. The good reader is versatile in the use of a variety of clues to word identification and does not slow his reading down by dwelling on either phonetic or structural analysis when he is able to determine the word quickly through an understanding of the context in which it is used, its configuration, the construction of the sentence it is in, an accompanying diagram or picture, the paragraph or section heading, or some other means. Careless or unskilled use of any word-recognition technique can lead to guessing, and to mistakes. However, the skillful reader uses the most appropriate technique and exerts the degree of caution in using any technique relevant to the purpose of his reading.

READING WITH UNDERSTANDING

Facility in word recognition, combined with wide experiences and the relating of those experiences to words, usually leads to understanding. As was implied in the preceding section, there is a danger present in many reading programs, however, that over-concern with word recognition may retard the child's attainment of reading maturity. Particularly, there is danger that undue emphasis on word recognition will lead to inattention to reading skills which aid understanding.

Comprehension, which is the ultimate goal of reading, is a complex activity. Comprehension comes from the reader's relating his own background of experiences to the words of the writer. The printed page itself contains no meaning; as someone has said, "It is just ink on paper." Meaning comes from the mind of the reader. Thus, the problem in teaching children to read with understanding becomes one of providing many and varied experiences, selecting reading materials which relate to experiences they have had, and making use of certain skills which facilitate the relating of the language on the printed page to their experiences.

A comprehensive reading program provides for instruction in reading to:

1. Get the main idea of a sentence, paragraph, or longer selection.
2. Select important details.

3. Follow directions.
4. Determine the organization of the selection.
5. Secure visual or other images from the material.
6. Draw inferences.
7. Anticipate meaning and predict outcomes and conclusions.
8. Summarize what has been read.
9. Discriminate between fact and opinion.
10. Gain information from specific kinds of materials such as encyclopedias, atlases, maps, graphs, etc.

ORAL READING

Oral reading has been de-emphasized in reading programs, because silent reading has greater social utility and because many poor reading habits develop when all members of a class silently "follow along" while "turns" are taken in reading aloud. Modern reading programs, however, recognize that oral reading is a form of communication and does have a place, though a minor one, in the total reading program.

Oral reading may be of two types: (1) sight reading in which no preparation has been made for the oral presentation, and (2) prepared oral reading for communication and/or enjoyment. The first type is used by a teacher to determine a pupil's ability in recognizing words, in phrasing, in enunciation, and the attention he gives to punctuation in his reading. This type of oral reading is done individually, without an audience in the usual sense except that of the teacher, and without the other children "following" the reader's efforts. The second type of oral reading calls for preparation and is used for true communication. There are many opportunities for such reading: proving a point in a discussion; sharing an exciting, happy or sad part of a story; answering specific questions; reading reports, directions, announcements, and creative products; and reading in choral and dramatic situations.

Oral reading is a complex skill demanding that the reader not only recognize the words and understand what he reads, but also convey this understanding to an audience. Because of this complexity, silent reading should always precede oral reading. Difficulties with vocabulary and with meaning can thus be worked out prior to facing the audience. A child who stumbles through unfamiliar material feels confused and inadequate, and not only fails to interpret the material to the audience but will likely be less willing to read or speak before the group again.

Oral reading has a particular place in the teaching of literature. The teacher reads orally to develop interest in reading, to develop appreciation, and to provide stimulation and excitement. Poetry, of course, should

411

be read aloud and the rhyme and rhythm savored and enjoyed. Many stories, too, are more effective when read aloud and accompanied by sound effects and changes in tone and speed. Every teacher should spend at least a few minutes each day reading aloud something which the children will enjoy. Generally for this reading the selection should be above the reading level of the class, but not above the comprehension level. For example, though few third-grade children would read *Rabbit Hill* for themselves, they will enjoy hearing it read.[10] Too, a child might read a selection from a story which he has particularly enjoyed but which others have not read. His choice might be appreciated by the other children, and some would be influenced in their reading by his presentation. It is a good practice to establish standards for oral reading in the same manner as standards are set for other oral and written language activities. One fifth-grade class developed these standards and a pupil wrote them on a chart:

When Reading Aloud

1. Make sure you have a good reason.
2. Prepare ahead of time.
3. Read carefully and clearly.
4. Be certain everyone hears you.
5. Pay attention to punctuation.
6. Try to read with expression.

INDIVIDUALIZED AND GROUP TEACHING APPROACHES

There are many ways to organize an instructional program in reading, but the traditional plan is to group the children within one classroom into two to five groups. The composition of the groups is determined by the pupils' reading levels as measured by standardized reading tests, plus informal appraisal of reading ability by the teacher, with the reading ability of all of the children in any one group being approximately the same. The principal advantage of this plan is that the range in abilities that the teacher must deal with at any one time is considerably narrowed from that which would be faced in teaching the entire class. Too, provision of material that each child may succeed in reading is facilitated, for each group can receive instruction in a book different from those used in the other groups.

The traditional plan has a number of limitations, however, which

[10] Robert Lawson, *Rabbit Hill*. Viking Press, New York: 1944.

have led to the advancement of other plans for instruction. One limitation is that such grouping does not really mean that the children in a group have the same reading ability, and thus the teacher is still faced with the problem of dealing with wide differences. Another is that the standardized reading tests and other means of appraisal may not reveal the various levels of reading abilities which the pupil may use, but rather gives only a composite picture which is not too meaningful for specific instructional purposes. The traditional plan has been criticized, too, because of the feeling that the stigma likely to be attached to those in the lower groups, or the lowest group, may retard instruction.

Other plans for instruction include grouping on the basis of interests rather than ability and grouping on the basis of social preferences. Both of these plans allow a teacher to deal with fewer children at a time, just as does the traditional plan. Both are likely, however, to result in an even wider range in reading abilities than would have been the case in the traditional plan.

An organizational plan that has received considerable recent attention is the individualized approach. According to this plan each child reads a book of his own choosing, at his own rate, and keeps his own records. The advantages claimed for the plan are that each child is truly instructed at his own level, that he is more interested in reading since he has chosen what he wants to read, and that such attributes as self-direction and self-confidence are fostered. Advocates of the plan also emphasize the elimination of competition among groups, though they admit to increased competition among individual pupils. Criticism of the individualized approach centers around the apparent lack of a systematic plan for teaching the various reading skills. It is obvious that a limited supply of books, an inexperienced teacher, and the number of pupils the teacher has in the average classroom would all reduce the effectiveness of the plan.

It would appear that the best teaching plan makes use of features from all of the plans described above. Dividing a class into groups, with as much attention to homogeneity as possible, is the most systematic way to teach the reading skills. The particular groupings may be modified from time to time to take care of special interests and specific problems. Such modification should prevent any stigma being attached to membership in a low group, for it would be recognized that a single pupil's abilities in reading may range rather widely. Under this plan individualized reading instruction can occur in the supplemental reading program and in the free reading and literature programs.

In planning for instruction in reading it is important for the teacher to recognize the purposes of such instruction and the range of differences among children. No simple plan will achieve these purposes, recognize these differences, and be compatible with every teacher's personality. As Betts has said, "To find one plan of class organization to be executed effectively by all teachers with all children is as difficult as finding a word to rhyme with *orange*." [11]

THE TEACHING OF LITERATURE

The ultimate goal of reading instruction in schools is the use of the reading skills for independent gaining of information and knowledge, and especially the gaining of pleasure and appreciation from reading. While the basic skills of reading must be taught, and independence in the use of these skills must be achieved, a reading program—a language arts curriculum—which does not provide children with ample opportunity to enjoy and explore literature is an impoverished one. An adequate and effective literature program provides children with knowledge, inspiration, pleasure, escape, satisfaction, and recreation. In the limited space available here it is not possible to present such a program, nor to indicate completely how literature may be taught. Some suggestions are in order, however, since literature is so intimately related to creative expression, choral speaking, and other aspects of the language skills program discussed in other sections of this volume.

THE TEACHER AND LITERATURE

The teacher is really the heart of the literature program. The teacher must know the reading levels and the interests of his class and of the pupils within that class; he must have an appreciation for fine literature; he must have enthusiasm and a genuine liking for and knowledge of children's stories, poems, and books. In addition, the teacher must be able to guide children's tastes in literature and to expand continually their reading horizons.

Much teaching of literature may be done incidentally by reading to the class, by casual suggestions, by comments made when children report on something they have read, and by making literature available

[11] E. A. Betts, "Developing Basic Reading Skills . . . Through Effective Class Organization," *Education*, 78:571; May, 1958.

for reading. Sometimes, however, the direct teaching of literature is needed. In such teaching, the teacher should always maintain the attitude that this is a happy experience. This calls for the careful choosing of selections for teaching—selections which the children can understand and appreciate because of experiences they have had. The analysis of poetry and prose has no place in the elementary school program. What a child thinks about the characters in a story, what pictures he visualizes from a poem, how he enjoyed the action of a story—these things represent appreciation of literature from the child's point of view. Most discussion will be spontaneous in a classroom with a climate that invites discussion. No probing on the part of the teacher should be necessary. The teacher may, however, ask for reasons for liking a story or a poem, or why the class wants to read or hear a story a second time. Too, the humor, the truth, the rhythm, the sound of the words, the word pictures suggested by a literature selection may be discussed—in fact, they should be.

READING PROSE AND POETRY

Because most children enjoy being read to, the time spent by a teacher in reading will pay good dividends in fusing the association between reading and enjoyment. The principal aim in reading to children is the building and maintenance of interest in reading; therefore, care should be given to the selection of material to be read and to the manner in which it is read. Material of poor literary quality and unsuited to the interest of the pupils may turn them against reading. Likewise, reading too rapidly and reading without proper interpretation will have little appeal and will not hold the interest of the class or achieve the goal desired.

It is often a good idea for the teacher to provide some introduction to the book he will read. The introduction may take the form of a discussion, the showing of pictures, a bulletin board display, or a film. The introduction should not be overdone, but in introducing *Pecos Bill and Lightning,* for instance, some discussion of other Pecos Bill stories and of tall tales in general may be all that is necessary.[12] As a general rule elementary school children are not interested in the life story of the author, although after a book sells itself to them, they may then be interested. Another poor practice in introducing a book is revealing too much of the story sequence before the reading, since this will satisfy

[12] Leigh Peck, *Pecos Bill and Lightning.* Boston: Houghton Mifflin, 1940.

curiosity rather than arouse it. Book reviewers, adult as well as child, often lose sight of the purpose of the review and dull the appeal by detailed accounts of the story itself.

The very dearth of poetry teaching in present-day schools is probably a commentary upon the nature of much of our living. Teachers, of course, have done much to kill a love of poetry and interest in it. As Huck and Young point out, they have done so in five ways: "required memorization, detailed analysis, inappropriate selection, dramatic presentation, and complete omission." [13] Poetry should be a natural part of the daily activities in the classroom. Time must be given to its reading, and its rereading. Reading poetry for any reason other than enjoyment is a mistake; this is a good rule to follow or test for the teacher to use. This does not mean that poetry will not be discussed, that it may not be memorized, that it may not be dramatized, or that some analysis may not be done. But none of these should constitute the purpose for the reading, and none should be attempted unless the interest for doing so comes from the pupils themselves.

DEVELOPING READING INTERESTS

Children's interests in reading are based upon their needs and are determined by many factors, among them age, sex, intelligence, and the experiences they have had. Of particular importance, too, as a factor influencing interest is the interest of their peers. Perhaps the most important fact for a teacher to recognize in developing children's reading interests is the individuality of each child, of his experiences, and of his interests. It is helpful to know that very young children are interested in stories about animals, people, and events near to their understanding and that gradually these interests broaden to include real and fanciful stories about people and faraway places and tales of mystery, adventure, and excitement; but it is even more helpful to realize that each child will turn to the types and kinds of literature which are compatible with his total experience and development at a particular time. This fact underlines the importance of (1) a wide variety of reading material, (2) adequate time for browsing, reading, and discussing, and (3) considerable insight on the part of the teacher.

Nancy Larrick, pointing to the uniqueness of each child and his read-

[13] Charlotte S. Huck and Doris A. Young, *Children's Literature in the Elementary School*. New York: Holt, Rinehart and Winston, 1961, p. 340.

ing interests and needs, suggests that the only way to capitalize on this uniqueness is by knowing him.[14] She suggests that this takes time and warmth but may be begun by having him write answers to such questions as: When do you have the most fun at home? What is your favorite sport? What is one thing you want to learn to make? Teachers, of course, get to know children through their many contacts in the classroom and on the playground. Conversation periods in which children may chat informally about books and interests may also be very enlightening. Other suggestions for fostering and developing interests are given later in this chapter.

METHODS AND MATERIALS FOR
TEACHING LITERATURE

Most persons have had some experience with children's literature. As children they have read many of the traditional classics, such as *Little Women, Black Beauty, Tom Sawyer,* and the *Mother Goose* tales; in addition, they may have read selections to their own children. Even so, their knowledge of children's literature may be somewhat "dated," and few will have had experience in presenting literature to a group of children and building their interest in it. This section presents suggestions for teaching literature in addition to those suggested in the sections in this chapter on oral reading, developing interests, and reading prose and poetry, and those suggested in other parts of this book for using literature in choral speaking, dramatization, and creative writing.[15]

WAYS OF PRESENTING LITERATURE

Basic in the teaching of literature are many books, readily available for children's use. A reading center consisting of table and shelves in one corner of the room is of immense value. Children may be encouraged to go to this center whenever they have a few moments as well as during regular periods set aside each week. Such a center may be attractively painted and will transform even home-made shelves and box tables into an appealing place. The children themselves will enjoy planning, making, and furnishing their "library."

[14] Nancy Larrick, *A Teacher's Guide to Children's Books.* Columbus, Ohio: Charles E. Merrill Books, Inc., 1960. p. 85.

[15] See also: Amy E. Jensen, "Attracting Children to Books," *Elementary English,* 33:332–339; October, 1956, for many other suggestions.

417

The story hour. A planned story hour in the week's program is important at every grade level. The teacher may vary this story hour from the customary reading of a story by the telling of one, by playing a story record, or by utilizing a story hour on radio or television.

Time for sharing. Time for children to discuss reactions, interpretations, and evaluations of books should be provided—preferably daily. The teacher may contribute to the exchange during this time by introducing new books or favorite poems and stories. Caution must be observed to avoid having a child stumble through the reading of sections of books and stories most of the children already know. Some reading aloud is appropriate, but it is best to have pupils who plan to read aloud practice with the teacher prior to the period. Usually showing a picture or two and briefly telling of one appealing incident is enough sharing.

Book exhibits. Children may be given opportunity to arrange exhibits of favorite books. Such exhibits may be part of the reading center, in the school's library, or in a corridor. One handbook suggests the following exhibits:[16]

Books on a certain subject with placards explaining what may be found in each book
Peep shows suggested by the book
Books exhibited with models and illustrations of different kinds—drawings, clay models, carved soap, or toys
Curios and specimens that show content of the book

Bulletin board displays. Children as well as the teacher may make bulletin board displays relating to books. Such displays may be in connection with units being studied, a book being currently read to the class, Children's Book Week, or of books relating to holidays and special events. Materials for display may include:

Jackets of newly purchased books
Posters made by children about books
Children's illustrations of favorite stories
Pictures from magazines relative to particular books and stories
Charts with questions to stimulate interest in a given book
Pictures of authors and of places related to the authors and their works

Memorization. Memorization of poems has fallen into disrepute in some schools and with many teachers. However, many children enjoy memorizing favorite poems and lines, and if this practice is not forced,

[16] *The Language Arts: A Handbook for Teachers in Elementary Schools.* New York: State Education Department, 1957, p. 94.

it can be a valuable activity. Children may share poems that they have learned during the sharing times and may write them in their personal poetry books. Choral speaking often leads to the memorization of appealing poems.

Free reading periods. Time allowed for children to read something they especially want to read or to go to the central school library, or the reading center for book selection and for browsing is important. Such activity not only stimulates habits of selection which may carry over into adult life, but it also gives the teacher the opportunity to provide individual help, suggestion, and guidance.

Reports and reviews. Written reports and reviews of books read provide the teacher with some check on the children's reading in addition to the more informal checks. Such reports may also be used on bulletin boards and in other ways to stimulate interest in books. These reports, however, should be brief and not burdensome to either the child or teacher and should not tell the whole story, give away the plot, nor include unimportant details.

Book clubs. Many children will become interested in literature through the incentive of membership in a book club. Sometimes a club may be only for the purpose of exchanging personal books the children have. Other clubs center around commercial distribution of books. The following are the names of some clubs, their addresses, and details of the age levels for which they are intended.

Arrow Book Club, 33 W. 42nd Street, New York 36, N.Y. Ages 9–11.
Catholic Children's Book Club, 260 Summit Avenue, St. Paul, Minn. Groups for ages 6 through 16.
Catholic Youth Book Club, Garden City, N.Y. Ages 9–15.
Junior Literary Guild, Garden City, N.Y. Groups for ages 5 through 16.
Parent's Magazine Book Club for Beginning Readers. Bergenfield, N.J. Ages 8–11.
Teen Age Book Club, 33 W. 42nd Street, New York 36, N.Y.
Weekly Reader Children's Book Club. Education Center, Columbus 16, Ohio. Ages 5–12.
Young People's Book Club. Spencer Press, Inc., 153 N. Michigan Avenue, Chicago 1, Illinois, Ages 8–13.
Young Readers of America (Division of Book-of-the-month Club). 345 Hudson Street, New York 14, N.Y. Ages 9–14.
Young Folks Book Club. 1078 St. John's Pl., Brooklyn 13, N.Y. Ages 5–12.

MATERIALS AND THEIR SELECTION

Few teachers have the time to keep up with children's books, since several hundred new books are published each year. Excellent anthologies of children's literature are available to help teachers choose selections for reading to children and to aid in the guidance of the children's individual reading.[17] Many of these anthologies provide additional aid by listing sources in which teachers can find information about books. The following suggestions concerning the selection of books, stories, and poems are representative of the aids which are given in volumes devoted entirely to children's literature.

Book selection aids. The most complete listing of children's books is found in *The Children's Catalog,* published by the H. W. Wilson Company (950 University Ave., New York, N.Y.) every five years and kept up to date with annual supplements. The American Library Association (50 E. Huron Street, Chicago 11, Illinois) publishes *Subject Index to Books for Primary Grades, Subject Index to Books for Intermediate Grades, Subject Index to Poetry for Children and Young People,* and *Subject and Title Index to Short Stories for Children.* This association also publishes booklists, as does the Association for Childhood Education International (3615 Wisconsin Ave., N.W. Washington 16, D.C.) and the Child Study Association of America (9 East 89th Street, New York 28, N.Y.).

Reports and reviews. A number of periodicals report on books published and review many of them. Some of these periodicals are:

Childhood Education Magazine, published by the Association for Childhood Education International, has reviews in each issue.
The Horn Book (Horn Book Inc., 585 Boylston Street, Boston 16, Massachusetts) is published six times each year and is devoted entirely to children's literature.
Elementary English has a monthly "Books for Children" section and often has additional articles on authors, illustrators, and special books.
Parents Magazine (Parents Institute, Inc., 52 Vanderbilt Ave., New York 17, N.Y.) regularly reports on children's books.
The New York Times has a column each week "For Younger Readers" and in the fall of each year devotes one issue of its book review section to children's books.

[17] For example: Huck and Young, *op. cit.;* May Hill Arbuthnot, *The Arbuthnot Anthology,* Chicago: Scott, Foresman and Company, 1953; Edna Johnson, Carrie E. Scott, and Evelyn R. Sickels, *Anthology of Children's Literature.* Boston: Houghton, Mifflin, 1948.

The New York Herald Tribune regularly reviews children's books in the Sunday edition. In addition, during Children's Book Week in the fall, and again in the spring, special sections are devoted to reviews of children's books.

Newspapers and magazines. There are many magazines and newspapers designed for children that are good sources of supplementary reading material and have special appeal for some readers in that they are different from books. A few of these are:[18]

Child Life (O. H. Rodman, 136 Federal Street, Boston, Mass.) Ages 5 to 9.
Jack and Jill (Curtis Publishing Company, Independence Square, Philadelphia, Penn.) Ages 6 to 12.
Story Parade (Story Parade, Inc., 200 Fifth Avenue, New York) Ages 5 to 8.
Highlights for Children (Highlights For Children, Inc., 37 East Long Street, Columbus, Ohio) Ages 8 to 12.
Young American (Eton Publishing Corp., New York) Ages 10 to 14.

Other materials. The possibilities for the use of inexpensive paperback books in the elementary school are only beginning to be realized. Some of the books in the book clubs mentioned above are being presented in paperback form and many familiar classics are now available in this form. *Paperbound Books in Print* (R. R. Bowker Co., 62 West 45th Street, New York 36, N.Y.), published semi-annually, and categorizing titles in sections such as "Juveniles," "Humor," and so forth, is a useful aid in selection of paperback books.

Teachers should also not overlook (1) reading books designed to supplement basal readers; (2) science series such as the "all about," "first book," and "landmark" books; and (3) supplementary social studies books, pamphlets, and biographies.

EXERCISES FOR THOUGHT AND DISCUSSION

1. Develop the idea of the basic dependence of the child's learning to read upon his listening and language background.
2. Outline the essential features of the modern reading program.
3. What differences do you see between ordinary silent reading and work-study type reading? Is work-study reading necessarily silent?

[18] For a detailed list of such periodicals see Laura K. Martin, *Magazines for School Libraries*, rev. ed. New York: H. W. Wilson Company, 1950.

4. Evaluate the essentials of an instructional plan for promoting directed-reading activities.

5. Discuss the interrelationship of reading readiness and physical and mental maturity.

6. Explain the essential differences in the two kinds of word analysis, structural and phonetic.

7. In terms of its limited social utility justify the de-emphasis of oral reading in the instructional program. On the other hand, justify some oral reading for communication and enjoyment.

8. Outline what seems to you to be the best teaching plan for taking care of wide individual differences in reading ability.

9. What is the teacher's most significant contribution in the teaching of literature?

10. Evaluate the numerous ways of presenting literature to children as outlined in this chapter.

11. How can teachers and children be kept well-informed in their selection of reading material?

12. As a result of your study of this chapter prepare a series of concise statements which might be used as principles of method to guide you in teaching reading and literature in your classroom.

SELECTED REFERENCES

ARBUTHNOT, MAY HILL. *Children and Books*. Revised Edition. Chicago: Scott, Foresman and Company, 1957.

———. *The Arbuthnot Anthology*. Chicago: Scott, Foresman and Company, 1953.

ARNSTEIN, FLORA J. *Adventure Into Poetry*. Stanford, California: Stanford University Press, 1951.

BETTS, EMMETT A. *Foundations of Reading Instruction*. New York: American Book Company, 1954.

DAWSON, MILDRED A., and BAMMAN, HENRY A. *Fundamentals of Basic Reading Instruction*. New York: Longmans, Green and Company, 1959.

DE BOER, JOHN J., and DALLMANN, MARTHA. *The Teaching of Reading*. New York: Holt, Rinehart and Winston, 1960.

FENNER, PHYLLIS. *The Proof of the Pudding, What Children Read*. New York: John Day Co., 1957.

GATES, ARTHUR I. *The Improvement of Reading*, Third Edition. New York: The Macmillan Company, 1947.

HEILMAN, ARTHUR W. *Principles and Practices of Teaching Reading.* Columbus, Ohio: Charles E. Merrill Books, Inc., 1961.

HUCK, CHARLOTTE S., and YOUNG, DORIS A. *Children's Literature in the Elementary School.* New York: Holt, Rinehart and Winston, 1961.

LARRICK, NANCY. *A Teacher's Guide to Children's Books.* Columbus, Ohio: Charles E. Merrill Books, Inc., 1960.

RUSSELL, DAVID H. *Children Learn to Read,* Second Edition, Boston: Ginn and Company, 1961.

TINKER, MILES A., and MC CULLOUGH, CONSTANCE M. *Teaching Elementary Reading,* Second Edition. New York: Appleton-Century-Crofts, Inc., 1962.

15

Selecting and Using

Language Textbooks

THE PURPOSE OF THIS CHAPTER IS TO PRESENT A CRITICAL DISCUSSION of the language textbook as an indispensible instructional instrument in the language classroom. Ways and means of selecting, evaluating, and effectively using language textbooks are summarized under the following general topics:

    a. The textbook in the language program.
    b. Functions of the language textbook.
    c. Using the language textbook.
    d. Factors in textbook selection.
    e. Practical problems of the language textbook committee.
    f. Factors of quality in language textbooks.
    g. Judging textbook quality.

The most readily accessible instructional aid for the teacher of the language skills is the textbook. To most teachers the textbook *is* the course of study, the guide on methods of instruction, and the source of language activities and practice exercises. It is important, therefore, for the language teacher to learn to use the textbook as effectively as possible and to become acquainted with the elements of quality of textbooks in the field of language.

THE TEXTBOOK IN THE LANGUAGE PROGRAM

In the ideal language program the course of study would be developed in conformity with the best modern philosophy of teaching. The learning situations would be set up in accordance with the best principles of learning. The class activities would be planned and directed by a superior teacher, well-trained in methods of teaching and a master of the subject-matter field. The children would come from excellent home environments with

424

well-established habits of good language usage. The school itself would be attractively furnished, artistically decorated, and properly equipped. Facilities for cultural contacts with the best in art, music, and literature would be available. The school library would be stocked with many interesting volumes of fiction and poetry suitable for children. The book shelves would be filled with colorful volumes on art, literature, music, science and related subjects. Encyclopedias, world almanacs, yearbooks, dictionaries, atlases, globes, and reference sources of all types would be available when needed.

In such a school the world of language would be so completely available to each child that there would be little use for a language textbook. Material needed for activities to stimulate language expression would be accessible in almost every area of interest. It would seem that in such an environment the child might acquire an adequate mastery of usage without ever realizing that he had been studying language at all.

The difficulty with this lovely picture lies in the fact that few such ideal schools, courses of study, teachers, and libraries exist except in our professional dreams. After all, schools are built, staffed, and operated with the typical child in the typical community in mind. Most of our teachers are members of that great middle group called average. They are normal or typical in their mental abilities, scholastic achievements, professional interests, and backgrounds of training and experience. Unfortunately, a few teachers must be classified as poor in most of these qualities. The inexperienced, poorly trained, overloaded teacher with a sketchy outline for a course of study and an inadequate library stands in real need of ready-made instructional help. For such teachers, the language textbook is an absolute necessity. In the hands of the able teacher, the textbook also serves a very useful purpose. In fact, the superior teacher may very properly wish to use, not a single textbook in the hands of the children, but several different sets of books as reference sources.

While there are wide differences in the quality of language textbooks, it may not be too much to expect that in general the textbook in language should represent the highest levels of curriculum development in the subject. It has been suggested that the language text should accomplish the following purposes: [1]

1. Reflect a defensible and modern point of view on language teaching and demonstrate its application in the instructional material presented;

[1] Harry A. Greene, "English—Language, Grammar and Composition," *Encyclopedia of Educational Research,* rev. ed. New York: The Macmillan Company, 1950.

2. Provide a well-organized and properly graded source of the expressional skills which bear the burden in social usage;
3. Present a rich, readable, and varied source of subject-matter content as the basis for suggested activity programs in which expressional skills are acquired under life-like conditions;
4. With its accompanying manual be the source of suggestions on method;
5. Provide the necessary initial fixation and maintenance drills;
6. Be a source of evaluation and remedial materials.

Teachers qualified by training and experience and with ample material at hand to teach written and oral expression without the use of a textbook are extremely rare. Few such superior classroom teachers can be found who have the point of view, the knowledge of the subject matter, not to mention the skill in organizing it, or the firsthand knowledge of the child's learning problems, to prepare a suitable instructional program in language without the use of a textbook. The average and the poor teachers would find the task impossible even if time permitted them to undertake it. In fact, most teachers find it sufficiently difficult to make the necessary adjustments in the textbooks available to them to meet the individual requirements of their classes without attempting to organize the entire instructional program.

FUNCTIONS OF THE LANGUAGE TEXTBOOK

The language textbook may serve several functions in the total language program, as suggested in the listing of purposes of a well-developed text in the preceding section. The language teacher should know and understand these functions as he develops his instructional program.

Consistent reflection of a point of view. An examination of sets of language texts with copyrights in each of the seven decades from 1890 to and including 1960 reveals in a striking manner the changes in point of view that have taken place in the teaching of language. In general, the trend has been away from the abstract and formal toward the functional, although in certain periods there have been surprising reversals in this general trend toward the functional and utilitarian elements in language, in spite of the demonstrated failure of formal methods to produce the expected improvements in expressional skills.

For the teacher who has not crystallized his own thinking on point of view in language teaching, the textbook may give just the assistance he needs in objectifying his own philosophy of language.

Serving as a source of content. The language program includes so many specific skills that only a highly trained subject-matter specialist could possibly keep them all in mind. For the typical teacher, overloaded with many other subjects, the textbook provides an organized and cataloged source of information on the language skills considered suitable for instruction in the particular grade. One writer has aptly described the textbook as "an assistant teacher in print." [2] Even the superior teacher finds the textbook an excellent means of checking the instructional emphasis on the language skills included in his own program, even though no textbook as such may be used in the classroom.

Language has been described in this volume as a skill field with little subject-matter structure of its own. Language skill is not developed economically by *talking about* language, but by *using* language in connection with other worthwhile classroom and life activities. Language activities arise out of pupil interests stimulated by contact with material and information in other areas. Unfortunately the library facilities in many schools are so limited that the information required for pupil activities is not available except as it is supplied in the language text itself. Too, many teachers do not understand this point of view, or are unwilling to accept it. Thus these two reasons apparently account for the surprisingly large number of pages in many of the current language textbooks. Hoping that the desired activities may take place, authors have been compelled to crowd the information necessary for an activity approach into the pages of the book with the result, it is feared, that considerable badly needed fixation and maintenance drill is crowded out. Because of this fact many teachers feel that they are forced to supplement the textbook drills with workbook and practice materials.

Serving as a source of teaching methods. Except for teachers fortunate enough to have had special training in methods of teaching elementary school language, the classroom teacher is compelled to depend almost entirely on the textbook for suggestions on teaching specific types of language lessons. While the instructions are written into each textbook lesson for the guidance of the pupil, they are often very frankly pointed in the teacher's direction. In addition to these indirect hints on methods of handling the lesson, the teacher is usually given extensive and timely suggestions on methods in the teachers' manuals prepared by most textbook publishers. These manuals are usually well written, and in many cases contain the benefit of the extensive knowledge and experience of successful teachers and supervisors. The teacher who, through his own indifference, does not secure and use the manual is not only making a

[2] Malcolm E. Melliott, "What to Look For in Choosing a Textbook." *N. E. A. Journal,* 44:158–159; March, 1955.

costly blunder, but is missing an effective means of simplifying his language teaching problems. In numerous surveys of special groups of teachers in this field, the authors have been amazed to learn how many teachers have not been made aware of the existence of these teacher guides for the textbooks they were using, or if they knew about them did not consider them important enough to study and follow in their teaching of language.

Providing fixation and maintenance drill. Economy of time is of such great importance to the language teacher that all available sources of material for the fixing of skills at the time of initial learning should be utilized. In language a great deal of such drill is required, and the textbook should supply it. Supplemental drill scattered through the instructional program is required for the maintenance of these skills. Modern textbooks in language are usually written around specifications calling for fixation and maintenance drills in amounts found to be adequate by experienced teachers; yet in the opinion of many teachers few language texts provide sufficient amounts of fixation and maintenance practice or drill materials. The teacher, then, must supplement the drill material with what he has made himself, or with that in the workbooks which are usually designed to accompany the language textbooks.

Providing sources of evaluation material. The textbook should supply the teacher with the materials for evaluating the results of the instructional program as well as with directions for their effective use in corrective instruction. While only a small part of evaluation in the language class consists in the use of informal objective types of tests, some recognition of the importance of teacher-made informal objective tests and standardized tests in language should be given in the textbook or in the teacher's manual. The use of inventory devices, either in the form of objective exercises or class-made standards, is recognized as a good technique for focusing the individual pupil's attention on the specific skills in the new unit, and for identifying the pupils who are in need of instruction on the skills involved. Pupils who make scores above a certain critical point may be excused from study or drill on the unit. They should, however, be expected to show that they have retained that mastery by making a similarly high score on the check test (or standards) following instruction. If such material does not form an integral part of the instructional program provided by the textbook, it would seem that in the interests of instructional efficiency the teacher might be compelled to secure it. In this event, economy of time would suggest that the evaluative programs provided in certain workbooks be utilized.

Below are sample items from a check test in a third-grade language textbook:

This test will help you see how much you have learned. It will show you what you need to practice. Use a sheet of paper for the test.

At the top of the page write a heading for this language paper. Number each exercise as you write it. (Score 4)

1.

Write *know* or *no* to show which word you would use in each of these blanks: (Score 4)

a) There is ——— book on that table.
b) Does Bob ——— this poem?
c) ——— one will ——— it.

2.

Write these four sentences. Use the correct short form for *is not* or *are not*. (Score 4)

a) May ——— going to school today.
b) The boys ——— going fishing.
c) We ——— quite ready.
d) ——— Joe helping you?

3.

In the proper place write a heading for a friendly letter. Use the name of your school, your city and state, and the date today. (Score 3)

8.

Read the following story. Choose a good title, such as *Up in the Air*. Write the title correctly. Then write in good paragraph form the sentences below. Correct all mistakes. (Score 5)

Yesterday I had a ride in an airplane and we went high up in the air and the houses all looked like doll houses.

How did you make out on the test? What was your score on these eight exercises? A perfect score, including the heading, is 42.

If you made any mistakes, correct them.[3]

USING THE LANGUAGE TEXTBOOK

For a teacher to begin on the first page of a language textbook and continue page by page through the entire book, is a procedure which fails to take into account the language abilities and needs of a particular class, to say nothing of the varying needs and abilities of the individuals in

[3] Harry A. Greene, Maude McBroom, Ruth Moscrip, and Norma Gillett. *Building Better English, Grade Three*. Evanston, Ill.: Row, Peterson and Company, 1947, pp. 122–124.

the class. Textbooks, in language as well as other subject areas, are used in a variety of ways. As has been suggested, perhaps an extremely capable teacher, teaching in a unique situation and with adequate resources, does not need to use a textbook. As has also been suggested, most teachers do not have the teaching resources and experience for teaching without the textbook. This does not mean, however, that a teacher needs to be a slave to the textbook and show no initiative or professional competence. It does not mean that the language assignment from day to day should consist merely of listing page numbers in the textbook.

The teacher should understand the functions of a language textbook, as developed in the preceding section. The teacher should know that a textbook presents a point of view toward language teaching, that it serves as a source of content for language activities, that teaching procedures are given in the textbook and in the teacher's manual, and that the textbook provides practice exercises and evaluative materials and suggestions. The competent teacher also knows that a textbook has limitations: (1) by itself it does not teach (although some learning may be achieved by reading it); [4] (2) the content presented as settings for language activities is bound to be artificial in nature for a particular class; (3) the practice exercises are likely to be inadequate because of limitations in the size of the textbook and because so much language practice needs to be done orally; (4) the teaching suggestions are also brief because of spatial limitations; and (5) the evaluation aids are also only suggestive and do not evaluate with the completeness required. Recognizing the shortcomings of a textbook is not to say that it is not useful; generally with this recognition, and with a recognition of the functions it does have, the textbook becomes extremely useful.

Classroom activities and textbook use. There are innumerable occasions for genuine language activities in the classroom as the teacher and children work, play, and study together. The teacher who has difficulty in recognizing the opportunities for language teaching in these activities may turn to the textbook for guidance. For example, if as the children return from recess they are discussing (perhaps arguing about) a misunderstanding of the rules of a game they were playing, this may be the ideal time for the teacher to teach about the giving of directions. He may suggest that the children look in their language textbooks for information on how to give directions. This should lead to the reading of the

[4] The authors recognize the current popularity of "teaching machines" and "programmed texts" for individual pupil use, particularly of information that perhaps may be "taught" by a straight stimulus-response approach, but insist that even such automation-oriented approaches call for the guidance of a teacher.

content in that particular section of the book (which thus becomes less artificial) and even to following all of the suggestions concerning practice for giving directions, setting of standards, usage items to receive special attention, and so forth.

In another instance the teacher may have observed that many of the children regularly used the expression, "We was going," and can then suggest referring to the textbook concerning this usage. This in turn might lead to an examination of the textbook's examples, practice upon the exercises for illustrating the usage, and use of the given drills for helping establish the correct habits of expression.

Other examples might be given, but all would relate to the use of the textbook as a source of help concerning language problems which have arisen in the regular classroom activities. Such a use of the textbook calls for a teacher's professional judgment and careful attention to language needs, but does recognize the functions that a textbook can perform.

The textbook as a guide. Teachers should also make use of the textbook as a guide to the language skills, abilities, and knowledges that should be taught and developed, and to the determination of the sequence of presentation of these skills, abilities, and knowledges. While the activities of a classroom would not likely coincide with the sequence of development of the activities presented in the textbook, and thus page by page use would be inappropriate, it is true that the activities and the skills and abilities suggested in the textbook for teaching at a particular grade level have been carefully selected and worked out and should not be ignored. A prudent teacher carefully and regularly checks his language teaching against the program in the textbook and plans for activities which will call for using those sections of the textbook which he has not already used and for which there is need with his group of children.

FACTORS IN TEXTBOOK SELECTION

Since language textbooks may be regarded as virtually indispensible teaching resources, it is important to give adequate attention to their selection.

PRESTIGE OF AUTHORS

There was a time when the reputation of the author as a scholar or as a highly successful teacher carried much weight in determining the quality of a textbook. In the field of language, this may have operated as a

431

disadvantage. In the early years of textbook production, few class-room teachers had the broad knowledge of subject matter, the under-standing of principles of learning, and the experience in organizing instructional material necessary to enable them to produce acceptable textbooks. This meant that the early texts in language were written by specialists in the history of language and in formal grammar. In the field of language, the early texts were written almost entirely by college teachers of English, individuals with the necessary scholarship, but with little interest in, or understanding of the learning problems of the ele-mentary school child.

The books produced during this period were generally at fault in two respects. First, they were factual, heavy, formal, and formidable. Second, the content and the presentation were poorly adapted to the needs of elementary school children. Being an authority in a subject-matter field does not necessarily unfit an individual for writing for the young and im-mature reader. The facts are, however, that most of these authors did not sense the problem, or were not interested in adapting their organization and style of presentation to the needs of their readers. In many such cases, the scholar knows his subject so thoroughly that it all seems very simple to him and beneath his dignity to present it in sufficient detail for the beginning student, or he becomes so interested in the subject itself that he neglects to consider his reader. Frequently he knows or cares lit-tle about how the beginning student learns a new subject and is unwilling (or unable) to adapt his presentation to the needs of his audience. It should be said in all fairness also that not all well-informed individuals are able to transmit to others the things they know. Moreover, relatively few of those who can do so are able to express this information in form that is attractive to the child of elementary school age.

One of the encouraging developments in the field of textbook pub-lication in recent years is the recognition that the best book is not neces-sarily the work of a single expert, but is the result of blending the efforts of several. Although one of the group might very properly be a well-known subject-matter authority in the field, others on the team of au-thors would be selected for their modern educational points of view, their understanding of the psychology of learning, their practical teaching or supervisory experience, or their ability to present difficult facts and skills in such a manner as to interest the young student.

REPUTATION OF PUBLISHERS

The selection of textbooks today is, as it should be, largely the responsibility of the professional staff of the school. In the days when the members of the board of education considered it their prerogative to choose the textbooks, the evidence shows that too often they were more concerned about the size and financial standing of the publishing company than they were about the book itself. The size, wealth, and prestige of the publishing company are unimportant elements in textbook production. A small and unknown publisher conceivably might secure the services of a group of relatively unknown authors and produce a text admirably adapted to the needs of a particular school or subject. As Maxwell pointed out many years ago, "The mere fact that a company has an excellent financial standing, that its imprint represents character, that it publishes many books, and all books it publishes are carefully edited, does not mean that it publishes necessarily the best . . . (book) . . . for a particular school system. . . . School officials investigating suitable texts should get in touch with all publishers who have the reputation of putting desirable books on the market in this particular field." [5] No better advice than this has been given relative to the selection of textbooks.

EXTENT OF USE

Extensive use of a textbook and its unit cost are two factors that have considerable weight in its selection even today. Both are factors of importance, but should be considered in the light of all of the facts. Publishers and book salesmen attempt to demonstrate the popularity of their product by showing that it is now adopted and in use in important cities across the nation. Such evidence may establish the quality of the product, or it may merely demonstrate the zeal of the publisher's sales force. A text may remain in use when it is not satisfactory for various reasons. Perhaps the school people have not found one with which to replace it, or lack the money to purchase new books. Sometimes political influences make a change impossible.

[5] C. R. Maxwell, *The Selection of Textbooks*. Boston: Houghton Mifflin Company, 1921.

COST

The real cost of a textbook is a very difficult matter to determine. Certainly it is not merely a matter of so many cents per volume. Cost is a relative matter to determine by all factors involved in the transaction. The language book submitted by one publisher at a net price of 53 cents per copy may be cheap when compared with a competitor's book priced at 48 cents per copy. Price comparisons must be made only with all other factors being equal. To the layman, doctor, banker, or business man, the five cent price differential may seem significant. To the professional educator, who knows what he is looking for in terms of the point of view, the suitability of the skills, the organization of the content, the psychology of learning employed in the lessons, the adequacy of the drill content, the recognition of individual differences within the class, and the methods of teaching presented for teacher guidance, the cheaper book may be the more expensive. Educationally, the cheapest language textbook is the one that provides the basis for the richest type of language program per unit of cost.

LOCAL OR LARGE UNIT ADOPTION

The size of the administrative or geographical unit to be considered in the adoption of a language textbook is a matter that is open to argument. There are those who hold that textbook adoption by the large unit, such as the state, results in economy to the schools due to the fact that the larger sales bring a lower unit-cost price from the publisher. Furthermore, there is greater economy for the individual child who is obliged to move from one school community to another within the state. A much stronger argument for larger units of adoption than that of economy, however, is that those selected to serve on state textbook committees are usually exceptionally competent authorities with high professional qualifications. Furthermore, these commissions, being made up of specialists, are able to give more time to the problems of textbook selection than could be given by a committee of teachers in a single school district. On the other hand, the opponents to state adoption hold that the use of a textbook uniformly throughout a large unit completely fails to take into account the varying local needs as found in large cities and in rural communities. Too often the members of state textbook commissions are political appointees who have little or no familiarity with the problems of textbook selection. Until this situation is corrected by limiting the membership of such commissions to educational specialists, the opponents of state adoption of textbooks have a very strong argument.

Improvement in the methods and results of textbook selection seems to hinge on the general acceptance of the principle that choosing the textbook suitable for use in a given grade, a specific subject, a particular school system is the responsibility of those qualified by professional training, experience, and service to the schools to make the technical decisions involved.

PRACTICAL PROBLEMS OF THE LANGUAGE
TEXTBOOK COMMITTEE

AVOIDING THE INFLUENCE OF
HIGH-PRESSURE SELLING

The production and sale of educational textbooks in recent years have become big business. The quality of the product has been greatly improved not only through the publishers' care in the selection of their authors for their professional qualifications, but also in the scholarly editing given the manuscripts submitted for publication. As the manufacture and distribution of textbooks have expanded, the competition has increased to the point that the textbook committee constantly faces the difficult problem of resisting the influence of high pressure selling. Yet the professional ethics of textbook publishers and representatives during recent years has been maintained at a high level. Book publishers today are represented by well-trained, professionally-minded educational experts. In fact, most of the representatives who call on supervisors and teachers to show the newest in textbook production are individuals who have themselves had extensive professional training and successful experience as teachers, supervisors, or administrators. They represent a highly selected, thoroughly capable professional group, who not only know the good qualities of the product they represent, but in many cases can go into the classroom and demonstrate its use.

The selection of a language textbook today is a difficult task. The desired qualities of the text must be clearly outlined in the mind of each member of the committee. The conditions of the selection must be so controlled that undue pressure may not be brought to bear by any one representative. Each textbook series under consideration must have the

435

same opportunity for presentation and demonstration as any other. Canvassing or contacting an individual teacher or member of the textbook committee outside of the specified committee meetings should constitute unprofessional conduct on the part of the representative. Every possible precaution should be taken to avoid the appearance of undue influence in connection with a textbook adoption, whether it be in a small local school system or in a state adoption.

SECURING OBJECTIVE EVIDENCE OF QUALITY

General statements concerning the special qualities of particular publications, must, of course, be considered, but the final and clinching argument should rest on the objective evidence that is made available in support of each textbook series. Publishers of textbooks in reading are careful, particularly in the beginning grades, to present a detailed tabulation showing the exact words comprising the basic vocabulary on which the reading program is based, as well as all new words added at each successive grade level. The buyer of a new spelling text is given the facts about the source of the writing vocabulary comprising the program. Many comprehensive writing vocabulary studies are available for general use, and credit to these sources should be given by the authors. Distributions showing frequencies of appearance of drill on certain basic facts in arithmetic are usually made by the authors as the examples and exercises are prepared. Ask for these distribution tables when examining an arithmetic text. If they are not available, try to discover why they are not. If you are still interested after being told that they were not available, it is, of course, possible for you to prepare them yourself, but it might be more profitable for you to examine more carefully another book whose authors and publishers have made data on frequency of drills available.

Tables showing the drill frequencies for language skills are difficult to prepare but they can be made. Ask to see these charts for the language books you are interested in examining. A substitute for drill distribution charts commonly featured by book representatives is the book index itself. Presumably each individual and successive appearance of a particular skill is indicated by separate page listings in the index. Where no other chart of drill appearances is available it will be profitable to make a careful check of the index listings to determine whether actual instructions on the skill appear on the pages indicated. Index listings sometimes appear when only a single word reference to the skill appears.

Tabulations showing the frequencies of appearance of certain mechanical skills in language, such as in capitalization and punctuation, should certainly be used in making comparisons of competing language texts. If this information is not available, some other objective means of comparison, such as the column-inch unit, should be adopted. The number of column-inches of drill on any given group of skills can be measured roughly by using a ruler to determine the total number of page-inches in each unit on each skill. Because of differences in lengths of lines the number of inches of drill per page will vary from book to book and must be equated before comparisons can be made.

CONSENSUS OF EXPERT JUDGMENTS

On all issues in textbook selection for which objective data are not available, the judgments of several qualified examiners should be followed. The more representative the membership of the textbook selection committee, the more likely it is that the books chosen will meet the local requirements. It is quite certain that at least one member should be chosen from the administrative or supervisory services of the school system, but the majority judgments should come from the teachers who will use the books in the classrooms.

Complete sets of texts with manuals should be collected well in advance by the administrative office for examination by the committee members prior to the presentation and demonstration meetings with the publishers' representatives. Publishers are most willing to work with properly constituted selection committees by making their publications available for examination and study.

FACTORS OF QUALITY IN LANGUAGE TEXTBOOKS

The critical examination and evaluation of the competing series of textbooks under consideration should be guided by carefully formulated statements setting forth the factors of quality expected of texts in this field. As a supplement to the textbook score card presented and explained later in this chapter, several of the more important general factors determining textbook quality are discussed in this section. This material should be of real assistance to teachers and any others who may be called upon to serve on a textbook selection committee.

437

INTEREST OF THE INSTRUCTIONAL MATERIAL

One test of a good textbook is its ability to arouse and hold a child's interest. Some of the factors that combine to make a book interesting to a child are discussed below.

Appeal to child interest. One of the most important factors determining the suitability and usability of a language textbook in a given grade is the appeal it makes to the interests of the children who are expected to study it. It is doubtful if third-grade children expect to find a series of sugar-coated morsels of language wisdom when they open their first book in the systematic language program. By the time they have completed kindergarten, first, and second grades, they are beginning to suspect that school life is real and earnest. They feel the importance of having a language book in their hands. They have grown up considerably in the last two years. They don't like to have older persons appear to talk down to them, but they still like to feel that their introduction to third grade language takes into account their own backgrounds of experience and interests. This places a very heavy burden of responsibility upon the early lessons in the program. The first sentences and paragraphs in a language book are critical ones; they are the real test of the author's ability to appeal to the child reader. They must pick him up at the opening of a series of new experiences in language and make him feel that profitable and enjoyable adventures lie ahead for him. It is no trade secret that authors of language books spend countless hours writing and rewriting these early lessons in the hope of awakening the interest of the children in the program of language activities that lies ahead.

Motivation. Another important element in the basic interest of the instructional program in the text is the manner in which it presents devices and procedures for stimulating each child to take an active personal interest in each of the new language activities undertaken by his group. The realization that a feeling of success is very important for the child undertaking new and difficult activities has encouraged authors of language textbooks to try to guarantee that his early activities result successfully. This is sound motivation provided it is not overdone. In his primary grade work, the child has had some experience with language as a tool of communication. The importance of this aspect of language must be constantly emphasized in the daily classroom activities. The child must be made to feel that his ideas and opinions are important to the members of his group. He must be given experiences of such richness, novelty, and interest that he feels a need to communicate his feelings and ideas to others.

The most important motivating forces for effective language expression arise from the well-planned class activity. The many group discussions in which the plans for the activity are developed, the committee meetings in which important decisions are reached, the class meetings in which standards of usage or personal conduct are formulated, all stimulate the individual to carry his share of the responsibility. To do this he must organize and present his ideas, criticize and disagree tactfully, assume leadership in areas in which he is qualified to lead. Modern textbooks in language place a great deal of emphasis on the importance of the activity program in motivating language expression and in providing opportunities for the effective mastery of language skills in life-like situations. It is suggested that the beginning teacher of language or the teacher who does not have well-developed projects of his own under way will do well to follow the plans outlined in textbooks in language. The experienced teacher may very properly substitute his own activity plans for those outlined in the textbook, but if he does so he must make a careful check of the language skills designated for teaching in order to guarantee that they are actually given the proper instructional emphasis.

Illustrations. Colorful and attractive illustrations scattered through the book add to the interest of the presentation and, if judiciously selected, may prove to be important motivational devices. The more physical activity the illustrations demonstrate, the more the children seem to like them. At times they are attracted by stick drawings depicting the human form in action as much as they are by finished art work. Children are attracted to the book with a colorful binding and like to turn through the pages admiring colorful art work. Perhaps of importance equal to the liberal use of color in the pictures and illustrations is the care with which the pictures are related to the activities they purport to illustrate. Charts and diagrams suggesting related activities for pupils are also important materials for motivation.

Style of presentation. Language is a technical subject which is difficult to discuss without the use of many terms that are new ones for the child. The explanations must be simply written and easily understood without appearing to talk down to the child. Technical or special words must be defined and illustrated in the context in which they appear. However, there is much more to style of presentation than a simple vocabulary.

Often it is difficult to discover just what makes the presentation in one textbook interesting and that in another boring. The answer probably lies in the individuals who do the writing. Some authors write in a style pleasing to children; others are unable to do so. It is probable that children are quite like most adults in that they find a light, vivacious, chatty style pleasing, and a dry, formal, heavy style boring. The language textbook is not designed to provide light and entertaining reading for the school child, but it must have enough interesting facts, activities, and bits of information scattered through its pages to keep the child hunting for more.

Relation to other subjects.   One of the very important advances in the language textbook of today over the one of yesterday is the fact that the new approach to language instruction relates language to practically all other school subjects and activities. Today the language program as presented in the modern textbook overlaps with practically every subject and classroom. It is in these other classrooms and subject-matter activities that the real motivation for language mastery is developed. Language skills are made habitual through use in practically all school activities. The use of correct oral and written expression is just as important in the science, mathematics, music, art, and social studies class as it is in the class in which language is supposed to be the central activity.

Stimulation of personal activity.   The interest of the language textbook is strengthened by the stimulation it provides for the individual child to become personally active in using the common forms of expression. Language skills may provide interesting topics for class discussion, but it is primarily through individual and personal activity in which they are *used* that they become a part of the child's ability and personality. Mastering language skills involves much more than merely keeping the learner active, the activity must be closely related to the desired language goals and objectives. The modern textbook in language provides the child with interesting information designed to stimulate each individual to express himself along the lines of his own interests. It sets up the standards by which he himself can improve his own language habits. The extent to which the text stimulates the child to culminate his activities in creative oral or written expression is one of the best measures of the quality of the book.

DIFFICULTY OF COMPREHENSION OF THE INSTRUCTIONAL MATERIAL

Language textbooks, in common with most other textbooks, reveal such wide differences in readability that it is recommended that no final adoption of a textbook series be made until tests have been run to determine the difficulty of the material for comprehension. In general, instructions to the child which cannot be followed without supplementary verbal explanations are too difficult and certainly should be rewritten. The only sure guide to this problem is found in the reactions of the pupils themselves. Other factors to be considered are the following.

Vocabulary. The suitability of a language textbook for use in a specific grade depends not only on the interesting manner in which the material is presented but also on the complexity of the organization of the material and the difficulties the children have in reading and in comprehending it. A language textbook written at a level of comprehension above that of the pupils who are expected to use it would have a limited usefulness. As a matter of fact, the textbook in language should use a vocabulary, style, and complexity of concepts at least one grade below the level of the children who are expected to study it. This presents a difficult writing problem for the author of the third grade book in which many new and special terms must be introduced. The first lessons in the third grade language book must be prepared with the realization that the children have but recently completed the second grade and do not read very well. All technical words and words with special meanings must be defined and explained in terms comprehensible to the beginning third grade reader.

Vague and unusual concepts. A common fault in the presentation of instructional material in textbooks is the use of novel and complex concepts which are often meaningless to the child. For example, what do expressions such as *several times a day, a high wind, a few miles away,* mean to the child? How many times is *several* times? How strong is a *high* wind? How far away is a *few miles?* In Maine a few miles might be two; in Ohio it might be twenty; in Texas it might be one hundred. The child of seven or eight has sufficient difficulty in comprehending instructional material written in concise language without being further confused by the introduction of vague and uncertain concepts. In the examination of language textbooks under consideration for adoption, a

441

careful check of the instructional material should be made for suitability of vocabulary and freedom from terms with vague and uncertain meanings.

IMPORTANCE OF THE SUBJECT MATTER

For a textbook to function as a useful instructional guide, its subject matter must not only be suited to the interests and abilities of pupils, but must also be acceptable in the light of the current educational point of view.

Point of view in selection. Authors and publishers of language textbooks may differ widely as to specific language skills and subject matter to be presented in a given grade, but most of the recent language texts are in reasonable agreement on general point of view. If the textbook under consideration does not make clear its general point of view on subject matter in its introductory statement, a careful check should be made of the teacher's manual for this information. It is the responsibility of the school to provide a language program that will enable the individual to meet all of the important expressional needs he is likely to encounter in his activities both in school and out of school. Considerable evidence supporting this point of view and instructional material illustrating its application in the language curriculum have been presented in this volume. In the event that the philosophy of the school interested in choosing a textbook in language is in disagreement with this point of view, the texts under consideration should be checked carefully to see that they consistently hold to their indicated point of view.

Consistency in emphasis on child and adult values. The author of a language textbook must present a consistent program in which both the child's immediate language needs and his ultimate language needs as an adult are given the proper instructional emphasis. Some language books appear to take an adult view looking completely past the child's present, school needs. They seem to assume that the needs for both ages are identical or that the child's school needs for language training will be met automatically in his other school activities. This is not entirely the case. Although many of the needs of the two groups are similar, the levels at which the emphasis is given are quite different. The effective language program is one in which instructional emphasis is adjusted to the maturity of the students as well as to their language needs.

Grade placement of subject matter. The grade placement of language skills and of the subject matter suitable for the language activities of a particular grade unfortunately depends much more upon the judgment and experience of teachers and textbook authors than upon experimental evidence. Unquestionably certain skills are more suitable than others for presentation and emphasis in certain grades. In general, skills which most often meet a child or adult language need should be taught early in the language program. Usually these frequently needed skills are among the easiest ones for the children to master. In certain areas it is apparent that some skills support those previously taught or simplify the mastery of those presented later in the sequence.

Adaptation of method to subject matter. The value of the subject matter in the language textbook is determined in a measure by the distribution of emphasis on different subject-matter units. A school system favoring a formal approach in language would not be interested in a program with little or no stress on rules, formal grammar, or diagramming. Those favoring a thoroughly functional activity approach would not be attracted to the formal and disciplinary treatment of language skills. The book with a heavy emphasis on oral expression would find favor with most well-trained, experienced teachers who would appreciate the adaptation of methods of teaching to the mastery of the essential skills of oral expression.

The content of the better language textbooks is selected with due consideration for the mental maturity of the individuals who are to use it. This is directly implied from the statements of the principles determining grade placement of subject matter. It must be remembered, however, that in spite of efforts to group children in accordance with their learning capacity within the grades, there is always a serious overlap from grade to grade. The most able individual in a fourth-grade class may far excel the poorest pupil in the grade next above. The actual range of mental maturity of learning capacity within a given grade, such as the sixth, may exceed five or six years or grades from the poorest to the best individual in the class group. This poses a serious problem for the author of the language textbook. Content that is suitable for the middle group in the class may be far too difficult for the slow learners and much too easy for the bright ones. No language book can be made large enough to provide suitable instructional material, drill, and evaluative devices for the entire range of ability of the class using the book. The teacher must be depended upon to make these important adjustments in emphasis and in methods of teaching under the guidance of helpful suggestions incorporated in the lessons and in the teaching manual.

443

Recognition of individual differences. The discussion in the preceding section on the relation of method to subject matter raises the problem of providing adjustments for individual differences in language instructional needs. Authors of language texts usually are forced by the limitations of space to adapt the content of the book for a specific grade to the abilities and interests of the large middle or average group of children. Some supplementary help must be provided for the rather sizable group that will not be able to work as rapidly as the average pupils. Another problem is what to do with the very active group of superior children who encounter little or no difficulty with the routine activities and lessons and are frequently bored by the useless waste of their time. They surely cannot be asked to do more of the same types of drills and exercises. The superior texts make a definite attempt to aid the teacher here by providing individualized enrichment activities utilizing language skills designed for the use of only the superior pupils who have met all minimum and average requirements. This program not only recognizes and encourages the superior pupils, but it also serves as a powerful motive for the less able children to strive to earn the privileges of doing the enrichment exercises.

Clear statement of procedures. Three different sources are noted for the presentation of suggestions to teachers on methods which have been found to be effective in the development of certain language skills and activities. An examination of many of the newer textbooks in language will reveal that quite often the directions to pupils include a suggestion that the teacher will probably wish to have the class proceed in a certain way. In other instances a footnote in the text itself will direct the teacher in the most effective procedures with a particular lesson or activity. The teacher's manual, of course, is the source to which the teacher should constantly turn for the best suggestions on methods of teaching each particular type of lesson unit.

Criteria for correct practices. Since there are so many language usages on which even the experts disagree, the textbook should give the teacher every possible assistance in settling such debatable issues. Naturally this means that if possible adequate criteria or standards for correct practices should be made available to the teacher.

Provision of suitable factual and content material. The importance of the activity program in the classroom as the means of motivating the mastery of language skills through their use in lifelike situations makes necessary the inclusion of extensive and suitable factual and content material in the language textbook of today. Provision of this material is certainly an important factor in determining the quality of the book.

JUDGING TEXTBOOK QUALITY

Teachers and supervisors confronted with the problem of selecting an elementary school language textbook must gather exact information on the specific factors which determine the quality of textbooks. Experience in determining the relative merits of farm grains or farm animals by the use of detailed score cards in the hands of expert judges has demonstrated the value of such devices. In the hands of the expert stock or grain judge, the score card may not be an indispensable instrument. If it is not useful to such a judge, it is because through his experience he is able to retain in his mind all of the essential elements of quality. For the inexperienced, the score card provides a reasonable guarantee that important elements of quality will be neither overlooked nor given weightings out of line with their relative importance. Score cards for the evaluation of handwriting, art products, machine-shop and wood-working shop products, printing and other educational products have demonstrated their usefulness. Being based on individual judgments, the results lack much of the objectivity and reliability desired in educational evaluation, but they are considerably better than no instrument whatever. The authors are convinced that in the same way a textbook score card can render a distinct and highly valuable service in a textbook adoption program. The quality of the service, of course, will depend upon the training the examiners are given in the use of the score card, and the conscientious care with which they apply their training in the analysis and evaluation of the textbooks they are asked to examine.

A SCORE CARD FOR EVALUATING
LANGUAGE TEXTBOOKS

The textbook score card presented here (pages 446–448) is the result of several years of effort to catalog the specific factors that teachers consider important in the production of a quality textbook and to arrive at independent estimates of the relative importance of each of these elements of quality. An examination of the available score cards and other devices for the evaluation of textbook quality was a first step. A tenta-

A Score Card for Use in Selecting Elementary Language Textbooks

	I	II	III
1. PRELIMINARY INFORMATION Name of book	*A superior language book* [6]		
Author's name			
Author's reputation in language in other fields	*Exc.* *Exc.*		
Publisher's name Reputation in language field Reputation in general	*Exc.* *Exc.*		
Copyright date, this edition first edition next revision	1963 1950 1955		

	Standard	I	II	III
2. SUBJECT-MATTER CONTENT	450			
a. General suitability	(150)	*(128)*		
Point of view	25	*22*		
Adaptation to course of study	35	*31*		
Authority for selection	25	*21*		
Interest	40	*34*		
Criteria for practices	25	*20*		
b. Difficulty	(75)	*(62)*		
Comprehension	20	*16*		
Vocabulary	10	*9*		
Concepts	15	*13*		
Style	15	*11*		
Complexity or organization	15	*13*		
c. Gradation and placement	(50)	*(42)*		
Suitability for grade	30	*25*		
Criteria used	20	*17*		
d. Organization of content	(40)			
Psychological, logical		*36*		
e. Emphasis on basic units	(35)			
Page and time allotments		*30*		

[6] Sample scoring of an excellent book.

	Standard	I	II	III
f. Adequacy of drill for initial learning	(40)	*(35)*		
Distribution	15	*14*		
Kind	10	*9*		
Amount	15	*12*		
g. Adequacy of drill for maintenance	(30)	*(25)*		
Distribution	10	*10*		
Kind	10	*8*		
Amount	10	*7*		
h. Adequacy of testing and diagnostic material	(30)	*(26)*		
Distribution	10	*9*		
Kind	10	*9*		
Norms	10	*8*		
3. METHODS	300			
a. General adequacy	(200)	*(180)*		
Recognition of individual differences	35	*33*		
Adapted to mental level of users	40	*36*		
Drill vs. rules	35	*31*		
Supplemental notes to teacher	20	*17*		
Correlated with life activities	35	*32*		
Correlated with subject matter	35	*31*		
b. Aides in use	(100)	*(84)*		
Teacher's manual				
Adequacy of	15	*13*		
Point of view	10	*9*		
Sources and authority	10	*8*		
Methodology	15	*13*		
Supplementary materials				
Index	10	*8*		
Tables of contents	10	*9*		
References to sources	10	*8*		
Selection of illustrations, charts, graphs, etc.	10	*8*		
Footnotes to pupil and teacher	10	*8*		
4. PHYSICAL AND MECHANICAL FEATURES	250			
a. Size of book	(20)	*(16)*		
Suitability for user	10	*9*		
Page size	5	*3*		
Thickness	5	*4*		

	Standard	I	II	III
b. Covers: title and decoration	(20)			
Suitability and attractiveness		*18*		
c. Binding	(20)	*(17)*		
Color	5	*5*		
Kind and quality	5	*4*		
Workmanship—durability	5	*4*		
Suitability	5	*4*		
d. Paper	(40)	*(33)*		
Color	10	*8*		
Quality	10	*9*		
Finish	10	*8*		
General suitability	10	*8*		
e. Typography	(100)	*(85)*		
General suitability	20	*18*		
Size of type	15	*14*		
Style	10	*8*		
Spacing—letters, words, lines	10	*9*		
Leading	10	*9*		
Length of lines	10	*7*		
Margins	10	*7*		
Marginal notes and heads	10	*9*		
Footnotes	5	*4*		
f. Illustrations	(50)	*(43)*		
Size	5	*4*		
Kind (bl.-wh., Color)	10	*9*		
Number	10	*9*		
Placement	10	*8*		
Suitability	15	*13*		
Total score	1,000	*860*		

5. OPTIMUM UTILITY OF THE BOOK
   Basic
   Supplementary source book
   Drill book
   Reference
   Teacher's handbook

448

tive listing of these elements was submitted to hundreds of teachers and graduate students in the classes of the senior author over a period of four or five years with the request that point-weights be assigned to each of the elements grouped under the three major headings, *Subject-matter Content, Methods,* and *Physical and Mechanical Features,* in the accompanying score card. The point values assigned represent the composite of all judgments adjusted to the nearest 5-point value for each factor. The weightings assigned each of the factors were combined to indicate the total weightings under the three main heads. In this manner *Subject-matter Content* was given 45% of the total score, *Methods* was given 30% of the total score, and *Physical and Mechanical Features* was given 25% of the total. In order to eliminate fractional scores for certain of the sub-points under each main head all values were multiplied by 10, thus raising the total possible score for an ideal and perfect textbook to 1,000 points. Considerable experience with this score card indicates that only very superior language texts deserve ratings as high as 860 points.

EXPLANATION OF THE SCORE CARD

An explanation of the way the score card is used is given below. The number of each item corresponds to the number of the item on the score card.

1. PRELIMINARY INFORMATION. Early experience with the development of this score card indicated that certain items are often improperly considered as elements in the quality of the book. This accounts for the assignment of no point values to the group of items included under *Preliminary Information.* Naturally the name of the book and the author's name should be entered on the score card as a matter of record. The remaining three items relative to the reputation of the author in the language field, his reputation in other fields, the publisher's reputation as a producer of language textbooks, and his general reputation as an educational publisher are included for the record but are unscored.

The copyright of the edition of the text under consideration, the copyright of the first edition, and the recentness of the next revision are included because they contribute significant data relative to the care and the rate of development of the book. For example, if a certain book in a current edition this year first appeared four years ago and was put through a revision the following year, some question might legitimately be raised concerning the care with which the original edition was prepared. Revisions in textbooks are necessary, of course, but if the first manuscript is carefully prepared and critically edited it should not be necessary to revise it so soon.

2. SUBJECT-MATTER CONTENT. In this score card, subject-matter content of a text, including suitability, difficulty, gradation and placement, organization, emphasis, and adequacy of drills and testing material, accounts for almost one-half of the points given to the book.

2. a. *General suitability.* General suitability of the content, represented by the acceptability to the scorer of the point of view presented by the book, its possibility of adaptation to the local course of study, the reasons given for the selection of the content, the general interest of the content, and the criteria or standards of practice presented in the book represents a total of 150 points, or one-third of the weight given to subject-matter content.[7]

2. b. *Difficulty.* General reading difficulty of the textbook is assigned a total of 75 points, of which 60 points are given to vocabulary, concepts, and style. Difficulty of the material, or readability, is discussed earlier in this chapter.

2. c. *Gradation and placement.* The proper application of the principles of grade placement in the individual textbook in relation to the entire series is assigned a total of 50 points, with 30 points assigned to suitability of the content for the grade, and 20 points for evidence of the proper use of the criteria for grade placement presented in this chapter.

2. d. *Organization of content.* Three general methods of organization of language skills for instruction are found in the available educational literature. These are: (a) logical, (b) psychological, and (c) sociological. When subject matter is organized on the logical plan, the skills that logically come first in the total process are placed in the lower grades. The skills that logically come last in the subject are placed in the higher grades. The difficulty with the theory lies in the fact that the logic of skill organization is often quite unrelated to the learning difficulty of the skills and thus does not take into consideration the natural interests or capacities of the child. In contrast with the logical plan, the psychological plan presents the skills at the time and place when the child's interests, needs, and abilities are best served. In theory the psychological plan has a much greater practical appeal than does the logical plan. The chief limitation to its general use is found in the fact that so little

[7] See column 1 of the score card for part scores assigned a superior language book.

is known about the interests, abilities, and needs of children. In actual practice the organization and grade placement of skills and subject matter in most language texts are a blending of the sociological principles for the selection of the subject matter with the psychological plan for grade placement. This factor is assigned 40 points.

2. e. *Emphasis on basic units.* The 35 points assigned this factor are concerned with the balance of the instructional emphasis as shown by page and time allotments in accordance with the sociological importance of the different skills, abilities, and activities presented at this particular grade level.

2. f. *Adequacy of drill for initial learning.* Drill is only one form of instructional emphasis but it is a very important element in fixing facts after initial presentation and in maintaining effective habit reactions. Three factors are considered here in the evaluation of drill for initial learning: distribution, kind, and amount of drill. Distribution refers to the adequacy of the skill coverage provided in the drill as well as to the periodic recurrence of the drill exercises throughout the language program for the grade. Kind of drill refers to the variety of drill forms used for accomplishing different specific goals of learning. Amount of drill may be determined by item tabulations showing frequencies of item and skill recurrences, or it may be measured roughly in column-inches of page space assigned to it.

2. g. *Adequacy of drill for maintenance.* The assignment of 30 points to this factor and 40 points for adequacy of drill for initial learning appears to indicate that in the opinions of the judges who assisted in assigning these weights, drill for maintenance was somewhat less important than drill for initial learning purposes. Perhaps the best way to view items 2.f. and 2.g. of this score card is that together they account for 70 points and in this manner receive emphasis in proportion to their importance.

2. h. *Adequacy of testing and diagnostic material.* The importance of the presence of a complete program of evaluation in a textbook naturally depends upon the point of view of the user. In the judgment of the authors, this factor is much more important than is indicated by the 30 points assigned to it.

3. METHODS. The importance of this main head is indicated by the assignment of a total of 300 points—200 points to the general adequacy of the methods program, and 100 to the specific aids to the teacher and pupils.

3. a. *General adequacy.* The responsibility of the textbook for the

451

presentation of adequate instructional assistance to the teacher has been discussed briefly in this chapter (pages 426–431).

3. b. *Aids in use.* Quite properly one-half of the 100 points assigned to this factor are related to the general adequacy of the teacher's manual. The authors consider that it is practically impossible to include within the covers of the textbook itself a sufficient selection of practical aids and suggestions to the teacher to justify the omission of a teacher's manual from the language program. The score of a textbook without a teacher's manual is automatically reduced 50 points.

The index is an important aid to the pupil and to the teacher in locating specific items. The index should be complete, but it should not be filled with duplicate classifications of the same items to give the appearance of a heavy maintenance program.

Illustrations, charts, and graphs presented in the context should have a direct relationship to the subject matter they accompany. Colorful art work is very attractive to children especially in the lower grades and, other things being equal, the textbook liberally illustrated with color work should rate higher than one using black and white illustrations.

The presence of footnotes and special instructional notes on the pages of the language textbook is a good indication that the authors are sensitive to the instructional problems involved. Frequently a note directed to the pupil is an effective way to suggest a desirable teaching or procedural technique to the teacher.

4. PHYSICAL AND MECHANICAL FEATURES. The physical and mechanical features of the textbook are important to the textbook buyer, especially in situations in which the book must survive several years of use. It is equally obvious that these elements are much less important to the child and the teacher than the content and the methods program presented in the book. In this score card 250 of the 1,000 score points are assigned to these factors.

4. a. Many factors enter into the determination of the suitability of the size of a language textbook. The old idea that the small child should have a small book has been made somewhat obsolete by the manufacturers of trade books for children. On the other hand the practical problems of boxing and shelving books for shipping and storage, and for placing them in desks, have definitely encouraged the production of language books that fit in with other textbooks in the school situation. Teachers quite correctly demand a book that lies open flat and presents a page surface free from extreme curvature. This means that manufac-

turers are tempted to produce books with wide pages and narrow type lines. This tendency has resulted in two types of page-sizes: (a) the traditional single-column page with wide gutter (margins next to the binding edge), (b) the double-column page with short type line. Books of both of these types, if properly bound, will lie open and will present a reasonably flat page surface. Some believe that the two-column page presents an easier reading problem for the child than does the longer type line. It is doubtful if this has been definitely demonstrated as a fact. It is certain, however, that locating a specific exercise on the two-column page involves more difficulty for the child than does the single-column page.

The thickness of the language book is another element in book size. Experiments with type sizes in lower grade textbooks have discouraged the use of very large type even in third-grade books. The practical effect of these findings has been to increase greatly the amount of printed matter in the book without increasing its thickness. Full advantage of this feature has been taken by textbook authors and publishers to provide the lengthy and detailed directions necessary for stimulating activity projects in the third and fourth grades.

Only 20 points are assigned to size of book. Perhaps this small weighting is difficult to justify in view of the above rather lengthy discussion of book size. The suitability of the book for the user is the important element, and it should be scored rather strictly.

4. b. *Covers: title and decoration.* Children instinctively choose books with bright and colorful covers. Publishers naturally have taken this into account in the manufacture of most recent language series. Suitability and attractiveness are highly subjective factors for the judge to evaluate.

4. c. *Binding.* The color, quality, and workmanship of the binding of a language textbook are probably more important features of textbook merit than is indicated by low weighting given them in the score card. The color of the binding appears as a factor in b. above. Light and colorful covers appeal to children but practically they may be undesirable. The quality of the cover is much more important than color. The bindings of competing textbooks for general classroom use should be subjected to a standard torture test to determine their durability.

The workmanship and the type of binding used are very important factors determining the usability and the length of life of the book. The pages of large books usually are printed on 16-page spreads which after folding are sewed for assembling and gluing along the backs of

453

the folios. Books in which the folios are sewed through the fold in the middle of the folio are said to be saddle-stitched. Folios which are folded flat and sewed or stitched along the folded edge are said to be singer-sewed. This latter process tends to hold the pages so tightly that they cannot be opened flat without a severe strain being put on the stitching. Saddle-stitched folios assemble readily with the threads projecting through the backs for tying and gluing. Folios sewed in this manner permit the book to lie flat open without a special strain on the binding. Quality of workmanship shows clearly in the tying, gluing, and binding. These are important elements in the quality and the life of the book and should be scrutinized sharply by the textbook examiner.

4. d. *Paper.* The color, quality, and finish of the paper stock used in a language textbook should be examined critically. Preferably the stock should be a flat-finished paper in a light ivory or just off-white color. Paper of this type is easy on the eyes because it does not reflect glaring lights. It is difficult to specify the exact weight of the paper but as a general guide it should be heavy enough to prevent the imprint on the back of the page from showing through.

4. e. *Typography.* The fact that the general typographical appearance of a textbook is the most important single feature of the physical makeup of a textbook is indicated by the assignment of 100 of the 250 points allotted to this section of the score card. Criteria for general suitability of the typography are difficult to set up objectively. Simplicity and clarity of letter form are not to be sacrificed for beauty, although some type styles are both simple and beautiful. Heavy black type in profusion becomes disturbing to the reader. The horizontal lines of a's and e's should be heavy enough that they stand out clearly in print.

The size of type for a particular book depends to a large degree upon the editorial policy of the publisher. Some will wish to set a third-grade book in 14 point type and reduce the size of the type to 12 point in the fourth grade. Experimental studies of the effects of type size indicate that children react favorably to type sizes indicated above provided there is sufficient leading or separation between the type lines.[8] This of course reduces the number of printed lines per page but does provide for more copy per page than a larger size of type would permit. In most textbooks using the single-column page, reasonably short type-lines are used, thus

[8] B. R. Buckingham, "New Data on the Typography of Textbooks." Thirtieth Yearbook of the National Society for the Study of Education, Part II. Bloomington, Illinois: Public School Publishing Company, 1931.

providing liberal margins on the outside as well as on the binding edge of page.

Instructional material in a textbook is usually rather difficult reading at best, but when the printed pages are not broken frequently by center heads, side heads, pictures, charts, and other devices, the solid page of printing presents a serious reading problem to the average child. Marginal notes and supplementary or explanatory heads should be used liberally. Pictures based on the content of the page should be inserted frequently. New printing processes have made possible some highly attractive art work flowing in and around the context.

4. f. *Illustrations.* The importance of illustrations in the language textbook has been discussed on page 439 of this chapter. General suitability of the size, kind, and number of illustrations is the most significant item here.

Total score. The total possible point score that can be assigned to a textbook considered to be absolutely perfect in every respect would be 1,000 points. Obviously no such textbook is in existence. Considerable experience in the use of this score card with groups of teachers trained in its use indicates that a text that scores as high as 860 points is a genuinely superior book. This is in no sense a norm score, but it does indicate something of the way in which an excellent product compares with the ideal as expressed by 1,000 points.

5. OPTIMUM UTILITY. The final evaluation of a textbook series is made with the idea that the best possible text for the purposes of the local school system may be found. The final point scores should rate the competing texts in the approximate order of their suitability as indicated by the judgment of the local selection committee. These final scores coupled with the scorer's personal impressions of the books in general should very properly culminate in a recommendation concerning the optimum utility of the book.

EXERCISES FOR THOUGHT AND DISCUSSION

1. Discuss and evaluate the major functions of the textbook as an instructional aid.
2. Criticize the typical use of the language textbook by the teacher in the classroom.

455

3. Discuss the relative importance of the five major factors usually considered in selection of textbooks.

4. Suggest a procedure for the selection and adoption of a series of language textbooks for a school system in which you are a teacher.

5. What are the essential factors of quality in language textbooks? How can the evaluation of these qualities be objectified in making a textbook selection?

6. How could you determine (1) the comprehension difficulty of directions, and (2) the vocabulary range of other content in the textbook?

7. Use the score card given in this chapter for the rating of two textbooks suitable for your use in teaching. How do your ratings compare with your general opinion of the books?

SELECTED REFERENCES

BAKER, ELIZABETH W. *The Development of Elementary English Language Textbooks in the United States.* Contributions to Education, No. 45. Nashville, Tenn.: George Peabody College for Teachers, 1929.

BETTS, EMMETT ALBERT. "Readability: Its Application to the Elementary School," *Journal of Educational Research,* 42:438–459; February, 1949.

BUCKINGHAM, B. R. "Textbooks." *Encyclopedia of Educational Research,* Third Edition (Chester W. Harris, ed.). New York: The Macmillan Company, 1960, pp. 1517–1524.

BUCKINGHAM, B. R., and DOLCH, E. W. *A Combined Word List.* Boston: Ginn and Company, 1936.

CHALL, JEANNE S. *Readability, and Appraisal of Research and Application.* Bureau of Educational Research, Ohio State University, 1958.

CLEMENT, J. A. *Manual for Analyzing and Selecting Textbooks.* Champaign, Ill.: Daniels Press, 1939.

CRONBACH, LEE J., and others. *Text Materials in Modern Education.* Urbana, Ill.: University of Illinois Press, 1955.

DE BOER, JOHN J., and YOAKAM, GERALD A. "Textbooks and the Educative Process." *Elementary English Review.* 22:333–336; December, 1945.

DOLCH, E. W. "Fact Burden and Reading Difficulty." *Elementary English Review,* 6:135–138; 1939.

DOLCH, E. W., and CLEMENTS, J. A. "Textbooks." *Encyclopedia of Educational Research,* rev. ed. New York: The Macmillan Company, 1950.

DURRANCE, VICTOR R. "Public Textbook Selection in Forty-eight States." *Phi Delta Kappan,* 33:262–266; January, 1952.

EDMONSON, J. B., and others. *The Textbook in American Education.* Thirtieth Yearbook of the National Society for the Study of Education, Part II. Bloomington, Ill.: Public School Publishing Company, 1931.

GRAY, W. S., and LEARY, BERNICE E. *What Makes a Book Readable?* Chicago: The University of Chicago Press, 1935.

HALL-QUEST, A. L. *The Textbook; How to Use It and Judge It.* New York: The Macmillan Company, 1918.

Instructional Materials for Elementary Schools. Thirty-fifth Yearbook number of *The National Elementary Principal,* XXXVI, No. 1, Dorothy Emig, chairman. Washington: National Education Association, September, 1956. The following articles particularly: Charlotte D. Davis, "Developing and Applying Criteria," pp. 38–40; Harry E. Houtz, "Score Sheets for Selecting Textbooks," pp. 31–37; Guy McNeil and D. H. Wilkinson, "Operation of a Textbook Selection Program," pp. 26–30; Richard M. Pearson and William E. Spaulding, "Textbook Publishers Look at Selection," pp. 18–25.

MELLIOTT, MALCOLM E. "What to Look for in Choosing a Textbook." *NEA Journal,* 44:158–159; March, 1955.

RINSLAND, HENRY D. *A Basic Vocabulary of Elementary School Children.* New York: The Macmillan Company, 1945.

Textbooks in Education. New York: The American Textbook Publishers Institute, 1949.

THORNDIKE, EDWARD L., and LORGE, IRVING. *The Teacher's Word Book of 30,000 Words.* New York: Teachers College, Columbia University, 1938.

TRABUE, M. R. "Significant Issues in Language-Arts Instruction." *Teaching Language in the Elementary School.* Forty-third Yearbook of National Society for the Study of Education, Part II. Chicago: The University of Chicago Press, 1944.

WHIPPLE, GERTRUDE, "Procedures Used in Selecting Schoolbooks." *Elementary School Journal,* 36:665–673, 760–775; 1936.

YOAKAM, GERALD A. "The Reading Difficulty of School Textbooks." *Elementary English Review,* 22:304–309; December, 1945.

16

Language Workbooks
and Practice Materials

THE NEED FOR SUITABLE SUPPLEMENTARY INSTRUCTIONAL MATERIAL to aid in the accomplishment of the objectives of the expressional language arts program is felt by every classroom teacher of the subject. Of particular importance in developing language skills are certain drill and practice materials which teachers are often called upon to construct or to select. This chapter, which deals with the functions of such material and with the problems of selecting, evaluating, and using it in the classroom, emphasizes the following topics:

    a. Workbooks and practice materials in the language program.
    b. The function of workbooks.
    c. Limitations and values of language workbooks.
    d. Selection and use of workbooks and practice materials.

WORKBOOKS AND PRACTICE MATERIALS
IN THE LANGUAGE PROGRAM

The part that workbooks and practice materials should play in the language program needs examination in the light of the answers to two broad but important questions. First, is there a real need for the kind of instructional material which workbooks and practice lessons purport to supply? Second, if this need is critical, do these instruments meet that need satisfactorily?

NEED FOR SUPPLEMENTARY
INSTRUCTIONAL AIDS

Workbooks and supplementary practice lessons have tended to emphasize the readily identifiable mechanical features of expression, such as punctuation, capitalization, usage, and matters of form. For the

458

teacher who believes that the development of such skills should not be a distinct phase of language teaching, but feels that these skills will be best attained through systematic emphasis in connection with much written expression, the workbook has little or no appeal. Another large group of teachers, however, while not denying the importance of the functional development of these skills in connection with expressional activities, considers that supplementary practice and drill are not only desirable but necessary to effective learning. The case for this group is well summarized as follows:

> To hold that the average school teacher in English can arouse and sustain enough interest in composition over a period of time that the typical pupil is stimulated to the point of so attending to the mechanics of composition that he writes correctly without direct teaching or organized drills, is simply to disregard the evidence, to assume that pupils recognize their own errors, and to confuse the ideal situation with the actual one.[1]

Thus for this rather large and important group of teachers, the problem is not one of deciding whether or not to *use* drills and practice material for certain learning purposes, but one of determining *which types* of materials appear most promising. Several sources of such materials, each undoubtedly capable of making its own worthwhile contribution, are available in the form of textbooks, workbooks, and teacher-made practice exercises.

The major source of skill and subject-matter content as well as instructional guidance for schools is now, and doubtless will continue to be, the language textbook. Within a limited number of pages, the language textbook for the given grade undertakes to introduce and teach to a point of mastery a large number of highly interrelated language abilities. Adequate mastery of these desired skills is developed, not by *talking about* them in the language class, but by *using* them in carefully planned, lifelike activities arising out of interests in experiences and information in other areas. Unfortunately, as was pointed out in Chapter 15, the provision of suggested activities in the textbook has crowded out much drill and practice material, leaving the teacher in need of a supplement to the program from other sources. If heavy teaching schedules and crowded classes did not place such a severe strain on the teacher's time and energy, the ideal procedure would be for the teacher himself to produce the material. However, the preparation of suitable drill material

[1] Mary Agnella Gunn, *A Technique for Improving Basic Skills in English in High School,* Studies in Education, Vol. 8, No. 7. Iowa City: State University of Iowa, 1934, p. 7.

459

is a very complicated and time-consuming process, calling for the abilities and experience of the specialist. Under these circumstances, it is quite natural for the teacher to turn to workbooks and practice exercises for the drills needed.

ADEQUACY OF TEXTBOOK DRILLS

No very recent data are available on the trends in language textbooks of emphasis on drills and practice materials. In connection with his own study of practice exercises in language, Leonard reported results from an early survey of ten texts published between 1877 and 1918.[2] The proportion of space given to drill varied from 17% in the 1877 text to 51% in the one published in 1918. When Leonard made an analysis of twelve textbooks published after 1918, he found three which gave less than 10% of their space to drill materials, only six that exceeded 20%, and two that exceeded 30%. While it is impossible to say that these results are indicative of the trend today, it does appear that the amount of drill material included within the typical language textbook is definitely limited. The reasons become obvious when we consider the large amount of subject matter included in the modern book in the interests of the activity projects designed to stimulate expression. In the face of all of the other demands for page space the author can scarcely hope to supply in a single text an adequate program of fixation, maintenance, and remedial exercises to meet the individual needs of all classes and pupils. The teacher seriously concerned with operating an effective instructional program in language is therefore inevitably driven to look to other sources than the textbook for the needed additional drill and practice materials.

TEACHER-MADE DRILLS AND PRACTICE EXERCISES

Aside from the workbook, the most common type of supplementary practice material in language is the teacher-made exercise. There is much to be said in its favor. Drill and practice exercises constructed by the teacher can be much more closely related to the activities of his class than any commercially prepared exercises are likely to be. The drills are in all likelihood ones for which some real need on the part of an individual pupil has been noted by the teacher. In theory at least they

[2] J. Paul Leonard, *The Use of Practice Exercises in the Teaching of Capitalization and Punctuation.* New York: Teachers College, Columbia University, 1930.

should excel in validity and functional value those found on the typical workbook page. Major factors limiting the quality of such practice exercises include the fact that their production is technical and extremely time consuming. The authors are inclined to believe that if the time required for the teacher to produce his own drill exercises were spent in the critical selection of exercises for specified purposes, the resulting practice exercises would be superior to any that he could make.

THE FUNCTION OF WORKBOOKS

SUPPLEMENTING THE TEXTBOOK PROGRAM IN SKILLS

Properly designed workbooks conform to the philosophy of the language program and provide supplemental identification of the specific facts, knowledges, and skills organized for instruction in the language textbook. In no sense should the workbook be considered or used as a substitute for the textbook. While the workbook may ease the teacher's mechanical burdens somewhat, it does not relieve him of his instructional responsibilities. Perhaps there would be as little need for the workbook as for the textbook in the ideal language program, but since so few ideal programs exist, it would seem that the busy teacher, no matter how able and experienced, needs the guidance and assistance of an organized program as presented by the modern textbook in language and as supplemented by the properly designed and correctly used language workbook.

AIDING IN MAINTAINING GOOD LANGUAGE HABITS

Acquiring acceptable habits of expression, like all other types of learning, requires extensive and repeated exercise of the desired responses until they become purely automatic. To achieve this end, strong initial presentation and explanation accompanied by motivated repetition to fix the first reactions must be followed by practice in the correct responses in lifelike language situations. To maintain the habit at an effective level, additional instruction and motivated practice in realistic language situations must be provided. Here again the workbook functions, not as a substitute for the textbook, the teacher, or the activity program, but as an effective supplementary instrument for the application of the principles of habit formation.

461

AIDING IN MEETING INDIVIDUAL DIFFERENCES

The language abilities of children within a given grade are known to vary widely; yet the classroom in which these individual language differences are systematically cared for is probably the exception rather than the rule. Properly designed workbooks provide suitable and extensive material for such a program through inventory tests, supplementary exercises, and self-checking devices, all designed to identify and to guide the individual child into the activities and experiences suited to his immediate needs. Used in this manner, the workbook is not merely a drill book to be assigned to the class lesson by lesson or page by page. It is rather a source of individual experience for the pupil who needs special assistance, and it becomes a valuable aid to the teacher in meeting individual differences within his class.

PROVIDING NEEDED SUPPLEMENTARY DRILLS

In order to maintain immediate and reasonably permanent mastery of language skills the teacher must have access to extensive drills suitable for at least three different types of uses. Immediately following the initial presentation of a new skill, the child should be called upon to use it as the first step in fixing the correct response as a habit. For this purpose extensive, interesting, and well-motivated drills are needed. Practice exercises are also valuable if a child is to secure a permanent mastery of language skills once used. The third use is in the correction of faulty language habits. This problem presents a constantly recurring need for exercises and activities designed to encourage and assist the child in developing correct habits. The modern workbook in language, if properly designed and used, enables the teacher to meet his class's needs for these three important types of drill activities and exercises.

PROVIDING SUPPLEMENTARY EVALUATIVE MATERIAL

Relatively few language textbooks are accompanied by testing and evaluative devices suitable for taking an accurate inventory of the class or of the individual pupil's mastery of language skills as a basis for the instructional program. Fewer still provide the teacher with comparable in-

Record of My Daily Drills [3]

Page	Drill	Best score	My score	Page	Drill	Best score	My score
	Unit 1				*Unit 4*		
2.	Inventory Test 1	35	—	65.	Inventory Test 4	36	—
3.	Using Alaphabetical Order	39	—	66.	Filling in Blank Forms	2	—
4.	Using Words Correctly	12	—	67.	Writing Titles of Books	6	—
5.	Using Words Correctly	30	—	68.	Using *Ran, Run; Went, Gone*	14	—
6.	Using Periods and Question Marks	14	—	69.	Using *A* and *An*	13	—
7.	Finding Complete Thoughts	11	—	70.	Writing a Letter of Invitation	10	—
8.	Correcting Run-on Sentences	8	—	71.	Using *Their* and *There*	10	—
9.	Copying a Paragraph	4	—	72.	Writing Your Own Outline	5	—
10.	Keeping to the Topic	3	—	73.	Changing Word Order in Sentences	4	—
11.	Writing a Paragraph	6	—	74.	Using *Teach* and *Learn*	12	—
12.	Spelling Useful Words	7	—	75.	Using *Took, Taken, Drank, Drunk*	13	—
13.	Studying Letter Form	5	—	76.	Using Apostrophes for Ownership	8	—
14.	Writing Headings, Letters	3	—	77.	Correcting Poor Sentences	12	—
15.	Writing Greetings, Closings	8	—	78.	Using Words Correctly, Review	17	—
16.	Using Commas in a List	17	—	79.	Writing Sentences in Paragraphs	6	—
17.	Making Sentences from Fragments	5	—	80.	Spelling—Using Hyphens	20	—
18.	Correcting Run-on Sentences	12	—	81.	Using Apostrophes for Ownership	9	—
19.	Correcting Poor Sentences	9	—	82.	Using Words Correctly, Review	18	—
20.	Using Capital Letters	30	—	83.	Changing Word Order in Sentences	4	—
21.	Using Capital Letters	26	—	84.	Check Test 4	36	—
22.	Using Punctuation	28	—		Mastery Test 4	55	—
23.	Using Words that Sound Alike	11	—				
24.	Check Test 1	35	—				
	Mastery Test 1	50	—				

[3] Emmett A. Betts and Harry A. Greene, *Daily Drills in Language Skills, Grade 4.* Evanston, Ill.: Row, Peterson and Company.

struments for later checks on the final mastery of the skills at the completion of the instructional program. It is regrettable that some textbook authors as well as some teachers and supervisors do not consider testing devices to be important instructional instruments. The language program that does not provide adequate tests of inventory, check, and mastery should be supplemented by evaluative instruments of these types found in the well-designed workbook.

The extent and nature of supplementary exercises provided in workbooks is illustrated on page 463 in the reproduction of the record sheet showing the drill lessons in two of the six units comprising this workbook. In addition to the 107 drills covering essential aspects of the fourth-grade language program, this 125-page workbook contains inventory tests and check tests and an additional general practice lesson for each of the six units. Six mastery tests are also supplied separately for use in this grade and in each grade for which the workbooks are available.

Part of an inventory test from a six-grade workbook is shown below:

Finding out what you need to learn [4]
(Inventory Test 1)

This is the first of several tests in this book. It will show what you know and what you need to learn in these language lessons. Do your best.

A. _____

B. _____ C. _____

1. Write the title "a language test" correctly on line A.   (Score 1)
2. Write your name correctly on line B, and the date today on line C.

                                                 (Score 2)

   ·

   ·

   ·

6. Punctuate these sentences correctly:
   a) When Bud left he said that he'd be in Kent Ohio on October 6, 1942
   b) When are you going to practice asked Pearl
   c) Jane answered I am going Sunday Monday Tuesday and Wednesday

                                              (Score 14)

7. Draw a line under the correct words to use in these sentences:
   a) (Whose, Who's) dog is this? (Its It's) collar is marked with a B.
   b) (Your, You're) going with us. (There, Their) is room in our car.
   c) (Whose, Who's) bringing (your, you're) glove, Jack?   (Score 6)

   ·

   ·

   ·

---

[4] Emmett A. Betts, Harry A. Greene, and Mabel-Louise Arey, *Daily Drills in Language Skills. Grade 6.* Evanston, Ill.: Row, Peterson and Company, p. 2.

10. Place capitals and periods where they belong in these sentences:
   a) father and mother came the monday after thanksgiving day with dr h v cole
   b) mr and mrs brown visited emerson school last friday   (Score 22)
   Proofread your test carefully.
   Correct every mistake you find in it.
   Your teacher will help you correct your paper.
          The best score is 100.   My score is —————

LIMITATIONS AND VALUES OF LANGUAGE
WORKBOOKS

Although there is widespread disagreement regarding the value of workbooks to the language teacher, there is general agreement that all learning is the result of personal and purposeful mental activity on the part of the learner, and that it takes place most readily when the individual has a clear understanding of what is expected of him. Most teachers would also agree that one of their most important instructional tasks is the provision of interesting situations of suitable difficulty to call forth these personal and purposeful mental activities and responses on the part of their pupils. The point on which they do not agree is the question of whether the workbook or some other device offers the best way to attain the objectives. It is unfortunate that much of the argument on both sides of the question appears to rest more heavily on subjective opinions than on the results of research. Furthermore, the picture is clouded by the fact that much of the available research evidence is inconclusive and often contradictory. The safest conclusion at this time is that much more research must be done before the problem can be resolved satisfactorily.

ARGUMENTS AGAINST LANGUAGE WORKBOOKS

Criticisms of workbooks fall into two general categories, those related to the content and the organization of the material, and those concerned with the manner in which the supplemental practice and test lessons are fitted into the total instructional program.

Workbooks restrict the educational program. Teachers may come to rely on the workbook and cease to use their own initiative in planning a stimulating instructional program. Thus the use of workbooks limits the initiative of the teacher and reduces the amount of planning in which children may participate. Too often the workbook becomes the textbook

465

in fact, even though it was not designed for the purpose. Trabue, apparently assuming that the workbook is generally accepted and used by teachers as basic rather than supplementary instruction material, criticizes workbooks on a number of counts. "The typical language workbook alone cannot provide an adequate instructional program . . . One of the most serious limitations of workbooks is that they can affect oral expression only slightly, if at all." [5] It would seem that his criticisms are not of the workbook itself, but of the manner in which it is used by some teachers.

Betts, in comments directed primarily at the use of workbooks in the field of reading, says, "If the workbook activities are to contribute to learner development, then it is essential that the pupil engage in those selected activities which meet his individual needs and interests . . . Teaching cannot be relegated to the sheer assignment of exercises and routine checking of results . . . Workbooks are not a cure-all for all pedagogical ills . . . One of the chief dangers from indiscriminate use of workbooks is that of regimentation." [6]

Workbooks are not educationally sound. Pooley attacks workbooks by saying, "The great majority of language workbooks and seatwork practice pads are educationally unsound in both material and method . . . The workbooks in language are generally unsound in method, in that the type of practice given is the filling in of blanks and the crossing out of alternative forms. Such practice may aid the brighter pupil to discover certain distinctions in usage, but it has very slight effect in the establishing of good habits or the breaking of undesirable habits. Such practice for the slower pupil often reinforces bad habits, as he tends to supply the familiar but undesirable form, or to cross off the desired form. Above all, such practice is futile because it is silent and detached from genuine communication." In an implied criticism of the tendency of workbooks to call for a written response in practice exercises designed to correct errors in oral usage, Pooley correctly points out that "usage practice must be heard and spoken to be effective, and it should always be in a setting of normal and natural use of language for a purpose recognized by the pupil." [7]

[5] M. R. Trabue, "Significant Issues in Language-Arts Instruction," *Teaching Language in the Elementary School.* Forty-third Yearbook of the National Society for the Study of Education, Part II. Chicago: University of Chicago Press, 1944, p. 225.

[6] Emmett A. Betts, "The Workbook Situation." *Education Administration and Supervision,* 27:561–577; Nov., 1941.

[7] Robert C. Pooley, *Teaching English Usage.* New York: Appleton-Century-Crofts, Inc., 1946, pp. 183–184.

Workbooks become "crutches" for the poor or lazy teacher. The ready availability of workbook exercises often tempts the poorly prepared teacher to make more use of these materials than is justified in the instructional program. According to Kerr, some administrators feel that "the use of workbooks is not professionally defensible because workbooks are often regarded as a kind of busywork that is relied on by inexperienced and lazy teachers. Frequently the children are required to work at more or less mechanical tasks which are not too closely related to their other learning activities." [8]

A number of important ways in which workbooks should *not* be used are suggested below. The teacher will do well to check with this list his own practices with respect to their use.

Do *not* fall back on the workbook when:
You have been unable to make a careful preparation due to extra duties.
You are transferred to a subject in which you have not studied.
You want a day off from teaching.
You neglected to make preparation the previous day.
Your principal or supervisor enters the room.
You do not know how to make proper preparation in the subject.
You find that thoughtful preparation is distasteful.[9]

The real implication of the above suggestions lies in the point that the continuous use of workbooks on every occasion and at every excuse or the use of workbooks in too many different subjects may cause them to become ineffective. Unpleasant or monotonous experiences with workbooks may readily make the teacher as well as the child allergic to them.

Workbooks are often used improperly by teachers. The workbook is a tool which may be used well or it may be used badly. Pupils may do the exercises mechanically and with little or no reflective thinking. They may work through an entire drill lesson without identifying what they are doing as being directly related to the important expressional skills stressed in the language class.

Tidyman and Butterfield point out that "the indiscriminate assignment of lessons to whole classes, and progression through the book page by page are not the best ways to use the [workbook] materials." [10] In using the workbook as a means to the mastery of skills, teachers should never

[8] Margaret Kerr, "Teaching with Workbooks." *Elementary School Journal,* 48:218–221; December, 1947.

[9] Adapted from George E. Carrothers, "Workbooks," *Education Digest,* 10:32–34; April, 1945.

[10] W. F. Tidyman and Marguerite Butterfield, *Teaching the Language Arts.* New York: McGraw-Hill Book Company, Inc., 1951, p. 302.

467

assign workbook drill lessons in sequence to all pupils regardless of individual needs. The workbook exercises should be checked through and assigned only as they give the needed drill. Teaching schedules and school programs can surely be made flexible enough to enable even the busiest teacher to tailor his workbook program to the needs of his pupils.

Workbooks fail to produce expected improvements in language as shown by scores on language tests. The effectiveness of certain practice materials and workbooks has been questioned as the result of contradictory evidence from numerous studies of their use in classrooms. The specific nature of learning in language should make it obvious that growth in mastery of skills as a result of drill would be revealed in the language test only if the same skills were involved. A check of the overlap of drill emphasis in commercial workbooks with the item content of an extensive sampling of standardized language tests indicated a serious lack of common content and emphasis.[11] These data strongly suggest the need for very careful cross-validation of skill and drill content of both tests and drills in any attempt to use standardized language tests to evaluate a special drive on language skills set forth in practice exercises and workbooks. It is quite probable that this factor alone would account for the indifferent results reported by Curtin following his experimental study of certain workbooks.[12] In fact, from the large number of different drill items appearing in only two or three of the sources one would sometimes imagine that the authors of each test, drill, and workbook were deliberately attempting to avoid practicing or testing on the same skills. Obviously there is need for greater cooperation on the part of the authors of language workbooks and language tests in the selection of drill and test content.

Workbooks fail to produce superior ability to write complete sentences. This statement seems to be justified by the evidence reported by Curtin, although its significance is limited by the various factors discussed above.[13] According to Curtin's data, workbooks produced only average gains in teaching sentence sense and word meaning, but showed some superiority in teaching such mechanical skills as capitalization and punc-

---

[11] Based upon data combined from two independent studies under the direction of the senior author at the State University of Iowa: J. P. Bunch, "An Analysis of Certain Standardized Language Tests"; J. R. Crawford, "The Drill Content of Certain Practice Exercises in Language."

[12] James Curtin, "Evaluation of Certain Language Workbooks." Unpublished master's thesis, State University of Iowa, 1950.

[13] *Ibid.*

tuation. To this indictment of the workbook as a device for the development of skills in constructing sentences, Madden, without offering supporting evidence, adds the statement that workbook-trained children "are often poor in written expression in general." [14]

Workbooks add unnecessarily to the outlay for instructional equipment. Whether the workbooks are purchased by the parents or by the school, their cost is an important item. The objection is not so serious if workbooks in many different subjects are not involved, but if a disproportionate share of school funds available for textbooks and library facilities goes for workbooks so that other important library equipment cannot be acquired, it becomes serious.

Workbooks fail to provide adequately for individual differences. In spite of the large amount and variety of practice material typically presented in workbooks, those opposed to their use hold that little or no differentiation in assignment of drill activities actually takes place. The fact that in many workbooks no real differentiation is made in lessons and in exercises for brighter children or for those needing special work makes this a serious criticism.

ARGUMENTS FAVORING LANGUAGE WORKBOOKS

Those who favor the use of language workbooks naturally question the validity of many of the arguments presented by those opposed to their use. They insist that the criticisms apply equally well to textbooks and other related instructional materials, and that, furthermore, the comments are not all unfavorable. In addition to the values of workbooks in relation to the broad philosophy of learning in language discussed in a preceding section of this chapter, the following points are among those most frequently presented in defense of their use:

Workbooks are useful educational tools; they need not be misused. "Teachers who cannot use workbooks properly usually do other things no better." [15]

Workbooks result in time-saving in securing pupil responses. Whether classes are large or small, the teacher can secure but one oral recitation at a time. With workbooks properly used and with individual assign-

[14] Richard Madden, "Workbooks! Tool or Crutch?" *NEA Journal,* 49:94–95, February, 1956.
[15] *Ibid.*

ments given as needed, as many responses as there are individuals in the class at the moment can be secured.

Workbooks encourage the establishment of good work habits.   By setting a specific task, a definite plan of attack, and a time to complete the task, workbook exercises aid pupils in establishing habits of thoroughness in their school work.

Workbooks aid in class control.   The readily available test and practice materials provided in the modern workbook in language enable the teacher to keep his class active and under control, thus discouraging disciplinary problems.

Workbooks provide meaningful practice or drill.   "Practice exercises can be used effectively if there is a recognized purpose in the mind of the learner. The value of the material depends in large part on the way in which it is used. In the skill subjects such as language, learning comes largely from doing, from repetition of the correct response time after time until it is firmly and permanently fixed as a habit." [16] The workbook meets this need for practice material which frequently is not available elsewhere.

Workbooks provide material for individual instruction.   One of the chief values of a satisfactory workbook lies in the amount and character of the drill material, in the advantage it offers in making individual assignments, and in its adaptability to individual instruction through material for individual practice. Workbooks provide a practical means of supplementing group instruction with individual instruction.

Workbooks provide a means of adjusting for individual differences. Workbook exercises of suitable content and difficulty give the slow student an opportunity to grow in mastery and in confidence in his own ability to improve his language skills. Controlled vocabulary and simple and clear directions enable him to proceed independently. He is directed to a wide variety of material designed for different types of needs. Adjusting instruction to the superior pupil is a more difficult problem for the busy classroom teacher to solve. While there is little point in rewarding the superior child with more practice on skills he has already mastered, workbooks, through a wide variety of exercises and supplementary drill, help the teacher to meet this problem satisfactorily.

[16] Tidyman and Butterfield, *op. cit.*

470

Workbooks provide a means of preserving pupils' work for review. According to many teachers, principals, and supervisors, the opportunity which the workbook offers for the preservation of their earlier work in convenient and attractive form has a very definite appeal for children.

Workbooks are useful in diagnostic and remedial work. Many modern workbooks in language contain or are accompanied by excellent inventory and mastery tests which if carefully analyzed will give the teacher a clear picture of the strengths and weaknesses of his pupils in many different aspects of language ability. They are not to be treated as substitutes for an adequate analytical testing program, but they certainly do provide valuable supplementary diagnostic information for the teacher's guidance. The modern practice of listing the specific practice lessons to be used by individuals making low scores on the inventory tests makes the administration of the remedial program quite simple.

Workbooks add variety and supplement instruction. Interesting activities and practice exercises that frequently are crowded out of the textbook itself find a useful place in the workbook. Such materials, written by the textbook authors themselves or under their direction, are likely to follow a similar organization to that of the textbook and compare favorably with the quality of exercises in the book itself. There is at least an even chance that they will be better prepared than the teacher's hurriedly duplicated exercises.

Workbooks save the teacher's time and energy. The time saved from preparing and duplicating teacher-made practice exercises may be used profitably in planning activities that will much more greatly enrich and extend the children's experiences as a basis for expression. The pupil's time is also saved by avoiding the endless copying of exercises from the textbook or from the blackboard. He writes only the words or responses that are the result of his own thinking and decision.

Workbooks provide savings on cost. The use of a workbook largely does away with mimeographed sheets, scratch pads, notebooks and the like. It provides each child with his own individual book at a cost actually below that of similar teacher-made materials. In his workbook the child can record and trace his own progress, his increase in maturity, his growth in mastery as shown by his responses in the workbook.

In a discussion dealing primarily with the value of workbooks in reading, Gray stated for the guidance of authors and teachers the following principles which, if carefully followed, would make workbooks valuable instruments in any skill area. It is believed that these principles apply equally well to workbooks in the language program:

1. Make each exercise fit the total skill program necessary for each level.
2. Provide varying types of exercises to fit the needs and interests of the child. Then supplement the materials with teacher-made material. It will prevent boredom.
3. Never let the material become an end in itself. Practice on skills should be a means to an end. The end is to use the skill in a functional situation . . . A transfer of learning takes place only when the teacher deliberately attempts to make it take place.
4. The material should be the basis for additional teaching. Every page should be checked so that the difficulties will be noted and removed through further teaching and practice. Every practice lesson should be a diagnostic lesson.
5. The children must be able to understand what, how, and why they are to do each thing they do. Seeing a reason facilitates a transfer of learning.[17]

SELECTION AND USE OF WORKBOOKS AND PRACTICE MATERIAL

The only defensible justification for the extensive production and widespread use of practice material and workbooks in the language classroom is that through their use the learning process is encouraged and strengthened. Once it is decided that a workbook or practice material is desirable, two additional problems confront the teacher: (1) How can I select a good workbook or practice material? (2) How can I use this material most effectively to help children learn?

SELECTING WORKBOOK OR PRACTICE MATERIAL

In addition to the large number of specific elements of textbook quality listed in the tentative score card on pages 446–448 of Chapter 15, there are a number of important factors to be considered in the selection of workbooks and practice materials. The following questions, which may be used to supplement the points in the score card, may also stimulate clear and critical thinking on the part of the teacher as he makes this important selection:

[17] W. S. Gray, *Basic Instruction in Reading in the Elementary and High Schools*. Chicago: University of Chicago Press, October, 1948, pp. 149–151.

1. Does this type of material support and strengthen the objectives of this subject?
2. Is the content organized to help the children attain these objectives?
3. Is it interesting to the pupils?
4. Is it attractively arranged?
5. Does it supplement and enrich what you are attempting to do in class?
6. Will the pupils gain a feeling of success in using this material?
7. Are the exercises varied and well motivated?
8. Does the material utilize sound principles of learning?
9. Is it based on sound pedagogical principles?
10. Is the vocabulary suitable for the pupils with whom it is to be used?
11. Are the directions simple, clear, and concise enough to permit pupils to work independently?
12. Does the material provide drills of the types needed by most pupils?
13. Does it provide practice material of a suitable range of difficulty?
14. Does it utilize a wide variety of suitable drill forms?
15. Does it contain material capable of stimulating expression for recording in other than mechanical forms?
16. Does it indicate that care and judgment were exercised in selecting the content?
17. Does it indicate that proper regard was given to scientific findings in the selection of content?
18. Is it organized in such a manner that pupils can proceed independently with a minimum of teacher guidance?
19. Does it provide adequately for all types of review?
20. Does it stimulate self-appraisal by the pupil?
21. Does it contain suitable inventory, check, and mastery test material for pupil guidance?
22. Does it stress the oral as well as the written approaches in exercises for usage and sentence development?
23. Can it be used effectively to provide for individual differences in children?
24. Can the material be objectively and rapidly scored to save the teacher's time for the preparation of other valuable learning activities for the children?
25. Is it economically priced?

While the use of these questions designed to identify the desirable qualities of workbooks and practice exercises has not been standardized in any experimental or statistical sense, it is believed that in the case of good or superior material at least twenty of the above twenty-five questions should be answerable by "yes."

USING WORKBOOKS AND PRACTICE MATERIALS

The danger of the misuse of workbooks and practice exercises as supplementary instructional materials has received repeated attention in this chapter and in the critical comments of those opposed to their use in the classroom. It is evident that if the teacher is to realize fully the advantages of these materials as instructional aids, he must give special attention to the manner in which they are used. As a first and general principle, caution should be exercised concerning the use of many different workbooks in many different subjects, and the use of any one too often. Leaning too heavily on such materials may cause the teacher to fail to do the best job of teaching of which he is capable. The following statements summarize concisely a number of other important principles which should be observed in this connection:

1. Before using any workbook or supplementary practice material, the teacher should determine just what he wants it to accomplish and then plan his teaching so that the workbook can be used to help reach this objective. Each particular practice lesson should be outlined with as much care as any other lesson. Careful planning is necessary if the pupils are to gain the greatest advantage from the practice lessons.

2. At the outset, the workbook or other practice material chosen should be carefully evaluated in terms of worthwhile criteria such as are suggested in this chapter. Acceptability of point of view, suitability of content, adequacy of methods, and desirable physical and mechanical features should all be considered. Special attention should be given to the ways in which accepted pedagogical and psychological principles are utilized.

3. Each workbook test or practice lesson should be checked and the results reported to the pupils as soon as possible. The children should always know exactly what errors they made and why the errors indicated are marked as errors. Furthermore, the pupils should correct their wrong answers. Some consider this an unduly time-consuming practice, but it is a good teaching technique.

4. Practice exercises and drills are required to aid the pupil in acquiring needed skills that he has not already developed. A pre-testing program consisting of informal tests made by the teacher or objective inventory tests such as accompany many modern workbooks provide a practical and economical means of identifying the individual pupils in need of further drill as well as the areas in which the drill is required.

5. It should be clearly understood that great individual differences in abilities and needs exist within every class. There is no justification, therefore, for assigning the same practice or workbook lesson for all pupils unless it is clear that it is actually needed by all.

6. Since adequate and permanent mastery of a skill cannot be ex-

pected to result from a single teaching or practicing of a skill, carefully chosen and properly distributed drills must be provided if the teaching and learning program is to be effective in producing the desired results.

7. The assignment of a carefully chosen lesson or practice exercise from the workbook does not in any sense conclude the teacher's responsibility. Its use must be properly motivated by showing the pupil the evidence of his needs and by convincing him that the proposed drill program is not a punishment but an interesting experience which is almost certain to help him individually in the development of habits of expression that are valuable and permanent social assets.

8. The interest of the pupil in the potential values of workbook and practice material may be aroused by a frank explanation, discussion, and demonstration of an easy sample lesson. This initial interest must be maintained for those pupils whose records indicate that they need considerable contact with drill and practice. The best way to accomplish this is by making sure that the child's experience includes a variety of types of drill (lest he grow into a bored "blank-filler"), that the materials are as functional as possible in relation to his other needs, and that he is constantly aware of the progress he is making through their use.

9. In addition to the basic drill exercises, workbooks and practice materials of the better type have many associated contributions to offer. These include inventory devices in verbal or test form, checklists and tests to measure progress, guide sheets for further practice, mastery tests, explanatory materials for teacher and pupil reference, suggestions for follow-up activities, progress charts, record blanks and the like. Both teacher and pupils should become familiar with all of these and be prepared to use them on every legitimate occasion.

10. In attempting to individualize the use of workbook and practice materials in the language class, the teacher is certain to encounter a number of problems of classroom management. Since many of these can be anticipated, time spent in developing a systematic plan for the handling of administrative details will be well rewarded. Administering the important inventory tests, carrying out diagnostic procedures, individualizing the actual drill assignments, checking and recording test scores and drill results, and handling the physical materials of the drill program can all be coordinated into a workable system by any competent teacher. Without such planning, workbooks and practice materials are likely to degenerate into merely another group of instruments in the regimentation of instruction.

EXERCISES FOR THOUGHT AND DISCUSSION

1. Discuss the major functions of workbooks as presented in this chapter.

2. What are the chief factors which have stimulated the development of the large amount of workbook and supplemental practice material in language now available?

3. Outline what you consider a proper method of using a workbook to supplement the basic language textbook.

4. Show how workbooks when properly used provide one excellent means of taking account of the wide individual differences in language mastery in the class.

5. Evaluate the arguments usually advanced against the use of language workbooks.

6. Which of the arguments advanced here in favor of the use of workbooks presents the strongest case for their use?

7. Use the textbook score card in Chapter 15 to rate two workbooks suitable for use in your classroom. Supplement these ratings with the results of applying the twenty-five questions on page 473. How do these two separate evaluations compare with your general judgment of the quality of the workbooks?

SELECTED REFERENCES

BETTS, EMMETT A. *Foundations of Reading Instruction.* New York: American Book Company, 1946, p. 530.

———. "The Workbook Situation." *Educational Administration and Supervision,* 27:561–578; 1941.

BROWN, FREDERICK S. "Workbook Wanted." *School Executive,* 61:30–31; February, 1942.

CARROTHERS, GEORGE E. "Workbooks." *Education Digest,* 10:32–34; April, 1945.

CURTIN, JAMES R. "An Evaluation of Certain Language Workbooks." Unpublished master's thesis, State University of Iowa, February, 1950.

DAWSON, MILDRED A. "Special Tools that Facilitate Expression." *Teaching Language in the Elementary School.* Forty-third Yearbook of the National Society for the Study of Education, Part II. Chicago: The University of Chicago, 1944, pp. 164–171.

GOODYKOONTZ, BESS. "Current Uses and Effects of Workbooks." *The Curriculum Journal,* 4:31; April 22, 1935.

GRAY, A. "Lift the Workbook Cover." *Phi Delta Kappan,* 33:286–287; January, 1952.

GREENE, HARRY A. "English—Language, Grammar, and Composition." *Encyclopedia of Educational Research,* rev. ed. New York: The Macmillan Company, 1950, p. 395.

JACKS, ROBERT W. "The Status of Workbooks in Classroom Instruction." *Educational Method,* 18:106–108; December, 1938.

JOHNSON, W. P. "Then Came the Workbook." *Journal of Education,* 131:64–66; February, 1948.

KERR, M. E. "Teaching With Workbooks." *Elementary School Journal,* 48:218–221; December, 1947.

MADDEN, RICHARD. "Workbooks! Tool or Crutch?" *NEA Journal,* 49:94–95, February, 1956.

MATTINGLY, E. H. "Meet the Modern Workbook." *Illinois Education,* 38:191; January, 1950.

MILLER, EDITH. "What About Workbooks?" 32:15–16, *American Childhood,* December, 1946.

RIGG, H. H. "Are We Making Blank Fillers Out of Students?" *School Executive,* 51:329; March, 1932.

SARTAIN, HARRY W. "Do Reading Workbooks Increase Achievement?" *Elementary School Journal,* 62, No. 3:157–162; December, 1961.

A Study of Reading Workbooks. Washington: Association for Childhood Education, 1939.

TIDYMAN, W. F., and BUTTERFIELD, MARGUERITE. *Teaching the Language Arts.* New York: McGraw-Hill Book Company, Inc. 1951.

WOLCOTT, FRED G. "The Use of Workbooks." *English Journal,* high school ed. 22:574–578; September, 1933.

part 5

Evaluating the Results of Language Teaching

THE TWO CHAPTERS COMPRISING PART FIVE BRING TOGETHER IN CONCISE form for teachers and supervisors many of the important tools, procedures, and materials needed in the proper evaluation of the results of the language teaching program in the elementary school.

17

Problems of Measurement

and Evaluation in Language

ONCE THE OBJECTIVES FOR THE LANGUAGE PROGRAM ARE SET UP IN keeping with sound educational philosophy and the methods for achieving these objectives are put into effect, the problem becomes one of evaluating the results, and of determining how effective the methods and techniques have been in attaining the established goals. This chapter, which is concerned primarily with the general aspects of measurement and evaluation as they are related to the language program in the elementary school, emphasizes the following topics:

    a. Evaluation as related to the language program.
    b. Types of measuring instruments and techniques.
    c. Kinds of measures of language.
    d. Qualities of the good measuring instrument.

EVALUATION AS RELATED TO THE LANGUAGE PROGRAM

Historically, language was one of the first school subjects to attract the attention of early workers interested in the evaluation of educational accomplishments. It is, therefore, somewhat disturbing to note that in spite of these early efforts to evaluate the results of language teaching, it still remains one of the slowest of the school subjects to respond to objective methods of evaluation. Just why this has been true is not entirely clear. Perhaps it may be traced to unfortunate experiences of teachers with certain of the early language scales and tests, many of which were admittedly lacking in validity, objectivity, and reliability. Perhaps a more reasonable explanation of the attitude of language teachers toward evaluation in language may be found in the extreme complexity of the expressional skills themselves with the resulting limitations on the production of efficient evaluative instruments. It is hoped that the use of more critical procedures in the analysis of language abilities and more refined techniques of evaluation may improve the situation in the future.

MEASUREMENT AND METHOD IN LANGUAGE

In the available literature on the teaching of language there is a surprising lack of critical discussion of the real significance of the evaluative and measurement techniques in the language classroom. Of the early writers in this field, McKee was almost alone in his recognition of the inseparable relation of methods and measurements in language.[1] Not only is this problem treated superficially or not at all by most of those who have written more recently on the subject, but the reader is left with the impression that any attempt at the objective measurement or evaluation of language achievement is not only futile, but runs counter to the best interests of the school, the teacher, and the pupil. In the judgment of the authors this conclusion is not in accord with the facts —a point which it is one of the purposes of this chapter to establish.

This discussion of the problems of evaluation and measurement in language in a chapter separate from those on methods of developing expressional power should not lead the reader to the erroneous conclusion that the two are distinct and unrelated activities. Measurement and evaluation appear constantly at all levels of instruction as essential elements of methods. They are treated in this special chapter in order to give full recognition to their important contributions to the teacher's classroom procedures and to prevent the teacher from drifting into the mistaken notion that measurement and evaluation may be considered as only minor or incidental aspects of language methods.

The importance of some form of objective evaluative equipment for use in the typical program of instruction and supervision is indicated by an examination of the following steps in such a program:

1. Administer initial or inventory tests to determine in advance of instruction the mastery of the individuals comprising the class. Such instruments should confront the individual with situations calling for responses to the precise abilities or skills included in the instructional program. This procedure is proposed in the interests of economy of learning resulting from having the learner waste no time on facts or skills he has already mastered, and

---

[1] Paul McKee, *Language in the Elementary School,* rev. ed. Boston: Houghton Mifflin Company, 1939.

having him focus his learning effort on only those elements he personally needs to master.

2. Teach the facts or develop the skills in ways designed to meet so far as possible each individual's needs. Develop the skills by oral presentation, discussion, and demonstration in realistic and lifelike situations.

3. Follow at once with valid, and properly motivated opportunities for each individual to repeat the desired reactions correctly as presented in 2 above. The purpose of this procedure is to fix the facts or the skills to the point that the correct responses may be maintained as habits. Short and frequent practice periods are most effective in habit formation.

4. Administer a check-test closely paralleling the content of the initial or inventory test to determine the extent of each pupil's improvement or growth.

5. Analyse each check-test as a basis for discovering each individual's existing difficulties.

6. Remedy the defects thus identified through re-teaching and further remedial practice.

7. Re-test, and if necessary, re-teach.

It will be noted that on at least three occasions in the foregoing seven steps some type of evaluative instrument is utilized in this instructional-learning cycle. It is recognized that not all learning situations may be as objective in content as the one presented above, but it is believed that some adaptation or modification of the instruments or the procedures may be followed in language as in most other fields of learning.

MEASUREMENT AND EVALUATION

Many teachers and educators seem to have been unnecessarily confused by the efforts of certain critics of measurement to introduce the term *evaluation* as representing processes quite different from measurement in the usual meaning of the term. The fact that measurement is recognized by most teachers and supervisors as only *one* of several techniques designed for use in evaluating individual pupil achievement, the success of special teaching procedures, or the success of the instructional program as a whole should not be overlooked here. It is true that evaluation does imply a more comprehensive approach and often a more individualized interpretation of results than does measurement. Evaluation in the broad sense includes more than the purely objective assessments of results implied by the traditional conception of measurement. It is the final step in appraisal applied to the individual pupil in terms of his total accomplishment; to the class and the school in terms of the success of teaching procedures; and to the success of the instructional program as a whole.

483

It has been somewhat disturbing to note that in an effort to secure this very desirable comprehensive and general picture, those who deny the values of measurement as a part of total appraisal seem quite willing to substitute the subjectivity and unreliability of teacher's opinions and estimates in place of well-established, objective, and reliable measures. Cook stresses the fact that "evaluation procedures are an inherent part of the language program and that no attempt to separate them in order to justify the use of poor or inadequate instruments for evaluation can change that fact. Certainly the most important factor in the learning situation is the goal of the learner." [2] Few would disagree with this. The assumption seems to be made, however, that goals and objectives stated and identified by the test-makers are fuzzy and false, while those of the less objective evaluative experts are clear and sound.

In a further statement, Cook attacks today's language program by saying that "in many schools [it] consists almost exclusively of isolated drill exercises in vocabulary, spelling, punctuation, capitalization, grammatical usage, and word usage. Perhaps the test-makers are not entirely responsible for this condition, but certainly they have done little to improve it. The standardized tests available in the language arts fields are almost exclusively limited to measures of these elements of correct form." It may not be unfair to point out here that measurable objectives in the field of language other than those of skills and form are extremely difficult to evaluate in a valid manner. Statements of guides, standards, checklists and the like for use in general evaluation procedures are of value but are largely a matter of the subjective judgment or personal opinion of the teacher. On the other hand, in most instances the establishment of the validity of the content of an objective test depends upon a critical analysis of the subject matter by a reasonably well-informed subject-matter expert supplemented by extensive statistical evidence—no guarantee of perfection, perhaps, but still much better than a series of guesses.

Recent writers on the use of certain of the less objective evaluative techniques appear to sense some of the limitations of evaluation through observation. Thorndike and Hagen suggest the following steps for the improvement of observational procedures:

1. Selecting the aspect of behavior to be observed
2. Defining the behaviors that fall within a category

[2] Walter W. Cook, "Evaluation in the Language Arts Program," In *Teaching Language in the Elementary School,* Forty-third Yearbook of the National Society for the Study of Education, Part II. Chicago: The University of Chicago Press, 1944, p. 195.

3. Training observers
4. Quantifying observations.
5. Developing procedures to facilitate recording [3]

To one experienced in the construction of objective instruments, the above steps for the improvement of observational procedures in evaluation will seem similar to the steps in test construction: (1) selecting outcomes important enough to be measured; (2) selecting the item forms suitable to be used; (3) validating the performance of the item content; (4) equating item difficulty; (5) mechanizing the item-marking and the scoring procedures. An additional item might well be added to the above; namely, (6) the interpretation of the meaning of the observations or scores.

Other critics of objective methods writing in support of observational forms of evaluation present the following timely "cautions to the observer":

1. The significance of observations depends upon the ability, understanding, and characteristics of the observer.
2. The observer needs to be conscious of the danger of misinterpretation through the confusion of symptoms with underlying causes.
3. Recordings of observations should be made promptly, so that none of the important details will be forgotten.
4. Generalizations from observation should be arrived at only after careful study. Such generalizations should be held to a minimum. [4]

With these observations the experienced maker of objective tests would agree, and, with slight re-wording, apply them directly to the more objective methods of observation:

1. The significance of a score on an objective test depends upon the validity, reliability, and suitability of the instrument.
2. Care is needed to avoid mistaken inferences from low scores.
3. Scoring and interpreting the results should be done promptly while the experience is still fresh in the mind of the pupil.
4. Results should be interpreted with care for the facts and conditions of the testing; generalizations and comparisons should be reduced to a minimum.

The apparent issues between the proponents of evaluation and of measurement largely disappear under the light of fair criticism and comparison. It is not a matter of evaluation only through subjective ap-

[3] Robert Thorndike and Elizabeth Hagen, *Measurement and Evaluation in Psychology and Education*. New York: John Wiley and Sons, Inc., 1955, pp. 312–314.
[4] J. Wayne Wrightstone, Joseph Justman, and Irving Robbins, *Evaluation in Modern Education*. New York: American Book Company, 1956, p. 122.

praisals; nor is it a matter of objective, analytical, diagnostic measurement alone. Actually, it is evaluation *and* measurement, not one *or* the other. Total evaluation of the language program of the school, evaluation of the effectiveness of the principles of learning or the methods of teaching, and evaluation of the accomplishments and limitations of the individual child are not obtainable through a single type of appraisal, but through the use of many different devices including inventory and appraisal charts, class and individual guides and standards, score cards, and merit scales, as well as standardized analytical objective tests.

TYPES OF MEASURING INSTRUMENTS
AND TECHNIQUES

Modern measuring instruments and evaluative techniques are so varied in type, structure, and function that it is difficult to arrive at an entirely acceptable basis of classification for purposes of description and discussion. Under the broad classification by function, most measuring instruments may be identified as evaluating educational accomplishments, mental abilities, and personality qualities. *Educational achievement tests,* as the name suggests, are designed to reveal the results of learning opportunity. *Mental ability tests* are used to evaluate the learner's capacity for learning without reference to what he has learned. *Personality instruments* attempt to evaluate certain of the intangible aspects of human behavior, such as interests, attitudes, and emotionality. Since measurement and appraisal in the expressional language arts are primarily concerned with the evaluation of individual and group acomplishments in their relation to instruction, it is natural that the large group of educational testing instruments should receive attention here somewhat to the exclusion of the other types of instruments.

When all types of educational examinations, tests, tools and techniques are classified by their form or structure, they fall quite readily into five main groups: (1) oral examinations, (2) essay examinations, (3) objective examinations and scales, (4) performance tests and scales, and (5) other evaluative instruments and techniques.[5]

[5] Adapted from J. R. Gerberich, Harry A. Greene, and A. N. Jorgensen, *Measurement and Evaluation in the Modern School.* New York: David McKay Company, Inc., 1962, pp. 38–44.

ORAL EXAMINATIONS

The use of oral questions with individuals or with groups is recognized as an essential phase of typical classroom procedure. Every language class makes extensive use of the oral question either as a probe for information or as a stimulus for discussion.

ESSAY TESTS

The essay examination is the widely-used, traditional, teacher-made, brief-discussion, recall form of test based on the subject matter of the course as taught. Some form of essay-type exercise appears almost constantly in either oral or written form for either oral or written response in every language class. As a matter of fact, a report, an announcement, or a story, in either oral or written form, is the common response to this type of exercise in the language classroom. The essay test has been brought under criticism as an evaluative technique in recent years because of the small number of individual responses that can be stimulated, and the inability of teachers to rate the results accurately for evaluative purposes. The introduction of the short-answer quiz question, affording a wider sampling of subject matter, and many more pupil responses, is thought by many to avoid the weaknesses caused by the broad and general coverage of the essay question as well as the extremely specific nature of the objective test item.

OBJECTIVE EXAMINATIONS AND SCALES

Informal objective tests and commercially available standardized tests utilize the same general principles of objective test construction, and are subject to the same general evaluative criteria discussed in a later section of this chapter. (Pages 493–500.)

Objective achievement tests, depending on their structure and content, may be used for *survey* purposes in certain specific school subjects or in broad, general areas of learning. Scores from such instruments have general significance in contrast with more concise results from *diagnostic* and *analytic* tests. Diagnostic tests are designed to identify individual pupil strengths and weakness, and within reasonable limits to point out the underlying causes of unsatisfactory accomplishment. Due to the difficulty or the impossibility of identifying the essential skills in certain subjects

487

and in constructing valid testing techniques, the diagnostic information afforded by many present-day tests is too general for critical use. For example, in the fields of reading and language it is possible to identify a number of different skill-areas which can be measured with reasonable objectivity and accuracy, but it is difficult to relate in any causal way the different phases of each subject on which achievement seems to depend. Although each can be measured objectively with high validity and reliability, causal relationships have not been established between such important language skill-areas as word choice, sentence sense, usage, capitalization, punctuation, or organizational abilities. Accordingly, it seems advisable in the language classroom to treat these individual measures of different abilities as unrelated aspects of the total ability, and to describe the tests as *analytic* rather than as diagnostic instruments.

The *product scale* is of importance to the teacher not because of its value as an objective instrument, but because it provides a useful source of material for the construction of tests. At the moment these source scales are limited to the field of spelling, although at one time product scales were available in other fields. The scales themselves are not for pupil use but provide a rich source of evaluated material for the teacher to use in constructing his own testing instrument. In the currently available source scales for spelling, two different plans of arranging the words have been followed. In the *Ayres Spelling Scale* [6] and in *Ashbaugh's Spelling Scale* [7] the spelling of words of a certain degree of difficulty comprising the vocabulary were grouped together and placed on a scale of difficulty from easy to difficult. In the newer scales, the words are arranged in alphabetical order with difficulty ratings given for each word for each grade.[8] Further explanation of the nature and uses of these scales appears in Chapter 18. (See pages 537–543.)

PERFORMANCE TESTS AND SCALES

The manner in which the individual performs or produces in a given life or test situation probably represents the most valid evidence of his capacity to learn or his ability to do. The problem is to secure and evaluate the

[6] Leonard P. Ayres, *Ayres' Spelling Scale*. New York: Russell Sage Foundation, 1915.

[7] Ernest J. Ashbaugh, *The Iowa Spelling Scales*. Iowa City: State University of Iowa, 1944.

[8] H. H. Bixler, *The Standard Elementary Spelling Scale*. Atlanta: Turner E. Smith and Company, 1940; Harry A. Greene, *The New Iowa Spelling Scale*. Iowa City: Bureau of Educational Research and Service, State University of Iowa, 1955.

product. In a broad sense every test is a performance test whether it be a written or oral response to questions, spelling a word, or writing a letter or a story. In general, oral and paper-and-pencil tests of factual knowledge are not regarded as performance tests. Gerberich clarifies this point in the accompanying statement: ". . . performance tests are here thought of, in accordance with usual practice, as requiring the use and perhaps the manipulation of physical objects or materials and the application of physical skills in situations not limited to oral or written responses by pupils." [9] Thus, a handwriting test calling for the production of a sample of standardized copy under time control is a performance test. Giving a speech or recording a sample of written expression under controlled conditions is a performance test, for speaking or communicating ideas by means of script writing both unquestionably require performance.

Performance testing in the classroom is concerned with the *procedures* followed in accomplishing a certain task and with the *product* resulting from the completion of the task. The actual performance of the individual is commonly evaluated by checklists closely identified with the process, while the product resulting from the performance is usually evaluated by means of quality scales, rating scales, score cards, and similar devices. In certain school subjects, such as handwriting and composition, the pupils produce tangible specimens differing in quality and in speed of production. Since the specimens are usually collected under controlled time and working conditions, the use of a checklist to evaluate procedures is not essential. From the point of view of appraisal the evaluation of the product itself is the next important step.

A quality scale consists of a series of previously evaluated specimen products representing varying degrees of quality from low to high, with each specimen carrying a numerical quality value. The scale values representing different levels of quality usually range from three to ten in number depending on the complexity of the skills and the exactness of the analysis attempted in the evaluation. Experience shows that it is doubtful if more than ten levels of quality can be distinguished by any except the most superior judges. In the evaluation of a given product, a scale of this type is used by matching the specimen with the one on the scale that most resembles it in quality. Considerable training and experience in the use of such a scale are required before teachers become sufficiently skilled in its use to secure reliable results.

[9] Raymond Gerberich, *Specimen Objective Test Items*. New York: Longmans, Green and Company, 1956, p. 379.

OTHER EVALUATIVE INSTRUMENTS
AND TECHNIQUES

The clear distinction between tests that measure and instruments that evaluate is as difficult to establish as is the difference between evaluation and measurement in appraisal. Perhaps the distinction may be made that evaluative instruments differ from tests that measure by the "greater emphasis on the less tangible or even intangible types of instructional outcomes, on the types of outcomes resulting from broad and varied learning experiences, and on the ability of the pupil to apply and to use information in reasoning and problem solving." [10] Such evaluative instruments include interpretive reaction tests, pupil records, reports to parents, checklists, pupil rating scales, questionnaires, and participation forms. In this same category, although not in the form of instruments, are observational records of various kinds kept by the teacher, interviews, teachers' logs, open-ended questions, diaries of pupils, and autobiographies.

KINDS OF MEASURES IN LANGUAGE

Measurement and evaluation in language are complicated by the fact that expression is both a process and a product, both of which are important outcomes in the language program. As a matter of fact, it was the problem of appraising the quality of the product that first stimulated workers in educational measurement to create quality scales for the evaluation of the merit of handwriting and written compositions. At the outset, the product was looked upon as direct and tangible evidence from which skill was inferred. A high quality written or oral production was taken as direct evidence that the individual who produced it possessed a superior mastery of the expressional skills. The mistake was in assuming that the individual utilized all of his skills at top efficiency. The subjective limitations of this approach also soon became apparent. The many difficulties in the way of evaluating the products with satisfying objectivity naturally stimulated the development of objective measures of the skills involved in producing the products. In this way, survey and analytical tests of such skills as capitalization, punctuation, usage, sentence sense, sentence structure, organization of ideas, word meaning, and

[10] Gerberich, Greene and Jorgensen, *op. cit.,* p. 283.

the like came into being. Here, too, a questionable assumption is involved, namely, that the ones who are superior in their use of the individual skills will also be superior in applying them to the production of superior written expression. Herein lies a serious limitation of the validity of these instruments.

Before any program of evaluation or corrective teaching can be undertaken, a critical analysis of the underlying skill-areas in the field and the accurate translation of these knowledges, skills, and abilities into instructional objectives are necessary. Even a superficial examination of any outline of language outcomes and objectives will indicate that there is a maze of highly complicated and interrelated skills. In one such outline designed as the basis for an analytical approach to measurement in language, twenty-four general and specific oral language outcomes and situations are listed, sixteen general and specific knowledges and outcomes peculiar to written expression are cataloged; and sixteen general outcomes involving correct usages and the rhetorical skills common to both oral and written expression are identified. This is by no means a complete list of language objectives.

Effective oral language depends upon the success with which the speaker chooses, arranges, and enunciates his words as symbols of his thoughts to secure the effect he desires. In teaching children to think and to talk under the conditions imposed by the audience situation, instructional emphasis must be placed on the development of pleasing voice qualities, clear enunciation of words, gracious manners, avoiding common language errors, careful choice of words, careful selection and arrangement of ideas, and skill in expressing ideas in exact words and effective sentences designed to lead the thinking of the speaker's hearers along the channels he has chosen to lead them. It is equally important that proper skills and attitudes be developed on the part of the listener. Effective audience-speaker relationships are the result of the interplay of the essential elements of communication. Many of these elements are so lacking in definition that thus far relatively little has been done to develop objective means of evaluating them.

Written language confronts the individual interested in evaluation with a threefold problem involving (1) the mechanical factors of expression, such as writing, spelling, punctuation, capitalization, form and general appearance; (2) the simple grammatical factors, such as common errors in language usage, sentence structure and form; and (3) the rhetorical factors, involving choice of words, interesting subject matter, and logical organization of the material within the sentence and in the larger

491

units. In a general way, the mechanical and grammatical factors constitute the raw material of written expression. They are tangible, objective, and measurable. The rhetorical factors are the results of the skillful manner in which the raw materials are utilized. They are the intangible qualities that make for interest, appeal, style, originality, and uniqueness in written expression; as such, they are exceedingly difficult to identify and to measure objectively. Thus far many of these elements have successfully eluded the best efforts of the evaluation experts.

In addition to the usual forms of objective informal and standardized survey and analytical tests, the instruments used most commonly for appraisal in the language field include a number of product and merit scales, score cards, checklists, and performance tests designed specifically to function in this field. To this list should also be added tests in underlying or related fields such as those measuring mental abilities, reading abilities, special interests and aptitudes, and personality qualities. Thus, contrary to the first impression the reader might have gained, the field of language expression appears to be rather well equipped with evaluative instruments qualified to contribute significantly to rounding out the total picture of the pupil's language abilities or limitations. The types of instruments which have been found to be especially useful for appraisal are discussed in detail and their use illustrated and demonstrated later in Chapter 18.

QUALITIES OF THE GOOD MEASURING INSTRUMENT

The selection of an evaluative or measuring instrument for instructional use in the classroom depends to a large degree upon the nature of the service it is expected to perform as well as the effectiveness with which it performs this service. The *good* measuring instrument is one that does what is expected of it in an accurate, dependable, and meaningful manner. This is a simple way of expressing the major criteria for the good evaluative instrument; it must possess the qualities of reliability, validity, adequacy, objectivity, administrability, scorability, economy, comparability, and utility. The first four of these major criteria are grouped together and discussed in detail here, not only because of their importance, but also because of their interdependence. Although the five supplemental criteria are much less involved and interrelated than the first group, they are nevertheless of considerable importance to the teacher in securing an accurate picture of the total suitability and quality of a measuring instrument.

Users of standardized tests and other commercially available evaluative devices have very properly adopted the practice of placing on the makers the responsibility for establishing the facts concerning the validity and reliability of these instruments. Examiners' manuals for the better types of measuring instruments contain complete statements concerning these factors. Teachers and others interested in the critical examination of such measuring devices soon learn where to look and how to interpret these facts.

INTERDEPENDENCE OF THE FOUR MAJOR CRITERIA

Reliability, validity, adequacy, and objectivity are related in ways which have only recently been made clear in the literature on measurement. The understanding of this interdependence requires careful consideration of each of these qualities, which in turn may be aided by a redefinition of each. Since the reliability of an evaluative instrument appears to be such an important factor in its validity it is well to define it prior to the discussion of the other major criteria.

Reliability.[11]   A simple synonym for reliability in the performance of a test is the word *consistency*. A reliable instrument is one that performs its function consistently. It may not measure what it claims to measure or what its maker designed it to measure (that is, it may lack validity), but whatever it does measure it measures consistently. The statement that *the reliability of an evaluative device depends upon the accuracy and the efficiency with which it measures what it does measure* may seem at first thought to conflict with the common notion of validity indicated above. This, however, is not the case when the statement is analysed completely. A test may be reliable without being valid, but its validity cannot be determined unless it is reliable. Thus, in a sense, reliability is an aspect of validity. A reliable instrument used with the type of individuals and for the purposes for which it was devised may be

---

[11] The definitions stated here are adapted from three sources: J. Raymond Gerberich, Harry A. Greene, and A. N. Jorgensen, *Measurement and Evaluation in the Modern School*, 1962; J. Raymond Gerberich, *Specimen Objective Test Items;* Carter V. Good, ed., *Dictionary of Education*. McGraw-Hill Book Company, 1945.

expected to be valid. Similarly, a reliable device used for wrong purposes or an unreliable instrument used for any purpose will be invalid. It is apparent that reliability and validity are not all or none qualities; measures may range from very high reliability and validity to almost complete invalidity and unreliability.

Reliability of a testing instrument is in a large measure a function of its length in terms of working time and the number of pupil reactions it calls forth. Through the use of objective item forms permitting short answers, many pupil reactions are possible in a given working period. Objective test forms also allow for an extensive sampling of important subject-matter areas. Thus, test reliability is affected by two additional aspects which need further definition. These are (a) adequacy and (b) objectivity, which are discussed later in this section.

The reliability of a measuring instrument is commonly expressed by the relationship (correlation) of the scores obtained by giving two equivalent forms of the instrument to the same pupils under the same conditions. The resulting measure, known as the *reliability coefficient,* constitutes a reasonably dependable index to reliability. Where only a single form of the instrument is available, other less satisfactory procedures may be followed. In the determination of the *retesting coefficient* the single form is given twice to the same pupils under the same conditions and the correlation of the scores on the first and second testing is determined. The second type of reliability measure on a single form of a test known as the *chance-half coefficient,* is obtained by correlating the scores on the odd-numbered items of the test and the scores on the even-numbered items. The two half-test scores when correlated give the reliability of a test one-half the length of the original test itself. A special formula is then applied to this measure to provide an estimate of the reliability of the complete test. Experience shows that while these last mentioned measures of reliability are much more easily obtained than the true reliability coefficient, they are likely to produce spuriously high estimates. Actually any reliability coefficient, in order to have significant meaning, must be based upon a large sampling of pupils of known and appropriate age and grade.

Validity. To be valid, a measuring instrument must give a direct and positive answer to the question, "Does it really measure the qualities, abilities, skills, or attitudes it attempts to measure?" An instrument is valid if it measures what its user intends to measure. A test may be adequately valid in one situation or with one group or level of pupils and be seriously lacking in validity in another. For example, a language test designed for use with upper-grade or high school pupils would obviously contain material unsuitable for use in the primary grades and would thus be lacking in validity at that level. A grammar information test might be highly valid for measuring knowledge of grammatical rules and at the same time be of low validity in measuring functional grammar as represented by language usage. *The validity of a measuring instrument depends upon the efficiency with which it performs whatever function it is designed for or claims to perform.*

The source from which the material in a test is selected frequently affords an index to the validity of the instrument. A spelling test composed of words selected from an unabridged dictionary by taking the first word at the top of the right-hand column of each tenth page would be lacking in validity for two very definite reasons. In the first place, the words thus selected at random would be unsuited for use in the test because they would be of unknown and uncertain social utility. In the second place, the test would be lacking in validity because pupils tested would probably have had no reason or opportunity to learn to spell these words. In other words the test would be directed toward an indefensible outcome. The test could be improved in validity for the class by selecting the test words from those words of known social utility which the individual pupils have had an opportunity to learn.

A testing instrument may be valid in a general sense, but may at the same time be lacking in validity for use in a specific situation. For example, a standardized survey test designed to measure achievement in certain language abilities must be validated in terms of the broad aspects of the course as it is taught in representative samplings of school systems, not in a single class or school. The result of attempting to cover only those objectives or to measure those specific skills common to the offerings of all types of schools is to narrow the content of the instrument and thus to limit its validity. A local teacher may prepare an instrument that will have much greater validity for his class, his point of view, and his purposes than any similar device intended for universal use could possibly have.

Validity in a measuring instrument is not a matter of all or none; it is a matter of degree, ranging from a very high validity in some to almost incomplete invalidity in others. The discussion of validity thus far has suggested a number of factors affecting the degree of validity of an instrument. Among those that should be specifically noted by the teacher as reducing the validity of measurement are:

1. The use of the instrument for purposes for which it was not designed.
2. The use of the instrument at improper levels of ability.
3. Content emphasis on wrong or indefensible objectives.
4. The item form in which the content is presented in the testing situation.
5. The adequacy of subject-matter sampling provided.
6. The reliability with which the instrument performs.

In a general way, validity may be expressed in terms of the extent to which the instrument sets up a situation calling for the use of the skills or abilities which experienced observers consider fundamental to success in a given field. Frequently such judgments are represented by the opinions of authors of textbooks, courses of study, special committees, or teachers and other qualified authorities. Validity may also be expressed statistically in terms of the relationship (correlation) found between the new measuring device and some other well-established and validated device in the same field.

Few classroom teachers have the time, interest, or technical skill required for the construction of their own languages tests or scales. However, the teacher can construct valid and reliable instruments for his own use if he will carefully follow these suggestions:

1. Clearly define the socially defensible objectives established for his class.
2. State the desired outcomes in terms of pupil behavior-reactions.
3. Select material for testing from content actually taught to the class.
4. Sample adequately all essential aspects of the subject matter.
5. Devise test items in appropriate objective form.
6. Include enough occasions for pupil-response to secure reliable measures.

The application of these steps should result in an instrument valid enough to be useful in a specific classroom situation, with sufficient objectivity and adequacy of sampling to be reliable, and in turn reliable enough to be valid.

Adequacy. Practically all tests and evaluative devices are merely more or less adequate samplings from the total behavior pattern which is considered essential to pupil mastery in the given field. The same principles of sampling regularly used in assaying ore or in determining the average quality of a carload of grain apply here. The maker of the device constructs items sampling extensively enough the widely different types of expected outcomes to justify him in accepting the resulting scores as representative of pupil achievement in the entire field. *Adequacy is the degree to which a measuring instrument sufficiently samples the subject so that the resulting scores are really representative of the rela-*

tive total performance in the areas measured.[12] It is relatively easy to demonstrate that if the sampling is small, the scores may be unfair to some individuals, while if the sampling is extensive (i.e. adequate), the scores are likely to be accurate measures of total accomplishment in the field. Thus adequacy of sampling is an essential factor in the reliability or the consistency of any instrument measuring performance.

Objectivity. Forms containing objective items with their short answers and key-scoring possibilities, not only eliminate much of the undesirable unreliability due to subjective scoring but contribute directly to reliability of testing. *Objectivity in a test makes for the elimination of the opinion, bias, or judgment of the person who scores it.* In general, objectivity is secured by wording items in such a manner that only one answer is acceptable for the statement, with the result that, aside from purely human or chance errors, scores assigned the test by different individuals or by the same scorer on different occasions should show no variation. Statistically, it is possible to express objectivity in terms of the correlation of scores resulting from different scorings, but this is rarely done because variations in scorings are readily noted by inspection. The relatively slight variations in objective scores on a specific instrument contribute significantly to the reliability of measurement afforded by the test. Adequacy and objectivity are thus important independent factors in the reliability of measurement.

Objectivity in a test item is secured by fitting the content to be tested into a number of different forms calling for a single brief answer, or for the recognition of the correct answer from several possible statements. The above statement classifies objective items into the two major forms, *recall* and *recognition.* Experience shows that, in general, recall items demand a somewhat longer working time and are more difficult in terms of pupil failure per item than the recognition forms.

Numerous variations of these basic objective item forms have been developed. A few of the more commonly used forms are illustrated here.

Recall

Simple recall:	What are words called that may be used in a sentence in place of nouns? *pronouns*
Completion:	A _____ is a word used in a sentence in place of a noun. (*pronoun*)

[12] Gerberich, Greene, and Jorgensen, *op. cit.,* pp. 62–63.

Recognition

Alternate response:	A pronoun may be used in a sentence in place of (1) a verb (2) a noun. <u>2</u>
True-false:	A pronoun is never used in a sentence in place of a noun. True False ( ) (x)
Multiple response:	A pronoun may be used in a sentence in place of (1) a verb (2) a noun (3) an adverb. <u>2</u>

The teacher of language will find many opportunities for the construction and use of informal objective instruments or for the selection of standardized objective tests. The following suggestions for the construction of objective items may be used as guides to the teacher in formulating his own test items or they may be used to sharpen his critical inspection of the quality of items in commercial testing devices.

General suggestions:

1. All test items should be carefully constructed using good language.
2. The use of difficult vocabulary should be avoided in test items.
3. The wording of the textbook should be avoided.
4. The test item should be open to only one interpretation.
5. Items having obvious answers are useless and should be avoided.
6. Items containing irrelevant clues and suggestions should be avoided.
7. Items that depend upon intelligence alone should be avoided.
8. Quantitative and definite words should be used as a control on items that depend upon opinion rather than facts.
9. Catch words and irrelevant and confusing statements should be avoided.
10. Each item should be independent of others in the test.
11. Answer spaces should be arranged to simplify answering and expedite scoring.

Recall items:

1. Lines for answers should be of adequate and uniform length.
2. Items should be stated to call forth a definite and brief response.
3. Only critical portions of the statement should be omitted in recall or completion forms.
4. Any correct answer should receive credit whether in the key or not.
5. There should be no penalty for spelling errors.
6. Whenever possible "a" or "an" before a blank should be avoided.
7. Statements should be formulated to bring answer space at end of the line.
8. Completion exercises should not obscure meaning by using too many blanks.

Alternate-response items:

1. Avoid statements involving double negatives.
2. Statements that are part true and part false should be avoided.
3. Avoid specific determiners, such as "always" or "never" in false statements.
4. Highly objective answers should be demanded, such as underlining T or F, or marking X in brackets under T and F columns at right.
5. Arrange true and false statements in random order and in approximately the same number within the test.

Multiple-choice items:

1. Include as much as possible of the statement in the stem of the item.
2. State all alternative answers in correct grammatical form.
3. Use only plausible incorrect alternative answers.
4. Avoid use of "a" or "an" to introduce alternative answers where possible.
5. Items of four or five plausible alternative answers are preferred.
6. Use the same number of alternatives within a single test.
7. Preferably alternatives should appear at the end of the statement.
8. Highly objective answer forms should be demanded.
9. Distribute correct responses approximately equally among possible answer positions.
10. Arrange correct answer responses in approximately random order of position.

SUPPLEMENTARY CRITERIA

In addition to the essential qualities of validity, reliability, adequacy, and objectivity, a good measuring instrument must possess elements of a practical nature which make it easy and economical to use in the classroom. These characteristics have to do with the ease of administering the instrument, and scoring and interpreting the results, as well as with the labor and financial outlay involved in using it.

Administrability is the characteristic of a testing instrument that is concerned with ease, clarity, and uniformity in its administration in the classroom and in preparation for its use. The essential aspects of administrability are usually concisely summarized in the manual of the better standardized tests and should be carefully studied by the classroom teacher before he attempts to use the test, or undertakes to construct an informal test of his own.

Scorability is the result of design in a measuring instrument which makes the results of its use available rapidly, accurately, and in usable form. Today most measuring instruments are accompanied by prepared answer keys, and many are provided with separate answer sheets which may be scored by hand or by machine.

Economy in a program of measuring and evaluating is best expressed in terms of the amount of useful and valid information secured per unit of cost. Cheap instruments do not necessarily result in economy, nor are the most expensive always the most economical.

Comparability is the quality resulting from the design of testing instruments in which two measures, such as scores on two different tests, are expressed in the same units with reference to the same zero point. Direct comparisons of achievements in different fields or on different forms of the instrument are thus possible. Without comparability, many of the real values of measuring are lost.

Utility in a measuring device is expressed by the extent to which the instrument makes available accurate, useful, and detailed information concerning the situation in which it is used. Evidences of status or of general growth in achievement may be shown by a survey instrument. For such a purpose the survey test possesses utility. For securing accurate information concerning the causes of individual difficulties or as the basis for a remedial program, the analytical-diagnostic type of instrument may possess the desired utility. "Utility may in a sense be considered a final master criterion. It is certainly not entirely distinct from the other criteria, but it may be an effective final check on the value of the test." [13]

EXERCISES FOR THOUGHT AND DISCUSSION

1. How do you account for the fact that while language was one of the first fields in which measurement was attempted, it has been slow to respond to modern methods of evaluation?

2. Evaluate the seven steps in the supervisory-evaluative program suggested in this chapter.

3. Discuss the meanings that the terms *measurement* and *evaluation* now have for you.

4. Show how the six steps involved in test construction would be carried through in some one limited area of language skill.

5. Which of the five types of measuring instruments and techniques lend themselves to use in the language classroom?

[13] *Ibid.,* pp. 67–68.

6. Define and discuss the major criteria for quality of the good measuring instrument.

7. Show how reliability, validity, adequacy, and objectivity are highly interrelated.

8. Discuss each of the supplementary criteria for a measuring instrument in terms of their practical aid to the classroom teacher in making or selecting a suitable instrument.

9. Show how utility is in a sense a master criterion of a good examination.

10. On the basis of your study of this and the preceding seventeen chapters on language what reasons can you now advance which account for the difficulties involved in producing good evaluative instruments in many language skill areas?

SELECTED REFERENCES

American Educational Research Association. "Methods of Research and Appraisal." *Review of Educational Research,* 3:327–362; December, 1951.

Commission on the English Curriculum, National Council of Teachers of English. *Language Arts for Today's Children.* New York: Appleton-Century-Crofts, Inc., 1954.

COYNER, N. IREAN. "Criteria for Evaluating Programs of Oral and Written Language." *Elementary English Review,* 27:323–329, 334; May, 1950.

GERBERICH, J. RAYMOND, GREENE, HARRY A., and JORGENSEN, A. N. *Measurement and Evaluation in the Modern School.* New York: David McKay Company, Inc., 1962.

GREENE, HARRY A. "English–Language, Grammar, and Composition." *Encyclopedia of Educational Research,* rev. ed. New York: The Macmillan Company, 1950, pp. 383–396.

GREENE, HARRY A., JORGENSEN, A. N., and GERBERICH, J. R. *Measurement and Evaluation in the Elementary School.* New York: Longmans, Green and Company, 1953.

THORNDIKE, ROBERT L., and HAGEN, ELIZABETH. *Measurement and Evaluation in Psychology and Education.* New York: John Wiley and Sons, Inc., 1955.

TORGENSON, T. L., and ADAMS, GEORGIA S. *Measurement and Evaluation.* New York: The Dryden Press, Inc., 1954.

WRIGHTSTONE, J. WAYNE, JUSTMAN, JOSEPH, and ROBBINS, IRVING. *Evaluation in Modern Education.* New York: American Book Company, 1956.

18

Measuring and Evaluating

Language Outcomes

THE SPECIFIC INSTRUMENTS AND TECHNIQUES FOR MEASURING AND evaluating the results of instruction in the elementary-school language program are discussed in this chapter. In addition, diagnostic and remedial procedures are suggested and ways presented in which the results of evaluation may be translated into greater accomplishment in the classroom. The discussion emphasizes the following specific topics:

a. Evaluating oral language skills and products.
b. Evaluating listening comprehension.
c. Measuring oral and silent reading abilities.
d. Evaluating written language products and skills.
e. Appraising general merit of written composition.
f. Measuring grammar and usage.
g. Evaluating letter-writing skills and products.
h. Evaluating handwriting quality and speed.
i. Measuring ability to spell.
j. Analytical and remedial procedures in language skill areas.

EVALUATING ORAL LANGUAGE SKILLS
AND PRODUCTS

In spite of the very great social importance of oral language and the long-time interest of teachers in the subject, evaluative instruments suitable for the reliable appraisal of either the skills or the products are extremely limited. Doubtless the difficulties involved in securing normal samplings of oral expression may also contribute to the limited production and use of measuring instruments in this area. At the present time there are no acceptable standardized instruments similar to the merit scales for written composition for use in evaluating the quality of oral expression. Today, however, the ready availability of high efficiency tape-recorders at relatively low cost should encourage the development of many different types of measures of oral expression.

In marked contrast with those of a previous decade, today's language textbooks for the elementary school provide systematic instructional emphasis on the development of the socially useful oral-language abilities. From these textbooks and the accompanying manuals, teachers should secure many helpful suggestions on effective teaching procedures as well as on the identification and correction of oral language disabilities.

THE TEACHER AND SPEECH DISORDERS

In attempting a practical approach to the instructional problems of oral expression, the teacher needs to keep at least two principles clearly in mind. First, he should never forget that the act of producing speech sounds calls for extremely accurate coordination of all of the mental, physical, and emotional aspects of the speech mechanism. Second, the teacher should not attempt to undertake corrective treatment for speech disorders. The most important function of the language teacher is to operate as an observer responsible for an immediate and non-technical report on all individuals showing noticeable speech difficulties in his classes. In cases of speech disorders, the treatment involves highly technical medical, mental, and hearing examinations which certainly should be undertaken only by a trained clinician in each field and should precede classroom attack upon the problem.

There are certain disorders which have such immediate and serious effects upon the individuals themselves that it is important for teachers to have at least some idea of their nature and extent. Surveys indicate that approximately one pupil per hundred will be a stutterer, with boys far outnumbering girls. There seems to be no relationship between the mental ability of the individual and the emotional disturbances causing him to stutter. The most important action for the teacher is to develop a proper understanding of the stutterer's outlook on life.

Speech pathologists and teachers of speech must be given much credit for the identification of oral language disabilities and the development of sound and practical corrective procedures. The advocate of one very helpful approach to speech problems encountered by the classroom teacher, classifies the major speech problems under the three main headings indicated in the accompanying outline. An examination of this out-

503

line should be a definite aid to the teacher in identifying the nature and possible causes of many of the common speech disorders.

Problems of Speech Pathology [1]

I. Functional Speech Disorders
    A. Baby talk (infantile speech sounds and substitutions)
    B. Defective phonation (faulty production of speech sounds)
        1. Inorganic lisping (impure production of sibilant sounds)
        2. Lingual protrusion (misplacement of tongue)
        3. Lateral emission (due to malformation of teeth and tongue placement)
        4. Nasal emission (poor control of soft palate causing sound to be emitted through the nose)
    C. Vulgar speech
        1. Foreign accent (omissions, substitutions, intonations due to influence of foreign language)
        2. Regional dialects (deviations that label speaker geographically)
II. Organic Speech Disorders
    A. Organic lisping (due to malformation of jaws or to failure of jaws to meet properly)
    B. Tongue-tie (tongue movement impeded)
    C. Cleft palate (defective palate or roof of mouth)
    D. Chronic hoarseness of voice (due to pathological condition, misuse, or to a neurotic condition)
    E. Nasality (too large a proportion of nasal resonance)
    F. Denasality (too little nasal resonance; from chronic catarrh, sinus infection, adenoids)
III. Emotional Disorders
    A. Stammering (habitual hesitation or repetition in forming speech sounds)
    B. Neurotic lisping (persists because individual desires to keep it in spite of lack of physical cause)
    C. Neurotic hoarse voice (may be due to nervousness or hysteria)

Many observable speech disorders are largely the result of habit or the lack of proper encouragement, and may be changed by retraining and the giving of a feeling of acceptance and security to the speaker. Although a trained speech teacher should work closely with the language teacher in providing the retraining, most classroom teachers with this direction can provide a service to the child with a speech disorder that a speech therapist alone cannot provide. The accompanying chart further suggests possible causes of many common speech disorders and indicates possible remedial approaches to the problems.

[1] Adapted from Dorothy I. Mulgrave, *Speech for the Classroom Teacher,* rev. ed. Englewood Cliffs, N.J.: Prentice-Hall Inc., New York, 1946.

Diagnostic and Remedial Speech Chart

Observable speech disorder	Possible causes	Suggested remedial treatment
1. Baby talk	1. Immaturity; home example; low mentality; defective hearing; inability to discriminate sounds accurately.	1. Set correct example; encourage home to do likewise; check hearing and discrimination; provide warm classroom climate.
2. Lisping	2. Malformation of teeth or jaws; loss of front teeth; hearing deficiency; immaturity.	2. Arrange for physical examination; teach formation of sounds; give breathing exercises.
3. Poor articulation	3. Carelessness; home background; defective hearing; inadequate knowledge of sounds.	3. Set correct example; give training exercises in making sounds; motivate class to set high standards in articulation; listen to recording of speech.
4. Excess nasality	4. Poor breathing habits; physical defects; home example.	4. Arrange for physical examination; give breathing exercises (panting, yawning, etc.), auditory discrimination exercises, exercises requiring blowing.
5. Breathiness	5. Emotional tension; improper breathing.	5. Give emotional security; prescribe deep-breathing exercises; check causes of excessive tension; arrange for choral speaking.
6. Stuttering	6. Physical defects; emotional problem.	6. Give security; avoid ridicule; arrange for physical examination; take part in choral speaking.

505

Diagnostic and Remedial Speech Chart (*continued*)

Observable speech disorder	Possible causes	Suggested remedial treatment
7. Stammering	7. Feelings of inferiority; physical defects.	7. Give encouragement and security; join group activities; focus on the thought rather than on manner of speech.
8. High pitch	8. Self-consciousness; insecurity; fatigue; faulty hearing and sound discrimination.	8. Prescribe adequate rest; give security; listen to recorded voice; do reading exercises.
9. Stridency	9. Poor social adjustment; home conditions; hearing defect; emotional problems.	9. Give security; listen to recorded voice; join in dramatization with need for soft voice, or choral speaking.
10. Low pitch	10. Physical defects; fatigue; emotional problems.	10. Arrange for medical examination; practice articulation and nonsense verse; provide security.

APPRAISING ORAL-LANGUAGE SKILLS AND PRODUCTS

The following functional objectives of oral expression, adapted from a statement by the senior author in collaboration with Dr. William S. Gray, provide the framework for a few selected samples of appraisal and evaluative techniques suitable for use in this area.[2] Many of the suggested procedures are quite general and most of them are highly subjective. It should be noted that to a large degree the final appraisal of expression, whether oral or written, involves devices for the evaluation

[2] Harry A. Greene and William S. Gray, "The Measurement of Understanding in the Language Arts," *The Measurement of Understanding,* Forty-fifth Yearbook of the National Society for the Study of Education, Part 1. Chicago: National Society for the Study of Education, 1946, pp. 175–180.

of the total product as well as of the skills and abilities related to the specific objectives.

Functional Objectives of Oral Expression

1. To greet others easily and courteously in social situations.
2. To use the telephone courteously and efficiently.
3. To tell a story or personal experience effectively and interestingly.

   The success of an oral story rests upon the audience appeal of the incident, the selection and arrangement of details, and the animation of the narrator. The following criteria may be used in evaluating pupil's presentations:

   a. Standards for selecting a good topic for an oral story:
      (1) Was the incident unusual, startling, or very amusing?
      (2) Did you see it, or take part in it yourself?
      (3) Can you make the characters of your story speak for themselves?
      (4) Does the story end well—a surprise, or a satisfactory outcome?
   b. Points for arranging the details of a story:
      (1) When, where, and under what circumstances did the incident take place?
      (2) Who were the characters? Did each one have a distinctive part?
      (3) What fact or happening started the incident?
      (4) What facts complicated the incident?
      (5) What did the incident lead to?
   c. Standards for judging the effective story teller:
      (1) He looks directly at the audience.
      (2) He speaks clearly and not too rapidly.
      (3) He avoids "and-uh" and other sounds between words and sentences.
      (4) He uses descriptive words.
      (5) His face reflects his thoughts and his interest.
      (6) He uses appropriate gestures.
      (7) He is relaxed and at ease.
4. To report information gained by observation, interview, or reading.
5. To give clear directions, explanations, or announcements.
6. To participate in conversation, group discussion, and meetings.

   Appraisal procedures involve consideration of attitudes as well as knowledge.

   a. Standards for checking participant in a conversation, meeting, or panel discussion:
      (1) Willingness to listen while others speak.
      (2) Courtesy in interrupting or correcting speaker.
      (3) Conciseness in presenting his own views.
      (4) Willingness to yield the floor, or give way in conversation, when it is appropriate to do so.
      (5) Willingness to accept and weigh opinions contrary to his own.

507

(6) Sensitivity to the rights of all in a group to participate freely and
equally.
  b. Checklist of parliamentary procedures for teacher or class.
    (1) To address the chair correctly.
    (2) To nominate a person to office.
    (3) To close nominations.
    (4) To make an original motion.
    (5) To second a motion which has been made.
    (6) To move to adjourn.
    (7) To amend a motion.
    (8) To refer to a committee, to postpone, or to lay on the table.
    (9) To rise to point of order, or to ask special privilege.
7. To take part in a dramatic production.

Teachers find that evaluation is an essential part of good classroom
method in language as it is in all other learning activities. The following
checklist for the evaluation of a discussion lesson is proposed in a recent
curriculum bulletin.[3] The teacher and student should compare this checklist with the standards in 6a in the foregoing statement of objectives.

1. For the group
  a. Was the problem suitable for class discussion?
  b. Was the problem stated clearly?
  c. Were all the terms defined?
  d. Was the topic of interest to all?
  e. Did the members display attitudes of sincerity and cooperation by
     listening attentively, keeping to the point under discussion, request-
     ing further information or clarification of information presented, per-
     mitting all members to participate?
  f. Were all members qualified to discuss the problem intelligently on the
     basis of indirect and direct preparation?
  g. Were the important issues discussed?
  h. Did the discussion promote a better understanding of the problem and
     of the members of the group?
  i. Were the voices audible and of good quality?
  j. Were the speech patterns acceptable? Did they permit free and easy
     exchange of ideas?
  k. Were the thoughts well organized and expressed in a convincing and
     concise manner?
  l. Was the discussion worthwhile in proportion to the amount and qual-
     ity of information gained and the time consumed?
2. For the discussion leader
  a. Did the leader guide the discussion wisely?
  b. Did he encourage all members to participate?
  c. Did he discourage individuals or small groups from monopolizing the
     discussion?

[3] *Toward Better Speech*, Curriculum Bulletin Number 5, 1952–1953 Series. New
York: Board of Education of the City of New York, 1955, pp. 81–82.

d. Did he keep the discussion on the point at issue?

e. Did he keep the discussion moving forward by raising a new issue as soon as the one under discussion seemed to have been handled adequately?

f. Did he focus attention on the important points by the use of a running summary?

g. Did he summarize at the close of the discussion period?

The following is an example of the excellent statements of goals and standards which pupils themselves can evolve for the evaluation of their own activities and products.[4]

1. The conversation should be kept going.
   a. Keep on main points.
   b. Change the subjects smoothly.
2. The people should be polite.
   a. Boys should stand when girls enter.
   b. If a boy and a girl start to talk at the same time, the boy should let the girl go ahead.
   c. If two girls or two boys start to talk at one time, the girl or boy who has talked more gives place to the one who has talked less.
   d. Only one person should talk at a time.
   e. Usually questions should be addressed to the group instead of to individuals.
   f. The people in the audience should not attract the attention of the people in the conversational group.
3. The host or hostess should be polite to the guests.
   a. The host or hostess should talk only to encourage the guests to talk.
   b. The host or hostess should talk only when the conversation drags.
   c. The host or hostess should greet the guests cordially.
4. Only people who have studied the *Weekly Reader* and read the local papers and listened to radio reports should accept an invitation.
   a. People should think as they read.
   b. People should be able to locate on the map places mentioned.
   c. People should look up difficult words.
   d. People should be able to give the source of their information.
5. People should talk about topics that are important now and will probably be important for some time to come.
   a. Talk about the causes of the war and how the war affects people.
   b. In connection with disasters, talk about means of preventing them.
6. People should discuss sensible, interesting, and pleasant topics.
7. People should use good English.
   a. People should make themselves heard.
   b. People should pronounce words correctly.
   c. People should use correct expressions, e.g., *the reporter* instead of *it,*

[4] Walter W. Cook, *Grouping and Promotion in the Elementary School.* Minneapolis: University of Minnesota Press, 1941, p. 14.

and *interesting conversation* or *a lively conversation* instead of a *nice time.*
  d. People should omit unnecessary words.
  e. People should try to add to their vocabularies.

EVALUATING LISTENING COMPREHENSION

Listening is now recognized as an area of major importance in the field of language arts. However, since this recognition has been slow in developing and because of the difficulties which have been encountered in specifically identifying the skills essential to good listening, the development of measuring instruments to determine the level of listening comprehension as well as measurable factors in the total skill has been delayed.

The skills involved in listening have been identified by Brown as follows: [5]

1. Identification and recall of details presented orally.
2. Ability to follow the sequence of details in the form of oral directions.
3. Retention of details long enough to answer questions about them.
4. Ability to listen reflectively for the purpose of identifying the central idea of the statement given orally.
5. Ability to draw inferences from the supporting facts presented in the statement.
6. Ability to distinguish relevant from irrelevant materials.
7. Use of contextual clues to word meanings.
8. Recognition of transitional elements in sentences.

Teachers may use this listing of skills as the basis for developing tests or standards to measure attainment of the various skills. The development by the pupils themselves of standards for listening which focus upon specific abilities or skills is also a useful evaluative technique.

The authors know of only one standardized listening test for use in elementary schools. This is the *Listening Comprehension* test of the *Sequential Tests of Educational Progress.*[6] This test, available in forms for four levels—grades 4–6, 7–9, 10–12, 13–14—attempts to measure simple comprehension, interpretation, evaluation, and application. The test is based upon oral presentation by the teacher with the pupil responding with one of four optional answers to each question given after the

[5] James I. Brown, "The Construction of a Diagnostic Test of Listening Comprehension." *Journal of Experimental Education,* 18:139–146; December, 1949.
[6] Educational Testing Service, Princeton, N.J., 1957.

presentation. The pupil has a copy of the question asked and the four options; hence certain elements of reading ability are involved.

MEASURING ORAL AND SILENT
READING ABILITIES

The measurement and evaluation of the skills and abilities necessary for effective reading have not raised the problems in development that have plagued the other receptive language skill of listening. Contrarily, measuring instruments and evaluative techniques have been developed further in the area of reading than perhaps in any other area of the school curriculum. For this reason, and because the teaching of reading is not the principal concern of this book, only a survey of the evaluation of this language skill is presented here. The student is referred to textbooks dealing with measurement and evaluation exclusively, or with reading exclusively, for complete discussion.[7]

SIGNIFICANCE OF THE RECEPTIVE
LANGUAGE SKILLS

A major purpose for teaching children to read is to enable them to understand and react intelligently to those things they have occasion to read in ordinary life situations. A comparable purpose exists for the teaching of listening skills. Thus much of the instruction in these areas should be built around purposeful situations in which the skills of reading and listening are needed. When considered from this point of view, the teaching of the receptive language skills becomes more than the development of ability to comprehend symbols rapidly and to memorize what has been read or heard. The receptive language skills should be taught as highly important tools of learning—tools by which information and pleasure are gained, tools which are useful in all activities both in and out of school.

Most of the advantages accruing from the receptive language skills are available only to the person who is thoroughly trained in their use. In order to adjust an instructional program in the receptive language

[7] For example: J. R. Gerberich, Harry A. Greene, and A. N. Jorgensen, *Measurement and Evaluation in the Modern School*, New York: David McKay Company, Inc., 1962; or David H. Russell, *Children Learn to Read*, second edition, Boston: Ginn and Company, 1961.

skills to fit the needs of individual children in using these tools, it is necessary to measure and appraise the various skills and abilities at particular times and intervals, and in particular areas of concern. Evidence of growth in reading abilities and skills are determined by: (1) observation by the teacher of the pupil's reading; (2) informal tests and check lists of material in readers and similar textbook materials; (3) standardized reading achievement tests; and (4) the pupil's work in other subject areas and records he may have kept of his reading. The informal aspects for appraising growth are usually dealt with in the teacher's manuals that accompany the textbooks in a basal reading series; therefore, principal consideration will be given here only to standardized tests.

MEASUREMENT OF READING READINESS

Readiness is an important factor in reading, as was pointed out in Chapter 14; not only at the first grade level, when instruction in reading is first given, but throughout the elementary school as children progress from one level of ability to the next. Readiness may be thought of as the maturity achieved or the specific ability acquired which is necessary for successfully learning a new skill or the attaining of a further goal. The belief that a pupil should be ready for any learning situation with which he is faced has long been an accepted principle of teaching and is neither unique to beginning reading instruction nor to any other aspect of reading instruction alone.

Readiness for a reading task is dependent upon many factors, among them: (1) intelligence, (2) the ability to perceive accurately written and oral symbols, (3) physical health and vigor, (4) background of experience, (5) an understanding and use of language, (6) emotional and social stability, and (7) interest in reading and learning. Equal or comparable development of each of these factors—and others—is not vital for attainment of success in every new reading task, but sufficient development in most factors is necessary. Certainly the factors making for success at each successive stage in reading must be appraised, and if deficiencies are found, they must be remedied. Appraisal is sometimes made by checklists but more often through the use of standardized tests which focus upon specific skills and abilities. While most reading tests can be thought of as diagnosing reading skills and therefore indicating readiness for certain reading tasks, the teacher's greatest concern about

512

reading readiness is concentrated at the beginning reading stage, for which specific reading readiness tests are available.

The *Harrison-Stroud Reading Readiness Tests* employ testing procedures which are representative of most such tests.[8] Instructions are given orally by the teacher, and readiness is measured by the pupil's ability to (1) use symbols, (2) make visual discriminations, (3) use context, (4) make auditory discriminations, (5) use context and auditory clues, and (6) give the names of letters.

The *Gates Reading Readiness Test* deals with picture directions, word matching, rhyming, and the identification of letters and numbers.[9] The *Lee-Clark Reading Readiness Test* is also widely used and measures (1) recognition of likenesses, (2) discrimination of differences, (3) experiential background, and (4) ability to discriminate among similar but different forms of letters and words.[10]

MEASUREMENT OF ORAL READING ABILITIES

Oral reading tests, such as the *Gray Oral Reading Paragraphs,*[11] the *Gray Standardized Oral Reading Check Tests,*[12] and the *Gilmore Oral Reading Test*[13] are an effective means for evaluating efficiency in the use of word-recognition clues and techniques. In addition, oral reading tests measure accuracy of oral reading, comprehension of material read, and rate of reading. Types of errors made by the pupil are usually recorded by the teacher, who is thus enabled to gain a concise picture of a pupil's particular difficulties with word recognition and pronunciation. The scores made on these tests and the analysis of errors made by the teacher do not, however, show certain factors which are important to reading aloud to an audience. Such factors as phrasing, volume, expression, voice quality, poise, and rhythm generally are best appraised by careful and systematic observation by the teacher.

[8] Lucille Harrison and James B. Stroud, *The Harrison-Stroud Reading Readiness Tests.* Boston: Houghton Mifflin Co.

[9] Arthur I. Gates, *Gates Reading Readiness Test.* New York: Bureau of Publications, Teachers College, Columbia University.

[10] J. Murray Lee and Willis W. Clark, *Lee-Clark Reading Readiness Test.* Los Angeles: California Test Bureau.

[11] William S. Gray, *Gray Standardized Oral Reading Paragraphs.* Indianapolis, Ind.: Public School Publishing Co.

[12] William S. Gray, *Gray Standardized Oral Reading Check Tests.* Indianapolis, Ind.: Public School Publishing Co.

[13] John V. Gilmore, *Gilmore Oral Reading Test.* New York: Harcourt, Brace and World, Inc.

513

MEASUREMENT OF SILENT READING SKILLS

Silent reading serves a number of purposes, not all of which are subject to testing. The two major types of silent reading tests are work-study tests and vocabulary or word-knowledge tests. At the secondary school level there are also standardized tests which measure the outcomes of the teaching of literature. In the elementary school, however, the evaluation of the literature aspects of the reading program are usually appraised or informally tested by the teacher.

Tests such as the *Gates Primary Reading Tests* and the *Gates Advanced Primary Reading Test* measure word recognition and paragraph meaning.[14] The *Gates Basic Reading Test,* for use in Grades 3 to 8, has five separate booklets designed to measure (1) appreciation or general comprehension, (2) understanding directions, (3) noting of details, (4) vocabulary, and (5) level of comprehension.[15] The *Iowa Silent Reading Test,* elementary edition, measures rate and comprehension, directed reading skill, word meaning, sentence meaning, paragraph comprehension, and skill in locating information.[16] In addition to tests specifically designed to measure reading skills, achievement tests such as the *California Achievement Tests* have sections which measure vocabulary, ability to follow directions, reference skills, and interpretative skills.[17]

EVALUATING WRITTEN LANGUAGE PRODUCTS AND SKILLS

The possibilities for the objective and reliable evaluation of pupil achievement and growth are much greater in the case of written expression than in oral expression—a result natural enough considering that the objectives of instruction in written expression are numerous and definitely stated, and that in written expression production assumes a tangible form relatively easy to secure and not too difficult to evaluate. The following list of

[14] Arthur I. Gates, *Gates Primary Reading Tests.* New York: Bureau of Publications, Teachers College, Columbia University.

[15] Arthur I. Gates, *Gates Basic Reading Test.* New York: Bureau of Publications, Teachers College, Columbia University.

[16] Harry A. Greene and Victor H. Kelley, *Iowa Silent Reading Tests.* Yonkers, N.Y.: World Book Co.

[17] Ernest W. Tiegs and Willis W. Clark, *California Achievement Tests.* Monterey, Calif.: California Test Bureau.

eight functional objectives of written expression includes samples of some evaluative techniques suitable for use in the area of written expression.[18]

Functional Objectives of Written Expression

1. To use correct form and content in all social and business correspondence. The sample exercises below illustrate evaluative techniques useful in help-ing determine the degree to which this objective has been achieved: [19]
   a. The following informal friendly letter is not written in good form. Study it carefully. Find the parts of the letter. Then write the letter correctly on a suitable sheet of paper. Sign your name.
   room 302, maplewood school pocono city texas june 11, 1958 dear mr royce our class voted your explanation of the way the atomic generator works one of the most interesting talks we have had in our room this year we would like to have you visit us again some time thank you so much for your trouble yours very sincerely
   b. Which of the following types of headings (A, B, or C) would be re-quired in a friendly letter from the Fourth Grade to the Third Grade in Lowell School?

(A)	(B)	(C)
1013 Market Street	Lowell School	1401 Cedar Street
Lansing, Georgia	Room 4	April 28, 1945
April 28, 1945	April 28, 1945	

   c. Which of the above headings (A, B, or C) would be suitable for use in a business letter?
2. To fill in certain forms and items of information as evidence of under-standing.
3. To write creatively a story, essay, or verse for personal pleasure, or for the entertainment or information of others.
   The success of creative writing rests upon (a) the selection of a suit-able topic or title, (b) the selection and organization of suitable and pleas-ing details, and (c) a spontaneous interest in the production and a desire to create for enjoyment. Results may be judged on the following bases:
   a. Standards for choosing a topic for a creative effort in writing.
      (1) Is the incident, the thought, or the plot unusual, startling, or amus-ing?
      (2) Is it real to you as an author?
      (3) Will its telling give you and others pleasure?
   b. Points for arranging the details of the story for effectiveness of pres-entation.
      (1) Who are the characters? Is each distinct?
      (2) When, where, and under what circumstances did the incident take place?
      (3) What started or complicated the incident?
      (4) What did it all lead to?

[18] Adapted from the statement by Greene and Gray, *op. cit.*, pp. 180–184.
[19] See also section on measuring letter writing, pp. 520–523.

515

4. To write a telegram, notice, announcement, or advertisement.

This type of writing is dependent upon the ability to select only the essential facts, and to choose words that express the meaning briefly and concisely.

5. To outline content and factual material from sources.

Evidence of understanding is best shown by skill in the use of correct outline form as required in the following exercises.

a. In making an outline, which should be used to indicate main heads?
(1) Roman numerals　(2) Capital letters　(3) Small letters

b. Which of the above (1, 2, or 3) should be used to indicate two or more subheads under a main head in an outline?

c. Read the following paragraph. At the right is an outline form partly filled in. Complete the outline.

Preparing Rice for Market

From the fields the grain is taken to the rice mills where it is threshed, cleaned, and husked. Next each little grain is polished by a special process. Finally the rice is graded, weighed, and packed for the market.

Many of the mills are small and limited in capacity, turning out less than 1,000 bushels of rice per day. Some of the larger ones prepare as many as 10,000 bushels of rice for the market every twenty-four hours.

Preparing Rice for Market

I. Functions of Rice Mills
A. _____
B. _____
C. _____
D. _____
E. _____
F. _____
G. _____
II. Capacity of Rice Mills
A. _____
B. _____

6. To prepare a bibliography or selected list of reference sources.

7. To keep records and minutes of group meetings.

Success in recording minutes of meetings depends upon an understanding of the essential facts and procedures in parliamentary practice. A checklist is a convenient device for testing understandings of this type.

Check each item below that must be included in the record or minutes of a club meeting in order that the full purpose of the meeting may be recorded exactly.

_____ a. The name of the club
_____ b. The name of the founder of the club
_____ c. Where or when the meeting took place
_____ d. Who presided at the meeting
_____ e. The name of the president and vice-president
_____ f. Reading and approval of minutes of last meeting
_____ g. The list of all members present
_____ h. Each motion with resulting action; the names of its maker and those who seconded it
_____ i. The nature of the program if one was given
_____ j. The time of adjournment
_____ k. The secretary's signature
_____ l. The president's signature

APPRAISING GENERAL MERIT
OF WRITTEN PRODUCTS

Like any evaluation based on individual judgments, the appraisal of the quality of written products by means of any of the available composition scales is subject to considerable unreliability, in part because of the subjectivity of the scorers' ratings and the limited samplings of the products on which the ratings are based. Thus composition scales operate most effectively in the evaluation of extensive samplings of the writing of large groups or classes. Reliable evaluation of the written products of an individual can be obtained only by (1) securing an extensive series of samples of his written expression; and (2) securing repeated ratings of the samples by an expert judge; or (3) securing many independent ratings by expert judges; or (4) by a combination of all three steps. By carefully collecting and scoring samples of the written products of his pupils under controlled conditions at the beginning and conclusion of an instructional period, the teacher can evaluate class and individual improvements as well as determine whether or not his pupils on the average are writing as well as they should at their present grade and maturity levels. If the teacher will remember the subjective character of the measures yielded by the scales, and avoid the error of thinking of them as having the accuracy of objective test scores, these measures of general merit of written expression can be valuable aids in the language classroom.

Hillegas early developed a scale (see Chapter 17) in which a pupil-written product may be compared with each specimen in the scale until a scaled sample is found that is of approximately the same general merit or quality as the pupil's product.[20] The scale value of the comparable scale specimen is then assigned to the pupil's theme. This type of instrument, while not generally accepted enthusiastically by English teachers, accomplished much good through focusing interest on the need for improved measures of written expression. This scale was later revised by Thorndike,[21] and while still considered by many to be a usable instrument, to the best of the authors' knowledge it is no longer published.

The Willing Scale for Measuring Written Composition is made up of 8 scaled specimens of composition ranging in scale values from 20 to

[20] Milo B. Hillegas, "A Scale for the Measurement of Quality in English Composition by Young People," *Teachers College Record,* Columbia University, September, 1912.

[21] Edward L. Thorndike, *Thorndike Extension to the Hillegas Scale for the Measurement of Quality in English Composition by Young People.* New York: Bureau of Publications, Teachers College, Columbia University, 1914.

90 all written on the subject, "An Exciting Experience." [22] The practical usefulness of this scale is increased by the introduction of two special features. The relation of form errors to the general quality of the written work is definitely recognized and included in the scoring. In addition, an excellent list of interesting topics is suggested as the basis for stimulating written expression. The use of the standardized list of topics and the control of the conditions under which the writing takes place both add distinctively to the reliability with which the written products may be evaluated.

Two specimens representing quality 20 and quality 60 on the Willing scale are reproduced here as illustrations of very poor quality (well down in the lower one-fourth of value scores for fourth-grade stories), and excellent quality (approximately median or average for fifth grade). It should be noted that the story values 20, 30, 40, 50, 60, etc., are given in the scale merely for practical purposes. Quality 20 should be interpreted as representing theme quality ranging from 15 to 24.9; 30 means 25 to 34.9, etc.

20

Deron the summer I got kicked and sprain my arm. And I was in bed of wheeks And it happing up to Washtion Park I was going to catch some fish. And I was so happy when I got the banged of I will nevery try that stunt againg.

(Number of mistakes in spelling, punctuation, and syntax per hundred words, 30.)

60

One time when mother, some girl friends and myself were staying up in the mountains. An awful storm came up. At the we were way up the mountain. The lightning flashed and the thunder roared. We were very frightened for the cabin we were staying at was at the foot of the mountain. We didn't have our coats with us for it was very warm when we started. There were a few pine trees near us so we ran under them. They didn't do much good for the rain came down in torrents. The rain came down so hard that it uprooted one of the trees. Finely it began to slack a little, So we thought we would try and go back. About half way down the mountain was a little hut. We started and when got about half way down it began to rain all the harder. We didn't know what to do for this time there wasn't any trees to get under. We decided to go on for the nearest shelter was the hut. Finely we got there cold and wet to the skin.

(Number of mistakes in spelling, punctuation, and syntax per hundred words, 11.)

[22] M. H. Willing, *The Willing Scale for Measuring Written Composition*. Bloomington, Ill.: Public School Publishing Company. Reported as being available through ETSA, 120 Detzel Place, Cincinnati, Ohio.

The directions call for the children's writing to be done in a twenty-minute period with five minutes additional time allowed for the pupils to complete the writing, to proofread and make corrections, and to record the number of words in their productions. Rating for *story value* follows the usual process of comparing the pupil's product with the scale specimens and assigning it the scale value of the specimen it most closely resembles. Following the assignment of the story value to a product, all errors in grammar, punctuation, capitalization, and spelling are marked and counted. This total number is multiplied by 100 and the result is then divided by the number of words written by the pupil. The resulting index is the *form value* score. Thus for each written product two separate scores are available. Expected end-of-grade scores for both story values and form values are given on the class record sheet for use with the scale.

The Hudelson English Composition Scale consists of sixteen scaled specimens of written expression spaced uniformly along a linear scale of values.[23] All except the two top value specimens were written by school children. Mid-year norms are provided for all elementary school grades above grade 4. One of the special advantages of this scale is the provision of three sets of sample compositions of known merit as assigned by experts for use in training teachers inexperienced in the use of the instrument.

The *STEP Essay Tests* [24] are devised for four different ability levels ranging from the fourth grade to the sophomore year of college. Pupils are directed to write essays on particular topics in a thirty-minute writing period. The pupil's paper is then matched with evaluated comparison essays on the same topic and assigned one of seven ratings. Each rating is weighted 50 per cent for quality of thought and content, 30 per cent for style, and 20 per cent for mechanics of writing.

MEASURING GRAMMAR AND USAGE

Relatively little has been done in recent years in the development of measures of usage and grammar. General achievement tests, such as the *Metropolitan Achievement Test* [25] and the *California Achievement Tests* [26] have sections which call for the identification of words used in context as nouns, pronouns, verbs, or adjectives. The pupil may also be asked to choose the correct word in a sentence without reference to

[23] Earl Hudelson, *Hudelson English Composition Scale.* Yonkers-on-Hudson: World Book Company.

[24] Educational Testing Service, *op. cit.*

[25] *Metropolitan Achievement Tests.* New York: Harcourt, Brace and World, Inc., 1958.

[26] *California Achievement Tests.* Monterey, Calif.: California Test Bureau, 1957.

519

grammatical terminology, as is the case in the *Iowa Language Abilities Test* discussed later in this chapter.

The *Kirby Grammar Test* is designed for those who believe that there is a formal as well as a functional aspect of usage.[27] This test calls on the pupil to (1) choose the correct one of two usages in a sentence situation and then (2) to recognize the correct grammatical reason for his choice. The usage exercises unfortunately are based on a rather old study of children's errors. Many believers in the contributions of grammar to correct usage are surprised and disappointed to find that the expected high relationship between usage and grammar does not exist. Another more recent instrument, the *Iowa Grammar Information Test* [28] makes no attempt to relate usage and grammatical knowledge, but measures purely informational aspects of grammar in eighty specific situations. In the current forms of this test the pupil answers the exercises by selecting the correct response from three choices and writes the number of that response on the line at the right margin of the test sheet. Sample items are reproduced here as examples of the types of grammatical information sampled in this test.

1. A sentence that makes a statement of fact is called (1) imperative
   (2) exclamatory   (3) declarative ...._____
2. The sentence, *"Who are you?" he asked,* is   (1) declarative
   (2) interrogative   (3) exclamatory ...._____
5. A sentence that has two clauses of equal rank is said to be
   (1) compound (2) simple (3) complex ...._____
76. What is the independent element in these sentences? *John, please
    tell George and Frank to come here. Thank you.* (1) John (2)
    Thank you (3) please ...._____
79. *Whether you can go or not depends on how much money you
    have by that time.* In this sentence, what is the use of the clause
    composed of the last eight words? (1) adverb modifier (2) base
    of prepositional phrase   (3) adjective modifier ...._____
80. *We thought him to be honest.* If we consider *him to be honest* a
    clause, in what case is its subject? (1) nominative (2) objective
    (3) possessive ...._____

EVALUATING LETTER-WRITING SKILLS
AND PRODUCTS

The writing of friendly and business letters is an exceedingly important form of language expression throughout the child's school and later life

[27] T. J. Kirby, "A Grammar Test," *School and Society,* 11:714–719, 1920. *The Kirby Grammar Test* is published and distributed by the Bureau of Educationtal Research and Service, State University of Iowa, Iowa City.

[28] Fred D. Cram and Harry A. Greene, *Iowa Grammar Information Test.* Iowa City: Bureau of Educational Research and Service, State University of Iowa, 1935.

activities. It rightly receives such heavy instructional emphasis in the elementary school that special attention to ways and means of evaluating the skills and the products is believed to be thoroughly justified.

In the primary grades, the chief emphasis in letter writing is on simple letter form and the correct use of the mechanics of placement, capitalization, and punctuation. Many simple notes and friendly letters are motivated by life situations and are written by the children both in and out of school. At the outset the letters usually are dictated by the class after a discussion of the content and are written on the board by the teacher to be copied by the children as a part of the learning process. In the third grade and above, letter writing becomes more of an individual effort with continued emphasis on forms and mechanics, but with special stress on the suitability and interest of the content.

Evaluation of letter writing as language expression consists largely in the appraisal of the quality of the product itself. From the start self-evaluation of his letter-writing efforts by the pupil is encouraged by providing each child with a model for guidance and comparison. When more exact measures of letter-writing abilities and products are desired, a copying test such as that comprising Part 8 of the *Iowa Primary Language Test* is suggested.[29] This letter-writing test, designed and standardized for use in the second and third grades, measures the child's ability to use and insert correct punctuation marks, greeting, and signature in a printed letter form. The teacher reads the letter aloud to the class before the test is begun, calling attention to the fact that some numbers, words, and punctuation marks are omitted in their copies. The pupils' test copy is scored on the following ten specific points, allowing one point for each correct response.

> *Comma* after city
> *Year* given correctly in date
> *Dear* written correctly in salutation
> *Comma* after name in salutation
> *Period* after first sentence
> *Capital M* Miss
> *Period* after last sentence
> *Comma* after sincerely
> *Whole name* written correctly
> *Name placed at right of paper and below closing*

A check sheet of the type reproduced here is suggested as a detailed and analytical form of evaluative device which teachers will find useful in appraising the quality of business letters. Pupils in grades four and

[29] Lou A. Shepherd and H. A. Greene, *Iowa Primary Language Test*. Iowa City: Bureau of Educational Research and Service, State University of Iowa, 1935.

EVALUATING THE RESULTS OF TEACHING

above will show surprising skill in developing similar check sheets for this and other language products.[30]

1. Is my whole letter brief, courteous, and easy to read?
2. Is the spelling correct?
3. Did I write the heading correctly at the upper right side of my paper?
4. Did I block the inside address even with the left margin?
5. Did I write the name of the person or firm correctly?
6. Did I give the street address and the name of the town and the state?
7. Did I use a greeting suitable for a business letter, such as "Dear Sir:" "Dear Madam:" "Gentlemen:" or "Dear Mr. Blye:"?
8. Did I make my meaning clear in the body of the letter?
9. Did I indent the first word, and write the body of the letter in good paragraph form?
10. Did I use a suitable closing, such as "Yours truly," or "Sincerely yours"?
11. Did I sign the letter correctly?
12. Did I use paper suitable for a business letter?
   (The pupils should be able to answer "yes" to each of the twelve questions above.)

The accompanying score sheet for evaluating friendly or informal letters provides a helpful appraisal and guidance device for use with pupils in the upper elementary grades. Attention is called to fifty specific details of good letter-writing form and content with certain crucial items being weighted heavily in terms of their social importance in the total product. The total possible point score on this check sheet is 100 points for a practically perfect letter.

Score on following points:

	Pupil Points:	Score:		Pupil Points:	Score:
1. Paper suitable, size, color	2	—	8. Space between paragraphs	1	—
2. Space at top of paper	1	—	9. Space between body and closing	1	—
3. At least inch margin, left	1	—	10. Space between closing and signature	1	—
4. Half-inch margin, right	1	—	11. No erasures (1), blots (2), soiled places (3)	3	—
5. Space at bottom of page	1	—	12. Penmanship legible (1), letters well-formed (2), on line (3), well-spaced (4)	4	—
6. Space between heading and salutation	1	—			
7. Space between salutation and body	1	—			

[30] Adapted from *Building Better English, Grade 5*. Evanston, Ill.: Row, Peterson and Company, 1947, p. 93.

522

Pupil
Points: Score:

13. Heading, right side of paper; not crowded — 1 —
14. Heading blocked or indented consistently — 1 —
15. Open punctuation in heading; no excess punctuation — 3 —
16. Heading on proper number of lines — 1 —
17. Heading in right order — 2 —
18. No required capitals omitted in heading (1 for each line) — 3 —
19. No abbreviations in heading — 1 —
20. Salutation even with left margin — 1 —
21. Appropriate salutation used — 1 —
22. First word only of salutation capitalized unless person's name is used — 1 —
23. Comma after salutation — 1 —
24. Closing in line with heading — 1 —
25. Word *from* not used in closing — 1 —
26. Appropriate closing used — 1 —
27. First word only of closing capitalized — 1 —
28. Comma after closing — 1 —
29. Signature at right of paper; in line with closing — 1 —
30. Signature not crowded — 1 —
31. First and last name in signature except for very close friends or relatives — 1 —
32. No misspelled words (1 off for each misspelled word up to and including 5) — 5 —

Pupil
Points: Score:

33. No hyphen mistakes — 1 —
34. No omissions or repetitions — 2 —
35. No abbreviations in body (except certain titles and initials with names) — 1 —
36. Punctuation in body (1 off for each error up to 5) — 5 —
37. Capitals in body (1 off for each error up to 5) — 5 —
38. Paragraphes indented correctly (1 point for each; limit 3) — 3 —
39. Lines filled within paragraphs — 1 —
40. No errors in usage or grammar (1 off for each up to 5) — 5 —
41. No run-on sentences — 3 —
42. Complete sentences (1 off for each unclear or incomplete sentence) — 3 —
43. Paragraph for each main topic — 3 —
44. Well-organized paragraphs — 1 —
45. Variety in sentences where possible — 2 —
46. Avoidance of slang expressions — 2 —
47. Subject matter content suitable and interesting — 3 —
48. Content clearly presented — 5 —
49. No use of trite phrases (I take my pen in hand, etc.) — 3 —
50. Additional points for outstanding content (upper five or six percent of the class) — 5 —

Total score — 100 —

EVALUATING HANDWRITING
QUALITY AND SPEED

Instruction in handwriting has as its major objective the development of the special skills enabling the individual to write with sufficient ease, legibility, and speed to meet his present needs and social requirements. Handwriting skills involve a very complex type of visual-muscular coordination. If the written product is to possess the desired legibility, speed of production, and general aesthetic qualities, a high level of this coordination must be developed. The close dependence of language expression in recorded form upon handwriting speed and legibility makes it important that a functional program of handwriting instruction be coordinated with the elementary language program. Legibility and physical appearance are both important elements affecting the quality of written expression. The language teacher is thus confronted with a real need for instruments to appraise the results of instruction in handwriting, as well as to diagnose the difficulties of individual pupils in writing.

Two factors constitute the chief approaches to the measurement of handwriting. These are (1) quality, or the degree of legibility, and (2) speed, or the quantity of writing produced in a given unit of time. The first of these factors is usually evaluated by means of quality or merit scales. The second is commonly expressed in terms of the number of letters per minute at which the copy was written.

QUALITY OR LEGIBILITY

The quality of the pupil's handwriting is usually determined by comparing the specimens to be evaluated with samples of established or known value. At one time this meant the comparison of the samples of the child's writing with the copy-book model. This procedure naturally resulted in an over-emphasis on the shape, size, and shading of the letters largely for decorative purposes. Under these conditions, quality and rate certainly were not the main objectives of writing instruction or measurement. With the appearance of scales for the evaluation of handwriting merit and legibility the teaching emphasis moved away from writing as a decorative art to writing as an effective tool of written communication. The speedy production of handwritten copy at a socially acceptable level

524

of legibility quite properly became the major goal of instruction in handwriting.

Handwriting scales in current use, of limited availability as parts of some achievement tests,[31] have been developed utilizing the theoretical approaches of two early scales. The *Thorndike Handwriting Scale* was designed to assist teachers in appraising the general merit of handwriting on the bases of three characteristics: namely, beauty, legibility and character.[32] The second type of scale, the *Ayres Measuring Scale for Handwriting*, was standardized solely on the basis of legibility.[33] Both of these scales are described more fully later in this chapter. The use of these scales has done much to improve the accuracy of the appraisal of handwriting quality, but as with all such instruments which require individual judgments, the results still lack much of the desired objectivity of measurement.

RATE

The ability to write rapidly at an acceptable level of legibility affords the individual an important advantage in most situations whether in school or outside. In such fields of written expression as in notetaking or in written examinations, the advantage is very real provided the speed of an individual's thinking keeps pace with his ability to transcribe his ideas. The measurement of rate of writing is easily accomplished by having pupils write for a specific period selections from standardized copy which they have previously read and memorized.

SECURING HANDWRITING SPECIMENS FOR EVALUATION

Handwriting specimens for evaluation on a quality scale and for deriving rate scores are affected by three factors which must be considered when they are being collected. The first of these is the suitability or the difficulty of the copy pupils are asked to write. Sentences from Lincoln's Gettysburg Address may be of suitable difficulty for fifth grade and above, but children in the lower grades are frightened by such unusual and long

---

[31] For example: *California Achievement Tests.*

[32] Edward L. Thorndike, "Handwriting," *Teachers College Record,* Columbia University, March, 1910.

[33] Leonard P. Ayres, *A Scale for Measuring the Quality of Handwriting of School Children.* Bulletin No. 113. New York: Division of Education, Russell Sage Foundation, 1912.

words as *fourscore, forefathers,* or *continent.* It is suggested that the teacher make use of some simple sentence which the pupils may have memorized and used on some other occasion, such as "Mary had a little lamb." The sentence, "The quick brown fox jumps over the lazy dog" is simple, and has the additional merit of making use of all of the letters of the alphabet. In any case, the sample should contain very few spelling or vocabulary difficulties and should be easily understood. The selected copy should be written on the blackboard several days prior to the test where it can be studied and where it can be seen during the writing test itself.

A second factor is the care with which the instructions for the writing test are given. Children are easily influenced in the quality and the rate of their writing by the wording of the directions and the manner of giving the test. The following directions are suggested: "When I say begin, start to write as well as you can and at your usual speed the copy you have read and memorized from the blackboard. Write your copy over and over until I say stop. When I say stop, you are to quit writing at once even though you are in the middle of a letter."

The third factor which must be controlled in the collection of writing specimens is the time allowance. In the standardization of his scale Ayres used the first four sentences of Lincoln's Gettysburg Address, allowing each pupil two minutes in which to copy as much of the material as possible. The two-minute period has been generally accepted as suitable for the writing of such samples.

SCORING HANDWRITING SPECIMENS

Before attempting to use a quality scale for the purpose of evaluating handwriting samples, the teacher should make a very careful study of the scale itself, the directions for its use, the norms, and the special functions which the scale is designed to perform. Elements of differences in quality apparent in the low value, average, and superior specimens comprising the scale should be especially noted.

Quality scores. The quality of the specimen being evaluated is determined by comparing it with the scale samples by moving it along the scale until a scale sample is found that closely matches it in appearance, quality, or legibility. The quality value of the matching scale sample is then assigned to the pupil's handwriting sample. As experience with the scale gives the user confidence, he may wish to increase the accuracy of his scoring by assigning intermediate values.

Because of the nature of the quality scale and the way in which it is used, objective and highly accurate ratings of handwriting samples are difficult to secure. However, experience shows that through the use of a training period as short as two hours spent in study of the scale samples, study of the grade norms and of colleagues' scores as a basis for adjusting the scorers own levels of expectancy, and directed practice with samples of known quality, the average teacher can learn to rate handwriting samples with sufficient accuracy and objectivity for survey use.

Rate scores. The accuracy with which handwriting rate scores may be obtained is largely determined by the care with which the samples are collected. Rate of writing may be expressed in either seconds per letter or in letters per minute, but the latter is the form most commonly used. The rate score is obtained by counting the total number of letters written by each child and dividing this number by the number of minutes allowed for the writing.

According to the directions on the scale the teacher is directed to secure the samples of handwriting by writing on the board the first three sentences of Lincoln's Gettysburg Address. The pupils are allowed to read and copy it until they are familiar with it. At the time of the testing they should copy the material in ink on ruled paper, beginning at a given signal and writing for precisely two minutes. The copy with the count of letters is as follows:

Four *4* score *9* and *12* seven *17* years *22* ago *25* our *28* fathers *35* brought *42* forth *47* upon *51* this *55* continent *64* a *65* new *68* nation *74* conceived *83* in *85* liberty *92* and *95* dedicated *104* to *106* the *109* proposition *120* that *124* all *127* men *130* are *133* created *140* equal *145*. Now *148* we *150* are *153* engaged *160* in *162* a *163* great *168* civil *173* war *176* testing *183* whether *190* that *194* nation *200* or *202* any *205* nation *211* so *213* conceived *222* and *225* so *227* dedicated *236* can *239* long *243* endure *249*. We *251* are *254* met *257* on *259* a *260* great *265* battlefield *276* of *278* that *282* war *285*.

QUALITY AND RATE STANDARDS

Handwriting quality and rate scores show slow but consistent growth from grade to grade. The accompanying table shows both quality and rate expectancies for grades 2 to 8 based on the scoring of many thousands of samples of the writing of school children on the Ayres Scale using the first three sentences of Lincoln's Gettysburg Address as the

527

test copy. These standards proposed by West and Freeman [34] do not agree with those appearing on the Ayres Scale itself. They have been modified upward in line with the evidence on the increased speed and quality of handwriting of school children since the standardization of the scale.

Handwriting quality and speed standards

Grade	2	3	4	5	6	7	8
Quality on Ayres Scale	44	47	50	55	59	64	70
Rate in letters per minute	36	48	56	65	72	80	90

This table indicates that pupils at the end of the second grade should write 36 letters per minute and that the typical quality of their samples should average approximately 44 on the *Ayres Scale*. By the end of the third grade they should write 48 letters per minute and increase to a rate of 90 letters per minute at the end of the eighth grade. Many teachers and handwriting experts feel that to press elementary school children to write faster than the sixth-grade norm rate of 72 letters per minute and at a quality above 60 on the Ayres Scale is to go beyond reasonable social requirements. There are some who feel that there is justification for setting the quality standard at 50. The writers are convinced that quality 60 meets all of the legibility requirement of social usage. Furthermore, except for purposes of over-learning to compensate for skill losses from lack of practice, there seems to be little reason why the pupil should spend the time necessary to learn to write better than the above standard of legibility.

SCALES FOR MEASURING HANDWRITING QUALITY

The currently available scales for evaluating handwriting may be divided into two groups in accordance with the purpose each instrument serves: (1) general merit scales, and (2) analytical and diagnostic charts and scales. In the first group, four scales for the measurement of general merit of cursive writing are sufficiently well known and widely used to justify description. One valuable scale for the use of teachers of manuscript-writing groups is also included in this list. The number of standardized charts or scales classifiable in the second group is limited to two very useful instruments.

[34] Paul V. West and Frank N. Freeman, "Handwriting," *Encyclopedia of Educational Research,* rev. ed. New York: The Macmillan Company, 1950, pp. 524–529.

The *Thorndike Scale for the Measurement of Merit of Handwriting* consists of 16 specimens of handwriting arranged in ascending order of merit from a lower scale value of 4 units above zero to a high of 18. The unit of measurement used in this scale was based upon the consensus of judgments of a large number of persons presumably qualified by training and experience to discriminate between minute levels of quality in handwriting specimens. These specimens, selected and described as being one unit apart, are arranged in order from poorest to best to constitute the rough scale. The poorest specimen is somewhat arbitrarily designated as representing a quality four judgment units above zero, zero representing just no handwriting quality whatever. A second specimen approximately one judgment unit better is assigned a scale value of 5.

The scaled specimens reproduced here represent scale values of 8 and 9 on the Thorndike Scale, and are defined as being one scale unit apart. According to the standards provided with the scale, quality 9 is approximately normal for fifth grade.

8

9

The *Ayres Handwriting Scale,* the second scale to be developed, was standardized on the basis of legibility alone. Ayres believed that the judgment unit used in the *Thorndike Scale* introduced many undesirable subjective elements and proposed to measure legibility in terms of the speed and ease with which samples of handwriting could be read by trained and competent readers.[35] This scale, known generally as the *Gettysburg Edition* because the specimens were based on the first four sentences of Lincoln's Gettysburg Address, has been one of the most widely used handwriting scales.

The accompanying sample represents quality 60 from the Ayres Scale.

[35] *Op. cit.*

This quality, according to modern standards, is approximately normal expectancy for sixth-grade pupils at the end of the year.

Four score and seven years ago our fathers brought for theupon this continent a new nation, conceived in liberty, and dedicated to the proposition that all men are created equal Now we are engaged in a great civil war, testing whether that nation, or any nation so con – ceived and so dedicated

The American Handwriting Scale, one of the most comprehensive of the general merit scales, provides a number of distinctive features of which at least two deserve special mention: (1) a separate scale is provided for each grade from two to eight; (2) the specimens have been scaled for both quality and rate taking into account the fact that the better writing is usually done at a more rapid rate and the poor writing at a slower rate.[36] The provisions of separate scales for each grade from two to eight makes possible a somewhat more accurate evaluation of quality of writing in its relation to the grade in which it is produced than is possible in a single scale.

The *Freeman Handwriting Measuring Scales* are similar in many respects to the scales designed by West.[37] Scales for each grade present specimens classified as poor, satisfactory, and good. The specimen reproduced here indicates the copy used in securing samples of the pupils' writing. It is classified as a "poor" fourth-grade product.

[36] Developed by Paul V. West. Published and copyrighted by A. N. Palmer Company, 1951.
[37] Frank N. Freeman and the Zaner-Bloser Staff, *Handwriting Measuring Scale for Grade 4.* Columbus, Ohio: The Zaner-Bloser Company.

530

Intelligent practice makes perfect
We learn by trying over and over
again. Each time we try to do little
better.

H O R J U V X Y

The almost universal practice of introducing the first-grade child to writing through the use of print script or manuscript writing has not resulted in the expected development of scales for the evaluation of this type of product. Only one instrument, The *Conard Manuscript Standards* appears to have been used widely enough to justify description here.[38] Two separate scales comprise this instrument. The scale used in scoring pencil-written forms contains 12 specimens ranging in quality from the undecipherable scrawl of the beginning first-grade child to excellent manuscript writing at the fourth-grade level. The specimen reproduced here is Sample 6 from the scale for pencil forms and represents a rather good second-grade product with a quality rating of approximately 27 on the scale.

6

Dear Miss Conard
I am glad that we cou
our writing.

The scale for scoring pen-written forms comprises 10 specimens ranging from beginning third-grade work in ink to excellent quality ink work produced by a sixth-grade child. The author points out that the rating of pencil forms extends from approximately zero to 60. The pen forms begin at 50 and extend to 100. The pencil and pen forms thus overlap between 50 and 60.

[38] Edith Conard, *Conard Manuscript Writing Standards.* New York: Bureau of Publications, Teachers College, Columbia University, 1929.

DIAGNOSIS AND REMEDIATION
IN HANDWRITING

At one time, instruments recommended for the location of specific faults in handwriting included both analytical scales and score cards, but today interest centers almost entirely on such devices as the *Freeman Chart for Diagnosing Faults in Handwriting* or the Zaner-Bloser Chart on *Handwriting Faults and How to Correct Them*.[39] Actually the Freeman Chart is five scales in one, each of which is designed to reveal whether or not the pupil's specimen of handwriting violates one or more of the following essential qualities: (1) uniformity of slant; (2) uniformity of alignment; (3) quality of line; (4) letter formation; and (5) spacing. Three levels of quality—excellent, mediocre, and poor—are shown for each trait.

The Zaner-Bloser Chart is essentially a revision and improvement of the Freeman Chart. In addition to the desirable qualities of the original chart it contains the following excellent suggestions on ways to test handwriting copy for such elements as legibility, slant, spacing, alignment, size of letters, and quality of line. This chart is helpful because it enables the teacher as well as the pupil to discover the special handwriting weaknesses that are in need of remedial treatment and gives excellent suggestions for correcting the defects.

How to test legibility: Make a letter finder by cutting a hole a little larger than the letter in a piece of cardboard. Place the hole of this finder over each letter in turn and mark the letters which are illegible. Have the pupils practice these letters separately, then write the word again and test as before.

How to test slant: Draw slanting lines through the letters and mark all letters which are off slant.

If the slant is too great, the paper is tilted too much. If the writing is too vertical, the paper is too

[39] Zaner-Bloser Staff, *Handwriting Faults and How to Correct Them*. Columbus, Ohio: The Zaner-Bloser Company.

upright and if the slant is backward, the paper is tilted the wrong direction.

How to test for spacing: Begin each new word in a sentence directly under the ending stroke of the preceding word.

correct   *incorrect*

How to test alignment: Alignment and size are closely integrated and should be studied together. Use a ruler (a diagnostic ruler is best) and draw a base line touching as many of the letters as possible. Also draw a line along the tops of the small letters. Mark the letters above or below these lines

How to test size of letters: Draw lines along the tops of the letters. Remember the minimum letters, i, u, v, etc., are ¼ space high; d, t, p are ½ space; capitals and l, h, k, b, d, are ¾ space high. All the lower loop letters extend ½ space below the line.

How to test for quality of line: Make a letter finder by cutting a hole a little larger than the letter in a piece of cardboard. Place the hole of this finder over each letter in turn and mark the letters which are illegible due to the quality of line. Have pupils practice these letters from their writing books separately until the letters are perfectly legible. Then have them write the whole word again and test as before.

One rather extensive investigation analysed the writing of children and adults and found approximately 3,000 different causes for illegibilities.[40] Of these illegibilities almost ten per cent were malformations of letters so serious that they interfered with reading. The following sum-

[40] L. C. and S. L. Pressey, "Analyses of Three Thousand Illegibilities in the Handwriting of Children and Adults," *Educational Research Bulletin*. Columbus: The Ohio State University, 6:270–273; September 28, 1927.

mary adapted from an extensive tabulation shows the twenty-three letter malformations with frequencies of ten or more identified in this study. These errors in the formation of fourteen letters used frequently in cursive writing undoubtedly account for a high percentage of all errors in letter formation.

Important types of letter malformations

a	made like	u	l	made like	uncrossed t
a	made like	o	m	made like	w
c	made like	e	n	made like	u
c	made like	i	n	made like	v
d	made like	cl	o	made like	a
e	closed		r	made like	i
g	made like	y	r	made like	s
h	made like	li	r	made like	n
i	made like	c	s	indistinct	
i	with dot right		s	made like	r
i	with dot left		t	made like	l
			t	with cross above	

The teacher will find that the following list of seven of the most common defects in writing, with their contributing causes will, if properly used, provide a useful supplement to the diagnostic information resulting from the use of Freeman's *Chart for Diagnosing Faults in Handwriting*.

Important defects in writing and their causes

Defect	Causes
1. Too much slant	a. Writing arm too near body
	b. Thumb too stiff
	c. Point of nib too far from fingers
	d. Paper in wrong position
	e. Stroke in wrong direction
2. Writing too straight	a. Arm too far from body
	b. Fingers too near nib
	c. Index finger alone guiding pen
	d. Incorrect position of paper
3. Writing too heavy	a. Index finger pressing too heavily
	b. Using wrong type of pen
	c. Penholder too small in diameter
4. Writing too light	a. Pen held too obliquely or too straight
	b. Eyelet of pen turned to side
	c. Penholder too large in diameter
5. Writing too angular	a. Thumb too stiff
	b. Penholder too lightly held
	c. Movement too slow
6. Writing too irregular	a. Lack of freedom of movement
	b. Movement of hand too slow

Defect	Causes
	c. Pen gripping
	d. Incorrect or uncomfortable position
7. Spacing too wide	a. Pen progresses too fast to right
	b. Too much lateral movement

REMEDIAL INSTRUCTION IN HANDWRITING

As in every other tool subject, corrective work in handwriting can be applied effectively only on an individual basis and following a careful individual diagnosis. Unfortunately only the briefest of suggestions on the problems of corrective teaching in handwriting can be presented here. Two groups of factors seem to affect improvement in handwriting most directly. These are (1) the provision of adequate physical conditions and materials and (2) the maintenance of the correct psychological conditions for effective learning.

Undoubtedly one of the most important *physical factors* affecting the individual's handwriting is the matter of his desk and his position with respect to it. The desk-seat and writing-top should both be adjusted to permit the pupil to sit comfortably with both feet touching the floor and with both arms resting in a relaxed position on the writing top. He should face the desk squarely, bending slightly forward at the hips. In the case of the *right-handed individual,* the right arm and hand should be placed in the proper writing position while the left should be used to hold the paper and to move it upward and to the left as the writing progresses. *The reverse of this position is taken by a left-handed individual.* There are wide differences of opinion about the position of the writing arm, the angle of the hand and wrist, and the use of arm and finger movements. There is rather close agreement on the recommendation that the paper be placed at such an angle with the body that the wrist of the writing arm is perpendicular to the line of writing. Most teachers of handwriting recommend that the writing instrument be held lightly by placing the forefinger nearer the point than the thumb, with both at least one inch above the writing point. They also agree in general that rapid and legible writing is the result of the smooth coordination of whole arm, forearm, wrist, and finger movements.

The provision of desirable *psychological conditions* is probably no less important than the control of physical factors in improving handwriting in the classroom. One simple and effective plan involves explaining one of the handwriting scales to the pupils and encouraging them to use it themselves in the appraisal of their own writing. For example, the

535

Ayres Handwriting Scale, or the scale designed to accompany the writing system in use in the local school system, might be made available to the pupils by placing it under glass or cellophane on the classroom bulletin board. If, in addition, some good diagnostic chart such as Freeman's can be made available, the pupils will be definitely encouraged to evaluate their own products and to identify their own handwriting defects. Another effective procedure used by many teachers is the practice of exempting from penmanship drill for a specific period all pupils who have attained the standards of speed and quality for the grade. This plan not only encourages the 50 to 75 per cent of the pupils who are able to attain these standards to try to maintain their superior ratings, but, equally important, it frees the busy teacher to devote more time to those who are still in need of remedial instruction.

MEASURING ABILITY TO SPELL

There is much more to being a good speller than merely being able to make a high score on a spelling test. Obviously a major objective of spelling instruction in the language program is to teach the child to spell the words he needs to use in expressing himself in written form. However, the good speller is the individual who recognizes the social importance of correct spelling in all of his written expression, makes a special effort to spell correctly each word he writes, and equips himself to learn independently how to spell the new words he encounters. These and other habits, skills, and attitudes combine to produce in the individual what is known as spelling ability.

Spelling is one of the fields in which learning is specific. The child does not just learn spelling; he learns to spell specific words. Naturally such factors as superior mental capacity, outstanding vividness in imagery, and an unusually retentive memory may all contribute to success in learning to spell. It is obviously impossible to secure objective measures of all of the elements that contribute to spelling success. The ability to spell in list or in context those words that are needed and used in the individual's written expression is relatively easy to measure by means of samples of words chosen from socially validated vocabularies. The ability to identify the correct and incorrect spellings of words is also quite readily measured by proofreading tests. Quite often ability to spell is inferred from scores on such tests. Obviously recognizing a correctly or incorrectly spelled word form does not require quite the same abilities as are required in spelling the word correctly. Good study habits in spelling are best revealed by the record of the child's daily work in spelling.

SPELLING ABILITY DEFINED

Spelling ability may be defined as the ability to spell specific words. Words vary in difficulty of spelling just as individuals vary in ability to use the skills required to spell the words. In fact, word difficulty and pupil ability are much like the opposite ends of a teeter-totter; as word difficulty goes up, what we describe as pupil ability goes down. On easy words, even a poor speller may show up favorably. Thus it is apparent that the term *spelling ability* demands much more exact definition than it is usually given. At any given time the spelling ability of the individual child depends upon his capacity and his opportunity for learning. Ability to perform on a given test, of course, varies in accordance with the testing conditions, and the difficulty of the items, in addition to the previously mentioned factors. With this in mind, it is important to point out early in the consideration of measuring spelling that there are at least two aspects of the pupil's acomplishment that must be determined: (1) the *present status* of his success in spelling certain words; and (2) the *growth* he makes in spelling success as a result of learning opportunity with these words.

The pupil's present status in spelling certain words presumably is determined prior to his study of the specific word list. As a matter of fact, more often than not such initial tests given for this purpose are administered without knowledge of the prior experience of the pupils with these words. The use of the second measure at the end of the instructional period reveals how much the individual has improved in his mastery of the selected vocabulary. Both of these measures are important in evaluating the child's ability to spell.

CONSTRUCTING OBJECTIVE MEASURES OF SPELLING

The specific nature of spelling makes it extremely difficult to guarantee the validity of a standardized spelling test. The words tested must be selected from those presented for instruction. This means, naturally, that the most common and useful measures of spelling are those constructed locally by the classroom teacher or supervisor. The following four problems require careful consideration in the development of such tests:

537

1. From what sources should the words be selected for use in the tests?
2. At what levels of difficulty should the words be selected for testing?
3. How many words are required to secure an accurate and reliable measure?
4. In what form should the selected words be presented for testing?

Sources of words. Since the values of spelling are almost entirely specific, it is important that the content of a spelling test be sampled from properly validated writing vocabulary lists comprised of words that are now and will be ultimately of greatest usefulness to the pupil. Many early sources of such word lists, such as the one by Anderson [41] used by Ashbaugh in constructing the *Iowa Spelling Scales*,[42] Horn's *Basic Writing Vocabulary*,[43] and Bixler's *Standard Elementary Spelling Scale* [44] have been used in the development of commercial spelling text-books. A valuable source of socially-evaluated and difficulty-rated spelling material for this purpose is *The New Iowa Spelling Scale*.[45] The 5,507 words comprising this list were screened from eight different valid vocabulary sources. "The sampling of pupils for the determination of the level of difficulty of the words was nation-wide. School systems from every state and from the District of Columbia participated in the study near the opening of the school year. Approximately 230,000 pupils in almost 8,800 classrooms in 645 different school systems were involved." Since each pupil undertook to spell one hundred words, over twenty-three million spellings comprise the data for this scale. If the directions accompanying the scale and those in the following paragraph are followed, this scale can be used as a source of material for spelling tests that will provide valid and reliable measures of spelling efficiency.

Teachers who are using no spelling textbooks or who are using texts whose vocabulary content is of unknown social importance will find these spelling scales valuable sources for use in selecting valid content for their own spelling tests. Words included in a spelling test should, of course, be sampled from those comprising the list studied by the pupils. "The most valid types of spelling words on which to test a pupil are also those words that have relatively high social usage. Thus,

[41] W. N. Anderson, *Determination of a Spelling Vocabulary Based Upon Written Correspondence.* Studies in Education, Vol. II, No. 1. Iowa City: State University of Iowa, 1917.

[42] E. J. Ashbaugh, *The Iowa Spelling Scale.* Bloomington, Ill.: Public School Publishing Company, 1919.

[43] Ernest Horn, *A Basic Writing Vocabulary.* Monographs in Education, First Series, No. 4. Iowa City: State University of Iowa, 1926.

[44] H. H. Bixler, *The Standard Elementary Spelling Scale.* Atlanta: Turner E. Smith and Company, 1940.

[45] Harry A. Greene, *The New Iowa Spelling Scale.* Iowa City: Bureau of Educational Research and Service, The State University of Iowa, 1955.

a cross check of the words common to the local spelling text and to a standardized spelling scale will reveal the high social frequency words that the pupils have had a chance to study and will at the same time give the teacher a measure of the relative difficulty of the words from their values in the scale itself." [46]

Difficulty of words. Words selected from a socially validated vocabulary source such as *The New Iowa Spelling Scale* should not only be found among those in the list studied by the pupils but they should be selected in terms of their known spelling difficulty.[47] Common sense dictates that the words included in a test for any grade should be adapted as closely as possible to the average ability of the group to be tested. Not much experimental evidence is available on this point, but many believe that classes of average ability appear to respond best to test words of approximately 50 per cent difficulty.[48] Some theoretical considerations suggest that test words ranging in difficulty from 14 to 86 per cent standard scale accuracy with a mean of 50 per cent tend to give a distribution of scores approximating the normal frequency curve with the pupil scores grouped closely around the mean. "In general, it is probably safe to say that the words to be included in a test for any grade should be those on which there are from 40 to 70 percent misspellings. Tests made up of such words will give a reliable measure of spelling ability, since the words will not be so easy that there will be many perfect scores nor so difficult that there will be many low scores." [49]

Number of words. Since the ability to spell one word is distinct from the ability to spell other words, it might seem necessary to test the pupil on several hundred words in order to obtain a reliable measure of his ability to spell the commonly used words. However, the principle of sampling commonly used in all other testing applies equally well in the field of spelling. The number of words required for adequately reliable results depends largely upon the purpose the test is to serve. For a survey of the status of spelling in an entire school system, a list

[46] Harry A. Greene, A. N. Jorgensen, and J. R. Gerberich, *Measurement and Evaluation in the Elementary School.* New York: Longmans, Green and Company, 1953, p. 442.

[47] Throughout this discussion, *spelling difficulty* should be understood to be best represented by the per cent of misspelling of a word in a given grade without regard to, or any information about, the previous opportunity the pupils may have had for learning the words. The quality as defined here is really "persistence of error" and should not be confused with "learning difficulty" as such.

[48] Walter W. Cook, *The Measurement of General Spelling Ability Involving Controlled Comparisons Between Techniques.* Studies in Education, Vol. VI, No. 6. Iowa City: State University of Iowa, 1932.

[49] Greene, *et al., op. cit.,* p. 443.

of twenty-five carefully selected words may be sufficient. A much larger list of words is required in a test intended to reveal the spelling ability of individual pupils, while fifty words may be adequate for use with a complete class group.

Form of the test. The form in which spelling words should be presented for testing has been subjected to considerable experimental investigation with results that are not entirely conclusive in the light of classroom practices. In life situations, words are almost never spelled orally or in list or column form. Aside from situations in school, spelling needs invariably arise when the individual is writing connected discourse in which he chooses his words and writes them without giving much thought to correctness. Because of this fact, many educators favor the teaching and testing of spelling in contextual form. They defend this practice on the ground that it provides valuable training on such mechanical aspects of written composition as handwriting, punctuation, capitalization, and manuscript form in addition to spelling. On the other hand, reasonably conclusive experimental evidence tends to indicate that for the teaching of spelling the column method is fully as effective as the context method.[50]

The instructional program in spelling should not ignore the pupil's need to spell words in context in all his normal writing activities in other school subjects. This suggests that in the classroom, a combination of list and context dictation exercises may provide the most effective instrument for the measurement of spelling ability. Numerous investigators have found that pupils almost uniformly spell with a higher per cent of accuracy words dictated separately in list form than they do words of similar difficulty presented in sentence form. While the spelling accuracy for words in list form will average from two to four per cent above words of similar difficulty in context form, the placement of pupils on the two forms of tests is so highly correlated that there is considerable question whether the additional time required for the timed-sentence tests is justified.

Horn has summarized the evidence on the question of the form in which spelling words should be presented in the following statement:

Written tests are to be preferred to oral tests. . . . Recall tests are superior to and more difficult than recognition tests. The evidence indicates that the most valid and economical test (in spelling) is the modified recall

[50] Paul McKee, "Teaching and Testing Spelling by Column and Context Forms." Fourth Yearbook. Washington, D. C.: National Education Association, Department of Superintendence, 1926.

form, in which the person giving the test pronounces each word, uses it in an oral sentence, and pronounces it again. The word is then written by the students.[51]

The following statement adapted from the introductory pages of *The New Iowa Spelling Scale* is presented as an example of the way in which a spelling test of the type described above may be prepared and administered.[52]

Let us assume that a fourth-grade teacher has checked the words presented in the local spelling textbooks against the vocabulary of *The New Iowa Spelling Scale*. This check has revealed the fact that the following words taught in this grade appear in the alphabetical list of this scale with the spelling accuracies given immediately following each word.

LIST A				LIST B			
grade	67	month	50	luck	67	inch	50
floor	57	army	48	miles	57	copy	48
able	46	evening	45	unlike	56	fighting	45
track	54	gloves	40	party	54	meetings	40
boots	50	office	35	mails	52	program	35

In practice, there would certainly be many more words common to both the spelling text and the scale, and naturally many more than ten words would be included in the spelling list. Lists A and B are shown here merely to indicate how two parallel and approximately equal word lists may be compiled. The words from List A only are presented in the sample dictation test below. The score expected on these words prior to study would be approximately 50 per cent for beginning fourth graders.

Directions: Write the following words as I read them to you. First you will hear a word, then a sentence in which the word is used, and then the word. Do not begin writing until you have heard the sentence and the word repeated. *Write only the word*. Do not write the sentence. Be careful of your writing and your spelling.

1. grade	I am in the fourth grade this year.		grade
2. floor	The floor of the room was covered with mud.		floor
3. able	Jim was able to work the puzzle.		able
4. track	A broken rail on the track caused the wreck.		track
5. boots	How did you get your boots so muddy?		boots
6. month	School started a month ago today.		month
7. army	My brother was in the army two years.		army
8. evening	Every evening Father reads me a story.		evening
9. gloves	You may wear your gloves to school today.		gloves
10. office	My sister works in an office in the city.		office

[51] Ernest Horn, "Spelling." *Encyclopedia of Educational Research*, rev. ed., The Macmillan Company, 1950, p. 1259.

[52] Greene, *op. cit.*, p. 13.

The rate at which spelling words should be dictated depends upon the writing rate of the children. Cook offered some evidence that eighth-grade pupils were best satisfied with a list test in which fifty per cent standard accuracy words were dictated at the rate of one word every eleven seconds.[53] In lower grades this rate of dictation would be reduced. In practice, the proper dictation rate for spelling lists is easy to determine with sufficient accuracy by observing the children at their work. In sentence dictation exercises the material should be dictated at a rate approximating the standard rate of writing for the grade. The rate of dictation is dependent upon: (1) the rate at which children of the grade normally write; (2) the number of letters in the exercises to be written; and (3) the time required for the examiner to dictate the exercise. Experience has shown that the addition of ten per cent of the writing time for the sentence will compensate for the dictation time. The accompanying table based on standard writing rates per letter *adjusted for the time required for dictation* gives the time allowance in seconds per letter for the different school grades.

Time in seconds per letter, adjusted for dictation time	Grade						
	2	3	4	5	6	7	8
	1.84	1.38	1.18	1.01	.92	.83	.73

The accompanying sample test of timed dictation designed for use in the seventh grade illustrates the way in which this table is used. The first sentence in the test, "He is evidently entitled to the money," is made up of 31 letters. The number of letters, 31, multiplied by the rate in seconds for the seventh grade (.83) gives 26 seconds in round numbers as the time required for this sentence. The time required for the dictation and writing of the second sentence of 30 letters is 25 seconds. In the administration of the timed dictation test the usual practice is to start the test with the second hand of the watch at 60. Read the first sentence. Then wait until the second hand of the watch reaches the time indicated at the left of the next sentence, then read the second sentence, etc. Thus the second sentence in this test is read when the second hand of the watch reaches 26. Since the second sentence requires 25 seconds, the third sentence will be read when the second hand reaches 51. Read each sentence only once. In beginning the test do not suggest that it is a spelling test. Something like the following is a good approach:

I am going to read to you some sentences which I wish you to write down. The sentences are not long and you need not hurry. Listen carefully and

[53] Cook, *op. cit.*

542

then write each sentence or word as I have read it. Be careful of your writing and spelling.

In scoring this type of spelling test only the words in italics are considered critical. In constructing the dictation exercises the critical words should not be placed at the ends of sentences since the pupil may not hear or understand the first word, or may not be able to complete the writing of the last word within the time limit.

Specimen dictation exercise and spelling list
50 word spelling test for grade 7

Start with
watch at

60   He is *evidently entitled* to the money.
26   Write a *brief description* of the man.
51   I *prefer* this *proposition* myself.
14   We have an *excellent commercial* club here.
43   We are *studying science* and *literature* today.
14   The city *council* will not *interfere* with the work.
48   We *acquire literary appreciation* through study.
22   The *annual agricultural demonstration* was held here.
59   The *university* is *altogether* too *crowded* this year.
35   The *superintendent authorized athletics* in the school.
14   Stop

Now have the children write the following words on the blank side of the paper. Pronounce these words as you would an ordinary spelling lesson at the rate of about one word every 12 seconds.

Spelling list

bargain	league	absence	pitcher	handkerchief
regardless	salmon	unusual	confident	magazine
remedy	quarrel	pleasant	whirl	operate
assure	scenery	graduation	carnival	kindergarten
equipment	opposed	positive	charity	temperature

DIAGNOSIS OF SPELLING DISABILITIES

The discovery from the results of repeated observations and testings that a pupil is seriously below his age and grade expectancy in spelling may be of considerable value, but unless it reveals to the pupils and his teacher the causes of his poor showing, it falls far short of its real value. Among the items of diagnostic information that may be procured through observation and measurement and are invaluable in identifying the pupil's disabilities and analysing his spelling habits are the following:

1. *General capacity*. Give a group or individual mental test or use results from such tests if available as measures of general learning capacity.

2. *Attitude toward spelling*. This is revealed most readily in the pupil's previous record in spelling and in his scores on a series of carefully validated spelling tests.

3. *Reading ability*. Secure results from silent reading comprehension tests emphasizing words and word meaning. In addition, oral reading tests should be given to reveal superficial speech defects as well as deficiencies in pronunciation and enunciation.

4. *Handwriting, legibility and speed*. Certain spelling difficulties arise through slow and faulty letter formation. Secure previous school records on handwriting as well as speed and quality ratings on standardized handwriting scales.

5. *Visual defects*. Use observation and superficial tests of binocular vision and visual acuity as the approach. If deficiencies are suggested, secure immediate medical examination.

6. *Auditory defects*. Use observation and superficial tests as approach. If necessary secure medical examination.

7. *School attendance*. Secure complete school history of attendance, age-grade-progress data.

8. *Speech defects and maturity*. If results in item 3 above suggest need, secure supplemental speech pathology data.

9. *General Health*. Secure and analyse data on general health from school medical or nursing service.

10. *Personality characteristics*. Collect and analyse data from observations on pupil's industry, aggressiveness, independence, attentiveness, exactness.

One of the most encouraging modern approaches to the identification of the causes of spelling deficiency seems to be found in the careful observation and testing of the work habits of the pupils. The failure of pupils to learn and utilize approved methods of learning to spell new or difficult words is one of the chief causes of poor achievement in spelling. Certainly, this is not always the fault of the pupil. Frequently he is not taught how to study, or the methods he is taught are not effective. Spelling success results from the process of forming correct and effective associations between the letters of words through the use of established techniques of habit formation. Frequently little more than general observation is required to reveal whether or not the pupil makes a systematic attack on his learning of new or difficult words. Does he definitely center his attention upon the word; does he try to visualize the word, i.e., close his eyes and attempt to recall its appearance; does he say the letters of the word softly to himself; does he pronounce the word correctly syllable by syllable and try to recall how each syllable appears; does he compare the word with the correct written or printed copy; does he watch for silent letters, double letters, different vowels having the same sound, and for different combinations of letters; does he recall the word repeatedly until he has mastered it; does he develop the meaning of the word by using the dictionary, and fix it in his experience by using it in sentences?

Very frequently, words are misspelled because they are spelled the way they are heard or pronounced. Improper pronunciation by the pupil himself is more likely to result in misspellings than in mispronunciation by the teacher either in teaching or in testing. Imperfect hearing or improper pronunciation or enunciation of the words by his associates thus becomes a contributing cause. It is therefore imperative that children form proper habits of pronunciation and enunciation.

The lack of a spelling conscience, or a critical sensitivity to correct spelling is a frequent cause of poor spelling in normal written expression. Pride in spelling ability and a sensitivity toward spelling errors must be developed to the point that it carries over into all of the normal writing activities in school and life. Pupils must come to feel a deep dissatisfaction every time a word is misspelled in their written work.

CORRECTIVE WORK IN SPELLING

Persistently poor spelling of common and frequently used words is due to inadequately formed associations during the learning process or perhaps to faults in the learning process itself. All spellers, good or bad, learn in the same way—through association. The study technique by which new words are mastered sets forth the methods by which these associations are formed. Actually the main differences between the good speller and the poor one are to be found in (1) the study technique he uses, (2) his mental and personality characteristics, and (3) the emphasis he gives to the subject.

The accompanying chart (pp. 546–548), adapted by the authors from a current language test manual,[54] provides an excellent summary of the many causes of spelling deficiency as well as remedial suggestions which the classroom teacher may profitably follow.

[54] *Manual for Interpreting Iowa Language Abilities Tests.* Yonkers-on-Hudson: World Book Company, 1948, pp. 24–25.

Diagnostic and Remedial Chart for Spelling

Possible causes of low test scores	Additional evidence of deficiency	Suggested remedial treatment
1. Lack of experience with the testing technique.	1. Low score on test contrasted with high score when words are given on dictation test.	1. Drills on choosing correct spellings from lists of errors of same word; choosing correct forms from long lists, some correct, some incorrect; proofreading own written work.
2. Emphasis on different or wrong vocabulary.	2. Low scores on test in contrast with good record for daily work.	2. Check words not taught in your course with lists of known social utility.
3. Failure to develop a critical attitude toward spelling.	3. Indifference to spelling errors in daily written work.	3. Emphasize proofreading of own work. Drill on choosing correctly spelled forms in lists. Check pupil's certainty of his judgment of correctness of spelling.
4. Lack of teaching emphasis on individual's own spelling difficulties.	4. Observation of pupil's misspellings in daily work.	4. Have pupils keep lists of misspellings in daily work as basis for individual study. Focus on pupil's own errors. Try for transfer to all written work.
5. Specific learning difficulties: a. Faulty pronunciation by the teacher.	5. a. Observation of speech habits; informal pronunciation tests based on spelling vocabulary.	5. a. Look up word in dictionary. Pronounce it distinctly for pupil. Have him repeat it while looking at word to associate sight and correct sound.

Possible causes of low test scores	Additional evidence of deficiency	Suggested remedial treatment
b. Limited power to visualize or "see" word forms.	b. Observation test. Have pupil try to visualize a 3-in. cube painted red. Ask questions: number of faces; number of planes necessary to cut it into 1-in. cubes; number of small cubes; number painted on one side, two sides, three sides, not painted, etc.	b. Emphasize the practice of looking at the word; closing eyes, and attempting to recall the word, as part of every spelling study period.
c. Difficulties in seeing or in hearing.	c. Observation; doctor's or nurse's examination.	c. Refer to nurse or medical service. Move pupil to front of room near window and blackboard. Stand near him in tests and spelling exercises. Make special effort to speak and write clearly.
d. Failure to associate sounds of letters and syllables with spelling of words.	d. Individual interview; analysis of spelling errors in tests and in daily work.	d. Go over words with child while he studies them. Teach him to analyse words himself.
e. Tendency to transpose, add, or omit letters.	e. Analysis of spelling papers; observation of daily work; pronunciation tests.	e. Emphasize visual recall of words. Have pupil practice writing the words, exaggerating the formation of the letters. Underline individual hard spots.

547

Diagnostic and Remedial Chart for Spelling (*continued*)

Possible causes of low test scores	*Additional evidence of deficiency*	*Suggested remedial treatment*
f. Tendency to spell unphonetic words phonetically.	f. Note types of errors made in spelling tests, especially insertion or leaving out letters.	f. Show that all words are not spelled as they sound. Each word must be learned individually. Emphasize steps in learning to spell. See *h* below.
g. Difficulties in writing; letter formation.	g. Observation of daily written work and spelling papers. Check writing with Ayres or Freeman writing scales.	g. Practice difficult letter formations and combinations. Emphasize need to avoid confusing letter forms, as *i, e, r,* and *t*.
h. Failure to master method of learning to spell.	h. Low scores on daily tests; observe the pupil's method of study in spelling; test on steps in learning to spell.	h. Check pupil's method of learning spelling. Teach steps in learning to spell until he uses them. Steps: (1) look at word, (2) listen as teacher pronounces it, (3) pronounce it by syllables then say the letters, (4) use it in a sentence, (5) close eyes and visualize it, (6) write it, (7) close eyes and recall, (8) write word. Repeat steps as necessary.

ANALYTIC AND REMEDIAL PROCEDURES IN LANGUAGE

In the light of the criteria for diagnostic measurement maintained by most critics today, the majority of language achievement tests fall far short of being really diagnostic. However, certain of the currently available language tests provide a program of analytical measurement in language that offers more than ordinary breadth in grade and content coverage.

ANALYTICAL MEASURES OF LANGUAGE SKILLS

The *Iowa Primary Language Test* mentioned briefly on page 521 enables the teacher in Grades 1, 2, and 3 to secure reasonably accurate analytical appraisal of pupil accomplishment in eight different oral and written skill and product areas.[55] The reproduction of the pupil's record sheet below shows the eight language areas sampled by the test with the number of points representing a perfect score at each grade level.

The tests may be administered in groups of six or eight by the time the pupils reach the maturity of the second semester of the first grade. No reading is required and the pupil reactions are simple and objective. The Examiner's Manual is a special feature of the test, presenting a useful inventory of primary language skills for these grades as well as a double-column set of directions determining the form of the test that is administered. Norms are given for September, February, and June results.

Individual Pupil's Test Record

Part	Test	Grade:	Perfect score One	Two	Three
1.	Filling in forms		4	15	15
2.	Conversation		14	14	14
3.	Oral Composition		12	12	12
4.	Telephone conversation		10	10	10
5.	Correct usage		40	40	40
6.	Recorded composition		6	6	6
7.	Miscellaneous social usage				
	A. Description		3	3	3
	B. Introduction		5	5	5
	C. Announcement, message, invitation		5	5	5
	D. Directions for finding a place		3	3	3
	E. Forms of courtesy		3	3	3
8.	Letter writing		—	10	10
Total			105	126	126

[55] Lou A. Shephard and H. A. Greene, *Iowa Primary Language Test.*

549

The *Iowa Language Abilities Tests* are available at two levels, the elementary battery for Grades 4, 5, and 6 with optional use in Grade 7, and the intermediate battery for Grades 7, 8, and 9 with optional use in Grade 10.[56] The elementary test booklet contains the following five sub-tests: (1) Spelling, (2) Word meaning, (3) Language usage, (4) Capitalization, and (5) Punctuation. In addition to these five tests the intermediate booklet contains tests on recognition of grammatical form and sentence sense. Specimens of these and other tests described in this volume are readily available from the publishers. The teacher will find a helpful list of publishers and distributors of educational tests on pages 596–597 of *Measurement and Evaluation in the Modern School* by Gerberich, Greene, and Jorgensen, which is listed in the selected references at the end of this chapter.

The language test booklet of the current *Iowa Every-Pupil Tests of Basic Skills* [57] possesses considerable analytical power. The skill coverage of this booklet closely parallels that of the *Iowa Language Abilities Tests;* although in most instances the actual testing techniques are different. The elementary booklet is designed for use in Grades 3, 4, and 5 and the advanced booklet is for Grades 5 to 9.

DIAGNOSTIC AND REMEDIAL PROCEDURES IN LANGUAGE

Effective corrective instruction in language will result only to the extent that pupils are made sensitive to the social importance of good usage and are stimulated to make the personal effort to use the best and most acceptable forms of expression and to formulate correct habits of usage. Teachers will find that tests of language abilities of the types now current will prove valuable in aiding their pupils in the development of this desirable self-critical attitude which leads in turn to the desire to develop correct habits of oral and written expression.

Extensive and doubtless adequate remedial materials in the areas of important language skills are provided in the many workbooks and practice exercises designed to supplement the instruction in current language textbooks. These are discussed in considerable detail in Chapter 16. For this reason, and because of space limitations in this chapter, specific ex-

[56] Harry A. Greene and H. L. Ballenger, *Iowa Language Abilities Tests.* Yonkers-on-Hudson: World Book Company, 1948.

[57] E. F. Linquist, general ed., *Iowa Every-Pupil Test of Basic Skills, Test C.* Issued annually in new and equated forms for use in the Iowa Every-Pupil Testing Program. Iowa City: State University of Iowa.

amples of types of remedial exercises in language are not presented here. However, the following general diagnostic and remedial suggestions presented in the *Manual for Interpreting the Iowa Language Abilities Tests* have proved so helpful to teachers and pupils that charts dealing with language usage, sentence sense, capitalization, and punctuation are reproduced here to supplement the remedial suggestions on handwriting and spelling given previously in this chapter.[58]

It has been emphasized repeatedly throughout this volume that the most effective remedial materials arise out of the language difficulties encountered by the individual children in their daily expressional activities. The remedial treatments suggested in the accompanying charts are admittedly general, but they should give the interested classroom teacher helpful assistance in the construction of remedial exercises in handwriting, spelling, language usage, sentence sense, capitalization, and punctuation which will directly aid the individual pupil in mastering these essential language skills.

[58] Reproduced here with the permission of the publishers, World Book Company, Yonkers-on-Hudson, New York.

Language Usage

Possible causes of low test scores	Additional evidence of deficiency	Suggested remedial treatment
1. Failure to comprehend testing technique.	1. Misunderstanding of method of recording responses to items.	1. Prepare and use drill exercises similar to those used in test. Work with pupil until he understands technique.
2. Poor control over special language usages.	2. Observation and check on daily habits or oral and written expression.	2. Check pupil's test paper to identify types of usages missed. Check with text and course of study for grade emphasis. Emphasize individual drill on specific errors. Contrast correct forms with those to be avoided. Supplement with oral drill.
3. Poor language background.	3. Careless, inaccurate usage in oral and written expression.	3. Corrective instruction is the only remedy here. Select a limited number of usages and proceed as in No. 2 above.
4. Foreign language in the home.	4. Observed foreign accents. Evidence of two languages in the home.	4. Use direct corrective instruction here. Follow suggestions in No. 2 above.
5. Poor general reading comprehension.	5. Erratic response to test items; poor reading ability in other subjects.	5. Drill on sentence and total meaning comprehension as required for general improvement in reading.
6. Low mental ability	6. Difficulty in following directions; erratic response to difficulty with common usages; low MA and IQ shown by reliable mental test.	6. Follow general procedure as outlined in Nos. 2 and 3 above. Have pupil prepare and memorize a key sentence for troublesome usages.

552

7. Careless language habits.	7. Erratic responses to test items; carelessness in informal expression.	7. Develop self-critical attitude toward usage errors. Bring pressure to bear favoring correct usages. Stress proofreadin all written work.
8. Confusion caused by emphasis on formal rather than functional usages.	8. Inaccurate responses to items emphasized mainly through rules.	8. Emphasize individual drills; stress definite habits of correct response to important usages.

Sentence Sense

Possible causes of low test scores	Additional evidence of deficiency	Suggested remedial treatment
1. Limited meaning vocabulary.	1. Low scores on vocabulary tests; observation of pupil's use of words in oral and written work.	1. Drill on meaning vocabulary. Develop different meanings of common words. Stress using words in sentences demonstrating differences in meanings.
2. Poor reading comprehension.	2. Low scores of information and on reading comprehension tests.	2. Drill on word meanings, sentence and paragraph meanings, and comprehension of total meaning of content suitable for the grade.
3. Inability to recognize subjects and predicates of sentences, and to sense what is missing in a fragment.	3. Note pupil's habits in speech and writing; individual work with pupils on analysis of sentences and fragments.	3. Drill on choosing complete subjects and predicates from pupil's own writing. Use matching exercises made up of complete subjects in one column and complete predicates in parallel column.

Sentence Sense (*continued*)

Possible causes of low test scores	Additional evidence of deficiency	Suggested remedial treatment
4. Failure to think of sentence as complete unit of expression.	4. Note pupil's spoken and written work for sentence errors.	4. Stress use of complete sentences in daily oral and written work. Point out that there are times when fragments may be used but that they must be recognized as such. Drill on completion of exercises in which subjects or predicates are missing. Drill on exercises calling for identification of fragments and sentences.
5. Use of "run-on" sentences; loose *and*.	5. Analysis of pupil's expression for use of loose *and's* and "run-on's."	5. Explain and illustrate various types of incorrect sentences. Stress individual practice in writing good sentences. Drill on identifying poor sentence structure and in recasting poor sentences.

Capitalization

Possible causes of low test scores	Additional evidence of deficiency	Suggested remedial treatment
1. Lack of knowledge of capitalization situations.	1. Analysis of pupil's test paper and other written work to determine types of errors made.	1. Check specific capitalization skills missed by pupil on test paper with textbook and local course of study. Stress proofreading drills on skills in which pupil is weak.
2. Limited knowledge of exceptions and irregularities in capitalization.	2. Analysis of test paper and daily written work; note tendency to over-capitalize.	2. Give direct drill on capitalization skills taught in this grade. Point out exceptions and irregularities in the use of capitals.

3. Tendency to over-capitalize.	3. High correction for over-capitalization in test.	3. Inspect test paper and written work for excessive use of capitals. Use dictation and proofreading designed to emphasize correct use of capitals.
4. Lack of self-critical attitude toward capitalization. Poor proofreading ability.	4. Erratic and careless work in daily written expression in other subjects; limited ability to note errors in own or other written copy.	4. Emphasize need for self-critical attitude toward pupil's own written work. Drill on proofreading exercises designed to emphasize use of capitals.
5. Poorly developed sentence sense.	5. Low scores on sentence sense tests.	5. Use suggestions in remedial chart for sentence sense.
6. Carelessness in writing.	6. Analysis of handwriting characteristics in daily work.	6. Drill on distinctive characteristics of capital letters and small letters which analysis shows cause trouble.

Punctuation

Possible causes of low test scores	Additional evidence of deficiency	Suggested remedial treatment
1. Lack of knowledge of specific punctuation skills.	1. Check test papers to determine types of skills missed; observation of daily written work.	1. Check punctuation items missed in test with textbook and course of study. Use proofreading drills on skills missed by pupil. Stress drills on correct punctuation, avoiding over-punctuation, and self-editing of own copy.
2. Tendency to over-punctuate.	2. Analysis of test and daily work for evidence of over-punctuation, especially commas.	2. Use dictation and proofreading drills for the elimination of improper or excessive punctuation.

Punctuation (*continued*)

Possible causes of low test scores	Additional evidence of deficiency	Suggested remedial treatment
3. Lack of self-critical attitude toward own written work.	3. Careless punctuation in daily work; fails to note errors in own or in other written copy.	3. Emphasize self-criticism of own daily written work. Use proofreading exercises to emphasize correct use of punctuation marks.
4. Poor general comprehension in reading.	4. Low scores on comprehension tests; poor reading in other subjects.	4. Drill on word meaning, sentence comprehension, and comprehension of total meaning in varied subject-matter fields.
5. Poor vision or hearing.	5. Observation of pupil at work; nurse's or doctor's examination.	5. Refer pupil to doctor for medical attention. Move pupil to front of room. Encourage pupil to make special effort to write carefully and to make punctuation marks distinctly.
6. Poorly developed sentence sense.	6. Observation of pupil's daily usage.	6. Explain types of sentences and the relation of sentence structure to punctuation. Stress practice in writing sentences and punctuating them correctly. Use dictation and proofreading exercises calling for punctuation.
7. Carelessness in matters of form in written expression.	7. Observation and analysis of characteristics of handwriting and punctuation.	7. Stress essentials of good form in written work. Insist that pupils edit and proofread all written work.

EXERCISES FOR THOUGHT AND DISCUSSION

1. Evaluate the social importance of listening as a language skill.
2. Discuss the relative demands made in life on the oral and the written language skills.
3. How are the quality of the product and ability in written expression measured?
4. Give examples of the more important problems of measuring oral expression.
5. What are the major measurable aspects of reading readiness?
6. What are the chief work-study testing techniques represented in the currently popular silent reading tests?
7. Discuss the nature of tests of listening comprehension.
8. Discuss the practical values of using tape-recorders for the study of deficiencies in oral expression.
9. What are the primary measurable objectives of oral expression?
10. Evaluate the listening skills identified by Brown in this chapter.
11. Use some one available scale for the measurement of merit of written composition to rate three compositions written by school children. How do your scores compare with your general judgment of the quality of the compositions?
12. Use the letter-writing scoring sheet in this chapter to rate a friendly letter you may have received. Does the score reflect the quality of the letter?
13. Rate a specimen of handwriting on a handwriting scale available to you. Follow the standard procedure in determining the rate score by having the subject write standard copy for two minutes.
14. Prepare a timed sentence dictation test based on ten words of difficulty suitable for the grade you expect to teach.
15. Show how a spelling test based on socially useful words can be validated for use with a class using a speller based on vocabulary of unknown social significance.

SELECTED REFERENCES

ASHBAUGH, E. J. *The Iowa Spelling Scales*. Journal of Educational Research Monographs, No. 3. Bloomington, Illinois: Public School Publishing Company, 1922.

AUSTON, JOHN T. "Methods and Levels of Measurement in Speech." *Educational and Psychological Measurement,* 13:228–247; Summer 1953.

AYRES, L. P. *A Measuring Scale for Ability in Spelling.* New York: Russell Sage Foundation, 1913.

Commission on the English Curriculum, National Council of Teachers of English. *Language Arts for Today's Children.* New York: Appleton-Century-Crofts, Inc., 1954. Chapter 13.

COOK, WALTER W. "Evaluation in the Language Arts Program." *Teaching Language in the Elementary School.* Forty-third Yearbook of the National Society for the Study of Education, Part II. Chicago: The University of Chicago, 1944. Chapter 9.

FREEMAN, F. N. "An Analytical Scale for Judging Handwriting." *Elementary School Journal,* 15:432–441; 1915.

———. "An Evaluation of Manuscript Writing." *Elementary School Journal,* 36:446–455; 1936.

GERBERICH, J. RAYMOND, GREENE, HARRY A., and JORGENSEN, A. N. *Measurement and Evaluation in the Modern School.* New York: David McKay Company, Inc., 1962.

GREENE, HARRY A. "English—Language, Grammar, and Composition." *Encyclopedia of Educational Research,* rev. ed. New York: The Macmillan Company, 1950, pp. 383–396.

———. *The New Iowa Spelling Scales.* Iowa City: Bureau of Educational Research and Service, State University of Iowa, 1955.

GREENE, HARRY A., and BALLENGER, H. L. *Iowa Language Abilities Tests.* Yonkers-on-Hudson: World Book Company, 1948.

GREENE, HARRY A., and BALLENGER, H. L. *Manual for Interpreting Iowa Language Abilities Tests.* Yonkers-on-Hudson: World Book Company, 1948.

GREENE, HARRY A., and GRAY, WILLIAM S. "The Measurement of Understanding in the Language Arts." *The Measurement of Understanding,* Forty-fifth Yearbook of the National Society for the Study of Education, Part I. Chicago: The University of Chicago Press, pp. 176–189.

GREENE, HARRY A., JORGENSEN, A. N., and GERBERICH, J. R. *Measurement and Evaluation in the Elementary School.* New York: Longmans, Green and Company, 1953. Chapter 16.

HARRING, SIDNEY. "A Scale for Judging Oral Composition." *Elementary English Review,* 5:71–73; 1928.

HARRIS, THEODORE L. "Handwriting." *Encyclopedia of Educational Research.* Third edition. New York: Macmillan Co., 1960, pp. 616–624.

HILDRETH, GERTRUDE. *Teaching Spelling.* New York: Henry Holt and Co., 1955. Chapter 11.

HILLEGAS, M. B. "Scale for the Measurement of Quality of English Composition by Young People." *Teachers College Record,* 13:331–384; 1912.

HORN, ERNEST. "Spelling." *Encyclopedia of Educational Research,* Third ed. New York: The Macmillan Company, 1960, pp. 1337–1354.

LINDQUIST, E. F., general ed. *Iowa Every-Pupil Tests of Basic Skills.* Iowa City: State University of Iowa, published annually.

NETZER, ROYAL F. *The Evaluation of a Technique for Measuring Improvement in Oral Composition. Studies in Education,* Vol. 10, No. 4. Iowa City: State University of Iowa, 1939.

NICHOLS, RALPH G. "Factors in Listening Comprehension." *Speech Monographs,* 15:154–163; 1948.

PETTY, WALTER T. *Improving Your Spelling Program.* San Francisco: Chandler Press, 1959.

————. *The Language Arts in Elementary Schools.* Washington, D.C.: The Center for Applied Research in Education, Inc., 1962. Chapter 6.

THORNDIKE, E. L. "A Scale for Merit in English Writing by Young People." *Journal of Educational Psychology,* 2:361–368; 1911.

THORNDIKE, ROBERT L., and HAGEN, ELIZABETH. *Measurement and Evaluation in Psychology and Education.* New York: John Wiley and Sons, Inc. 1955. Chapter 2.

VARTY, J. W. *Manuscript Writing and Spelling Achievement.* Teachers College Contributions to Education. New York: Columbia University, 1938.

WEST, PAUL V., and FREEMAN, F. N. "Handwriting." *Encyclopedia of Educational Research,* rev. ed. New York: The Macmillan Company, 1950, pp. 524–529.

WILLING, M. H. "The Measurement of Written Composition in Grades IV to VIII." *English Journal,* 21:290–296; 1920.

ZEDLER, EMPRESS YOUNG. *Listening for Speech Sounds.* Garden City, N.Y.: Doubleday and Company, Inc., 1955.

Index